Berlin

Potsdam & Dresden

Derek Blyth

Prentice Hall Travel

New York • London • Toronto • Sydney • Tokyo • Singapore

THE AMERICAN EXPRESS ® TRAVEL GUIDES

Published in the United States by
Prentice Hall General Reference
15 Columbus Circle
New York, NY 10023

PRENTICE HALL is a registered trademark and colophon is a trademark of Prentice-Hall, Inc.

First published 1992 in the United Kingdom by Mitchell Beazley International Ltd, Michelin House 81 Fulham Road, London SW3 6RB and Auckland, Melbourne, Singapore and Toronto as *The American Express Pocket Guide to Berlin*. This edition, revised, updated and expanded, published 1994.

Edited, designed and produced by Castle House Press, Llantrisant Mid Glamorgan CF7 8EU, Wales

Contact Library of Congress for full CIP data.
ISBN 0-671-86826-8

The editors thank Neil Hanson, Alex Taylor and Steve Ramsay of Lovell Johns, David Haslam, Anna Holmes and Sylvia Hughes-Williams for their help and co-operation during the preparation of this edition. Special thanks are also due to the staff of the German National Tourist Office in London and Berlin.

Thanks to Dell Publishing Co. (USA) and Jonathan Cape Ltd (UK) for permission to reproduce the extract from *Slaughterhouse-five* by Kurt Vonnegut, Jr., published 1969 (US) and 1970 (UK).

Some illustrations in this book were first used in *The Mitchell Beazley pocket guide to Architecture* by Patrick Nuttgens (1980).

FOR THE SERIES:
Series Editor:
David Townsend Jones
Map Editor: David Haslam
Indexer: Hilary Bird
Gazetteer: Anna Holmes
Cover design:
Roger Walton Studio

FOR THIS EDITION:
Edited on desktop by:
Eileen Townsend Jones
Art editors:
Castle House Press
Illustrator:
Sylvia Hughes-Williams
Cover photo:
Britstock – IFA/Aberham

FOR MITCHELL BEAZLEY:
Art Director: Andrew Sutterby
Production: Katy Sawyer
Publisher: Sarah Bennison

PRODUCTION CREDITS:
Maps by Lovell Johns, Oxford, England
U-Bahn & S-Bahn map by TCS, Aldershot, England
Typeset in Garamond and News Gothic
Desktop layout in Corel Ventura Publisher
Reproduction by M & E Reproductions, Essex, England
Linotronic output by Tradespools Limited, Frome, England

Contents

How to use this book 6
Key to symbols 7
About the author: A message from the editors 8

Foreword — Cities of *die Wende* 11
The Porcelain Cities 14
Visiting Northern Germany: practical information
Before you go 16
Getting there 19
On-the-spot information 20
Emergency information 23

Berlin

Introduction — The War, the Wall, the Change 25

Culture, history and background
Landmarks in Berlin's history 31
Who's who in Berlin — a gallery of historical personalities 36
The architecture of Berlin 42
Art in Berlin 47
Film in Berlin 48
Suggested reading 52

Practical information
Getting there 53
Getting around in Berlin 55
On-the-spot information 59
Useful numbers and addresses 61
Business in Berlin 63
Emergency information 64

Planning your visit
Orientation; When to go; The Berlin calendar 65
Organizing your time 67

Sightseeing
An overview of the city 71
Berlin expeditions — walks; tours by S-Bahn,
bus and steamer 74
Exploring Berlin — an introduction 89
Sights classified by type — a practical checklist 90–91
A to Z of Berlin sights 92

Berlin: living in the city

Where to stay	161
Berlin hotels A to Z	164
Eating and drinking in Berlin	168
Berlin restaurants A to Z	170
Cafés and fast food	175
Berlin cafés A to Z	177
Beer halls and beer gardens	179
Berlin after dark; The performing arts	181
Nightlife	187
Where to shop	191
What to buy	192
Berlin for children	201
Sports and activities	202

Potsdam

Introduction — The Prussian paradise	205
Landmarks in Potsdam's history	207
Potsdam's architecture	208
Practical information	
Getting there	211
Getting around in Potsdam	212
On-the-spot information	214
Emergency information; Useful numbers and addresses	215
Planning your visit; The Potsdam calendar	216
Organizing your time	217
Sightseeing — an overview of the city	219
Exploring Potsdam — walks; bus tour	220
A to Z of Potsdam sights	227
Where to stay in Potsdam	240
Eating and drinking in Potsdam	242
Shopping	244
Potsdam after dark	245
Sports and activities	247

Dresden

Introduction — The ruins, the riches, the rebuilding	248
Landmarks in Dresden's history	250
Who's who in Dresden	
A gallery of historical personalities	252
Architecture in Dresden	254
Books about Dresden	257

Practical information
Before you go; Getting there 258
Getting around in Dresden 259
On-the-spot information; Business in Dresden 261
Useful numbers and addresses 262
Emergency information 263
Planning your visit; The Dresden visitor's calendar 264
Organizing your time 265
Sightseeing — an overview of the city 268
Exploring Dresden — walks; tram tour 269
A to Z of Dresden sights 278
Where to stay in Dresden 304
Eating and drinking in Dresden 308
Dresden entertainment 311
Performing arts 312
Dresden by night 314
Shopping 315
Sports and activities 316
Spectator sports 317
Dresden for children 318

German in a nutshell — a vocabulary 319
Index 323
List of street names 336
International clothing sizes near back of book

Maps

Germany 13
Berlin walk: the Spree 76–77
Berlin walk: Kreuzberg 79
Berlin walk: Scheunenviertel (the Old Jewish Quarter) 81
Berlin walk: Grunewald 83
Potsdam 220–21
Potsdam: Park Sanssouci 223
Dresden environs 266–67
Walk: heart of Dresden 271
Dresden walk: across the Blaues Wunder bridge 275

Color maps:
Key to main map pages
Berlin city Maps **1** to **4**
Berlin U-Bahn & S-Bahn
Berlin environs Maps **5** to **7**
Dresden Maps **8** and **9**

How to use this book

Few guidelines are needed to understand how this book works:

- For the general organization of the book, see CONTENTS on the pages preceding this one.
- Wherever appropriate, chapters and sections are arranged alphabetically, with headings appearing in **CAPITALS.**
- Often these headings are followed by location and practical information printed in *italics.*
- Subject headers, similar to those used in telephone directories, are printed in CAPITALS in the top corner of each page.
- If you still cannot find what you need, check in the comprehensive and exhaustively cross-referenced INDEX at the back of the book.
- Following the index, a LIST OF STREET NAMES provides map references for all streets, squares etc. mentioned in the book that fall within the Berlin and Dresden maps (color maps **1–4** and **8–9** at the back of the book).

CROSS-REFERENCES
These are printed in SMALL CAPITALS, referring you to other sections or alphabetical entries in the book. Care has been taken to ensure that such cross-references are self-explanatory. Often, page references are also given, although their excessive use would be intrusive and ugly.

FLOORS
We use the European convention for the naming of floors in this book: "ground floor" means the floor at ground level (called by Americans the "first floor").

AUTHOR'S ACKNOWLEDGMENTS
Derek Blyth would like to thank the German National Tourist Office in Berlin, Gutenberg Buchhandlung in Brussels, the Goethe Institut in Brussels, Henriette Heimgärtner and Doug and Cathy Hutchinson for their invaluable help.

Key to symbols

- Telephone
- Facsimile (fax)
- Recommended sight
- Good value (in its class)
- Tourist information
- Parking
- Building of architectural interest
- Free entrance
- Entrance fee payable
- Guided tour
- Cafeteria
- Good view
- Special interest for children
- Hotel
- Simple hotel
- Luxury hotel
- American Express
- Diners Club
- MasterCard/Eurocard
- Visa
- Facilities for disabled people
- Air conditioning
- Secure garage
- Quiet hotel
- Garden
- Good beach nearby
- Swimming pool
- Elevator
- TV in each room
- Telephone in each room
- Dogs not allowed
- Gym/fitness facilities
- Sauna
- Conference facilities
- Business center
- Bar
- Mini-bar
- Restaurant
- Simple restaurant
- Luxury restaurant
- Good wines
- Open-air dancing
- Disco dancing
- Live music
- Dancing
- Casino/gambling

PRICE CATEGORIES

- Cheap
- Inexpensive
- Moderately priced
- Expensive
- Very expensive

Our price categories for **hotels** are explained on page 163. Those for **restaurants** are explained on page 170.

About the author

Born in Scotland, **Derek Blyth** is a European writer, translator and journalist. During more than a decade spent exploring the art and culture of Northern Europe, he has written several travel books, including *Flemish Cities Explored,* and, in this series, *American Express Amsterdam, Rotterdam & The Hague* (1992), and, in 1993, *American Express Brussels,* co-written with Rory Watson.

He is currently based in Brussels, where he writes for *The Bulletin* magazine, although his travel writing often takes him on trips around the Low Countries and beyond. Returning frequently to Berlin to keep abreast of the changes, he particularly looks forward to strolling around Potsdamer Platz after dark, and to spending time in the Café Einstein.

A message from the editors

Months of concentrated work were dedicated to making this edition accurate and up to date when it went to press. But time and change are forever the enemies, and between editions we are very much assisted when you, the readers, write to tell us about any changes you discover.

Please keep on writing — but please also be aware that we have no control over restaurants, or whatever, that take it into their heads, after we publish, to move, or change their telephone number, or, even worse, close down. Some restaurants are prone to menu notices like the following genuine authenticated example: "These items may or may not be available at all times, and sometimes not at all and other times all the time." As to telephone numbers, everywhere on earth, telephone authorities seem to share a passion for changing their numbers like you and I change shirts.

My serious point is that we are striving to tailor the series to the very distinctive tastes and requirements of our discerning international readership, which is why your feedback is so valuable. I particularly want to thank all of you who wrote while we were preparing this edition. Time prevents our responding to most such letters, but they are all welcomed and frequently contribute to the process of preparing the next edition.

Please write to me at **Mitchell Beazley**, an imprint of Reed Illustrated Books, Michelin House, 81 Fulham Road, London SW3 6RB; or, in the US, c/o American Express Travel Guides, **Prentice Hall Travel**, 15 Columbus Circle, New York, NY 10023.

David Townsend Jones, Series Editor, American Express Travel Guides

Berlin

Potsdam & Dresden

Cities of *die Wende*

In November 1989, a new German word entered the world's vocabulary: *die Wende*— the turning point. It referred to the enormous changes that swept through East Germany in the final months of 1989, beginning with peaceful demonstrations in Leipzig and other cities, and ending in the fall of the Berlin Wall.

The three cities described in this book have changed dramatically as a result of *die Wende.* Before 1989, they were difficult to reach and all too often inhospitable. But Berlin, Potsdam and Dresden are now once again routine stops on the Grand Tour of Europe. East and West Berlin have merged into a single fascinating city; Potsdam has seen the Soviet garrison depart and the tourists arrive; and Dresden is rapidly rebuilding its ruined historic buildings in a bid to regain its former title of "Florence on the Elbe."

THE TRIUMPH OF THE WEST

Nobody can fail to be impressed, and occasionally appalled, by the changes that have happened in the few years since unification. It is still fascinating simply to sit on a tram in Potsdam, Dresden or eastern Berlin and look at the changes. The differences can be seen everywhere: in clothes, shop windows, driving habits, restaurant interiors, advertising slogans. The developments are almost too complex to describe, but it may be worth listing a few of the changes, major and minor, that have occurred in former communist Germany.

They include such innovations as the arrival of travel agents, English lessons, key-cutting shops, lock-opening firms, insurance companies, street markets, improved traffic markings on the roads, traffic jams, mountain bikes, cycle lanes, car auctions, video stores, "adult stores," bananas on sale, Soviet uniforms on sale, factories for sale, development companies, management companies, French lingerie, techno-house music, Rio bikinis, new bus shelters, listings magazines, squatters, fast cars, political parties, mass tourism, the *Tag der Unie* (Day of Unity public holiday), graffiti, new yellow Telekom telephone booths, direct trains to Paris from Alexanderplatz, unemployment, new registration plates on East German cars (P for Potsdam, DD for Dresden), skips, *Bild* and *Die Zeit* on sale, and so on.

The changes that have occurred in former West Germany have been far less profound. They include such things as day trips to Potsdam, higher taxes, slow cars on the *Autobahns,* government offices moving (although slowly and often reluctantly) from Bonn, and mounting *Angst.*

There are good changes and bad happening in Germany. It is not an easy period of transition, but the inquiring tourist will find an enormous wealth of interest in our three cities. It is a rare opportunity to see history in the making.

THE PEOPLE

It hasn't been easy. The transition from decaying communism to aggressive capitalism has created stresses in the cities of *die Wende.* Under the old regime, people may have grumbled, but they were guaranteed a job and a house for life, as long as they didn't make trouble. It is no longer so. Many have lost their jobs, and some have even had their homes repossessed by former owners. Many of the big East German factories that once supplied the communist world are suddenly empty and becoming derelict.

Meanwhile, Western entrepreneurs pour into the cities. They drive flashy cars and stay at the best hotels in town (often the ones formerly reserved for Communist Party bosses). Western businessmen have virtually colonized certain areas of East German cities: the Gendarmenmarkt in East Berlin; the Münzgasse in Dresden. Local people can no longer afford to eat out in these areas; they are often stuck in the monotonous suburbs, eating cheap sausage and drinking beer. The cities of *die Wende* are in danger of becoming divided into enclaves of privilege and vast pools of poverty.

The people of East Germany share the lot of the Czechs, the Slovaks, the Poles and the Hungarians. They are having to adapt fast to the capitalist system, or go under. Their lives were once stable, if monotonous, governed by the plodding pace of "five-year plans." Now everything is in turmoil. A local restaurant quadruples its prices overnight; a corner shop that once stocked a few packs of butter is suddenly taken over by Benetton; an ugly but familiar statue of Lenin is hoisted off its pedestal by a crane one day; a street name changes from "Lenin Street" to "King Street" the next.

The East Germans are having to adapt to a new set of rules. The orders once came from Moscow, but they come now from Bonn, Frankfurt and New York. There are new jobs in rising businesses, but they tend to go to applicants from western Germany. The East Germans do not have the right skills, or the right power-clothes, or the right eye-contact. They are out in the cold. Some who want to succeed have started to learn English, but many have drifted to western Germany in search of work. For those over 50 looking for work, the future looks bleak.

The West Germans have not always been very sympathetic. They complain that East Germans are lazy and stupid, but it is, of course, not that simple. East Germans have a different set of priorities, more old-fashioned ideas. They like to talk about their family, or their favorite forest walk. They don't get excited by BMW Series 5 cars, or the latest Nintendo game. They don't expect that much out of life, having perhaps inherited something of the fatalism of the Russians. They are perhaps also wary. They had Hitler, followed by Stalin. They might well ask themselves if capitalism is just another false dream.

It will change. Young people are now flocking to see Hollywood movies, where they pick up the latest ideas about fashion, fast cars and careers. People are traveling, too, to cities like Paris and Los Angeles — cities that once seemed as remote as the moon. It will not take long for the cities of *die Wende* to become carbon-copies of Frankfurt and Munich.

But maybe not. It may be that the people of *die Wende* will hold onto a different vision of society, and resist some of the changes that are being forced upon them. It would be good if something positive could be salvaged from all those years of communist rule.

GERMANY
DENMARK
Baltic Sea
North Sea
Schleswig - Holstein
Kiel
Rostock
Lübeck
Mecklenburg
HAMBURG
Bremerhaven
Oldenburg
Bremen
Brandenburg
POLAND
NETHERLANDS
Niedersachsen
BERLIN
Potsdam
Osnabrück
Hannover
Sachsen -
Braunschweig
Magdeburg
Münster
Bielefeld
Nordrhein - Westfalen
Anhalt
Duisburg
Dortmund
Halle
Essen
Kassel
Leipzig
Sachsen
Düsseldorf
Dresden
Erfurt
KÖLN
Chemnitz
Aachen
Bonn
Thuringen
BELG.
Hessen
Koblenz
Rheinland -
Frankfurt
CZECH REPUBLIC
Mainz
Würzburg
LUX.
Pfalz
Mannheim
Nürnberg
Saarbrücken
Heidelberg
Karlsruhe
Bayern
Baden -
Regensburg
Stuttgart
FRANCE
Augsburg
Wurttemberg
MÜNCHEN
AUSTRIA
Freiburg
0 50 100 150km
0 50 100 miles
SWITZERLAND

The Porcelain Cities

Porcelain is a curious rarity. Some people loathe it, but others will pay a fortune to own one tiny Rococo figurine. The cities of Berlin, Potsdam and Dresden were all major centers of porcelain manufacture in the 18thC, and their decorative arts museums are crammed with examples. Some of the work is good, and some is plain ugly, but it provides a fascinating reflection of 18thC taste.

The history of porcelain is teeming with intrigues and adventures. The secret Chinese formula for manufacturing white porcelain was discovered in Dresden in 1709 by Johannes Böttger. Augustus the Strong, his employer, promptly imprisoned Böttger, in order to keep the secret, or *arcanum,* from being discovered by anyone else. Despite the strictest security, the process was leaked by Böttger's assistant, and rival factories were soon founded in 1719 at Vienna and Venice.

MEISSEN
Augustus the Strong founded the first porcelain factory in Europe at Meissen, 23km (14 miles) downstream of Dresden on the River Elbe. The Meissen factory produced ornate porcelain dinner services for some of the great royal families of Europe. The whimsical figurines depicting pale-faced women had the same Rococo charm as Watteau's paintings. Augustus the Strong was the first compulsive collector of porcelain, and he conceived a bold plan to create a Japanese Palace in Dresden that would be crammed with the finest porcelain, and little else. He began to order objects from Meissen, including life-sized animals. This sparked off a trend throughout the royal palaces of Europe. Most rulers could not afford to fill an entire palace, but they could at least create a *Porzellanzimmer,* a porcelain room.

The Meissen factory continued to turn out traditional porcelain during the communist era, earning the country much-needed foreign currency. Other East German industries failed soon after reunification, but the **Meissen** factory is still flourishing.

BERLIN
Berlin's porcelain industry began in 1751 with the foundation of a factory by Wilhelm Caspar Wegeley, a local merchant. Johann Benckengraff, an arcanist trained at the Höchst porcelain works, was put in charge of the factory, which produced ware (marked with the letter W) imitating the elegant Rococo style of Meissen porcelain.

The Wegeley factory was patronized by Frederick the Great, who created a "Porcelain Room" at Schloss Charlottenburg. Inspired by Augustus the Strong's Porzellanzimmer at Dresden, it was filled from floor to ceiling with precious vases. The Prussian ruler lost interest in the Berlin factory after gaining control of the Meissen factory early in the Seven Years' War. Deprived of royal patronage, the business collapsed in 1757.

A second factory was founded in 1761 by a Berlin banker, Johann Ernst Gotzkowsky. Frederick the Great bought the business in 1763, renaming it the **Königliche Porzellan-Manufaktur**, or **KPM**. The Royal Porcelain

Factory moved from its original site in Leipziger Strasse to its present location near S-Bahnhof Tiergarten in 1870.

The enthusiasm for Classical Antiquity in early 19thC Berlin led KPM to produce large Grecian urns modeled on Classical amphora. Known as *Ansichtsporzellan,* the vases were hand-painted with miniature scenes of Neoclassical Berlin or Potsdam. The factory also produced copies of Neoclassical works, such as Schadow's famous statue of the Princesses Luise and Friederike (the original is now on view in Berlin's ALTE NATIONALGALERIE). After the Battle of Waterloo, KPM made a dinner-service (now in Apsley House, London) to present to the Duke of Wellington as a token of Anglo-Prussian friendship.

Jugendstil (Art Nouveau) ceramics were introduced at KPM by Theodor Hermann Schmuz-Baudiss, while in the 1920s prominent Bauhaus artists designed simple modern Berlin porcelain.

With the foundation of the Weimar Republic in 1918, the factory was renamed the **Staatliche Porzellan-Manufaktur** (State Porcelain Factory). Destroyed during an air raid in 1943, the factory was rebuilt in 1953, and the name KPM restored in 1988.

PORCELAIN COLLECTIONS IN BERLIN, POTSDAM AND DRESDEN

The largest collection of porcelain on view in Berlin is at the KUNSTGEWERBEMUSEUM. The BERLIN-MUSEUM, the MÄRKISCHES MUSEUM and the Schinkel-Pavillon at SCHLOSS CHARLOTTENBURG have a number of 18thC and 19thC works originating from KPM, while the BRÖHAN-MUSEUM has some striking Art Nouveau and Art Deco porcelain.

In Dresden, an exquisite collection of porcelain, mainly Meissen ware, is displayed in the PORZELLANSAMMLUNG. The CHINESISCHES TEEHAUS in Potsdam displays a small collection of Chinese and German porcelain in a glittering Rococo interior.

Visiting Northern Germany: practical information

This chapter contains four sections:

- BEFORE YOU GO, below
- GETTING THERE, page 19
- ON-THE-SPOT INFORMATION, page 20
- EMERGENCY INFORMATION, page 23

Each section is organized thematically rather than alphabetically. Summaries of subject headings are printed in CAPITALS at the top of most pages. For more localized information on Berlin, Potsdam and Dresden, see pages 53, 211 and 258.

Before you go

GERMAN NATIONAL TOURIST OFFICES
UK 65, Curzon St., London W1Y 7PE ☎(071) 495 3990
USA 747 3rd Ave., 33rd floor, New York, NY 10017 ☎(212) 308 3300

- There are also offices in **Los Angeles** ☎(213) 688 7332 and **Toronto** ☎(416) 968 1570.

DOCUMENTS REQUIRED
US citizens need a valid **passport**, while for citizens of countries of the European Union, a passport or **national identity card** is the only document required, if your visit to Berlin does not exceed three months.

If you intend to drive in Germany, you must have a valid national **driver's license**, and, if taking a vehicle into the country, you will need a **national identity plate** and the **vehicle registration certificate**.

TRAVEL INSURANCE
It is advisable to travel with an insurance policy that covers loss of deposits paid to airlines, hotels, tour operators, etc., and the cost of dealing with emergency requirements, such as special tickets home and extra nights in a hotel. To obtain on-the-spot cover, contact your local travel agent before departure.

MEDICAL EXPENSES
It is worth making arrangements before departure to cover costs in case you fall ill while in Germany. **Citizens of the European Union** are entitled to the same cover as Germans, provided that they can produce an

E111 form. This document, valid for a specified period, can be obtained before departure from a Social Security office in an EU country.

US nationals need private medical insurance when traveling to Germany, to avoid the risk of a large hospital bill. Most travel agents sell policies for short trips abroad, and American Express can offer a range of policies for cardholders.

IAMAT, or the International Association for Medical Assistance to Travelers, has a list of English-speaking doctors who will call, for a fee. The organization has member hospitals and clinics throughout Europe, including a number in Berlin and other parts of Germany. Membership of IAMAT is free. For further information on worldwide traveling, and a directory of doctors and hospitals, write to **IAMAT** *(417 Center Street, Lewiston, NY 14092, USA, or 57 Voirets, 1212 Grand-Lancy, Genève, Switzerland).*

MONEY

The unit of currency is the *Deutschmark* (DM), divided into 100 *Pfennige* (Pf). There are coins for 1, 2, 5, 10, 20 and 50 *Pfennige,* as well as DM1, DM2 and DM5. Banknotes are issued in denominations of DM10, DM20, DM50, DM100, DM500 and DM1,000. East German currency is no longer valid. Old East German banknotes weighing 2,000 tonnes were stored in a disused mine, to be turned ultimately into compost.

The banknotes issued by the Deutsches Bundesbank bear the portraits of illustrious Germans. The troubled face of Luther graces the old DM50 note, while the more recent notes in this denomination show the smiling face of Rococo architect Balthasar Neumann. The attractive woman on the DM20 note is Annette von Dröste-Hülshoff (1797-1848), considered to be Germany's greatest woman writer.

Eurocheques are the normal method of settling bills in Germany. The use of charge or credit cards is not as common as in the US or UK, although hotels, upmarket restaurants and large stores will normally accept the major cards, such as American Express, Diners Club, MasterCard and Visa. Lower-priced restaurants often do not accept payment by card.

Travelers without Eurocheques may find it useful to obtain travelers checks from one of the major issuing companies. American Express travelers checks can be obtained on the spot in any local office, although it may take several days to order them through an agent. **It is important to note separately the serial numbers of your checks and the telephone number to call in case of loss.** American Express also provide a fast refund of lost or stolen checks through their local offices or agents.

Currency may be changed and travelers checks and Eurocheques cashed at all banks, and at *Wechselstube* in major railway stations and airports, which have the advantage of longer opening hours. Some department stores, such as **KaDeWe** in Berlin, will also handle foreign exchange.

American Express also has a **MoneyGram®** money transfer service, making it possible to wire money worldwide in just minutes from any American Express Travel Service Office. This service is available to all customers and is not limited to American Express Card members.

CUSTOMS ALLOWANCES

Since January 1, 1993 there has been no restriction on the quantities of duty-paid goods you can take **from one European Union country to another**, provided they are for your own use and not for resale. In practice, this means that quantities must be reasonable and not excessive.

- **For travel within the EU**, allowances considered to be "reasonable" for personal use are very generous indeed; any person over 17 may import 60 liters of champagne or 90 liters of table wine, *plus* 110 liters of beer, *plus* 10 liters of spirits or 20 liters of fortified wine, *plus* 800 cigarettes or one kilogram of tobacco.
- **Visitors traveling from countries outside the EU**, such as the US, will still have to declare any goods in excess of the German Customs allowances: these vary according to whether you are an EU or non-EU national. The duty-free limit for a non-EU national is very much lower: 2 liters of table wine *plus* one liter of spirits, or two liters of sparkling wine, *plus* 200 cigarettes or 250 grams of tobacco, *plus* 50 grams of perfume.
- **For all travelers**, the import allowance for all other goods (such as perfume, electrical goods and gifts bought tax-free) brought into Germany is set for all EU countries at ECU 90 (about DM171 or $100). This figure may increase in response to pressure from business.
- **Goods bought in duty-free shops within the EU** will continue to be subject to much stricter limits until June 30, 1999, so do not rely on being able to buy large supplies at the airport or on the boat.
- Fuller details are available at ports and airports or, for British residents, from their local Customs and Excise office. It is advisable to carry dated receipts for new or more valuable items (e.g., portable computers, cameras etc.) to avoid the remote possibility of being charged duty.

VAT REFUNDS

Visitors are exempt from paying Value-Added Tax (*MWS* or *Mehrwertsteuer*) on purchases above a certain value, on completion of a simple form and presentation of a passport at the time of purchase. However, to validate the refund, which will be made to you at your home address, or through a charge or credit card refund, you must present the paperwork and goods at a checkpoint before the passport control on leaving the country. Allow enough time to do this.

TIME ZONES

Germany, like most Western European countries, observes **Central European Time**, which is one hour ahead of **Greenwich Mean Time** in the winter and two hours ahead in the summer, i.e., one hour ahead of Great Britain most of the year. It is six hours ahead of (US) **Eastern Standard Time** and 7–9 hours ahead of the other US time zones.

CLIMATE

Northern Germany has a continental climate, with cold winters (hovering around 2°C/35°F from November to February), hot summers (rising to around 25°C/77°F in July), and rain throughout the year.

The best times for visiting are spring and early summer. *Berliner Luft* (Berlin air) has been praised in song for its invigorating qualities, but it now suffers the pollution typical of most large cities.

WHAT TO WEAR

Pack some warm clothes if you are visiting Berlin, Potsdam or Dresden in winter, and take strong shoes if you intend to walk in the woods. Germans tend to wear casual clothes, and there are no rigid rules about dress.

GENERAL DELIVERY (POSTE RESTANTE)

Letters to be collected should be marked *Hauptpostlagernd* and sent to the main post office *(Hauptpostamt)* of the relevant city. See PRACTICAL INFORMATION for each city for fuller details.

Getting there

Northern Germany is readily accessible to travelers from the US by air and from the UK and Continental Europe by air, sea, coach and rail.

BY AIR

Berlin is served by a large number of international and domestic flights at its three airports. The airport at **Dresden** is small, and most services are short-hop flights to other German cities. There are also direct international connections to Paris, Zurich, Moscow and Budapest.

BY RAIL

The German railway network is currently run by two separate organizations: the former West German network **Deutsche Bundesbahn** (DB) and the former East German network **Deutsche Reichsbahn** (DR).

These networks have been rapidly improved in recent years, and fast, comfortable international trains now run direct to Berlin from many capital cities including Paris (13–14 hours), Brussels (11–12 hours), Copenhagen (8 hours), Warsaw (10 hours), Moscow (31 hours), Prague ($6\frac{1}{2}$ hours), Vienna (12 hours), Budapest ($16\frac{1}{2}$ hours), Sofia (23 hours) and Belgrade ($22\frac{1}{2}$ hours).

Sleek new **Inter City Express (ICE)** trains now run on the major routes through Germany. These luxurious high-speed trains travel at up to 250kph (155mph) and feature airline-style seats, a conference room, on-board phone and fax, and a smart restaurant. Tickets are more expensive than on other trains. Comfortable **EuroCity (EC)** trains run directly to Berlin, Potsdam and Dresden from major European cities. **InterCity (IC)** trains run on other international routes. Overnight services use rather older **Schnellzug (D)** trains.

The much-delayed opening of the Eurotunnel, now expected on May 6, 1994, will eventually cut the journey time from Britain by several hours, although this will offer a more useful time-saving once the rail lines in Britain, Belgium and Germany are better developed.

BY SEA

From Britain to Germany, regular train-and-ferry services operate from London's major railway stations. There are two main ferry routes: from Harwich to Hoek van Holland (crossing time 6 hours) and from Ramsgate to Ostend (crossing time 4 hours).

The fastest sea crossing is by Jetfoil from Ramsgate to Ostend (crossing time 1 hour 45 minutes).

One way to arrive in Dresden is to take a cruise ship down the Elbe from Hamburg to Dresden. This new inland route was opened soon after German reunification. The seven-day trip takes you through former East Germany, past the historic towns of Wittenberg and Meissen. See page 259 for fuller details.

BY COACH

Direct coaches run to Berlin from many major European cities, including London, Paris, Brussels, Amsterdam and Frankfurt. They offer a slightly cheaper and sometimes faster alternative to train travel.

On-the-spot information

PUBLIC HOLIDAYS

January 1; Easter: *Karfreitag* (**Good Friday**), *Ostersonntag* (**Easter Sunday**) and *Ostermontag* (**Easter Monday**); May Day, **May 1**; *Himmelfahrt* (Ascension — **6th Thursday after Easter**); *Pfingstsonntag* (Whit Sunday — **second Sunday after Ascension**) and *Pfingstmontag* (Whit Monday — **second Monday after Ascension**); *Fronleichnam* (Corpus Christi — **first Thursday after Whitsun**); *Gesetzlicher Feiertag*, **June 17**; Day of German Unity, **October 3**; *Allerheiligen* (All Saints' Day), **November 1**; *Busstag* (Day of National Repentance), **3rd Wednesday in November**; *Weihnachten* (Christmas Day — **December 25**) and *2 Weihnachten* (**December 26**).

BANKS AND CURRENCY EXCHANGE

Currency transactions are dealt with at the desk marked *Devisen,* and the money is handed over at the *Kasse* (cash desk). Banks in Germany are normally open Monday to Friday 8.30am–1pm and 2.30–4pm, and two afternoons a week until 6pm. See also MONEY on page 17.

SHOPPING HOURS

Shop opening hours in Germany are strictly regulated by law. Normally, stores are open Monday to Friday 9am–6pm, Saturday 9am–1pm and, often, Thursday until 8.30pm, although department stores may stay open Monday to Friday until 6.30pm and Saturday until 2pm. Shops remain open until 4pm on *langer Samstag,* the first Saturday of the month, and the four Saturdays before Christmas.

Only florists and bakers may open on Sunday, the latter perhaps because many Germans could not face a day without *Kuchen* (cake).

MUSEUM OPENING HOURS

Museums in Germany are normally open Tuesday to Sunday 9am–5pm. Most museums are closed on Monday. Large museums normally stop admitting visitors about 30 minutes before closing time. In this book, specific details are given with each A to Z entry, but all such information can be liable to change and you are advised to check ahead.

MAIL SERVICES AND POST OFFICES

Post offices Marked *Post* or *Postamt,* post offices are usually open Monday to Friday 8am–6pm, Saturday 8am–noon.
Postcodes A national five-digit system was introduced in East and West Germany in 1993.
General Delivery (poste restante) See previous page.

TELEPHONE AND FAX SERVICES

To call Germany from abroad Dial the international code (US/Canada **011**, UK **010**) then **49** (for Germany) and then the telephone number, leaving off the initial 0 on the area code.
Public telephones Marked *Fernsprecher,* public phones are usually found at main squares, railway and U-Bahn stations, cafés and department stores. Phones take 10 Pfennige, DM1 and DM5 coins. Phones marked *Kartentelefon* or *Telefonieren ohne Münzen* are operated by a phonecard *(Telefonkarte),* which are sold at post offices.
To make a call The telephone networks of East and West Germany have now been merged. The notoriously inefficient East German telephone network is currently being improved by Telekom. Until completion (and no date is yet fixed) you may have some difficulty reaching numbers in eastern Berlin, Potsdam or Dresden. Keep dialing until you get a connection.
Toll-free numbers These numbers start with the digits **0130**.
To call home from Germany Key the international code (**00**) then the country code (**1** for US, **44** for UK), and then the telephone number, leaving off any initial 0 on the area code.
Home Direct While in Germany, if you wish to call home, key the Home Direct number for your country and you will be connected (toll-free) with a local operator. You then agree the method of payment (charge/credit card, AT&T card etc) and the call is made for you.

- **AT&T USA Direct** ☎0130-0010
- **MCI US Direct** ☎0130-0012
- **Sprint US Direct** ☎0130-0013
- **BT Direct UK** ☎0130-80 0044

Faxes Urgent documents can sometimes be sent from the public fax at a large post office. Most major hotels will send faxes for non-residents.
Telegrams ☎1131. These can be sent from any post office or by telephone.
Directory inquiries (Germany) ☎1188
Directory inquiries (abroad) ☎00118

ELECTRIC CURRENT

The electric current in Germany is 220V. Plugs are standard European, with two round pins. Take an adaptor with you.

PUBLIC LAVATORIES (REST ROOMS)

Public lavatories are located on main squares, in department stores, fast-food outlets and railway stations, and, in Berlin, at U-Bahn and S-Bahn stations. A charge of about 50 Pfennige is normally made.

The German word is *Toilette*, although you will often see the letters **WC** on the door. Men's lavatories are often marked with **H** *(Herren)* or **M** *(Männer)*; women's toilets are marked **F** *(Frauen)* or **D** *(Damen).*

LAWS AND REGULATIONS

Look at Germans standing at cashpoint machines. They routinely stand two meters back from the person at the till to ensure privacy. That tells you something about Germans. They respect rules, and expect visitors to do the same. You may be scolded for jaywalking, loitering at a shop entrance or even taking a baby out without a hat. This somewhat nagging tone is reflected in the signs that appear at almost every flight of steps in German parks, warning users *Betreten bei Schnee und Glätte auf eigene Gefahr* (use in snow and ice at own risk). German intolerance is at its worst on autobahns, where it is customary for cars to flash their headlights angrily at slower vehicles blocking their lane.

Germans are deeply fond of their pine forests, and strict laws are enacted, to prevent environmental damage. Ramblers in the woods are expected to keep to the marked paths and to avoid smoking in summer.

So many activities in Germany are *streng verboten* (strictly forbidden) that it comes as a shock to many visitors to discover that nudist sunbathing is widely tolerated on beaches and in parks and forests. Officially permitted only in areas designated **FKK** *(Freikörperkultur),* nudity can sometimes occur in unofficial places without apparently causing offense.

DRIVING IN GERMANY

You should have no need ever to use a car in Berlin, Potsdam or Dresden, but, if you do drive, remember that it is strictly prohibited to pass a stationary tram. The minimum age for driving in Germany is 18.

ETIQUETTE

It is normal to shake hands when you meet someone in Germany. Say *Guten Tag* when you enter a store and *Auf Wiedersehen* as you leave. Be sure to apologize with *Entschuldigen Sie* or *Pardon* (sorry) if you accidentally tread on someone's foot. Men and women should always cover their heads when entering a Jewish cemetery or synagogue, out of respect for religious custom.

TIPPING

In restaurants and cafés, service charges are almost always included in the check, although the sum is rounded up to the nearest DM.

Taxi drivers will expect about 10 percent of the fare.

Emergency information

EMERGENCY SERVICES

Coins are not needed for emergency calls from public telephones.

- **Police** ☎110
- **Fire** ☎112
- **Ambulance** ☎112 in West Berlin; ☎115 in East Berlin, Potsdam and Dresden

AUTOMOBILE ACCIDENTS

- Do not admit liability or incriminate yourself.
- Ask any witness(es) to stay and give a statement.
- Contact the police.
- Exchange names, addresses, car details and insurance company details with any other drivers involved.
- Give a statement to the police, who will compile a report acceptable to insurance companies.

CAR BREAKDOWNS

- Put on flashing hazard warning lights, and place a warning triangle 50 meters (55 yards) behind the car.
- ☎ police, or the **ADAC** (road patrol). For ☎ numbers, see under the relevant city.

LOST PASSPORT

Contact the local police and your consulate immediately.

LOST TRAVELERS CHECKS/CHARGE/CREDIT CARDS

Notify the local police immediately, then follow the instructions provided with your travelers checks, or contact the issuing company.

Contact your consulate *(addresses on page 62)* or **American Express** *(☎0130-853100; 24-hours, toll-free)* if stranded with no money.

LOST PROPERTY

Report all losses to the police immediately, as insurance claims may not be accepted without a police report.

EMERGENCY PHRASES

Help! *Hilfe!*
There has been an accident. *Ein Unfall!*
Where is the nearest telephone/hospital? *Wo ist das nächste Telefon/Krankenhaus?*
Call an ambulance! *Bitte, einen Krankenwagen, schnell.*
Call the police! *Die Polizei, bitte.*

- See also GERMAN IN A NUTSHELL on page 319.

Berlin is a city with two centres — the cluster of expensive hotels, bars, cinemas, shops round the Memorial Church, a sparkling nucleus of light, like a sham diamond in the shabby twilight of the town; and the self-conscious civic centre of buildings round the Unter den Linden, carefully arranged. In grand international styles, copies of copies, they assert our dignity as a capital city — a parliament, a couple of museums, a State bank, a cathedral, an opera, a dozen embassies, a triumphal arch; nothing has been forgotten. And they are all so pompous, so very correct — all except the cathedral, which betrays in its architecture, a flash of that hysteria which flickers always behind every grave, grey Prussian facade.

Christopher Isherwood, *Goodbye to Berlin* (1939)

Berlin

The War, the Wall, the Change

There were once two cities called Berlin, but now there is just one. That, anyway, is the story you are told. The Wall that for 38 years divided communist East Berlin from capitalist West Berlin has gone for good. The concrete slabs daubed with graffiti were hoisted by crane and shipped off long ago to the auction houses and museums of the West. The rest was gradually broken apart by "the woodpeckers" — people who knocked off rough lumps with hammers, and sold them to tourists at the Brandenburg Gate.

Gone are the days when you would come across military signs printed with the scary warning: "You are leaving the American sector." You can now walk from the leafy villa quarters of Dahlem in the west to the tatty apartments of Köpenick in the east without anyone asking to see your passport. That was not possible before November 1989 — a trip across Berlin was once fraught with difficulties.

The rules were strict. You had to go through the underground checkpoint at Bahnhof Friedrichstrasse, changing 25 Deutschmarks into 25 East German Marks. You had to spend the East German money before you left, which was not easy. Museum entry cost a few Pfennige; a beer-and-sausage lunch (it was hard to find anything else) used up about one Mark at most. The bookstore on Unter den Linden stocked little except for some guidebooks to the Black Sea resorts and a stack of Russian–Dutch dictionaries. The only luxury was ice cream, so you would order the biggest *Eis* on the menu in the most expensive hotel in town, and you would still have money to burn and nowhere to burn it. You had to leave East Berlin by midnight, but most visitors ran out of enthusiasm by about nine o'clock, when the streets were already empty apart from the occasional puttering Trabant car. You would hunt for the transit hall (a sign hidden in the shrubbery pointed simply to *Ausgang,* exit), and take the U-Bahn back to Bahnhof Zoo. It was just a few stops on the subway, but it felt as if you had arrived in a different country — which it was, in those days. You emerged from the U-Bahn to find that the nightlife on Kurfürstendamm had not yet even begun.

Berlin was simple to understand in those days. The divided city was a miniature version of the postwar world. The Wall provided a visual aid to the politics of the period. East Berlin represented drab, regimented communism; West Berlin symbolized the dynamism and freedom of capitalism. The two sides of the great political divide could scowl at each other across the barbed wire at Checkpoint Charlie. It felt dangerous, the mood resembling that in an espionage movie, especially in Kreuzberg district, where many streets came to an abrupt end at the Wall. Tourists and politicians went to Berlin to see the Wall, to stand on the wooden platform near the Tiergarten and look into the East Berlin, watching the guards watching them through binoculars.

TWO CITIES OR ONE?

And now? What is Berlin like without its famous Wall? Like Venice without its canals, say some. Others claim that the city has lost its edge. A few Germans say, only half joking, that the Wall should be rebuilt, and a section was actually reconstructed near the Spree, to satisfy the wishes of tourists. But the truth is that the Wall never played a big part in the lives of most Berliners. It was often nothing more than a minor irritation, like a river or a highway running through the city. A few in the East tried to jump it; some artists in the West attempted to improve it with graffiti. But most people on both sides ignored it, and simply carried on with their lives.

The demolition of the Wall has actually made Berlin a much more interesting city to visit. The combined metropolis now sprawls across an area of roughly 1,000 square kilometers (386 square miles), with a fast-growing population of already well over three million. In cultural terms, the merger of the two Berlins has created an embarrassment of riches. No other European city — no other city in the world, perhaps — can match Berlin's three opera houses, two national art galleries, two zoos and three international airports.

This richesse is not likely to last forever. Money is much scarcer in Berlin these days, and many cultural organizations face painful cuts. Theaters and concert halls may close, and many art galleries will have to merge at some time. Yet whatever happens, Berlin will still have one of the greatest concentrations of culture in the world. The sights every visitor should try to see include the reconstructed Greek temples in the Pergamon-Museum and the steam locomotives in the transport museum; the palaces of Charlottenburg and Grunewald; the art treasures of the Gemäldegalerie and the Bode-Museum; the head of Nefertiti and the paintings in the Brücke-Museum; the handsome architecture on Gendarmenmarkt and Unter den Linden; the Grunewald forest and the Wannsee lake.

ISOLATION

Berlin is not always an easy city. Sometimes it can feel hostile and vaguely threatening. This is partly because its past still haunts Berlin. The city is littered with the relics of the Imperial past, of the Nazi regime, and of the communist era too. But it is more than just history that makes Berlin a hostile place. The city is isolated by its location, stranded in the midst of dank marshes and gloomy pine woods, far from the mainstream of Europe.

It is not a natural capital; the major trade routes by land and sea do not touch Berlin, and it seems a long way from anywhere important. The nearest big city is run-down Leipzig, a 183-kilometer drive down the *Autobahn*. The closest city with a healthy economy and any significant nightlife is Hamburg, which lies to the north, on the far side of a 289-kilometer stretch of flat nothingness.

It took an outsider like Christopher Isherwood to sense the isolation. Describing the winter of 1932 in *Goodbye to Berlin,* he wrote, "Outside, in the night, beyond the last new-built blocks of concrete flats, where the streets end in frozen allotment gardens, are the Prussian plains. You can feel them all around you, tonight, creeping in upon the city, like an immense waste of unhomely ocean — sprinkled with leafless copses and ice-lakes and tiny villages which are remembered only as the outlandish names of battlefields in half-forgotten wars."

Paintings, too, sum up this spirit, and many are to be found in Schloss Charlottenburg. Not the whimsical Watteaus collected by Frederick the Great, but the moody works by Caspar David Friedrich, in which one dead tree or a solitary monk stands for the human condition. Even today, in this city of many millions, you can find yourself quite alone on the deserted shore of the Tegeler See watching the sun set, or in the depths of the Grunewald, where the only sound is the distant cry of a bird.

The movies shot in Berlin in the 1920s tell the same story. They were frequently thrillers or horror movies, featuring a solitary murderer on the loose, or a single woman, like Marlene Dietrich or Brigitte Helm, exerting a fatal attraction. The songs by Kurt Weill were likewise dark and melancholy. Berlin was an edgy city long before the Cold War.

It took enormous energy and willpower to create a capital city in this dank region. Founded in the 13th century, Berlin was an insignificant dot on the map until the Hohenzollern rulers made it their capital. The Electors of Brandenburg gave the town a Baroque flavor that was calculated to rival Dresden and Munich. The Great Elector laid the basis for a cosmopolitan capital by his enlightened (and, no doubt, self-interested) toleration of Huguenot refugees. By the 18th century, one in five Berliners was of French origin.

But it was Frederick the Great who turned Berlin into a dazzling capital. Inspired by Louis XIV, he created a palace to rival Versailles in the watery landscape outside Potsdam. Later Kings of Prussia added to the allure of Berlin by building opera houses, theaters and monumental streets.

Yet another Berlin lay beneath the civilized veneer. The bullying Friedrich Wilhelm I — Frederick the Great's father — was driven by an obsessive militarism. He built up the army, exchanging porcelain for soldiers, and forced every male Berliner to drill on vast parade grounds such as the one at Tempelhofer Feld.

A more appealing Berlin developed in the 19th century under Friedrich Wilhelm IV. A romantic traveler with a deep love of Italy, he built ocher villas in Tuscan Renaissance style on the lakes to the southeast of Berlin — the setting for the genteel rituals of the Biedermeier era.

But the creation of the German Reich in 1871 brought an end to Biedermeier civility. The German Kaisers transformed Berlin into a fearful city, with massive government buildings designed to overwhelm (some are still standing in Mauerstrasse, looking as grim as ever). Factories boomed, and the German capital was transformed into one of the most modern cities in the world. The world's first electric tram ran through the

Berlin streets, and the U-Bahn (underground) and S-Bahn (overground) railways were models of Prussian efficiency. But it all ended with a mighty war that left millions dead, and the Kaiser in exile.

The Weimar Republic that followed seemed briefly to offer a new beginning. Berlin was no longer the seat of government, but it was still an exciting and dazzling city, and provided the setting in the 1920s for the most explosive era in modern European culture. German Expressionist painting flourished alongside decadent cabaret acts; Brecht wrote *The Threepenny Opera* and Dietrich sang *Falling in Love Again.* The world was mesmerized by the daring and decadence of Berlin, yet there was still something rotten in the state of Weimar. It showed up in the paintings of Otto Dix and the movies of Fritz Lang. The corruption spread inexorably under the Nazis, finally engulfing almost an entire continent. As Nazi torchlight parades marched through the Brandenburg Gate, Berlin was no longer admired, but feared as a cradle of evil. When the airmen of the British Bomber Command were ordered to strike Berlin in 1944, they did so with few regrets.

Berlin was carved up after the war into four sectors. The British held onto the western edge around Spandau, with its famous prison, while the Americans were concentrated in the leafy suburb of Zehlendorf, where they introduced an annual rodeo show, and stores selling *Hungry Jack Pancake Mix* and the like. The French kept a low profile out in Tegel, but the Russians in East Berlin played rough from the start. West Berlin was an irritating enclave in their sector of Germany, and they wanted it all. For nearly half a century, they tried every trick they could devise to squeeze out the Allies. They blockaded the road links, built the Wall and cut the telephone lines. But it did not work. The West hung onto Berlin, and pumped in money and troops to ensure its survival.

The Wall finally fell, one chilly night in November when nobody was expecting it. The regime that had seemed so tough suddenly fell apart. It was the most peaceful revolution in German history. The night in 1989 when the guards at the Berlin Wall unexpectedly began to allow people to cross the border *without* formalities was a rare moment of joy in German history. The world was briefly thrilled by the dramatic images of young Berliners scrambling onto the Wall that had divided their city for as long as they could remember. Scenes of East Berliners flooding through the breached Wall into the glare of television floodlights seemed unreal, like the moment in Beethoven's opera *Fidelio* when the prisoners emerge from captivity into the blinding daylight.

Berlin is now one city. Or is it? With the euphoria gone, some people say that there are still two Berlins. The concrete Wall may have gone, they say, but there still remains "a Wall in the head," dividing *Ossis* (East Germans) from *Wessis* (West Germans). There are grumblers, that's true, but for most Berliners the end of the Wall means a return to normal life. Which, being Berlin, means tough times.

BERLIN TODAY

Everyone has an image of Berlin, usually a wrong one. It maybe comes from watching old spy movies, or looking at Expressionist paintings, or listening to cabaret songs. Berlin is sometimes seen as a sinister, seedy and wickedly sexy place. People picture spies lurking in the shadows of the S-Bahn viaducts, smoke-filled cabarets, and tanks lined up at Checkpoint Charlie. The city isn't at all like that. You have to sketch in the Poles selling cartons of orange juice at the Brandenburg Gate; the property speculators in shiny Porsches cruising past apartment blocks in Prenzlauer Berg; the kids riding mountain bikes on the dusty strip where the Wall used to run.

Berlin is an odd city, where you find yourself doing unexpected things, at unlikely hours. Take eating. You tend not to eat at regular hours. You might eat two breakfasts, no lunch, and a big slice of cake in the afternoon. Or you may be hit by hunger pangs at two in the morning, having forgotten to eat since lunchtime. Never mind. There's always a sausage stand glowing in the dark, or a café that stays open until dawn.

Berlin is odd, too, in that it preserves the ragged wastelands left behind from 1945. Other German cities have been carefully rebuilt, like a smashed porcelain vase, but Berlin still shows the cracks. There is a certain raw edge to this city that you do not find in Cologne or Frankfurt. The broken spire of the Kaiser-Wilhelm-Gedächtniskirche and the wasteland at the Anhalter Bahnhof are permanent mementoes of the war. It is as if Berliners need a reminder of the city's earlier *Sturm und Drang*.

Berlin is full of surprises. The forest is one. You can stay in a hotel deep in the pine woods, and be in downtown Berlin for a nine o'clock meeting. Ten minutes out of Zoo station on the S-Bahn, you might look out of the carriage window and see someone riding a horse along a sandy forest track. Ten minutes later, the S-Bahn stops at Wannsee, where people pile out with buckets and towels to grab a space on the beach.

The beach? . . . Yes, there are beaches in Berlin, dozens of them, complete with straw chairs to keep off the wind. Berlin is still half wilderness. Almost a third of the city is covered with placid lakes, dark forests and muddy moorland. You can even board a steamer at Wannsee to visit the Pfaueninsel follies, or sit on deck as a boat chugs through the heart of the city.

You see the contrasts best from the S-Bahn. In one hour, you can ride across the entire city, from east to west. You board at Erkner, deep in the birch woods, not far from reed-fringed lakes with nesting waterfowl. The people in the carriage are perhaps dozing, or grumbling about rising rents, or reading one of the many sex-and-scandal magazines that have flooded eastern Germany. The doors shut and the train moves off, slowly, creakily, through the forests that were once East German, past little allotment gardens with leeks and cabbages, and crumbling factories that nobody wants to buy. You glimpse the shape of Trabbis abandoned in the fields; signs advertising cars and beer; a mixture of communist wreckage and capitalist glitz. Look carefully—for in a few years all will be different again.

The train goes through one grimy station after another, then there is a lot of movement at Bahnhof Friedrichstrasse. One batch of people in shabby clothes gets off the train, and a different batch of smartly dressed people gets on. This is still a sort of frontier between East and West. By the time the train pulls into Bahnhof Zoo, you are in a different city. East

Berlin is still shabby and clapped-out, whereas West Berlin looks clean and orderly, like a piece of West German electronic equipment. The people look more awake. They are maybe talking about the latest play at the Hebbel-Theater, or reading the *Wall Street Journal.* They don't worry about rents, or jobs, or the price of 4711 perfume.

BERLIN TOMORROW

As soon as the Wall fell, people were busy inventing scenarios for the future. Germany was to be the capital of Germany, the meeting place of West and East, the ultimate city of the 21st century. Others saw Berlin as the movie capital of Europe, or the music capital of the world.

But these are only plans. In Berlin, people have come to be wary of predictions. No one in 1871 could have predicted that the second Kaiser of Germany would end his days in exile in the Netherlands, or that women would toil throughout the 1950s shifting the rubble of the bombed metropolis. Karl Marx, who studied law at Berlin University, once made the famous prediction that capitalism would wither away, but the reality was exactly the opposite. East German socialism collapsed almost overnight, and pieces of the Berlin Wall became mere souvenirs.

The politicians now hesitate, as if afraid of going forward. They long ago decided to move the parliament from Bonn to Berlin, but then they froze the process, as if afraid of going too far, too fast. The last thing Germans now want is to go back to 1871 when Berlin became the capital of Imperial Germany. The city has even been slow to change the old communist street names in East Berlin. Marx-Engels-Platz has gone back to being Lustgarten, but Karl-Marx-Allee (known as Stalinallee until the leader fell from grace) has retained its old name.

What now? You will have to look for yourself. Go to Potsdamer Platz, which was the busiest square in Europe in the 1930s. Have the cranes and construction trucks arrived, or is it still a vast wasteland with a circus tent and the ruins of an old hotel? Wander down Unter den Linden. Some people predicted a line of fashionable shops reaching from the Brandenburg Gate to the Spree, but it hasn't happened yet. Check to see if the Aeroflot office and the Skoda showroom are still there.

Another test is to look at the Reichstag. Is anything being built nearby to accommodate the German members of parliament? If not, why not? And is the old East German parliament building still standing on Lustgarten? Or have they started rebuilding the old royal palace on the site?

Changes are happening, but much more slowly than people predicted. The politicians from the wealthy West Berlin districts are now adapting to the routine of working in the Rote Rathaus on bleak Alexanderplatz instead of the cozy Rathaus Schöneberg. And at some point in the future, the civil servants and politicians will have to sell their villas in Bonn and hunt for something similar in Berlin. There are already plans underway for a major new international airport to the south of Berlin, a new station building at Bahnhof Zoo, and an entire new government quarter near the Reichstag. But nobody can say when it will happen. After the fall of the Berlin Wall, nothing seems certain any more. You can only guess.

Berlin: culture, history and background

Landmarks in Berlin's history

ELECTORS OF BRANDENBURG

c.1230: Two small settlements were established on the Spree River: Berlin, a trading outpost on the right bank, and Cölln, a fishing village on the island opposite. **1369**: Berlin became a leading member of the Hanseatic League, a powerful group of German trading towns. **1380**: Robber barons terrorized Berlin, and trade declined. **1414**: Robber barons crushed by Burggraf Friedrich of Nuremberg, of the House of Hohenzollern.

1415: Friedrich elected *Kurfürst* (Imperial Elector) of the North German region of Brandenburg. **1440**: Elector Friedrich II built the Stadtschloss on the island town of Cölln. Berlin became a royal residence and administrative center. Medieval privileges were eroded, but prosperity increased.

1517: Martin Luther led the Reformation in Germany, nailing 95 anti-Catholic theses to the door of the Schlosskirche at Wittenberg, 78km (48 miles) sw of Berlin. **1539**: Elector Joachim II introduced the Reformation to Berlin.

1618–48: The Thirty Years' War, a struggle between Protestant and Catholic states, was fought mainly on German soil. Berlin was repeatedly plundered by Swedish troops.

1640: The succession of the Great Elector, Friedrich Wilhelm I of Brandenburg. He trebled the strength of the army from 8,000 to 23,000 and increased the state's power by eroding civil liberties and granting privileges to the nobility. **1675**: The Swedish army was defeated at the Battle of Fehrbellin. Brandenburg became the strongest German state after Austria.

1685: The Great Elector enacted the Potsdam Edict, opening Berlin to Huguenots driven from France by the Revocation of the Edict of Nantes. Some 20,000 Protestant exiles settled in Brandenburg, including 5,000 in Berlin (mainly in the suburbs of Friedrichswerder and Dorotheenstadt), where they worked as merchants, artists, inventors and linen manufacturers. The Great Elector modeled Berlin on the mercantile cities of the Dutch Republic, where he had spent his youth. Quays were constructed along the Spree waterfront, and a canal was built between the Spree and the Oder.

1688: Friedrich III succeeded his father, and engaged Baroque architects to embellish the city, while Queen Sophie Charlotte, a friend of Descartes and Leibnitz, encouraged art, philosophy and the sciences.

Berlin became known as the Athens on the Spree. **1695**: The Baroque *Zeughaus* (arsenal) was built by Andreas Schlüter. **1696**: The Academy of Art was founded in Berlin.

THE KINGDOM OF PRUSSIA

1701: The Kingdom of Prussia was founded, combining Brandenburg and the duchy of Prussia. Friedrich Wilhelm III was crowned King Friedrich I at Königsberg, East Prussia (now Kaliningrad). The Academy of Science founded in Berlin, based on a proposal by the philosopher Leibnitz, who was appointed its first director.

1709: Berlin was expanded to include the settlements of Cölln, Friedrichswerder, Dorotheenstadt and Friedrichstadt. **1713**: King Friedrich Wilhelm I, the "Soldier King," succeeded his father, and devoted his energies to building up the army to 83,000 soldiers. Austere and devout, he was the first European king to wear uniform constantly, and elevated the Prussian officer corps to the highest rung of the aristocracy. Friedrich Wilhelm laid out large parade grounds such as Pariser Platz, Leipziger Platz, Mehringplatz and the Tempelhofer Feld (now Tempelhof airport). The parade grounds were linked by broad streets named Friedrichstrasse and Wilhelmstrasse in honor of the king.

1730: The future Frederick the Great rebelled against his father's strict regime. He attempted to flee Prussia, but was captured. **1735**: The city was encircled by a wall to facilitate the collection of tolls.

1740: King Frederick II — known as Frederick the Great — succeeded his unloved father. Pursuing a more enlightened policy, he embellished Berlin, building the Forum Fridericianum, Unter den Linden, the Alte Königliche Bibliothek and the Staatsoper.

1740–48: The War of the Austrian Succession was sparked off by Prussia's invasion of Silesia. Austrian troops occupied Berlin briefly in 1742.

1756–63: The Seven Years' War, during which Austria, France, Russia and Saxony combined forces against Prussia. **1759**: Prussia narrowly avoided defeat at the Battle of Kunersdorf. **1760**: Frederick the Great bombarded Dresden and occupied Saxony, gaining control of the Meissen porcelain factory. Russian troops occupied Berlin, but Russia dropped out of the alliance in 1762 and the war ended through exhaustion, leaving Prussia intact as one of the five major European powers.

1786: Friedrich Wilhelm II succeeded his father. **1791**: The Brandenburg Gate was built. **1792**: The Prussian army was defeated by the French at the Battle of Valmy. **1797**: Friedrich Wilhelm III succeeded his father.

1806: Napoleon defeated the Prussian army at the Battles of Jena and Auerstadt, and entered Berlin in triumph through the Brandenburg Gate. He then abolished the Holy Roman Empire, a loose German confederation founded in the 10thC. **1813**: Wars of Liberation. Napoleon was defeated at the Battle of Leipzig. The French occupation ended, and Prussia recovered the Ruhr. **1815**: The timely arrival of General Von Blücher's Prussian army played a decisive role in the defeat of Napoleon at Waterloo. A German Confederation under Hapsburg rule was established at the Congress of Vienna. **1838**: The first train ran from Berlin to Potsdam.

1840: Friedrich Wilhelm IV succeeded his father. **1848**: The German Revolution was sparked off by the overthrow of the French King Louis Philippe. Demonstrations in Berlin and elsewhere led to the drafting of a German constitution in Frankfurt. The Assembly asked Friedrich Wilhelm IV of Prussia to become king of a united Germany, but he refused.

1862: Bismarck was appointed Chancellor of Prussia. **1866**: The Prussian army led by Count Helmuth von Moltke defeated the Austrians at the Battle of Königgrätz.

1870–71: The Franco-Prussian War was sparked off by Napoleon III. Germany encircled the entire French army at Sedan, leading to a humiliating defeat and the German occupation of Alsace and Lorraine.

IMPERIAL GERMANY

1871: Bismarck forged a united German Empire (the Second Reich) out of 39 independent kingdoms and principalities that once belonged to the Holy Roman Empire. The Second Reich was proclaimed at Versailles. Wilhelm I, King of Prussia, was crowned Emperor, and Berlin became the imperial capital of an increasingly authoritarian society. Bismarck's policies ensured peace in Europe for 20 years, but German military build-up continued.

1878: The attempted assassination of Kaiser Wilhelm I in Berlin provided Bismarck with an excuse to persecute socialists. **1888**: Kaiser Wilhelm II succeeded his father. He dismissed Bismarck and assumed control of the army.

1914: Austria attacked Serbia, in response to the assassination of Archduke Franz Ferdinand at Sarajevo. Germany entered World War I to protect its ally Austria against a threatened attack from Russia. Germany attacked France, Russia's ally, through neutral Belgium, drawing Britain into the four-year carnage.

1917: The film studios Universal Film AG (UFA) were founded at Babelsberg, sw of Berlin, to produce German war propaganda movies.

1918: The German spring offensive on the Western Front failed. Realizing the inevitability of defeat, the German generals persuaded the Reichstag to negotiate for peace. Under the Treaty of Versailles, Germany was forced to pay massive war reparations. A naval mutiny at Kiel garrison sparked off the November Revolution, leading to anarchy in Berlin as Social Democratic Party (SPD) followers fought with communists. Kaiser Wilhelm II fled to the Netherlands.

THE WEIMAR REPUBLIC

1919: In the elections, the SPD gained a majority of seats, and Friedrich Ebert was elected President of the new republic. The Reichstag moved from Berlin to Weimar, where a model federal constitution was drawn up. The Spartacus Revolt crushed. **1920**: The National Assembly returned to Berlin. The Law of April 27 created the metropolis of *Gross-Berlin* (Greater Berlin), with a population of four million, through the fusion of seven towns, 59 villages and 27 estates. The Kapp Putsch, led by a Prussian civil servant, failed to topple the government.

1922: Walter Rathenau, the Jewish foreign minister, was assassinated by right-wing extremists angered by a treaty signed with Russia.

1923: France and Belgium occupied the Ruhr after Germany defaulted on reparations payments. A general strike in Germany led to massive inflation. A right-wing military putsch failed in Munich, led by Göring, Ludendorff and Hitler (who was imprisoned for 8 months for high treason).

1924: Generous US loans to Germany led to a brief economic boom. The French occupation of the Ruhr ended. Painting, theater and cabaret flourished in Berlin in conditions of relative political stability. **1925**: General Field Marshal von Hindenburg succeeded Ebert as president. **1926**: Joseph Goebbels, appointed by Hitler as Nazi party chief in Berlin, orchestrated clashes between Nazi stormtroopers and local communists. **1927**: Fritz Lang's movie *Metropolis* was released.

1929: The Wall Street Crash in October halted US loans to Germany, and unemployment soared to 3 million. **1930**: Marlene Dietrich became an overnight star, following the Berlin premiere of *The Blue Angel* on April 1. The Nazi party gained 107 seats in the Reichstag. **1932**: The Nazis gained 230 seats, to become the largest party in the Reichstag. Street violence in Berlin escalated, and Jewish businesses, theaters and cabarets were attacked. The Nazis suffered a setback, but only temporarily, when they lost 34 seats in the November elections. Hitler was appointed Chancellor of Germany in December.

NAZI GERMANY

1933: The German nightmare began. The Reichstag was burned down on February 27. The Weimar Republic was suspended in March. Jewish shops were boycotted in April, and Nazis burned books on the Opernplatz in May. Trade unions and opposition oolitical parties were outlawed. Countless artists, directors and writers fled from Berlin, among them Bertolt Brecht, Wassily Kandinsky and Billy Wilder. **1934**: The Night of the Long Knives (June 30), during which SA officers were murdered by Nazis.

1936: Hitler cut the ribbon on the first German *Autobahn.* The Berlin Olympics were exploited for Nazi propaganda. To Hitler's dismay, the Black American athlete Jesse Owens beat the allegedly invincible German runners, to win four gold medals at the games. **1938**: The Generals' Plot, an attempt on Hitler's life led by General Ludwig Beck, ended in failure. Hitler invaded the Sudetenland region of Czechoslovakia. Jewish properties in Berlin were destroyed in widespread riots in November.

1939: Britain and France declared war on Germany after the invasion of Poland in September. **1943–44**: The Battle of Berlin, during which the RAF dropped more than 30,000 tons of bombs on Berlin in an attempt to crush civilian morale. **1944**: The Von Stauffenberg Plot, in which Colonel Von Stauffenberg planted a bomb under Hitler's conference table at Rastenberg in East Prussia. Hitler survived the assassination attempt and the conspirators were executed.

1945: Soviet troops led by Marshal Zhukhov entered Berlin on April 21. Hitler shot himself in his underground bunker nine days later. The German army surrendered on April 30, after fierce street fighting. This was the moment Germans came to call *Stunde Nul* (Zero Hour). A few months after Germany's surrender, the Potsdam Agreement was signed by the US, Russia and Britain. Germany was divided into four sectors under US, British, French and Soviet control. Berlin was stripped of its status as capital of Germany. The Nuremberg Trials, held from **November 1945 to October 1946**, led to the execution of many prominent Nazis for crimes against humanity. Rudolf Hess and Albert Speer were imprisoned in Spandau prison for their role in the Nazi war machine.

DIVIDED GERMANY

1948: The Berlin Blockade was imposed in June by the Soviet Union, in an attempt to starve West Berlin into submission. Road and rail links through East Germany were closed, preventing essential supplies from reaching US, British and French sectors of the city. The Berlin Airlift was immediately organized by General Lucius D. Clay, to land essential supplies at Tempelhof airfield. Some 2.2 million tons were landed in 274,418 flights. East and West Berlin became increasingly polarized.

1949: The Soviet Blockade was lifted in May. The division of Germany was formalized by the enactment of the Basic Law in May, creating the German Federal Republic (West Germany), with Konrad Adenauer as the first Chancellor. The German Democratic Republic (East Germany) was established in October, with Otto Grotewohl as its first prime minister. Ernst Reuter was elected the first Mayor of West Berlin.

1950: A constitution was drawn up for Berlin as a special West German *Land* (state) under the control of the four powers. It became the *de jure* capital of West Germany, with Bonn as the *de facto* capital. The Berlin Film Festival was launched as part of a plan to rebuild Berlin's movie industry. **1952**: East Germany cut the telephone links between East and West Berlin.

1953: The East German government insisted on a 10 percent increase in productivity for no increase in pay, prompting strikes. The rebellion was crushed by Soviet troops — a foretaste of things to come in Prague and Budapest.

1961: Fearing war between US and Soviet Union, East Germans flooded into West Berlin. Walter Ulbricht ordered the construction of the 47km (29-mile) Berlin Wall as an "antifascist defense barrier" along the boundary of the Soviet sector.

1963: US President John F. Kennedy expressed solidarity with West Berliners in speech at Rathaus Schöneberg, West Berlin's town hall.

1969: Chancellor Willy Brandt, a former West Berlin mayor, launched *Ostpolitik,* a policy of reconciliation with East Germany.

1971: The Four Powers Agreement on Berlin reduced Cold War tension by improving access to West Berlin through East Germany, and easing restrictions for West Berliners visiting relatives in East Berlin.

1987: Major celebrations were organized in East and West Berlin to mark the 750th anniversary of the foundation of the city. The planned joint celebrations were scrapped because of political differences, and each city marked the anniversary according to its own ideas. The Nikolaiviertel was constructed in East Berlin, and the Prinz-Albrecht-Gelände became a protected site in West Berlin.

GERMAN UNIFICATION

Late 1989: This was the period of change known as *die Wende* (the turning point). The border between Hungary and Austria opened, leading to an exodus of East Europeans to the West. The 40th anniversary of the foundation of the DDR was marred by the weekly demonstrations in Leipzig, led by the pastor of the Nikolaikirche. Protest groups formed in other East German cities, including Dresden and Berlin. The Communist Party leader Erich Honecker was removed from office and the entire East German government resigned. The Berlin Wall was opened to East Germans on November 9.

1990: Border checks between East and West Berlin were abolished. The West German Deutschmark became the sole legal tender in both countries. Fears of mass unemployment in East Germany led to acceleration of the unification process. East and West Germany were formally united on October 4.

1991: The *Bundestag* (parliament) restored Berlin as capital of Germany. Many street names honoring communist heroes were changed: Marx-Engels-Platz reverted to Lustgarten, and Otto-Grotewohl-Strasse became Toleranzstrasse. Karl-Marx-Strasse escaped the purge, but a colossal granite statue of Lenin was removed.

1992: The world was shocked by scenes of racist violence in Rostock and other German cities. Some 17 people were killed in racist attacks in that year, including a Turkish woman and two children at Mölln. At Christmas, a large crowd held a candlelit demonstration at the Brandenburg Gate to protest at *Fremdenhass,* or hatred of foreigners. Marlene Dietrich, who died in Paris, was buried in Berlin.

1993: The director Billy Wilder, who fled from Berlin in 1933, was mobbed by movie fans when he returned to the Babelsberg Studios to collect an award during the Berlin Film Festival.

Who's who in Berlin

Many Berliners have made their mark on the world, for better or worse. Some famous Berliners are commemorated in street names; others have been erased from the city's memory. The list below features politicians, industrialists, movie stars, philosophers, scientists, architects and writers. Most were not born in Berlin, and many did not linger long, but all have helped to shape the city.

The Hohenzollern rulers are covered separately on page 41.

• **Behrens, Peter** Born in Hamburg in 1868, Behrens trained as a painter, but later worked as an architect and designer for the AEG electrical company in Berlin. He designed a turbine factory and many of the products manufactured by AEG. He died in Berlin in 1940.

• **Bismarck, Otto von** The German politician known as the Iron Chancellor was born near Berlin in 1815. He became Chancellor of Prussia in 1862 and played a major role in the unification of Germany in 1871. He is seen as something of a villain, having used war to achieve his political ends, but he was also instrumental in introducing social welfare legislation. He resigned in 1890 in protest at the policies of Kaiser Wilhelm II and died eight years later at Friedrichsruh.

• **Brandt, Willy** The greatest German statesman of the 20thC was born at Lübeck in 1913. Active in the resistance to Hitler, he fled in 1933 to Norway. Brandt returned to Germany in 1945 and served as mayor of West Berlin from 1957–66. As Chancellor (1969–74), his policy of *Ostpolitik* led to peace talks with East Germany and other communist countries.

• **Brecht, Bertolt** Berlin's most famous playwright and theater director was born at Augsburg in 1898. His first success came in 1928 with the *Threepenny Opera* (*Die Dreigroschenoper*). Brecht fled from the Nazis in 1933, living in exile for the next 15 years. Some of his greatest works date from this period, including *Mother Courage and her Children* (1938) and *The Caucasian Chalk Circle* (1945). He returned to East Berlin in 1948 to direct the Berliner Ensemble. Brecht died at Eutin in 1956, and was buried alongside notable Berliners in the Dorotheenstädtischer Friedhof. His former home next to the cemetery is now a museum.

• **Dietrich, Marlene** Perhaps the most famous Berliner of all time, Marlene Dietrich was born in 1901 (although in later years she often tried to pretend otherwise) at Leberstrasse 65 in Schöneberg district. Originally named Maria Magdalene von Losch, Dietrich rose to movie stardom after playing the sensual Lola-Lola in *Der Blaue Engel* (1930). She was lured to Hollywood that same year, starring in Josef von Sternberg's *Morocco* (1930) and *Shanghai Express* (1932).

Hitler tried to seduce her back to Germany, but she refused, and even put on a US army uniform during World War II to entertain the Allied troops. She died in Paris in 1992 and was buried in a cemetery in Friedenau district. *Wann wird man je versteh'n?* (When will they ever learn?), reads the inscription on her tomb. It is a line from one of her favorite anti-war songs.

• **Einstein, Albert** The German physicist Einstein, born at Ulm in 1879, is famous for his theory of relativity. He was director of the Kaiser Wilhelm Physical Institute in Berlin from 1914–33, and carried out research in Potsdam at the Einsteinturm, a tower specially designed for him by Expressionist architect Eric Mendelsohn. He fled from Hitler's Germany in 1933 and died in the US in 1955.

• **Fichte, Johann Gottlieb** Born in Saxony in 1762, Fichte became one of the great German philosophers. He drafted the constitution of the new University of Berlin, founded in 1810, and served as the first rector. He died in Berlin in 1814 and is buried in the Dorotheenstädtischer Friedhof.

• **Goebbels, Joseph** The notorious Nazi Minister of Propaganda was born at Rheydt in 1897. He and his wife committed suicide in Hitler's Berlin bunker in 1945, after killing their six children.

• **Hegel, Georg Wilhelm Friedrich** The immensely influential German philosopher Hegel was born in 1770 in Stuttgart. He taught at several German universities, developing the theory of the dialectic, which influenced Marx and other philosophers. He was appointed professor of philosophy at the University of Berlin in 1818, and died there of cholera in 1831. He is buried in the Dorotheenstädtischer Friedhof next to his colleague Fichte.

• **Hess, Rudolf** A close friend of Hitler, Hess was sent on a strange mission to Scotland in 1941 to negotiate peace with the British government. Sentenced for war crimes at Nuremberg in 1946, he was imprisoned at Spandau. After the release of Speer in 1966, Hess was Spandau's sole prisoner. He died there in 1987.

• **Hitler, Adolf** Born in Austria in 1889, and originally named Schicklgrüber, Adolf Hitler became Chancellor of Germany in 1933, in the wake of the Reichstag fire. He toyed with grandiose ambitions to turn Berlin (which was to be renamed Germania) into a monumental Nazi capital, but little was ever achieved. He led Germany into World War II (see LANDMARKS IN BERLIN'S HISTORY on page 34).

As Allied troops marched on Berlin, he retreated to a concrete air raid shelter under the Chancellery. Hitler and his mistress Eva Braun committed suicide in the bunker on April 30, 1945. The site of the bunker is marked by a mound of earth in the former death strip separating East and West Berlin. Hitler's body was apparently burned and buried in the Chancellery garden by Soviet troops, but a Soviet archivist announced in 1993 that the skull was still being kept in the Russian State Archives in a cardboard box labeled "blue ink for pens."

• **Hoffmann, Ernest Theodor Amadeus** Born in 1776, Hoffmann was the author of Gothic horror stories. Three of his macabre tales formed the basis of Offenbach's 1881 opera *Tales of Hoffmann.* Hoffmann died in Berlin in 1822.

• **Humboldt, Alexander von** Born in Berlin in 1769, Alexander von Humboldt studied at several German universities before setting out to explore South America with Aimé Bonpland. He died in Berlin in 1859 and was buried in the family cemetery at Schloss Tegel. An ocean current off the west coast of South America is named in his honor.

• **Humboldt, Wilhelm von** The elder brother of Alexander von Humboldt, Wilhelm was born in Potsdam in 1767. He was a statesman and a gifted scientist, studying various languages including Basque. He founded Berlin University on Unter den Linden in 1809 and commissioned Schinkel to build him a house (see SCHLOSS TEGEL) in 1820. He died near Berlin in 1835. The communist authorities renamed Berlin's university the Humboldt-Universität in his honor.

• **Isherwood, Christopher** Born in 1904, Isherwood worked as an English tutor in Berlin from 1930–33. His experiences of the decadent Weimar years provided material for two of the great English novels of the Thirties: *Mr Norris Changes Trains* (1935) (published in the US as *The Last of Mr Norris*) and *Goodbye to Berlin* (1939). The stage musical and the movie *Cabaret* were loosely based on *Goodbye to Berlin.*

• **Kennedy, John F.** The former US president joined the ranks of *Wahlberliners* (Berliners by choice) when, in his famous speech at Schöneberg in 1963, he declared, in rather shaky German, "Ich bin ein Berliner."

• **Karajan, Herbert von** Born in Salzburg in 1908, von Karajan was conductor of the Berlin Staatsoper on Unter den Linden from 1938–1942. After the war, he stood accused of belonging to the Nazi Party and was forbidden from working until 1947. Despite his tainted past, von Karajan was the highly acclaimed principal conductor of the Berlin Philharmonic from 1955 to 1989. He died near Salzburg in 1989.

• **Kleist, Heinrich von** The German dramatist and poet Heinrich von Kleist was born at Frankfurt an der Oder in 1777. He served briefly in the Prussian army, before turning to poetry and drama. Von Kleist is best remembered for the play *Prinz Friedrich von Homburg* and the novel *Michael Kohlhaas.* He committed suicide on the shore of the Wannsee in Berlin in 1811.

• **Kollwitz, Käthe** Born in 1867, Käthe Kollwitz worked in Berlin's Prenzlauer Berg district as a graphic artist and sculptor. An ardent socialist and pacifist, she was deeply affected during World War I by the suffering of Berlin's women and children. She lost her own 17-year-old son Peter in the early months of the war when he was killed at Diksmuide in Flanders. A wooden cross that once marked his grave is now in the Salient Museum in Ypres.

After the war, Kollwitz carved a statue of *The Mourning Parents* for the German military cemetery at Vladslo, near Diksmuide. She died in 1945 in Rüdenhof, near Schloss Moritzburg. Some of her best works are now to be seen in the Käthe-Kollwitz-Museum in Berlin.

• **Lang, Fritz** The great Berlin movie director of the 1920s was born in Vienna in 1890. Originally a painter, he moved to Berlin to work at the Babelsberg Studios, where he made *Metropolis* in 1926. He fled from Berlin in 1933, and spent the rest of his life in Hollywood.

• **Lenné, Peter Josef** Born in 1789, Peter Lenné introduced Italian landscape gardening to Berlin and Potsdam. He landscaped the gardens around Schloss Klein-Glienicke in Berlin, and Schloss Charlottenburg and the Neuer Garten in Potsdam. Lenné died in 1866 and was buried in the Bornstedter Friedhof in Potsdam.

• **Lilienthal, Otto** Born in 1849 at Anklam, the German engineer Otto Lilienthal was one of the pioneers of unpowered flight. In the 1890s he designed various gliders similar to Leonardo da Vinci's flying machines, and meticulously recorded the results of more than 2,000 glider flights. He also constructed an artificial hill on the outskirts of Berlin to carry out some of the test flights. Using a man-powered glider, Lilienthal flew a distance of 100 meters in 1894, nine years before the Wright brothers' first flight. He crashed to his death in 1896 after flying a distance of 200 meters. The 11-meter high (36ft) *Fliegeberg* (flight hill) built by Lilienthal now stands in the small Lilienthalpark *(Schütte-Lanz-Strasse, Lichterfelde).* The memorial on the summit was erected in 1932. Tegel airport was named Otto-Lilienthal-Flughafen in 1988 in honor of the German aviator.

• **Luxemburg, Rosa** Born in 1871 in Russian Poland, Rosa Luxemburg was one of pioneers of German socialism. She and Karl Liebknecht formed the revolutionary Spartacus League, which later became the German Communist Party. They were both arrested and murdered during the Spartacus revolt in 1919. A memorial on the Lichtensteinbrücke marks the spot where the two bodies were dumped into the Landwehrkanal.

• **Nicolai, Friedrich** One of the leading figures of the German Enlightenment, Friedrich Nicolai (1733–1811) worked in Berlin as a bookseller, writer and critic. His former home at Brüderstrasse 13 is still standing.

• **Nicolai, Otto** Born in 1810 at Königsberg, Nicolai studied music in Berlin and Rome. He became conductor of the Berlin Opera in 1847 and composed his popular opera *The Merry Wives of Windsor* in Berlin shortly before his untimely death in 1849.

• **Reinhardt, Max** One of the most innovative theater directors of the 20thC, Reinhardt was born at Baden in 1873. He became an immensely influential figure in Berlin theater life, running the Deutsches Theater, the adjoining Kammerspiele and the Grosses Schauspielhaus, where he staged spectacular performances involving hundreds of actors. He fled from Berlin in 1933 and died in New York ten years later.

• **Schinkel, Karl Friedrich** The main architect of Neoclassical Berlin was born at Neuruppin in 1781. He studied in Berlin and Italy, becoming state architect of Prussia in 1815. Schinkel designed many of the squares and public buildings in central Berlin, including the Altes Museum and the Schauspielhaus. He was also a talented Romantic artist and stage designer. He died in Berlin in 1841, and is buried in the Dorotheenstädtischer Friedhof. His architectural drawings are found at the Schinkelmuseum in the Friedrichswerdersche Kirche and the Schinkel-Pavillon at Schloss Charlottenburg; some of his paintings hang in the Galerie der Romantik.

• **Siemens, Werner von** The founder of the Siemens electrical company was born near Hannover in 1816. Werner von Siemens enlisted in the Prussian army, and was put in charge of the artillery workshops in Berlin. He developed a galvanometer and founded a telegraph manufacturing company in 1847. Von Siemens died in Berlin in 1892.

• **Speer, Albert** Born in Mannheim in 1905, Speer became Hitler's chief architect in 1934. He was tried at Nuremberg in 1945, and imprisoned at Spandau in Berlin for 20 years. He died in London in 1981.

• **Weigel, Helene** Born in Austria in 1900, Weigel worked in Berlin as an actress. She married Bertolt Brecht in 1929 and acted in many of his plays. She ran the Berliner Ensemble after Brecht's death in 1956, and organized the Ensemble's influential international tours during the Cold War. She died in 1971 and is buried alongside Brecht in the Dorotheenstädtischer Friedhof.

• **Weill, Kurt** Berlin's most famous composer was born at Dessau in 1900. He moved to Berlin to study and work, writing the music for Brecht's *Threepenny Opera* (1928). He fled from the Nazis and settled in the US in 1934. He continued to write music, but his work lost its early Berlin edge. He died in New York in 1950.

• **Wenders, Wim** Born in Düsseldorf in 1945, the movie director Wim Wenders has long been fascinated by Berlin. He shot two movies there: *Summer in the City* (1970) and *Wings of Desire* (1987).

THE HOHENZOLLERN

Most people are confused by the fact that the Hohenzollern rulers were all named Friedrich, or Wilhelm, or various combinations of the two. This chronological guide may help sort out the muddle.

- **Friedrich Wilhelm** *(1620-88)* The Great Elector, as he was known, enacted the Edict of Potsdam, which offered asylum to French Huguenot refugees.
- **Friedrich I** *(1657-1713)* He became Elector Friedrich III in 1688, and was crowned the first King of Prussia in 1701. Friedrich I gave Berlin many of its Baroque buildings.
- **Friedrich Wilhelm I** *(1688-1740)* Known as the Soldier King, he was a brutal father and fanatical disciplinarian who laid the foundations of the Prussian military state. The size of the army was increased and enormous barracks were erected in Berlin and Potsdam. Tall men were press-ganged into military service and all Prussian males were required to attend military drill on Sundays. Friedrich Wilhelm even imprisoned his son (the future Frederick the Great) for trying to escape from the tedium of Berlin, and forced him to watch the execution of a young officer suspected of being his lover.
- **Frederick the Great** *(1712-86)* Frederick the Great (Friedrich der Grosse in German) inherited something of his father's militarism, waging four major wars to make Prussia one of the great European powers. Yet he was a deeply civilized man, building the Rococo palace at Sanssouci, debating with Voltaire in French, and playing the flute. He died at Potsdam in 1786. The communists tried to erase his memory, removing his statue from Berlin to a corner of Sanssouci Park in Potsdam, but the statue is now back in its old place on Unter den Linden. His bones were reburied at Sanssouci in 1991.
- **Friedrich Wilhelm II** *(1744-97)* Another Prussian military leader, who waged war against Poland, capturing Warsaw.
- **Friedrich Wilhelm III** *(1770-1840)* Led Prussia in the war against Napoleon.
- **Friedrich Wilhelm IV** *(1795-1861)* King of Prussia during the German Revolution. A deep romantic, Friedrich Wilhelm IV introduced Italian Renaissance architecture to Berlin and Potsdam.
- **Wilhelm I, Kaiser** *(1797-1888)* The first Emperor of Germany, Kaiser Wilhelm was the second son of Friedrich Wilhelm III. He became King of Prussia in 1861 and first *Kaiser* (Emperor) of the new German state ten years later. He built up the German army and suppressed socialism.
- **Wilhelm II, Kaiser** *(1859-1941)* The Emperor who brought Germany into World War I was born at Potsdam in 1859. He was the son of Friedrich II and Victoria (the daughter of Queen Victoria of Britain), and a grandson of Kaiser Wilhelm I. He was a mere figurehead during the war, and fled to the Netherlands after the German army collapsed in 1918.

The architecture of Berlin

The bombing raids on Berlin during World War II destroyed a massive stock of palaces, churches, cinemas and apartments, leaving little of the old city. The Nikolaikirche and the Marienkirche are the only medieval buildings still standing in central Berlin, and virtually all the Renaissance architecture commissioned by Joachim II, Berlin's first Protestant Elector, has disappeared, except for the Jagdschloss in the Grunewald.

BAROQUE

Nor have many buildings survived from the long reign of Friedrich Wilhelm, the Great Elector (from 1640–88), who rebuilt Berlin at the end of the Thirty Years' War in a Baroque style, modeled on the Dutch towns where he had spent his youth. The principal mementos of the Great Elector are the monumental 17thC urban spaces such as **Unter den Linden** and the **Lustgarten**.

The formal Baroque new towns of Friedrichswerder (W of Cölln) and Dorotheenstadt (N of Unter den Linden) were laid out at this time to accommodate Berlin's rapidly growing population of Huguenot craftsmen, although most of the buildings now standing were built in the 19th or 20thC.

Berlin continued its westward push in the era of Friedrich III (reigned 1688–1713), the first king of Prussia, who created the suburbs of Friedrichstadt (S of Unter den Linden) and Charlottenburg (W of the Tiergarten).

The reconstruction of **Schloss Charlottenburg** for Sophie Charlotte, the king's second wife, turned the former village at Charlottenburg into one of Berlin's most elegant suburbs. Johann Arnold Nering's compact palace, built 1695–99, came to mirror the growth of Prussian power in the extensions that were soon added. Courtyards, wings, a cupola and

Schloss Charlottenburg

an orangery were completed within 30 years, while Georg Wenzeslaus von Knobelsdorff's new wing was added in 1740–46 for Frederick the Great, and additions were still being made 100 years later.

Many new buildings were designed for Friedrich III by Andreas Schlüter (1664–1714), a Polish architect and sculptor invited to Berlin in 1694. After a two-year study tour of France and Italy, he returned to Berlin to complete the royal arsenal, or **Zeughaus** (now the Deutsches Historisches Museum) on Unter den Linden, a monumental Baroque building begun by Johann Nering. Schlüter subsequently reconstructed the **Stadtschloss** (city palace) or **Berliner Schloss** on the Spree; it was bombed in 1945, and finally demolished in 1950. A scale model in Schloss Charlottenburg shows the grandeur of Schlüter's Baroque design, but all that now remains is a few charred Baroque statues in the Bode-Museum.

Schlüter's most famous sculptural work — an equestrian **statue of the Great Elector**, made in 1700 — stood until World War II on the bridge beside the palace. It now graces the courtyard of Schloss Charlottenburg. Schlüter was dismissed from his post following the collapse of a tower of the Stadtschloss, and his last completed work in Berlin was the Villa Kamecke in Dorotheenstadt. It, too, was destroyed in 1945, and all that remains are some sculptures from the balustrade, which are to be seen in the Bode-Museum.

Friedrich Wilhelm I, the Soldier King (reigned 1713–40), had little time for architecture. Interested only in expanding the Prussian army, he laid out the Pariser Platz and the Tempelhofer Feld (now an airport) as military parade grounds. His son, Frederick the Great, was a keen soldier too, but nurtured grand architectural schemes for the capital. He turned **Unter den Linden** into one of Europe's finest streets, lined with monumental Baroque edifices such as the **Staatsoper**, designed by Georg Wenzeslaus von Knobelsdorff (1699–1753), the **Palais des Prinzen Heinrich** by Johann Boumann (1706–76), and the **Alte Königliche Bibliothek** by Christian Unger (1743–1812). Karl von Gontard (1731–91) built the **Deutscher Dom** and the complementary **Französischer Dom** (the cathedral of the Huguenot community) on the Gendarmenmarkt, and Georg Wenzeslaus von Knobelsdorff designed **St Hedwigskirche** (later the Catholic cathedral) in the style of the Pantheon in Rome. **Schloss Bellevue** was built on the edge of the Tiergarten in 1785, prompting the development of an elegant residential quarter around the woods.

Frederick the Great flirted briefly with the Rococo style at his summer palace, **Schloss Sanssouci**, at Potsdam. The palace and its terraced grounds were designed by Knobelsdorff, while Johann Gottfried Büring created the **Chinesisches Teehaus** (1745), a delightful Rococo whimsy (see illustration on page 228).

NEOCLASSICAL

Neoclassical architecture proved more suited to the stern Prussian temperament than flighty French Rococo. The **Brandenburger Tor**, erected in 1793 by Carl Gotthard Langhans (1732–1808), was Berlin's first Neoclassical building, in Classical Athenian style. The Greek revival was developed by Friedrich Gilly (1772–1800), who abandoned Neo-Gothic in favor of Neoclassical in his 1796 design for a national monument to Frederick the Great. After completing a study tour of France and England, Gilly was appointed Professor of Optics and Perspective at the newly-founded Academy of Architecture.

SCHINKEL

Karl Friedrich Schinkel (1781–1841), a pupil of Gilly's, designed much of Neoclassical Berlin. A German Romantic at heart, Schinkel was fond of painting melancholy scenes of Gothic churches. But he later adopted a disciplined, Neoclassical style exactly suited to the quiet mood of confidence in Berlin that followed the defeat of Napoleon in 1815.

Appointed to the public works department in 1815, Schinkel designed the Neoclassical **Neue Wache** on Unter den Linden in 1816. Two years later, he resorted to his beloved Neo-Gothic style in a **War Memorial** on the Kreuzberg. But he returned to sober Neoclassicism with the **Schauspielhaus** on the Gendarmenmarkt in 1818–21, the exquisite **Schinkel-Pavillon** at Schloss Charlottenburg (1824), and **Schloss Tegel** (1822–24), built for his scholarly friend Wilhelm von Humboldt. He also completed several buildings at Potsdam, including **Schloss Charlottenhof** (1826) and the **Nikolaikirche** (1830), and he designed a Neoclassical palace and other smaller buildings in the nearby **Volkspark Klein-Glienicke**.

Schinkel's **Altes Museum** on Museumsinsel

Schinkel's masterpiece was the **Altes Museum** on the Spree (1823–30), a handsome museum incorporating a domed hall modeled on the Pantheon in Rome. But medieval architecture never entirely lost its hold on him, and his designs for the **Friedrichswerdersche Kirche** (1824–30) and **Schloss Babelsberg** near Potsdam (1833) are pure Neo-Gothic.

WILHELMINE

The Wilhelmine period at the end of the 19thC led to the development of a heavy, bourgeois style for hotels, government offices and apartment blocks in Mitte, Charlottenburg and other prosperous districts.

Meanwhile, speculators were erecting massive tenement blocks or *Mietskaserne* in the poorer districts of Kreuzberg, Neukölln, Wedding and Prenzlauer Berg. Many of these grim apartments were lit only from deep courtyards — the notorious *Hinterhöfe,* as they were known.

A new simplicity of design was introduced by Peter Behrens (1868–1940), a disciple of William Morris. After producing Art Nouveau posters, he was appointed chief architect for the giant Berlin electricity company AEG in 1907. Behrens developed a unified modern corporate design for AEG's factory buildings, electrical products (such as kettles and fans), canteen cutlery and stationery.

BAUHAUS

Walter Gropius (1883–1969), who worked in Peter Behrens' firm until 1910, built factories in a severe functional style that heralded the Modern Movement. In 1919, he moved to Weimar, 262km (164 miles) SW of Berlin, to replace the Belgian architect Henry Van de Velde as director of the School of Arts and Crafts. Renaming it the *Bauhaus* (House of Building), Gropius transformed it into a revolutionary school based on medieval ideals of craftsmanship. Although it lasted only 14 years, the Bauhaus had an enormous influence on 20thC architecture and design, employing Paul Klee, Wassily Kandinsky and Theo van Doesburg as teachers.

Harassed in Weimar by the Nazis, the Bauhaus moved in 1925 to the left-wing town of Dessau, midway between Weimar and Berlin. But even here Gropius was harangued, and he was finally forced to resign in 1928.

After the Dessau Bauhaus was closed down in 1933, the school moved to Berlin, but lasted there only a few months. Although finally crushed in Germany, Bauhaus architects such as Walter Gropius and the last director, Mies van der Rohe, went on to play a major role in the development of postwar American architecture. Several American skyscrapers were the realization of Bauhaus projects for Berlin frustrated by the Depression and the Nazi regime.

The closure of the Bauhaus marked the beginning of a dark age in German architecture. Adolf Hitler outlawed modern design in Germany, and conspired with the architect Albert Speer to create a terrifying Neoclassical Nazi capital to be called Germania. Few of his megalomaniacal plans were ever realized, and almost all traces of Germania have vanished.

POSTWAR RECONSTRUCTION

The first task after World War II was to shift the millions of tons of rubble. Reconstruction of the devastated city began in the Soviet sector, where a heroic attempt was made at Stalinallee (later Karl-Marx-Allee) to create a modern Berlin in harmony with Schinkel's Neoclassicism. Driven by the tense rivalry of the Cold War, West Berlin responded by commissioning a team of international architects to design new apartments in the devastated **Hansaviertel**.

Gropius returned to Berlin in 1957 to submit a design for the competition. He also designed the **Bauhaus-Archiv** on the edge of the Tiergarten. Mies van der Rohe was invited back to the city that he had fled, to design the **Neue Nationalgalerie** (pictured on following page), a strikingly simple square structure with glass walls overhung by a black steel roof, which was completed in 1968, only a year before his death.

Mies van der Rohe's **Neue Nationalgalerie**

The nearby **Kultur-Forum** was begun in 1960 by Hans Scharoun as a new cultural quarter comprising several major museums, the **Philharmonie** concert hall, the **Kammermusiksaal** and the **Staatsbibliothek**. Scharoun's Philharmonie concert hall won worldwide acclaim for the radical design of the auditorium, in which the audience surrounds the orchestra on staggered tiers of seating. Its tent-like aluminum roof makes the Philharmonie one of Berlin's most distinctive modern buildings.

The overall design of the Kultur-Forum was less well received. Critics complained about the brutality of the concrete construction and the seemingly incoherent plan, and the project is still unfinished.

IBA ARCHITECTURE

These postwar styles largely failed to create a livable city out of the rubble. A major turning point came in 1979, when the International Building Exhibition (IBA) was set up by the West Berlin *Land* (state) to transform the inner city into an attractive environment for living. The IBA sponsored imaginative schemes in Kreuzberg, employing international architects to create colorful and quirky apartment blocks alongside the gloomy buildings of the Wilhelmine age. Sometimes the new buildings incorporate fragments of old houses or Neoclassical touches, generating the rudiments of a recognizable Berlin style once again.

Now that Berlin is capital of Germany once more, grand architectural projects have been mooted, to adapt the city to its new role. The planned developments range from the rural idyll of creating a park along the strip of wasteland left by the Wall, to Daimler-Benz's massive office complex on **Potsdamer Platz**. The plans to transform Berlin have sparked off fierce controversy among architects and politicians, which adds immensely to the current mood of excitement in the changing metropolis, but little has been built so far.

Art in Berlin

The great movements of German Gothic and Renaissance art did not touch Berlin, and the city only became an important center of European painting in the early 20thC, when a succession of radical art movements created a climate of bold experimentation. Artistic groups in Berlin tended to be short-lived and explosive, and artists often participated in several different movements.

The revolt against the established art of the 19thC began with the **Berliner Secession**, a group inspired by radical artists in Munich and Vienna who had seceded from the official art exhibitions. Max Liebermann (1847–1935), the foremost of the German Impressionists, founded the Berliner Secession in 1899 and served as its first president.

An idealistic group called **Die Brücke** (The Bridge) was founded at Dresden in 1905 by a group of art students that included Ernst Ludwig Kirchner (1880–1938), Emil Nolde (1867–1956) and Max Pechstein (1881–1955). Inspired by German woodcuts and the ethnography collection in the Zwinger Palace at Dresden, Die Brücke sought to express human emotions through violent colors and jarring compositions. The group dissolved in 1913, just three years after its move to Berlin.

Meanwhile, the Secession had become rather too staid for the most radical of Berlin's artists, and in 1910 a new splinter group, the **Neue Secession**, was founded. Led by Max Pechstein, it drew recruits from Die Brücke, including Kirchner and Nolde.

The artists of the various German art movements that challenged 19thC Impressionism became collectively known as the **Expressionists**. Inspired by Munch and Van Gogh, they evolved a highly emotional, anxious style, employing vivid colors and distorted forms. Expressionism had a profound influence on early German cinema and (to a lesser degree) architecture.

The utopian ideals of Expressionism were dashed by World War I. The **Novembergruppe**, founded in Berlin in 1918 by disillusioned Expressionist artists and architects such as Max Pechstein and César Klein, sought to heal a world broken by war through a socialist unification of art, architecture and town planning. Some of the group's members later joined the Berlin **Dada** movement, founded in 1918 after the German poet Richard Huelsenbeck proclaimed an irrational Dada speech in Berlin. A reaction against German Expressionism, Berlin Dada was a provocative and revolutionary art movement born out of the savagery of war. But it lasted only a few years; after a brief explosion of creativity, Berlin Dada was officially pronounced dead in a meeting at Weimar in 1922.

John Heartfield (1891–1968), a communist and founding member of the Berlin Dada movement, continued to create biting photomontages ridiculing Hitler and the Nazis in the 1920s. He fled to England in 1938 and returned to East Berlin in 1950.

German **Impressionism** resurfaced in the 1920s, when Lesser Ury painted attractive Berlin street scenes, but the most powerful art movement in the Weimar Republic was **Neue Sachlichkeit** (New Objectivity), led by Georg Grosz (1893–1959) and Otto Dix (1891–1969). Scarred by their experiences in World War I, Grosz and Dix painted savage caricatures of the corrupt businessmen and generals of the Weimar Republic.

Neue Sachlichkeit and German Expressionism became prime targets for Hitler's notorious vilification of "decadent art" in the 1930s. Expressionist artists and galleries were hounded, modern paintings were ridiculed in exhibitions of decadent art staged by the Nazis, and the bulk of the works were sold abroad. What little remained was mostly burned in Berlin in 1939, in a sequel to the notorious book-burning. All that survives in Berlin of those astonishing years of creativity from 1899–1933 are the depleted collections in the Alte Nationalgalerie, the Neue Nationalgalerie and the Brücke Museum in Dahlem.

German art took a long time to recover from the Nazi years. In the late 1970s, the Expressionism of the 1910s resurfaced in West Germany under the group known as **Die Neue Wilden** (the New Wild Ones). The permanent collection of 20thC Berlin paintings in the Martin-Gropius-Bau illustrates modern Berlin artists' understandable obsession with themes of violence and terror.

But the most famous works of postwar Berlin art were the spontaneous murals sprayed onto the Wall by numerous artists. Now that the Wall has come down, little remains in Berlin of this playful and irreverent art — apart from fragments in the Berlin-Museum and the Deutsches Historisches Museum — although these extraordinary works of graffiti art have been placed on permanent record in several published books of photographs.

Berlin is now rapidly regaining the status it enjoyed 60 years ago as the avant-garde capital of Europe. After the Wall came down, some 20 new galleries sprang up in just two years. The city currently boasts more than 130 commercial art galleries, some well-established in handsome villas, others eking out a precarious existence in squatted factories. Almost every modern art form is flourishing in Berlin — painting, sculpture, ceramics and photography are all to be found. A list of selected galleries can be found in SHOPPING IN BERLIN on page 193.

Film in Berlin

FILMSTADT BABELSBERG

Movie history was made in Berlin. The husky voice of Marlene Dietrich and the dizzying camera angles of *The Cabinet of Dr. Caligari* are among the lasting mementoes of the Berlin movie industry.

For a brief period in the 1920s and '30s, the film studios at Babelsberg, just outside Berlin, produced some of the most exciting movies of the age. American audiences were enthralled by the technical sophistication and sultry sex-appeal of German cinema. But the golden age of Berlin cinema ended abruptly in the early 1930s, and all that remains today are the old studios outside Potsdam (see DEFA FILM- UND TV-ERLEBNIS on page 229).

The first flickering movies were screened in Berlin by Max Skladanowsky in 1895. The new art fired the imagination of the modern-minded Berliners, and film studios were founded in a Potsdam suburb in 1911.

Originally called the Filmstadt Babelsberg, and renamed the **UFA** *(Universum-Film-Aktiengesellschaft)* in 1917, the film studios (by then the largest in Germany) turned out a series of government propaganda movies during World War I.

Recovery was rapid after the war, and the studios provided glamorous work for hungry Berliners. The sophisticated audiences of the Twenties flocked to the movies that poured out of the Berlin studios. The German Expressionist directors of the 1920s had a profound influence on Hollywood style, with their experimental use of unusual camera angles, tracking shots, and *chiaroscuro* (dramatic light and shade) to achieve heightened suspense.

The Berlin film industry began to fall apart in the 1920s when many of its greatest stars and directors were lured to Hollywood by the promise of big fees and fame. The early deserters included the beautiful Polish star Pola Negri, the director Ernst Lubitsch and the actor Emil Jannings. The rise of the Nazis turned the trickle into a flood; the directors Fritz Lang and Billy Wilder were among those that fled.

Yet others who had been lured by Hollywood dollars returned to Berlin in the 1930s. Pola Negri and Emil Jannings found their careers in Hollywood talkies hampered by their strong German accents, and both went back to Germany to star in Nazi propaganda films.

THE COLD WAR MOVIE

Berlin no longer had much of a film industry after World War II, but the bleak, bombed ruins of the city provided the background for melancholy films such as Roberto Rossellini's *Germany, Year Zero* (1947), in which a 13-year-old boy is haunted by the Nazi past, and Robert Stemmle's *Ballad of Berlin* (1948), telling of a defeated soldier returning home to be preyed upon by criminals and bureaucrats. Carol Reed's *The Man Between* (1953) was a Berlin spy thriller modeled on his famous *The Third Man,* while Sam Fuller's *Verboten!* (1958) is an unusual story of a US soldier's relationship with a German woman who saved him from sniper fire in occupied Berlin.

The division of Berlin by the Wall offered an edgy setting for a number of 1960s Hollywood spy thrillers such as *The Spy Who Came In From The Cold* (1965) and Hitchcock's *Torn Curtain* (1966). Berlin is the setting, too, for several movies based on British author Len Deighton's thrillers, which include *Funeral in Berlin* (1966), starring Michael Caine, and *The Quiller Memorandum* (1966).

DECADENT BERLIN REVISITED

Bob Fosse's *Cabaret* (1972) is the screen version of a stage musical of the same name, based on Christopher Isherwood's *Goodbye to Berlin.* Set in the tormented late years of the Weimar Republic, the Hollywood movie stars Liza Minnelli as a sexy singer in a louche Berlin cabaret. The smoky, sinful setting is similar to that in *The Blue Angel,* but Michael York remains almost untainted by the corruption all around.

Swedish director Ingmar Bergman's *The Serpent's Egg* (1977) was a later attempt to re-create the atmosphere of Berlin in the early 1920s.

RECENT TRENDS

The realistic school of the 1970s, labeled New German Cinema, was developed by West German directors such as Rainer Werner Fassbinder and Werner Herzog. Their studios were based in Munich, dubbed "Hollywood on the Iser," but Berlin sometimes provided a bleak setting. *Berlin Alexanderplatz,* the classic novel set in 1920s Berlin, was made into a 15-hour television movie by Fassbinder in 1980. Set in the late years of the Weimar Republic, the film deliberately evoked the smoky, seedy atmosphere of *The Blue Angel.*

Contemporary Berlin was portrayed as a drab and menacing metropolis in *Christiane F* (1981) by German director Ulrich Edel. Filmed in the squalor of the Bahnhof Zoo (nowadays far less sinister) and the modern tower blocks of the Märkisches Viertel, it recounts the true story of a 13-year-old heroin-addict-turned-prostitute. The Berlin gay world has been affectionately filmed by Rosa von Praunheim, a male American, in movies such as *City of Lost Souls* (1983). *Rosa Luxemburg* (1986) by the feminist director Margarethe von Trotta tells the moving tale of the Polish-born co-leader of the Spartacus revolt, who was brutally murdered in Berlin in 1919.

THE BABELSBERG STUDIOS TODAY

East Germany's state-run film industry (DEFA) was based at the old UFA studios at Babelsberg, where some 5,000 people were employed in the production of television shows, documentaries and feature films. Like much industry in the eastern part of Germany, DEFA was threatened with closure following reunification, but the studios have been reprieved by an injection of Western capital, and Berlin looks set to become a popular location for German and foreign directors.

Some of the old Babelsberg studios have been converted into a tourist attraction (see DEFA FILM- UND TV-ERLEBNIS on page 229), but the more modern facilities there are still utilized for movie and television productions.

Berlin cinemas still offer a broad choice of movies, and the annual festival in February proves that Berliners are still enraptured by the art form pioneered in their city.

TEN BERLIN MOVIES TO SEE

There are various movie theaters that screen German movie classics. Several regularly offer such titles as *Der Blaue Engel* or *Das Kabinett des Dr. Caligari.* The most likely places to catch a Dietrich movie are the BERLINER KINOMUSEUM and the TRÄNENPALAST. The simplest way to find out what's on is to look up the film title in Zitty's *Film ABC.*

Here follows a personal selection of ten all-time greats.

• **Berlin: Die Sinfonie der Grossstadt** *(Berlin: Symphony of a Great City)* Filmed in Berlin in 1927, Walter Ruttmann's experimental documentary gives a fragmentary portrait of one day in the life of the modern metropolis, from the break of dawn to a late-night fireworks display. Technically brilliant in its shots of factories and machines, it has been criticized for its cold vision of human life.

• **Der Blaue Engel** *(The Blue Angel)* Filmed by Josef Von Sternberg in the winter of 1929 at the UFA studios in Babelsberg, Der Blaue Engel was based on the Heinrich Mann novel *Professor Unrat.* Set in the smoke-filled Blue Angel Cabaret, the movie portrays the moral decline of a respectable German professor captivated by the Berlin cabaret singer Lola-Lola, played by Marlene Dietrich.

Von Sternberg had returned to Europe from Hollywood to direct this film, which was the first sound production in Germany, making an international star of both him and Dietrich. The premiere on April 1, 1930, at the Gloria Palast cinema in Berlin, was a sensation. The same night, Dietrich and Von Sternberg boarded a steamer bound for America, to begin a long moviemaking collaboration.

• **A Foreign Affair** The ruins of Berlin provide the backdrop for Billy Wilder's 1948 movie. Marlene Dietrich (then a grandmother) plays a former mistress of a Nazi officer forced to earn her living as a cabaret singer. Not a particularly great movie, but interesting for its Berlin locations and songs.

• **Die Himmel über Berlin** *(Wings of Desire)* Wim Wenders' affectionate movie about Berlin, filmed in 1987. It tells the story of an angel who looks down on the city from the Siegessäule, then longs to become human when he falls in love with a melancholy trapeze artist at the Tempodrom circus. Set mainly on the desolate wasteland around Potsdamer Platz, the film has lingering shots of the Wall, the Staatsbibliothek, and the ruins of a World War II concrete bunker.

• **Das Kabinett des Dr. Caligari** *(The Cabinet of Dr. Caligari)* Made by Robert Wiene, with substantial contributions from Fritz Lang, at Berlin's Decla Studios in 1919, this movie marked the beginning of German Expressionist cinema. Dr. Caligari runs a fairground booth in a small German town where several murders have taken place.

Lang was responsible for the movie's innovative "frame" structure and for the late revelation that we have been watching a tale told by a madman.

• **M** The story of a child murderer, played by Peter Lorre, set in the moral chaos of the Weimar Republic. Filmed in Berlin in 1931 by Fritz Lang.

• **Metropolis** An early science fiction film set in a visionary city in the year 2000. Directed by Fritz Lang, the movie was filmed in 1925–26 on a set constructed in UFA's Babelsberg studios. It still has enormous impact and relevance today.

• **Nosferatu** The first screen version of Bram Stoker's 1890 novel *Dracula.* Shot in Berlin's Jofa studios in 1932 by F.W. Murnau.

• **Olympia** Leni Riefenstahl's masterful movie of the 1936 Olympics, involving remarkable sequences filmed from a zeppelin, and others filmed underwater. The premiere was screened on Hitler's birthday in 1938. Riefenstahl's reputation was tainted for life as a Nazi sympathizer, despite the fact that her earlier film of the 1934 Nuremberg Rally *(Triumph of the Will)* had offended the Nazis.

• **Das Testament des Dr. Mabuse** *(The Last Will of Dr. Mabuse)* Fritz Lang filmed this thriller in 1932 in Berlin. The evil Dr. Mabuse was intended to represent Hitler. Goebbels banned the film.

Suggested reading

FOUR BERLIN NOVELS TO READ

If you fancy fiction with a Berlin setting, try dipping into one of the following:

- **Berlin Alexanderplatz** *(publ. 1929)* Long enough to last the train journey from Paris to Berlin, Alfred Döblin's great Berlin novel was inspired by James Joyce's *Ulysses.* Set in the 1920s amid squalor and corruption, it tells the story of Franz Biberkopf, a worker imprisoned for battering his wife to death, who tries to make a new beginning, but is dragged down into crime and madness. The plot infuriated the Nazis, and they added the book to the pyre of decadent literature burned on the Opernplatz.
- **Funeral in Berlin** *(publ. 1964)* A thriller for the airplane journey from New York to Berlin. Len Deighton is an expert on the politics of Cold War Berlin. His other Berlin novels include *Berlin Game* and a more highbrow novel *Winter: A Berlin Family 1899–1945,* chronicling the fortunes of a prosperous Berlin industrialist's family.
- **Goodbye to Berlin** *(publ. 1939)* Christopher Isherwood based two novels on his experiences as a teacher in Berlin in 1929–33. *Mr Norris Changes Trains* (published in the US as *The Last of Mr Norris*) (1935) is a sinister tale of a seedy communist activist in late Weimar Berlin, while the more famous *Goodbye to Berlin* (1939) contains a collection of evocative reminiscences of Berlin people, including Sally Bowles, the flighty cabaret singer, who inspired a play, a stage musical and the movie *Cabaret.* You can read the short story "Sally Bowles" in the time it takes to ride the S-Bahn from Alexanderplatz to Potsdam.
- **The Innocent** *(publ. 1990)* A chilling espionage story by Ian McEwan, set in Berlin in the 1950s. A gullible English engineer is sent to Berlin to work on a secret tunnel that is being dug into the Soviet sector. He falls in love with a German woman, and accidentally kills her drunken husband during a quarrel. The account of the disposal of the body is perhaps the most gruesome ten pages in modern literature.

OTHER BOOKS

- **The Berlin Diaries** This is an account of wartime Berlin by Marie Vassiltchikov, a woman who knew several of the conspirators in the failed Von Stauffenberg Plot.
- **The Berlin Raids** *(publ. 1988)* Martin Middlebrook's story of the bombardment of Berlin is recounted in detail, and includes eye-witness accounts by both bomber crews and Berliners.
- **Weimar Culture** *(publ. 1969)* This is a fascinating account of the politics and art of the 1920s, written by Peter Gay, a Berliner who fled from the Nazis.

Berlin: practical information

This chapter is organized into six sections:

- **GETTING THERE**, below
- **GETTING AROUND IN BERLIN**, page 55
- **ON-THE-SPOT INFORMATION**, page 59
- **USEFUL NUMBERS AND ADDRESSES**, page 61
- **BUSINESS IN BERLIN**, page 63
- **EMERGENCY INFORMATION**, page 64

Each section is organized thematically rather than alphabetically. Summaries of subject headings are printed in CAPITALS at the top of most pages. See also **VISITING NORTHERN GERMANY: PRACTICAL INFORMATION** on page 16.

Getting there

BY AIR

International and domestic flights arrive at three Berlin airports.

- **Berlin-Schönefeld** *(☎(030) 67870)*. Formerly the airport of East Berlin. International airlines flying to former Communist countries often use Schönefeld. Located SE of central Berlin (off map **7**F7). There is an S-Bahn station at Flughafen Berlin-Schönefeld. Allow about 40 minutes to get from the airport to Bahnhof Friedrichstrasse. The **Airport-Transfer bus** runs between Tegel and Schönefeld airports, stopping at Bahnhof Zoo and other central locations.
- **Berlin-Tegel** *(☎(030) 41011)*. Formerly the main airport of West Berlin. Most major international airlines use Tegel. Located NW of central Berlin (map **6**C4). Bus 109 links the airport with Budapester Strasse, stopping at Adenauerplatz, Uhlandstrasse, Kurfürstendamm and Zoologischer Garten station along the way. Allow 30 minutes for the bus journey. For bus times ☎(030) 2165088. The **Airport-Transfer bus** runs between Tegel and Schönefeld airports, stopping at Bahnhof Zoo and other central locations.
- **Berlin-Tempelhof** *(☎(030) 69091)*. A small city airport, becoming increasingly popular with airlines using small jets for short-haul flights. Located S of central Berlin (map **6**D5). The U-Bahn station Platz der Luftbrücke is opposite the airport terminal. Allow 10–15 minutes for the U-Bahn journey to central Berlin.

BY RAIL

The railway network in Germany is currently run by two separate organizations: the former West German network **Deutsche Bundesbahn (DB)**, and the former East German network **Deutsche Reichsbahn (DR)**.

The railway network has been rapidly improved in recent years, and fast, comfortable international trains now run direct to Berlin from many capital cities including Paris (13–14 hours), Brussels (11–12 hours), Copenhagen (8 hours), Warsaw (10 hours), Moscow (31 hours), Prague ($6\frac{1}{2}$ hours), Vienna (12 hours), Budapest ($16\frac{1}{2}$ hours), Sofia (23 hours) and Belgrade ($22\frac{1}{2}$ hours).

The much-delayed opening of the Eurotunnel, now seriously promised for May 1994, will eventually cut the journey time from Britain to Berlin by several hours, although dramatic changes are not likely for several years, due to the slower rate of progress in developing the necessary high-speed rail lines.

Sleek new **InterCity Express (ICE)** trains were recently introduced on the route from Frankfurt to Berlin via Hannover. These luxurious high-speed trains travel at up to 250kph (155mph) and feature airline-style seats, a conference room, on-board phone and fax, and a smart restaurant. Tickets are more expensive than on other trains. Comfortable **EuroCity (EC)** trains run directly to Berlin from major European cities. **InterCity (IC)** trains run on other international routes. Overnight services use rather older **Schnellzug (D)** trains.

The main railway line runs straight through Berlin from SW to NE. Trains from Paris, Brussels, Amsterdam, Cologne and other northern cities normally stop at all four mainline stations. Trains from Budapest, Bucharest, Warsaw, Dresden and Leipzig usually terminate at either Bahnhof-Lichtenberg or Berlin-Hauptbahnhof. See page 56 for details of the four main Berlin stations serving the international and long-distance lines.

In Berlin, for information on both DB and DR train services ☎(030) 19419. Information can also be obtained from the **German National Tourist Offices** in London or New York (see page 16 for addresses). Tickets can be bought at railway stations or, to avoid a long wait, in offices of the travel agency **DER-Reisebüro**. Check about any special deals such as *Super Sparpreis* tickets.

BY SEA

From Britain, regular train-and-ferry services operate from London's major railway stations. There are two main ferry routes: one crosses from Harwich to Hoek van Holland (6 hours) and the other crosses from Ramsgate to Ostend (4 hours).

The fastest sea crossing is by Jetfoil from Ramsgate to Ostend (1 hour 45 minutes). The total journey time to Berlin from London is 17–19 hours via Ostend and about 30 hours via Hoek van Holland.

BY COACH

Direct coaches run to Berlin from many major European cities, including London, Paris, Brussels, Amsterdam and Frankfurt. They offer a slightly cheaper and sometimes faster alternative to train travel.

Getting around in Berlin

GETTING FROM THE AIRPORTS TO THE CITY

See GETTING THERE BY AIR on page 53.

GETTING AROUND BY PUBLIC TRANSPORT

Berlin has an excellent public transportation network, run since 1929 as an integrated system by **BVG** *(Potsdamer Strasse 188, map 3E6 ☎(030) 2165088).*

The *Region Berlin Fahrplan* is a bulky tome listing the times of all public transport services in Berlin. Although rather heavy to carry around, it is an immensely useful tool, and is available from BVG *(address above).*

See our full-color U-BAHN & S-BAHN MAP at the back of the book.

The U-Bahn

The U-Bahn (subway/underground), founded in 1896, is the fastest means of getting around. Trains run from 4.30am–1am, and lines U1 and U9 continue through the night. Stations (marked at street level with a white **U** on a blue background) tend to be clean and are well designed.

See also U-BAHN on page 152, for a description of interesting sights on the U-Bahn network.

The S-Bahn

The S-Bahn *(Stadtbahn)* elevated railway network was begun in 1875. The main routes are the *Ost-West* and *Nord-Süd* lines, which intersect at Friedrichstrasse station. Administered by East Germany after 1945, the S-Bahn became rather dilapidated, and many stations were closed after the Wall was built, resulting in a boycott by West Berliners. Now run by BVG, the system has greatly improved.

The S-Bahn is useful for getting to outlying districts such as Wannsee, Potsdam and Köpenick. Trains normally run at 10-minute intervals from 4.30am–1am, and line S3 from Charlottenburg to Friedrichstrasse continues through the night. Stations (many of them impressive 19thC iron-and-glass structures) are marked by a white **S** on a green background.

See also BERLIN BY S-BAHN on page 84.

Buses

Buses are slower, but useful for reaching remote corners of the city. You enter the bus at the front, using the door marked *Kasse* if you need to buy a ticket, or *Sichtkarten* if you have a pass (which must be shown to the driver). You leave by the rear door, using the stairs at the back on double-decker buses. Buses are well designed for wheelchairs and baby-carriages, which use the rear door to get on and off. Safety belts are provided to help secure wheelchairs.

Bus stops are marked with a green **H** on a yellow background. **Night buses**, indicated by a yellow number on a green background, continue on several routes throughout the night.

See also BERLIN BY BUS on page 86.

Ferries and trams

BVG also operates a regular **ferry** service across the Havel from Wannsee to Kladow. Some antiquated **trams** *(Strassenbahn)* still rumble through the streets of East Berlin, offering a slow and rather bumpy ride.

Tickets

Tickets are issued for one-way trips *(Normaltarif)* and multiple journeys *(Sammelkarte).* A *Normaltarif* ticket allows you unlimited travel on the BVG network for two hours from the time stamped. Children aged 6–14 years pay a reduced rate *(Ermässigungstarife).* A *Sammelkarte* covers five separate journeys.

The *Ku'damm-Ticket* offers a reduced fare for travel along Kurfürstendamm on buses (except number 109) between Rathenauplatz and Wittenbergplatz. The *Kurzstrekenfahrausweise* is a reduced rate for short journeys by bus, not valid for transfers. Timetables posted at bus stops indicate the zone in which the ticket is valid.

If you are planning to make four or more journeys in a single day, it is cheaper to buy a *Berlin-Ticket (24-Stunden-Karte),* which is valid for 24 hours on all U-Bahn, S-Bahn, bus and tram services. It is also valid on the Wannsee to Kladow ferry run by BVG, and on S-Bahn and bus services from Berlin to Potsdam. It is not valid on special excursion buses from Wannsee (marked with a triangle) or local buses and trams in Potsdam.

The *Familien-Tageskarte* is a one-day ticket valid on weekends, entitling a family of two parents and all children under 16 to unlimited travel.

The combined day ticket *(Kombi-Tageskarte)* is valid for 24 hours on all BVG services, and on scheduled steamer services (known as *Linienverkehr*) run by Stern und Kreisschiffahrt from April to October. It can also be used on certain excursions on the paddle steamer *Havel Queen.* Steamers sail from Tegel, Spandau, Wannsee, Pfaueninsel, Glienicker Brücke and other major landing stages on the Havel. For sailing times ☎(030) 8100040.

Tickets can be bought from counters marked *Fahrausweise* at U-Bahn and S-Bahn stations, and from automatic machines.

Tickets, maps and timetables are sold at the **BVG-Pavillon** *(Hardenbergplatz, opposite Bahnhof Zoo, map* **2***D4* ☎*(030) 2562462, open Mon–Fri 8am–6pm, Sat 7am–2pm, Sun 9am–4pm).*

All tickets, including 24-hour passes, must be stamped in the red *Entwerter* on station platforms and in buses.

The main Berlin stations

The four major Berlin stations are:

- **Bahnhof Zoologischer Garten** (usually known as **Bahnhof Zoo**, map **2**D4). Linked to U-Bahn, S-Bahn and bus routes. Use this station for destinations in the Tiergarten, Charlottenburg and Kreuzberg districts.
- **Bahnhof Friedrichstrasse** (map **4**B8). Linked to U-Bahn, S-Bahn and bus routes. Use this station for addresses in Mitte or Prenzlauer Berg. Friedrichstrasse was formerly the main railway station of East Berlin. While the Wall stood, Friedrichstrasse was the main entry point for travelers arriving from West Berlin. The gloomy waiting room where people were questioned by the East German guards is still standing behind the station.
- **Berlin Hauptbahnhof** (map **7**C5). Linked to S-Bahn and bus routes, but not on the U-Bahn. Despite the name, this is not a station that many international travelers will want to use.

- **Bahnhof-Lichtenberg** (map 7D6). Linked to U-Bahn, S-Bahn and bus routes. Some services from Dresden and Leipzig terminate here.

GETTING AROUND BY TAXI

Taxis can be ordered by telephone *(☎6902, 240024, 240202 or 261026)*, or picked up at one of the taxi stands at Bahnhof Zoo, Savignyplatz and other central locations.

GETTING AROUND BY CAR

There should be no need ever to use a car in Berlin, but, if you have to drive, remember that it is strictly prohibited to pass a stationary tram. The legal minimum age for driving is 18, throughout Germany.

RENTING A CAR

A car is likely to be a hindrance in Berlin, although you might find private transport useful to get out of the city. Most major international car rental firms have branches at Tegel and Schönefeld airports, and in central Berlin. Payment is almost always made by credit card; take along a passport and current driver's license.

Some car rental firms do not allow their cars to be driven in Eastern European countries; check with the rental company before you think of setting off on a trip to Prague or Warsaw.

- **Avis** ☎(030) 0130-7733
- **Europcar** ☎(030) 41013354
- **Hertz** ☎(030) 0130-2121

See also DRIVING IN GERMANY on page 22.

USING A BICYCLE

West Berlin has an extensive network of bicycle lanes (the lanes often run along the sidewalk), and there are numerous attractive routes in the Grunewald to follow. Bicycles may be taken on the S-Bahn (use the doors marked with a bicycle symbol), and on the U-Bahn *(Mon–Fri 9am–2pm and 5.30pm–closing time)*. You use the reduced rate ticket *(Ermässigungstarif)* for a bicycle.

Bicycles can be rented for one or more days at the **Fahrradbüro** *(Hauptstrasse 146, Schöneberg, map* **3** *E6 ☎(030) 7845562, closed Tues, Sat pm, Sun)*, or **Harry's Fahrrad Shop** *(Grolmanstrasse 46, Charlottenburg, map* **2** *D4 ☎(030) 8833942)*. In the summer months, bicycles are rented at Grunewald S-Bahn station and in the Freizeitpark at Tegel.

New destinations can be reached now that the western part of the city is no longer encircled by the Wall. The best map for serious cycling around Berlin is the 1:100,000 Radtourenkarte, which covers *Berlin und Umgebung* (Berlin and environs).

GETTING AROUND ON FOOT

Distances in Berlin are often too great to cover on foot, but some districts are pleasant for wandering, such as Tiergarten, Kreuzberg and Prenzlauer Berg. The Grunewald is the main forest where Berliners stretch their legs on weekends.

For suggested walks and rambles (with maps) see also WALKS on pages 74–84. The Falkplan patent folded map of Berlin is indispensable for rambles in the city and forests. See our color maps **1–4** for a detailed look at the streets of central Berlin.

When out and about on foot, remember that pedestrians who jaywalk can expect to be harangued by drivers, policemen, and old ladies eager to uphold the law.

NAME CHANGES OF BERLIN STREETS AND STATIONS

Many street names in eastern Berlin have changed in the wake of reunification. Most of the streets named in honor of Communist leaders have reverted to their former names, although Karl-Marx-Allee has so far survived the purges. If asking directions, remember that many East Berliners are still more familiar with the old street names.

Among the names that have vanished from Berlin maps, the following are the most important:

- **Platz der Akademie** (now **Gendarmenmarkt)**
- **Heinrich-Rau-Strasse** (now **Märkische Allee)**
- **Klement-Gottwald-Allee** (now **Berliner Allee)**
- **Leninallee** (now **Landsberger Allee**)
- **Marx-Engels-Brücke** (now **Schlossbrücke)**
- **Marx-Engels-Platz** (now **Lustgarten**)
- **Otto-Grotewohl-Strasse** (now **Toleranzstrasse)**
- **Otto-Nuschke-Strasse** (now **Jägerstrasse**)
- **Wilhelm-Pieck-Strasse** (now **Elsässerstrasse)**

You can't rely on out-of-date transport maps either, as some station names have also changed. For example, you now take the S-Bahn to **Hackescher Markt** (formerly **Marx-Engels-Platz**) and the U-Bahn to **Mohrenstrasse** (formerly **Otto-Grotewohl-Strasse**).

MAPS

Even Berliners need a good map to get around the city these days. Most people are at a loss when they venture into the parts of the city that were once forbidden territory. To make matters worse, street names have been changed, although signposts often still bear the old name. The best you can do is to buy an up-to-date map with the new street names. As a test, look up "Toleranzstrasse" (see our map **3**C7) in the index. If you can't find it, don't buy the map.

The most reliable large map is the latest edition of the Falkplan map of Berlin. On a smaller scale, our full-color U-BAHN & S-BAHN MAP and city maps **1–4** at the back of the book are up to date as at January 1994.

On-the-spot information

BANKS AND CURRENCY EXCHANGE

Banks in Berlin are normally open Monday to Friday 9am–3.30pm, and two afternoons a week until 6pm.

Banks with slightly different opening hours include the following:

- The **Berliner Commerzbank** *(at Maison de France, Kurfürstendamm 211, map 2D4)* remains open Monday to Friday until 6pm, Saturday 10am–1pm.
- Branches of the **Sparkasse der Stadt Berlin** *(at Kurfürstendamm 11, map 2D4 ☎(030) 8827671, at Savignyplatz 9, map 2D4, at the Internationales Congress Centrum (ICC), and at other locations where a Spätservice (extended service) operates)* are open similar hours.
- The bank at the **KaDeWe** department store *(Wittenbergplatz, Schöneberg, map 2D5 ☎(030) 2114182)* is open Monday to Friday from 10am–6.30pm, Saturday 10am–2pm, or until 6pm on the first Saturday of every month.
- The *Wechselstube* (currency exchange) at **Bahnhof Zoo** *(map 2D4 ☎(030) 8817117)* is open Monday to Saturday 8am–9pm, Sunday 10am–6pm, and at **Tegel airport** *(☎(030) 4135049)* daily 8am–10pm.

SHOPPING HOURS

For details of German shopping hours, see page 20.

Turkish-run stores in Kreuzberg and Neukölln are sometimes open on Saturday and Sunday, while shops in a few U-Bahn stations such as Kurfürstendamm open late and on weekends.

MAIL, TELEPHONE AND FAX SERVICES

For further information, see also page 21.

Postcodes A national five-digit system has now been introduced in East and West Germany. Addresses in Central Berlin begin with a **10**, northwestern districts with a **13**, southwestern districts with a **14**, and southeastern districts with a **12**.

Post offices Marked *Post* or *Postamt,* post offices are usually open Monday to Friday 8am–6pm, Saturday 8am–noon. The **Main Post Office** *(Hauptpostamt)* at Bahnhof Zoo *(map 2D4 ☎(030) 3139799)* has one counter that never closes.

General Delivery (poste restante) Letters to be collected should be marked *Hauptpostlagernd* and addressed to Bahnhofpostlagernd, Postamt 120, Bahnhof Zoo, 10623 Berlin. Collect at the desk marked *Postlagernde Sendungen* and take a passport for identification.

American Express offers a mail-holding service to its customers. Write to: Client Mail, American Express Travel Service, Uhlandstrasse 173, 10719 Berlin *(map 2D4 ☎(030) 8827575)*.

Making a telephone call Calls between West and East Berlin used to be treated as international calls, but the two networks are now merged. The former East German telephone network is currently being modernized. Until completion (no date is yet fixed), be patient, as you may have difficulty dialing to or from former East Berlin.

- **Berlin area code** The national area code for Berlin is **030.**
- **To call Berlin from the UK** ☎010-49-30 + number
- **To call Berlin from the US** ☎011-49-30 + number

Faxes Urgent documents can be sent from a fax machine located at **Bahnhof Zoo post office** *(map **2**D4),* or from **Trigger** *(Pohlstrasse 69, map **3**D6).* Most major hotels will send faxes for nonresidents.

WOMEN

Berlin boasts a well-developed network of organizations for women. The **Fraueninfothek** *(Leibnitzstrasse 57, map **1**D3 ☎(030) 3245078, open Tues–Sat 9am–9pm, Sun 9am–3pm)* provides useful information for women visiting Berlin.

Women can chat together at several women-only cafés such as **Dinelo** *(Vorbergstrasse 10, map **3**E6).* A small hotel in Wilmersdorf is run exclusively for women tourists: the **Frauenhotel Artemisia** *(Brandenburgische Strasse 18, map **1**E3 ☎(030) 878905 Fx(030) 8618653).*

DISABLED VISITORS

The provision for disabled people in Berlin is generally good. Buses have specially designed rear doors for wheelchair access, and safety straps to attach a wheelchair firmly. A booklet, *Berlin-Stadtführer für Behinderte,* available free from **Landesamt für Zentrale Soziale Aufgaben** *(Sächsische Strasse, 10707 Berlin, map **1**E3 ☎(030) 8676114),* contains detailed information on facilities available for handicapped people in Berlin.

LOCAL PUBLICATIONS

The monthly *Berlin Programm,* available from tourist offices, provides a comprehensive listing of theater, opera, dance, music, cabaret, museums, exhibitions and other events in Berlin and Potsdam, plus international train and airline timetables. German tourist offices abroad also often stock a few copies.

Two thick magazines publish comprehensive listings of events in Berlin. *Zitty,* printed on recycled paper, is the more comprehensive, with long lists of movies, plays, children's events, workshops and television programs. *Tip,* its glossy rival, contains the same basic information in a more user-friendly format. Each magazine covers two weeks of events. They are both targeted at youthful Berliners; for information on opera and classical music, *Berlin Programm* is the better buy.

Unlike many major European cities, there is currently nothing published in the English language in Berlin. For **international and English-language publications**, see SHOPPING on page 199.

Several **German newspapers** are published in Berlin. The weighty leftish weekly *Die Zeit* is written in ponderous prose that even Germans sometimes find daunting. *Tageszeitung,* known as *TAZ,* is a serious alternative daily, but the best paper for local news is the *Berliner Morgenpost.*

Useful numbers and addresses

TELEPHONE SERVICES

- **Directory inquiries** (Germany) ☎1188
- **Directory inquiries** (abroad) ☎00118
- **Telegrams** ☎1131

TOURIST INFORMATION

The main tourist information office **(Verkehrsamt Berlin)** is situated in the **Europa-Center** *(use the Budapester Strasse entrance, map **2**D5 ☎(030) 2626031),* open daily 8am–10.30pm.

Other information offices, open daily from 8am–11pm, are located at **Tegel airport** *(map **6**C4 ☎(030) 41013145)* and **Bahnhof Zoo** *(map **2**D4 ☎(030) 3139063).* Another, open 8am–8pm, is situated at the base of the **Fernsehturm** *(Alexanderplatz, Mitte, map **4**B9 ☎(030) 2424675).*

Good general information can be had from the **Informationszentrum** *(Hardenbergstrasse 20, 2nd floor, map **2**C4 ☎(030)310040, open Mon–Fri 8am–7pm, Sat 8am–4pm).* See also WOMEN opposite.

American Express Travel Service *(branches at Uhlandstrasse 173, Charlottenburg, map **2**D4 ☎(030) 8827575, open Mon–Fri 9am–5.30pm, Sat 9am–noon; and Friedrichstrasse 172, map **4**C8 ☎ (030) 2150, open same hours)* is an invaluable source of information for any traveler in need of help, advice or emergency services.

BOAT TOURS

Boat excursions in Berlin are organized by the following companies:

- **Berliner Geschichtswerkstatt** ☎(030) 2154450. Boat tours (May–Sept) through the heart of Berlin on the Spree and Landwehrkanal, focusing on Berlin's history.
- **Reederei Bruno Winkler** ☎(030) 3917010. River trips from Schloss Charlottenburg.
- **Reederei Horst Schlenther** ☎(030) 4162732. Daily six-hour Havel cruise from Tegeler Weg in Charlottenburg to Potsdam.
- **Reederei Triebler** ☎(030) 3315414. Trips from S-Bahnhof Wannsee to Potsdam.
- **Spreefahrt Horst Duggen** ☎(030) 3944954. Trips on the Spree and Landwehrkanal, departing from the Kongresshalle.
- **Stern und Kreisschiffahrt** ☎(030) 8100040. Regular services on the Havel between Tegel, Spandau, Wannsee and Pfaueninsel, and trips to Potsdam and Tempelhof.
- **Weisse Flotte Berlin** ☎(030) 2712327. Cruises in East Berlin from Treptow pier.

BUS TOURS

Departure times and dates of bus tours appear in *Berlin Programm.* The following companies run bus excursions:

- **BBS** Buses leave from Gedächtniskirche *(map **2**D4 ☎(030) 2134077)* and Alexanderplatz *(map **4**B9 ☎(030) 2124362).* Tours of Berlin and day trips to Dresden and the Spreewald.

- **BVB** ☎(030) 8859880. Buses from Kurfürstendamm 225 *(map 2D4)*. Tours of Berlin and day trips to Dresden and the Spreewald.
- **BVG** ☎(030) 2567039. Tours of Berlin in a replica 1920s bus with an open roof. Bus departs from Gedächtniskirche *(map 2D4)*.
- **Berolina Sightseeing** ☎(030) 8822091. Buses from Kurfürstendamm 220 *(map 2D4)* and Karl-Liebknecht-Strasse *(map 4B9)*. Tours of Berlin and day trips to Dresden and the Spreewald.
- **Kultur Kontor** ☎(030) 310888. Informed cultural tours on topics such as 1920s Berlin, architecture and literature. Buses leave from Savignyplatz 9 *(map 2D4)*.
- **Severin & Kuhn** ☎(030) 8831015. Buses from Kurfürstendamm 216 *(map 2D4)*. Tours of Berlin and Spreewald day trips.

AIRLINES

- **Air France** Europa-Center, map **2**D5 ☎(030) 261051
- **British Airways** Europa-Center, map **2**D5 ☎(030) 691021
- **Delta Air Lines** Europa-Center, map **2**D5 ☎(030) 0130-2526 (toll-free)
- **Lufthansa** Kurfürstendamm 220, map **2**D4 ☎(030) 88755

MAJOR LIBRARIES

- **Amerika-Gedenkbibliothek** Blücherplatz, Kreuzberg, map **4**E8 ☎(030) 69050
- **Staatsbibliothek Preussischer Kulturbesitz** Potsdamer Strasse 33, Tiergarten, map **3**D7 ☎(030) 2662303. Also at Unter den Linden 8, Mitte, map **4**B8 ☎(030) 203780

PLACES OF WORSHIP

Churches are listed in the Berlin telephone directory under *Kirchen.*

- **Französischer Dom** (Französische Friedrichstadtkirche) Gendarmenmarkt, Mitte, map **4**C8 ☎(030) 2291522.
- **Kaiser-Wilhelm-Gedächtniskirche** Breitscheidplatz, Charlottenburg, map **2**D4 ☎(030) 2185023. Service in English every Sunday at 9am.
- **St David and St George** Preussenallee 16–17, Charlottenburg, off map **1**C1 ☎(030) 3091. Anglican service.
- **St. Hedwigs-Kathedrale** Bebelplatz, off Unter den Linden, Mitte, map **4**C8 ☎(030) 2004761. Catholic service.

CONSULATES IN BERLIN

Other countries are listed in the telephone directory under *Konsulate.*

- **Canada** Friedrichstrasse 95, map **4**B8 ☎(030) 2611161
- **Ireland** Ernst-Reuter-Platz 10, map **2**C4 ☎(030) 34800822
- **Japan** Wachtelstrasse 8, Dahlem, map **6**E4 ☎(030) 8327026
- **United Kingdom** Unter den Linden 32–34, map **4**C8 ☎(030) 2202431
- **United States** Neustädtische Kirchstrasse 4–5, Mitte, map **4**B8 ☎(030) 2385174

Business in Berlin

Many new facilities are currently being developed in Berlin.

CONFERENCE HOTELS

Berlin's new-found role as an international business city has prompted the development of sophisticated in-hotel conference facilities, and the best hotels now offer the latest technology for showing transparencies, transmitting messages and interpreting languages. The following can be counted on to meet most needs. For fuller accommodation details, see pages 161–67.

- **Berlin Hilton** Mohrenstrasse 30, 10117 Berlin. Map 4C8 ☎(030) 23820 Fx(030) 23824269. Ten conference rooms available, including five smaller rooms. Maximum capacity 400.
- **Grand Hotel Esplanade** Lützowufer 15, 10785 Berlin. Map **3**D6 ☎(030) 261011 Fx(030) 2651171. Eight conference rooms are available; the largest seats 450, while the intimate library holds 30. A river boat can also be rented for a canal-cruise.
- **Inter-Continental Berlin** Budapester Strasse 2, Charlottenburg, 10787 Berlin. Map **2**D5 ☎(030) 26020 Fx(030) 260280760. See also entry below. There is a choice of ten conference rooms, including the renovated Congress Center, which seats 1,250. The hotel works in cooperation with the nearby **Schweizerhof** *(Budapester Strasse 21, 10787 Berlin, map* ***2****D5* *☎(030) 26960).* The two hotels together can deal with up to 2,000 delegates.

BUSINESS CENTERS

A handful of Berlin hotels now have business centers equipped, at the very least, with word processors, faxes and photocopiers, but the best is undoubtedly in the hotel INTER-CONTINENTAL BERLIN (see below, plus entry in HOTELS A TO Z, and also CONFERENCE HOTELS above).

- **Inter-Continental Berlin Business Center**, Budapester Strasse 2, Charlottenburg, 10787 Berlin ☎(030) 26020 Fx(030) 260280760. Map **2**D5. Business center open Mon–Fri 9am–5.30pm. This center is equipped with state-of-the-art Philips personal computers, desktop publishing facilities, laser printers, portable telephones and photocopiers. You can hire an in-house secretary by the hour. Some executive bedrooms are equipped with two telephone numbers, four outside lines and a fax.

EXHIBITIONS AND CONFERENCES

The vast **Messegelände** *(Hammarskjöldplatz, map* ***5****D3),* comprising two dozen halls, is the main venue for exhibitions. The adjoining **Internationales Congress Centrum (ICC)** *(Messedamm 19, U-Bahn to Theodor-Heuss-Platz for both centers)* can host up to 20,000 delegates.

CONFERENCE ORGANIZATION

CPO Hanser Service Schaumburgallee 12, Charlottenburg, 14052 Berlin ☎(030) 3053131 Fx(030) 3057391. Organizes conferences, group excursions and special theme evenings in Berlin and Potsdam.

Emergency information

For advice on **automobile accidents**, **lost passport** and **emergency phrases**, see EMERGENCY INFORMATION on page 23.

EMERGENCY SERVICES

Coins are not needed for emergency calls from public telephones.

- **Police** ☎110
- **Fire** ☎112
- **Ambulance** ☎112; ☎115 in East Berlin.

MEDICAL AND DENTAL EMERGENCIES

- **Doctors' emergency service** (24 hours) ☎310031
- **Dentists' emergency service** (24 hours) ☎1141
- There is no English or American hospital in Berlin, except those that cater solely to the military.

FIRST AID

- **First-aid assistance** ☎310031

PHARMACIES

Pharmacies are open during normal shop hours. A list of those open at night and on Sunday is placed in the window of every pharmacy. For information on all-night pharmacies ☎(030) 1141.

- **Europa-Apotheke** Tauentzienstrasse 9, map **2D5** ☎2614142. Open daily 9am–9pm.

CAR BREAKDOWNS

- ☎ police (110), or the **ADAC** (road patrol) ☎(030) 19211
- See also EMERGENCY INFORMATION on page 23.

LOST PROPERTY

Report all losses to the police immediately, as insurance claims may not be accepted without a police report.

- For lost items, contact the police lost property office (**Fundbüro der Polizei**) *(Tempelhofer Damm 3, off map* ***4****F8* ☎ *(030) 6990).*
- For items lost on **public transport**, go to the **Fundbüro der BVG** *(Potsdamer Strasse 184, Schöneberg, map* ***3****E6* ☎ *(030) 2161413).*
- If you have lost **American Express travelers checks** ☎0130-853100 (24 hours, toll-free).

Berlin: planning your visit

Orientation

Berlin (population 3.2 million) is located on the River Spree, 40 meters (131 feet) above sea-level. The countryside around is mainly flat, dotted with lakes and woods. **Potsdam** is 24 kilometers (15 miles) to the southwest; **Hamburg** is 289 kilometers (180 miles) to the northwest; **Dresden** is 198 kilometers (123 miles) to the south. The **Polish border** lies 105 kilometers (65 miles) to the east at Frankfurt/Oder. The nearest coastal town is **Rostock**, on the Baltic, 222 kilometers (138 miles) to the northwest.

When to go

A lively, cosmopolitan city all year long, Berlin has much to offer by day and night, as well as superb churches, palaces, museums and galleries.

Spring in Berlin tends to be mild, while summers are hot. Early summer is the time to see the lime trees in blossom on UNTER DEN LINDEN. From about May to September, you can sit in the leafy TIERGARTEN or enjoy open-air concerts in the parks and zoos. Berlin does not suffer from the "dead" spell that afflicts some other European capitals during July or August.

The beech and oak woods to the west of the city look their best in fall, while Berlin's winters, although often severe, offer an excellent opportunity to take full advantage of the city's uncrowded museums.

The Berlin calendar

It is worth consulting a checklist of annual events due to take place in the city. You may want to be sure to catch a particular attraction — or you may wish to avoid the crowds at all costs. Some events span two or more months, and the exact date may vary from year to year. Check with the **German National Tourist Office** *(addresses on page 16)*.

Berlin has several annual **music festivals**, a major **film festival** and various **theater festivals**. For information on forthcoming events in Berlin, contact **Infoladen und Galerie der Berliner Festspiele** *(Budapester Strasse 50, Tiergarten, map* ***2****D5* ☎ *(030) 254890)*. Information on all the festivals is also listed in *Berlin Programm*.

See also PUBLIC HOLIDAYS on page 20.

JANUARY
January to February: **Berliner Musiktage**: three-week festival of experimental music.

FEBRUARY
Mid-February: **Festival des politischen Liedes**. Festival of Political Song. • Late February: **Internationale Filmfestspiele Berlin**. Several hundred movies from every continent are screened at the two-week Berlin Film Festival. Berlin was once the place to catch urgent political films. The program is more eclectic these days, but Berlin still remains a forum for bizarre and off-beat movies, usually screened in the original language and carrying subtitles. Winning films receive the Golden Bear award.

APRIL
Easter: Parents take their children to look at **KaDeWe's window displays** featuring mechanized scenes from nature. • Early April to early May: **Freie Berliner Kunstausstellung** (FBK). This major show of works by Berlin artists takes place at the Messegelände exhibition center.

MAY
May: **Theatertreffen Berlin**. Berlin Theater Festival, featuring experimental German theater, pantomime, dance and circus at various venues. • Whitsun: Early morning **classical music concerts** in the zoo and at various parks. • May to September: **Spandauer Sommerfestspiele**. Summer festival of theater and music at Spandau *(for information ☎(030) 3316920)*.

JUNE
All month: **International jazz** in the garden of the Neue Nationalgalerie. • Early June: **Festival of Traditional Music**. • Mid to end June: **Festival of classical music** in Sanssouci Park, Potsdam. • End June: **Köpenicker Sommer**. Commemorative parade and festival at Köpenick.

JULY
July to August: Open-air **classical concerts by the Berlin Philharmonic** at the Waldbühne amphitheater. • July to August: **Organ concerts** in the chapel at Schloss Charlottenburg *(Sat, Sun ☎(030) 8173364 for dates)*. • Early July: **Internationales Drehorgelfest**. Whimsical street festival of barrel organs from Berlin and other places. • Second week: **Berliner Bachtage**. Bach festival *(details from: Büro der Berliner Bachtage, Bismarckstrasse 73, 10627 Berlin; map **1** C3 ☎(030) 3123677)*.

AUGUST
End August: **Berliner Tierparkfest**. Events for children at Tierpark Friedrichsfelde.

SEPTEMBER
Berliner Festwochen. Berlin Festival. Extended festival celebrating the culture of a particular period through a varied program of opera, dance, classical concerts, theater, painting, film and literature.

OCTOBER
October: **Berliner Festtage**. Theater and film festival. • First Sunday in October: **Berlin Marathon**. • Mid-October: **Orangerie**. A major art and antiques fair held every two years (next in 1995). Originally held in the Orangerie at Schloss Charlottenburg, the fair caused a stir in the dusty world of antique dealers by displaying the works in a museum setting. • End October to early November: **JazzFest Berlin**. International jazz festival held in the Philharmonie concert hall and the Delphi-Filmpalast.

DECEMBER
December: **Christmas markets** at Breitscheidplatz and below the Funkturm.

Organizing your time

Berlin is a big city, with an overwhelming list of sights. If you are visiting for only a few days, you must accept that you won't see everything. Even if you managed four museums a day, it would take almost a month to see them all.

Don't be put off. You can get a fair bite at the city in a brief visit, particularly if you make good use of the public transport system (see the color map of the U-BAHN & S-BAHN at the back of the book).

The following pages offer some suggested itineraries and ideas for themed visits. Turn to page 90 for the LIST OF SIGHTS CLASSIFIED BY TYPE, which may help you focus on specific themes. Suggestions for enthusiastic walkers are given on pages 74-84, and a one-day visit to POTSDAM is also well worth the effort.

WHAT TO SEE; WHAT TO DO

- There are some Berlin visual experiences that should not be missed. They include, in no particular order: the bust of Nefertiti, the Gendarmenmarkt, the Pergamon altar, the Flemish Masters at the Gemäldegalerie, Schloss Charlottenburg, Unter den Linden, the Brücke-Museum and the Museum für Verkehr und Technik. New sights are being added to the stock every day. Art lovers are particularly looking forward to the return of the Trojan treasure, which has been hidden in a vault in Moscow since the end of World War II. If the Russians keep their promise and the treasure is returned, it should be added to that list of unmissable sights.
- Other experiences to be savored if at all possible include: a concert by the Berlin Philharmonic Orchestra, a walk in the Tiergarten, a visit

to the excellent delicatessen on the 6th floor of the KaDeWe department store, a taste of *Currywurst* and *Eisbein*, a glass of *Berliner Weisse* beer, a ride on the S-Bahn through central Berlin from Savignyplatz to Hackescher Markt, an evening on Kurfürstendamm, and breakfast in a café.

- Try to keep back some energy for the Berlin night. Reserve ahead on the day you arrive for any shows or plays that you want to see. Tickets can be ordered at *Theaterkassen* throughout the city (details on page 181). The night mood is special, especially on long summer evenings. See BERLIN AFTER DARK, starting on page 181, for some ideas.
- When it comes to the evening, you might find it difficult to linger for long over a meal. People tend to eat a rapid meal — probably something Italian — before hitting the cinemas and theaters.

SOME DO'S AND DON'TS

- **Don't** be tempted to bet on a street game called *Hütchenspiel* (hat game), in which a little ball is concealed under one of three boxes. You always lose, even when you are sure you have cracked the secret.
- **Don't** visit Alexanderplatz after dark. There is no one around and nothing to do.
- **Do avoid** the bars in the Sperlingsgasse — unless you want to spend a noisy evening among parties of tourists.
- **Don't** wait in the crowded main hall of Bahnhof Zoologischer Garten. The InterCity Restaurant is comfortable.
- **Hold onto** your handbag and wallet as you would do in New York or Rome. Berlin is not a particularly unsafe city, but crime is on the rise.

A FIVE-DAY VISIT

Day 1 — Finding your feet; first impressions

- Travel by S-Bahn from Savignyplatz to Friedrichstrasse. The overground railway takes you straight through the heart of the city, where the biggest changes are taking place.
- Spend the morning at the MUSEUMSINSEL, visiting one or two (but probably not all) of the museums. Despite the daunting crowds, the PERGAMON-MUSEUM is a must for anyone interested in the ancient civilizations of Babylon, Rome and Greece. The collection includes entire buildings shipped from the Mediterranean to Berlin.
- Lunch in the NIKOLAIVIERTEL.
- Stroll along UNTER DEN LINDEN to admire the carefully reconstructed Baroque and Neoclassical buildings. Cross Friedrichstrasse, and go on down Unter den Linden to the BRANDENBURGER TOR, a Neoclassical monument which has been adopted as the symbol of reunited Berlin. Turn right beyond the gate to reach the REICHSTAG, where the German parliament sometimes assembles.
- Take bus 100 to the terminus at Bahnhof Zoo, and walk along Hardenbergstrasse to find the KAISER-WILHELM-GEDÄCHTNISKIRCHE, left as a ruin to remind future generations of the devastation of war. The church makes a suitable departure point for a stroll along KURFÜRSTENDAMM, Berlin's elegant shopping street, which runs to the W.

Day 2 — The green spaces (for sunny days)

- Visit the ZOOLOGISCHER GARTEN and walk in the TIERGARTEN. Take the S-Bahn to GRUNEWALD and walk in the forest. Try to end up at one of the rustic country inns tucked away in the woods.
- Alternatively, follow WALK 1, along the banks of the SPREE (see page 74), making a three- to four-hour walk last all day by taking time out to visit the TIERGARTEN.

Day 3 — Berlin art (good for a rainy day)

- Spend the morning at SCHLOSS CHARLOTTENBURG, visiting the ÄGYPTISCHES MUSEUM, the GALERIE DER ROMANTIK and the Goldene Galerie. Lunch at Luisen-Brau, just outside the grounds of the Schloss (details in BEER GARDENS on page 180).
- In the afternoon, take the U-Bahn from Richard-Wagner-Platz (a 5-minute walk from Schloss Charlottenburg) to Dahlem-Dorf. Look at the collection of Old Masters at the GEMÄLDEGALERIE.

Day 4 — Becoming a Berliner

- Lie in bed until 11am. Eat breakfast in a Kreuzberg café. Go to the Viktoriapark. Eat a sausage at a stand-up stall and drink a *Berliner Weisse.* Stay up late.

Day 5 — Goodbye to Berlin

- Visit one last sight, such as the BRÜCKE-MUSEUM, with its almost unknown collection of 20thC German art, or any other sight that appeals (see the LIST OF SIGHTS on page 90; recommended sights are marked with the ★ symbol). Write postcards home in a café on Kurfürstendamm. Buy any souvenirs you need at the KaDeWe.
- Climb the tower of the FRANZÖSISCHER DOM for a last view of the city. Repeat to yourself as you leave the city, *Ich habe noch ein Koffer in Berlin* (I still have a suitcase in Berlin.) The catch phrase, from a Marlene Dietrich song, is the exiled Berliner's way of saying he will be back one day.

A THREE-DAY ARCHITECTURE TOUR

See ARCHITECTURE on page 42 for a brief introduction to the architecture of the city. Several excellent guides to Berlin architecture can be bought in the Bücherbogen bookstore (address on page 195).

Day 1

- Visit Schinkel's ALTES MUSEUM, then walk down to UNTER DEN LINDEN to look at Schinkel's Schloss Brücke and the Neue Wache.
- Go to the Schinkel Museum in the FRIEDRICHSWERDERSCHE KIRCHE.
- Walk to GENDARMENMARKT to climb the tower of the FRANZÖSISCHER DOM. This is a good vantage point to survey the harmonious proportions of the Gendarmenmarkt square.

Day 2

- Visit SCHLOSS CHARLOTTENBURG in the morning, looking especially at the Goldene Galerie and the Schinkel-Pavillon.
- Stroll through Kreuzberg (see WALK 2 on page 78) in the afternoon, to see some of the best new architecture in Berlin, such as the Wohnpark am Berlin Museum *(Lindenstrasse 15-19),* and the nearby Wohnanlage Ritterstrasse *(Ritterstrasse 55-60 and 61-65).*

- Visit the Aedes gallery, where various models and plans of utopian architectural projects are displayed (see ART GALLERIES on page 193).

Day 3

- Visit POTSDAM (see pages 205-247), particularly the Baroque old town, SCHLOSS SANSSOUCI, the Rococo CHINESISCHES TEEHAUS, and Schinkel's SCHLOSS CHARLOTTENHOF.

A THREE-DAY GERMAN ART TOUR

For a brief introduction to the subject, turn to ART IN BERLIN on page 47.

Day 1

- Study the German Renaissance art in the GEMÄLDEGALERIE (Wing B) and the SKULPTURENGALERIE, both at Dahlem.

Day 2

- Look at the 19thC Romantics in the GALERIE DER ROMANTIK in the morning.
- Take bus 110 to Clayallee and walk through the woods to the JAGDSCHLOSS GRUNEWALD to discover an unexpected collection of German Renaissance art displayed in a historic hunting lodge. Visit the BRÜCKE-MUSEUM for a glimpse of one of the few collections of early 20thC Berlin art to have survived the Nazi purges of "decadent art."

Day 3

- Look at the postwar art in the NEUE NATIONALGALERIE in the morning, then go to the ALTE NATIONALGALERIE on MUSEUMSINSEL to see a small but captivating collection of German art ranging from the Baroque to the early 20thC.

A TWO-DAY BERLIN HISTORY TOUR

Day 1

- Follow the Kreuzberg walk (see WALK 2 on page 78) as far as the BERLIN-MUSEUM. Look around the museum's fascinating collection, and be sure not to miss the toys in the attic. Then stop for lunch in the museum's *Weissbierstube*.
- Visit the MÄRKISCHES MUSEUM in the afternoon to look at Berlin's second historical museum. Many of the oldest relics of Berlin are displayed in a fascinating old building standing near one of the last fragments of the medieval city wall.
- Take the U-Bahn to Kochstrasse to visit the HAUS AM CHECKPOINT CHARLIE, located near a former border crossing on the Wall. It remains open until late in the evening.

Day 2

- Visit the REICHSTAG in the morning (if it is not being used by the German parliament). Take lunch in one of the restaurants in the building.
- In the afternoon, take bus 100 to UNTER DEN LINDEN and visit the revamped DEUTSCHES HISTORISCHES MUSEUM for an informative insight into German history.

Berlin: sightseeing

An overview of the city

The brutal Cold War division of Berlin into East and West, Communist and Capitalist, no longer exists. The Wall that once ran through the city from north to south has gone, although you can still instinctively tell whether you are in the old East or West sector. The architecture, the shops and the lifestyles remain different. Yet Berlin has become far more complex since the Wall vanished, and it takes some time to get to grips with the 883 square kilometers (341 square miles) of urban area.

NATURAL FEATURES
Berlin stands on an area of flat land drained by several sluggish rivers. There are few natural hills to climb for a view, and the best vantage points tend to be man-made structures, such as church towers, broadcasting masts and hills built from the rubble of buildings bombed in World War II. Turn to VIEWPOINTS on page 155 to find where to go to get an aerial view of Berlin.

The most prominent natural features are the rivers that meander through Berlin. The River Spree flows through Berlin from the Müggelsee on the SE edge of the city to the River Havel on the W edge, while the River Havel skirts the W edge of the city through a series of large lakes. The other river to note is the Dahme, which flows from the S to join the Spree near the Müggelsee. You may also come across a canal, the Teltowkanal, which runs from the Spree through the southern quarters of Berlin to link with the Havel near Potsdam.

THE STREETS
More impressive than the rivers are the wide streets that cut across the city. The main arteries to identify on the map are the stately Unter den Linden in the historic heart of Berlin, which runs from the Brandenburger Tor to the Spree, and the lively Kurfürstendamm, which cuts through the prosperous western districts of the city in a frenzy of neon and noise.

Other streets to look up for future reference are Friedrichstrasse, which crosses Unter den Linden, and Kantstrasse, a busy artery running parallel to Kurfürstendamm.

Finding an address in Berlin can be difficult if you are not familiar with the German system of street numbering. The general rule is that numbers run consecutively down one side of the street and back along the other side. A single number often refers to an entire block and, to make matters even worse, many Berlin buildings are often not numbered at all. The best way of finding an address is to head for a major intersection, where the street signs usually indicate the direction in which the numbers run.

DISTRICTS

Berliners tend to break down the sprawling metropolis into districts *(Bezirke).* There are 23 official districts, each one with a town hall *(Rathaus)* symbolizing its political power. Tourists are most likely to find themselves in the central districts of Charlottenburg, Tiergarten, Schöneberg and Mitte. Trips to the forest may involve traveling to outlying districts such as Spandau, Zehlendorf or Köpenick, while quests after dark in search of throbbing clubs or bars may lead down streets in Kreuzberg and Prenzlauer Berg.

The Wall may have gone for good, but the districts which lay in East Berlin still differ from those of West Berlin. The division is bound to become more blurred as time passes, but it is still useful to be able to distinguish the respective districts of West and East Berlin.

The 12 districts which once formed West Berlin are Charlottenburg, Kreuzberg, Neukölln, Reinickendorf, Schöneberg, Spandau, Steglitz, Tempelhof, Tiergarten, Wedding, Wilmersdorf and Zehlendorf. The 11 districts in the former Soviet sector are Friedrichshain, Heinersdorf, Hohenschönhausen, Köpenick, Lichtenberg, Marzahn, Mitte, Pankow, Prenzlauer Berg, Treptow and Weissensee. A brief introduction to the main districts is given below.

For an overview of the city, see color maps **5–7**, and for detailed maps of the central districts, see color maps **1–4**.

• The central districts

These districts lie at the heart of Berlin, and tend to have the best of the hotels, restaurants, museums and nightlife.

CHARLOTTENBURG *(map **1**; W of the old city).* An elegant 19thC district that developed around SCHLOSS CHARLOTTENBURG and KURFÜRSTENDAMM. It was the heart of West Berlin, and still has the city's most fashionable stores, cafés, hotels, galleries and movie theaters.

KREUZBERG *(map **4**; S of the old city).* A 19thC district of large apartments and factories. Partially destroyed by wartime bombardment, it has become an animated quarter settled by migrants, political activists, punks and artists. Dotted with radical galleries and chic restaurants.

MITTE *(map **4**; Central Berlin).* A strange mixture of Old Berlin and Moscow. This was the heart of the old city, and you can still find many traces of Imperial Berlin. There are splendid architectural creations such as UNTER DEN LINDEN, MUSEUMSINSEL and GENDARMENMARKT, but you will also find ugly Communist blocks, plots of wasteland untouched since 1945, and shabby streets. Mitte is in the throes of change, but the transformation is going slowly, and there is still a shortage of good hotels, cafés and restaurants.

PRENZLAUER BERG *(map **7**; N of the old center).* A fascinating 19thC working-class district of apartment blocks and factories, with a typical

East Berlin mix of dilapidated grandeur and prim restoration. Alternative cafés, art galleries and 1950s milk bars generate an atmosphere akin to that in Kreuzberg.

TIERGARTEN *(map 3; between Mitte and Charlottenburg).* An elegant quarter bordering Berlin's principal park. Badly bombed in World War II, it is now a mixture of 19thC villas and modern apartment blocks. A major cultural quarter, the KULTUR-FORUM, stands on the S edge of the park, and the ZOOLOGISCHER GARTEN is located in its SW corner.

WEDDING *(map 6; N of Tiergarten).* A working-class 19thC district of grim apartment blocks and factories. Interesting historically as the scene of many clashes between Communists and Nazis.

• The outer districts

These are the districts where you find forests, open fields and village churches.

KÖPENICK *(map 7; SE corner of the city).* An appealing, although somewhat run-down old town, set among forests and lakes.

SPANDAU *(map 5; W edge of the city).* A historic town on the Havel, with an attractive old center.

TEGEL *(maps 5 to 6; N of Charlottenburg).* A pleasant old town surrounded by forests and lakes.

WILMERSDORF *(maps 1 to 2; S of Charlottenburg).* A prosperous residential quarter where elderly ladies appear to pursue a lifestyle based on walking the dog and eating cake. As it approaches Charlottenburg, the district becomes thick with cafés, restaurants and art galleries.

NEIGHBORHOODS

Berliners, like other urban dwellers, like to think in terms of compact neighborhoods rather than large administrative districts. With the aid of a map, the visitor can track down the most intimate corners of Berlin, where locals linger over a beer in a favorite café, or sit on a bench in the sun watching their children play.

DAHLEM *(Zehlendorf; map 5 E3).* This old village on the edge of the Grunewald still retains a rural air around the village church. Elsewhere, you find grand 19thC villas, university buildings and museums.

NIKOLAIVIERTEL *(Mitte; map 4 C9. U-Bahn to Alexanderplatz).* A postwar reconstruction of an Old Berlin neighborhood, with cafés, restaurants and craft shops. Some Berliners admire the mock Hanseatic architecture; others dismiss the exercise as "Honecker's Disneyland." Yet it does offer a refuge from the ghastly modern architecture on nearby Alexanderplatz.

SAVIGNYPLATZ *(Charlottenburg; map 2 D4. S-Bahn to Savignyplatz).* Ten years ago, Savignyplatz was a rather seedy area, but it has been imaginatively transformed into an upmarket neighborhood. The brick arches under the S-Bahn station are now occupied by fashion boutiques, bookstores, tapas bars and cafés.

SCHEUNENVIERTEL *(Mitte; map 4 B9. S-Bahn to Oranienburger Strasse).* This was the former Jewish Quarter. It suffered only minor damage during World War II, but was left to rot by the Communist government. Only a few streets were restored, such as Sophienstrasse.

Since the Wall came down, an extraordinary transformation has occurred. Dozens of new cafés and galleries have sprung up in dusty old buildings near the restored NEUE SYNAGOGUE. Explore Oranienburger Strasse and Tucholskystrasse to get an impression of the neighborhood.

WINTERFELDTPLATZ *(Schöneberg; map* ***3*** *E6).* A lively and youthful neighborhood thick with cafés and fashion shops. The atmosphere is particularly genial on market days (see SHOPPING on page 199).

GREEN SPACES

Berlin is blessed with vast tracts of green space, including pine woods, moorland, landscaped parks, botanical gardens and zoos. When packing a suitcase for Berlin, remember to take along a sturdy pair of shoes.

GATOWER HEIDE *(Spandau; map* ***5*** *D2. Bus 134 from U-Bahnhof Rathaus Spandau to Breitehornweg).* An area of moorland lying W of the Havel.

GRUNEWALD *(Wilmersdorf and Zehlendorf; map* ***5*** *D3. S-Bahn to Grunewald or Nikolassee).* A huge expanse of pine woods and lakes, where energetic Berliners go to walk, jog, swim or cycle, while the less energetic sit around on café terraces drinking *Berliner Weisse* beer.

MÜGGELBERGE *(Köpenick; off map* ***7*** *E7. Bus 169 from S-Bahnhof Köpenick to Rübezahl).* A region of rolling hills on the edge of Köpenick, which most West Berliners have still to discover. The restaurants and cafés remain rudimentary.

TIERGARTEN *(map* ***2*** *C5-* ***3*** *C7. S-Bahn to Tiergarten or U-Bahn to Hansaplatz).* A huge park in the heart of Berlin, dotted with statues and fountains. The ideal place to escape from the crowds.

Berlin expeditions

Although the enormous size of Berlin discourages walking tours, several compact areas are fascinating to explore on foot. Described in the following four walks are some of the best of these: the quiet quays along the Spree, the leafy residential districts of Kreuzberg, the developments in the old Jewish Quarter of Scheunenviertel and the extensive lakes and forests of the Grunewald.

Other, less strenuous exploratory journeys then follow; take a trip by S-Bahn (page 84), or by bus (page 86), or experience the Havel on a steamer trip (page 87).

WALK 1: THE BANKS OF THE SPREE

See map on following pages, and color maps ***1*** *A1–* ***4*** *C10. Allow 3–4 hours.*

Berlin first developed from a settlement on the River Spree, and several important buildings still overlook its quiet quays *(Ufer),* including the REICHSTAG, the DOM cathedral and the museums on MUSEUMSINSEL. The tree-lined waterfront offers a peaceful and unusual route through the heart of Berlin, past historic buildings and handsome 19thC bridges.

Take the S-Bahn to Tiergarten, turn left along Strasse des 17. Juni, then left into Klopstockstrasse past the **BERLIN-PAVILLON** with its curious collection of Old Berlin street lamps. Now turn left again into Haydnstrasse, walk under the elevated railway, and continue down Siegmunds Hof to reach the Spree. Turn right along Schleswiger Ufer, an attractive quay shaded by weeping willows.

Just beyond the **Hansabrücke**, you see some handsome *Jugendstil* houses on the opposite quay. Soon you reach the **Lessingbrücke**, a graceful iron structure with four red sandstone piers decorated with tragic scenes from such 18thC dramas as Lessing's *Emilia Galotti.* The parapet is adorned with figures of Neptune, frogs, and cats gnawing mice.

Continue along Holsteiner Ufer to the **Moabiter Brücke**, a low, black bridge built in 1894, decorated with four bears. Farther on, the **Gerickesteg** is an attractive *Jugendstil* footbridge with a sweeping staircase, built in 1914. Walk below the S-Bahn bridge and continue along Bellevue Ufer to the 18thC **Schloss Bellevue**, the German president's official Berlin residence. The nearby **Luther Brücke** — a stone bridge with obelisks at the corners — was built in 1892, bombed during World War II and rebuilt in 1951.

John-Foster-Dulles-Allee leads straight ahead through the Tiergarten to the semicircular **Grossfürstenplatz**. Four statues representing the great German rivers were moved here from the Königsbrücke in 1880. Damaged by shrapnel in the fierce fighting here in 1945, they have been left in ruins, the Rhine without a head, the Elbe riddled with bullet holes.

Continuing along the waterfront, you come to the **KONGRESSHALLE**, a now rather dated symbol of American-fired 1950s optimism. Beyond here, you may see obsolete signs warning that the end of the British Sector is approaching. The frontier between East and West Berlin lay just beyond the **Moltke Brücke**. Named after the general who commanded the victorious Prussian armies in 1866 and 1870, the red sandstone bridge is a rare relic of Prussian military pride, decorated with eagles poised on military trophies, and grief-filled women's faces. The street lamps on the bridge continue the military symbolism, in the form of cherubs laden with drums, swords and trumpets. Erected in 1886–91, the bridge was destroyed in 1945 and rebuilt in 1986.

Kronprinzen Ufer, once on the edge of the British sector, still remains an eerie wasteland, although the area is earmarked for new government offices. The land to the S of here was to have been the site of a vast Nazi assembly hall designed by Albert Speer. An overgrown footpath leads along the waterfront to the **REICHSTAG**, an isolated, melancholy building, carefully repaired after the war with thousands of tiny blocks of stone. The Wall used to halt further progress along the Spree, but there is nothing now to stop you continuing along Reichstagufer to the **Marschallbrücke**. The decaying building that houses the physics department of **Humboldt University** is to the right.

Bahnhof Friedrichstrasse spans the Spree a short distance farther on. Cross the river by the footbridge, and turn right along Schiffbauerdamm. The **Köpjohan Stiftung** *(#8)* is a handsome Old Berlin charitable institution decorated with boat-building cherubs. The quay leads to

WALK 1
The Spree

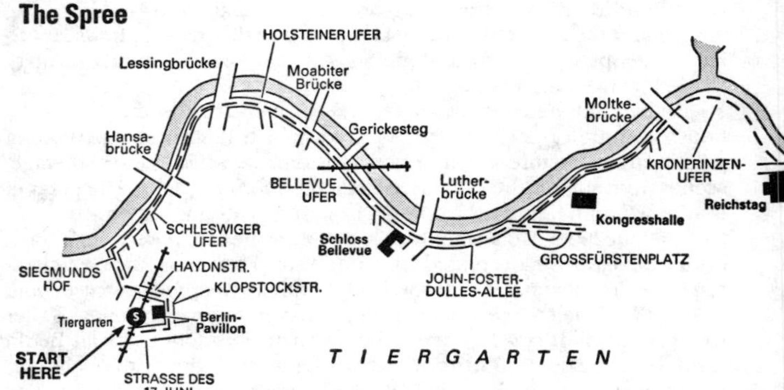

the **Berliner Ensemble** at Bertolt-Brecht-Platz, the theater where Brecht's *The Threepenny Opera* was first performed in 1928. The square opposite contains three pillars bearing quotations from his works, and a statue of the affable playwright seated on a park bench.

Now cross **Weidendammer Brücke**, an elegant *Jugendstil* iron bridge decorated with Hapsburg eagles and ornate lamps. Turn left along Am Weidendamm until you come to the **Monbijou Brücke**, a small stone bridge named after the Hohenzollern palace that stood here until its destruction in 1945. Continue along Am Kupfergraben, an arm of the Spree flowing along the s side of MUSEUMSINSEL. The S-Bahn elevated railway runs noisily along its track between the BODE-MUSEUM and the PERGAMON-MUSEUM, shaking the precious vases within.

Turn left at the **Eiserne Brücke**, a stone bridge built in 1914–16. It is named after Berlin's first iron bridge, which spanned the river in 1797. Bodestrasse leads past the NEUES MUSEUM and the ALTE NATIONALGALERIE on the left, and the ALTES MUSEUM on the right. At the handsome **Friedrichsbrücke**, designed in 1892 with four monumental flanking columns, turn right along the Spree. The DOM (cathedral) rises out of the water, a scene reminiscent of Venice. Once through the tunnel under Karl-Liebknecht-Strasse, you can see, on the right, the bronze-windowed **Palast der Republik**, formerly the seat of the East German parliament. It stands on the site of Schlüter's Baroque Stadtschloss, which was bombed in 1945 and demolished five years later.

Beyond the **Rathausbrücke** (the statue of the Great Elector now at Schloss Charlottenburg once stood on this bridge), the Spreeufer runs along the s edge of the NIKOLAIVIERTEL, a moderately successful reconstructed quarter of Old Berlin. An interesting statue near the site of Berlin's first bridge shows a woman poring over a map of medieval Berlin, as if trying to make sense of the enormous changes that have occurred here.

Another underpass brings you to the quiet Rolandufer, lined with weeping willows. Benches are conveniently placed beside a large lock, the **Mühlendamm-Schleuse**, which is still in use by huge Polish barges laden with gravel. A chart attached to the Neoclassical **lock-keeper's house** gives current water-levels on the Elbe, Oder and Havel rivers.

Continue to the **Jannowitzbrücke**, cross the Spree and turn right along the Märkisches Ufer, past the **MÄRKISCHES MUSEUM.** Make a brief detour by crossing the Classical **Insel Brücke**, which leads you across the Spree to **Fischerinsel**, a drab East German housing development. From the quay, you can obtain a good view of a row of restored 18thC buildings, including the **OTTO-NAGEL-HAUS** and the **Ermelerhaus** (see RESTAURANTS on page 172).

At the next bridge, cross the river again, and continue along the waterfront to the **Gertrauden Brücke**. Numerous bronze rats scuttle around the base of a statue dedicated to Gertraud, the patron saint of travelers.

Oberwasserstrasse brings you to Berlin's oldest surviving bridge, the **Jungfernbrücke**, a curious wooden drawbridge built in 1798. The next bridge, the **Schleusenbrücke**, is an elegant Neoclassical design, decorated with medallions showing 17thC and 18thC views of Berlin. The last bridge you come upon is the **Schloss Brücke**, a majestic structure designed by Schinkel in 1820–22. Decorated with a cast-iron frieze of sea-horses and figures of battling warriors, it terminates Unter den Linden in heroic style.

Continue along Am Zeughaus past what is now called the **DEUTSCHES HISTORISCHES MUSEUM**. The building, whose frontage is decorated with giant plumed helmets, was formerly the arsenal *(Zeughaus)*. Several old cannon are lined up along the waterfront, including a weapon with the letters H and VOC symbolizing the Hoorn chamber of the Dutch East

India Company. A Renaissance cannon bears the motto *Saturnus Frißt die Kind Allein, Ich Freß Sie Aller Groß und Klein* (Saturn devours only children, I devour everyone both large and small). Weapons such as this one (cast in 1617) were to devour one half of Berlin's population in the Thirty Years' War (1618–48).

Go back to the Schloss Brücke and turn right down Unter den Linden. At Friedrichstrasse turn right, to board the U-Bahn or S-Bahn at Bahnhof Friedrichstrasse.

WALK 2: KREUZBERG

See map opposite and color map ***4****. Allow 2–3 hours.*

Kreuzberg is interesting for its diverse architectural styles encompassing massive 19thC offices, fragments of war-damaged buildings and boldly experimental apartment blocks. A lively, bohemian district, it is teeming with art galleries, cafés and bars.

Take the U-Bahn to **Gleisdreieck**, then walk down Schönebergerstrasse and cross the Landwehrkanal. Curious fragments of statues damaged in the Battle of Berlin (1943–44) can be seen in the courtyard of the **LAPIDARIUM** (an old pumping house). Continue down Schönebergerstrasse to Askanischer Platz. The **ANHALTER BAHNHOF** once stood on this square, but all that remains is a token fragment of dusty brown brick wall. Descend to the ticket office of the renovated S-Bahnhof to see enlarged photographs of the 19thC station.

Take the exit signposted Stresemannstrasse, and turn left down this street to reach the **MARTIN-GROPIUS-BAU**, a 19thC museum still surrounded by an eerie landscape of rubble and weeds. Cross the square to reach a concrete building containing the **TOPOGRAPHIE DES TERRORS** exhibition. Stand on the hill of rubble (once an art school), to look on the wasteland known as the **PRINZ-ALBRECHT-GELÄNDE.** Study the plan of the site to identify the location of prewar buildings such as the Prinz-Albrecht-Palais and the Hotel Excelsior. Encouraging signs of urban renewal can be seen all around, notably the 12-story tower built by Pietro Derossi *(Wilhelmstrasse 120)*.

Turn left down Wilhelmstrasse; all that remains of the government offices of Imperial Germany that once lined this street is the massive **Air Ministry**. This grim building is now the headquarters of the Treuhandanstalt, the vast organization responsible for the privatization of the East German economy.

Now turn right along Zimmerstrasse, once a front-line street divided by the Wall. You may notice a few buildings on the left side of the street with their windows barred to prevent East Germans escaping. Turn right at Friedrichstrasse 990, past the **HAUS AM CHECKPOINT CHARLIE**. The former military checkpoint is nowadays a fascinating museum devoted to the history of the Wall.

A left turn on Kochstrasse takes you through the prewar center of Berlin's newspaper publishing industry. A towering office building *(Kochstrasse 50)* was built in 1961 by the Axel Springer publishing group as a defiant gesture aimed at the East German authorities just across the Wall.

WALK 2
Kreuzberg

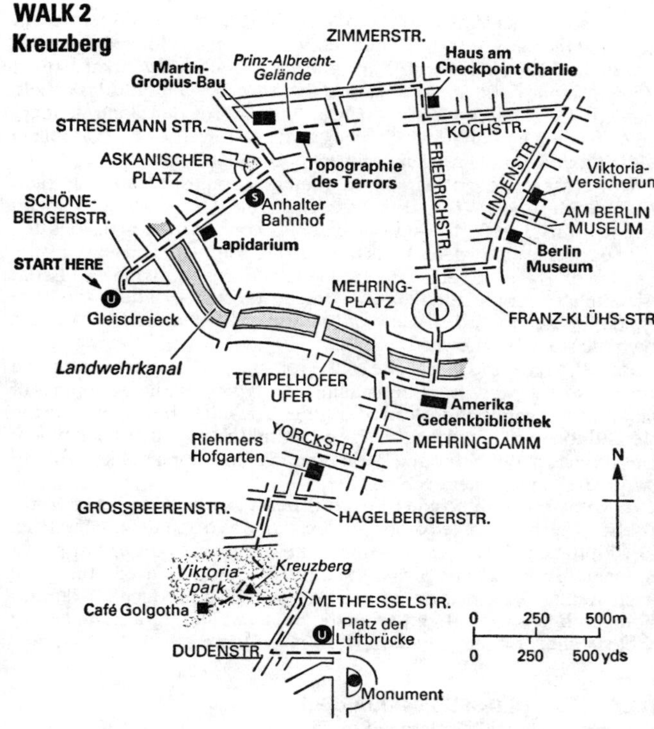

Turn right at Lindenstrasse, where some of the most sensitive recent architecture in Berlin has been built under the guidance of the Internationale Bauausstellung (International Building Exhibition or IBA), sometimes incorporating fragments of old buildings. A striking, modern apartment block is to be found, situated in the courtyard of the **Viktoria-Versicherung**, a massive rusticated insurance office laden with thick columns and heavy statues *(Lindenstrasse 20-25)*. Completed in 1913, it seems to reflect the brutal strength of Berlin on the eve of World War I. A dark, menacing portal leads into the courtyard, where a colorful Post-Modern apartment block designed by Arata Isozaki provides a measure of the new spirit in Berlin architecture.

Walk into the second courtyard and turn right, then right again on Am Berlin Museum, an attractive street with compact Post-Modern apartment blocks loosely modeled on suburban Berlin villas. Back on Lindenstrasse, turn left past the Baroque **BERLIN-MUSEUM**, where you can sample good local cooking in a reconstructed old *Weissbierstube*.

Just beyond the museum, turn right along Franz-Klühs-Strasse, then left down Friedrichstrasse to reach **Mehringplatz**, one of the squares laid out in the early 18thC by Friedrich Wilhelm, the Soldier King.

Walk under the elevated U-Bahn and across the Landwehrkanal, then turn right along Tempelhofer Ufer, past the **Amerika-Gedenkbibliothek,** a modern library built with US funding in 1952–54. Turn left along Mehringdamm, past a huge barracks with mock medieval towers *(#20-25),* built in 1850–53 for the Royal Prussian Regiment of Dragoon Guards.

Now cross Yorckstrasse, a broad tree-lined boulevard, and turn right to reach **Riehmers Hofgarten** *(Yorckstrasse 83).* Built by Wilhelm Riehmer in 1881–1900, the unusual complex consists of 20 mansions that look out over leafy gardens. Walk through the courtyard and leave by the entrance on Hagelbergerstrasse, beside an attractive-looking Old Berlin restaurant. Turn right, then left up Grossbeerenstrasse, where you have a splendid, almost surreal view of the artificial waterfall that cascades down the slopes of the **VIKTORIAPARK.**

Enter the park and climb one of the romantic paths that wind up the Kreuzberg. The view from the summit is a typical Berlin panorama of chimneys and spires, industry and culture. You might be tempted by the café **Golgotha**, situated on the slope behind the war memorial, where from 10pm fashionable young Berliners and aging hippies alike dance to disco music on summer evenings.

Leave by the path beside the **Schultheiss brewery** to get to Methfesselstrasse, then turn left along Dudenstrasse to reach U-Bahnhof Platz der Luftbrücke. Before leaving, notice the **Airlift monument** opposite Tempelhof Airfield symbolizing the three air corridors used during the Berlin Airlift. On a nearby information sign is reproduced a famous photograph, showing Berlin schoolboys scrambling up a mountain of rubble to cheer on the fully-loaded Douglas Dakotas.

WALK 3: THE OLD JEWISH QUARTER

*See map opposite and color map **4**B8. Allow 2 hours.*

There is change in the air everywhere in Berlin, but nowhere is it more acutely felt than in the former Jewish quarter known as the SCHEUNENVIERTEL to the N of ALEXANDERPLATZ. It was here in the 1930s that the Nazis demonstrated their deep hatred of Jews by setting fire to synagogues and daubing slogans on Jewish shops. After the war, the neighborhood was left to rot by the Communists, and even now, almost 50 years on, many apartment blocks remain pitted with bullet holes.

But not for much longer. The **NEUE SYNAGOGUE** is being restored to pristine condition and many of the abandoned buildings are now being renovated by squatters. For many people, the Scheunenviertel is currently the most exciting part of Berlin. Follow the route of this walk for a glimpse of some of the enormous changes that have happened since 1989. Expect wild art, bare cafés and scaffolding.

Begin at **Café Zeughaus** (see page 179) on the quay Am Zeughaus, next to the Schloss Brücke. Walk along the quay toward **MUSEUMSINSEL,** turn right across the Eisernebrücke and follow Bodestrasse. The building on the left, probably still covered in scaffolding, is the **NEUES MUSEUM.** The

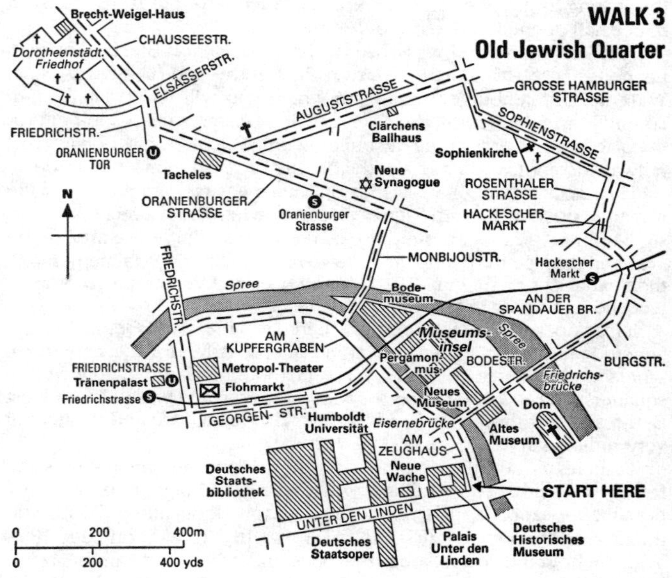

ALTES MUSEUM is on the right (see detailed plan of the MUSEUMSINSEL on page 135).

Stop in the middle of the Friedrichsbrücke. The **DOM**, freshly restored, is to the right. On the left, you may spot the gilded dome of the **NEUE SYNAGOGUE**, which you will reach in about 30 minutes. Go straight ahead down Burgstrasse, past grim apartment blocks that date from the Communist era. Turn left along An der Spandauer Brücke and go under the Hackescher Markt S-Bahn station (still known by many local people as the Marx-Engels-Platz station). Cross Hackescher Markt.

Go up Rosenthaler Strasse, but not for long, and turn left into Sophienstrasse, an unexpectedly pretty street lined with Old Berlin apartment buildings, their walls painted pink and pale yellow. This was one of the showpiece streets of Mitte, restored by the Communists in order to impress visiting diplomats. One shop sells wooden toys and another repairs brass instruments, but it all feels like a film set somehow.

One building was left to rot. It was the **Sophienkirche**, a Baroque church built in 1712. Wander into the churchyard, then continue down the street. The nearby small museum *(#23)* often has interesting exhibitions on the local history of Mitte.

Turn right on Grosse Hamburger Strasse, and left along Auguststrasse, a street that has barely been touched since the end of the war. But that is now changing slowly. A shop sells kosher food *(#78)* and a boutique stocks fashionable clothes *(#86)*. One old institution that has been here for as long as anyone can remember is **Clärchens Ballhaus** *(#25),* a dance hall opened on the eve of World War I.

The Scheunenviertel was once the haunt of Bertolt Brecht. To reach his house (BRECHT-WEIGEL-HAUS), turn right at the end of Auguststrasse. Walk up Oranienburger Strasse (to which you will return later), then continue up Friedrichstrasse. After crossing Elsässerstrasse, look out for the plaque commemorating the building, in 1842, of August Borsig's first railway locomotive, named Beuth after the Prussian minister of trade.

The **BRECHT-WEIGEL-HAUS** stands on Chausseestrasse, right next to the romantic **DOROTHEENSTÄDTISCHER FRIEDHOF** where both Brecht and Borsig lie buried. Wander around the cemetery, visit the house and, if you are interested, go further up the street to find a memorial commemorating the Spartacist uprising in 1919. Now go back to Oranienburger Strasse, reached by turning left off Friedrichstrasse.

It may not look much in broad daylight, but, after dark, Oranienburger Strasse is teeming with activity. Some people come for the new cafés, others to experience **Tacheles**, a vast abandoned factory taken over by squatters. The facade is decorated with scrap-iron and graffiti, like a West Berlin squat of the 1970s. Inside, there's a cinema, café and theater, all very rudimentary.

Tacheles is not all that's new. Farther down the street stands the freshly-restored **NEUE SYNAGOGUE**, guarded day and night to prevent any possible repeat of 1930s-style incidents. A few doors along *(#27),* you find a brutally modern café called **Silberstein** (see BARS on page 189). You might stand inside, drinking beer and talking art, amid bizarre sculptures made from scrap metal. For a more comfortable ambience, try the **Café Oren** *(#28),* described in CAFÉS on page 178.

Turn right down Monbijoustrasse, which leads back to the Spree. Cross the river at the **BODE-MUSEUM** and turn right along Am Kupfergraben. Follow the Spree until you come to Friedrichstrasse. Turn left. The modern building on your right holds sad memories for many Berliners. This was the transit hall for people traveling to West Berlin by the U-Bahn. Once a forbidding place filled with armed guards, the **TRÄNENPALAST** (palace of tears) is now used for wild discos and movie screenings.

Next to Friedrichstrasse station is a rather grand 19thC building known as the **Admiralpalast**. It is home to the Metropol-Theater, which stages German versions of old American musicals. A small cabaret next door has been poking fun at German politicians for years.

Go through the tunnel, and turn left on Georgenstrasse. A surprising development has taken place here. The arches under the elevated railway line have been turned into fashionable cafés and shops, like the ones under Savignyplatz station. The flea market, or **BERLINER FLOHMARKT**, once to be found at Nollendorfplatz station, now has its home under the arches. Follow the railway viaduct, and pause at **Kiepert's** bookstore. The building you can see through the gap on the right is the **Humboldt University**.

Carry on walking until you reach the Spree, then turn right along the waterfront, past the coaches dropping visitors at the **PERGAMON-MUSEUM**. This circular walk most conveniently ends here. The nearest stations are the S-Bahn at Hackescher Markt and the S- or U-Bahn at Friedrichstrasse. If time allows, you might either visit one of the museums on **MUSEUMSINSEL** or stop for a coffee at the **Café Zeughaus**.

WALK 4: GRUNEWALD

*See walk map below and color map **5**. Allow 3–4 hours.*

The extensive woods, lakes and nature reserves of the Grunewald are within easy reach of the city by public transportation. The route described below follows the shores of four lakes, from S-Bahnhof Grunewald to S-Bahnhof Nikolassee, a distance of about 8km (5 miles).

At S-Bahnhof Grunewald, an attractive rural station, take the exit signposted **Hundekehlesee** and turn right along Auerbacher Strasse, a leafy suburban street. Descend the cobbled lane to the left (beside some tennis courts) to reach the Hundekehlesee (dog-neck lake), a peaceful stretch of water lined with reeds and water lilies.

At the end of the lake, cross the Koenigs Allee, turn left and then right

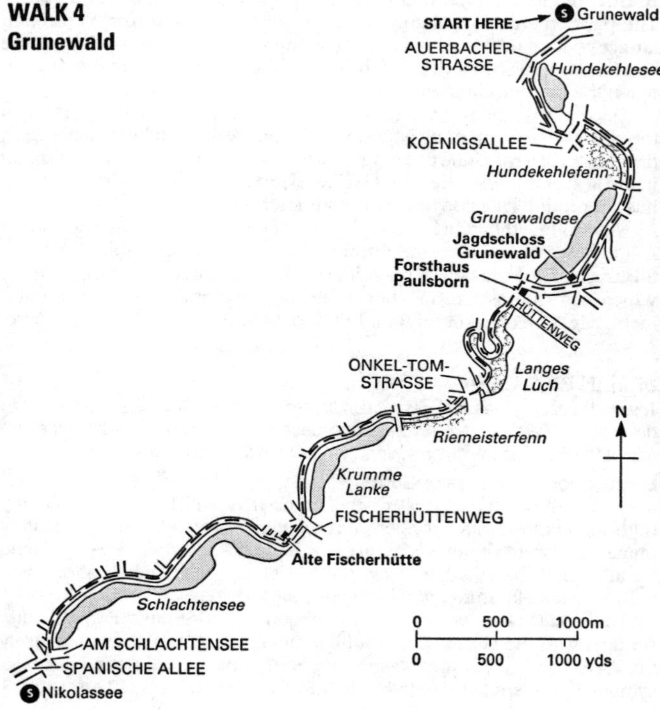

into the **Hundekehlefenn nature reserve**. The path follows a stream through a typical Brandenburg landscape of woods and marshes. Soon you come to the **Grunewaldsee**, a pleasant lake fringed with sandy beaches. Take the lakeside path to the left to reach the JAGDSCHLOSS GRUNEWALD, an old Hohenzollern hunting lodge on the waterfront. For a lunch of trout with a glass of dry Frankish wine, head to the **Chalet Suisse restaurant** *(Im Jagen 5, off Chalet-Suisse-Weg ☎(030) 8326362),* a rustic Alpine chalet set amid flowers and fountains: follow the sign to Dahlem, then Clayallee.

Continue along the lakeside, past the **Forsthaus Paulsborn**, a rural restaurant, and cross Hütten Weg. A narrow path winds through the undulating sand hills of the **Langes Luch** (long lynx) **nature reserve**. The path emerges on a main road in the forest, where you see a totally unexpected sign pointing to a U-Bahn station named Onkel-Toms-Hütte (Uncle Tom's Cabin). The station is named after an old country inn, as is a nearby modern housing estate designed by Bruno Taut during the Weimar Republic.

The footpath plunges into the woods again, skirting the edge of the **Riemeisterfenn**, a dark, eerie marsh populated by ducks and swans. The path emerges eventually on the edge of the **Krumme Lanke**, an attractive lake that is popular with swimmers. Take the fork along the right shore, cross the bridge at the end of the lake and climb the steps to reach the Fischerhüttenweg.

Once across the road, you disappear into the woods again to reach the shores of the ominous-sounding **Schlachtensee** (lake of slaughter), the subject of a romantic painting by Walter Leistikow, which is on display in the BERLIN-MUSEUM. The **Alte Fischershütte**, a long-established tavern, has a tempting lakeside terrace for summer days.

Now follow the right bank to the end of the lake, then turn right along Am Schlachtensee and straight ahead along Spanische Allee to reach **S-Bahnhof Nikolassee**, a magnificent Neo-Gothic station, built in 1901, which looks almost like a Hohenzollern hunting lodge. Return by S-Bahn in the direction of Erker for Bahnhof Zoo, or Frohnau for Friedrichstrasse.

BERLIN BY S-BAHN

It's worth reading the route description before departing. Choose a quiet time of day, such as 9am–noon. Allow 2–3 hours depending on how far you go at the far end of the line. See the color U-BAHN & S-BAHN MAP at the back of the book.

Forget about bus tours of Berlin. The best way to see the city is to take a trip on the S-Bahn. Most of the trains may still be old and creaky (although not for much longer), but the journey by S-Bahn immediately immerses you in the everyday lives of Berliners. *Zurück bleiben!* "Stand back!" shouts the guard, at every station. It's the one German phrase you will remember long after you have gone back home.

The **Stadtbahn**, or city railway, begun in 1875, links Berlin's outer suburbs with the center. Built on high, brick viaducts, with consecutively numbered arches often containing cafés or shops, the S-Bahn became a symbol of modernity for such Berlin Impressionist painters as Lesser Ury.

After World War II, the S-Bahn was administered by the East Germans, and the trains and stations became rather dilapidated, although the network has improved greatly since it was merged with BVG, the Berlin transportation authority.

Quiet Savignyplatz station on line S3 and S5 is a good departure point, its walls decorated with provocative works of art highlighting global pollution. Take the S-Bahn in the direction of Friedrichstrasse — and for the best view, sit, if possible, on the side opposite the opening doors. Soon you'll see, on the left, the **Theater des Westens**, built in 1896. With its flamboyant turrets and medieval-style German details, it looks totally out of place in the otherwise modern quarter.

The **zoo** is on the right after Bahnhof Zoologischer Garten. On the left, overlooking an idyllic stretch of the Landwehrkanal, is a striking modern blue building on stilts with a giant pink water duct. Designed by Ludwig Leo in 1971, it is used for fluid mechanics experiments carried out by Berlin technical university.

Now look right down the Strasse des 17. Juni and you will glimpse the **SIEGESSÄULE**, a Prussian victory column placed at the Grosser Stern intersection. The apartment blocks to your right beyond Tiergarten station are part of the 1950s-built **HANSAVIERTEL** quarter. After Bellevue station, you may see the 19thC **Luther Brücke** on the right as the S-Bahn crosses the Spree.

Did you notice the strip of wasteland next to the Spree? Maybe not, but that was where the Wall once ran. The S-Bahn trains stopped running along this line in 1961. This area, once a death strip, is set to change when the German government moves to Berlin, if it ever does, but for the moment the rabbits have the run of the place. Can you see the 19thC building on the right with the German flag flying? That is the **REICHSTAG**. It will one day stand at the heart of a new government district. Enjoy the view while it lasts.

In the distance, you can see the winking lights of the television tower (**FERNSEHTURM**) built by the East Germans near ALEXANDERPLATZ. It used to take a couple of hours to get from Bahnhof Zoo to Alexanderplatz, going through the checkpoint at Friedrichstrasse. It's now just a ten-minute hop, but you still notice the difference between west and east. The Wall has gone, but the divide of wealth still exists. The people who get on the S-Bahn at Bahnhof Friedrichstrasse don't look nearly as wealthy as those who got off at Bahnhof Zoo.

The elevated railway then cuts across **MUSEUMSINSEL**, passing between the **BODE-MUSEUM** and the **PERGAMON-MUSEUM**. You may spot the statue heads of Greek warriors through the windows of the Pergamon-Museum on the right. After crossing the Spree again, the S-Bahn follows the line of the medieval city walls, stopping at **Hackescher Markt**, a dusty old brick station. The next halt, **Alexanderplatz**, is bright and modern, with glass walls looking out on the rather bleak square.

Beyond here, the railway skirts the **NIKOLAIVIERTEL**; it is on the right, an area of reconstructed houses painted in pastel colors. Farther S, the **MÄRKISCHES MUSEUM** is the striking brick building on the opposite bank of the Spree.

Leave the train at **Jannowitzbrücke**, an elevated iron station built above the Spree. You now have to take the S-Bahn back to Friedrichstrasse, and change to the *Nord-Süd S-Bahn* (north–south line), following signs for Anhalter Bahnhof. Again, sit opposite the opening doors if possible. The line runs through a tunnel built in 1934–39, emerging at Grossgörschenstrasse station in Schöneberg district. You might decide to break the journey here and look at **KLEISTPARK**, a 5-minute walk from the station.

Soon, you pass dusty Old Berlin blocks with *Hinterhöfe* (back courts), alternating with well-designed modern apartments — a typical Berlin mixture. Farther S, the S-Bahn stops at several former villages, now leafy suburbs, such as **Steglitz**, **Lichterfelde** and **Zehlendorf**. The **BOTANISCHER GARTEN** is a 10-minute walk from the station of the same name. Later, the train stops at S-Bahnhof **Mexicoplatz**, a curious *Jugendstil* rotunda surmounted by a dome, built in 1905. A 2-minute walk from S-Bahnhof **Schlachtensee** brings you to the shores of an attractive Grunewald lake.

The S-Bahn trains used to stop at Wannsee and go no further. The next stop down the line was Griebnitzsee, on the other side of the Wall. It might as well have been the other side of the world. In those days, it was easier for West Berliners to travel to Paris than to get to Potsdam. But all that has changed and the S-Bahn now continues unhindered to Potsdam-Stadt station.

You have various options at Wannsee. You can stroll to the beach and take a steamer trip on the Havel, if there is time. Or you can go on to Potsdam. The best way back to central Berlin is to take line S3, which runs through the Grunewald. The S-Bahn viaduct passes through **Charlottenburg** district to our starting point, S-Bahnhof **Savignyplatz**. This is a good place to get off the train to avoid the crush at Zoologischer Garten station.

BERLIN BY BUS

Allow 1 hour to complete the trip.

Bus 100 is the line recommended by the BVG for tourists to get a first impression of the city. The line 100 was only created in 1991, providing a useful link between the centers of East and West Berlin, and taking in some of the most famous sights along the route. Get onto the bus at Bahnhof Zoo and sit on the top deck to see the recent developments that have followed upon reunification. The journey takes between 40–60 minutes from Bahnhof Zoologischer Garten to Alexanderplatz.

The bus leaves from Hardenbergplatz, opposite Bahnhof Zoologischer Garten. Look right to see the splintered profile of the **KAISER-WILHELM-GEDÄCHTNISKIRCHE**, now surrounded by modern buildings. The **ZOO** and **AQUARIUM** are on the left.

After crossing the Landwehrkanal, you head into the **TIERGARTEN**, a romantic park in the city center. The **SIEGESSÄULE** victory column stands in the middle of the Grosser Stern traffic intersection. The bus then turns down Spreeweg, past **Schloss Bellevue** (over to the left).

On John-Foster-Dulles-Allee, you will notice a semicircle of ruined statues on **Grossfürstenplatz** (to the right), a relic of the fierce fighting in the Tiergarten in 1945. The bus makes a sharp left turn to drop passengers beneath the soaring roof of the **KONGRESSHALLE**, and continues to the **REICHSTAG.**

Now the bus follows the former course of the **BERLIN WALL** to the **BRANDENBURGER TOR**, which once stood within the Soviet sector. You travel along the length of **UNTER DEN LINDEN**, passing the **Humboldt-Universität** (to the left) and the **Staatsoper** (on the square to the right). Look left to see Schinkel's **Neue Wache**, modeled on a Greek temple, and the huge Baroque **Zeughaus**, formerly an arsenal and now used as the **DEUTSCHES HISTORISCHES MUSEUM.**

The bus crosses the Schloss Brücke, built by Schinkel, to reach the island in the Spree where the village of Cölln was founded. At the far end of the **Lustgarten** (the square on the left) stands Schinkel's **ALTES MUSEUM**, one of five museums forming the **MUSEUMSINSEL** complex. The **DOM** stands on the same square. The Stadtschloss, a huge Baroque palace demolished in 1950, occupied the square to the right.

The bus now crosses the Spree to the site of the original settlement of Berlin. The brick **Marienkirche** (on the right) is one of the last relics of Hanseatic Berlin. The route terminates near the **FERNSEHTURM** on **ALEXANDERPLATZ**, where you can pick up the S-Bahn or U-Bahn.

THE HAVEL BY STEAMER

From Tegel to the Glienicker Brücke; daily, April to October. For sailing times ☎(030) 8100040. Allow 6–8 hours for the entire trip.

Berliners in search of *Lebensraum* (living space) tend to flock to the lakes, rivers and canals around Berlin. Several Berlin companies run boat trips on the Havel and Spree rivers, on the Potsdam lakes, and on the canals that run through the old city (see USEFUL ADDRESSES on page 61). The main departure points are **Tegel**, **Wannsee**, **Spandau**, the **Kongresshalle**, the Schlossbrücke at **Schloss Charlottenburg**, and **Treptow harbor**.

To take full advantage of convenient ticket combinations, buy a BVG *Kombi-Tageskarte,* a day-pass covering S-Bahn, U-Bahn, bus and tram services in Berlin, plus regular Havel river services *(Linienverkehr)* operated by **Stern und Kreisschiffahrt**. The pass can also be used on *Havel Queen* paddle steamer cruises.

Take the U-Bahn to Tegel and walk down Alt-Tegel to the pier at **Greenwichpromenade**. **Line 1** *(normally departs 10.25am)* weaves between some small islands in the **Tegeler See** to reach the Havel. The boat continues past the **Eiswerder**, an island with movie studios, then through a lock, to arrive at the **Lindenufer** pier on the SPANDAU waterfront.

The cruise continues down the Havel to the **Freybrücke** pier, a 5-minute walk from a strange area of marshes and lakes known as the *Tiefwerder.* To the S of here, the boat enters a broad expanse of the Havel bordered to the E by the GRUNEWALD. You'll see the 19thC **Grunewald-**

turm rising above the trees on the left and, farther S, **Lindwerder** island, which has a small restaurant. The boat moors at **Kladow**, a former fishing village in the dunes, then continues to the Pfaueninsel pier, where you should disembark. Take the ferry to **PFAUENINSEL** to wander among King Friedrich Wilhelm III's Gothic follies.

Back on the mainland, take a **Line 2** boat to **Wannsee** via **Glienicker Brücke**. The boat stops at **Moorlake** pier, where you might decide to get off to visit the curious Russian wooden cabin at **NIKOLSKOE**, a 10-minute walk from here. The boat continues to the **Glienicker Brücke**, the main bridge between Berlin and Potsdam, which remained virtually closed to traffic throughout the Cold War. Disembark to visit the **VOLKSPARK KLEIN-GLIENICKE** (next to the pier), a romantic park with a Schloss designed by Schinkel. **PARK BABELSBERG** (see POTSDAM on page 235), once cut off by the Wall, is now just a 10-minute walk from Klein-Glienicke.

The boat rounds the headland and turns into the **Griebnitzsee**, which once marked the frontier. Three stops later, the boat ties up at **Wannsee** pier, a 2-minute walk from the S-Bahnhof.

Berlin: sights and places of interest

HOW TO USE THE A TO Z SECTION

All the sights, including **museums** and **galleries**, **famous buildings** and **monuments**, are arranged alphabetically from pages 92–160.

- The list of SIGHTS CLASSIFIED BY TYPE on pages 90–91 should help you to pursue a particular interest or theme.
- Words in SMALL CAPITALS indicate a **cross-reference** to another section of the book or to a full entry in SIGHTSEEING.
- If you only know the name of a museum or other sight in English and cannot find it in the A TO Z OF BERLIN SIGHTS, try looking it up in the INDEX. Other sights that do not have their own entries may be included in a district entry; look these up in the INDEX too.
- The ★ symbol identifies the most important sights.
- The 🏛 symbol indicates buildings of particular architectural interest.
- The ⋞ symbol identifies a good view. There is also a special entry, called VIEWPOINTS, which gives the low-down on high places.
- The ♣ symbol pinpoints places of special interest for children.
- **For a full explanation of all the symbols used in this book, see page 7.**

Exploring Berlin

No visit to Berlin would be complete without exploring the treasures housed in a few of the hundred or so serious museums in the city. Afterward, you can unwind in the parks, beach resorts, woods and zoos with which the city is so well endowed.

The museums, palaces, picture galleries and gardens of Berlin have even now not fully recovered from the *Sturm und Drang* of World War II. Works of art were irreparably damaged or looted, and many buildings were destroyed by bombs. The postwar division of Berlin created an unhappy situation in which the main 19thC museums lay in East Berlin, while most of the art treasures were in West Berlin, shipped by the Americans from remote hiding places in southern Germany. New museums were built in the West to hold masterpieces of painting and sculpture, whereas the monumental Old Berlin museums in the East remained empty and neglected.

The construction of the Wall added a further complication, for West Berliners could no longer visit the historical museum or the opera, while people living in the Soviet sector were cut off from the zoo. Two independent cultural cities developed, each with a historical museum (the MÄRKISCHES MUSEUM and the BERLIN-MUSEUM), a national gallery (the NATIONALGALERIE [now called the ALTE NATIONALGALERIE, on MUSEUMSINSEL] and the NEUE NATIONALGALERIE), a museum of Classical arts (the PERGAMON-MUSEUM and the ANTIKENMUSEUM), an Egyptian collection (the BODE-MUSEUM and the ÄGYPTISCHES MUSEUM) and a zoo (the TIERPARK FRIEDRICHSFELDE and the ZOOLOGISCHER GARTEN).

The reunification of Berlin has created a situation of deep uncertainty, as proposals are mooted to move or merge collections. Collections that were split 50 years ago may be reunited, although the logistics of such an exercise, not to mention the funding needed, will make this a long-term plan.

Berlin's main museums and galleries are currently concentrated in four major clusters. The oldest group of buildings is the MUSEUMSINSEL complex, comprising five institutions holding some 12 separate collections. Six more museums and galleries are located at SCHLOSS CHARLOTTENBURG, while eight modern museums form the DAHLEM complex. The more recently built KULTUR-FORUM, to the S of the Tiergarten, now has three museums, with a further four planned.

Gone are the days when you could breeze into the Gemäldegalerie or the Neue Nationalgalerie without paying a *Pfennig*. The Prussian Cultural Foundation (**Staatliche Museen Preussischer Kulturbesitz** or **SMPK**), which runs the major museums in Berlin, can no longer afford to be generous. It faces enormous costs for relocating collections and modernizing the neglected museums of East Berlin, and an admission charge is now made except on Sundays and holidays.

The one sight you will *not* find is the BERLIN WALL. The concrete structure has all been dismantled, section by section. All that remains is a small stretch of reconstructed Wall, but without the armed guards in dark glasses, it has lost its significance.

Sights classified by type

All entries listed here can be found arranged alphabetically in the A TO Z OF BERLIN SIGHTS that follows on pages 92–160.

MAJOR MUSEUMS & GALLERIES
Ägyptisches Museum † ★
Alte Nationalgalerie † ★
Altes Museum 🏛
Bode-Museum † ★ 🏛
Gemäldegalerie † ★
Neue Nationalgalerie † ★ 🏛
Neues Museum 🏛
Pergamon-Museum † ★
Schloss Charlottenburg ★ 🏛

OTHER COLLECTIONS
Antikenmuseum †
Bauhaus-Archiv
Berlin-Museum ★
Berliner Kinomuseum
Brecht-Weigel-Haus
Bröhan-Museum
Brücke-Museum ★
Deutsches Historisches Museum 🏛
Deutsches Rundfunk-Museum
Ephraimpalais 🏛
Gal. der Romantik † ★
Georg-Kolbe-Museum
Haus am Checkpoint Charlie
Käthe-Kollwitz-Museum
Knoblauchhaus
Kunstgewerbemuseum †
Kunstgewerbemuseum Schloss Köpenick † 🏛
Kupferstichkabinett †
Märkisches Museum
Martin-Gropius-Bau 🏛
Mus. für Deutsche Volkskunde †
Mus. für Indische Kunst †
Mus. für Islamische Kunst †
Mus. für Naturkunde ♣
Mus. für Ostasiatische Kunst †
Mus. für Verkehr und Technik ★ ♣
Mus. für Völkerkunde †
Mus. für Vor- und Frühgeschichte †
Museumsdorf Düppel
Musikinstrumenten-Museum †
Otto-Nagel-Haus
Postmuseum
Reichstag
Schloss Charlottenburg ★ 🏛
Skulpturengalerie †
Topographie des Terrors
Zille-Museum

CHURCHES
Dom
Französischer Dom 🏛 ≪
Friedrichswerdersche Kirche 🏛
Kaiser-Wilhelm-Gedächtniskirche
Maria Regina Martyrum
Marienkirche
Neue Synagogue
Nikolaikirche

PALACES & CASTLES
Jagdschloss Glienicke
Jagdschloss Grunewald 🏛
Schloss Charlottenburg ★ 🏛
Schloss Friedrichsfelde
Schloss Klein-Glienicke ★ 🏛
Schloss Köpenick 🏛
Schloss Tegel
Zitadelle Spandau ≪

MEMORIALS
Gedenkstätte Deutscher Widerstand
Gedenkstätte Haus der Wannsee-Konferenz
Gedenkstätte Plötzensee

RUINS AND RELICS
Anhalter Bahnhof
Kaiser-Wilhelm-Gedächtniskirche
Lapidarium
Naturdenkmal "Alte Potsdamer Strasse"

HISTORICAL INTEREST
Berlin-Museum ★
Berlin Wall
Berliner Panoptikum ♣

USEFUL TO KNOW

- **Opening hours** Museums in Berlin are normally open Tuesday to Sunday 9am–5pm. All museums are **closed Monday**, except the ÄGYPTISCHES MUSEUM, ANTIKENMUSEUM, BAUHAUS-ARCHIV, BRÜCKE-MUSEUM, DEUTSCHES HISTORISCHES MUSEUM and the ZILLE-MUSEUM.
- A few museums stay **open in the evening**. These include the MARTIN-GROPIUS-BAU, the BERLIN-MUSEUM and the HAUS AM CHECKPOINT CHARLIE. Opening hours in East Berlin and Potsdam are likely to change as they become more harmonized with those in the West.
- The vast majority of sights are **closed on public holidays**.
- **Admission is free** to SMPK-run museums on Sundays and holidays.

Deutsches Historisches Museum 🏛
Dorotheenstädtischer Friedhof
Haus am Checkpoint Charlie
Märkisches Museum
Mus. für Vor- und Frühgeschichte †
Museumsdorf Düppel
Prinz-Albrecht-Gelände
Reichstag
Russischer Orthodoxe Friedhof
Topographie des Terrors
Tränenpalast

SCIENCE AND TECHNOLOGY
Archenhold-Sternwarte ♣
Mus. für Naturkunde ♣
Mus. für Verkehr und Technik ★ ♣
Mus. für Völkerkunde †
Planetarium am Insulaner ♣
Zeiss-Grossplanetarium ♣

GENERAL INTEREST
Berliner Schloss
Berlin-Pavillon
Brandenburger Tor 🏛
Brecht-Weigel-Haus
Fernsehturm ⋞
Funkturm ⋞
Hamburger Bahnhof
Kongresshalle 🏛
Neptunsbrunnen
Nikolskoe
Olympia-Stadion
Reichstag
Siegessäule ⋞

ZOOS
Aquarium ♣
Tierpark Friedrichsfelde ♣
Zoologischer Garten ★ ♣

DISTRICTS, SQUARES, STREETS
Alexanderplatz
Breitscheidplatz
Britz
Charlottenburg
Dahlem
Friedrichshagen
Gendarmenmarkt 🏛
Hansaviertel 🏛
Karl-Marx-Allee 🏛
Köpenick
Kreuzberg
Kultur-Forum
Kurfürstendamm
Lübars
Mitte
Museumsinsel ★ 🏛
Nikolaiviertel
Potsdamer Platz
Prenzlauer Berg
Prinz-Albrecht-Gelände
Scheunenviertel
Spandau
Tegel
Unter den Linden ★

SHOPPING CENTERS AND MARKETS
Berliner Flohmarkt ★
Europa-Center
Friedrichstadt-Passagen

FORESTS, RIVERS, PARKS, BEACHES
Botanischer Garten ★
Grunewald
Havel ♣
Kleistpark
Müggelsee
Pfaueninsel ★ 🏛
Spree
Tiergarten ♣
Treptower Park
Viktoriapark ⋞
Volkspark Friedrichshain
Volkspark Klein-Glienicke ★ ♣ 🏛
Wannsee ♣

OTHER THEMES
Allotments
Street lamps
U-Bahn
Viewpoints

The symbol † indicates establishments run by the **Staatliche Museen Preussischer Kulturbesitz**. These museums are normally open free of charge on Sundays and holidays.

- Several **cut-price tickets** *(Sammelkarte)* have been introduced. A combined ticket, or *Tageskarte,* gives access to the MUSEUMSINSEL (ALTE NATIONALGALERIE, BODE-MUSEUM and PERGAMON-MUSEUM), SCHLOSS CHARLOTTENBURG (ÄGYPTISCHES MUSEUM, ANTIKENMUSEUM, GALERIE DER ROMANTIK and MUSEUM FÜR VOR- UND FRÜHGESCHICHTE), and the KULTUR-FORUM (KUNSTGEWERBEMUSEUM, NEUE NATIONALGALERIE and MUSIKINSTRUMENTEN-MUSEUM).
- **Last entry** to the large museums is usually about 30 minutes before closing time.
- Be sure to deposit coats, large bags and umbrellas in the cloakroom, and always keep well back from paintings to avoid triggering invisible alarms.

A to Z of Berlin sights

ÄGYPTISCHES MUSEUM (Egyptian Museum) ★

*Schlossstrasse 70, Charlottenburg. Map **1**B2 ☎(030) 32091261 ▣ (▣ Sun and hols). Open Mon–Thurs 9am–5pm; Sat, Sun 10am–5pm; closed Fri ♿ (☎ ahead). U-Bahn to Richard-Wagner-Platz or Sophie-Charlotte-Platz; bus 121, 145, 204 to Schloss Charlottenburg.*

The Egyptian collection is currently split between Charlottenburg and Museumsinsel, but this is the main collection, housed in a handsome Neoclassical building opposite Schloss Charlottenburg. One of two identical guard houses (the other contains the ANTIKENMUSEUM) built by Friedrich August Stüler in 1851–59, the eastern Stüler building *(Ostlicher Stülerbau)* boasts a beautiful round stairwell with a domed roof. A darkened room on the first floor contains the hauntingly beautiful painted limestone **bust of Nefertiti** (or Nefretete), the aunt of Tutankhamun, discovered by a Berlin archeologist in 1912. The exquisite skin tones and vivid tints of blue and red have been untouched since c.1340BC, and virtually the only damage to the head is the missing left eye, making the right profile now the more striking. A damaged bust of her husband, King Echnaton, shows the same jutting profile and elegant features. Across the stairwell from Nefertiti is the **Berlin Green Head**, carved a millennium later. Influenced by Greek art, the gnomic green head (depicting an unknown Egyptian priest) has a sinister look.

The adjoining **Marstall** (stables) is an impressive gallery, with slender iron columns supporting a vaulted roof. The **Kalabsha temple gate**, built in 20BC, provides a handsome entrance to the exhibit. After admiring the antiquities, you might be tempted to visit the nearby **Gipsformerei** (see page 199) to buy a plaster cast bust of Nefertiti to ship home.

ALEXANDERPLATZ

*Mitte. Map **4**B9. U-Bahn or S-Bahn to Alexanderplatz.*

The bleak and windswept Alexanderplatz is a sad legacy of Soviet planning in Berlin. Named after Czar Alexander I — who visited Berlin in 1805 — Alexanderplatz was one of prewar Berlin's busiest squares. Alfred Döblin's 1929 novel *Berlin Alexanderplatz* captured the feverish vitality of the square under the Weimar Republic, but it had already begun to lose its cosmopolitan allure by 1933 when Nazis attacked the Jewish-owned Wertheim department store. There is little to see on this bleak square, unless you are an aficionado of modern television towers. Some people have even talked of tearing down the Moscow-style buildings on the square, but that seems a distant dream.

ALLOTMENTS

As you travel on the S-Bahn, look out for the little colonies of summer houses next to the railway tracks, known as *Kleingartenkolonien.* The city is dotted with hundreds of these tiny allotment gardens, created to answer the Berliners' deep need for a cottage in the country. You see the allotments alongside the railway in the Grunewald and near Plötzensee prison, where they are divided into districts named *Gemütlich-*

keit (perfect bliss) and *Jungbrunnen* (fountain of youth). Used for cultivating vegetables during World War II, they now tend to be crammed with flowers, sun umbrellas and cute gnomes.

ALTE NATIONALGALERIE ★

Bodestrasse 1–3, Mitte ☎(030) 20355530. Map **4**B8 *(Sun and hols). Open Wed–Sun 9am–5pm ♿ S-Bahn to Friedrichstrasse or Hackescher Markt.*

Der Deutschen Kunst (For German Art), declares a ponderous inscription on the pediment of the Alte Nationalgalerie. The stern Neoclassical art gallery was built in 1867–76 on the MUSEUMSINSEL to house a collection of 19thC German art donated by Joachim Wagener, a Berlin merchant. The gallery became less Germanic in the early 20thC, when it acquired a small number of works by Chagall, Goya, Rodin and Cézanne.

But in the 1930s, the Nationalgalerie became fiercely nationalistic once more. Its collection of 20thC German paintings — displayed in the Kronprinzenpalais (now the **Operncafé**) on Unter den Linden — was purged of many works vilified by the Nazis as decadent art.

The Nationalgalerie was rapidly repaired after World War II, and reopened in 1949. Although many of its finest works have been destroyed or dispersed, the gallery is still worth visiting, both for its elegant Neoclassical interiors, and its still distinguished 19th–20thC collection of painting and sculpture.

The lobby contains the attractive 18thC *Prinzessinnengruppe* (The Two Princesses), set in a gilded niche. Modeled on a Classical work, this early stone sculpture by Johann Gottfried Schadow shows Princesses Luise and Friederike, the daughters of Herzogs von Mecklenburg-Strelitz. The drapery is beautifully folded, although the girls' faces are rather idealized. There is a more convincing bust of Friederike elsewhere in the collection. Notice, too, the *Victory* statue by Christian Rauch, blackened from the fires of World War II.

The contented glow of the 19thC Biedermeier period is reflected in the portrait of Wilhelmine Begas by Johann Erdmann Hummel, and the portrait of Marie, wife of Karl von Preussen. Early 20thC paintings are hung in galleries whose dark green walls are decorated with Classical motifs. Von Lenbach's portraits of Richard Wagner and Otto von Bismarck are somewhat stiff and somber, but there are delightful Impressionist portraits including Max Liebermann's *Wilhelm von Bode* (1904), depicting the first director of the Bode-Museum, and Franz Skarbina's *Woman on a Sofa* (1881).

Several paintings by the Austrian Expressionist Oskar Kokoschka reflect the shifting mood of Berlin, from the edgy, jagged portraits painted before World War I, to the dark, morbid intensity of *The Hunt* (1918). The vibrant colors and nervous brush-strokes of *Pariser Platz* (1926) capture the surging crowds and roaring vehicles in Berlin at the height of the Weimar years. The view was painted from Kokoschka's bedroom at the fashionable Hotel Adlon, showing the Brandenburger Tor, the Siegessäule (which had not yet been moved to the Grosser Stern), and the dark mass of the Reichstag.

The blue and green interior in Lesser Ury's *Woman at a Writing Desk*

(1898) reflects the mood of the late Empire, while *Nollendorfplatz at Night* (1925) shows the incessant movement of the 1920s. Painted from the artist's studio window (a popular vantage point in the 1920s), it shows cars and trams speeding along the rainswept boulevards, while couples stroll beneath the trees. Ury's *Verkehrsturm at the Potsdamer Platz* shows Berlin's busiest square in 1925.

Otto Nagel's *Park Bench in Wedding,* painted in 1927, is a more melancholy Berlin scene illustrating the grim poverty of a Berlin working-class district. The first clashes between Nazis and communists took place in Wedding in the same year as this painting was executed.

ALTES MUSEUM 🏛

*Lustgarten, Mitte. Map **4**B8 ☎(030) 203550. Open Tues–Sun 10am–6pm. U-Bahn or S-Bahn to Friedrichstrasse or S-Bahn to Hackescher Markt.*

Berlin's oldest museum, the Altes Museum was built in 1824–30 by Karl Friedrich Schinkel in a handsome Neoclassical style modeled on Greek temples (see illustration on page 44). The lofty rotunda, with its busts of philosophers and poets, was, like St. Hedwigs-Kathedrale, inspired by the Pantheon in Rome. A polished granite basin was made for the center of the rotunda, but was too heavy to be lifted into place, and it remains in front of the museum, where it still mirrors the DOM on its dazzling surface.

Originally called the Museum am Lustgarten, the Altes Museum stands on the Spree island, now known as the MUSEUMSINSEL, which faces the former *Lustgarten* (pleasure garden) of the Prussian kings (see the plan of MUSEUMSINSEL on page 135). Built to display a collection of paintings donated by King Friedrich Wilhelm III, the building eventually became too small, and the pictures were rehoused in the BODE-MUSEUM.

The main attraction for many, at present, is the **Sammlung Ludwig**, a large collection of postwar international art which includes works by Beuys, Picasso, and the Cobra group. Until recently, part of the Prussian state collection of old prints and drawings was housed here, although this has now been relocated to the new KUPFERSTICHKABINETT at the KULTUR-FORUM complex.

ANHALTER BAHNHOF

*Askanischer Platz, Kreuzberg. Map **3**D7. S-Bahn to Anhalter Bahnhof.*

This was once the largest railway station in Central Europe. August Borsig's locomotive *Beuth* steamed out of the Anhalter Bahnhof in 1841, marking the beginning of the railway age in Germany. Trains used to leave from this station, bound for Dresden, Prague, Rome, Paris, Vienna and even Constantinople. The station was bombed in 1945, but trains continued to use it up until 1952.

Despite much opposition, it was decided to demolish the station in 1959. All that now remains is a fragment of the station entrance on Askanischer Platz.

The Askanischer Hotel, where Kafka stayed, has also gone from the square, and all that remains of the past are some enlarged photographs in the booking hall of the Anhalter Bahnhof S-Bahn station.

ANTIKENMUSEUM

*Schlossstrasse 1, Charlottenburg. Map **1**B2 ☎(030) 320911 ▣ (▣ Sun and hols). Open Mon–Thurs 9am–5pm; Sat, Sun 10am–5pm ♿ (☎ ahead). U-Bahn to Richard-Wagner-Platz or Sophie-Charlotte-Platz; bus 121, 145, 204 to Schloss Charlottenburg.*

Slender Cretan vases, Etruscan mirrors, and a Roman gladiator's helmet smashed in combat are among the antiquities displayed in one of two identical guard houses facing Schloss Charlottenburg (the other contains the ÄGYPTISCHES MUSEUM).

The collection once formed part of the Antiquarium, a department of the Neues Museum dispersed during World War II. Now divided between the PERGAMON-MUSEUM and the Antikenmuseum, the Antiquarium will eventually be reunited in the NEUES MUSEUM on Museumsinsel, when the restoration of the war-damaged building is completed (scheduled for the end of the century). Until then, the western Stüler building *(Westlicher Stülerbau)* provides a handsome setting for an important collection of **Greek vases** painted with black-figure and red-figure designs representing mythological gods and heroes. Look out in particular for the Greek classroom scenes on a unique red-figure Athenian drinking cup painted by Duris in the 5thC BC, and the slender satyr on a red-figure amphora decorated by the anonymous artist known as the "Berlin painter."

The **Schatzkammer** (treasure chamber) contains the Silberschatz von Hildesheim, a collection of Roman silver discovered in 1868. Probably made at the end of the 1stC BC, the treasure includes a gilded silver dish embossed with the goddess Minerva. Notice the curious clay figure of the *Dornauszieler,* a Negro boy carefully removing a thorn from his foot.

ANTIKENSAMMLUNG (Classical Antiquities Collection)

The collection of Classical antiquities is currently split between Charlottenburg and Museumsinsel. See ANTIKENMUSEUM and PERGAMON-MUSEUM.

AQUARIUM

*Budapester Strasse 32, Tiergarten. Map **2**D5 ☎(030) 254010 ▣ Open daily 9am–6pm; last Sat in month, 9am–9pm ✱ U-Bahn or S-Bahn to Zoologischer Garten.*

Established in 1869 on Unter den Linden, the Berlin aquarium moved in 1913 to a large new building next to the ZOOLOGISCHER GARTEN. Destroyed in World War II, the aquarium has been rebuilt and restocked with rare fish, reptiles and insects from every continent. It is now one of the world's largest and most modern collections of aquatic animals.

ARCHENHOLD-STERNWARTE

*Alt-Treptow 1, Treptow. Map **7**D6 ☎(030) 2728871 ✗ available ▣ Collection of telescopes open Wed–Sun 2–4.30pm. Guided tours of planetarium and telescope Wed 6pm, Sat, Sun 4pm ✱ S-Bahn to Plänterwald.*

This modern observatory for tracking the planets is located in Treptower Park. The Zeiss planetarium next to the observatory shows projections of the night sky on a large dome. Look out for special shows explaining such matters as extra-terrestrial life, horoscopes or the reason why the sky is blue.

BAUHAUS-ARCHIV

Klingelhöferstrasse 13–14, Tiergarten. Map **3D6** *☎(030) 2540020 ▬ Open 10am–5pm (Thurs to 8pm); closed Tues ♿ Bus 106, 129, 219, 341 to Lützowplatz.*

Bauhaus teapots from the 1920s, sleek steel chairs, architectural plans, paintings and models are displayed here in this white, functional museum overlooking the Landwehrkanal. The building was designed by Walter Gropius, the Berlin architect whose teaching methods revolutionized the Bauhaus school of design in Weimar. Originally a private collection, the archives are full of works by Gropius, Kandinsky, Klee, Schlemmer and Moholy-Nagy, with only a small number on display at any one time.

BERLIN-MUSEUM ★

Lindenstrasse 14, Kreuzberg. Map **4D8** *☎(030) 25862839 ▬ Open 10am–10pm; closed Mon ♿ ═ U-Bahn to Hallesches Tor or Spittelmarkt.*

One year after the Berlin Wall was built, a group of local history enthusiasts set up a museum in West Berlin as a substitute for the old MÄRKISCHES MUSEUM in the Soviet sector. The Berlin-Museum moved in 1971 to the law courts *(Kammergericht),* a handsome yellow and white Baroque building commissioned in 1735 by King Friedrich Wilhelm I to embellish Friedrichstadt new town. Badly damaged in World War II, the building was restored to almost perfect condition, while the rest of the neighborhood was torn down and reconstructed in Post-Modern style.

Although the MÄRKISCHES MUSEUM still owns the most important historical relics, the Berlin-Museum has rapidly amassed an impressive alternative collection of maps, paintings, models, porcelain, toys and furniture. You can even sample Berlin's culinary history in the Old Berlin **Weissbierstube** *(open Tues–Fri 11am–6pm, Sat, Sun 11am–4pm).* A friendly Berliner with a handsome mustache pours you a glass of Berliner *Kindl Weisse* with a dash of *röt* or *grün* (see page 180 for more about this custom). You then help yourself, at the antique buffet, to Berlin specialties such as *Boulette* (cold hamburger), *Rollmops* (pickled herring) and *Soleier* (pickled eggs). The nostalgic Berlin atmosphere is sometimes rounded off by a tape of Marlene Dietrich singing husky 1930s songs.

One room in the museum contains a fascinating **collection of maps and plans of the city**, including a detailed scale model from 1688. The only two buildings to have survived from this period are the Nikolaikirche and the Marienkirche. A glance at the maps shows that the explosive growth of Berlin has happened only in the last 100 years. Before then, the area between Charlottenburg and Tiergarten was open countryside, as Carl Oesteld's 1786 map shows, while Kurfürstendamm was just a winding country lane as late as Major Sineck's 1856 plan.

The period rooms offer a chance to glimpse changing styles of interior decoration. The restrained elegance of early 19thC Berlin is reflected in a Neoclassical interior and a Biedermeier room from the 1830s, while the more pompous style of the *Gründerzeit* — when Berlin became capital of the Second Reich — can be seen in the 1870s Neo-Renaissance interior rescued from a Kreuzberg mansion. Notice a photograph of a stern-faced Johann Kranzler, who in 1830 opened the famous Café Kranzler at the corner of Friedrichstrasse and Unter den Linden. A wartime photograph elsewhere in the museum shows the café in flames.

The Berlin-Museum has built up an excellent collection of paintings to reflect the changing character of the city. The harmonious scale of the early 19thC Prussian capital is illustrated by Eduard Gaertner's panoramic views painted in 1832 from the roof of Schinkel's Friedrichswerdersche Kirche. But the elegant Neoclassical city was ruptured by modern industrialism, as is clear from the paintings by the Berliner Secession artists Lesser Ury, in his view of *Bahnhof Friedrichstrasse* (1888), and Curt Herrmann, in his study of Savignyplatz in 1912.

Nollendorfplatz particularly appealed to *fin-de-siècle* Berlin artists such as Max Beckmann, who painted an attractive Impressionist view of the elevated station in 1911. An Expressionist work by Ernst Kirchner shows yellow trams converging on the square. Relentless industrialization is reflected in the American Lyonel Feininger's *Gasometer in Berlin-Schöneberg* (1912), a dramatic Cubist painting by an artist who later taught at the Bauhaus.

The wild Expressionism that flourished in the final years of Imperial Berlin resurfaced in the postwar period. A favorite subject was the Berlin Wall, as in Rainer Fetting's *Mauer* (wall). When the Wall started to come down in 1990, the Berlin-Museum lost no time in salvaging two concrete sections from Kreuzberg decorated with expressive graffiti by Kiddy Citny.

The Berlin-Museum boasts an extensive collection of KPM porcelain, including some large Neoclassical amphorae decorated with landscape paintings of the Spree and the Potsdam lakes. The museum's attic contains the sort of dusty curiosities you might expect to come upon in an abandoned Prussian mansion. There is a delightful collection of toys made in Berlin, including angelic Biedermeier dolls, a stuffy Gründerzeit dollhouse, some well-thumbed children's books, a miniature theater, complex working machines, a miniature grocery store, and a regiment of marching tin soldiers. Note too the reconstructed 1870s intarsia workshop and antique Kaiserpanorama with stereoscopic views of Imperial Berlin.

BERLIN-PAVILLON

Strasse des 17. Juni 100, Tiergarten. Map **2C5** ☎*(030) 8677080*
Open 11am–7pm; closed Mon. S-Bahn to Tiergarten.

Built at the same time as the nearby HANSAVIERTEL, the Berlin-Pavillon is a rather neglected relic of the 1957 International Building Exhibition. The little white pavilion on the edge of the Tiergarten (next to S-Bahnhof Tiergarten) is now used for temporary exhibitions on modern Berlin architecture, town planning and ecology.

The pavilion contains a curious Old Berlin *Kneipe* where you can sample typical Berlin specialities such as *Boulette* and *Sülze*. In the summer, you can eat at tables set out in the courtyard amid a clutter of 19thC fire alarms and gas lamps.

The sidewalks around the pavilion are lined with a bizarre collection of 22 historic gas lamps, which are lit at twilight. The lamppost from Riehmers Hofgarten in Kreuzberg *(#16)* is a superb example of Berlin ironwork, while a rather eccentric invention *(#11)* was designed by Franz Schwechten, the architect of the Grunewaldturm.

BERLIN WALL

*Original course of the Berlin Wall shown on color map **6** and **7**.*

The double concrete wall that once divided Berlin has vanished, although a strip of wasteland still cuts through the city like an operation scar. Single sections of the graffiti-daubed Wall were auctioned to art collectors in 1990, while smaller lumps of concrete were patiently chipped off by souvenir-hunters.

Local historians pleaded for sections of the Wall to be preserved, and finally persuaded the city to rebuild a short stretch near the HAMBURGER BAHNHOF. Some painted sections of the Wall have been preserved for posterity in the BERLIN-MUSEUM and the DEUTSCHES HISTORISCHES MUSEUM; the rest lies abandoned in scrap yards near Gleisdreieck and elsewhere.

BERLINER FLOHMARKT (Berlin Flea Market) ★

*S-Bahnbogen 190–203, Bahnhof Friedrichstrasse, Mitte. Map **4**B8 Open 11am–6pm; closed Tues. S-Bahn or U-Bahn to Friedrichstrasse.*

This bizarre flea market used to be located in an abandoned railway station at Nollendorfplatz. It was forced to close soon after reunification, when the Berlin transport authority decided to resurrect the U4 line from Nollendorfplatz to Mohrenstrasse, which had been shut down when the Wall was built. The flea market found a new location under the arches of the S-Bahn *(#190–203)* at Friedrichstrasse station.

Sixteen mustard-colored 1920s U-Bahn carriages have been converted into shops selling tin train sets, ancient typewriters, faded postcards of Old Berlin sights, and cheap jewelry. Many dealers have huge stocks of banknotes that were printed during the inflation years: a 2 million Mark note bearing the date 1923 is now worth a mere 15DM. There's also a photographer's studio where you can have your portrait done wearing period costume, while an artist in another railway carriage will cut your silhouette in one minute flat.

The ZILLE-MUSEUM is another nostalgic attraction at the flea market.

BERLINER KINOMUSEUM (Berlin Cinema Museum)

*Grossbeerenstrasse 57, Kreuzberg. Map **3**E7. No telephone inquiries (exhibitions) (movies). Screenings Wed, Fri 7pm, Sat 5pm. Check in the listing magazines for the current program. U-Bahn to Mehringdamm.*

The tiny 25-seat Cinema Museum can be counted on to show classic Berlin movies such as *Der Blaue Engel, Metropolis* and *Das Kabinett des Dr. Caligari.* The museum displays a small collection of memorabilia, including old Berlin film posters and publicity photographs.

BERLINER PANOPTIKUM

*Ku'damm-Eck center, 3rd floor, Kurfürstendamm 227–228, Charlottenburg. Map **2**D4 ☎(030) 8839000 Open daily 10am–11pm ✱ U-Bahn to Kurfürstendamm.*

A collection of some 200 waxwork figures displayed in a brash modern shopping center, the Panoptikum is inspired by Madame Tussaud's in London, but the special effects are far less dazzling. The show's only real appeal is the lifelike quality of the dummies. You will see the good and the bad from Berlin's past, including Frederick the Great, Napoleon and Kaiser Wilhelm II.

BERLINER SCHLOSS

*Formerly in Lustgarten, Mitte. Map **4**B9.*

The Berliner Schloss (royal palace) stands no longer. The main buildings were designed by Schlüter at the end of the 17thC in a heavy Baroque style, and a vast dome was added in the 19thC. The palace was hit by bombs in World War II, although the damage was no worse than to any other building in Mitte. It could have been restored, like Unter den Linden and Museumsinsel, but the East German government saw it as "a bastion of feudalism." It had to go, and in 1950 the building was dynamited. That was the mood of the time. The West Berlin government was guilty of much the same indifference when it demolished the ANHALTER BAHNHOF nine years later.

There has been much talk, since the Wall came down, of rebuilding the Schloss. If that were to happen, unlikely though it seems, it would require the demolition of the tinted-glass **Palast der Republik**, home of the East German **Staatsrat** (Council of State) until 1989. The building now lies empty and few Berliners would be sorry to see it go.

But the Berliner Schloss has not vanished completely. Fragments are scattered through the city, often in unlikely locations. One balcony was piously preserved by the communists because Karl Liebknecht stood on it to address the crowds during the Spartacus revolt in November 1919. It was incorporated into the facade of the former East German parliament building, on the S side of Lustgarten. Some dusty statues can be tracked down in the BODE-MUSEUM, and there are even a few fragments to be seen in the courtyard of an apartment building in Prenzlauer Berg.

But most of the building has gone, and the enormous task of reconstruction can be imagined by simply looking at the scale model in SCHLOSS CHARLOTTENBURG. Given Germany's current financial worries, it is likely that the ambitious rebuilding plan will be quietly shelved.

BERLINISCHE GALERIE

See MARTIN-GROPIUS BAU.

BODE-MUSEUM ★ 🏛

*Monbijou Brücke, Bodestrasse 1–3, Mitte. Map **4**B8 ☎(030) 20355444 🎫 (🎫 Sun and hols). Open 9am–5pm; closed Mon, Tues ♿ ☕ U-Bahn or S-Bahn to Friedrichstrasse or S-Bahn to Hackescher Markt.*

The handsome dome of the Bode-Museum rises above the Spree at the W tip of the MUSEUMSINSEL. Built in 1897–1904 by Ernst von Ihne, the Bode-Museum was originally called the Kaiser-Friedrich-Museum, but the imperialistic overtones of its name clashed with East German ideology, and in 1956 the museum was renamed after Wilhelm von Bode, the first director.

The museum once boasted one of Europe's greatest collections of paintings by Flemish and German Old Masters, but most of the works were dispersed during World War II to end up in the Dahlem GEMÄLDEGALERIE. Although the collection may never return, the Bode is worth a visit if only to savor the impressive Neo-Baroque interior, with its two monumental staircases surmounted by lofty domes. Damaged by wartime bombardment, the museum was lovingly restored by the East German government.

The museum currently contains five collections, although some major changes are probable in the coming years. The first room of the **Skulpturensammlung** (sculpture collection) contains a haunting collection of war-damaged Baroque sculpture. The Greek philosophers and plump cherubs were dug from the rubble in the nearby Dorotheenstrasse (now Clara-Zetkin-Strasse) after World War II. They are all that remain of Schlüter's final architectural masterpiece, the Villa Kamecke, built in 1711 in what was then a leafy Berlin suburb. The same room contains fragments of Baroque sculpture salvaged from the gutted shell of the Stadtschloss on the Lustgarten.

The collection of Late Gothic and Renaissance sculpture was also depleted when a bomb hit the bunker at the zoo, where many of the works had been concealed. Many of those works that did survive the war are now in the SKULPTURENGALERIE at Dahlem, but the Bode-Museum still owns some remarkable medieval German carvings from Swabia and Franconia, including a delicately carved Late Gothic Adoration by Tilman Riemenschneider.

The highlight of the **Frühchristliche-byzantische Sammlung** (Early Christian and Byzantine Collection) is a vibrant 6thC Byzantine mosaic removed from the apse of San Michele in Africisco, a ruined church in Ravenna. Sold in 1843 to King Friedrich Wilhelm IV, the work was damaged during shipment to Berlin, and again in 1945, but it has been restored to its original luster.

Created in 1850 as part of the Neues Museum, the spectacular Ägyptisches Museum was gutted in World War II. The best part of the collection is now at the ÄGYPTISCHES MUSEUM in Charlottenburg, but several beautiful works are to be seen in the rather old-fashioned cabinets in the **Egyptian rooms** at the Bode-Museum, including the serene head of a queen thought to be Nefertiti. The museum's large collection of mummies includes an embalmed crocodile and even an egg. A small study room devoted to the **Papyrus Collection** reflects the profound German scholarship encouraged by Wilhelm von Bode. The Egyptian collection will eventually return to the NEUES MUSEUM when restoration work is completed in the late 1990s.

Once Germany's greatest picture gallery, the **Gemäldegalerie** (picture gallery) of the Bode-Museum lost many works in World War II, including almost all the Rubens paintings it owned, as they were too large to be moved to safety. The masterpieces that survived are currently in the GEMÄLDEGALERIE at Dahlem, leaving the magnificent rooms at the Bode filled with minor works that had not been considered worth shipping out of the city. The most interesting works left here are the 17thC Dutch and Flemish Masters, hung in a series of intimate picture cabinets.

With only a few masterpieces left to admire, the gallery has a profoundly melancholy atmosphere, especially as several of the sculptures on view are still blackened by smoke from the wartime firestorms. The scarred marble faces in Donatello's *Virgin and Child* are a moving testament to the savagery of war. You will also see a 15thC angel by Antonio Rizzo which has lost both its arms, and the head of a cupid by the Flemish sculptor François Duquesnoy, which was shattered by a stray bullet.

Founded in the 16thC by Elector Joachim II, the **Münzkabinett** (Coin Cabinet) is the oldest collection in Berlin. A small room is devoted to temporary exhibitions of coins and medallions, but most of the collection remains locked away. Among the exhibits in the **Museum für Vor- und Frühgeschichte** (Museum of Prehistory and Early History) is a collection of Trojan finds donated by the German archeologist Heinrich Schliemann.

Don't miss the museum **café** *(open Wed-Sun 10am-5pm).* Situated amid palms on the balcony below the airy dome *(Grosse Kuppel),* the café is one of the last spots in Mitte where you can savor the grandeur of Old Berlin.

BOTANISCHER GARTEN ★

*Königin-Luise-Strasse 6 (N gate) or Unter den Eichen 5 (south gate), Dahlem. Map **6**E4 ☎(030) 830060 ▣ Open daily May–Aug 9am–8pm; Apr, Sept 9am–7pm; Mar, Oct 9am–5pm; Nov–Feb 9am–4pm. Greenhouses close Apr–Sept 5.15pm; Mar, Oct 4.15pm; Nov–Feb 3.15pm ♿ (☎(030) 83006119 ahead). U-Bahn to Dahlem-Dorf; S-Bahn to Botanischer Garten.*

Rolling lawns and exotic trees make Berlin's botanical garden one of the most romantic spots in the city. The first botanical garden in Germany (now the KLEISTPARK) was laid out in the 17thC to supply Frederick the Great's court with flowers, medicinal herbs, vegetables, and hops for brewing beer.

This newer garden, laid out at Dahlem in 1897, now boasts one of the world's largest botanical collections, with more than 18,000 different types of plants and flowers systematically arranged according to geographical regions. Sections are devoted to the vegetation of the Alps, the Steppes, the Balkans, the Himalayas and North America. But perhaps the most striking features are the vast greenhouses, landscaped with artificial waterfalls and exotic lily ponds.

BRANDENBURGER TOR (Brandenburg Gate) 🏛

*Pariser Platz, Tiergarten. Map **3**C7. S-Bahn to Unter den Linden, or bus 100 to Brandenburger Tor.*

The Brandenburger Tor, built in 1789–91 by Carl Gotthard Langhans at the W end of Unter den Linden, was designed to provide an imposing Neoclassical entrance to the city. Modeled on the Propylaea on the Athens Acropolis, the Doric-style gate was surmounted by a copper *quadriga* (a chariot drawn by four horses), made to a design by Gottfried Schadow. Although the figure in the chariot symbolizes peace, the Brandenburg Gate has long been associated with militarism. The armies of Napoleon, Prussia, Imperial Germany and the Third Reich have all marched in triumph beneath the majestic bronze chariot.

With the construction of the Berlin Wall, the gate became isolated in no-man's-land. Immediately after the Wall was breached in 1989, the Brandenburg Gate became the scene of immense celebrations marking the end of the Cold War. The postwar grime has now been scraped off, and the Brandenburger Tor has become a symbol of peace once more.

BRECHT-WEIGEL-HAUS

Chausseestrasse 125, Mitte. Map ***3****A7 ☎(030) 2829916 ✉ Open Tues–Fri 10am–noon (Thurs also 5–7pm); Sat 9.30am–noon, 12.30–2pm. U-Bahn to Zinnowitzer Strasse.*

The house where Bertolt Brecht (1898–1956) spent the last three years of his life has been turned into a small museum. The rooms are stocked with memorabilia of the German communist playwright and theater director who fled from Hitler in 1933 and spent 15 years in exile before returning to Berlin's Soviet sector. There he worked with the Berliner Ensemble, in the theater where his first major musical stage success, *Der Dreigroschenoper* (*The Threepenny Opera*) opened in 1928.

The house now contains a small bookstore stocked with Brecht's works, and a basement restaurant that is popular with writers and artists (see page 171).

On leaving, allow enough time to wander down the lane next to the house to enter the romantic cemetery, the DOROTHEENSTÄDTISCHER FRIEDHOF, where Brecht and Weigel are buried.

BREITSCHEIDPLATZ

Charlottenburg. Map ***2****D4. U-Bahn to Kurfürstendamm.*

The open space below the broken spire of the KAISER-WILHELM-GEDÄCHTNISKIRCHE became West Berlin's main square after World War II. Breitscheidplatz remains one of the most animated areas of central Berlin, with its teeming crowds of street musicians, toddlers and tourists. The main attraction is the EUROPA-CENTER, topped with a revolving Mercedes symbol.

On hot summer days, Berliners cool off in the **Weltkugelbrunnen** (world fountain), a bizarre fountain designed by Joachim Schmettau. Every hour, some 400,000 liters of water cascade over polished bronze statues representing crocodiles, apes, trees, and a sunbathing woman with a bottle of beer by her side.

BRITZ

Neukölln. Map ***7****E6. U-Bahn to Parchimer Allee.*

The old village of Britz has been absorbed into Berlin, but there are still attractive buildings such as a 13thC village church next to a pond *(Backbergstrasse 40),* and a castle, the **Schloss Britz** *(Alt-Britz 73 ☎(030) 6066051 ✗ Wed 2-5.30pm),* which was built in the 18thC and reconstructed between 1880 and 1883. But the main attraction is the **Britzer Garten** *(entrances at Mohriner Allee or Buckower Damm, map* ***6****E5* *☎(030) 7009060 ▪ open daily 9am-8pm),* Berlin's newest park, created by Wolfgang Miller for the 1985 National Garden Show.

Ingeniously landscaped to give an impression of open fields, the park features three hills and an artificial lake. Open-air concerts are staged by the lakeside throughout the summer, ranging from police brass bands to pop music. Children can clap at puppet shows or clowns at the playground *(Spiellandschaft)* or gulp down a drink in the milk bar *(Milchbar).* The **Café am See** *(open 10am-6pm ☎(030) 7036087),* a bizarre concrete grotto overlooking the lake, offers a family Sunday brunch.

BRÖHAN-MUSEUM

Schlossstrasse 1a, Charlottenburg. Map ***1****B2 ☎(030) 3214029 ▪ Open 10am–6pm (Thurs to 8pm); closed Mon ♿ (☎ ahead). Bus 145, 204 to Schloss Charlottenburg.*

This small museum near Schloss Charlottenburg is filled with fragile Art Nouveau and Art Deco vases and furniture, and although mainly of specialist interest, the museum conveys something of the spirit of early 20thC Berlin. What's more, the virtually deserted rooms provide a restful retreat from the crowded Schloss.

Formerly a private collection belonging to Karl Bröhan, the museum owns some exceptional Art Nouveau vases, mostly from France, although a few were manufactured in the KPM factory in Berlin. Several rooms are furnished in 20thC styles, including the **Salon Hector Guimard**, which is filled with Art Nouveau works, and the **Salon Henry van de Velde** containing furniture by the Belgian director of the Weimar school of design (which became the Bauhaus under Walter Gropius).

The museum owns a collection of 20thC Berlin paintings, ranging from the placid Impressionism of Karl Hagemeister's 1902 *Seerosen* (water lilies), to the restless urban Expressionism in Willy Jaeckel's *Im Café* (1912), which shows the seething interior of the Romanische Café (situated where the Europa-Center now stands).

BRÜCKE-MUSEUM ★

Bussardsteig 9, Dahlem. Map ***6****E4 ☎(030) 8312029 ▪ Open 11am–5pm; closed Tues ♿ (☎ ahead). Bus 115 to Pücklerstrasse, then a 5min walk.*

One of Berlin's most appealing art galleries stands in a quiet cul-de-sac on the edge of the Grunewald. Devoted to the artists of *die Brücke* (see ART IN BERLIN on page 47), the Bauhaus-style museum was built in the 1960s, and has large windows opening onto the pine woods. The setting is perfect for paintings such as Otto Mueller's *Zwei badende Mädchen* (1921), a powerful work of primitive energy depicting two naked girls beside a lake.

Founded in Dresden in 1905 by Erich Heckel, Ernst Ludwig Kirchner and Karl Schmidt-Rottluff, *die Brücke* represented the first wave of

German Expressionism. The jagged outlines and vibrant colors of the movement were inspired by artistic rebels such as Van Gogh, Gauguin and Munch, but there were also hints of primitive art and German Renaissance woodcuts in the style. The group was officially disbanded in 1913, and many of their paintings perished at the hands of the Nazis.

Heckel's works illustrate the evolution of his style from the tranquil *Laute spielendes Mädchen* (Girl playing a lute) of 1913 to harrowing paintings executed during World War I. Many artists never recovered from the two world wars, but Heckel regained his early lyrical style in an exquisite still life painted in 1949.

Kirchner's 1913 *Berlin Street Scene* is a somber, almost primitive portrait of a crowded Berlin street on the eve of World War I. Struck down by a nervous breakdown during this war, Kirchner was sent to Davos to convalesce. He continued to live in the Swiss resort after the war, and his painting became more calm and abstract. But the serenity was apparently deceptive, for in 1938 he committed suicide. The bizarre yellow sheep of *Schafherde* were painted shortly before his death.

Karl Schmidt-Rottluff used vivid colors: blood red in *Dreidurchbruch* (1910), bright green in a 1911 portrait of Rosa Schapire, and a melancholy blue in *Weinstube* (1913).

Although off the beaten track, the Brücke-Museum is an essential place to visit if you wish to understand one of the most exciting periods in German art. Afterward, you can wander through the GRUNEWALD to discover earlier German artists in the JAGDSCHLOSS GRUNEWALD.

CHARLOTTENBURG

*Center west. Maps **1**C2 and **5**C3–**6**C4.*

Named after the Baroque palace built for Sophie Charlotte, Charlottenburg is an elegant quarter of spacious tree-lined boulevards and solid 19thC apartments. Most of Berlin's best hotels, restaurants, stores, cafés and cinemas are located in this district. After World War II, numerous archeological relics and paintings from the MUSEUMSINSEL ended up at SCHLOSS CHARLOTTENBURG.

KURFÜRSTENDAMM, the main artery, is a bustling street from early morning until long after midnight, but it sometimes pays to explore streets "Off-Ku'damm," where there are intimate restaurants and original shops. The area around Savignyplatz is dotted with modern cafés that begin to buzz around 10pm.

DAHLEM

*In the sw suburb of Zehlendorf. Map **5**E3. U-Bahn to Dahlem-Dorf.*

The leafy suburb of Dahlem still has something of the character of a north German village, especially around the 14thC brick **church of St Annen** *(Königin-Luise-Strasse 55).* Shaded by old yew trees, the churchyard contains decayed Neoclassical tombs of scientists, opera singers, sculptors, actresses and World War I soldiers. A map at the entrance lists the most important occupants.

The U-Bahnhof at Dahlem-Dorf adds to the rural atmosphere, with half-timbered walls and thatched roof. Built in 1913 in the style of a Lower

Saxony farmhouse, the station has a painted wooden ceiling and a rustic station clock.

A **major museum complex** was built at Dahlem after 1945, to display works of art displaced from the MUSEUMSINSEL. The museums currently at Dahlem are the **GEMÄLDEGALERIE** (Germany's greatest collection of Old Masters), the **SKULPTURENGALERIE** (German and Italian sculpture), the **KUPFERSTICHKABINETT** (prints and drawings), the **MUSEUM FÜR VÖLKERKUNDE** (a modern ethnography collection), the **MUSEUM FÜR DEUTSCHE VOLKSKUNDE**, and museums of Indian, Islamic and Far Eastern Art.

The **Freie Universität** is a large, modern university campus at Dahlem. Originally established in a building on Unter den Linden late in 1945, the Free University sought to restore intellectual freedom, which had been crushed by the Nazis. But the early idealism quickly faded as the university came increasingly under Communist Party control, and a group of disillusioned lecturers and students moved to the new campus at Dahlem in 1948.

DEUTSCHES HISTORISCHES MUSEUM (Museum of German History)

*Unter den Linden 2, Mitte ☎(030) 215020. Map **4**B8 Open 10am–6pm; closed Wed on the waterfront. S-Bahn to Hackescher Markt or Friedrichstrasse.*

Begun by Johann Nering in 1695, the massive Baroque Zeughaus (arsenal) was completed by the architect and sculptor Andreas Schlüter in 1699. The courtyard known as the **Schlüterhof** (where concerts take place in the summer) is surrounded by 22 arches whose keystones bear Schlüter's expressively carved heads of dying warriors. In the 1880s, the building was turned into a bombastic Military Museum, complete with a Hall of Fame of the Prussian Army.

The communist government created a Museum of German History in the Zeughaus in 1952. The museum provided its visitors, not that there were many, with a blunt Marxist interpretation of German history from the Stone Age to the Nazi years. All this became an embarrassment when the Wall came down. The rooms dealing with the Soviet period were closed soon after the communist government fell, and exhibits such as Russian tractors and Vietnamese peasants' hats were quickly moved to the store rooms.

The revamped collection still has a strong military bias, with menacing pikes from the Peasants' Revolt, moldering red and blue Prussian uniforms, and dioramas of battles modeled with tin soldiers. Some of the old exhibits have been spared, such as a detailed reconstruction of the Bastille made by an enthusiastic East German, and a model of Karl Marx's house in London. The battered suitcase carried by the left-wing leader Karl Liebknecht on his journey to America in 1886 has also survived *die Wende*.

The most interesting rooms at present deal with 19thC Berlin history, with exhibits such as scientific equipment, an early automobile built in 1900, and a model of a grim *Mietskaserne* (tenement) of the 1880s.

Several rooms on the Nazi period contain a harrowing collection of documents, photographs and other relics, revealing that many East German leaders were active opponents of Hitler. A small section covers the history of postwar Germany, and pride of place is given to three concrete slabs from the Berlin Wall, bearing the lament "13 August 1961 — Walled in for 28 years!"

DEUTSCHES RUNDFUNK-MUSEUM (German Broadcasting Museum)
Hammarskjöldplatz 1, Charlottenburg. Map ***5**D3* *☎(030) 3028186. Open 10am–5pm; closed Tues ♿ (ground floor only). U-Bahn to Theodor-Heuss-Platz; S-Bahn to Westkreuz.*

Radio hams might enjoy the small German museum of broadcasting situated in a former studio at the foot of the FUNKTURM. Polished wood wirelesses from the 1920s are displayed in a period room amid potted plants, while a mock 1930s shop is crammed with radios once used to pick up Hitler's speeches or Marlene Dietrich songs.

DOM
Lustgarten, Mitte. Map ***4**B9* *☎(030) 2469134 ✉ Open Mon–Sat 9am–noon, 1–5pm, Sun noon–5pm ⇚ S-Bahn to Hackescher Markt.*

The massive hulk of Berlin's Baroque Dom (cathedral) stands on the site of an old Dominican church on the Spree island. Begun next to the royal palace during the reign of Frederick the Great, the old cathedral was finally completed by Schinkel in 1822. But the building was not grand enough for Kaiser Wilhelm II, who commissioned the present edifice in Italian High Baroque style. Blasted by bombs in 1944, the cathedral was left a ruin until 1975. The restoration of the building took 18 years to complete.

The cathedral contains a small exhibition documenting the destruction and rebuilding of the Dom. There is a good view of the nave from the gallery at the top of the Kaiserliches Treppenhaus (Imperial Staircase).

DOROTHEENSTÄDTISCHER FRIEDHOF (Dorotheenstadt Cemetery)
Chausseestrasse 126, Mitte. Map ***3**A7* *☎(030) 2826119. Open daily 8am–6pm (May–Sept 7pm). S-Bahn to Friedrichstrasse, or U-Bahn to Zinnowitzer Strasse.*

Many eminent Berliners are buried in a picturesque cemetery hidden down a narrow lane near Bahnhof Friedrichstrasse. Founded in 1762 for the new towns of Dorotheenstadt and Friedrichswerder, it contains the overgrown tombs of many of Berlin's celebrities over the years.

A plan at the entrance pinpoints the graves of the sculptor Johann Gottfried Schadow, the architect Karl Friedrich Schinkel, the author Heinrich Mann and the industrialist August Borsig. A striking monument of glazed Neo-Renaissance tiles commemorates inventor Friedrich Hoffmann, and the philosopher Hegel is buried, as he requested, next to his colleague Fichte.

The tombs of Marxist dramatist Bertolt Brecht and his wife, actress Helene Weigel, are also side by side. John Heartfield, the radical photomontage artist, is commemorated by a simple monument marked with his monogram, an H. The adjoining **Französischer Friedhof** is an old burial-ground of Berlin's Huguenot community.

EPHRAIMPALAIS 🏛
Poststrasse 16, Mitte. Map ***4**C9* *☎(030) 23809021 ✉ Open Tues–Fri 9am–5pm, Sat 9am–6pm, Sun 10am–5pm; closed Mon. U-Bahn or S-Bahn to Alexanderplatz.*

An elegant Rococo palace on the edge of the NIKOLAIVIERTEL was built in 1760 for Veitel Heine Ephraim, the court jeweler to Frederick the Great. The house used to stand farther E, but it had to be demolished in 1935 during the construction of the Mühlendamm-Schleuse, a large lock. The city authorities carefully stored about 2,000 blocks of masonry, and many years later the palace was rebuilt to something of its former splendor.

A restaurant currently occupies the ground floor, while the elegant upstairs rooms contain a department of the MÄRKISCHES MUSEUM. Once you have put on enormous felt slippers to protect the precious floors, you can glide through the palace looking at maps, plans and paintings covering the history of Berlin from the 17thC to the 19thC.

EUROPA-CENTER

*Breitscheidplatz, Charlottenburg. Map **2**D5. U-Bahn to Kurfürstendamm.*

The Europa-Center complex was built in the 1960s, on the site of the destroyed Romanische Café, as a glittering symbol of West Berlin's prosperity. Modeled on American shopping malls, the complex boasts more than 100 shops and restaurants, set amid landscaped ponds and waterfalls. A most captivating feature is the thermal clock, which resembles a huge chemistry experiment, with water bubbling through glass pipes and jars to mark the hours and minutes. For a view of Kurfürstendamm, take the elevator to the 22nd-floor terrace (⋞ ▣).

Unlike many modern malls, the Europa-Center remains bustling after the shops have closed. Some come to buy a magazine at the **Europa Presse Center** (see page 199) or to visit the **tourist information office**. Others are there for the **Casino** (see page 190), or to eat in one of the restaurants. The center remains lively deep into the night, as large and loud groups head off to watch the topless floor show at **La Vie en Rose**, or to hoot at the humor of the cabaret **Die Stachelschweine**.

FERNSEHTURM (Television Tower)

*Alexanderplatz, Mitte. Map **4**B9 ☎(030) 2423333 ▣ Open daily, May–Sept 8am–11pm, Oct–Apr 9am–11pm. Opens at 1pm on 2nd and 4th Tues of month ▬ ■ ⋞ U-Bahn or S-Bahn to Alexanderplatz.*

Built in the 1960s in the center of East Berlin, the 362-meter/1,187-foot Fernsehturm (television tower) is one of the city's landmarks. Long lines wait to take the high-speed elevator up to the observation deck and revolving restaurant, located in a steel-clad sphere resembling a Soviet sputnik. Perched 204 meters/670 feet above Alexanderplatz, you can gaze across the apartment roofs of Berlin to the flat plains beyond.

FRANZÖSISCHER DOM (French Cathedral) 🏛

*Gendarmenmarkt 5, Mitte. Map **4**C8 ☎(030) 2292042 ⋞ ♿ ■ U-Bahn to Französische Strasse.*

The Französischer Dom (French Cathedral) on GENDARMENMARKT, with its identical counterpart the **Deutscher Dom** (German Cathedral), flanks Schinkel's magnificent **Schauspielhaus** theater to form one of Germany's most splendid examples of the Neoclassical style. It was built in 1701–8 for the French Protestant community, and lofty towers were added to both cathedrals in 1780–85 by Karl von Gontard. The dome contains a small museum of Huguenot mementoes *(☎(030) 2291760, open Tues-Sat 10am-5pm, Sun 1-5pm).*

It is worth the toil up the spiral stair to the balustrade *(open Mon-Sat 10am-4pm)* to admire the heart of the reunited city, although the view back down the stairwell is not for the faint-hearted.

One last flight of steps leads up to the **Glockenspiel**, where you can sit and listen to the *carillon* chime automatically each day *(noon, 3pm and 7pm).* Twice a week *(Tues 2pm, Sat 3pm),* the *carillonneur* climbs a spiral stair and crosses a narrow iron bridge to reach the keyboard, which is enclosed in an iron structure suspended from the dome.

FRIEDRICHSHAGEN

Köpenick. SE *Berlin. Off map* ***7E7****. S-Bahn to Friedrichshagen.*

This is a strangely captivating quarter of Berlin that few tourists ever discover. Once a town in its own right, Friedrichshagen was incorporated into Greater Berlin at the end of World War I. After 1945, as part of the Soviet sector, it slowly fell into decay.

Leave the S-Bahn station and walk down Bölschestrasse, the main street, which is lined with a few dusty trees. Notice the neat little houses with Classical details, often crying out for restoration. The restaurant DIE SPINDEL (see page 174) occupies one of the old houses.

The sprawling **Berliner-Bürger-Bräu brewery** stands at the end of the street. If you turn left down Josef-Nawrocki-Strasse and right down a lane, you come to a little park overlooked by rambling old villas. The entrance to the **Spreetunnel** is tucked away in a corner of the park. Built in 1926, the 160-meter/525-foot tunnel goes under the River Spree. It takes two minutes to get to the other side, where you have a good view of the brewery, with its tall brick chimney marked "BBB."

The tunnel gets you out of the city into the Brandenburg countryside. The vast **Müggelsee** stretches away to the E, dotted with sailboats and steamers in the summer. A 20-minute hike along the quiet lakeside brings you to the **Rübezahl** restaurant. You can then take bus 169 to KÖPENICK.

FRIEDRICHSTADT-PASSAGEN

Friedrichstrasse, Mitte. Map ***4C8****. Currently being constructed. U-Bahn to Stadtmitte.*

One of the biggest construction projects in Berlin, the 3-block development just W of Gendarmenmarkt will, when completed (in early 1995 according to the latest reports), add a vast complex of shops, offices and apartments to the historical heart of Berlin. Some of the best architects from Paris, New York and Cologne have worked on the design, which promises to be spectacular. The fashionable French Galeries Lafayette plans to open a department store in the new complex.

FRIEDRICHSWERDERSCHE KIRCHE 🏛

Werderstrasse, Mitte. Map ***4C8*** *☎ (030) 2081323 ▣ (▣ Sun and hols) ♿ (ground floor only). Open 9am–5pm; closed Mon, Tues. U-Bahn to Hausvogteiplatz.*

The Friedrichswerdersche Kirche (1824–30) was built by Schinkel in an elegant Late Gothic style inspired by English Perpendicular churches. Blasted by wartime shrapnel, the red-brick building was expertly restored in 1982–87. The slender Neo-Gothic arches now provide an elegant backdrop for a collection of Neoclassical sculptures on loan from the ALTE NATIONALGALERIE on Museumsinsel. The works include Johann Gottfried Schadow's model for *The Two Princesses,* and Christian Tieck's statue of Schinkel holding a plan of the Altes Museum. Notice Rudolf Schadow's statue of a spinner unwinding an imaginary thread.

Situated on the wooden gallery, the **Schinkelmuseum** contains architectural plans and photographs of Schinkel's principal buildings. Although interesting, the exhibition does not possess the same wealth of material as the **Schinkel-Pavillon** at SCHLOSS CHARLOTTENBURG.

Another small exhibition in the gallery shows the ruined church after the war. A photograph showing the neighborhood after a bombing raid reveals that the only building left intact was a newsstand.

Schinkel enthusiasts should not miss the ornate doorway on a building N of the church, leading into the **Café Schinkel-Klause**. The door was designed in 1836 by Schinkel for the Bauakademie (Academy of Architecture), an imposing Neoclassical building that once stood on the Spree waterfront near the church. Bombed during World War II, the academy was razed to the ground by the East Berlin authorities in 1961 — the same year that West Berlin tore down the gutted shell of the Anhalter Bahnhof.

FUNKTURM (Radio Tower)

*Messedamm, Charlottenburg. Map **5D3** ☎(030) 30381 ▣ Open daily 10am–11pm ⇚ U-Bahn to Theodor-Heuss-Platz; S-Bahn to Westkreuz.*

Not far from the **Messe** exhibition center, the Funkturm is an impressive radio mast built in 1925. The steel tower is redundant now, but you can still take the elevator up to the observation deck 125 meters/410 feet above street level, to obtain a dizzying view of tangled roads and railway lines.

GALERIE DER ROMANTIK (Gallery of Romantic Painting) ★

*Neuer Flügel (new wing) at Schloss Charlottenburg. Map **1B2** ☎(030) 2662650 ▣ (▣ Sun and hols). Open Tues–Fri 9am–5pm; Sat, Sun 10am–5pm ♿ Bus 145, 204 to Schloss Charlottenburg.*

Romantic 19thC German paintings of jagged peaks and solitary abbeys are currently displayed in the E wing of SCHLOSS CHARLOTTENBURG. Once displayed in the NATIONALGALERIE on Museumsinsel, the works found a home in Charlottenburg after World War II. The collection is scheduled in the long term to move to a new gallery at the KULTUR-FORUM.

The main glory of the Galerie der Romantik is a collection of 23 works by Caspar David Friedrich. Paintings such as *Solitary Tree* and *Monk Beside a Lake* illustrate the German Romantic love of solitude and nature, while the 19thC nostalgia for the Middle Ages can be seen in a painting of the gloomy moonlit ruins of Eichwald Abbey.

The gallery owns a sizeable collection of moody Romantic paintings by Karl Friedrich Schinkel, the architect of Neoclassical Berlin. His early Neo-Gothic architectural aspirations are mirrored in an emotional study of an imaginary medieval church perched on a rock by the sea, painted in 1815. The Classical world seized his imagination in later life, as seen in his *Golden Age of Greece.*

The stately elegance of 19thC Berlin is captured in the panoramic view of *Unter den Linden,* painted by Eduard Gaertner in 1853. A curious painting by Johann Hummel shows the highly polished granite basin that still stands in front of the ALTES MUSEUM.

GEDENKSTÄTTE DEUTSCHER WIDERSTAND (German Resistance Memorial)

*Stauffenbergstrasse 13, Tiergarten. Map **3D6** ☎(030) 26542202. Open Mon–Fri 9am–6pm; Sat, Sun 9am–1pm. U-Bahn to Kurfürstenstrasse or bus 129 to Stauffenbergstrasse.*

A memorial to Graf von Stauffenberg and other army officers who attempted to assassinate Hitler on July 20, 1944 stands near the site of the German army headquarters where many of the conspirators were summarily executed.

An exhibition of photographs and documents gives an insight into the history of the unsuccessful coup, which led to thousands of people being arrested on the slightest suspicion of involvement. Another exhibition charts the tragic history of resistance in Nazi Germany.

GEDENKSTÄTTE HAUS DER WANNSEE-KONFERENZ (Memorial in the House of the Wannsee Conference)

*Am Grosser Wannsee 56–58, Zehlendorf. Map **5E2** ☎(030) 8050010 ✗ available 🎞 Open Tues–Fri 10am–6pm, Sat, Sun 2–6pm. Bus 114 from S-Bahnhof Wannsee to Haus der Wannsee-Konferenz. Ring the bell marked Besucher at the front gate, and then the bell at the front door.*

One of the most evil plots in human history was hatched in an elegant Neoclassical villa on the shores of the Wannsee. This building, the location of the Wannsee Conference, was where prominent Nazis gathered on January 20, 1942, to plan the so-called "Final Solution," aimed at the extermination of the 11 million Jews living in Europe.

Built in 1914–15 for a Berlin merchant, the villa has been sensitively converted into a permanent museum of the holocaust. Enlarged black-and-white photographs are hung on glass screens in the ground-floor rooms. Those in rooms 1–5 show the gradual unfolding of hatred and persecution, from petty notices banning Jews from public parks to the mass executions in occupied countries.

Room 6 is where the Nazis met to hasten the policy of extermination. This bright Neoclassical room looking out on the Wannsee seems an unlikely setting for such a horrendous plan. You can still see the table where the Nazi officials sat down to discuss such details as railway timetables and concentration camp design.

The remaining rooms from #7 onward are hung with photographs illustrating the consequences of the Wannsee Conference. You see the train timetables from Berlin to Auschwitz, deportations from Amsterdam in the summer of 1942, and the terrible scenes that the Allies found when they liberated the concentration camps in 1945.

The presentation is restrained and yet deeply moving. Sometimes a single face of a child stands out in the crowd, or perhaps the figure of an old woman on a railway station platform catches your eye. That is when the full horror of the Wannsee Conference is felt. This is a place where people are often reduced to tears.

GEDENKSTÄTTE PLÖTZENSEE

Hüttigpfad, Charlottenburg. Map **6***C4* ☎*(030) 3443226* ▣ *Open daily Mar–Sept 8am–6pm; Feb, Oct 8.30am–5.30pm; Jan, Nov 8.30am–4.30pm; Dec 8.30am–4pm. Bus 123 from S-Bahnhof Tiergarten to Plötzensee.*

A cobbled lane leads past a modern prison to the site of Plötzensee prison, where thousands were tortured and murdered by the Nazis from 1933–45. Many of those involved in the Von Stauffenberg Plot died here in 1944. The dimly lit shed where the executions took place has been kept as a memorial, and a small exhibition of official documents provides a harrowing glimpse of the Nazi period.

If you take bus 123 from S-Bahnhof Tiergarten to Plötzensee, you will also pass a **memorial** on the left side of Levetzowstrasse (just after the Hansabrücke, map **2**B4). Not marked on any maps, the monument stands on the site of the building where many of Berlin's Jews were brought before deportation. A large iron monument lists the destinations and dates of the trains from Berlin. The MARIA REGINA MARTYRUM, another monument to Nazi victims, can also be reached by bus 123.

GEMÄLDEGALERIE (Picture Gallery) ★

Arnimallee 23, Dahlem. Map **6***E4* ☎*(030) 83011* ▣ *(▣ Sun and hols). Open Tues–Fri 9am–5pm, Sat, Sun 10am–5pm* ♿ *U-Bahn to Dahlem-Dorf.*

This is one of the world's greatest collections of paintings, the result of the 19thC merger of the Prussian royal collection with several private collections, including that of Edward Solly, a British merchant in Berlin.

The Gemäldegalerie (Picture Gallery) has had a troubled history. The collection was originally housed in Schinkel's ALTES MUSEUM on Museumsinsel, but the works were later transferred to the more spacious Kaiser-Friedrich-Museum (now renamed the BODE-MUSEUM). The collection of artistic treasures was dispersed during World War II, and some works were destroyed when fire swept the bunker in which they were stored. Others survived the war in deep salt mines, and were eventually returned in 1957 to West Berlin from the US army's art collection depot at Wiesbaden, to be hung in the former Asiatic Museum at Dahlem.

The Gemäldegalerie at the Bode-Museum still has a few minor paintings from the original collection, but the best works are at this museum in Dahlem. How long they will remain there is anyone's guess. A new building to house the entire collection was planned for the KULTUR-FORUM, but the unification of the city has now cast some doubt upon the project.

Orientation

The **scale model** in the main entrance hall may help you find your way around, but probably not. The museum at Dahlem is vast and baffling. The Gemäldegalerie is just one of eight museums housed in the modern complex. Other collections such as the Asiatic Art contain many other exquisite works, but most people take the U-Bahn out to Dahlem-Dorf solely for the paintings. Yet it isn't easy to keep to the picture gallery, however much you try. You often end up straying from Flemish paintings into Polynesian canoes, or jumping from the German Renaissance portraits to Islamic prayer rugs. This can yield unexpected surprises, although you can easily miss entire sections of the Gemäldegalerie, such as the elusive Canalettos. There are a few signposts pointing the way, but it somehow seems to remain a maze. The **short gallery guides in English** are immensely useful if you can't manage the German labels.

People generally go to galleries to look at paintings, but this is one place where it is worth looking at the walls themselves. In each room the walls are clad in a different fabric shade, to set off the paintings: fiery red for the Canalettos, soft green for the German Renaissance, and a light blue for the Dutch landscape paintings.

Early German painting

Following the signs from the lobby brings you into in a room of 18thC English paintings. Don't get bogged down here, as the real treasures come much later. There are some interesting medieval Italian paintings by Botticelli (**rm 114**) and Raphael (**rm 111**), along with two exquisite 16thC miniature Renaissance portraits hung on red velvet walls (**rm 109a**), but the best medieval works here come from N of the Alps.

You will probably find yourself in among the Cranachs (**rm 134**) and Holbeins (**rm 133**) before too long. Lucas Cranach the Elder was the court painter to the Electors of Saxony in Wittenberg. He was one of the first German artists to paint the female nude. Look at Cranach's paintings of Venus, Lucretia and Eve. It is hard to decide whether this is art or soft porn. The most bizarre painting by Cranach is the *Jungbrunnen* (fountain of youth), in which the rejuvenating waters transform wrinkled old women into sexy young girls, who take off into the woods with old men. There's endless material for a feminist thesis here.

Hans Holbein the Younger was not interested in flesh. The people he painted may even seem over-dressed, such as the merchant *Georg Gisze* (**rm 133**). Wearing a dark cloak and hat, this German Hanseatic merchant stands in his office in the Steelyard in London surrounded by bills and ledgers. He looks like a man who would drive a hard bargain.

The Dürers are a long trek from the Cranachs, and you may well be side-tracked down the stairs into the Flemish rooms. But try not to miss the works by Dürer (**rm 138**), especially his portrait of Hieronymus Holzschuher, burgomaster of Nuremberg. German artists tended to excel at male portraits, and Dürer was no exception; his *Virgin and Child,* painted in Venice in 1506, is not one of his great works, although he painted a more successful portrait of a young Venetian woman in the same year.

Early Flemish painting

Now go down the stairs into the Flemish rooms. This is one of the highlights of the collection, so it will pay to take your time. The German art critic Max Friedländer played a major role in building up Berlin's collection of works by 15thC Flemish Primitives, but two world wars have taken their toll. The biggest blow to the department came after World War I when the Treaty of Versailles called for Germany to give several Flemish paintings to Belgium, by way of compensation for four years of carnage. Two wings from Jan van Eyck's Ghent altarpiece left on a train to Belgium. But all was not lost, and the Gemäldegalerie still boasts three miniature works by Jan van Eyck (**rm 143**). One of the paintings is a portrait of the Italian merchant Giovanni Arnolfini, painted in about 1440. This is the same man that also figures in the famous Arnolfini *Wedding Portrait* in London, looking a few years older, and slightly more cunning. The *Virgin in the Church,* an earlier work, was painted in the 1420s.

Baudouin de Lannoy, the subject of a later Van Eyck portrait, wears the collar of the order of the Golden Fleece, and a large green hat. De Lannoy was appointed Governor of Lille in 1423, and later accompanied Van Eyck on a diplomatic mission to Portugal. The slightly sinister *Man with the Carnation* was once believed to be by Van Eyck, but a recent study of the wood on which it is painted proves that it came from a tree felled after the artist's death. A painting of Christ on the Cross has also been dropped from Van Eyck's *oeuvre* on stylistic grounds.

The Flemish painters knew how to paint women. Petrus Christus, a pupil of Van Eyck's, painted an extraordinary *Portrait of a Young Girl.* While not as famous as the bust of Nefertiti at Charlottenburg, it is every bit as mysterious. The girl looks sulky and sullen, as well she might, having presumably posed for hours on end dressed in the tight fashions of the Burgundian court.

There are other works by Christus to linger over, such as the *Exeter Madonna,* an exquisite miniature barely larger than a postcard, showing a detailed view of tiny figures crossing the bridge over the Minnewater in Bruges. The *Madonna of Jan Vos* could almost be a Van Eyck, except that the faces are softer, more Italian in style.

Now look out for the paintings by Roger van der Weyden of Brussels **(rm 144)**. The *Bladelin Altarpiece* includes a portrait of the donor, Pieter Bladelin, kneeling at prayer before the Nativity. Bladelin, an official at the court of Philip the Good in Bruges, amassed sufficient private wealth to found the new town of Middelburg in Flanders, seen in the background. The *Miraflores Altarpiece* is a more complex work, with a frame that seems almost part of the Gothic church.

The *St John Altarpiece* features a lovingly-painted landscape of wheatfields and rocky outcrops, with three scenes from the life of St John the Baptist. The statues of saints with swords poised behind the executioner suggest the inevitability of retribution. Don't miss Van der Weyden's *Portrait of a Young Lady* **(rm 143)**. She is not as withdrawn as the girl in the Christus painting, and her eyes sparkle with humor.

Now look for the paintings by the Flemish painter Hans Memling. The *Portrait of an Old Man* once hung alongside a portrait of the man's wife, but the couple parted company long ago, and her portrait is now in Paris. The *Virgin and Child,* painted in 1487, is seen without its side wings, which are now in the Uffizi in Florence.

Part of the *Altarpiece of St Omer* by Simon Marmion has ended up in Berlin (**rm 144**), but it is only a small part, as the diagram on the wall opposite illustrates. (Don't go to St Omer looking for the other panels; nothing at all remains except for the ruins of the abbey where the altarpiece once hung.) If you have time to spare, you might pause in the little room with the painting by the Master of the *St Barbara Legend* (**rm 145**) to read the 12 Latin inscriptions translated into German. But it's perhaps better to hurry on to the next room.

We begin to see the Renaissance creeping into Flemish painting in the works of Hugo van der Goes (**rm 146**). His ambitious *Monforte Altarpiece* is named after a Spanish monastery where it once hung. It is an early work, not as tormented as the later paintings, with superb portraits of the Magi, and a giant cluster of lilies that might have been painted by an Impressionist. For a later work by the same artist, look at the *Adoration of the Magi,* a more ambitious composition that strives to convey drama and psychological tension.

The Dutch begin to appear in this room. Look out for the painting of *John the Baptist in the Wilderness* by the Haarlem artist Geertgen tot Sint Jans (**rm 146**). A melancholy St John is shown in a lush landscape filled with rabbits and deer. You are then plunged into the thick of the Flemish Renaissance with Quinten Metsys' *Throned Madonna* (**rm 148**). A few paintings later, you come upon one of the great works by Pieter Bruegel the Elder, illustrating *The Dutch Proverbs.* Everyone can spot the man hitting his head against a brick wall (bottom left corner), and the blind leading the blind (top right), but a lot of the other proverbs are obscure. Buy a 10-Pfennig leaflet for an explanation of all 118 proverbs depicted in the painting.

You can ignore the paintings by Van Hemessen, but don't miss the other painting by Pieter Bruegel in the glass cabinet (**rm 150**). It is called *Two Chained Monkeys* and its meaning is anyone's guess. Recent research has proved that the animals are long-tailed African monkeys, introduced to Antwerp (the city in the background) by 16thC Portuguese traders. But that doesn't help explain the riddle.

In the days when entrance to the Gemäldegalerie was free, you could leave at this point for a leisurely lunch at Alter Krug (page 170), or something simpler in a beer garden. But if you want to pause for lunch, you now have to use the museum restaurant — good enough if all you need is two Wiener sausages and some potato salad, or Sachertorte and coffee. Still, it has a terrace, which can be pleasant on sunny days.

17thC Flemish and Dutch painters

Back to the picture gallery, the next department is one flight up from Bruegel. You are very likely to arrive among the Rubens (**rms 240–241**). There used to be many more works by Rubens in Berlin, but some were too big to move during the war, and they perished in the bombardment. What remains are some small Baroque works in the *Rubenshalle* (**rm 240**), including a portrait of his frail first wife, Isabella Brant (**rm 241**). When Rubens remarried after his first wife's death, he chose a more robust mate in Hélène Fourment. You can see her posing as the captive Andromeda, and again as the music-loving St Cecilia (**rm 240**). Rubens seems to have liked the Andromeda legend, as he painted it on an earlier occasion in 1622, but this time with a different model chained to the rocks.

The Gemäldegalerie owns three works by the Dutch painter Vermeer, two masterpieces and one disappointment. The most striking painting is the *Young Girl with Pearl Necklace,* in which the light falling on the wall is painted with extraordinary skill (**rm 242**). Look closely at the wall in the background of Vermeer's *Couple Drinking Wine*; it is the same tint of green as the fabric covering the wall of room 242.

The same attention to decor crops up in a later room (**rm 237**), where low-horizon Dutch landscape paintings are hung against a pale blue background. The color exactly matches the sky in Esaias van de Velde's 1618 view of *Zierikzee.* There are views of various Dutch cities, including *Haarlem* and *Amsterdam* by Jacob van Ruisdael, and *Arnhem* by Jan van Goyen.

Two entire rooms are filled with works by Rembrandt (**rms 235–6**), including a portrait of Saskia, his delicate first wife, painted the year after she died. Rembrandt seems to have gone for the same robust female physique as Rubens when he sought a new wife. He chose Hendrickje Stoffels, the voluptuous woman seen in a portrait dated 1659. Other portraits by Rembrandt include a striking *Head of Christ* and a youthful self-portrait wearing a fur coat and black hat.

But now for the bad news. The famous *Man in the Golden Helmet* was recently exposed as a fake by the Rembrandt Research Project in Amsterdam. The Berlin gallery was devastated by the news. It was as if the Louvre had found out that the *Mona Lisa* was a fake. The Gemäldegalerie had no option but to alter the label to read "After Rembrandt."

GENDARMENMARKT 🏛

*South of Unter den Linden, Mitte. Map **4**C8. U-Bahn to Französische Strasse.*

The Gendarmenmarkt (where King Friedrich I built a guard house for his Gendarmes regiment) was laid out in the 17thC at the heart of the new town of Friedrichstadt. Gradually enhanced with grand Baroque and Neoclassical buildings, the square became one of Berlin's most handsome locations. It was severely bombed in the Battle of Berlin, and remained in ruins until well into the 1980s.

But the communists, who renamed the square Platz der Akademie in 1950, finally found the political will to reconstruct the old buildings using historical plans and fragments of rubble. The square (now renamed the Gendarmenmarkt), has become one of the most elegant urban spaces in Berlin, with its graceful arcades sheltering academic bookstores and cafés.

Two identical churches were built on the square in the first decade of the 18thC. The FRANZÖSISCHER DOM to the N was built for the Huguenots, while the **Deutscher Dom** to the S served the German Lutherans. The two churches were later elevated to cathedral status, and lofty domed towers were added by Karl von Gontard. It is worth slogging to the top of the tower in the Französischer Dom (⚞) for the view of central Berlin.

A theater, the **Schauspielhaus**, was built between the two churches. Gutted by fire in 1817, it was replaced by an elegant Neoclassical edifice designed by Schinkel. This, in turn, was destroyed during World

The Gendarmenmarkt **Schauspielhaus**

War II. The East German government carefully rebuilt the fabric, but converted the interior into a large hall for classical concerts and a small room for chamber music.

GEORG-KOLBE-MUSEUM

*Sensburger Allee 25, Charlottenburg. Map **5**C3 ☎(030) 3042144 ▣ Open Tues–Sun 10am–5pm ♿ (☎ ahead). Bus 149 to Raussendorffplatz.*

A collection of bronze nudes and sketches by Georg Kolbe (1877–1947) and other 20thC Berlin sculptors. The works are attractively displayed in the atelier and garden of a villa built for Kolbe in the 1920s.

GRUNEWALD

*E of the Havel. Wilmersdorf and Zehlendorf. Map **5**D3. S-Bahn to Grunewald or Schlachtensee; U-Bahn to Onkel-Toms-Hütte; bus 218 from Theodor-Heuss-Platz to the Grunewaldturm. See also WALK 4, with map, on page 83.*

The mystical Germanic love of forests has ensured the preservation of the extensive Grunewald on the W edge of Berlin. Writing in the early 1930s, Christopher Isherwood described the Grunewald as a "dank, dreary pinewood" in *Goodbye to Berlin,* but much of the old forest was felled for firewood after the war, and the pines have been replanted with a more agreeable mixture of oak and ash. You can wander for hours through the dark woods, disturbed only occasionally by the roar of traffic on the Avus, Germany's oldest race track, now an autobahn, built through the Grunewald in 1912–21.

The ancient forest, known as the *Grünen Wald* (Green Forest), was a favorite hunting ground of Elector Joachim II, who built a handsome Renaissance hunting lodge on the edge of a dark lake. The JAGDSCHLOSS GRUNEWALD now contains a somber collection of German Renaissance paintings depicting Hohenzollern rulers and hunting scenes.

A 19thC Romantic urge led to the construction of the **Grunewaldturm** *(Havelchaussee ☎ (030) 3041203; open daily 10am-9pm; closes at dusk in winter ⋞ ☰).* Designed in 1897 by the architect of the KAISER-WILHELM-GEDÄCHTNISKIRCHE, the Neo-Gothic tower was built in memory of Kaiser Wilhelm I. Perched on a hill overlooking the Havel, the 55-meter/180-foot-high balcony offers a view of thick forests and vast expanses of water.

You can also climb to the top of the **Teufelsberg** (devil's mountain) for a different view of the forest *(Teufelsseechaussee, S-Bahn to Grunewald, then a 20min walk through the woods ⋞).* The 115-meter/377-foot Teufelsberg is one of eight artificial hills built in Berlin from the rubble left behind after World War II. Most of the laboring was carried out by women *(Trümmerfrauen),* due to a chronic shortage of able-bodied men. An American radar station at the summit strangely resembles some extravagant castle built by King Ludwig of Bavaria.

The Grunewald is easily reached by S-Bahn or U-Bahn. S-Bahnhof Grunewald is a good starting point for rambles in the forest. You can follow a string of lakes to the S (see WALK 4, page 83), or wander along one of the meandering paths leading to the Grunewaldturm — about an hour's walk. Areas designated as nature reserves *(Naturschutzgebiet)* are worth exploring; the low hills rising E of the Havel provide marvelous panoramic views.

The woods are dotted with rustic country inns *(Wirtshäuser)* offering good beer and basic German food, and many are situated in historic buildings overlooking the lakes or the Havel.

HAMBURGER BAHNHOF

Invalidenstrasse 50-51, Tiergarten. Map ***3****A7 ☎(030) 3941438 ■ Closed for reconstruction. S-Bahn to Lehrter Bahnhof or U-Bahn to Zinnowitzer Strasse.*

The Hamburger Bahnhof was briefly the main station for trains traveling from Berlin to Hamburg. The handsome Neo-Renaissance edifice was built in 1845–47 as one of five great termini on the edge of the old city. It closed down in 1884, however, when the more modern Lehrter Bahnhof began operating, and since then, the former station has gone through various transformations.

Conversion is currently underway for its latest role, which is to house the Nationalgalerie's contemporary art collection currently housed in the ALTE NATIONALGALERIE on Museumsinsel. The old station had already served as a museum of transport and building (the forerunner of the MUSEUM FÜR VERKEHR UND TECHNIK) and as a center for temporary art exhibitions. Once it reopens (no one yet dares to guess when), the new art gallery may rival the museum at the old Gare d'Orsay in Paris.

HANSAVIERTEL 🏛

Altonaer Strasse, Klopstockstrasse and environs, Tiergarten. Map ***2****C5. S-Bahn to Tiergarten or Bellevue; U-Bahn to Hansaplatz.*

Situated on the N edge of the Tiergarten, the Hansaviertel was once one of Berlin's most elegant districts. Devastated in World War II, it was rebuilt in 1957 as West Berlin's response to the acclaimed Stalinallee (now KARL-MARX-ALLEE) in the Soviet sector. A team of 53 international architects was commissioned to design a modern residential quarter, with shops, a cinema and a day nursery. Set in landscaped grounds, the buildings range in height from one to fifteen stories.

The architecture may now look slightly dated, but the apartment blocks are still an interesting compendium of postwar styles. A rusted enamel sign outside U-Bahnhof Hansaplatz gives the locations of the 36 projects, and the names of the architects.

HAUS AM CHECKPOINT CHARLIE

Friedrichstrasse 44, Kreuzberg. Map ***4****D8 ☎(030) 2511031 ■ ■ Open daily 9am–10pm. U-Bahn to Kochstrasse.*

Now that the Berlin Wall has come down, the Haus am Checkpoint Charlie has lost its dramatic impact. During the Cold War, the Wall could only be crossed at three posts, named Alpha, Bravo and Charlie. Checkpoint Charlie, situated in the American sector, was the most volatile of the border posts, where US and Soviet tanks occasionally stood ready for war. But in 1990, the military checkpoint became redundant; the guard post went to the MUSEUM FÜR VERKEHR UND TECHNIK, and the Haus am Checkpoint Charlie became something of an anachronism.

Originally set up in a café near the border post, the Haus am Checkpoint Charlie (or Mauermuseum) charts the history of the 165km (102 mile) concrete wall built around West Berlin in 1961. On show is a curious collection of makeshift vehicles made by inventive East Berliners for escaping to the West. They include a tiny bubble car, two hot-air balloons, a radiogram (a radio-cum-phonograph) in which a lithe 24-year-old girl curled up, and a welding machine with a compartment hidden by coils of wire.

Now dusty and dated, the museum somewhat resembles a 1970s student apartment that hasn't been cleaned up in a long time. Newspaper cuttings glued to the walls, threadbare carpets and a scruffy café create an air of nonchalant anarchy intended perhaps to appeal to the young visitors who flock here from all over the world.

A newly-created section covers the events of 1989–90. There are banners carried by protesting East Berliners, and some impressive works of East European art, including Daniel Mitlijanskij's *Requiem for Sacharov,* which features a procession of mourners carved from solid tree trunks.

HAVEL

W suburbs, Zehlendorf and Spandau districts. Map **5***B3–E2* ✱ *S-Bahn to Wannsee; U-Bahn to Altstadt-Spandau.*

The river Havel creates an attractive landscape of lakes fringed with dunes and woods, in the W suburbs of Berlin. Rising in an area of lakes to the N of the city, the Havel flows through a lock at the old town of SPANDAU, then widens into a broad lake, with the GRUNEWALD on the E bank and the former fishing villages of Gatow and Kladow on the quiet W bank. Farther S, the river laps the shores of PFAUENINSEL, then flows under the **Glienicker Brücke** to **Potsdam**. After passing through the town of **Brandenburg**, the Havel finally enters the River Elbe.

Stern line steamers first began operating on the Havel in 1888, and the **Stern und Kreisschiffahrt** line now runs regular summer sailings between TEGEL (on the Tegeler See inlet), SPANDAU, WANNSEE (on the Grosser Wannsee inlet), PFAUENINSEL and the Glienicker Brücke.

The W bank of the Havel *(reached by bus 134 from U-Bahnhof Rathaus Spandau)* is dotted with old villages and quiet nature reserves. The former village of **Gatow** boasts a 14thC church with a wooden roof.

The only landing stage for steamers on the W bank is at **Kladow**, which has an attractive tree-lined waterfront with an extensive Biergarten in the summer. A leafy country lane climbs up to the old village church.

JAGDSCHLOSS GLIENICKE

S of Königstrasse, Zehlendorf. Off map **5***E1 and see map on page 221* ▣ ⋞ *Hunting lodge closed, but park open daily, dawn–dusk. S-Bahn to Wannsee, then bus 116 to Glienicker Brücke, or line 1 boat to Glienicker Brücke.*

A 17thC Baroque hunting lodge erected by the Great Elector near the SCHLOSS KLEIN-GLIENICKE was rebuilt in the 19thC by Prince Friedrich Karl. The Jagdschloss (now a college) is not open to the public, but you can wander in the 19thC gardens on the banks of the Havel (see VOLKSPARK KLEIN-GLIENICKE). Like so many parks in SW Berlin, it was landscaped by Lenné in the informal style of English country house gardens.

A good view of Potsdam is seen from a little promontory to the W.

JAGDSCHLOSS GRUNEWALD 🏛

*Am Grunewaldsee 29, Zehlendorf. Map **5**D3 ☎(030) 8133597 ▣ Closed Mon; open Apr–Sept, Tues–Sun 10am–1pm, 1.30–6pm; Mar, Oct closes 5pm; Nov–Feb closes 4pm. Bus 115 to Pücklerstrasse, then a 10min walk through the woods.*

The Renaissance Jagdschloss Grunewald, designed in 1542 by Caspar Theiss for Elector Joachim II, stands on a lake in the depths of the woods. The former hunting lodge was altered by later Prussian rulers, but the original 16thC **Grosse Saal** (Great Hall) on the ground floor has survived intact. With red sandstone floors and painted ceilings, this is now the sole surviving Renaissance interior in Berlin.

The Jagdschloss was one of several royal palaces in Berlin to be seized by the state after Kaiser Wilhelm II fled to the Netherlands in 1918. The rooms are now hung with landscape paintings from various royal palaces, including some from the now demolished Schloss Monbijou.

Dappled sunlight falls on 16thC paintings by Lucas Cranach the Elder. The mystical Germanic attachment to dark forests is revealed in *The Water Nymph,* while a painting of Judith with the head of Holofernes demonstrates Cranach's obsession with female cruelty.

A room overlooking the lake contains nine paintings from a *Passion Cycle,* painted for the Berlin Dom. The upstairs rooms contain some 17thC Dutch landscapes by the Haarlem School, and a painting showing the elderly Kaiser Wilhelm I arriving at the Jagdschloss in 1887. Don't miss the 19thC *trompe l'oeil* rusticated stonework as you leave, or the painted hunting scene beneath the interlocked antlers above the door.

KAISER-WILHELM-GEDÄCHTNISKIRCHE

*Breitscheidplatz, Charlottenburg. Map **2**D4 ☎(030) 2185023 ▣ Open Tues–Sat 10am–6pm. U-Bahn and S-Bahn to Zoologischer Garten.*

The E end of Kurfürstendamm is dramatically terminated by the shattered spire of the Kaiser-Wilhelm-Gedächtniskirche, one of ten Berlin churches gutted by fire during a single air raid on November 22, 1943. The church was built in 1891–95, in the Romanesque style of the Rhine, as a memorial to Kaiser Wilhelm I. Most of the church was demolished after the war, leaving just the jagged spire, and a portico decorated with glinting mosaics illustrating episodes of Hohenzollern history. Intended as a somber reminder of World War II, the church has, in recent years, been irreverently nicknamed the *hohler Zahn* (rotten tooth).

A modern hexagonal church, bathed inside with mysterious blue light, was constructed in 1959 where the nave of the Gedächtniskirche once stood. Impish Berliners call it "the makeup box," while a modern bell tower erected nearby is colloquially known as the "lipstick tube."

KARL-MARX-ALLEE 🏛

*Map **4**B10. U-Bahn to Alexanderplatz or Frankfurter Tor.*

Karl-Marx-Allee is the best example of postwar communist architecture in Berlin. Originally called the Frankfurter Allee, the 3-kilometer street in the Soviet sector was renamed Stalinallee by the communists. But in 1961, when the Soviet dictator fell from grace, the avenue became Karl-Marx-Allee. The name has survived the collapse of communism.

Stalinallee was designed in 1952 by Hermann Henselmann, who had already built an impressive tower block just S on the Weberweise. The monumental building blocks were intended to mirror the Neoclassical style of Schinkel's Berlin, and they incorporated elegant arcades, and loggias with slender columns on the top floor. Two matching tower blocks on the Strausberger Platz (modeled on Karl von Gontard's two church towers on the GENDARMENMARKT) provide an impressive entry to the street. The project included a children's store — **Das Haus des Kindes** — and the restaurant **Haus Berlin**. Bertolt Brecht, a close friend of Henselmann, was inspired to compose a verse which now adorns the Haus Berlin entrance.

The prestigious project later ran into difficulties; by the time work began at the Frankfurter Tor, the East Berlin authorities were beginning to complain about the high cost of the design. Labor relations worsened when production quotas on the project were raised, and on June 16, 1953, the Stalinallee workers staged a strike, which quickly turned into a general demonstration for democratic rights in East Germany. The next day, the Soviet Union sent in the army to crush the revolt.

KÄTHE-KOLLWITZ-MUSEUM

*Fasanenstrasse 24, Charlottenburg. Map **2**D4 ☎(030) 8825210 ▣ Open 11am–6pm; closed Tues. U-Bahn to Kurfürstendamm.*

This museum, devoted to the graphic art and sculpture of Käthe Kollwitz (1867–1945), occupies several rooms of a palatial Charlottenburg mansion built in 1897. As a doctor's wife in the impoverished district of Prenzlauer Berg, she sketched harrowing scenes such as *Woman with Dead Child* (1903). Kollwitz continued to portray the suffering of women and children during World War I and into the 1920s. Her poster *Nie wieder Krieg* (Never Again War) was an attempt to combat growing militarism in 1923, while *Brot* highlighted poverty in the inflation-ridden years between the wars.

In 1922–23, she produced the cycle of woodcuts titled *Krieg* in memory of her son, Peter, who had died in Flanders in World War I. A second cycle of eight woodcuts entitled *Tod* was produced in the early years of Nazi rule.

KLEISTPARK

*Potsdamer Strasse, Schöneberg. Map **3**E6. Open dawn–dusk. U-Bahn to Kleistpark.*

A small formal park named after the German Romantic dramatist Heinrich von Kleist. Originally a hop garden for the royal brewery, the site became Berlin's first botanical garden in 1679.

Two Baroque colonnades lend elegance to an otherwise rather dull quarter of Schöneberg. Designed by Karl von Gontard in 1777 for Frederick the Great, they originally flanked the Königstrasse (now the Rathausstrasse), which led from the royal palace to Alexanderplatz. Removed in 1910 to improve traffic flow along the important artery, the 18thC Königskolonnaden (king's colonnades) were rather confusingly renamed the **Kleist Colonnades**.

Two statues depicting men taming wild horses are copies of works on the Anitschkoff Bridge in St Petersburg. A gift from Czar Nicholas I to his brother-in-law Friedrich Wilhelm IV, they stood in the Lustgarten before being moved here in 1945.

The park is overlooked by the imposing Neo-Baroque **Kammergericht** (now the BERLIN-MUSEUM), the former German supreme court of appeal, built in 1913 to replace the 18thC court in Lindenstrasse. The Allied Control Authority was established here in 1945, and the flags of the four powers flew from the balcony until 1948, when the Soviet Union withdrew from the alliance following a dispute about currency controls. Three flags have flown since then, all probably to disappear when the Allies finally quit Berlin.

KNOBLAUCHHAUS

Poststrasse 23, Mitte. Map ***4C9*** *☎(030) 24313392. Open 10am–5pm; closed Mon. U-Bahn or S-Bahn to Alexanderplatz.*

A Baroque house built for Johann Knoblauch in 1760 has been carefully reconstructed in the NIKOLAIVIERTEL. Rebuilt in 1835 in a Neoclassical form, the house boasts handsome rooms furnished in Biedermeier style. The building now contains a collection of family mementoes including relics of Eduard Knoblauch, architect of the NEUE SYNAGOGUE, and Armand Knoblauch, founder of Berlin's Böhmische brewery.

KONGRESSHALLE 🏛

John-Foster-Dulles-Allee 10, Tiergarten. Map ***3B6*** *☎(030) 397870 ⚌ Open Tues–Thurs 2–6pm; Fri, Sun 10am–8pm; closed Mon, Sat. Bus 100 to Kongresshalle, or S-Bahn to Unter den Linden.*

Situated in a corner of the Tiergarten overlooking the Spree, the Kongresshalle was built in 1957 as America's contribution to the International Building Exhibition (IBA). Designed by Hugh Stubbins as a symbol of international friendship, the Kongresshalle is a striking example of 1950s futuristic design, with a remarkable concrete roof that inspired wry Berliners to dub the edifice the *Schwangere Auster* (pregnant oyster).

Surrounded by a bleak, windswept promenade deck, the Kongresshalle is now rather melancholy, although the 1950s chairs and lamps may appeal to design enthusiasts. Recently renamed the **Haus der Kulturen der Welt** (House of World Culture), it currently stages temporary exhibitions on aspects of life in the Third World, as well as occasional concerts and plays.

A gaunt black tower stands near the Kongresshalle. Built in 1987 by the Daimler-Benz company, it contains a 68-bell **carillon** *(concerts daily at noon and 6pm).*

KÖPENICK

*SE Berlin. Map **7**E7. S-Bahn to Köpenick, then tram 25 to Alt-Köpenick.*

Surrounded by lakes and forests, Köpenick is a wistful old town standing on a peninsula at the confluence of the Dahme and Spree rivers. The old quarter of Alt-Köpenick still has the neglected look of most former East German towns, with dusty brick churches and derelict Baroque houses, but once the grime has been scraped off, it could well be as attractive as Spandau.

A fortress was erected on this strategic site in the 12thC, and by the 13thC the town was important enough to receive a charter. The **castle** was rebuilt in Renaissance style by Joachim II, but only the foundations now remain. The present edifice was built in an intimate Dutch Baroque style for a son of the Great Elector, and currently houses a museum of decorative arts, the KUNSTGEWERBEMUSEUM SCHLOSS KÖPENICK. The attractive **Rathaus** (town hall) on Alt-Köpenick was built in 1903–5, in the style of a northern German brick church.

The annual *Köpenicker Sommer* festival in June commemorates the events chronicled in Carl Zuckmayer's play *Der Hauptmann von Köpenick* (The Captain of Köpenick). The play tells of a shoemaker disguised as a captain, who orders a group of soldiers to travel by train to Köpenick to arrest the Bürgermeister.

You can take a creaky East Berlin tram (#25) from Platz des 23 April in Köpenick to **Rahnsdorf** on the edge of the MÜGGELSEE. The tram rumbles past crumbling country villas surrounded by apple orchards, and then turns down the main street of FRIEDRICHSHAGEN, a pleasant old town with dusty 18thC Neoclassical dwellings. There are convenient S-Bahn stations at Rahnsdorf (a 10-minute walk through the woods from the tram terminus) and at Friedrichshagen.

KREUZBERG

*S of Mitte. See map for WALK 2 on page 79 and color map **4**.*

Named after a natural hill (now the VIKTORIAPARK), Kreuzberg district is a 19thC quarter S of Mitte. Parts of the district are heavily industrialized, such as **Gleisdreieck**, with its railway yards, pump house (now the LAPIDARIUM) and factories, but elsewhere you can find attractive tree-lined avenues with solid Old Berlin apartments.

Kreuzberg was badly damaged in World War II, and remained largely derelict afterward. Its vast, dilapidated apartments were settled by a cosmopolitan mix of Turkish immigrant workers, avant-garde artists and students. With the construction of the Berlin Wall, the quarter developed something of a frontier spirit, providing an exciting setting for social experiments, radical art galleries, cafés and theaters. Many flourished briefly, but a few, such as the **Künstlerhaus Bethanien** *(Mariannenplatz),* have become Berlin institutions. This is an ornate Neo-Gothic hospital converted into an alternative center. It contains artists' studios and craft workshops. The stretch of Oranienstrasse between Oranienplatz and Heinrichplatz has several bars for wild nights, while the waterfront cafés along Paul-Lincke-Ufer are quiet places for a late breakfast.

In recent years, Kreuzberg has looked less shabby, as old apartment blocks such as Riehmers Hofgarten *(Yorckstrasse 83-86, map 3E7)* have been renovated. Some of Germany's best modern architecture has been recently constructed in areas of Kreuzberg bordering the Wall, in an attempt to repair the urban fabric.

The demolition of the Wall is likely to make the district increasingly desirable (and, no doubt, expensive), although hopefully a few green and purple spotlights will continue to glow in apartment windows to symbolize Kreuzberg's radical spirit.

See also WALK 2 on page 78.

KULTUR-FORUM

*s of Tiergarten. Map **3**C6. Bus 129, 148, 187, 248, 341 to Kultur-Forum.*

The cluster of museums and concert halls on the s edge of the Tiergarten was planned as a center of the arts by the architect Hans Scharoun in 1960–63. The buildings are grouped rather randomly around the **St Matthäi-Kirche**, designed by August Stüler in 1844. The isolated Byzantine-style church is all that remains of an old neighborhood destroyed in World War II.

Scharoun set the tone for the Kultur-Forum with his design for the remarkable PHILHARMONIE concert hall, which received worldwide fame for its excellent acoustics. He later added the **Kammermusiksaal** and the nearby **Staatsbibliothek** to the scheme. The MUSIKINSTRUMENTEN-MUSEUM and the KUNSTGEWERBEMUSEUM subsequently fueled local wrath with their brutal style. A new KUPFERSTICHKABINETT was added in 1993, and a GEMÄLDEGALERIE (incorporating an 1895 villa that survived World War II) is planned.

Although still rather bleak and disconnected, the Kultur-Forum has several excellent museums run by the Prussian Cultural Foundation. The Musikinstrumenten-Museum stages occasional jazz concerts, while the nearby NEUE NATIONALGALERIE boasts a lively café.

KUNSTGEWERBEMUSEUM (Museum of Arts and Crafts)

The Kunstgewerbemuseum is currently split between two sites — one at the KULTUR-FORUM and the other at Schloss Köpenick.

Inspired by the Victoria & Albert Museum in London, the Kunstgewerbemuseum was founded in 1867 as a museum of decorative arts. A magnificent building (now the MARTIN-GROPIUS-BAU) was built in 1881 to house the collection of ceramics, tapestries, furniture, glass and metalwork. In 1920, the museum moved to the BERLINER SCHLOSS, vacated after the Kaiser fled to the Netherlands. Dispersed during World War II, the works are now divided between two sites.

Kunstgewerbemuseum Tiergarten

*Matthäikirchstrasse 10,. Map **3**C6 ☎(030) 2662911 ✉ (✉ Sun and hols). Open Tues–Fri 9am–5pm; Sat, Sun 10am–5pm; closed Mon ♿ ☕ Bus 129, 148, 187, 248, 341 to Kultur-Forum.*

Built in 1978–85 near the Philharmonie, the Kunstgewerbemuseum Tiergarten is part of the unfinished KULTUR-FORUM. The virtually windowless concrete design deters all but the most determined of visitors, yet it is worth penetrating the bunker-like building, as it contains an exceptional collection of European arts and crafts. Although the concrete-walled rooms seem sterile, the display techniques are generally excellent.

A small **Medieval collection** (Rm I) includes ornate reliquaries andg other religious works. The more extensive **Renaissance rooms** (Rms II and III) are hung with large Brussels tapestries depicting Classical legends and Biblical stories. Cabinets filled with Venetian glass, Nuremberg silverware and Florentine majolica show 16thC craftsmen's skills. Don't miss the ornate objects belonging to the **Lüneburger Ratssilber**, a collection of 15th–16thC silver vessels bought to symbolize the wealth of the Hanseatic port of Lüneburg. The sale of the town silver to the Berlin-Museum in 1874 sadly reflects the decline of the proud merchant town situated SE of Hamburg.

The **Baroque collection** (Rm IV) contains a fascinating collection of 17thC "cabinets of curiosity" *(Kunstkammern).* Crammed with secret boxes and drawers and encrusted with silver and precious stones, the **Pommersche Kunstschrank** was assembled in Augsburg in 1610–16 for the duke of Pommern-Stettin. Although the cabinet was destroyed in World War II, the contents survived, and they now fill three glass cases in the museum. The objects include erudite games, miniature books, medical instruments, razors, hair brushes, tools and even a tiny Renaissance fruit press.

A display of elegant **18thC porcelain** manufactured in Meissen, Nymphenburg and Berlin (including a magnificent KPM amphora painted in 1840 with a view of the Russian Orthodox church in Potsdam) is on view in Rm V. The **Chinesenzimmer**, an intimate 18thC room decorated with chinoiserie motifs, comes from the Palazzo Graneri in Turin. Rm VI is devoted to Biedermeier and Art Nouveau works, while Rm VII has sleek Art Deco vases.

Kunstgewerbemuseum Schloss Köpenick 🏛

Schloss Köpenick, Schlossinsel, Köpenick. Map ***7**E7* ☎*(030) 6572651.* ***Open*** *9am–5pm; closed Mon, Tues* 🚇 *S-Bahn to Köpenick or Spindlersfeld.*

Tucked away on a wooded peninsula at the confluence of the Spree and Dahme rivers, the old Schloss at Köpenick now contains an attractive museum of decorative arts. The intimate Baroque palace was built in 1678–90 for Prince Friedrich, the Great Elector's son, by the Dutch architect Rutger van Langevelt. A **chapel** on the opposite side of the courtyard was added by Johann Nering in 1682.

With its ornate ceilings and creaking wooden stairs, the former Hohenzollern palace makes an idyllic setting for a collection of Renaissance cabinets, Nuremberg pewter, Augsburg gold chalices and Berlin porcelain. The works came from the old Kunstgewerbemuseum, founded in 1867. Originally housed in a former panoramic picture gallery, the collection was moved to an abandoned porcelain factory, then to a custom-built museum of decorative arts (now the MARTIN-GROPIUS-BAU). After the 1918 Revolution, the ever-growing collection moved to the

Baroque royal palace facing the Lustgarten. Shipped out in crates during World War II, the collection was reassembled in the Kunstgewerbemuseum in the western sector and Schloss Köpenick in the Soviet zone. The Köpenick museum is much smaller than its counterpart near the Tiergarten, but the intimate Baroque setting is more pleasing. The only disappointment is that the museum café overlooking the river has not yet shaken off its dour Eastern Bloc atmosphere.

A dark **Renaissance room** from Schloss Haldenstein, near the Swiss town of Chur, was acquired by the museum in 1884. Built in 1548 by a craftsman who signed himself H.S., the room is decorated with elaborate *intarsia* representing perspective views of Renaissance cities.

The Baroque **Wappensaal** (coats-of-arms chamber) on the second floor was added to Schloss Köpenick in the late 17thC. Designed as a ballroom by the Italian architect Giovanni Carove, it is lavishly decorated with huge coats-of-arms of the Prussian provinces. The fireplaces are surmounted by masked savages supporting helmets laden with feathers and bizarre beasts. It was in this room bristling with Prussian pomp that Friedrich Wilhelm I conducted the court-martial of his son, the future Frederick the Great, for desertion.

The adjacent room contains relics of the **Silberbuffet**, a collection of gold and silver vessels. Commissioned by Elector Friedrich III, the ornate pieces were made in Augsburg in 1695–98 by the Biller family of goldsmiths. The works were shown to the public for the first time in 1982, in a room modeled on the Rittersaal at the Stadtschloss (where they were originally displayed). Some of the objects in the room were made by Berlin silversmiths, such as an overscaled 18thC silver tankard decorated with hundreds of coins.

KUPFERSTICHKABINETT (Engravings Collection)

*At the Kultur-Forum, Matthäikirchplatz, s of Tiergarten. Map **3C6** ☎(030) 8301228 ▣ (▣ Sun and hols). Open Tues–Fri 9am–5pm; Sat, Sun 10am–5pm. Bus 129, 148, 187, 248, 341 to Kultur-Forum.*

The Great Elector's collection of drawings and watercolors formed the basis of Berlin's print cabinet. Moved to the Altes Museum in 1831 and later to the Neues Museum, the collection ended up after the war split between the Kupferstichkabinett at Dahlem and the Altes Museum. The collections have finally been reunited at the KULTUR-FORUM.

The print collection has major works by Dürer, Grünewald, Cranach, Pieter Bruegel the Elder, Rubens, Rembrandt, Kandinsky and Dix. The prints are normally kept in storage, but you can ask to look at particular works. The museum shows a changing selection of prints taken from the collection, in an exhibition called *Im Blickpunkt* (At a Moment's Glance).

KURFÜRSTENDAMM

*Charlottenburg. Map **1**E1–**2**D4. U-Bahn to Kurfürstendamm.*

Extending 3.5km/2 miles from the KAISER-WILHELM-GEDÄCHTNISKIRCHE to the Halensee, the Kurfürstendamm (Ku'damm to Berliners) is a broad, leafy avenue modeled on the Avenue des Champs-Élysées in Paris. Created in 1882 by Otto von Bismarck to connect the city with the

Grunewald, Kurfürstendamm follows an old route from the BERLINER SCHLOSS to the Grunewald hunting lodge used by Electors *(Kurfürsten).* Wealthy Berliners began to build opulent villas on the avenue in the 1880s, and fashionable cafés and restaurants later sprung up, rivaling those on Unter den Linden. The avenue was shortened in 1886 at the time when the Kaiser-Wilhelm-Gedächtniskirche was built, and the final stretch became Budapester Strasse.

Most of the hotels and cafés on Kurfürstendamm were destroyed by bombing, but a few prewar buildings still stand. These include the former Chinese embassy *(#218),* and the ornate 1905 *Jugendstil* corner block *(#59-60).* Most of the avenue has been rebuilt in a sober modern style, but a few buildings preserve a little of the flavor of Old Berlin, notably the **Hotel Bristol Kempinski** and the **Café Möhring** *(#234).*

Kurfürstendamm is still Berlin's liveliest street, with cafés, hotels, stores, theaters and cinemas stretching along its entire length. The flamboyant street lamps, large clocks and Neoclassical newsstands (the best two, located at the corner of Uhlandstrasse, are tiny Neoclassical buildings) create a distinctive Berlin atmosphere that draws crowds from dawn until long after midnight.

LAPIDARIUM

*Hallesches Ufer 78, Kreuzberg. Map **3**D7. Open only during temporary exhibitions. U-Bahn to Gleisdreieck.*

A curious collection of war-damaged Berlin sculpture has been abandoned in the courtyard of a former 19thC pumping house on the Landwehrkanal. Known as the Lapidarium, it is rarely open, but you can peer through the iron gate to the right of the building to see a row of damaged statues striking preposterous poses. They are all that remain of a double avenue of 27 statues of Prussian rulers, commissioned by Wilhelm II to line the Siegesallee (Victory Avenue) in the Tiergarten. Most Berliners considered the Siegesallee merely comic, and dubbed it the *Puppenallee* (dolls' avenue).

The Siegesallee stood in the path of a much grander avenue planned by Albert Speer, and the statues were removed to the perimeter of the Grosser Stern. Here they were shelled in World War II, losing fingers, arms and even heads. Now abandoned in a damp courtyard, the Prussian dolls are rather melancholy symbols of Berlin's history.

LÜBARS

*Reinickendorf. Map **6**A5. Bus 222 from U-Bahnhof Tegel to Alt-Lübars.*

Surrounded by flat fields and farmhouses, the former village of Lübars is a surprisingly rural corner of Berlin. The Wall used to cut across the fields just N of the village, but life in the farming community is now back to normal. The village church — a modest Baroque edifice — was rebuilt in the 1790s after a fire.

The little village gets rather crowded in the summer, but out of season it still has a rural air. You can lunch on Lübars ham, the local speciality, at an old village inn, the **Dorfkrug zum lustigen Finken** *(Alt-Lübars 20 ☎ (030) 4027845),* which has a terrace.

MARIA REGINA MARTYRUM (Martyrs' Memorial)

Heckerdamm 230, Charlottenburg ☎(030) 3826011. Open daily 9am–5.30pm (Nov–Mar closes 4.30pm). U-Bahn to Jacob-Kaiser-Platz; bus 121, 123, 221 to Heckerdamm.

Built in the middle of a postwar housing estate in 1960–63, a bleak Catholic church commemorates victims of the Nazis. The empty courtyard hemmed in by concrete walls is meant to recall the concentration camps, as is the menacing Glockenspiel tower, where the church bells are hung.

MARIENKIRCHE

Karl-Liebknecht-Strasse 8, Mitte. Map ***4****B9 ☎(030) 2424467 ▣ Open Mon–Thurs 10am–noon, 1–4pm; Sat noon–4pm; closed Fri, Sun. S-Bahn or U-Bahn to Alexanderplatz.*

The attractive 13thC Marienkirche, now stranded in the middle of a bleak square near the FERNSEHTURM, was the second church to be built in Berlin. Destroyed by a fire in 1380, the red brick edifice was rebuilt in a simple, north German Late Gothic style. The elegant Neoclassical spire was added in 1790 by Carl Gotthard Langhans, architect of the BRANDENBURGER TOR.

A large 15thC *Totentanz* (dance of death) fresco was uncovered in the 19thC. The church has some striking tombs, including a 17thC memorial to Feldmarschall Otto von Spar. Laden with flags and cannon, the tomb was designed by Artus Quellien the Elder. Restored after World War II, the Marienkirche now contains a collection of religious paintings and sculptures dug from the rubble of bombed Berlin churches.

MÄRKISCHES MUSEUM

Am Köllnischen Park 5, Mitte. Map ***4****C9 ☎(030) 2700514. Open 10am–6pm; closed Mon, Tues. U-Bahn to Märkisches Museum; U-Bahn or S-Bahn to Jannowitzbrücke.*

The Märkisches Museum was founded in 1874 as a historical museum for Berlin and the Mark of Brandenburg. It now occupies an eccentric early 20thC building based on copies of historical buildings in the Mark of Brandenburg.

The brick choir is modeled on the 15thC Katharinenkirche in Brandenburg, W of Berlin, while the tower is copied from the Bischofsburg in Wittstock, NW of Berlin. The colossal figure by the entrance is modeled on the medieval Roland statues that symbolize municipal liberty in many Brandenburg towns.

Virtually destroyed in World War II, the museum was carefully rebuilt by the East Germans. Boasting a large collection of historical relics from prehistoric times to the 20thC, the museum has a rather melancholy air, with empty, echoing cloisters and cold stone stairs. The atmosphere is now somewhat less grim, since explanatory texts throughout the museum have been purged of their hectoring Marxist tone.

The **prehistoric collection** in the basement includes conjectural reconstructions of ancient northern German dwellings. The first documents to refer to Berlin and Cölln are also here; Cölln is mentioned in a 1237 document, and the name Berlin crops up for the first time in a deed penned in 1244.

Neoclassical monuments by Gottfried Schadow are displayed in a gloomy corridor. There is a tomb of a 6-year-old boy, and a memorial to Marianne Schadow, the sculptor's wife. Several rooms are filled with Berlin porcelain, including sentimental Rococo figures modeled on Meissen ware, imitation Delftware of the 1770s, and handsome Neoclassical *Ansichtsporzellan* (porcelain decorated with miniature landscapes and townscapes) produced at the KPM works in 1815–32.

The Industrial Revolution in Berlin is symbolized by a powerful series of four large **murals** that once decorated the Villa Borsig. The works were commissioned by the German industrialist to illustrate iron production. Two more panels from the series are displayed in the MUSEUM FÜR VERKEHR UND TECHNIK.

The museum has some attractive **paintings** of Berlin, including views of the Tiergarten, Treptow, Unter den Linden and a remarkable rural view of *Kreuzberg* (1847) by Adolph Menzel. Eduard Gaertner's view of the Garrison Church in Potsdam shows the church, destroyed in World War II, where the Nazis staged a sham parliament in 1933. *Monday Morning* (1898) by Hans Baluschek is a sad, sensitive study of four young Berlin women, the morning after a riotous night. The Norwegian Edvard Munch, a leading Berlin Expressionist, painted a striking portrait of Walther Rathenau, the Jewish government minister murdered by extremists in 1922.

The most delightful room contains a collection of **antique mechanical musical instruments** *(played Wed 3-4pm, Sun 11am-noon)*, which includes curiosities disguised as wardrobes, clocks or cabinets to blend in with Berliners' Biedermeier furniture. A Neoclassical *Flöttenuhr* plays Mozart melodies with a rather tinny sound, but the Polyphone from Leipzig has a marvelous liquid tone. A street organ made in the Schönhauser Allee in Prenzlauer Berg emits lusty, nostalgic tunes.

The park behind the museum stands on the site of a Renaissance bastion, but, confusingly, contains an 18thC round turret moved here from another part of the city defenses in 1893. Dotted among the trees are odd, old statues, including one of Hercules wrestling with a lion.

MARTIN-GROPIUS-BAU 🏛

*Stresemannstrasse 110, Kreuzberg. Map **3**D7 ☎ (030) 254860 🎫*
Open 10am–8pm; closed Mon ♿ (☎ ahead) 🚇 U-Bahn to Kochstrasse or Mohrenstrasse; S-Bahn to Anhalter Bahnhof.

Surrounded by the eerie wasteland of the PRINZ-ALBRECHT-GELÄNDE, the Martin-Gropius-Bau once housed Berlin's museum of decorative art (now in the KUNSTGEWERBEMUSEUM). Built in 1877 by Martin Gropius (uncle of Walter Gropius), the museum closely resembles Schinkel's 1836 Bauakademie (bombed in 1945 and demolished in 1961). The ornate Italian Renaissance museum incorporates an airy, glazed courtyard surrounded by arcades, and heavy ceilings decorated with war-damaged mosaics and frescoes, including one ironically entitled *Pax*.

Reconstructed in 1979–81, the building currently houses the modern art collection of the Berlin Gallery, the archives of the Werkbund movement and the Jewish historical museum. Temporary exhibitions are sometimes staged in the museum's palatial rooms.

The **Berlinische Galerie** on the first floor exhibits a selection of works from its extensive collection of 19th and 20thC Berlin painting, sculpture, photography and architecture. Lesser Ury's *Leipziger Strasse* (1898) depicts a rainy night on one of Berlin's fashionable arteries, while a sinister 1920s atmosphere is reflected in Conrad Felixmüller's *Boxer at a Fairground Booth.* The devastating impact of World War II haunts postwar works such as Hans Scheib's harrowing statue of *Christ in Torment,* and Wolf Vostell's giant canvas covered with bones and severed limbs titled *Die Schlacht* (Slaughter). But there's a kind of impish Berlin humor, too, in Ines Berger's *Picnic for Vincent,* showing Van Gogh in a wood with three naked prostitutes.

A trip to the attic (simplest by elevator) lets you see the impressive double-skin roof above the courtyard. The **Werkbund-Archiv** found there contains a collection of works of the *Deutscher Werkbund,* a federation of architects and craftsmen formed at Munich in 1907 to promote high-quality industrial design. The museum organises stimulating temporary exhibitions based on the Werkbund collection, and other 20thC artifacts.

The **Jüdische Abteilung des Berlin Museums** *(☎(030) 25486516)* is a rather forgotten and forlorn collection of Jewish mementoes. Founded in 1933, the museum illustrates the role of Jews in Berlin's history. There is a gravestone from Spandau's Jewish quarter dating back to 1320, found during excavations at ZITADELLE SPANDAU, and a 19thC map showing the 30 different synagogues in Berlin.

Sobering statistics reveal that Berlin's Jewish population dropped from 170,000 in 1933 to just 5,000 in 1945. The stories of just a few of the victims can be pieced together from several files crammed with their personal documents.

MITTE

Central Berlin, E of the Tiergarten. See map for WALK 3 on page 81 and map **4C8.**

Mitte (meaning middle), the historic heart of Berlin, covers the former settlements of Old Berlin, Cölln, Dorotheenstadt and Friedrichswerder. Berlin's principal museums, theaters, government buildings and churches were built here, from the 18thC onward.

Bombed in World War II, Mitte became the center of the East German capital after 1945. The buildings of the Second and Third Reich were demolished, and much was rebuilt in a cold official socialist style, although some handsome 18th and early 19thC buildings were restored, such as Schinkel's ALTES MUSEUM and his FRIEDRICHSWERDERSCHE KIRCHE. Several quarters were rebuilt in Old Berlin style, including the GENDARMENMARKT, the NIKOLAIVIERTEL and the MUSEUMSINSEL.

With the collapse of the old order in 1989, the character of Mitte has been rapidly changing. The district boundary to the S and W is still clearly defined by a broad strip of wasteland, but nearby streets such as Friedrichstrasse and Unter den Linden are becoming fashionable again after four decades of communist neglect.

The old Jewish quarter of Mitte is explored in greater depth in WALK 3 on page 80.

MÜGGELSEE

Köpenick. SE *Berlin. Off map* ***7****E7. Bus 169 from S-Bahnhof Köpenick to Rübezahl (for* S *shore); tram 25 from S-Bahnhof Friedrichshagen to Rahnsdorf (for* N *shore) or Weisse Flotte steamer from the Luisenhain pier in Köpenick to one of the stops on the lake (summer only).*

A fascinating area of lakes and woods lies just beyond the old town of KÖPENICK. This region was East Berlin's answer to the WANNSEE in the west — it offered to urban dwellers such attractions as steamer trips, lakeside restaurants, inland beaches and woodland walks. Berliners from the west are now flocking to the Müggelsee to discover a forgotten part of their city.

Most people head for the shores of the Grosser Müggelsee, Berlin's largest lake. You don't run any risk of going hungry on a trip to the Müggelsee. The wooded fringes of the lake are dotted with restaurants offering basic German cooking, such as **Rübezahl** *(Am Grossen Müggelsee; open 10.30am-6.30pm)* and **Müggelseeperle** *(Am Grossen Müggelsee; open 10.30am-11.30pm),* both with big outdoor terraces.

The woods of the Berliner Stadtwald extend to the south of the lake. A short hike from Rübezahl gets you to the **Teufelssee**, a little lake with a curious legend involving a princess imprisoned in a glass bell. A country inn, **Gaststätte Teufelssee** *(open Wed-Sun 10am-6pm),* overlooks the lake.

The rolling hills to the S of the lake rise to a low summit, 115m (377ft) high, crowned by the **Müggelturm**, a 1950s tower. You descend from the hills to the **Marienlust** restaurant *(Am Langer See; open Mon-Fri 11am-7pm, Sat, Sun 10am-8pm).* This is the most attractive of the lakeside restaurants, with a leafy garden looking out on the narrow **Langer See**. You might feel that you have hiked into the wilds here, but there are trams, boats and buses back to the city. Turn right along the lakeside to reach Wendenschloss, and take tram 83 to S-Bahnhof Köpenick. An alternative is to take the ferry F12 from Wendenschloss to Grünau, then walk to the S-Bahn station.

The lazy way to discover the Müggelsee is to cruise on one of the steamers of the Weisse Flotte line. They depart from the Luisenhain pier on the Dahme in Köpenick *(map 7E7)* for a 3-hour tour of the inland lake. You can step off at various piers to go for rambles in the woods.

MUSEUM FÜR DEUTSCHE VOLKSKUNDE (Museum of German Folklore)

Im Winkel 6, Dahlem. Map ***6****E4 ☎(030) 8390101 ▣ (▣ Sun and hols). Open Tues–Fri 9am–5pm; Sat, Sun 10am–5pm ♿ U-Bahn to Dahlem-Dorf.*

Northern German folk costumes and painted farmhouse furniture are displayed in a modern museum in Dahlem. Inspired by the Norse Museum in Stockholm, the Museum of German Folklore was founded in 1889, but much of the original collection was lost during World War II. Some of the surviving works are now in the PERGAMON-MUSEUM, but the majority are displayed in this rather sterile environment at Dahlem.

MUSEUM FÜR INDISCHE KUNST (Museum of Indian Art)

Lansstrasse 8, Dahlem. Map ***6****E4 ☎(030) 83011 ▣ (▣ Sun and hols). Open Tues–Fri 9am–5pm; Sat, Sun 10am–5pm ♿ ▣ U-Bahn to Dahlem-Dorf.*

Spotlit Buddhas, miniature paintings and bronze figures of gods are dramatically displayed in this museum, which forms part of the complex at Dahlem. Founded in 1963, the museum boasts an acclaimed collection of ancient Hindu and Buddhist statues from India, Tibet, Nepal, Indonesia, Thailand and Burma.

MUSEUM FÜR ISLAMISCHE KUNST (Museum of Islamic Art)
*Lansstrasse 8, Dahlem. Map **6**E4 ☎(030) 83011 ▣ (▣ Sun and hols). Open Tues–Fri 9am–5pm; Sat, Sun 10am–5pm ♿ ▣ U-Bahn to Dahlem-Dorf.*
The Islamic Art Museum at Dahlem has a rich collection of miniature paintings, ceramic bowls, carpets and books. Founded in 1904 as part of the Kaiser-Friedrich-Museum (now the BODE-MUSEUM), the Islamic museum has grown into one of the most important collections of Muslim art in the world. Even though many of the treasures belonging to the Museum of Islamic Art are currently in the PERGAMON-MUSEUM, there is enough to see in Dahlem to enthral admirers of Persian miniatures and Iranian mosaics.

MUSEUM FÜR NATURKUNDE (Museum of Natural Science)
*Invalidenstrasse 43, Mitte. Map **3**A7 ☎(030) 28972540 ▣ Open 9.30am–5pm; closed Mon ✱ U-Bahn or S-Bahn to Friedrichstrasse; S-Bahn to Lehrter Stadtbahnhof or U-Bahn to Zinnowitzer Strasse.*
Berlin's natural history museum was built in 1875–89 by August Tiede to display the Humboldt University's collection of minerals and fossils. The East Germans allowed the building to become rather dusty and dilapidated, and many of the rooms have been closed for years.

The collection is still worth a glance, particularly for the dinosaur skeletons in the lofty main hall. Excavated in East Africa in 1909–12, they include the world's largest assembled skeleton — a Brachiosaurus that fills much of the hall. The mineral collection is housed in beautiful antique wooden cases.

MUSEUM FÜR OSTASIATISCHE KUNST (Museum of Oriental Art)
*Lansstrasse 8, Dahlem. Map **6**E4 ☎(030) 83011 ▣ (▣ Sun and hols). Open Tues–Fri 9am–5pm; Sat, Sun 10am–5pm ♿ ▣ U-Bahn to Dahlem-Dorf.*
Chinese porcelain, red lacquered furniture and Japanese woodcuts are among the treasures currently in Dahlem's Museum of Oriental Art. Founded in 1906, this was the first museum in Germany devoted to the art of the Far East, and it gradually assembled a small but exquisite collection of works from China, Japan and Korea. Berlin's Oriental collection was split in two by World War II, however, and many of the works must now be viewed in the PERGAMON-MUSEUM.

MUSEUM FÜR VERKEHR UND TECHNIK (Museum of Transport and Technology) ★
*Trebbiner Strasse 9, Kreuzberg. Map **3**D7 ☎(030) 254840 ▣ (the entrance ticket is good for the main museum and the Spectrum workshop). Open Tues–Fri 9am–5.30pm; Sat, Sun 10am–6pm. Allow at least two hours to see everything ✱ ♿ ▣ U-Bahn to Gleisdreieck or Möckernbrücke.*

Berlin's vast museum of transport and technology displays a fascinating and varied collection of trains, cars, bicycles, steam engines, model ships, typewriters, printing presses and computers. The museum was opened in 1983, within a complex of 19thC industrial buildings in the war-torn Gleisdreieck quarter, and incorporates several prewar collections, including this one, which was formerly in the HAMBURGER BAHNHOF. As befits a science museum, the complex is constantly improved and expanded, although it still does not quite measure up to the exciting center portrayed on the mural facing the Landwehrkanal.

The **Eingangsgebäude** (entrance building) was built in 1908 as an ice-storage depot. Horse-drawn wagons were kept in the *Hof* (courtyard), where a door marked *Ausgang 6* leads to the *Pferdetreppe,* an old spiral ramp that gave access to the stables on the upper floors. Tethering rings can still be seen in a second-floor room containing old printing presses.

The **ground floor** is a marvelous clutter of old technology. A collection of historic planes includes a rare 1917 Fokker triplane and a 1941 Junkers Ju 52. Among the many vintage vehicles (some of them parked in the basement garage) are several gleaming German automobiles built by Karl Benz and Gottlieb Daimler, and a smart 1904 fire engine.

A demonstration of suitcase manufacture is staged in a reconstructed 19thC factory, while the technology of housework is illustrated in an old German kitchen. The museum even has a reconstructed ladies' hairdressing salon full of menacing gadgets used to create the sleek permanent waves of the 1920s.

The former locomotive works of Anhalter Bahnhof accommodate another department of the museum complex. A magnificent collection of old German steam trains and scale models is displayed in two huge 19thC **Lokomotivschuppen** (locomotive sheds). These are entered through the *Fürstenportal,* a monumental gateway saved when the Anhalter station ruins were demolished in 1961.

Two large murals showing a locomotive assembly works and a railway bridge were painted in 1876 for the Villa Borsig in the suburb of Moabit. They formed part of a cycle of seven works commissioned by August Borsig, Imperial Germany's foremost locomotive manufacturer. The MÄRKISCHES MUSEUM has four more panels salvaged from the villa.

Several railway coaches (including a well-padded Prussian model from 1898) are ranged around two locomotive turntables outside the sheds. The nearby open land is a bomb-site that has been left in its wild state as an ecological museum. Experiments on wind and solar energy are carried out in this romantic urban wilderness. Two historic windmills have been reconstructed nearby, while an abandoned water tower to the S adds an eerie note.

Most visitors are worn out by the time they reach the manager's office *(Beamtenwohnhaus)* situated between the two locomotive sheds, but it is worth climbing the stairs to explore the handsome wood-paneled rooms crammed with models of German ships, many constructed in Berlin, including Germany's first steamship and iron steamship. The collection also includes superb scale models of Berlin locks and bridges, such as the Charlottenburger Brücke and the Oberbaumbrücke.

A curious scale model of medieval Berlin in ruins incorporates trickling water to represent the Spree. The FERNSEHTURM has been added as a useful if anachronistic orientation point. Energetic travelers who reach the third floor will find a bizarre collection of 19thC stereoscopes, including an antique *Kaiserpanorama* fitted with a row of binoculars for viewing three-dimensional scenes of European capitals.

A nearby industrial building has been converted to house the **Spectrum** exhibition. This high-tech experimental workshop *(Versuchsfeld)* allows children to play with prisms, pulleys and other gadgets. The computer gallery has several demonstration models programed to play chess or compose music.

The museum has a technical bookstore with a large stock of nostalgic prewar Berlin postcards. The old-fashioned museum café recalls a vanished era, with its clutter of antique tin signs and other relics.

MUSEUM FÜR VÖLKERKUNDE (Museum of Ethnography)

*Lansstrasse 8, Dahlem. Map **6**E4 ☎(030) 83011 ▣ (▣ Sun and hols). Open Tues–Fri 9am–5pm; Sat, Sun 10am–5pm ♿ U-Bahn to Dahlem-Dorf.*

A 17thC "cabinet of curiosities" created by the Great Elector was merged with numerous 19thC private collections of German folk art to form the Museum für Völkerkunde.

Originally housed in a museum on Stresemannstrasse, the collection was moved to Dahlem in 1912. Some of the exhibits were later moved back to the former museum, and many of the treasures were destroyed by wartime bombing. The main collection is now housed in this modern complex at Dahlem, but a few objects rescued from the Stresemannstrasse museum are occasionally shown in the basement of the PERGAMON-MUSEUM.

Now one of the world's largest ethnographic collections, the museum in Dahlem covers Africa, America, Polynesia, the Near East, South Asia and the Far East.

The Africa collection, built up during Germany's brief colonial period, contains beautifully lit masks and sensual wooden statues. The South Asia department has a marvelous display of Burmese and Indonesian puppets. A superb Polynesian collection includes several reconstructed houses, and a basement hall is filled with replica boats, including a catamaran built from a sketch made by Captain James Cook.

MUSEUM FÜR VOR- UND FRÜHGESCHICHTE (Museum of Prehistory and Early History)

*Langhansbau at Schloss Charlottenburg (w wing), Spandauer Damm, Charlottenburg. Map **1**B2 ☎(030) 320911 ▣ (▣ Sun and hols). Open Mon–Thurs 9am–5pm; Sat, Sun 10am–5pm; closed Fri ♿ Bus 145, 204 to Klausener Platz.*

Berlin's museum of prehistory and early history is more interesting than its ponderous name might suggest. A "cabinet of curiosities" owned by the Hohenzollern family formed the nucleus of the original museum, established in Schloss Monbijou in 1829. Almost 100 years passed before a permanent museum of prehistory and early history was opened in 1930. The new building was gutted by fire in World War II, and the collection ended up split between Schloss Charlottenburg and the BODE-MUSEUM. The collection is superbly displayed and attractively lit, and there are occasional humorous touches such as the toilets labeled *homo sapiens.*

The **prehistoric collection** at Charlottenburg has relics from Germanic tribes, including a heap of ornamental buttons found at a Bronze Age site in the Berlin district of Lichterfelde. The metalworking skills of the Bronze Age are illustrated by the exquisite spiral necklaces and swords found in the Carpathian Mountains.

The centerpiece of the old museum was a collection of almost 10,000 Trojan antiquities gifted in 1880 by the German archeologist Heinrich Schliemann. While excavating the site of Homeric Troy (near Hisarlik, Turkey) in the 1870s, Schliemann uncovered a hoard of gold jewelry which he called Priam's treasure. Schliemann smuggled the collection of gold necklaces, earrings and beads back to Berlin, where it was displayed in the Museum of Early History, but an equally unscrupulous Soviet looter stole many of the works.

The objects now on display are mostly copies, while the originals gather dust in a government bank vault in Moscow. The treasure is due one day to be returned to Berlin under a German-Russian agreement signed in Dresden in 1983, although no date for the return was set.

MUSEUMSDORF DÜPPEL

Clauertstrasse 11, Zehlendorf. Map **5***E3* ☎ *(030) 8026671. Open May–Sept, Thurs 3–7pm, Sun and holidays 10am–5pm* ♿ *Bus 211 to Clauertstrasse from S-Bahnhof Wannsee.*

A stray bomb that fell on the Krummes Fenn in World War II revealed the remains of a lost medieval village. A group of archeologists resolved to reconstruct the 13thC village using replica medieval axes and local wood. On summer Sundays, the smoke rises from the cluster of wooden huts, as volunteers clad in medieval skins demonstrate primitive techniques of spinning, weaving, pottery and bread-making.

MUSEUMSINSEL ★ 🏛

In Mitte. Map **4***B8. S-Bahn to Hackescher Markt.*

The Museumsinsel was conceived in 1841 by the romantically-inclined Friedrich Wilhelm IV, as an island devoted to the arts and sciences. Occupying the W tip of the Spree island, the "museum island" was designed as a harmonious assembly of five buildings filled with an extraordinary wealth of paintings and antiquities from Hohenzollern and private bequests.

The oldest is the ALTES MUSEUM, built by Schinkel in 1824–30, long before the idea of a Museumsinsel had taken shape. August Stüler's NEUES MUSEUM rose to the W in 1843–59, in a Neoclassical style that blended with Schinkel's building. The NATIONALGALERIE (now called the ALTE NATIONALGALERIE) was added, to the N, in 1867–76, modeled on a Classical temple.

The fourth museum, the Kaiser-Friedrich-Museum (now the BODE-MUSEUM), broke the pattern with its Neo-Baroque pomp, and gave the Museumsinsel a striking dome at the W tip of the island.

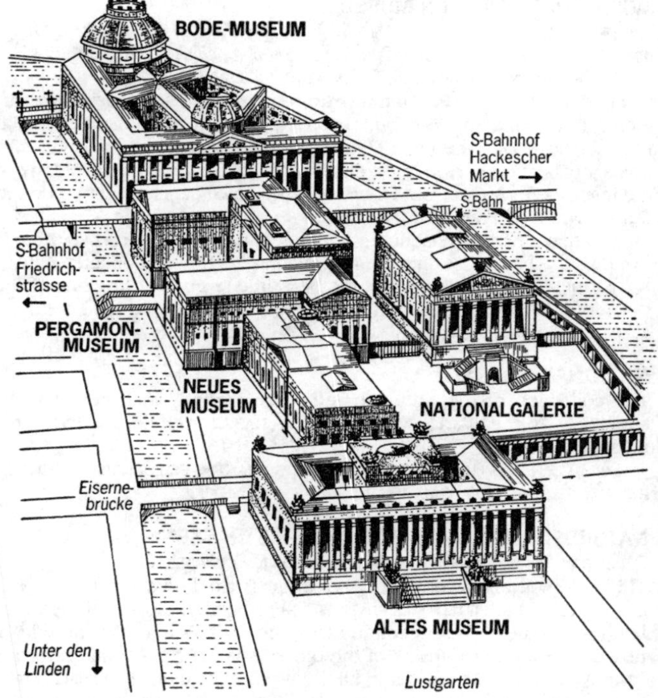

The PERGAMON-MUSEUM, begun in 1909, was not completed until 1930, exactly 100 years after the Altes Museum was first opened.

Friedrich's Museumsinsel was then complete, but it did not survive intact for long. Many modern paintings in the Nationalgalerie were removed in the 1930s as "decadent," and when war broke out, the principal treasures were shipped to secure hiding places in the Bavarian Alps. Some paintings and sculptures that were too large to move were destroyed during the wartime bombing.

The Museumsinsel was reduced to a melancholy shambles of gutted buildings after 1945, but the East German government began reconstruction almost at once, and by 1949 several rooms of the Nationalgalerie had reopened. The task was enormous, however, and the Neues Museum was still in ruins when the East German government collapsed in 1989.

Many of the major works from the Museumsinsel are now located in the collections at DAHLEM, SCHLOSS CHARLOTTENBURG or the KULTUR-FORUM, but some treasures may eventually be returned to the island site.

As things stand at present, the Pergamon-Museum and the Bode-Museum offer the most interesting collections.

MUSIKINSTRUMENTEN-MUSEUM

Tiergartenstrasse 1, Tiergarten. Map ***3****C7 ☎(030) 254810 ▣ (▣ Sun and hols). Open Tues–Fri 9am–5pm; Sat, Sun 10am–5pm; closed Mon ♿ ▣ Bus 148 to Philharmonie, or bus 129, 248, 341 to Kultur-Forum.*

Situated next to the **Philharmonie**, the museum of musical instruments is an airy, modern building forming part of the controversial KULTUR-FORUM. Designed in 1979–84 by Edgar Wisniewski, the museum owns a collection of rare lutes, clavichords, violins and pianos. Many of the instruments come from Hohenzollern palaces, including two boxed flutes owned by Frederick the Great.

You may find the museum rather lifeless unless you go when there is live music. A gaudy Wurlitzer organ built in 1929 fills the concert hall with lusty tunes *(Sats at noon).* But the best time to go is during one of the occasional performances of chamber music, jazz or folk, held amid the cases of precious instruments.

NATIONALGALERIE

The collection of the National Gallery is currently split between the MUSEUMSINSEL, the KULTUR-FORUM, SCHLOSS CHARLOTTENBURG and two other museums in Mitte.

See ALTE NATIONALGALERIE, GALERIE DER ROMANTIK, FRIEDRICHSWERDERSCHE KIRCHE, NEUE NATIONALGALERIE and OTTO-NAGEL-HAUS.

NATURDENKMAL "ALTE POTSDAMER STRASSE"

Potsdamer Platz, Tiergarten. Map ***3****C7. S-Bahn to Potsdamer Platz.*

This is something you might easily miss. Tucked away on the edge of the wasteland at POTSDAMER PLATZ is a short stretch of old cobbled road lined with lime trees and antique lamp-posts. This road that now leads nowhere is all that remains of the old Potsdamer Strasse that once ran from the royal palace in Berlin all the way to Potsdam. The road is now a protected natural site, so it stands some chance of not disappearing during the reconstruction of Potsdamer Platz.

NEPTUNSBRUNNEN (Neptune Fountain)

Rathausstrasse, Mitte. Map ***4****B9. U-Bahn or S-Bahn to Alexanderplatz.*

The Neptune fountain facing the MARIENKIRCHE once stood opposite the now destroyed BERLINER SCHLOSS. The elaborate structure, built by Reinhold Begas in 1891, is adorned with four female figures representing the Rhine, Elbe, Oder and Weichsel rivers. Water gushes out of vases, and spurts from the mouths of crocodiles, making the fountain one of the coolest spots in town.

NEUE NATIONALGALERIE ★ 🏛

Potsdamer Strasse 50, Tiergarten. Map ***3****D6 ☎(030) 2666 ▣ (▣ Sun and holidays) ▣ Open Tues–Fri 9am–5pm; Sat, Sun 10am–5pm ♿ U-Bahn to Kurfürstenstrasse; bus 129, 148, 248, 341 to Kultur-Forum.*

Situated on windswept wasteland near the Landwehrkanal, the Neue Nationalgalerie perfectly expresses the spirit of postwar Berlin. With its low, hovering roof and almost black exterior, the art gallery is a beautiful example of modern German architecture (see illustration, page 46).

The steel and glass building was constructed in 1965–68 by Mies van der Rohe, the last director of the Bauhaus, who had fled to the US in 1938. It was the only building he executed in Germany after the war.

The basement level of the art gallery houses a small, permanent collection of modern paintings removed from the NATIONALGALERIE on the Museumsinsel during World War II, and returned to West Berlin by the Allies in 1953–57.

The 19thC German works include Arnold Böcklin's dark, romantic *Die Toteninsel* (The Island of the Dead), and tranquil, domestic paintings by Adolph von Menzel such as *Das Balkonzimmer, Das Flötenkonzert* (Frederick the Great playing the flute at Schloss Sanssouci), and the *Palaisgarten des Prinzen Albrecht* (showing the garden of the Prince Albrecht Palace, now reduced to a desolate wasteland, known as the PRINZ-ALBRECHT-GELÄNDE). The Neue Nationalgalerie has a small but excellent collection of 19thC French art, including Manet's *In the Winter Garden,* Courbet's *Wave* and Monet's vibrant *St Germain l'Auxerrois.*

Much of the Nationalgalerie's prewar collection of 20thC art was disposed of by the Nazis under their policy of banning allegedly "decadent" art, but a few condemned paintings survived, such as Erich Heckel's *Village Dance,* Otto Dix's 1926 portrait of the art dealer Alfred Flechtheim, and Max Beckmann's grim 1938 painting *Tod.*

Temporary exhibitions of painting and sculpture usually occupy most of the gallery space. The museum bookstore has a wide range of art books and cards, and the crowded basement café serves hearty North German food.

NEUE SYNAGOGUE

*Oranienburger Strasse 30, Mitte. Map **4**B8. S-Bahn to Oranienburger Strasse; U-Bahn or S-Bahn to Friedrichstrasse.*

The Neue Synagogue is one of the few surviving synagogues in Berlin. Attacked by Nazis on *Kristallnacht* in November 1938 and gutted in an air raid in 1943, the domed building, designed by Eduard Knoblauch and built by Friedrich August Stüler in 1859–66, remained derelict until recently. A Jewish Studies center *(Zentrum Judaicum)* will open in 1995.

NEUES MUSEUM 🏛

*Museumsinsel, Mitte. Map **4**B8. Currently being rebuilt. No date set for reopening. S-Bahn to Friedrichstrasse or Hackescher Markt.*

The Neues Museum remained a bombed ruin until a few years ago. The Neoclassical building (built by Stüler in 1843–59) is now slowly being restored and its murals painstakingly retouched, although the future role of the museum remains uncertain.

Commissioned by Friedrich Wilhelm IV as the second phase of his MUSEUMSINSEL plan, the "New Museum" housed a remarkable Egyptian collection, in a colossal reconstructed temple.

The works once displayed there are now divided between the BODE-MUSEUM and the ÄGYPTISCHES MUSEUM, but the museum's former treasures (including the famous bust of Nefertiti) will probably be returned to the island in the Spree when the museum reopens.

NIKOLAIKIRCHE

Nikolaikirchplatz, Mitte. Map **4**C9 ☎ *(030) 24313146* *Open Tues–Fri 9am–5pm; Sat 9am–6pm; Sun 10am–5pm; closed Mon* ♿ *S-Bahn or U-Bahn to Alexanderplatz.*

Founded early in the 13thC, the Nikolaikirche is the oldest surviving edifice in Berlin. It is dedicated to St Nicholas, the patron saint of merchants and children. The church was rebuilt in the 15thC as a Late Gothic hall church with nave and aisles of equal height. Destroyed in World War II, the twin-towered ruin was painstakingly restored, and reopened recently as a branch of the MÄRKISCHES MUSEUM.

The airy, white interior contains several old tombs, including a monument to the Berlin goldsmith Daniel Männlich, which was designed in 1699 by Andreas Schlüter. The exhibits from the Märkisches Museum cover the history of Berlin up to the end of the Thirty Years' War in 1648.

You can hear the *carillon* playing automatically every day *(noon, 3pm and 6pm),* and a *carillonneur* also gives a weekly concert *(Sat 11am).*

NIKOLAIVIERTEL

In Mitte. Map **4**C9. *S-Bahn or U-Bahn to Alexanderplatz.*

A waterfront district of old houses clustered around the NIKOLAIKIRCHE was carefully rebuilt after World War II to provide a whiff of Old Berlin. Some of the houses are exact copies of Berlin buildings destroyed in World War II, such as the *Zum Nussbaum* tavern on Poststrasse, but most were built from prefabricated concrete sections designed to evoke Hanseatic gabled houses.

There are new museums in the EPHRAIMPALAIS and the KNOBLAUCHHAUS, while other houses contain shops, cafés and restaurants. Some people may dismiss the entire quarter as kitsch, but it does at least provide an escape from the bleak concrete buildings nearby.

NIKOLSKOE

Nikolskoer Weg, Zehlendorf. Map **5**E1 *Bus 216 from S-Bahnhof Wannsee to Nikolskoer Weg.*

Two curious Russian-looking buildings overlooking the river Havel are souvenirs of the marriage between Charlotte, a daughter of Friedrich Wilhelm III, and the future Czar Nicholas I. The romantic spot in the Düppel woods became generally known by the familiar Russian name of Nikolskoe (property of Nicholas).

A picturesque wooden chalet known as the **Blockhaus Nikolskoe** was built by the Prussian king in 1819, when the couple visited Berlin. Modeled on a log cabin near St Petersburg (Leningrad) where Friedrich Wilhelm had been guest at a feast, the Blockhaus now contains a rustic restaurant (described in RESTAURANTS on page 171).

Perched on a nearby wooded hill, the **Kirche St Peter und Paul** was built in 1834–37 by Friedrich August Stüler. The building is a scaled-down version of a church in St Petersburg admired by Friedrich Wilhelm during a visit to his daughter Charlotte in 1817.

When Charlotte (Czarina Alexandra) died in 1860, her brother Prince Karl (who lived nearby in SCHLOSS KLEIN-GLIENICKE) erected a memorial pavilion, the *Loggia Alexandra,* on the summit of the Böttcherberg.

OLYMPIA-STADION

Olympischer Platz, Charlottenburg. Map **5**C3 ☎*(030) 3040676* ▣ *Open daily 9am–5pm (closes at dusk in winter). U-Bahn to Olympia-Stadion.*

Familiar from Leni Riefenstahl's heroic film *Olympia* (included in TEN BERLIN MOVIES TO SEE, page 51), the Olympic stadium was built as a Nazi show-piece for the 1936 Berlin Olympics. Modeled on the architecture of Classical Greece, the elliptical arena seating 76,000 spectators is an awesome edifice, with massive stone columns and rugged male statues.

Rising up to the W, the **Glockenturm** (bell tower) *(Am Glockenturm ☎(030) 3058123, open Apr-Oct, daily 10am-5.30pm* ◁≤*)* offers a panoramic view of the Olympic site and the Grunewald. A lane runs through the woods to the **Waldbühne**, an open-air amphitheater built on a sloping site for the Olympics. The amphitheater was restored after its wartime bomb damage, and is now used in the summer for classical concerts and films (see page 183).

OTTO-NAGEL-HAUS

Märkisches Ufer 16–18, Mitte. Map **4**C9 ☎*(030) 2791424* ▣ *Open Sun–Thurs 9am–5pm; closed Fri, Sat. U-Bahn to Märkisches Ufer; S-Bahn to Jannowitzbrücke.*

Two reconstructed Baroque houses overlooking the Spree now house part of the Nationalgalerie collection. Named after the radical Berlin artist Otto Nagel (1894–1967), the museum is currently devoted to communist artists and photographers from the November Revolution to the present day, including Otto Nagel, John Heartfield, Käthe Kollwitz and Otto Dix.

PERGAMON-MUSEUM ★ ✓

Am Kupfergraben, Museumsinsel, Mitte. Map **4**B8 ☎*(030) 20355444. Open 9am–5pm; closed Mon, Tues* ♿ *S-Bahn to Friedrichstrasse or Hackescher Markt.*

Extraordinary architectural relics from ancient civilizations are displayed in the Pergamon-Museum. Opened in 1930, the museum contains four important collections of antiquities, covering Classical Greece and Rome, the Middle East, Islam and the Far East. There is also a small collection of German folklore.

A vast hall in the **Classical collection** *(Antikensammlung)* is taken up with the **Pergamon Altar**, a colossal monument from the ancient Greek city of Pergamon (now Bergama in Turkey), the capital of the Attalid dynasty. Built in 180–159BC on a hillside above the Aegean Sea, the altar was one of the architectural masterpieces of the Hellenistic Age. Excavated in 1878–86 by the dashing German archeologist Carl Humann, the entire edifice was shipped back to Berlin for reconstruction, which took some 20 years. Magnificent marble friezes of figures in high-relief decorate the bases, including Hercules being savaged by a lion, Eros entangled with a snake, and Athena clad in a flowing robe. One of the few incomplete figures is Aphrodite, whose head is now on display in a museum in Istanbul.

An interesting exhibition behind the altar shows old photographs of the ruined altar, with buffalo being used to transport massive relics from the site. The city of Bergama recently appealed for the return of the altar to the bare hillside where it once stood, but for the time being, this exceptional work of art remains in Berlin.

A room of Roman relics includes the huge **Miletus Market Gate**, strikingly displayed against an azure background. The gate was built in the reign of the Emperor Hadrian at the entrance to one of the markets in Miletus, a prosperous port on the W coast of Asia Minor. A detailed scale model shows the former location of the gate.

The **Vorderasiatisches Museum** (Middle East Museum) contains a remarkable reconstruction of the **Ishtar Gate**, based on fragments excavated in 1899. One of the eight city gates of Babylon, it was built c.580BC by King Nebuchadnezzar. Faced with glazed tiles adorned with enameled bulls and dragons, the gateway leads to a **Processional Way** flanked by high walls of glazed tiles decorated with lions. The ceremonial street originally led from the temple of the god Marduk through the Ishtar Gate to the Akitu House, where the golden image of Marduk was taken in procession every New Year. Nebuchadnezzar's throne room has been diligently reconstructed near the gateway.

Besides manuscripts, Persian carpets and ceramics, the **Islamisches Museum** (Islam Museum) contains the impressive facade of Mschatta, an 8thC castle in the Jordanian desert, SE of Amman, presented by Sultan Abdul Hamid to Kaiser Wilhelm II in 1903. The **Ostasiatische Sammlung** (Far East Collection) was founded by Wilhelm von Bode in 1906 and contains a wealth of Chinese porcelain.

The **Museum für Volkskunde** (Folklore Museum) has never recovered from the devastation of World War II, when the old museum in Mitte was bombed and most of the collection destroyed. Now rather forgotten in the basement of the Pergamon, the museum valiantly tries to stage interesting temporary exhibitions based on a small selection of its surviving collection of German farmhouse furniture and folk costumes.

PFAUENINSEL ★ 🏛

Wannsee, SW Berlin. Map ***5E1*** *☎(030) 8053042 🎫 Open daily, May–Aug 8am–8pm; Apr, Sept 8am–6pm; Mar, Oct 9am–5pm; Nov–Feb 10am–4pm. No smoking on island. Keep to the footpaths and try not to startle the peacocks. Bus 216, 316 from S-Bahnhof Wannsee to Pfaueninsel, then take the ferry (five minutes); or take steamer line 1 from Wannsee to Pfaueninsel, then the ferry.*

A ferry plies across the narrow strait to Pfaueninsel (peacock island), a romantic island where the peacocks strut among mock ruins. Johann Kunckel rowed across here in the 17thC to carry out chemical experiments that led to the invention of ruby glass, but the island remained a wilderness until the late 18thC, when Friedrich Wilhelm II built a fantastic ruined castle there to amuse his mistress, the beautiful Countess Lichtenau.

The island became dotted with curiosities built by Friedrich Wilhelm III in the 19thC, including a palm house, which provided 19thC painters with an exotic setting for Oriental fantasies. The glass building burned down in 1880, but most of the other follies have been zealously maintained.

Like many aristocratic parks on the Havel, Pfaueninsel was landscaped in 1822 by Lenné in romantic English style. A few elderly Berliners still

The Pfaueninsel **Schloss**

recall that the island provided the setting for a spectacular Nazi party organized by Dr Goebbels during the 1936 Olympics. The island is now a peaceful nature reserve, offering a rare opportunity to wander undisturbed by any noise except the screeching of peacocks. On arrival, look at the map near the pier to plan a route. Allow at least one hour to walk around the island; follow the signs to the *Fähre* (ferry) if you lose your way.

The **Schloss** located at the S end of the island is an eccentric folly constructed from 1794–99 by Johann Brendel for Friedrich Wilhelm II. A cabinet-maker by trade, Brendel used his joinery skills to build a wooden ruined castle, expertly painted white with mock joints. Many mistake it for a stone edifice. The gateway contains a *trompe l'oeil* landscape to add to the deception. The wooden bridge that once linked the twin round towers was replaced in 1807 by Berlin's first iron bridge.

The Schloss *(open Apr-Oct, Tues-Sun 10am-12.30pm, 1.30-4.30pm; closed Nov-Mar)* contains rare 19thC furniture and faded murals installed by Friedrich Wilhelm III.

Brendel created another fantasy ruin at the N end of the island. Known as the **Meierei** (dairy farm), the building is adorned with Gothic arches and trefoil windows. Notice the chandelier glinting in a first-floor room. A nearby mock Gothic farm known as the **Rinderstall** (cattle shed) has real geese clucking in the yard.

The portal of the **Luisen-Tempel** standing to the N formed the original facade of Queen Luise's mausoleum at SCHLOSS CHARLOTTENBURG. When Schinkel constructed a more imposing temple front in 1829, the old portal was rebuilt amid the follies on Pfaueninsel.

Schinkel also designed the **Kavalierhaus** (gentleman's house) in the middle of the island in 1824. A six-story Late Gothic house, bought in Danzig (Gdansk) by the Crown Prince, is carefully fused into the fabric. King George IV of Britain presented Friedrich Wilhelm III with a miniature frigate for his fantasy island. It was moored in a little boat house known as the **Fregattenschuppen**, near the landing stage.

An 1830 map hanging in the house by the pier reveals that the island once had a zoo. The animals were moved in 1842 to the new ZOOLOGISCHER GARTEN in Charlottenburg, leaving only some exotic birds on Pfaueninsel. Follow the signs (or the screechings) to the **Vogelhaus**, a netted bird reserve where noisy parrots perch above artificial waterfalls.

PLANETARIUM AM INSULANER

*Munsterdamm 90, Schöneberg. Map **6**E4 ☎(030) 7900930 ✗ available ▭ ☎ for times of demonstrations ✱ S-Bahn to Priesterweg.*

A modern planetarium built on top of a 75-meter/246-foot-high hill created from the rubble of Berlin buildings destroyed in the World War II. This is a good place to go with children on a rainy day, to introduce them to astronomy. Look out for special programs, which might include video screenings, classical music and poetry readings.

POSTMUSEUM (Postal Museum)

Leipzigerstrasse 16, Mitte. Map ***4****C8* ☎ *(030) 22854710* ▣ *Open Tues–Sat 10am–6pm* ♿ *(☎ ahead). U-Bahn to Stadtmitte.*

Built in 1889 around a vast Neo-Renaissance courtyard, the German postal museum was bombed in World War II, and remained a ruin for several decades. Recently restored, the building contains a nostalgic collection of jaunty antique mail boxes and franking machines.

POTSDAMER PLATZ

Map ***3****C7. S-Bahn to Potsdamer Platz.*

There is currently almost nothing to see at Potsdamer Platz, yet to Berliners it is one of the most poignant spots in their city. Considered the busiest square in Europe in the 1930s, it was reduced, in the bombardment, to a bleak tract of wasteland overshadowed by the Berlin Wall. All traces of the concrete wall have now been removed, and the square looks likely to be redeveloped as a giant office and shopping complex.

PRENZLAUER BERG

Map ***7****C6. U-Bahn to Eberswalder Strasse.*

The 19thC district of Prenzlauer Berg has scarcely changed since the end of the World War II and, even now, you can come across derelict breweries, neglected graveyards and crumbling apartment blocks riddled with shell holes. A few streets have been primly restored by the East German authorities, but the most interesting sights in Prenzlauer Berg are the streets that have not been touched for more than half a century.

To explore the district on foot, walk along Danziger Strasse from Eberswalder Strasse U-Bahn station, then turn right into **Husemannstrasse**. While most of Prenzlauer Berg under East German rule was left to rot, Husemannstrasse was given the sort of lavish treatment usually reserved for Neoclassical opera houses. The tree-lined street has, as a result, an odd air of unreality, with its grand 19thC houses, handsome old street lamps and iron pumps. Here, you can stroll along a broad Berlin sidewalk as it once was: a wide strip of flagstones flanked by cobbles.

The **Friseurmuseum** (hairdressers' museum) *(Husemannstrasse 8 ☎ (030) 4495380, open Mon-Thurs 10am-6pm, Sun 10am-4pm)* contains an eccentric assortment of gadgets that were once used to cut and perm chic Berliners' hair. A few doors down *(#10),* there's a real barber's shop that looks as if it has been stocked from the museum collection.

Berlin's working-class history is documented at the **Museum Berliner Arbeiterleben um 1900** *(Husemannstrasse 12 ☎ (030) 4485675, open Tues-Thurs 10am-6pm, Fri 10am-3pm).* You might pause for coffee at the *Kaffeestube (#6),* an attractive café that was formerly the haunt of serious-minded East Berliners.

Husemannstrasse leads into Käthe-Kollwitzplatz, a leafy triangular space with a few cafés. The Berlin artist Käthe Kollwitz (see KÄTHE-KOLLWITZ-MUSEUM) lived in a nearby apartment from 1891 to 1943. In the square, a statue, *die Mutter,* is based on one of her many drawings of suffering women.

Now turn right down Wörther Strasse and left along Schönhauser Allee. The U-Bahn rattles along an elevated viaduct here, creating a rather dismal atmosphere. On the left, behind an iron gate that is normally locked, you will see a large Jewish cemetery packed with overgrown tombs that have not been tended for several decades. You can pick up the U-Bahn just beyond here at Senefelder Platz.

PRINZ-ALBRECHT-GELÄNDE (Prince Albrecht Terrain)

Wilhelmstrasse, Kreuzberg. Map 3D7. U-Bahn to Kochstrasse, S-Bahn to Anhalter Bahnhof.

Rabbits flit across a desolate inner-city wasteland that marks the site of the Gestapo headquarters. Before World War II the notorious building at #8 Prinz-Albrecht-Strasse (renamed Niederkirchnerstrasse after the war) had been the School of Arts and Crafts. More than a thousand Gestapo workers were based in the former classrooms, plotting Nazi policies of genocide and terror. Jews and communists summoned to the building in the 1930s had little chance of survival. They were interrogated, tortured and often murdered in the cellars.

A nearby building known as the Prince Albrecht Palace was one of Berlin's most distinguished 19thC residences. It was designed by Schinkel in 1830 for Prinz Albrecht, the son of Friedrich Wilhelm III, and set in gardens landscaped by Lenné. It was here that the Nazi security service headquarters were located, providing information for the notorious SS, whose headquarters were also nearby, in the former Hotel Prinz Albrecht.

Almost all traces of these three notorious buildings have vanished. Everything was demolished after the war, leaving a rubble-strewn wasteland known as the Prinz-Albrecht-Gelände. For years the city debated ways of transforming the area (a heliport was once mooted), and in 1987 it was decided to turn the site into a memorial park. Several notice boards were put up, showing the location of the buildings that once housed the apparatus of Nazi terror. The rest was left to grow wild, except for the cellars of the art school, which were excavated and became an exhibition center, TOPOGRAPHIE DES TERRORS, housed in a temporary building.

REICHSTAG

Platz der Republik, Tiergarten. Map **3***B7* ☎ *(030) 39770* ♿ 🚌 ☕ *Open Tues–Sun 10am–5pm; closed Mon and when German parliament meets in the Reichstag. Bus 100, 248 to Reichstag, or S-Bahn to Unter den Linden.*

Curiously isolated at the E end of the Tiergarten, the Reichstag was built in 1884–94 by Paul Wallot as a parliament for the Second German Empire. Inscribed in 1916 with the bold motto *Dem Deutschen Volke* (For the German People), the Reichstag became a gloomy symbol of failed German democracy after an arsonist gutted the building in 1933. The construction of the Berlin Wall a few feet from the derelict parliament added a further note of foreboding.

Shell holes from the bitter last weeks of fighting in 1945 were carefully patched up with thousands of tiny blocks, which still remain clearly visible, and the echoing, defunct building was reconstructed; the reunited German parliament met there for the first time in October 1990.

A permanent historical exhibition was opened in 1971 to mark the centenary of the foundation of the Second Empire. Titled *Fragen an die deutsche Geschichte* (Questions on German History), the exhibition chronicles the development of democracy and the rise of fascism in Germany. As well as old documents and historic photographs, there are reconstructed street scenes showing wartime Berlin, when people chalked urgent messages to relatives on the walls of their burned-out homes. Other scenes show Berlin youths protesting in the 1960s.

The Reichstag has a typical Berlin cafeteria, where you can eat *Bockwurst* (boiled sausage) and cold potato salad. Another café serves coffee and cake in a more elegant setting.

The square in front of the Reichstag was laid out by Schinkel in 1840 as a military parade ground, "to educate the Prussian people to be soldiers and loyal subjects." Hitler had much the same aim in mind when he planned to build a broad avenue across the square, lined with monumental buildings and including the world's largest assembly hall, two railway stations and a triumphal arch.

A new museum of German history, designed by Aldo Rossi, is scheduled to be built near the Reichstag, probably opening around the year 2000.

RUSSISCHER ORTHODOXE FRIEDHOF (Russian Orthodox Cemetery)

*Wittestrasse, Reinickendorf. Map **6**B4. U-Bahn to Holzhauser Strasse. From station, turn right along Holzhauser Strasse, and right down Wittestrasse after about 10mins.*

A rustic gateway hung with a cluster of heavy bells leads into the Russian Orthodox Cemetery. Tucked away in an industrial district on the edge of an autobahn, this is a sad and forgotten spot, overgrown with trees and shrubs. Yet the cemetery is a strangely fascinating place to wander. Its tombstones commemorate people whose lives brought them to Berlin from the farthest corners of Russia, including the Russian composer Mikhail Glinka, who died in Berlin in 1857.

Some of the graves have ornate marble memorials, but many are marked by simple wooden crosses. A Russian Orthodox Church stands in the midst of the tombs, topped with blue onion domes and large iron crosses.

SCHINKELMUSEUM See FRIEDRICHSWERDERSCHE KIRCHE.

SCHLOSS CHARLOTTENBURG ★ 🏛

*Luisenplatz, Charlottenburg. Map **1**B2 ☎(030) 320911 🎫 Open Tues–Fri 9am–5pm; Sat, Sun 10am–5pm. Buy a combined ticket (Sammelkarte) to visit all the museums at a reduced rate ≡ (in grounds) ☕ U-Bahn to Richard-Wagner-Platz or (armed with a good map) U-Bahn to Jungfernheide, then cross the Spree by the footbridge to enter the Schlosspark by the N gate; Bus 109, 121, 145, 204 to Schloss Charlottenburg.*

An old stone pillar opposite Schloss Charlottenburg gives its location as being *1 Meile von Berlin* (1 mile from Berlin). Originally named Schloss

Lietzenburg, the palace was built in the old village of Lietzow to the W of Berlin, as a summer residence for Sophie Charlotte. The spirited wife of Friedrich III, and great-granddaughter of James VI of Scotland, Sophie Charlotte passed her days at Charlottenburg debating with Leibnitz on profound philosophical problems.

The emphasis in 17thC German philosophy on reason and harmony is neatly reflected in the architecture of Johann Nering's compact palace, built in 1695–99. From the palace gates you can see the original Schloss, measuring just 11 bays across. The growth of Prussian power is mirrored in the subsequent extensions to the building. Two wings enclosing the courtyard were begun in 1701, the same year that the Kingdom of Prussia was founded, while Eosander von Goethe later added the lofty cupola and the long **orangery** to the W.

The composition was balanced by the **new wing** *(Neuer Flügel)* to the E, built in 1740–46 by Georg Wenzeslaus von Knobelsdorff for Frederick the Great, while a final Rococo flourish was added in 1787–91 by Carl Gotthard Langhans, who conceived the **theater** at the W end of the orangery. Facing the palace, two identical **guard houses** flanking the Schlossstrasse were constructed in 1851–59 by Friedrich August Stüler. The Schloss is illustrated on page 42.

Badly damaged in an air raid in November 1943, Schloss Charlottenburg underwent a massive postwar restoration, to emerge in the 1960s in almost mint condition as a major new museum complex for West Berlin. The GALERIE DER ROMANTIK currently occupies the ground floor of the new wing, while the MUSEUM FÜR VOR- UND FRÜHGESCHICHTE is established in the Langhans wing to the W. The ÄGYPTISCHES MUSEUM and the ANTIKENMUSEUM are located in the two guard houses, and the BRÖHAN-MUSEUM in a former infantry barracks nearby.

The **equestrian statue** of the Great Elector was moved to the main courtyard in 1950. Designed by the architect Andreas Schlüter and cast in bronze by Johann Jacobi in 1700, the colossal work shows its subject in a heroic pose, with his frock-coat flying in the wind. The statue originally stood on the Lange Brücke (now the Rathausbrücke), but was moved during World War II. The boat on which it was being transported sank in the Tegeler See, and the statue was not recovered until 1950.

The **Neringbau** and **Eosanderbau** — the original Schloss — can be visited only on a guided tour. Totally reconstructed after World War II, the palace now contains only a few relics of Sophie Charlotte. The main attraction is an 18thC **Porzellanzimmer**, crammed to the ceiling with blue and white Chinese porcelain from various Berlin collections. Chamber music concerts are held in the intimate wood-paneled **Eichengalerie** *(☎(030) 3005395)* or the **Schlosskapelle** *(☎(030) 8173364)*.

If the line of people waiting to visit the Neringbau is too daunting, head for the Neuer Flügel to wander through the glittering Rococo rooms designed by Knobelsdorff, on the upper floor *(Obergeschoss)*. The **Goldene Galerie** is a 42m (138ft) Rococo ballroom overlooking the garden, with pale green walls encrusted with gilded stucco. A bold decision was taken to replace the Rococo ceiling in the *Weisser Saal* (White Hall), destroyed by fire in 1943, with a modern abstract painting in a vaguely Rococo style.

Several smaller rooms contain delightful 18thC Rococo paintings, including works by Watteau from Frederick the Great's Schloss Sanssouci collection. Inspired by an 18thC play, Watteau's shimmering *Embarkation for Cythera* (1720) depicts young women in crisp silk dresses preparing to board a ship that will take them to the temple of love on the Greek island of Cythera. The frothy Rococo works are a far cry from Jacques Louis David's heroic painting of *Napoleon crossing the St Bernard Pass.*

An entire room of Frederick the Great's apartments is taken up with a scale model of the BERLINER SCHLOSS. Demolished in 1950, the old Imperial palace occupied the square now known as Lustgarten. The detailed model shows the former position of the statue of the Great Elector and the 19thC NEPTUNSBRUNNEN. An adjoining room contains a reconstruction of Kaiser Wilhelm's bedroom in the BERLINER SCHLOSS.

Laid out in 1701 by Simon Godeau, the **Schlosspark** *(open dawn-dusk)* was the first geometrical Baroque garden in Germany. Sentimental 19thC taste turned it into a rambling English-style park landscaped by Lenné, but the formal garden behind the Schloss has been recently restored to its original design. The clipped hedges and gravel paths soon give way to meandering paths, and one leads to a *Spielplatz* where children can play.

Suffused with the warmth of Berlin Neoclassicism, the **Schinkel-Pavillon** *(open Tues-Sun 10am-5pm)* is a peaceful place to retreat from the crowds. Almost no one visits the Italianate villa built by Schinkel in 1825 for King Friedrich Wilhelm III, yet it is one of his most elegant interiors. The delicate pavilion, with its frail iron balconies and *trompe l'oeil* murals, took ten years to restore and now houses a superb collection of early 19thC Berlin paintings and porcelain. There are numerous sketches and architectural plans by Schinkel to pore over, including some elaborate theater sets for a production of *The Magic Flute.*

One room with warm red walls contains the Romantic *Panorama of Berlin,* painted by Eduard Gaertner from the roof of the FRIEDRICHSWERDERSCHE KIRCHE in 1834. Gaertner was also enlisted to produce the *Panorama of Moscow.* Yet another panorama, painted from the Kreuzberg summit by Hintze, shows a rural landscape that is now totally buried by apartment blocks and railway yards. There are also some KPM porcelain vases decorated with Potsdam and Havel landscapes.

Hidden in the trees near the Spree, the three-story **belvedere** was designed in 1790 by Langhans. Originally a tea-house, the elegant green and white Rococo edifice was reconstructed after World War II to hold a collection of porcelain dinner-services from the palace.

A path lined with yew trees leads to the **mausoleum**, built after the untimely death of Queen Luise in 1810. The original portico (now among the follies on PFAUENINSEL) was replaced by Schinkel, who executed a design suggested by the bereaved King Friedrich Wilhelm III. The temple contains a melancholy marble monument of the young queen, carved by Christian Rauch in 1811–14.

You will need to spend at least a day at Charlottenburg to visit the main sights. Pause for coffee in the elegant **Café Möhring** *(Luisenplatz),* or at the **Orangerie** in the palace grounds. For good beer and plain German cooking, try **Luisen-Brau** (described on page 180).

SCHLOSS FRIEDRICHSFELDE

Am Tierpark 125, Lichtenberg. Map **7***D7 ☎(030) 51531136 ✗ available June–Sept, Tues–Sun 11am, 1pm, 3pm; Oct–May Tues–Fri 3pm, Sat, Sun 11am, 1pm, 3pm. U-Bahn to Tierpark.*

A 17thC country house built for a naval officer in Dutch Baroque style now stands in the grounds of TIERPARK FRIEDRICHSFELDE. Restored in 1981, the Schloss has 16 Neoclassical rooms furnished with tapestries and paintings, and provides a rare opportunity to glimpse the interior of a Prussian country retreat.

SCHLOSS KLEIN-GLIENICKE See VOLKSPARK KLEIN-GLIENICKE.

SCHLOSS KÖPENICK See KUNSTGEWERBEMUSEUM SCHLOSS KÖPENICK.

SCHLOSS TEGEL

Adelheidallee 19–20, Reinickendorf. Map **5***B3 ☎(030) 4343156. U-Bahn to Alt-Tegel, then a 5min walk.*

Deep in the woods NW of Berlin, the Neoclassical Schloss Tegel was built in 1820–24 by Schinkel for Wilhelm von Humboldt, the founder of Berlin University. An attractive family cemetery at the end of an avenue of lindens planted in 1792 contains the tombs of von Humboldt and his brother Alexander, a scientist and South American explorer.

SIEGESSÄULE

Grosser Stern, Tiergarten. Map **2***C5 ☎(030) 3912961. Open Apr to mid-Oct Tues–Sun 9am–6pm. Last entry 5.30pm ⋖ Bus 100, 106, 341 to Grosser Stern, or U-Bahn to Hansaplatz.*

The Siegessäule (Victory Column) was originally erected on the square in front of the Reichstag in 1873 to commemorate a series of German victories over Denmark, Austria, and France. Designed by Heinrich Strade, the 67m/220ft column, surmounted by a gilded angel, was decorated with reliefs showing scenes from the three wars.

The pompous column became a hated symbol of Prussian militarism after World War I, and in 1921 a group of local anarchists almost succeeded in blowing it up. The column stood in the way of Hitler's projected monumental avenue through the Tiergarten, and in 1939 it was rebuilt on the Grosser Stern — a broad traffic circle in the middle of the Tiergarten — where it now looks perfectly at home.

Some 285 steps inside the column lead the visitor up to a cramped viewing platform, from where there is a dizzying view of the five avenues radiating out through the Tiergarten.

SKULPTURENGALERIE

Arnimallee 23–27, Dahlem. Map **6***E4* ☎*(030) 83011* ▪ (▪ *Sun and hols). Open Tues–Fri 9am–5pm; Sat, Sun 10am–5pm* ♿ ▪ *U-Bahn to Dahlem-Dorf.*

The modern sculpture gallery at the Dahlem museum complex contains works from the former gallery of Christian art on the Museumsinsel. The collection was created in 1883 by Wilhelm von Bode, who fused Early Christian and Byzantine sculpture with German and Italian works. Some of the works were destroyed or stolen in World War II, while others (including statues charred in the firestorms of 1944–45) are now in the BODE-MUSEUM. But many of the finest works were shipped from the city during the war, and later returned to the Allied sector. The works are currently displayed in a museum built at Dahlem in 1966.

The **Early Christian and Byzantine Collection** is smaller than the corresponding department at the Bode-Museum, although it has some interesting Roman altars and Byzantine mosaics. The collection of **Medieval German Sculpture** contains melancholy oak statues of pious women. The exquisite Late Gothic craftsmanship of Tilman Riemenschneider is shown in the *Four Evangelists,* carved for a church altar in 1491.

The **Renaissance Collection** has two giant wooden figures from a church in the Bavarian town of Wasserburg. Carved by Martin Zürn, they represent St Sebastian (invoked against plague) and St Florian (a protector against fire). The sculptures date from the Thirty Years' War (1618–48), when fire and plague were constant perils. The rather sad face of St Florian is apparently a likeness of Kaiser Ferdinand III, while the figure of St Sebastian was modeled on Elector Maximilian of Bavaria.

The **Italian rooms** contain some exceptional Renaissance busts, such as Desiderio da Settignano's 15thC bust of Marietta Strozzi, a Florentine girl. Notice also Francesco Laurana's impressive bust of Ferdinand II of Aragon, which stands on a Florentine pedestal carved at roughly the same time, imitating a display technique pioneered by Wilhelm von Bode.

The **Neoclassical collection** is dominated by Antonio Canova's overscaled *Dancer with Cymbals,* carved in 1809–12 for a Russian diplomat living in Vienna.

SPANDAU

W edge of Berlin. Map **5***C2. U-Bahn to Altstadt-Spandau.*

Situated at the confluence of the Spree and the Havel, the old town of Spandau was founded in 1232. Commanding an important river crossing, it grew into a strategic military town. The imposing 16thC ZITADELLE SPANDAU still stands to the E of the old quarter. Although Spandau lost its independence when Greater Berlin was created in the 1920s, the district still retains some of the atmosphere of a small Prussian town.

Devastated in World War II both by Allied bombers and Russian tanks, the old streets of Spandau have been lovingly reconstructed with a mixture of old and new buildings painted in pastel tones. An attractive quarter surrounds the squat 15thC **St Nikolai-Kirche** *(off Carl-Schurz-Strasse),* dedicated to the popular 4thC St Nicholas of Myra, patron saint of merchants and children. The cobbled Ritterstrasse to the W contains old half-timbered houses and handsome Baroque buildings. Kinkelstrasse, known as the Judenstrasse (Jews' Street) until the Nazis renamed it in 1938, leads N to the busy street Am Juliusturm. Cross the road to reach the pleasant old quarter around the Schleuse Spandau, a lock on the Havel.

Spandau district includes a vast area of open fields and rustic summer houses to the S. Not widely known, the **Rieselfelder** is a quiet area of farmland crossed by straight footpaths *(bus 134 from Rathaus Spandau).*

From May to September, the *Spandauer Sommerfestspiele,* a summer festival with classical and jazz concerts, takes place in an open-air theater.

THE SPREE

*See map for WALK 1 on pages 76–77 and color maps **1–7**.*

Rising in the forests to the SE, the Spree meanders through Berlin from KÖPENICK to SPANDAU, where it enters the Havel under the shadow of Spandau's citadel. Gravel barges still occasionally negotiate the lock opposite the Märkisches Museum, but the main river traffic now consists of tour boats and motor cruisers.

Just beyond the lock, the river splits into the Spree and the Kupfergraben, forming the long island on which the 13thC settlement of Cölln grew up. The Spreeinsel (Spree Island) became the site of the DOM, MUSEUMSINSEL and the now destroyed BERLINER SCHLOSS.

There are attractive stretches of the river to the E of Köpenick, N of the Tiergarten and behind SCHLOSS CHARLOTTENBURG park. A series of elegant iron and stone bridges span the river in the Tiergarten and Mitte districts. See WALK 1 on page 74 for a fuller description and for directions for a half-day stroll along its banks.

STREETLAMPS

It can be amusing to look out for unusual Berlin streetlamps as you travel through the city. Highly ornate iron streetlamps are found on KURFÜRSTENDAMM and in the heart of KÖPENICK, while stylish modern lamps illuminate the leafy streets of the HANSAVIERTEL.

The city takes such pride in its streetlamps that an open-air collection of old lamps has been assembled outside the BERLIN-PAVILLON.

TEGEL

*Reinickendorf, NW Berlin. Map **5**B3 ✱ U-Bahn to Alt-Tegel.*

Overlooking a sweeping bay at the N end of the Tegeler See, Tegel is one of Berlin's most attractive districts. Alt-Tegel is an attractive street with 19thC houses, cafés and restaurants, running from the U-Bahnhof to the waterfront. The old harbor to the N of Alt-Tegel is overlooked by elegant Post-Modern apartments built in the 1980s as part of the IBA plan to revitalize Berlin.

Alt-Tegel leads down to the **Greenwichpromenade**, an attractive lakeside promenade where steamers depart for Spandau and the Havel resorts. The meandering paths are lined with British red telephone booths and Victorian mailboxes to evoke the jaunty atmosphere of an English seaside resort. A café even organizes genteel Sunday tea-dances.

To the S of the old quarter are the giant Borsig engineering works, where steam locomotives were once built. Berlin's first skyscraper, constructed here in 1922–24, still dominates the neighborhood. The 11-story edifice has a curious top tier that combines jagged German Expressionism with Gothic tracery.

The nearby RUSSISCHER ORTHODOXE FRIEDHOF (Russian Orthodox Cemetery) lies to the SE of the Borsig factory, on the far side of an elevated highway. A richly carved wooden gatehouse leads to a 19thC Russian church with onion domes. A wistful cemetery is filled with the graves of Russian emigrés including the composer Mikhail Glinka, who died in 1857.

An idyllic wooded walk follows the shore of the Malchsee, an inlet N of the Greenwichpromenade reached by a handsome red iron bridge. Pause to admire the view from the promontory at the S end of the bay, then continue to the **Freizeitpark**, where children can romp in a big adventure playground while their parents fry *Bratwürste* on the park's open-air barbecues. A little wooden cabin signposted **Fahrrad und Spiele-verleih** rents bicycles and seats for children, footballs, croquet sets, giant chessmen, skipping ropes and a host of other toys. Energetic parents can rent rowboats at the **Tretbootverleih** *(open summer, daily 10am-7pm).*

Serious ramblers can strike off into the forest along the Mühlenweg, while swimmers should continue along the waterfront to the **Strandbad Tegel**, a quiet beach with old-fashioned wickerwork beach chairs *(Strandkörbe)* like those on the windy Baltic coast. The path ends at the **Tegelort-Seeterrassen** landing stage, where you can pick up a steamer to Tegel or Spandau. To pick up bus 222 back to Tegel, continue to the terminus at Tegelort.

Established in about 1724, **Alter Fritz** *(Karolienstrasse 12)* is Berlin's oldest surviving inn. Situated just N of Tegel, it was visited by Goethe and Frederick the Great. The restaurant serves traditional Berlin food, and there is a pleasant beer garden for idle summer days.

TIERGARTEN

*Map **2**C3–**3**C7 ♣ ▀ S-Bahn to Tiergarten or U-Bahn to Hansaplatz.*

"The real heart of Berlin is a small, damp black wood — the Tiergarten," ruminated Christopher Isherwood in 1932. Extending from the BRANDENBURGER TOR to the ZOOLOGISCHER GARTEN, the Tiergarten was originally a private hunting estate for Elector Friedrich III, situated outside the city walls. Overlooking the river Spree, **Schloss Bellevue** was built in the 18thC on the N edge of the Tiergarten. The Baroque palace is now the official Berlin residence of the German president.

In 1838, the Tiergarten became Berlin's first public park, with rambling paths and ponds laid out in romantic English style by the landscape gardener Peter Lenné. The park lost some of its quiet seclusion in 1936 when the Charlottenburger Chaussee (renamed the Strasse des 17 Juni to commemorate the 1953 East Berlin workers' uprising) was widened to provide a fast road from Mitte to the prosperous western suburbs. Another road-building scheme commissioned by Hitler in 1939 cut through the Tiergarten from N to S near the Reichstag.

The park was destroyed during the fighting at the end of World War II, and the elegant quarter of diplomatic residences on the Tiergartenstrasse to the S was left totally gutted. The former Japanese embassy now houses the **Japanisch-Deutsches Zentrum** *(Tiergartenstrasse 24-27),* which promotes cooperation between Japan and Germany. Several foreign governments are now looking at the idea of rebuilding their embassies at their prewar locations.

The few trees that remained after the fierce fighting were felled to provide fuel during the harsh winter of 1946, and the land was then used to grow potatoes. About one million trees were later replanted and many of the 19thC statues were restored, so that now you are hardly aware of the damage, except for the blackened statues around the Grossfürstenplatz, on the N edge of the park near the Kongresshalle.

Massive stone blocks from Hitler's Imperial Chancellery were used to build the **Sowjetisches Ehrenmal** (Soviet war memorial), at the point where the two main axes meet. The American-funded KONGRESSHALLE was built in the park, while the British contributed the **Englischer Garten**, to be found behind the statue of Bismarck at the SIEGESSÄULE.

The Tiergarten is a pleasant place to while away a sunny afternoon. You will find rhododendron (rosebay) beds S of the Grosser Stern, several children's playgrounds, and cafés hidden in the trees. Rowboats can be rented at the Neuer See. Be sure to keep off the grass except at areas designated *Liegeweise.*

The park is dotted with picturesque 19thC statues representing mythological scenes as well as eminent Germans. The statues of Bismarck and Von Moltke, now on the Grosser Stern, were moved from the Platz der Republik in front of the Reichstag in 1939. The figures of Friedrich Wilhelm II, Queen Luise and Prinz Wilhelm are grouped together around an island to the S, while Goethe and Lessing lurk in the trees near the former site of the Berlin Wall.

TIERPARK FRIEDRICHSFELDE (Zoo)

*Am Tierpark 125, Friedrichsfelde. Map **7**D7 ☎(030) 515310. Open daily 9am–dusk* ☕ ♣ *U-Bahn to Tierpark.*

Founded in 1954 as East Berlin's answer to the ZOOLOGISCHER GARTEN, Friedrichsfelde zoo has rapidly built up a remarkable collection of 900 different species of animals. Rare antelopes, llamas and buffaloes roam contentedly in spacious enclosures, while special windows allow observation of the polar bears swimming at close quarters. There is a playground where children can imitate the antics of the monkeys, and two cafés with the added interest of tropical fish in tanks.

The zoo stands within an old country estate, landscaped in 1695 in the formal style of Dutch gardens then in vogue. The grounds to the N were later transformed by Peter Lenné into a romantic 19thC English garden landscape. A spacious café terrace overlooks the formal Dutch gardens, where deer graze and water fowl splash in the canals. The Baroque SCHLOSS FRIEDRICHSFELDE houses a small museum showing the Prussian country lifestyle.

TOPOGRAPHIE DES TERRORS

*Stresemannstrasse 110, Kreuzberg. Map **3**D7 ☎(030) 25486703* 🎫 *Open Tues–Sun 10am–6pm. U-Bahn to Kochstrasse; S-Bahn to Anhalter Bahnhof.*

A bleak tract of wasteland known as the PRINZ-ALBRECHT-GELÄNDE marks the site of the Gestapo headquarters and other Nazi institutions. The old buildings were eventually razed to the ground, and the area has remained a rubble-strewn wasteland ever since. Excavations near the MARTIN-GROPIUS-BAU uncovered the cellars of the former School of Applied Arts, where thousands had been tortured at the hands of the Gestapo.

A shed constructed on top of the cellars contains a moving exhibition of photographs and documents illustrating the Nazi terror and the destruction of the government quarter of Berlin.

Wooden steps lead to the top of a hillock constructed from the rubble of the art school. From here you can look across the eerie inner city wasteland where rabbits still run wild.

TRÄNENPALAST

Reichstagufer 17, Mitte. Map ***4****B8 ☎(030) 2386211*

A modern iron and glass building is tucked away behind Bahnhof Friedrichstrasse. It never had a name and it was marked simply by a sign that said *Ausgang* (exit), but for older Berliners it was the *Tränenpalast,* the palace of tears. It was here, and only here, that Berliners from the west could cross the Wall to visit relatives in the east. There were long queues, petty bureaucratic squabbles, and sometimes tearful farewells.

The building is now the setting for concerts featuring the wildest of music, and there are also occasional movie screenings.

TREPTOWER PARK

Treptow. Map ***7****D6. S-Bahn to Treptower Park.*

Laid out on the S bank of the Spree, Treptow's public park was landscaped in romantic English style in 1876. The park is now dominated by the **Sowjetisches Ehrenmal**, a colossal war memorial built to commemorate some 5,000 Russian soldiers who died fighting in the streets of Berlin at the end of World War II. Monumental gates and windswept flights of steps lead to a heroic 13-meter/42-foot-high statue of a Russian soldier rescuing a German child.

U-BAHN

See Berlin U-Bahn & S-Bahn color map at the back of the book.

Berlin's U-Bahn is one of the world's great subway systems, providing rapid access to large areas of the city. Some of the lines run above ground on elevated bridges, offering intriguing glimpses of the city, while others have handsome underground stations that survived World War II intact. Each line has its own character, and you can observe a lot about the lifestyles of Berliners by traveling different routes.

Avoid the rush hours if you want to explore the U-Bahn network; the quietest times are in mid-morning and mid-afternoon, while a late-night trip lets you glimpse Berliners of all types in a party mood. A Berlin-Ticket gives you 24 hours of unlimited travel.

The oldest subway line in Germany, built in 1896–1902, ran from Warschauerstrasse to Richard-Wagner-Platz. A stretch of this line in Kreuzberg is now known locally as the Orient Express because of the exotic mix of Turks and punks living along the route. It's worth getting off at **U-Bahnhof Wittenbergplatz**, opened in 1913, to admire the polished wooden ticket booths, ornate clocks and iron columns topped with Ionic capitals. The giant posters are designed to look ancient, although they advertise contemporary Berlin shops. The weighing machines on the station platforms are genuine antiquities. You can eat something quick at the **Mini Bistro** at Wittenbergplatz U-Bahnhof before continuing your journey.

An interesting ride to take is on the northern stretch of line U2, which runs from Mohrenstrasse in Mitte to Pankow. Begun in 1913, the line was completed in 1930. An interesting station to visit is **U-Bahnhof Klosterstrasse**, which features paintings of Old Berlin views in the ticket hall and tiled walls modeled on the Processional Way of Babylon (copied from the PERGAMON-MUSEUM).

N of Alexanderplatz, the yellow U-Bahn trains clatter along a graceful iron viaduct past the upper windows of dusty mansions in Prenzlauer Berg. The high-level stations at Eberswalder Strasse and Schönhauser Allee are masterpieces of engineering, designed by the architects Alfred Grenander and Johannes Bousset.

The southern section of the line U1 runs from U-Bahnhof Wittenbergplatz to U-Bahnhof Krumme Lanke in wooded Zehlendorf. The trains on this line are frequented by women in hats who travel in from the leafy suburbs to take coffee and cake at the KaDeWe. It is also the line tourists tend to use to get to the museums at Dahlem. Some of the finest stations in Berlin are on the U1. Look out for the station at **Hohenzollernplatz**, where the walls are decorated with tiled pictures showing scenes from the lives of the Hohenzollern family. Two stops down the line, **U-Bahnhof Heidelberger Platz** is one of the most handsome stations in Berlin, decorated with Neoclassical vaults, ornate iron lamps and romantic scenes of Heidelberg.

Farther out, the U1 has several romantic suburban stations built in the style of traditional German farmhouses. The most notable is **Dahlem-Dorf**, the station for the Dahlem museums. The station is built in farmhouse style with a thatched roof, and a painted ceiling in the booking hall. Notice the wooden benches on the station platform carved in the form of naked men and women. They are intriguing to look at, but enormously uncomfortable to use.

The middle section of line U2 was closed down when the Berlin Wall was built, but the derelict stations between Wittenbergplatz and Mohrenstrasse have been rebuilt, and the stretch is operational again. Many other stations that were closed when the Wall went up have also been reopened. Travelers who visited Berlin during the Cold War might remember the eerie, darkened stations on the stretch of line U6 that passed through East Berlin. These stations, such as Oranienburger Tor and Französische Strasse, have emerged after renovation, although they still sometimes sport the old metal signs bearing the station names in Gothic script.

UNTER DEN LINDEN ★

Mitte. Maps 3C7–4B8. U-Bahn to Französische Strasse; S-Bahn to Unter den Linden.

Berlin's famous avenue lined with linden or lime trees was a 17thC creation of the Great Elector to link the royal palace with the forests to the W (now the Tiergarten). The street was enhanced in the 18thC by Frederick the Great, who commissioned the Forum Fridericianum (now known as Bebelplatz), a square in the style of a Roman forum with the Staatsoper as the centerpiece. The W end of the street (between Friedrichstrasse and the BRANDENBURGER TOR) became the glittering hub of Imperial Germany at the end of the 19thC, and fashionable Berliners flocked to the famous Café Kranzler and the Hotel Adlon.

Unter den Linden lost its allure after World War II, when the East German government tore down anything that smacked of the Second or Third Reich, and put up bland modern office buildings in their place. The stretch to the W of Friedrichstrasse, once lined with ponderous Wilhelmine-style buildings, was wrecked by the socialist planners, but many of the older Neoclassical and Baroque buildings E of Friedrichstrasse were judiciously rebuilt to their old splendor.

Although Unter den Linden has lost its former allure, it is still a handsome and harmonious avenue, thanks to the East Germans' resolve to maintain the 19thC scale. Now that the old regime has shuffled off, the mile-long street is poised to become the most elegant thoroughfare in Germany's capital, although this has not happened as fast as some had expected.

It is no longer possible to stroll down the middle of the street, as rich Berliners did in the 19thC, but you can still wander along the broad sidewalks under the lime trees, which flower in early summer. Beginning at Friedrichstrasse (King Friedrich Wilhelm I's military road to the Tempelhofer Feld parade ground), head away from the Brandenburger Tor, keeping to the S side of the street. The curvaceous **Alte Königliche Bibliothek** (royal library), built in 1775, was modeled on the Hofburg in Vienna. But the voluptuous Baroque style did not impress Berliners, who dubbed it the *Kommode* (chest of drawers).

The library stands at the W end of Frederick the Great's Roman forum (formerly the Opernplatz, renamed Bebelplatz in honor of an East German socialist leader). The Enlightenment ideals symbolized by the square were brutally crushed when a gang of Nazi students gathered there in 1933 to set fire to a stack of books from the university library.

The elegant Neoclassical **Staatsoper** (State Opera House) stands in the middle of the square. Built by Knobelsdorff in 1742 for Frederick the Great, it burned down in 1843 but was rebuilt in its original style. It was hit by a bomb in 1941 and rebuilt immediately, only to be destroyed again in 1945. The East Germans carefully rebuilt it again, to provide East Berlin with a far more dazzling opera house than West Berlin could hope for.

The Catholic **St Hedwigs-Kathedrale** stands in the corner of the square. Modeled on the Pantheon in Rome, it was built in 1747, probably by Knobelsdorff, who perhaps followed sketches by Frederick the Great. The E side of the square is occupied by the **Prinzessinnenpalais** (Palace of the Princesses), now the Operncafé, and the **Palais Unter den Linden**, built by Langhans for the future Kaiser Wilhelm I.

Walk to the end of Unter den Linden and cross the Spree by the **Schloss Brücke**, built by Schinkel in 1822–24. This leads to the windswept **Lustgarten**, which marks the site of the BERLINER SCHLOSS, the city palace of the Electors of Brandenburg. Rebuilt in Baroque style by

Andreas Schlüter, the palace was devastated by bombs in World War II.

In 1950, the East Berlin mayor Walter Ulbricht ordered the palace to be demolished on the grounds that it symbolized Imperial Germany. All that now survives are some Baroque sculptures in the BODE-MUSEUM, and the palace balcony (where Karl Liebknecht proclaimed the German revolution in 1918), which has been piously incorporated into the facade of the **Staatsrat** (Council of State) building on the E side of the square. The modern building on the N side, the **Palast der Republik**, was once the seat of the East German parliament.

Cross the road and go back along the N side of Unter den Linden, past the DEUTSCHES HISTORISCHES MUSEUM, situated in the former arsenal. You come to the **Neue Wache**, a compact Neoclassical temple designed by Schinkel in 1816–18. Formerly a guard house, it was rebuilt after World War II as the *Mahnmal für die Opfer des Faschismus und Militarismus,* a memorial to the victims of fascism and militarism. Schinkel also designed the nearby **Maxim Gorki Theater**, originally a concert hall called the Sing Akademie, where performances were given by Brahms, Liszt and Paganini.

The dusty buildings of the **Humboldt-Universität** are farther along the avenue, located in the **Palais des Prinzen Heinrich**, a palace built in 1748 for Prince Heinrich, brother of Frederick the Great. The diplomat Wilhelm von Humboldt founded a school here in 1809 which later became Berlin University. Hegel and Einstein taught at the university, and communist leaders such as Marx, Engels and Liebknecht were students there. Renamed after its founder in 1946, the Humboldt University lost its academic edge in 1948 when many disillusioned teachers left to found the Free University in Dahlem.

The nearby **Deutsche Staatsbibliothek** (National Library of Germany) was built in Neo-Baroque style by Ernst von Ihne in 1903–14. There are a few benches in the secluded courtyard, offering a moment's rest.

VIEWPOINTS ⋞

Berlin lies in a flat region that offers few natural viewpoints. The only hill of any interest within city limits is the Kreuzberg in VIKTORIAPARK, which offers a panoramic view of central Berlin much loved by Romantic artists.

The FERNSEHTURM boasts a revolving observation room situated 204 meters/670 feet above Alexanderplatz; the view is best on days of clear air. The less elevated observation deck of the FUNKTURM (125 meters/410 feet up) offers a dizzying view of the Messegelände, the vast exhibition and conference center directly below.

For the best view of the old city, you must toil up the tower of the FRANZÖSISCHER DOM on Gendarmenmarkt. Another interesting view, not for the nervous, is from the top of the SIEGESSÄULE, looking toward the Brandenburger Tor. An elevator takes you up to the top of the EUROPA-CENTER for a view of western Berlin.

VIKTORIAPARK

*Kreuzbergstrasse, Kreuzberg. Map **3**E7–F7 ⋞ ▇ ♣ U-Bahn to Möckernbrücke.*

The Viktoriapark is a romantic, landscaped park with ponds, a children's playground and a small zoo, but its most alluring feature is an artificial waterfall constructed on the N slope. Some 13,000 liters (2,860 gallons) of water tumble down the rocky clefts every minute, presenting an unusual sight as you approach the park along Grossbeerenstrasse.

The park was created in 1888–94 on the slopes of the Kreuzberg (Cross Hill), a natural hill named after a Neo-Gothic war memorial on the summit. Designed by Schinkel in 1818–21 to commemorate the Wars of Liberation, the memorial stands on a base modeled on the Iron Cross, a German military decoration first awarded during the Napoleonic Wars.

The park is a romantic place for wandering, although some of the paths are steep. At the summit, you can enjoy the typical Berlin skyline of church spires mingled with chimneys. You'll find a beer garden named **Golgotha** on the S slope of the hill.

VOLKSPARK FRIEDRICHSHAIN

*Am Friedrichshain. Off map **4**A9, or map **6**C5. Tram 24, 28, 58 to Am Friedrichshain, or U-Bahn to Strausberger Platz.*

An attractive public park with a rose garden and a lake graces the former East Berlin district of Friedrichshain. The grand Neo-Baroque fountain near the main entrance was built in 1913. Known as the **Märchenbrunnen** (Fable Fountain), it is surrounded by statues of characters from traditional German fairy tales.

The two artificial hills in the park reflect the darker side of Berlin's history; they were created from the rubble left behind after World War II.

VOLKSPARK KLEIN-GLIENICKE ★ 🏛

*To the N of Königstrasse, Zehlendorf. Off map **5**E1 ☎(030) 8053041. Park open daily, dawn–dusk ☰ ✱ S-Bahn to Wannsee, then bus 116 to Glienicker Brücke, or Line 1 steamer to Glienicker Brücke.*

On the old road from Berlin to Potsdam, the Volkspark at the Hohenzollern Schloss Klein-Glienicke is one of the most romantic spots along the River Havel. The grounds extend down to the water's edge, where steamers call in summer. Laid out in a picturesque English style by Peter Lenné, the head gardener at Sanssouci, Klein-Glienicke is landscaped in rolling parkland, with spreading chestnut trees and extensive lawns.

- **Exploring the park**

Schloss Klein-Glienicke (★ 🏛) *(Königstrasse 36 ☎(030) 8053041. Open Tues-Fri 2-6pm, Sat, Sun 10am-6pm ☰).* An old villa on the site was bought in 1824 by Prince Karl von Preussen, the brother of the future Kaiser Wilhelm I. Infatuated with Italy, Prince Karl commissioned Schinkel to rebuild Schloss Klein-Glienicke in the style of an Italian villa.

Prince Karl amassed a considerable collection of Classical spoils during his tour of Italy. Capitals, torsos, mosaics, doorways and gravestones were incorporated into the walls of several buildings, to form a curious open-air museum of antiquities. An unexpected heap of broken Classical columns in the park is intended to suggest a ruined temple, but the most eccentric building is the **Klosterhof**, designed by Ferdinand von Arnim in 1850. Hidden in a clump of trees near the Casino, it was constructed using architectural fragments from northern Italian churches. The cloister came from a Carthusian monastery on an island near Venice, the lion on a pillar is Venetian, while the strange capital decorated with a chained ape once adorned the campanile at Pisa.

The **Remise**, the former coach house, has been converted into a restaurant with a large terrace *(☎(030) 8054000 ▥ open Tues-Sun 10am-6pm).* The Italianate **Casino**, also designed by Schinkel, commands a sweeping view of the reed-fringed lake. Flanked by pergolas, the ocher building is decorated with *trompe l'oeil* frescos evoking Pompeian art.

Other Italianate buildings are clustered around the main entrance on Königstrasse. When it rains, you can take shelter in the **Stibadium**, a semicircular Neoclassical pavilion designed by Ludwig Persius in 1840. The nearby **fountain**, designed by Schinkel and modeled on a fountain at the Villa Medici in Rome, is flanked by two gilded lions on pedestals.

Lenné's park is dotted with elegant little buildings modeled on Classical architecture. The **Kleine Neugierde** (Little Curiosity) was built in 1825 as a teahouse standing beside the Potsdam road. Facing the Glienicker Brücke, Schinkel's **Grosse Neugierde** (Large Curiosity) is an eye-catching rotunda surmounted by a tall lantern modeled on an Athenian monument. The view from the platform (⋞) takes in the GLIENICKER BRÜCKE and SCHLOSS BABELSBERG (see POTSDAM). Until recently, the prospect was marred by the blazing floodlights and tall observation towers along the nearby Berlin Wall, but all traces of the frontier have now gone.

The park is a pleasant place to wander in search of architectural curiosities or glimpses of the Havel. Exploring the woods to the E, you may stumble upon the *Maschinenhaus* (pump house) and the *Matrosenhaus* (boatmen's house), both common features of 19thC Potsdam summer residences.

Another Hohenzollern retreat, the JAGDSCHLOSS-GLIENICKE, stands on the opposite side of the road. Only the gardens are open to the public.

- **A half-day ramble**

Take the Uferweg along the Havel shore (following the little white stone signs to Moorlake) to reach the **Teufelsbrücke** (Devil's Bridge). Spanning a deep ravine, the bridge was built in 1838 in the form of a ruin. The effect was so convincing that the city authorities took it for a real ruin and rebuilt it entirely, much to the dismay of local folly-lovers.

Continue past the **Jägertor**, a gate built by Schinkel in English Gothic style, and follow the path down to **Moorlake**. The **Wirtshaus Moorlake** *(Pfaueninselchaussee 2 ☎(030) 8052509 ▥ closed Tues)* is an attractive country inn occupying Prince Karl's 19thC hunting lodge. A beguiling beer garden overlooks the Havel. A gentle stroll along the shore brings you soon to NIKOLSKOE and PFAUENINSEL.

WANNSEE

Zehlendorf. Map **5**E2 ✱ *S-Bahn to Nikolassee or Wannsee.*

An inlet of the Havel river, the Wannsee became a fashionable resort in the 19thC, after Carl Conrad, a government official, built a villa here. Wealthy Berliners, including the artist Max Liebermann, built summer residences on the W side of the sea, while in recent years, yacht harbors have been squeezed into every available inlet.

The waterfront near Wannsee S-Bahn station is constantly bustling with cruise boats, including an old steamship, a Mississippi paddle steamer called the *Havel Queen,* and a bizarre vessel built to resemble a large black whale. Boats regularly sail from here to SPANDAU, SCHLOSS KLEIN-GLIENICKE, POTSDAM and PFAUENINSEL.

For details of the various boat tour operators, see page 61.

Berliners also flock to the Wannsee to bask on the longest inland beach in Europe, the Strandbad Wannsee, which stretches along the E shore of the lake (bus 513 runs from S-Bahnhof Nikolassee to the beach on sunny days).

To the N lies a tiny, wooded peninsula called the **Schwanenwerder** (Swan Island), dotted with elegant villas. The little wooded island of **Lindwerder** lies farther N *(S-Bahn to Wannsee, then bus 218 to Lindwerder, followed by a short ferry crossing, or steamer from Wannsee harbor to Lindwerder island).* The sole building on the island is the rustic restaurant **Insel Lindwerder** *(☎(030) 80365840, open Easter-Oct, Tues-Sun, from 10am),* set in an idyllic garden overlooking the Havel.

A string of narrow lakes runs S from the Wannsee to enter the Havel at the Glienicker Brücke. A silent, wooded park on the shore of the Kleiner Wannsee contains the **Kleistgrab** (follow the wooden sign on Bismarckstrasse marked *Zum Kleistgrab*). The grave marks the spot where the dramatist Heinrich von Kleist shot himself in 1811. "Now, Immortality, you are entirely mine," proclaims the inscription.

The Griebnitzsee used to be forbidden territory between East and West Berlin, but cruise boats now ply regularly between Wannsee and the Glienicker Brücke.

ZEISS-GROSSPLANETARIUM

*Prenzlauer Allee 80, Prenzlauer Berg. Map **6**C5 ☎(030) 4200916. Open daily. For information and times of cinema screenings ☎(030) 42284156 ✱ Tram 20, 71 or S-Bahn to Prenzlauer Allee.*

Berlin has three planetariums, but this is the most lively. The stars at night are projected onto a dome, to illustrate topics such as space travel and the winter sky. Look out for special screenings featuring music.

ZEUGHAUS

See DEUTSCHES HISTORISCHES MUSEUM

ZILLE-MUSEUM

*S-Bahnbogen 201 (at Bahnhof Friedrichstrasse), Mitte. Map **4**B8 ☎(030) 2082590 ▣ Open 11am–7pm, closed Tues. U-Bahn or S-Bahn to Friedrichstrasse.*

A reconstructed apothecary's shop located in the arches under Friedrichstrasse station provides an appropriately eccentric setting for a collection of etchings, drawings and paintings by Heinrich Zille (1858–1929). The cluttered interior is full of humorous, compassionate portraits of impoverished Berliners at the turn of the century.

Zille's fame rests on works such as *Zur Mutter Erde* (To Mother Earth), with its brawny Berlin matrons, drunken husbands and grubby children (including one dragging along a dead mouse on a string). When swimming became fashionable in 1907, Zille immediately captured the ridiculous appearance of plump Berlin women in bathing costumes. He continued to

delight Berliners during World War I with strip cartoon tales of Vadding, a soldier in the trenches.

ZITADELLE SPANDAU

Am Juliusturm, Spandau. Map **5***C3* ☎*(030) 3391212. Open Tues–Fri 9am–5pm; Sat, Sun 10am–5pm. Last entry 4.30pm* ♿ *(☎ ahead) U-Bahn to Zitadelle, then a 5min walk.*

A giant reproduction of Cranach's painting of Joachim II greets you upon arrival at Zitadelle U-Bahnhof, a modern U-Bahn station near Zitadelle Spandau built in the style of the old fortress, with handsome red brick pillars and doors painted with black and white diagonal lines. It is rather useful to study the enlarged 16thC Renaissance plans and maps in the station before visiting the citadel.

Standing at the confluence of the Spree and Havel rivers, Spandau citadel was built in the 14thC on an important trade route from Western Europe to Poland. The fortress was rebuilt in 1560–83 in a mighty Renaissance style, with acute-angled bastions projecting into the moat like arrow heads. The building was completed by the military architect Graf Rochus von Lynar, whose bust glowers down at you from the U-Bahn entrance.

A small museum with scale models, paintings, tin soldiers and old guns occupies the restored **Torhaus** (gatehouse). A passage leads from there to the **Juliusturm**, a round brick tower dating from the 14thC. A sturdy wooden stair winds up to the battlements, which once offered a sweeping view of the medieval river and land routes. The prospect now takes in Spandau old town, the Grunewald and clusters of industrial chimneys.

A few old cannon are left in the citadel courtyard, along with a 19thC statue of a rather demonic-looking Albrecht the Bear of the House of Askanier, who drove the Slavs out of Brandenburg in the 12thC. The statue, and others now in the LAPIDARIUM, stood on the Siegesallee in the Tiergarten until World War II.

A restaurant within the fortress walls has a heavy medieval atmosphere, with food to match. After visiting the citadel, you can stroll into a rambling nature reserve created on a neck of land that is overgrown with wild flowers.

ZOOLOGISCHER GARTEN ★

Entrances at Hardenbergplatz 8, or Budapester Strasse 26, Tiergarten. Map **2***D4* ☎*(030) 254010* *Open daily 9am–6.30pm (closes at dusk in winter). U-Bahn or S-Bahn to Zoologischer Garten.*

Berlin boasts one of the world's biggest and best-kept zoos, situated next to the main railway station in the very heart of the metropolis. Its animal population increases every year, and at the last count there were 14,600 animals, representing 1,700 different species.

The zoo has been expertly designed to create habitats that are remarkably close to the natural environment. Monkeys perform wild acrobatics on the **Affen Insel** (monkey island), which is surrounded by water to prevent escapes, while the biggest collection of crocodiles in Europe bask in the sultry heat of the **Reptilienhaus** (reptile house).

You can eavesdrop on the nocturnal activities of bats, owls and other creatures of the night in the eerie **Nachttierhaus**, which is artificially darkened by day and lit by night. Rare antelopes roam in unfenced enclosures near the Landwehrkanal, while beautiful Przewalski's horses from the Russian steppes are among the animals inhabiting an enclave on the other side of the canal. Finally, children can pet donkeys, sheep and chickens at the **Tierkinderzoo**.

The Zoologischer Garten dates back to 1841, when King Friedrich Wilhelm IV presented the city with his menagerie of beasts from Pfaueninsel to form Germany's first zoo. Built on the site of the royal pheasantry on the edge of the Tiergarten, the zoo was beautifully landscaped by Lenné with lakes and winding paths, and stocked with an impressive variety of rare species.

The zoo animals suffered alongside the Berliners during World War II. Martin Middlebrook's *The Berlin Raids (Viking Penguin, 1988)* recounts a young Berlin woman's sadness on visiting the zoo the day after a devastating air raid in November 1943. "A terrible smell lingered above the total destruction of my beloved zoo. There were blasted and dead animals everywhere. The only living thing, in his big pond, was a big bull hippopotamus called Knautschke, still swimming while above him his shelter burned down."

The famous Knautschke was one of only 91 animals to survive the war, from a collection that in peacetime had numbered 4,000 mammals and birds, and 8,000 fish.

Berlin: living in the city

Where to stay

The hotel business has boomed in Berlin since reunification, as tourists and business travelers flock to the city. Whereas some features of life have not improved since *die Wende,* the hotel sector has made enormous investments in interior design and staff training. The highest standards used to be found in West Berlin, but many of the hotels in East Berlin have been modernized by international chains to provide a level of service equal to the western hotels.

LOCATION

The location of a hotel is often the most important consideration. Those who come to Berlin on business may need a base close to the airport or the Messegelände exhibition center off Theodor-Heuss-Platz, whereas tourists are more likely to prefer a location in the vicinity of Kurfürstendamm or Unter den Linden.

A room in central Berlin

Before reunification, most visitors to West Berlin stayed in **CHARLOTTENBURG** district in one of the low-rise modern hotels built after World War II. Most of the hotels are located on **KURFÜRSTENDAMM** or one of its side streets, in what is still the liveliest quarter of Berlin. Some hotels, such as the BRISTOL KEMPINSKI, have tried to re-create an Old Berlin atmosphere, but most are sober modern buildings in the Bauhaus style. A few small hotels occupy old mansions that survived the bombardment, such as the picturesque KRONPRINZ.

In recent years, a hint of the Post-Modern style has crept into the interior design of hotels such as the CURATOR and the ART-HOTEL SORAT.

A room in historic Berlin

Hotels in the **historic heart** of Berlin were virtually out of bounds to travelers during the Cold War, but you can now stay in comfortable modern hotels in **MITTE**, such as the MARITIM GRAND HOTEL on Unter den Linden or the RADISSON PLAZA near Alexanderplatz. These hotels provide a good base for discovering the historic relics of old Berlin, such as Museumsinsel and the Staatsoper. Bear in mind that Mitte remains rather quiet after dark; the choice of restaurants and cafés is still limited.

A room in Kreuzberg

A few hotels are located in other districts of Berlin, but you must count on using the U-Bahn or S-Bahn to get around. The most bohemian atmosphere is found in **KREUZBERG**. There you will find several hotels located in grand mansions, the most appealing of which is RIEHMERS HOFGARTEN.

A room in the suburbs

If you want peaceful nights, you can choose from an increasing number of hotels located in Berlin's leafy suburbs. The new SORAT HUMBOLDT-MÜHLE at **TEGEL** is the most spectacular out-of-town hotel, but some people may prefer the intimacy of smaller hotels located in suburban villas, such as the VILLA TOSCANA in **Lichterfelde** or the FORSTHAUS PAULSBORN in the depths of the **GRUNEWALD**.

A room in Potsdam

Another possibility, at least for Baroque enthusiasts, is to stay in a hotel in **POTSDAM**. Recommended hotels there are listed on page 240. Count on about 30 minutes to travel from Potsdam to central Berlin by S-Bahn.

A room near the airport

Travelers arriving on late flights or departing in the early morning may want to spend a night close to the airport.

The most convenient hotel for **Berlin-Tegel** airport is the **Novotel Berlin Airport**, 1km from the airport *(Kurt-Schumacher-Damm 202, 13405 Berlin ☎(030) 41060 Fx(030) 4106700 181 rms shuttle bus to airport).*

The attractive hotel RIEHMERS HOFGARTEN is about 1km from the terminal building at **Berlin-Tempelhof** airport. There are as yet no hotels conveniently located for **Berlin-Schönefeld** airport.

Conference hotels

The choice of conference locations has increased dramatically since reunification. Several international hotels in Berlin have large conference rooms and business centers (see BUSINESS IN BERLIN on page 63). Those organizing a small meeting may prefer a more modest business hotel, such as the SORAT HUMBOLDT-MÜHLE, only 5 minutes by cab from Berlin-Tegel airport. It can accommodate up to 90 people in a purpose-built center.

RESERVING A ROOM

It hardly needs to be said that Berlin has boomed as a tourist and business destination since 1989, and it is now often impossible to find a hotel room on short notice.

If you have difficulties, call **First Hotel Reservierung** *(Kurfürstendamm 180, 10707 Berlin ☎(030) 8811515 Fx(030) 8826644),* a free service that will try to find a room in one of several modern and well-situated hotels in Berlin or Potsdam. If you have no luck there, try the **tourist office** at the EUROPA-CENTER *(Budapester Strasse entrance, Charlottenburg, map **2**D5 ☎(030) 2626031 Fx(030) 21232520),* or one of the other tourist offices (for addresses see page 61), where the service offered is also free. Both will handle advance reservations as well as on-the-spot inquiries, but try **First Hotel Reservierung** first.

The demand for rooms in large hotels often falls off on weekends and during vacation periods, prompting many branches of international hotel chains to offer lower rates on weekends or during the slack season. The SORAT HUMBOLDT-MÜHLE has a special *Wochenende in Berlin* (Weekend in Berlin) arrangement, and the BERLIN HILTON sometimes offers a special half-price weekend rate in its "Two for One" deal.

Some hotels let one (or possibly two, but seldom more) children share the parents' room at no additional charge, which can represent a considerable saving for a family.

BREAKFAST

In most hotels breakfast is included in the price of the room. In a large hotel, you can expect a generous buffet breakfast, with various types of German bread and rolls, *croissants,* cold hams, spicy salamis, cereals, muesli and sometimes even German pastries and cakes. Many hotels will offer British-style bacon and scrambled egg as well, while the ART-HOTEL SORAT even provides Japanese specialities.

It helps to be aware of the difference between *Vollmilch* (unskimmed milk) and the *Karnemelk* (buttermilk) that many tourists innocently add to their muesli.

A CHOICE OF STYLES

Only a few international hotels chains were represented in Berlin before unification, but you now find many familiar names, including **Hilton** and **Radisson**. There is also an **Ibis** *(Messedamm 10, 14057 Berlin ☎ (030) 303930 Fx (030) 3019536),* convenient for the Messegelände exhibition center, and a **Novotel Berlin Airport** (see opposite) close to the airport.

These hotels guarantee travelers a high standard of service, but have scarcely any local character. If you want to experience the solemn grandeur of an old Berlin mansion, or stay in a room with a view of the Spree, or wake up in the depths of the Grunewald, you should select one of the hotels listed on the following pages.

HOW TO USE THIS CHAPTER

- **Location:** Each entry shows the nearest U-Bahn or S-Bahn stations or other transportation details. Map references are given for the color maps at the back of the book.
- **Symbols:** The symbols show price categories and credit cards, as well as giving a résumé of available facilities. See the KEY TO SYMBOLS on page 7 for an explanation of the full list.
- **Prices:** The price categories given for each hotel are intended as a rough guide to what you can expect to pay, and are **based on average charges for two people staying in a double room with bathroom/ shower, inclusive of breakfast and Value-Added Tax** (*MWS* in German). You will find that in practice, charges for one person are not much cheaper.

Although actual prices will inevitably increase, our relative price categories are likely to remain the same.

Symbol	Category	Current price
/////	very expensive	more than DM 450
////	expensive	DM 350–450
///	moderate	DM 250–350
//	inexpensive	DM 150–250
/	cheap	under DM 150

Berlin hotels A to Z

ART-HOTEL SORAT

Joachimstaler Strasse 28–29, Charlottenburg, 10719 Berlin. Map **2***D4* *(030) 884470* *(030) 88447700* *75 rms* *U-Bahn to Kurfürstendamm.*

Location: Off Kurfürstendamm. A modern hotel, decorated with style and flair. Rooms are furnished with quirky, modern furniture and striking lithographs of Berlin. The works of art (including the metallic discus thrower on the hotel roof) were designed by the German artist Wolf Vostell, who earned notoriety in the Sixties for his subversive "happenings." The buffet breakfast offers a tempting range of breads, German cold meats, and even Japanese dishes. A personal favorite of the author.

ASKANISCHER HOF

Kurfürstendamm 53, 10707 Berlin. Map **1***D3* *(030) 8818033* *(030) 8817206* *17 rms* *U-Bahn to Uhlandstrasse or S-Bahn to Savignyplatz.*

Location: In the heart of Charlottenburg, near theaters and cinemas. Franz Kafka stayed in Berlin in 1914 at a hotel called the Askanischer Hof. It was there that he broke off his engagement to Felice Bauer, a few days after the assassination of the Archduke Ferdinand and his wife at Sarajevo. The building has long since gone, but this postwar hotel has kept up the name. The Askanischer Hof also retains something of the atmosphere of Old Berlin, with its breakfast room filled with evocative furniture and photographs. The bedrooms have an old-fashioned charm, each with its own random collection of furniture: an antique desk in one room, a potted fern in another. The bathrooms are modern, and offer small extras such as a free toothbrush. This is not an unduly expensive hotel, and a copious buffet breakfast is included in the price.

BERLIN HILTON

Mohrenstrasse 30, 10117 Berlin. Map **4***C8* *(030) 23820* *(030) 23824269* *505 rms* *U-Bahn to Stadtmitte.*

Location: Facing the Gendarmenmarkt, 5 minutes' stroll from Unter den Linden. The Berlin Hilton stands on a beautiful square in the heart of historic Berlin. Formerly the Domhotel, it was built by the East German government in a style that harmonizes with the noble architecture around. Compared to the modest exterior, the lobby seems unexpectedly grand, with an opera-house-style flight of stairs, and cascading greenery. The Hilton has no less than six restaurants under one roof, which is something of a blessing in an area where good places to eat are still a rarity. Among the choices are international *nouvelle cuisine* at **La Coupole**, regional dishes at **Mark Brandenburg**, or a sandwich in the **Wintergarten**. The choice of drinking dens is almost as varied: one, furnished like an English club, has bookshelves and a blazing fire; another has the mood of a rustic German beer cellar. The hotel pool is large enough for a serious swim, and the Tiergarten is nearby, for an early-morning run. There are ten attractive meeting rooms of varying sizes available to business users. Located close to the new center of German government, as well as to the treasures on Museumsinsel and Unter den Linden, this could become the best-sited hotel in the city within a few years.

BRANDENBURGER HOF

Eislebener Strasse 14, 10789 Berlin. Map **2***D4* *(030) 214050* *(030) 21405100* *to* *88 rms* *U-Bahn to Augsburgerstrasse.*

Location: In a quiet street 5 minutes' walk from Kurfürstendamm. Those looking for the grandeur of Old Berlin will find it here. Located in a handsome, turn-of-the-century mansion, this hotel preserves a hint of Wilhelmine Berlin. Rooms are bright and spacious, some with balconies, others with bay windows. There is an elegant winter garden in the glass-roofed courtyard, which provides the setting for the occasional concert, art exhibition or auction.

BRISTOL KEMPINSKI BERLIN

*Kurfürstendamm 27, Charlottenburg, 10719 Berlin. Map **2**D4 (030) 884340 (030) 8836075 to 325 rms U-Bahn to Kurfürstendamm.*

Location: On the smartest stretch of Kurfürstendamm. The rounded modern facade of the Kempinski is one of the landmarks on Kurfürstendamm. Built in 1952, the hotel was named after the prewar Kempinski Haus Vaterland on Potsdamer Platz. This legendary establishment, run by Berthold Kempinski and his wife, had contained a ballroom, numerous restaurants and two hotels. The interior of its successor is tastefully decorated with antique furniture, and guests have the run of three restaurants, a hairdresser, an indoor pool, sauna and gym.

CURATOR

*Grolmanstrasse 41–43, Charlottenburg, 10623 Berlin. Map **2**D4 (030) 884260 (030) 88426500 to 100 rms U-Bahn to Uhlandstrasse, S-Bahn to Savignyplatz.*

Location: Off Kurfürstendamm. A well-designed, modern hotel situated in a leafy street off the fashionable stretch of Kurfürstendamm. You can breakfast outdoors in the summer, or bask on the roof terrace seven floors above the street. There is also a sauna where you can lose some of the pounds put on in the nearby German restaurants. The Curator is in the heart of an increasingly attractive neighborhood of stylish boutiques and cosmopolitan cafés, while Savignyplatz S-Bahn station is convenient for getting to the ICC and Mitte.

FORSTHAUS PAULSBORN

*Am Grunewaldsee, Zehlendorf, 14195 Berlin. Map **5**D3 (030) 8141156 to 11 rms (closed Mon) Taxi, or bus 115 to Pücklerstrasse, then a 10-minute walk through the woods.*

Location: In the forest, to the sw of central Berlin. This attractive hotel is located in the depths of the Grunewald, not far from the Jagdschloss Grunewald. Ideally situated for long rambles in the forest, but rather far from the main sights. The hotel has a rustic restaurant, closed on Monday.

FORSTHAUS AN DER HUBERTUSBRÜCKE

*Stölpchenweg 45, Wannsee, 14109 Berlin. Map **5**F2 (030) 8053054 (030) 8053524 22 rms Bus 118 to Hubertusbrücke.*

Location: On a lakeside on the sw edge of the city. This is a small, family-run hotel for those who want to escape from the city. It stands on the edge of the Berliner Forst overlooking a small lake. In summer, steamers bound for Potsdam occasionally sail past the hotel garden. Bedrooms are bright and elegant, with balconies overflowing with geraniums. The hotel is well located for walks in the woods or along the lakeside. The sights of the Wannsee, Klein-Glienicke and Potsdam are also nearby. A car would be useful, although not absolutely essential.

GRAND HOTEL ESPLANADE

*Lützowufer 15, 10785 Berlin. Map **3**D6 (030) 261011 (030) 2651171 402 rms Bus 106, 129, 219, 341 to Lützowplatz.*

Location: On the Landwehrkanal, a few minutes on foot from the Tiergarten. This new and stylish hotel near the Neue Nationalgalerie has invested heavily in modern art and high-tech decor. The corridors and bars are dotted with zany contemporary sculptures and stylish metal spotlamps. The bedrooms are more muted, with the emphasis more on comfortable beds, elegant furniture and all the necessary accessories. Those facing the canal often have interesting views of the Bauhaus-Archiv and the Tiergarten, and the hotel also has a medium-sized river boat. Breakfast at the Esplanade is an impressive feast even by Berlin standards. For business users, there are eight conference rooms ranging from a 450-seater hall to an intimate library seating just 30.

INTER-CONTINENTAL BERLIN

Budapester Strasse 2, Charlottenburg, 10787 Berlin. Map **2**D5 ☎(030) 26020 Fx(030) 260280760 582 rms Bus 109 to Budapester Strasse; U-Bahn to Wittenbergplatz.

Location: In central Berlin, near the zoo. A large modern hotel on the edge of the Zoologischer Garten, with airy and comfortable rooms (some with a view of the captive zebras). The hotel boasts excellent fitness facilities including a gym, sauna and a large swimming pool overlooking a garden. You can jog and rent boats in the Tiergarten, a 5-minute walk away.

The **Brasserie** offers Berlin specialities, while the old-style restaurant ZUM HUGENOTTEN sets the right tone for a serious business lunch. You can meet for drinks in the mock wood-paneled country inn, or sit by an open fire in the rooftop bar, watching the neon lights winking on Breitscheidplatz. A good base for a serious business trip, the Inter-Continental boasts a very well-equipped business center (see BUSINESS IN BERLIN and CONFERENCES on page 63). The airport bus stops at the hotel door, but the U-Bahn is a good 10-minute walk away.

KRONPRINZ

Kronprinzendamm 1, Wilmersdorf, 10711 Berlin. Map **1**E1 ☎(030) 896030 Fx(030) 8931215 53 rms Bus 104, 105, 110, 119, 129, 219 to Henriettenplatz.

Location: At the W end of Kurfürstendamm. An attractive, family-run hotel in a large Old Berlin mansion that dates from 1894. There is a small garden sometimes used for sculpture exhibitions. Rooms are comfortable, and some have balconies where you can sit out on summer evenings. The hotel is located in a quiet street, not far from Schloss Charlottenburg, the Grunewald and the ICC conference center.

MARITIM GRAND HOTEL

Friedrichstrasse 158–164, Mitte, 10117 Berlin. Map **4**C8 ☎(030) 23270 Fx(030) 23273362 350 rms U-Bahn to Stadtmitte, S-Bahn to Friedrichstrasse.

Location: In the heart of historic Berlin. Dominating the corner of Unter den Linden and Friedrichstrasse, the Grand Hotel was built by the East Germans in 1987. With its airy, fern-filled lobby and sweeping staircase, the hotel attempts to evoke a sense of prewar comfort and *Jugendstil* grandeur, although the service tends to be rather dour. Rooms are tastefully furnished in Old Berlin style, and there are several theme suites for those who would like to imagine themselves in the role of Frederick the Great or Wilhelm von Humboldt. The hotel boasts a spacious swimming pool, a gym and three restaurants. Although ideally located for strolling to the Museumsinsel, the hotel is in a neighborhood that does not swarm with activity after dark. But in a few years, Unter den Linden may well be *the* place to stay.

MEINEKE

Meinekestrasse 10, 10719 Berlin. Map **2**D4 ☎(030) 882811 or 8834063 to 68 rms U-Bahn to Kurfürstendamm.

Location: Off Kurfürstendamm, in the midst of shops and restaurants. A small, family-run hotel occupying an Old Berlin house in a quiet street off Kurfürstendamm. Rooms are spacious and elegantly furnished.

MONDIAL

Kurfürstendamm 47, 10707 Berlin. Map **1**D3 ☎(030) 884110 Fx(030) 88411150 to 75 rms U-Bahn to Uhlandstrasse, S-Bahn to Savignyplatz.

Location: Central Berlin, near theaters and restaurants. A friendly hotel on Kurfürstendamm where you can recover totally from the city's hectic pace. Rooms are comfortably furnished, and there is a small swimming pool with a gym and medicinal baths. Conference facilities are also available. This is one of a very small number of hotels in Berlin equipped to accommodate disabled visitors.

NOVA
*Weitlingstrasse 15, 10317 Berlin. Map **7**D6 (030) 5252466 (030) 5252432 33 rms U-Bahn or S-Bahn to Lichtenberg.*
Location: In a suburb of eastern Berlin. This is a modern hotel for the budget traveler. The rooms are simply furnished, but comfortable. Some travelers may find the location unduly far from the bright lights of Ku'damm, but other, more adventurous souls may appreciate the location in the heart of the east, close to Treptower Park and Köpenick.

RADISSON PLAZA HOTEL BERLIN
*Karl-Liebknecht-Strasse 5, 10178 Berlin. Map **4**B9 (030) 23828 (030) 23827590 600 rms U-Bahn or S-Bahn to Alexanderplatz.*
Location: On the Spree, a 5-minute walk from the Museumsinsel. This was the Palasthotel when the communists ran East Berlin. The Radisson group has pumped in millions of dollars to smarten up the decor and train the staff in customer service. The bedrooms are tastefully styled, and the restaurant looks inviting. The hotel has everything you need to keep fit, including a big pool looking out on the garden. Ask for a bedroom on the Spree side, for a spectacular view of the restored Dom.

RESIDENZ
*Meinekestrasse 9, 10719 Berlin. Map **2**D4 (030) 884430 (030) 8824726 88 rms U-Bahn to Kurfürstendamm.*
Location: Off Kurfürstendamm. This is a friendly hotel for travelers who want to savor the grandeur of Old Berlin. You stay in a white mansion laden with heavy balconies and Classical details. The lobby is grand, and most bedrooms have lofty stucco ceilings and big windows. The Residenz is in an ideal location for dancing and dining out in Kreuzberg, and its prices are low for this quarter.

RIEHMERS HOFGARTEN
*Yorckstrasse 83, Kreuzberg, 10965 Berlin. Map **3**E7 (030) 781011 (030) 7866059 to 21 rms U-Bahn or bus 119 to Mehringdamm.*
Location: In a smart part of Kreuzberg. In a handsome Old Berlin mansion overlooking a leafy avenue near the Viktoriapark, this small hotel is part of a residential complex designed in 1881–1900 by Wilhelm Riehmer. The rooms have a spacious elegance, with such useful gadgets as a trouser-press. This is a fine base for exploring Kreuzberg and Mitte.

SCHLOSSPARK
*Heubnerweg 2a, 14059 Berlin. Map **1**B2 (030) 3224061 (030) 3258861 39 rms Bus 204 to Mollwitzstrasse.*
Location: In a quiet street, two minutes' walk from Schloss Charlottenburg. A small, modern hotel with a leafy garden and an indoor swimming pool. The bedrooms are spacious and tranquil, some with balconies overlooking the Schlosspark. Breakfast consists of a substantial spread of cold meats and cheeses served in a rustic restaurant. The hotel is within walking distance of Schloss Charlottenburg, and a short taxi ride from Tegel airport or the Messegelände exhibition center. However, the journey into central Berlin by public transport can take some time.

SEEHOF
*Lietzensee Ufer, Charlottenburg, 14057 Berlin. Map **1**C2 (030) 320020 (030) 32002251 78 rms U-Bahn to Sophie-Charlotte-Platz, or bus 110 to Kuno-Fischer-Strasse.*
Location: Overlooking a lake at the W end of Kurfürstendamm. This comfortable, quiet, modern hotel on the shores of the Lietzensee is popular with musicians performing in Berlin. Bedrooms are furnished with elegance; most have a view of the lake. The well-designed swimming pool is generous in size, with large windows looking out onto the park.

The hotel is a 10-minute walk from the ICC conference center, and Savignyplatz is easily reached by bus.

SORAT HOTEL HUMBOLDT-MÜHLE
An der Mühle 5–9, Tegel, 13507 Berlin. Map ***5****B3 ☎(030) 439040 Fx(030) 43904444 107 rms*
U-Bahn to Tegel.
Location: On an inlet of the Tegeler See in NW *Berlin.* An unusual and striking hotel located in a converted grain warehouse on the waterfront in Tegel. Opened a few years ago, the hotel offers well-equipped and tastefully decorated bedrooms (some with waterfront views). The hotel has a fitness center and sauna, and you can look forward to an ample Continental breakfast. The particular attraction of the Humboldt-Mühle is its almost rural setting. You have a lake nearby with a long sandy beach, and extensive woods where you can ramble or run (see TEGEL on page 149 for other sights in the neighborhood). The hotel has some sturdy bikes for rent if you want to explore the woods. You can also hire a private yacht, 10-seater Chevrolet van, Harley-Davidson bike, or a mean red Ferrari. Parents can keep children amused at the nearby lakeside park and beach, or take the steamer from Greenwichpromenade to Wannsee. A 5-minute taxi ride gets you to Tegel airport, while Kurfürstendamm is about 30 minutes away by U-Bahn.

STEIGENBERGER BERLIN
Los-Angeles-Platz 1, Charlottenburg, 10789 Berlin. Map ***2****D4 ☎(030) 21080 Fx(030) 2108117 397 rms U-Bahn to Kurfürstendamm.*
Location: Off Kurfürstendamm. A low-rise, modern hotel with a grand reception lobby and elegant rooms, facing a small park near Kurfürstendamm. The hotel has a sauna and an attractive circular swimming pool that looks out over a leafy courtyard. The wood-paneled **Berliner Stube** restaurant serves local specialities, while the more elegant **Park-Restaurant** offers well-prepared modern cuisine. Guests have the opportunity to borrow Siemens portable computers as well as software for use in their rooms.

VILLA TOSCANA
Bahnhofstrasse 19, 12207 Berlin. Map ***6****E4 ☎(030) 7723961 Fx(030) 7734488 15 rms*
U-Bahn to Rathaus Steglitz, then 10mins by bus 180 or 186 to Bahnhofstrasse.
Location: In a suburban street in SW *Berlin.* This small hotel is located in an elegant villa with an idyllic Italianate garden. The bedrooms are comfortable and bright, although the bathrooms tend to be rather small. The leafy garden, filled with statues and fountains, is evocative of Tuscany. One disadvantage of this suburban retreat, although only a minor one, is that it can take some time to travel to central Berlin by public transport. You may not find many good restaurants in the neighborhood, although one solution to this would be to reserve one of the apartments that has a kitchen.

Eating and drinking in Berlin

WHAT TO EAT

Don't expect an abundance of sophisticated restaurants. The Berliner tends to like regional food, well-cooked but simple. You can look forward to eating Berlin specialities such as *Eisbein* (boiled knuckle of pork) served with sauerkraut, or *Boulette* (cold hamburger). *Schweinefleisch* (pork) is the main meat served in German restaurants, but you might balance your diet by ordering the occasional Havel trout or North Sea fish.

Dishes labeled *Berliner Art* should be treated cautiously, as Berliners sometimes have a rather strange art with cooking. When a restaurant advertises *burgerliche Küche,* take it as a warning not to expect anything refined. Many of the country inns on the shores of the Havel or the Grunewald lakes fall into this category; you go there to appreciate the rural setting or the amiable atmosphere rather than the cuisine.

Much of the best cooking in Berlin currently goes on in the kitchens of Italian restaurants. Some offer old-fashioned Italian pasta dishes, while others prepare the more refined meat-and-sauce inventions of the northern cities. Young, sophisticated Berliners adore Italian food, and many modern café menus will feature pasta dishes rather than heavy German food.

See also CAFÉ TERRACES, ICE CREAM BARS and FAST-FOOD STALLS on page 176.

WHERE TO EAT

Berliners have always been impressed by spectacular restaurants. They flocked in the 1920s to the Haus Vaterland on Potsdamer Platz, where they could sample various national cuisines in *ersatz* settings, or sit on a mock terrace overlooking a Rhine panorama, where the big attraction was an artificial thunderstorm staged every hour. Haus Vaterland has gone, but Berliners can still eat in exotic settings such as the mock tropical island in the EUROPA-CENTER, or the spacious Wintergarten on the top floor of the KADEWE department store.

The business lunch is not a Berlin tradition, and most good restaurants, including those in major hotels, open only for dinner. Exceptions are the out-of-town ROCKENDORF'S, ZUM HUGENOTTEN at the INTER-CONTINENTAL BERLIN, and ANSELMO, which is close to the ICC conference center.

Eating out in former East Berlin is still a risky undertaking unless you have a reliable recommendation. Some restaurants E of the Brandenburg Gate have improved since reunification, but others leave much to be desired in their standards of cooking and service. Many of those living in eastern Berlin prefer *Imbiss* stands to restaurants; cheapness is the most important factor.

The eating habits of four decades will not change overnight, and the most sophisticated cooking is still found in the west.

RESERVING A TABLE

You can just turn up at a restaurant and ask if they have a table free, but the chances are that the best restaurants in town will be fully booked. It generally pays to call ahead, especially if a long journey is involved. This not only secures a table, but confirms that the establishment is still in business. Restaurants in any city can go bust, or move location, or close for vacations. It's a risky business, especially in Berlin, where rents are now soaring and fashionable folk are abandoning old haunts.

When you call, ask whether payment by charge or credit card is accepted. Restaurants in Berlin often only accept Eurocheques or cash. And don't forget to cancel your reservation if you decide not to go. Restaurants need all the help they can get to stay in business.

HOW TO USE THIS CHAPTER

- **Location:** Each entry shows the nearest U-Bahn or S-Bahn stations or other transport details. Map references are given for the color maps at the back of the book.
- **Symbols:** The symbols show price categories and credit cards. See the KEY TO SYMBOLS on page 7 for an explanation of the full list.
- **Times:** Times are specified when restaurants are **closed**.
- **Tipping:** In restaurants and cafés in Germany, service charges are almost invariably included in the bill, although it is customary to round up the sum to the nearest DM.
- **Prices:** The price categories given for each restaurant are intended as a rough guide to what you can expect to pay. They are **based on the approximate cost of a meal for one person, inclusive of wine, Value-Added Tax** (*MWS* in German) **and service**.

Although actual prices will inevitably increase, our relative price categories are likely to remain the same.

Symbol	Category	Current price
[IIIII]	very expensive	more than DM 100
[IIII]	expensive	DM 80–100
[III]	moderate	DM 60–80
[II]	inexpensive	DM 40–60
[I]	cheap	under DM 40

Berlin restaurants A to Z

ALFONS ***Italian***
Wilmersdorfer Strasse 79, Charlottenburg. Map ***1****D3 ☎(030) 3242282 [II] [AE] [DC] [MC] [VISA] Closed Mon, lunch. U-Bahn to Adenauerplatz.*

A spacious, modern Italian restaurant decked with chrome and mirrors. Chef Alfons Brosius offers a varied menu, with both traditional regional cooking and modern Italian dishes.

ALTER KRUG ***Traditional German***
Königin-Luise-Strasse 52, Dahlem. Map ***5****E3 ☎(030) 8325089 [II] to [III] [car] [AE] [DC] [MC] [VISA] [garden] Closed Thurs. U-Bahn to Dahlem-Dorf.*

This restored 19thC country inn with ocher walls stands in an almost rural setting opposite the old village church of Dahlem. Tastefully furnished with antiques, it offers traditional northern German cooking, but with a few unusual choices, such as deer and pheasant. The wines come mainly from German vineyards. The rambling garden at the back is popular with everyone from elderly professors' wives to local students.

ALT LUXEMBURG ***Sophisticated German***
Windscheidstrasse 31, Charlottenburg. Map ***1****C2 ☎(030) 3238730 [IIII] to [IIIII] [DC] [VISA] Closed Sun, Mon, lunch. U-Bahn to Sophie-Charlotte-Platz, then a 5-min walk.*

A comfortable, old-fashioned restaurant, with mirrors, chandeliers and paintings to lend an air of elegance. The chef fastidiously prepares daring dishes such as catfish in curry sauce or breast of guinea-fowl. Reservations are advisable.

ANSELMO ***Italian***
Damaschkestrasse 17, Wilmersdorf. Map ***1****D2 ☎(030) 3233094 [II] to [III] Open noon–midnight; closed Mon. Bus 110 or*

204 to Holtzendorffplatz; S-Bahn to Charlottenburg.
Anselmo Bufacchi's modern Italian restaurant is one of the few in Berlin where you can eat throughout the day. The cooking is classical Italian, with dishes such as quail with olives, or breast of duck simmered in dark, sweet Marsala wine. The wide choice of fish dishes includes sole with salmon in white wine.

BAMBERGER REITER ***Austrian***
Regensburgerstrasse 7, Schöneberg. Map ***2****E5 ☎(030) 244282 ▥ No cards. Closed Sun, Mon, lunch, first 2wks Jan and first 2wks Aug. U-Bahn to Viktoria-Luise-Platz.*
Franz Raneburger's sophisticated cuisine combines traditional recipes from his native Tirol with the best elements of *nouvelle cuisine.* Whether the dish is goose liver served in pastry, or almond soufflé with fruits, Raneburger prepares the finest ingredients with consistency and flair. The handsome rustic interior is decorated with antiques, and you can linger over brandies until long after midnight. Reservations a must.

BLOCKHAUS NIKOLSKOE ***Traditional German***
Nikolskoer Weg, Wannsee. Map ***5****E2 ☎(030) 8052914 ▭ No cards Closed Thurs. Bus 216 from S-Bahnhof Wannsee.*
The Blockhaus Nikolskoe is just the sort of eating place that Berliners hope to find after a brisk walk through the forest. Perched on a hill above the Havel, the restaurant occupies an imitation Russian log cabin in the Düppel woods. This curious edifice was built by the sentimental Friedrich Wilhelm III for his daughter, Charlotte, who married Czar Nicholas I. With its ornate balconies laden with geraniums, it still has a hint of old Russia, although the red and white cloths add a Bavarian feel.

The solid, North German style of cooking is better than in many restaurants dotted along the Havel shore. Try the homemade *Eisbeinsülze* (pork in jelly), washed down with a glass of Charlottenburger Pilsner. For those who have seen enough pork in Berlin, there is trout or *Matjes* (Dutch cured herring) on the menu. The waiters are polite, if rather solemn. Should the weather be mild, you can sit out on a terrace for a superb view of the Havel.

BRECHT-KELLER ***Traditional Viennese***
Basement of the Brecht-Weigel-Haus, Chausseestrasse 125, Mitte. Map ***3****A7 ☎(030) 2823843 ▭ No cards. Closed lunch. U-Bahn to Oranienburger Tor.*
This intimate restaurant is tucked away in the cellar of Brecht's former home. The two rooms are decorated in the style of an old student *Kneipe,* with solid wooden tables, heavy metal lamps, and candles flickering in dark alcoves. The walls are crammed with Brechtian memorabilia, including framed photographs faded with age, miniature stage sets lit from within, and even an old guitar. The cooking is based on Viennese recipes served to Brecht by his actress wife Helene Weigel. You can try her onion soup, followed by beef stew cooked in beer, served with homemade noodles. The house beer is Berliner Bürgerbräu, a well-made *pils* brewed in Friedrichshagen. The wines come from France, Italy and California.

LE BUFFET ***Traditional German***
KaDeWe, Tauentzienstrasse 21–24 (7th floor). Map ***2****D5 ▭ Open Mon–Fri 9am–6.30pm, Sat 9am–2pm; closed Sun. U-Bahn to Wittenbergplatz.*
The KADEWE department store recently opened a big new restaurant to woo Berliners. Located one floor above the famous gourmet-delicatessen floor, the FEINSCHMECKERETAGE (see separate entry), the restaurant sets out to re-create the atmosphere of a 19thC winter garden. A vaulted iron-and-glass roof extends over most of the top floor, with striking modern lighting adding to the effect. You can eat under a pergola, beside a fountain, or next to a big arched window looking down on the rooftops of Charlottenburg. The restaurant is self-service, with just about everything the Berlin gourmet might need, including pork cutlets, *Wurst,* Scandinavian Smørrebrød, salads, cakes and Berlin-

style donuts. It makes a good stop for lunch, and there's plenty of room for kids to roam around. But remember that doors close at 6.30pm sharp.

ERMELERHAUS ***Traditional German***
Märkisches Ufer 10–12, Mitte. Map ***4C9*** *☎(030) 2794028 ▭ No cards. U-Bahn to Spittelmarkt.*
When hunger strikes on a stroll through Mitte, you might try one of the restaurants in the Ermelerhaus, a pale yellow Neoclassical mansion on the Spree waterfront. Built by a Berlin coffee merchant in 1808, it is decorated with friezes illustrating the owner's trade. The **Raabediele** restaurant in the cellar is done out in German farmhouse style, with pine walls and painted chairs. Friendly and relaxed, it offers warming North German winter cooking, such as *Berliner Kohl-roulade mit Speckwickel* (pork wrapped in cabbage with bacon), or unwieldy hunks of *Eisbein*. The building also houses an elegant **Weinrestaurant** *(☎(030) 2755103 ▭)* at the top of a grand Baroque staircase, and a café on the ground floor.

FIORETTO IM CARMER'S ***Italian***
Carmerstrasse 2, Charlottenburg. Map ***2C4*** *☎(030) 3123115 ▭ to ▭ AE VISA Closed Sat lunch, Sun. S-Bahn to Savignyplatz, U-Bahn to Ernst-Reuter-Platz.*
Before the Wall came down, Fioretto was one of the culinary landmarks of East Berlin. Foreign diplomats in need of good food would regularly brave the bumpy streets of Köpenick in search of this restaurant. But *die Wende* has filled chef Doris Burneleit with *Wanderlust,* and she has moved from shabby Köpenick to prosperous Charlottenburg. Her new restaurant is elegant and spacious, and the Italian cuisine is as delicious as ever. But something of the old magic has gone, and the restaurant is now just one among many good Italian establishments in the neighborhood.

FOFI'S ESTIATORIO ***Greek***
Fasanenstrasse 70, Charlottenburg. Map ***2D4*** *☎(030) 8818785 ▭ No cards Closed lunch. U-Bahn to Uhlandstrasse.*
A bustling, informal Greek restaurant, with polished wooden floors, and white walls hung with vibrant abstract paintings. It is perhaps the Mediterranean atmosphere, rather than the plain Greek-style cooking, that draws Berlin artists and businessmen here. It is certainly fascinating to watch as the waiters dash around recklessly with tureens of cream of scampi soup or plates of bubbling moussaka. Fofi's attracts a fashionable crowd all year, especially on summer evenings, when the terrace is always full.

FRANZÖSISCHER HOF ***French***
Jägerstrasse 56 (at the Gendarmenmarkt), Mitte. Map ***4C8*** *☎(030) 2293969 ▭ to ▭ AE CB MC VISA U-Bahn to Französischer Strasse.*
This is an attempt to create a grand restaurant in the historic heart of Berlin. It has the sort of trappings you expect to find in the palaces of minor European royalty, including sweeping staircases, marble statues and potted ferns. The restaurant even has a cloakroom. The window tables have a good view of the restored grandeur of Gendarmenmarkt. You can eat a reasonable meal here, based on upmarket French cuisine, or simply stop in the afternoon for coffee and *Apfelstrudel*. The service remains as stiff as it was in the days when the State ran the restaurants, although this may change with time.

HARDTKE ***Traditional German***
Meinekestrasse 27–27b, Charlottenburg. Map ***2D4*** *☎(030) 8819827 ▭ No cards. Open daily 9.30am–midnight. U-Bahn to Uhlandstrasse.*
An Old Berlin restaurant just off Kurfürstendamm, decorated in rustic style with heavy wooden tables and antique lamps. This is the place to go for hearty Berlin specialities such as *Boulette* and *Eisbein*. Hardtke is enormously proud of its homemade *Wurst* (sausage), prepared according to traditional methods.

KADEWE FEINSCHMECKERETAGE
Traditional German
KaDeWe, Tauentzienstrasse 21–24 (6th floor). Map ***2D5*** *▭ to ▭ Open Mon–Fri*

9am–6.30pm, Sat 9am–2pm; closed Sun. U-Bahn to Wittenbergplatz.

Even the most sophisticated Berliners love to perch at the crowded counters in KaDeWe's huge delicatessen department to sample the *Feinschmecker* (gourmet) dishes. A rather noisy crowd gathers around the beer pump, while smart executives congregate after work at the champagne bar. The atmosphere is informal, like a good beer garden, but the food far superior. One stand (**Le Nôtre**) offers coffee, *croissant* and *brioche* for breakfast *(9am-11am)* or rich *Heidelbeeretorte* (bilberry tart) to bolster your strength mid-afternoon. A sausage counter sells plump *Münchener Weisswurst* to expatriate Bavarians requiring their traditional mid-morning snack. Those wanting to try genuine Berlin food can start at the soup counter with a bowl of *Erbsensuppe* (thick pea) or *Kartoffelsuppe* (potato), then wander across to the **Zum Hackepeter** kitchen, which doles out *Eisbein mit Sauerkraut, Bouletten* (cold hamburgers), *Kartoffelsalat* (potato salad) and *Lübars Landschinken* (Lübars country ham), washed down with a glass of *Berliner Weisse.* To complete the Berlin eating experience, try a *Kartoffelpuffer mit Apfelmus* (potato pancake with apple sauce) at the **Kartoffelacker** counter.

Sitting at the fish counter (which has a view of the Gedächtniskirche), you can sample *Rotbarschfilet* (fillet of red perch), served with a glass of 1987 Riesling Kabinett. Or order half a dozen Sylt oysters with a glass of 1984 Riesling at the elegant **Austernbar** (oyster bar). Other counters offer Dutch raw herring served with a glass of Bremen-brewed Beck's beer, Normandy *crêpes* accompanied by French cider, or a selection of ice creams. The only drawback of this wonderful Berlin institution is that it all shuts down at 6.30pm sharp.

LUTTER & WEGNER ***Traditional German***

Schlüterstrasse 55, Charlottenburg. Map ***1****D3 ☎(030) 8813440 ▭ AE ⦿ ⦿ VISA Closed lunch. Bus 109 to Bleibtreustrasse or S-Bahn to Savignyplatz.*

A convivial Berlin *Weinstube* where the candles flicker until 3am. The wine bar was founded in 1811, although the wood-paneling and mottos in Old German Gothic script are not original. The cooking here has become more refined in recent years, and portions have dwindled somewhat. A good place to drop into for a light supper or a glass of wine.

MAHACHAI ***Thai***

Schlüterstrasse 60, Charlottenburg. Map ***1****D3 ☎(030) 310879 ▭ No cards. S-Bahn to Savignyplatz or bus* ***149*** *to Schlüterstrasse.*

A well-run Thai restaurant that is always crowded. The bamboo hut style of decor may not be to everyone's taste, but the cooking is excellent, with specialities such as crispy fried duck served with bamboo shoots and almonds. The service is efficient and friendly. Reserve ahead, unless you are prepared to perch on a bamboo bar stool.

MEINEKE X ***Traditional German***

Meinekestrasse 10, Charlottenburg. Map ***2****D4 ☎(030) 8823158 ▭ U-Bahn to Kurfürstendamm.*

A friendly, crowded Berlin restaurant just off Kurfürstendamm, with a sidewalk terrace, and attractively decorated with dark wooden furnishings, antique clocks and flickering candles. It offers solid, reliable German dishes daily from noon until 1am. Try *Leber "Berliner Art"* (liver garnished with sliced onion and apple).

MING'S GARDEN ***Chinese***

Tauentzienstrasse 16 (entrance around the corner at Marburger Strasse), Charlottenburg. Map ***2****D5 ☎(030) 2118728 ▭ No cards. U-Bahn to Kurfürstendamm.*

This is Chinese cooking at its best. Situated not far from Bahnhof Zoo, Ming's provides an unexpected haven of Oriental calm. It is a big and bustling place, but the interior is divided into compartments to create a sense of intimacy. The rich decor of red velvet, black wood and polished brass adds to the exotic allure. The menu draws on a broad range of Oriental recipes from Singapore, Mongolia, Canton and Szechuan. The *dim sum* arrives piping hot in a silver pot, and the "Chicken Ming's Garden" is prepared in a delicate caramelized sauce with beans and nuts. The staff is earnestly attentive. This is a good place to eat before catching a late train or a night flight: the cloakroom attendant will look after your suitcase.

PARIS BAR ***French***
Kantstrasse 152, Charlottenburg. Map ***2****D4* *☎(030) 3138052* ▥ *No cards. Closed Sun. Bus 149 to Uhlandstrasse.*
An attractive restaurant off Savignyplatz that emulates a Parisian Left Bank brasserie. Plain French cooking is served from noon until after midnight by waiters dressed in traditional long aprons. The straight rows of tables are covered with starched white cloths, while the yellowing walls are hung with Surreal art, including a bizarre painting with an overflowing ashtray and a dusty wine bottle glued to it. Paris Bar attracts an unusually broad range of customers, from radical artists dressed entirely in black to prim folk up from Bavaria. Solitary diners can come to eat here armed with a novel. Charge and credit cards are not accepted.

PEPPINO ***Italian***
Fasanenstrasse 65, Charlottenburg. Map ***2****D4* *☎(030) 8836722* ▥ AE *Closed Mon. U-Bahn to Uhlandstrasse.*
An intimate Italian restaurant with two small rooms and a covered terrace. The interior is furnished simply with white tablecloths and a few potted plants. Berliners like the traditional Italian cooking such as *Saltimbocca alla Romana.*

PONTE VECCHIO ***Italian***
Spielhagenstrasse 3, Charlottenburg. Map ***1****C2* *☎(030) 3421999* ▥ ◙ *Closed lunch. U-Bahn to Bismarckstrasse.*
Careful and creative Italian cooking based on the regional specialities of Tuscany. The decor is plain and old-fashioned by Berlin standards, but dishes such as skewered fillet of lamb or *ricotta* in zucchini flower provide more than enough visual excitement.

ROCKENDORF'S RESTAURANT
Sophisticated German ⏏
Düsterhauptstrasse 1, Waidmannslust. Map ***6****A4* *☎(030) 4023099* ▥ AE ◙ ◙ VISA
Closed Sun, Mon. S-Bahn to Waidmannslust, or bus 222 from U-Bahnhof Tegel. By taxi, allow about 20 mins from Kurfürstendamm.
Siegfried Rockendorf's restaurant is situated in an elegant villa in a quiet North Berlin suburb. Combining French style with the best German ingredients available, Rockendorf's creates exquisite dishes such as quail mousse with artichoke and truffle salad, or breast of wild duck with grated apple. Despite the remote location, the small restaurant is constantly full, so reservations are essential.

DIE SPINDEL ***Traditional German***
Bölschestrasse 51. Off map ***7****E7* *☎(030) 6452937* ▭ AE ◙ VISA *Closed Tues. S-Bahn to Friedrichshagen, then a 5-min walk down Bölschestrasse.*
This friendly little restaurant is one of the best to be found E of the Brandenburg Gate. It occupies an old inn with a pale green facade, on the main street of Friedrichshagen. You sit in one of three small rooms decorated with wood paneling, thick drapes and antique lamps. In the summer, a few tables are squeezed onto the terrace outside. The restaurant's strength is in preparing plain Berlin dishes such as *Berliner Kohlroulade* (minced beef wrapped in cabbage, cooked with salami and cream). The wine list features bottles from vineyards throughout Europe, but you might prefer to sample a beer from the Berliner Bürgerbräu brewery, which stands on the waterfront at the end of Friedrichshagen's main street. Local ladies in hats gather here at lunchtime to sample the good-value dish of the day *(Tagesangebot).* You can usually find a table for lunch, but it makes sense to reserve ahead for dinner, especially on weekends. Not a restaurant to go to specially for the food, but a pleasant place to stop if you are looking at FRIERICHSHAGEN's old architecture, or hiking along the shores of the nearby MÜGGELSEE.

TAVOLA CALDA ***Italian***
Leibnitzstrasse 45, Charlottenburg. Map ***1**D3 ☎(030) 3241048 ▭ No cards. S-Bahn to Savignyplatz.*
An intimate Italian restaurant off Savignyplatz, offering traditional Italian dishes with pasta and *scaloppine* (scallops). Decorated in a tasteful modern style, this is one of the few good restaurants in Berlin where you can meet for lunch.

TRIO ***Italian***
Klausenerplatz 14, Charlottenburg. Map ***1**B2 ☎(030) 3217782 ▭ to ▭ No cards. Closed Wed, Thurs, lunch. Bus 145 or 204 to Klausenerplatz.*
On a leafy square near Schloss Charlottenburg, Trio is an elegant restaurant, decorated with modern paintings hung on white walls. The handwritten menu (fiendishly difficult to read) features modern Italian dishes such as veal cutlets in mustard sauce. Worth reserving a day or so ahead.

TUCCI ***Italian***
Grolmanstrasse 52, Charlottenburg. Map ***2**C4 ☎(030) 3139335 ▭ to ▭ S-Bahn or bus 149 to Savignyplatz.*
A fashionable café-restaurant off Savignyplatz, with bare wooden floors, wiry black chairs and artificially aged walls. Run by friendly young Berliners, it offers simple, well-prepared Italian regional cooking, such as *pappardelle con ragù.* Tucci appeals especially to Berliners in their thirties, reminding them perhaps of lingering summers in Tuscany.

ZUM HUGENOTTEN ***French***
Hotel Inter-Continental Berlin, Budapester Strasse 2, Charlottenburg. Map ***2**D5 ☎(030) 26020 ▭ to ▭ AE ◫ ◫ VISA Last orders 11pm.*
With its wood-paneled walls and old paintings, the INTER-CONTINENTAL BERLIN'S elegant restaurant is an ideal location for a business lunch or a lingering dinner. Taking its name from the Huguenots who settled in Berlin in the 17thC, Zum Hugenotten offers fastidiously prepared French *nouvelle cuisine* dishes, together with a few specialities of the German kitchen. Some rare vintages have been maturing in the hotel's extensive wine cellar.

Cafés and fast food

Expressionist artists of the 1920s depicted Berlin cafés such as the Romanische (destroyed in 1943) as chaotic, somewhat seedy venues frequented by artists, prostitutes and businessmen. Almost all the legendary cafés were destroyed during World War II, but you may still find a hint of *fin-de-siècle* Berlin at the branch of CAFÉ MÖHRING at Kurfürstendamm 234.

Today's most exciting meeting places tend to be modern, cosmopolitan cafés off Savignyplatz or in Kreuzberg. Most of the cafés in Mitte and other former East Berlin districts retain the rather dreary imitation 19thC interiors of the communist era, with wooden furnishings and a few wilting ferns, although some have been revamped to fulfil Western demands. Those looking for fashionable, buzzing cafés should head to Prenzlauer Berg, to places such as **Kaffeestube** *(Husemannstrasse 6).*

BREAKFAST

Breakfast *(Frühstück)* is the meal that Berliners take most seriously. You can expect a generous buffet breakfast if staying in a large hotel. This will include various types of German bread and rolls, *croissants,* as well as cold ham and salami, cereals, muesli and even German pastries and cakes. Some hotels offer British-style bacon-and-egg breakfasts as well. Although most hotels include breakfast in the price of the room, you can still indulge in the Berlin custom of *Zweite Frühstück* (second breakfast) at a café, and many cafés in Berlin offer excellent breakfasts, not just in the morning but all day.

Open for early risers at 7am is CAFÉ MÖHRING *(corner of Kurfürstendamm and Uhlandstrasse),* but many fashionable cafés don't begin serving until 10am or later, while **Café Nolle** continues serving breakfast until 6pm. The restaurant **Fasanerie** *(Uhland-Passage, Charlottenburg, map* ***2****D4* AE ◐ ◉ VISA*)* lays on a vast buffet breakfast *(Mon-Sat 7.30am-noon, Sun 9am-1pm),* with smoked trout, salmon, cold meats and cheeses. Breakfast is served in an elegant winter garden filled with ferns, or on the terrace when the sun shines.

CAFÉ TERRACES

Berliners like to sit out on café terraces whenever the weather permits. The terrace of the **Mövenpick** on Breitscheidplatz is a popular place to bask in the sun, but it's hardly a peaceful spot. The OPERNCAFÉ terrace on Unter den Linden is likewise rather a noisy location.

For more restful cafés, head out of the city center. Some of the city parks have cafés with terraces. The romantic VIKTORIAPARK has a beer garden with a big terrace in summer. Elsewhere in Kreuzberg, several cafés on Paul-Linke-Ufer have canalside terraces overlooking the Landwehrkanal.

COFFEE AND CAKE

You might revisit a favorite café in the afternoon for *Kaffee und Kuchen* (coffee and cake). This admirable German habit is followed by young and old Berliners alike, and the chocolate cake to be had in austere Kreuzberg artists' cafés can sometimes prove even better than the *Kuchen* eaten by ladies at the KADEWE department store or CAFÉ MÖHRING.

ICE CREAM BARS

Ice cream bars once flourished in East Berlin, offering a whiff of Western decadence, although sadly they are more difficult to track down these days. Those that survive are often a touching last reminder of the innocent optimism of the socialism of the 1950s. You might be tempted to try the decadent ice cream sundaes at the **Milch-Mix-Eis-Mocca-Bar** *(Karl-Marx-Allee 35, Mitte),* a spacious modern milk bar, painted in pastel tints and filled with rampant greenery.

Delicious Häagen-Dazs ice cream is sold at a shop on Kurfürstendamm *(#224),* too small unfortunately to have space for tables and chairs.

FAST-FOOD STALLS

Berliners tend to pursue hurried lives that do not allow much time for eating. They like to crowd around informal street stalls to snatch a sausage and coffee. These stand-up stalls (called *Imbiss* or *Schnellimbiss*) offer different types of sausage, such as *Bratwurst* (fried sausage), *Bockwurst* (boiled sausage) or *Currywurst.*

Berliners are particularly lyrical about the sausage served at **Konnopke** *(under Eberswalder Strasse U-Bahn station, open daily 6.30am-7pm).* Located under a noisy viaduct in the heart of Prenzlauer Berg, Konnopke was opened in 1930 by Max Konnopke. During the communist era, his was one of only two sausage stalls in East Berlin. Now run by his daughter, Konnopke is the place to sample a Berlin *Currywurst*— a plump pork sausage sliced in half, served with a squirt of ketchup and a dusting of curry powder.

Even when indulging in gourmet food at the KADEWE, Berliners eat at a remarkable tempo. If you find yourself hit by a sudden craving, you can pick up a sandwich or cheese cake at the **Mini Bistro** *(in the ticket-hall at Wittenbergplatz U-Bahnhof)* before rushing off to catch the U-Bahn.

Berlin cafés A to Z

ADLER

Friedrichstrasse 206, Kreuzberg. Map ***4****D8.*
Open 10am–1am. U-Bahn to Kochstrasse.

This attractive café is located in a handsome Baroque building dating from 1735, near the site of Checkpoint Charlie. The café takes its name from an ancient Berlin pharmacy known as Zum Weissen Adler (At the White Eagle). Founded back in 1696, the pharmacist moved to this building in 1829. The business survived the war, but failed after the construction of the Wall in 1961.

The building, now fastidiously restored, contains a café that is popular with tourists who come in search of the Wall. They may find nothing left except for a museum, but Café Adler's cakes offer some consolation.

AEDES

Stadtbahnbogen 599, off Savignyplatz, Charlottenburg. Map ***2****D3.*

Situated in one of the brick arches under Savignyplatz S-Bahnhof, this modern café is popular with young bohemians. The café forms part of the Aedes architecture gallery (see ART GALLERIES on page 193) and the walls are crammed with utopian projects. Aedes is a good spot for quiet conversation in the evening, although the entire building shudders every time a train passes overhead. Open for breakfast.

DEPONIE

Georgenstrasse 5 (look for it in the arches of the S-Bahn viaduct), Mitte. Map ***4****B8.*
Open Mon–Fri 9am–late; Sat, Sun 10am–late. S-Bahn or U-Bahn to Friedrichstrasse.

A fashionable new café built into the arches of the S-Bahn. The décor evokes the cafés of Old Berlin, with bare wooden tables and metal coat racks salvaged from flea markets. The atmosphere is relaxed and friendly, especially on jazz concert nights.

EINSTEIN STADTCAFÉ

Kurfürstenstrasse 58, Tiergarten. Map ***3****D6*
☎(030) 2615096 ❀ U-Bahn to Nollendorfplatz.

A vast café situated in an Old Berlin villa that was once the home of a star of the silver screen, Einstein has the faded elegance of a Viennese coffee house, with its huge mirrors, plump sofas and marble-topped tables. Serious, fashionable Berliners wearing the maximum of black clothing come here to drink coffee, read the newspapers and feast on the moist, delicious *Apfelstrudel.* The geranium-filled garden at the back is the perfect place to while away a summer afternoon in the city, and the restaurant *(same ☎ ▯ AE ◎ ● VISA)* stays open until 2am. There are occasional piano concerts and literary readings.

HARDENBERG

*Hardenbergstrasse 10, Charlottenburg. Map **2**C4. U-Bahn to Ernst-Reuter-Platz.*

A spacious café on the ground floor of an old mansion, popular with students and travelers of every nationality. A good place for breakfast or a last drink before you depart from Berlin on the night train.

KRANZLER

*Kurfürstendamm 18, Charlottenburg. Map **2**D4 ☎(030) 8826911. Open 8am–midnight. U-Bahn to Kurfürstendamm.*

Like CAFÉ MÖHRING, the Kranzler was one of the great cafés of prewar Berlin. It was rebuilt in the 1950s in a jaunty modern style, with a round pavilion on the roof and striped awnings covering the pavement terrace. German tourists flock here in search of Old Berlin ambience, but most find to their chagrin that it has fled, leaving just cakes and memories.

LEYSIEFFER

*Kurfürstendamm 218, Charlottenburg. Map **2**D4. Open Mon–Sat 9am–10pm, Sun 10am–10pm. U-Bahn to Uhlandstrasse.*

A delicatessen and café situated in an 1897 building that once housed the Chinese embassy. With its stucco ceilings and ornate wood-paneling, the first-floor café is one of the few relics of Old Berlin still standing on Kurfürstendamm. Order a breakfast of *croissants* with honey and jam, or a pastry and coffee, and you can perch at the bay window table to watch the street life of Berlin teeming below.

MOCCA-MILCH-EIS-BAR

*Karl-Marx-Allee 35, Mitte. Map **6**C6.*

Situated on a spectacular boulevard built in the socialist era, this coffee bar and ice cream shop is a marvelous relic of the 1950s. The huge glass walls and curving mezzanine floor symbolize the mood of confidence in East Berlin society before the Soviet tanks rolled in. Painted pink and filled with plants, coffee bars such as this one were where young East Berliners once came to have some innocent fun.

MÖHRING

*Kurfürstendamm 234, Charlottenburg. Map **2**D4. Open 7am–midnight. U-Bahn to Kurfürstendamm.*

Situated near the Gedächtniskirche, Möhring evokes the atmosphere of Old Berlin, with its spacious Neoclassical interior decorated with nostalgic photographs of Kurfürstendamm in the 1930s. The first Café Möhring — opened on the Kurfürstendamm in 1898 — was destroyed in World War II. There are now four successors to choose from, although this branch is the most authentic. An elegant spot for breakfast *(from 9am)* or *Kaffee und Kuchen* (coffee and cake).

MÖHRING

*Kurfürstendamm 213, (at Uhlandstrasse) Charlottenburg. Map **2**D4. Open 7am–10pm. U-Bahn to Uhlandstrasse.*

Rebuilt on the site of the famous Berlin café frequented by Maxim Gorki, this branch of Möhring serves five different types of breakfast. The *kleines Frühstück* is enough to sustain most people, while the *Berliner Frühstück* is best left to Berliners — unless you seriously want to start the day with *Solei* (pickled egg).

OPERNCAFÉ

*Unter den Linden 5, Mitte. Map **4**C8. Open daily 11am–midnight. S-Bahn to Hackescher Markt.*

West Berlin ladies dressed in furs and hats are slowly finding their way across town to Unter den Linden. The old haunts of the rich have gone, but the ladies are content to settle into the comfort of the Operncafé. This grand café is situated in the Kronprinzenpalais, where the young Frederick the Great once lived. The unfriendly chill of State control still hangs around the building, but the coffee and cakes are as good as most on Kurfürstendamm. In addition to the café, the building contains two restaurants and a disco.

OREN

*Oranienburger Strasse 28, Mitte. Map **4**B8. Open daily 10am–1am. U-Bahn to Oranienburger Tor.*

This is a friendly refuge for those who do not feel at ease in the hard-edged café scene of Scheunenviertel. Oren is located in the Jewish community center, next to the NEUE SYNAGOGUE. The interior is white, with black tables, tall ferns and candles that flicker throughout the day. Oren serves breakfast, vegetarian dishes, kosher specialities and some Moroccan food.

SLUMBERLAND

Goltzstrasse 24, Schöneberg. Map ***3****E6. U-Bahn to Nollendorfplatz.*

An amiable local café on Winterfeldtplatz with sand scattered on the floor and exotic ferns in pots. Best on a Saturday morning during the weekly market (see page 199) when potato sellers rub shoulders with the quarter's anarchists. This is a café for those who want to chat with the locals, but maybe not for those who don't speak German.

ÜBERSEE

Paul-Lincke-Ufer 44, Kreuzberg. Off map ***4****E10* ✿ *Open 9am–2pm U-Bahn to Kottbusser Tor.*

A fashionable Kreuzberg café with modern art on the walls and a shady terrace looking out on the Landwehrkanal. Frequented by the sort of people who often don't go to bed much before 5am, which is why breakfast is served until 4pm. If the terrace is full, try **Café am Ufer** *(#42-43).*

CAFÉ WINTERGARTEN

Fasanenstrasse 23, Charlottenburg. Map ***2****D4* ✿ *Open 10am–1am U-Bahn to Uhlandstrasse.*

A few steps from the crush of Kurfürstendamm, this elegant café, located in the conservatory of a mansion dating from the days of Imperial Berlin, projects the aura of a less hurried world. Literary editors pore over the cultural supplement of *Die Zeit* at its marble-topped tables, while book-lovers discuss the latest outpourings on German unification by Günter Grass. A little terrace offers a place to bask on sunny days. The café belongs to the **Literaturhaus**, which runs a bookstore in the basement and organizes highbrow literary evenings.

ZEUGHAUS

Am Zeughaus, Mitte. Map ***4****B8. Open daily from 10am. S-Bahn to Hackescher Markt.*

One of the attractive new cafés in Mitte is located in the Zeughaus with its entrance on the Spree waterfront (see DEUTSCHES HISTORISCHES MUSEUM, page 105). The café occupies two airy halls decorated with statues and palms. Serving breakfast (French, German or American), traditional Berlin food and rich cakes, the Zeughaus is the perfect place to recover from the endless rooms of paintings and sculptures on Museumsinsel. The hall at the back has lots of space for children to roam.

Beer halls and beer gardens

Berlin beer halls are generally less boisterous than their Bavarian counterparts, perhaps because the beer is normally served in modest 20-centiliter glasses rather than the one-liter *Mass* jugs common in Southern Germany. A waitress serves you at the table; pay as you leave.

The list of dishes is chalked up on a blackboard; you order at the counter. Expect to be served hearty German specialities throughout the year, such as knuckle of pork *(Eisbein),* meatballs *(Bouletten),* eel in herb sauce *(Aal grün),* mashed peas *(Erbspüree),* and potato pancake dusted with sugar *(Kartoffelpuffer).* Beer halls are normally open noon–midnight.

The beer in Berlin, and throughout Germany, is of excellent quality, due to the 1516 *Reinheitsgebot* (Pure Beer Law), which forbids the use of chemicals in the brewing process. *Schultheiss* and *Kindl* are the largest Berlin brewers, but a few small independents have recently launched new brands of beer brewed by traditional Berlin methods.

Berliner Weisse (Berlin white beer) is the local drink for hot summer days. A light wheat beer, it comes in a chalice-shaped glass, and is served with a slice of lemon and a straw. Berliners, never timid in their tastes, traditionally order it *mit Schuss* — a dash of red or green syrup. A *Rote Weisse,* laced with *Himbeere* (raspberry syrup), has a sparkling, fruity character. The *Grüne* version, served with a squirt of *Waldmeister* (the herb woodruff), is a peculiar taste unique to Berlin.

A *Weizenbiere* (not to be confused with *Berliner Weisse*) is a Bavarian wheat beer, which often features on lists of beers in Berlin cafés. You may be offered the choice of *Hefe* (yeasty) or *Kristall* (clear).

ASCHINGER
Kurfürstendamm 26, Charlottenburg. Map ***2****D4* ☎*(030) 8816966. U-Bahn to Kurfürstendamm.*
The old Berlin brewery of Aschinger makes a pleasant, light-brown house brew, which can be sampled in an elegant tiled basement beer hall filled with gleaming copper brewing equipment. The food is of the plain, North German type, and the Bavarian background music is almost unobtrusive, making this a pleasant place for quiet conversation.

GOLGOTHA
Viktoriapark, Kreuzberg. Map ***3****F7. U-Bahn to Möckernbrücke.*
An enormously popular beer garden situated on the heights of the Viktoriapark. A cramped disco plays the latest dance music until dawn.

LORETTA AM WANNSEE
Kronprinzessinnenweg 26, Zehlendorf. Map ***5****E2. S-Bahn to Wannsee.*
A rambling beer garden shaded by trees. A pleasant place to take kids after a steamer trip on the Havel.

LORETTA IN DER CITY
Lietzenburgerstrasse 87, Wilmersdorf. Map ***2****D4. U-Bahn to Uhlandstrasse.*
A spacious beer garden not far from Kurfürstendamm, with a fairground Ferris wheel, and strings of lights dangling from the trees. The food is simple, but the festive mood is appealing, especially to children.

LUISE
Königin-Luise-Strasse 40, Dahlem. Map ***5****E3. U-Bahn to Dahlem-Dorf.*
A popular beer garden near the Dahlem museums, where you can sip a *Berliner Weisse* after a long day looking at paintings. Children are welcome in the small playground.

LUISEN-BRAU
Luisenplatz 1, Charlottenburg. Map ***1****B2. U-Bahn to Richard-Wagner-Platz.*
Founded in 1987, the **Luisen-Brau** brewery has a beer hall with a Neoclassical interior and long wooden benches. One of Berlin's most alluring brews, Luisen-Brau, is produced on the premises, using Bavarian hops and soft Brandenburg water. The kitchen prepares plain German specialities such as *Lamm Haxe* (knuckle of lamb) or *Spiessbraten* (roast pork stuffed with chopped ham). Its location near Schloss Charlottenburg makes this an ideal place to pause for lunch during a tour of the treasures. On summer days you can sit outside on a small terrace.

Berlin after dark

Nights in Berlin are never empty. From the impeccable acoustics of the Philharmonie concert hall to radical plays set in abandoned factories, reunited Berlin is one of the world's most exciting cities after dark. The city has three opera houses, 85 movie houses, 30 theaters, 20 cabarets, and at least one circus. You can browse through the daily listings in *Zitty* (thick and radical) or *Tip* (glossy and mainstream) to find out what's happening in Berlin, or just stroll down Kurfürstendamm to join in the fun.

Plenty of movies and plays occupy the early evening, but the serious nightlife does not begin until much later. Most fashionable bars remain empty before 10pm, visited only by a few disoriented tourists wondering if they have the right address. By the time the action starts, the tourists may have trudged back to their hotels to watch the in-house video.

TICKETS

Reserve well ahead for classical concerts, plays, cabarets and dance events. This can conveniently be done at one of the many *Theaterkassen* in the city.

Many department stores have a *Theaterkasse;* others are located on main shopping streets.

- **Europa-Center** Tauentzienstrasse 9, map **2**D5 ☎(030) 2617051
- **Hertie** Wilmersdorfer Strasse, map **1**D3 ☎(030) 3129497
- **KaDeWe** Tauentzienstrasse, map **2**D5 ☎(030) 241028
- **Karten-Service** Hardenbergstrasse 6, map **2**C4 ☎(030) 3137007
- **Theaterkasse Zehlendorf** Am Rathaus, Zehlendorf, map **5**E3 ☎(030) 8011652. Also handles concerts in Potsdam, Dresden and Vienna.
- **Wertheim** Kurfürstendamm 24, map **2**D4 ☎(030) 8825254

The performing arts

Berlin offers the visitor a vast range of performing arts, although movies and theater are mostly in German.

ALTERNATIVE CENTERS

Germany's radicals, alternative thinkers, pacifists, dissidents and environmentalists have flocked to Berlin since 1945, setting up various alternative cultural centers that challenge mainstream society.

KUNSTHAUS TACHELES

Oranienburger Strasse 53–56, Mitte. Map **4***B8* ☎*(030) 2826185* ▣ *U-Bahn to Oranienburger Tor.*

Tacheles took root in a ruined East Berlin department store in the heady days after reunification. The squatted building may not survive for many years, but it is currently one of the most exciting alternative venues in Germany. The warren of rooms — some without outside walls — are occupied by half a dozen discos, a rudimentary cinema, a makeshift theater, and various savage art installations.

Café Zapata in the basement has become a favorite haunt of wild young Berliners.

MEHRINGHOF

*Gneisenaustrasse 2 (at Mehringdamm). Map **4**E8. U-Bahn to Mehringdamm.*

The alternative culture of the 1970s survives in this huge old Kreuzberg building. The Mehringhof houses, among other things, a school of adult education, a socialist group, a wholefood store, an anarchist bookstore and a bike workshop. You can turn up at any time of the day to rent a bike, or drink a beer with lefties in the **EX** bar.

UFA-FABRIK

*Viktoriastrasse 10–18, Tempelhof. Map **6**E5 ☎(030) 755030. U-Bahn to Ullsteinstrasse.*

Offers circus acts, radical theater, children's shows and offbeat movies (original-language versions) in a converted former UFA film studio.

CINEMA

Berliners have been in love with the movies since the first flickering film was screened in the city in 1895. Glamorous stars such as Marlene Dietrich and Pola Negri launched their careers in Berlin, before being lured by the salaries and status of Hollywood.

The legendary Babelsberg Studios are still standing, in a suburb near Potsdam (see DEFA FILM- UND TV-ERLEBNIS, page 229), and the BERLINER KINOMUSEUM (page 98) regularly screens Berlin movies of the 1920s and 1930s, along with Charlie Chaplin and Buster Keaton classics.

The city now has more than 80 cinemas offering films from every continent. The latest Hollywood hits can usually be found in the big movie theaters clustered around **Bahnhof Zoo** and along **Kurfürstendamm**, but one of the great pleasures in Berlin is to come across a movie you haven't seen for years, in one of the small independent film theaters *(Off-Kinos)*. If you're in luck, the film will even be screened in the original language.

Many of the big names in the movie business descend on Berlin each February for the **International Film Festival**, when several hundred films are screened in a two-week period.

Sadly for non-German-speaking movie fans, Berlin cinemas tend to show foreign films dubbed into German. Those rare cases in which a cinema shows a film in the original language are listed as **OF** *(Originalfassung)*, and **OmU** *(Originalfassung mit Untertiteln)* if German subtitles are used.

See also TEN BERLIN MOVIES TO SEE on page 50.

Movie theaters worth noting are as follows:

- **Arsenal** Welserstrasse 25. Map **2**D5 ☎(030) 2186848. U-Bahn to Wittenbergplatz. An adventurous cinema with some films screened in the original language.
- **Filmkunst 66** Bleibtreustrasse 12. Map **1**D3 ☎(030) 8815510. An avant-garde cinema with a daring choice of new movies.
- **Gloria-Palast** Kurfürstendamm 12. Map **2**D4 ☎(030) 2611557. U-Bahn to Kurfürstendamm. Mainstream movies in a renovated cinema with state-of-the-art sound and vision.

- **Schlüter** Schlüterstrasse 17, Charlottenburg. Map **1**D3 ☎(030) 3138580. Bus 249 to Schlüterstrasse. An intimate Art Deco cinema run by an affable bearded Berliner who occasionally delivers a brief talk before the film. The owner's passions range from the Marx Brothers to the latest Wim Wenders movie.
- **Steinplatz** Hardenbergstrasse 12, Charlottenburg. Map **2**C4 ☎(030) 3129012. U-Bahn to Ernst-Reuter-Platz. Committed cinema, sometimes screening films in the original language. The cinema café is popular with students from the nearby art college and technical university.
- **Tränenpalast** Reichstagufer 17, Mitte. Map **4**B8 ☎(030) 2386211. Classic films like *The Blue Angel* are screened in the former East Berlin transit hall behind Bahnhof Friedrichstrasse.
- **Waldbühne** Glockenturmstrasse, Charlottenburg ☎(030) 3055079. Bus 249 to Scholzplatz. Open-air amphitheater built in the forest for the 1936 Olympics. Now used in the summer months for screening cult movies like *The Rocky Horror Picture Show.*
- **Zeughaus-Kino** Unter den Linden 2, Mitte. Map **4**B8 ☎(030) 215020. Classic German movies screened in the cinema of the DEUTSCHES HISTORISCHES MUSEUM.

CIRCUS

Berliners, otherwise an urbane crowd, still seem to retain a naive affection for circus acts.

- **Tempodrom** In den Zelten, Tiergarten. Map **3**B6 ☎(030) 3944045. Bus 100 to Kongresshalle. Closed winter. A unique mix of traditional circus acts, alternative cabaret and live bands, in a tent pitched next to the Kongresshalle.

CLASSICAL AND POPULAR CONCERTS

Berlin has long been one of the world's foremost cities for classical music, drawing the greatest conductors and musicians. For most of the postwar period, Herbert von Karajan dominated the Berlin music world as conductor of the Berlin Philharmonic Orchestra. After von Karajan's death in 1989, this prestigious post passed to Claudio Abbado.

But classical music is currently in trouble in Berlin. The city cannot afford to run three prestigious opera houses and several full orchestras. Cuts are going to have to be made, and nobody knows quite what will be lost. But whatever happens, Berlin will continue to offer a seemingly vast choice of concerts, from the grandest operas to intimate chamber music.

Venues range from grand concert halls, restored churches, libraries or Baroque palaces to art schools and open-air theaters. Watch out for occasional concerts of Baroque chamber music held in the old palaces of BRITZ, FRIEDRICHSFELDE and SANSSOUCI, or in the scintillating Eichengalerie at SCHLOSS CHARLOTTENBURG. The monthly *Berlin Programm,* available at most German tourist offices, has all the details.

- **BKA** Mehringdamm 32. Map **4**E8 ☎(030) 2510112. U-Bahn to Mehringdamm. Radical Berliners flock to performances of *Unerhörte Musik* (Outrageous Music) in a candlelit Kreuzberg venue every Tuesday at 8.30pm. The music may sound weird, but Berliners claim to love it.

- **Eissporthalle Jafféstrasse** Charlottenburg ☎(030) 30384387. S-Bahn to Westkreuz or (better) bus 219 to Messedamm. Concerts by famous rock bands.
- **Hochschule der Künste** Hardenbergstrasse 33, Charlottenburg. Map **2**C4 ☎(030) 31852374. U-Bahn to Zoologischer Garten. Classical concerts and jazz performances.
- **Kammermusiksaal** Map **3**C7 ☎(030) 254880. Bus 148 to Philharmonie. Concert hall for classical and modern chamber music, built in the 1980s next to the Philharmonie.
- **Loft** Nollendorfplatz 5, Kreuzberg. Map **2**D6 ☎(030) 2161020. U-Bahn to Nollendorfplatz. Innovative rock groups.
- **Philharmonie** Matthäikirchstrasse 1, Tiergarten. Map **3**C7 ☎(030) 254880. Bus 148 to Philharmonie. The world's greatest orchestras and conductors regularly perform in this striking in-the-round concert hall designed in the 1960s by Hans Scharoun. The main concerts of the year are performed by the Berlin Philharmonic Orchestra, the resident orchestra directed by the mighty Herbert von Karajan until his death in 1989, and now under the direction of Claudio Abbado. Advance sales begin 2–3 weeks before the concert, and tickets sell out almost at once.

CULTURAL INSTITUTIONS

Several national centers in Berlin actively promote the film, theater and literature of their respective countries. They often have large libraries, recorded music collections, and videos for rent.

- **Amerika-Haus** Hardenbergstrasse 22, Charlottenburg. Map **2**C4 ☎(030) 8197661. U-Bahn to Zoologischer Garten. The program features classic US movies and theater.
- **British Centre** Hardenbergstrasse 20, Charlottenburg. Map **2**C4 ☎(030) 3110990. U-Bahn to Zoologischer Garten. This is a likely place to catch a screening of *Brief Encounter,* and other such classic English movies.
- **Deutschlandhaus** Stresemannstrasse 90, Kreuzberg. Map **3**D7 ☎(030) 2611046. S-Bahn to Anhalter Bahnhof. A serious cultural institution with a program of German music and talks.
- **Haus der Kulturen der Welt** Kongresshalle, John-Foster-Dulles-Allee 10. Map **3**B6 ☎(030) 397870. Bus 100 to Kongresshalle. Non-European music and theater, staged in a futuristic 1950s building.
- **Institut Français de Berlin** Kurfürstendamm 211, Charlottenburg. Map **2**D4 ☎(030) 8859020. U-Bahn to Uhlandstrasse. French films and plays.
- **Jüdisches Gemeindehaus** Fasanenstrasse 79–80, Charlottenburg. Map **2**D4 ☎(030) 88420333. U-Bahn to Uhlandstrasse. Jewish plays and concerts.

FOLK

At the last count there were 17 Irish bars in Berlin.

- **Highlander** Yorckstrasse 75, Kreuzberg. Map **3**E7 ☎(030) 7858745. U-Bahn to Yorckstrasse.

- **Go In** Bleibtreustrasse 17, Charlottenburg. Map **1**D3 ☎(030) 8817218. S-Bahn or bus 149, 249 to Savignyplatz. Folk groups from every continent.
- **Oscar Wilde Bar** Friedrichstrasse 112a, Mitte. Map **4**B8 ☎(030) 2828166; open daily 11am–2am. U-Bahn to Oranienburger Tor. One of the most civilized, with folk music for homesick Dubliners spilling out into the Berlin night.
- **The Shannon** Apostel-Paulus-Strasse 34, Schöneberg. Map **2**E5 ☎(030) 7818676. U-Bahn to Eisenacher Strasse.

JAZZ

Jazz cafés must be one of the best bets for anyone hunting for live entertainment in a strange town. Jazz is an art without language barriers, dress codes or complicated booking systems. Nobody fights or gets too drunk in a jazz café. The mood is inevitably relaxed, cosmopolitan and (to use the jazzmen's favorite word) cool.

Big, friendly international jazz festivals happen in June and from late October to early November (see THE BERLIN CALENDAR on page 66), but folk and blues sounds can be heard throughout the year in dimly-lit cafés. Concerts usually begin as late as 10–11pm. In the summer, jazz bands can be heard at the **Naturtheater Hasenheide** and other open-air venues.

- **Blues Café** Körnerstrasse 11, Tiergarten. Map **3**D6 ☎(030) 2613698. U-Bahn to Kurfürstenstrasse. Classic blues.
- **Flöz** Nassauische Strasse 37. Map **2**E4 ☎(030) 8611000. U-Bahn to Hohenzollernplatz. Berlin bands improvising jazz and salsa.
- **Lohmeyer** Eosanderstrasse 24, Charlottenburg. Map **1**B2. U-Bahn to Richard-Wagner-Platz. Jazz fans crowd into this intimate club to hear Berlin bands playing nostalgic numbers.
- **Quasimodo** Kantstrasse 12a, Charlottenburg. Map **2**D4 ☎(030) 3128086. U-Bahn to Zoologischer Garten. Top international musicians playing all styles of jazz.

OPERA AND BALLET

Opera- and dance-lovers in Berlin have an enviable choice of classical and modern performances in three opera houses.

- **Deutsche Oper Berlin** Bismarckstrasse 35, Charlottenburg. Map **1**C3 ☎(030) 3410249. U-Bahn to Deutsche Oper. Austere postwar concert hall for opera and modern dance.
- **Deutsche Staatsoper** Unter den Linden 7, Mitte. Map **4**C8 ☎(030) 2004762. U-Bahn to Französische Strasse. This was the opera house founded by Frederick the Great, not to be confused with the Deutsche Oper, which was built after the Wall went up. It occupies a handsome 18thC opera house, bombed during the war, but recently restored by the East German government to provide a glittering Baroque setting for classical opera and ballet. The repertoire was once solidly German, but a more international program is now on offer.
- **Komische Oper** Behrenstrasse 55–57, Mitte. Map **4**C8 ☎(030) 2292555. U-Bahn to Französische Strasse. Operettas and ballet in a concert hall modeled on the Paris Opéra Comique.

THEATER

Theater has changed, like everything in Berlin, since the Wall came down. During the Cold War, West Berlin theaters were bastions of the avant garde, while venues in the East performed turgid plays designed to promote communist ideology. But no more. The most exciting dramatic performances now tend to be staged in the eastern districts, whereas theaters in the West are struggling to keep their audiences.

The heyday of Berlin theater was in the 1920s, when playwrights such as Erwin Piscator and Max Reinhardt used theater as a form of social criticism. This radical tradition was crushed by the Nazis, and many of Berlin's great actors and directors fled to the US. A revival began with Bertolt Brecht's return to East Berlin in 1949, and the city now hosts numerous groups performing classical German theater and modern experimental works.

Berliners are addicted to big Broadway-style musicals. It might be an old show of Cole Porter songs or the latest Stephen Sondheim musical. Whatever it is, Berliners are likely to rave. Even shows that have flopped in New York or London sometimes draw big crowds in Berlin.

The range of venues is vast. You will find plays performed in art schools, cellars, former cinemas, converted factories and open-air amphitheaters. Anything is possible. You might even catch a play in English (signaled in the *Berlin Programm* as *in engl. Sprache*).

- **Berliner Ensemble** Bertolt-Brecht-Platz, Mitte. Map **4**B8 ☎(030) 2888155. U-Bahn or S-Bahn to Friedrichstrasse. Gone are the days when the Berliner Ensemble faithfully staged Brecht's repertoire. The spirit of *die Wende* has swept through the company founded by Bertolt Brecht, and it now stages provocative modern plays in its theater near the Spree. Even the comfortable old seats have been ripped out, and the audience has to sit on hard wooden boxes, like it or not. It seems likely that Brecht would have applauded the radical changes.
- **Deutsches Theater** Schumannstrasse 13a, Mitte. Map **3**B7 ☎(030) 2871225. U-Bahn or S-Bahn to Friedrichstrasse. This is the famous theater run by Max Reinhardt from 1905–33. Movie stars such as Pola Negri and Marlene Dietrich began their acting careers in Reinhardt productions. That was a long time ago, but the Deutsches Theater still has a reputation for staging bold productions of contemporary drama.
- **Hebbel-Theater** Stresemannstrasse 29, Kreuzberg. Map **3**D7 ☎(030) 2510144. S-Bahn to Anhalter Bahnhof. Some of the most exciting theatrical experiences in Berlin are staged here. Plays are put on by groups from Berlin and abroad, sometimes in English. There are also occasional performances by the Dance Berlin group.
- **Schaubühne am Lehniner Platz** Kurfürstendamm 153, Wilmersdorf. Map **1**D2 ☎(030) 890023. Bus 119 to Lehniner Platz. A restored 1920s cinema designed by Erich Mendelsohn, now home to one of Germany's most innovative theater companies.
- **Theater am Kurfürstendamm** Kurfürstendamm 206, Charlottenburg. Map **2**D4 ☎(030) 8823789. U-Bahn to Uhlandstrasse. The Marlene Dietrich musical *Sag mir wo die Blumen sind* (Where have

all the flowers gone?) is booked to run in this theater until the year 2000, unless (as some critics predict) the show flops sooner.

- **Theater des Westens** Kantstrasse 12, Charlottenburg. Map **2**D4 ☎(030) 31903193. U-Bahn to Zoologischer Garten. Broadway-style musicals in a flamboyant 19thC theater.
- **Vaganten Bühne** Kantstrasse 12a, Charlottenburg. Map **2**D4 ☎(030) 3124529 U-Bahn or S-Bahn to Zoologischer Garten. The itinerant Vaganten troupe emerged from the ruins of World War II to stage plays that explored the psychological damage of war. Now based in the Delphi-Haus, where they perform modern literary plays.

Nightlife

The flashing neon around the spotlit spire of the Gedächtniskirche marks the hub of Berlin's nightlife. Stroll down the broad, tree-lined Kurfürstendamm to savor the irresistible allure of Berlin after dark, then explore the streets radiating from Savignyplatz to find the *Off-Kinos* (independent cinemas) and sleek cafés where fashionable Berliners gather in the evening.

DIE SZENE

Looking for nightlife used to be easy in Berlin. In West Berlin, you would head off to Ku'damm or Kreuzberg; in East Berlin, you would go to bed. It has all changed now. Kreuzberg is out, Prenzlauer Berg is in. The followers of *die Szene* (the in scene) have crossed to East Berlin, where rents are cheaper, buildings are there for the squatting, and the atmosphere is that bit more edgy.

You won't find *die Szene* listed in any Berlin guidebook. The hottest addresses are known only to a faithful few — passed on by word of mouth or scribbled on the back of a beer mat. Clutching your scrap of paper, you take the S-Bahn several stops beyond Alexanderplatz, walk along a pot-holed street lined with crumbling apartments, until you come to a building scrawled with graffiti. You see a long line of people (most dressed in black) waiting to get past the bouncer. Some get in; others are sent away.

You may not even want to be part of *die Szene.* The places everyone raves about are often startlingly dingy. They are abandoned factories, derelict apartment blocks, even former Secret Police buildings. You have to be part of Berlin's subculture, or you will feel most uncomfortable.

If you want a glimpse of *die Szene,* wander along Oranienstrasse in Kreuzberg, or join the *Wessis* currently sniffing out the fashionable cafés on Oranienburger Strasse. But the first thing you must get straight is that Oranienstrasse (Kreuzberg) is different from Oranienburger Strasse (Mitte).

BARS

Berlin bars come in any style you might crave. Some evoke New York, others strive for the Barcelona look, and a host of places reproduce the relaxed bonhommerie of an Irish bar. But the true spirit of Berlin is found in the *Kneipen,* or local bars. The interiors tend to be dark, with heavy wooden furniture and old lamps. The one rule of etiquette is that strangers must not sit down at the *Stammtisch.* This is the table reserved for regulars, which is likely to be larger than the other tables and occupied by a group of old men.

Do not fret if your beer takes a long time to arrive. That is the Berlin way. It is not that the waiter has forgotten you, but simply that the barman needs five minutes or longer to pour out the beer. He pulls the tap and fills the glass to the brim with foam, then waits for it to settle, pulls again, pauses again, chats to a customer, draws some more foam, chats some more, and so on. Berliners are often in a hurry, but when it comes to beer they apparently have all the time in the world.

The licensing laws in Berlin are more relaxed than elsewhere in Germany, and bars can stay open up to 23 hours per day (with one hour off, to clean up). Most places keep fairly normal hours, but you can, if you have the stamina, while away the night in the bustling bars at Savignyplatz, Nollendorfplatz or Oranienburger Strasse.

Here are some of the best addresses in Berlin. Some you'll love; others you'll let pass.

- **Carpe diem** Savigny-Passagen 576–577, Charlottenburg. Map **2**D4. Open Mon–Sat 11am–1am. S-Bahn to Savignyplatz. A stylish *tapas* bar inspired by the Barcelona look, located in the arches under the S-Bahn viaduct.
- **Filmbühne** Steinplatz, Charlottenburg. Map **2**C4. U-Bahn to Zoologischer Garten. A friendly bar attached to a cinema that screens innovative films. Overcrowded during the Berlin Film Festival.
- **Harry's New York Bar** Grand Hotel Esplanade, Lützowufer 15, Schöneberg. Map **3**D6 ☎(030) 261011. U-Bahn to Nollendorfplatz. Venice has one, Paris has another, and so it was almost inevitable that Berlin would end up with a Harry's Bar. And a very stylish place it is, complete with tomato-red seats and a piano player. Harry's Bar became fashionable from the moment it opened, attracting the sort of Berliners whose talk is more about BMWs than Brecht.
- **Hegel** Savignyplatz 2, Charlottenburg. Map **2**D4. Open Mon–Sat 6pm–3am. S-Bahn to Savignyplatz. This small bar is where Berlin's intellectuals like to gather in the evening. It's run by a Russian exile who has hung a 1945 framed copy of *Pravda* above the bar. The collected works of Hegel are kept on a shelf, ready to settle any dispute that might arise over the meaning of the dialectic. The list of cocktails includes one called *Glasnost* and another named *Red October.* There's live music most evenings, and the place is generally packed.
- **Jahrmarkt** Bleibtreustrasse 49, Charlottenburg. Map **1**D3. S-Bahn to Savignyplatz. A friendly bar with aged wooden furniture and an overgrown garden at the back. The food is plain.
- **Kaffeestube** Husemannstrasse 6, Prenzlauer Berg. U-Bahn to Dimitroffstrasse. Handsome bar in a restored East Berlin street.
- **Kaminbar** Hotel Inter-Continental, Budapester Strasse 2, Tiergarten. Map **2**D5. Bus 109. Elegant penthouse bar with a blazing winter fire.

- **Leydicke** Mansteinstrasse 4, Schöneberg. Map 3E6. U-Bahn to Kleistpark. Ancient bar crammed with nostalgic Berliners sipping liqueurs and fruit wines.
- **The Oscar Wilde Bar** Friedrichstrasse 112. Map 4B8. Open daily 11am–2am (stays open until 3am on Fri and Sat). U-Bahn to Oranienburger Tor. This strangely authentic Irish pub has brought Guinness and televised Sunday soccer to former East Berlin. You can eat Irish breakfast, drink Murphy's and "crack" until the small hours. Wonders never cease.
- **Silberstein** Oranienburger Strasse 27, Mitte. Map 4B8. Open Mon–Fri 4pm–4am; Sat, Sun noon–4am. U-Bahn to Oranienburger Tor. One of several hip bars that sprang up in the former Jewish quarter after the Wall came down. Decorated in a grim Post-Industrial style, it is filled with bizarre sculptures. The word on the street is that Silberstein is now a little too well-known to be part of *die Szene,* but it's still a good place to go.
- **Zur Letzten Instanz** Waisenstrasse 14–16, Mitte. Map 4C9. Open Mon 4pm–midnight, Tues–Sun 11am–midnight. U-Bahn to Klosterstrasse. This is the oldest bar in town, and it looks it. Zur Letzten Instanz (ask a friendly Berliner to explain the name) dates back to 1621. Its ancient iron stove has warmed such famous Berliners as Heinrich Zille. Try the *Eisbein* (knuckle of pork) with a beer.

DANCE CAFÉS

Nostalgia-prone Berliners now flock to run-down quarters of former East Berlin to savor the old-fashioned charm of the *Ballhaus.* Back in the Twenties, almost every quarter in Berlin had its Ballhaus, where you could drink, dine and perhaps dance with a stranger. Those in West Berlin closed down, one by one, after the war, but a handful have survived in former East Berlin.

Grand yet shabby, the dance cafés attract those who shy away from the shiny new discotheques of the West. There is usually a band playing melodies of the 1920s and '30s, or, more often these days, slow versions of pop hits. Some places still have telephones on the tables so that you can dial the number of some good-looking stranger across the room. Many old Berliners met their partners in a Ballhaus; young Berliners have taken up the tradition.

- **Ballhaus** Berlin Chausseestrasse 108, Mitte. Map 3A7 ☎(030) 2827575. U-Bahn to Zinnowitzer Strasse. An ancient neon sign lights up the word *Tanz* (dance) in a grim street N of Friedrichstrasse station. The old building doesn't look much from the outside, but it conceals a grand Ballhaus from the 1930s, with mirrors, velvet curtains and a sweeping wrought iron staircase. Each of the tables has a round lamp with a black number on it. You pick up the phone to call the table of your choice, if you dare.
- **Clärchens Ballhaus** Auguststrasse 24–25, Mitte. Map 4B8 ☎(030) 2829295. U-Bahn to Oranienburger Tor. Opened on the eve of World War I and still run by the Clärchen family, it has kept most of the original decor, including Art Deco mirrors and smoke-stained posters.

- **Prater** Kastanienallee 7–9. U-Bahn to Eberswalder Strasse. A run-down old dance café in Prenzlauer Berg modeled on the Prater in Vienna. The Prater has a rambling garden where you can drink a beer on a sunny afternoon. Look out for posters announcing pantomime shows in the garden. Arrive early, as tickets sell out fast on the day. The Prater Ball, held every month, attracts elderly romantics.

CABARETS AND REVUES

Berlin cabaret is all about fast talk, political in-jokes and street slang. If you don't speak fluent German, you won't get the gags, but it can still being fun going to a late-night show. You might, if you are lucky, come across a show that captures the wickedly sexy atmosphere of 1920s Berlin. Some Germans are particularly fond of transvestite acts featuring men dressed up in feathers and frocks. Others prefer the sharp wit of political cabaret.

- **BKA** Mehringdamm 32. Map **4**E8 ☎(030) 2510112. U-Bahn to Mehringdamm. The **Berliner Kabarett Anstalt** (Berlin Cabaret Institution) stages avant-garde cabaret five nights a week in a converted 19thC Kreuzberg apartment block.
- **Chez Nous** Marburgerstrasse 14. Map **2**D4 ☎(030) 2131810. U-Bahn to Augsburgerstrasse. A transvestite show applying a formula that has changed little in a hundred years.
- **Die Distel** Friedrichstrasse 101, Mitte. Map **4**B8 ☎(030) 2004704. U-Bahn or S-Bahn to Friedrichstrasse. Classic Berlin cabaret now seen casting a sardonic eye on 40 years of socialism.
- **Friedrichstadtpalast** Friedrichstrasse 107, Mitte. Map **4**B8 ☎(030) 2836474. U-Bahn or S-Bahn to Friedrichstrasse. Released from the straitjacket of State control, this once-drab theater now stages spicy satirical reviews playing on the preoccupations of *Ossis* and *Wessis* (East and West Germans).
- **Mehringhof Theater** Gneisenaustrasse 2a. Map **4**E8 ☎(030) 6915099. U-Bahn to Mehringdamm. Sharp political cabaret in an alternative cultural center.
- **Wintergarten** Potsdamer Strasse 96, Tiergarten. Map **3**D6 ☎(030) 2629016 ▭ Shows start every day at 8.30pm. U-Bahn to Kurfürstenstrasse. The hugely successful Wintergarten opened in 1992. Modeled on a famous 19thC Berlin entertainment palace located in the Central Hotel on Friedrichstrasse, it draws nostalgia-hungry crowds with variety acts mimicking the style of the 1920s. The walls are hung with old posters and props salvaged from defunct cabaret theaters.

CASINO

For those with Deutschmarks to burn, the **Spielbank Berlin** *(Europa-Center, map* ***2****D5, open daily 3pm-3am)* runs roulette, poker and baccarat games. Another casino is located in the **Forum Hotel** on Alexanderplatz.

DISCOS

The dance scene in Berlin has changed since *die Wende.* A few years ago, Dschungel was *the* address for dancing, but the fashion pack have moved on elsewhere, and Dschungel has closed down. Young Berliners now dance to the latest sounds in cramped clubs in Mitte and Prenzlauer Berg, although mainstream revelers still boogie the night away in the big discos near Bahnhof Zoo.

Discos in Berlin, as in every city, are often choosy about whom they admit. If you aren't sure what to wear, dress in black. Most discos don't begin to get busy until after midnight, and some don't shut until dawn. Here are two places to ponder.

- **Metropol** Nollendorfplatz 5, Schöneberg. Map **2**D6 ☎(030) 2164122. Open Friday, Saturday 10pm–4am. U-Bahn to Nollendorfplatz. Dancing to chart hits in a spectacularly-lit former Art Deco theater.
- **Tresor** Toleranzstrasse. Map **3**C7. U-Bahn to Mohrenstrasse. You won't find Tresor without a good map. It's situated in a street in former East Berlin which most taxi drivers still think of as Otto-Grotewohl-Strasse. But the street name has changed and so has the neighborhood. Once part of the death strip, it is now visited by the youth of the world in search of thrills. Hitler's bunker lies somewhere nearby, and the vaults of the former Wertheim department store, destroyed in the war, have been turned into a disco. Techno-house music fans dressed in baseball caps and leisure suits mill around the vast, moldering basement. The flash of strobes briefly illuminates metal grilles and safe-deposit boxes last used during the war. Don't expect to get past the doorman if you're not wearing the right clothes.

Where to shop

In the matter of shopping, Berlin is still very much a divided city. While West Berliners feasted on the products of the Federal Republic's economic miracle, those in the Soviet sector had to make do with drab clothes, and Trabant cars powered by two-stroke engines. Although the Wall dividing the city has now vanished, there still exists an invisible division between the poor East and the rich West, and although a few smart stores have now opened on Friedrichstrasse, it will be some years before East Berlin is a place for serious shopping.

West Berlin's best stores proudly display their merchandise along **KURFÜRSTENDAMM**, a leafy avenue with broad sidewalks stretching W from the broken spire of the Gedächtniskirche. You can satisfy every whim and desire in the countless stylish shops specializing in clothes, shoes, porcelain, art books or kitchen accessories. Original fashion stores are found in the streets that intersect Kurfürstendamm — they tend to become more unconventional as you travel west.

Fasanenstrasse, **Uhlandstrasse** and **Uhland-Passage** *(at Uhlandstrasse 170)* stock dresses and shoes for flaunting at the theater or opera house, while **Bleibtreustrasse** boutiques offer a more raw chic for wild parties. As if that were not enough, there are elegant shopping streets in many West Berlin suburbs, such as **Schlossstrasse** in Steglitz, where you will find major department stores and stylish fashion shops.

In recent years, some unusual boutiques have opened up in the arches under the S-Bahn viaducts. The first shops were established in the arches of the S-Bahn at **Savignyplatz**, between Uhlandstrasse and Grolmanstrasse. A new cluster of shops, some more fashionable than others, has recently opened in the arches along **Georgenstrasse**, between Friedrichstrasse and Kupfergraben.

When the Wall came down, there was much talk about new stores opening on **Unter den Linden**. The chic jeweler Tiffany opened a branch there, but it has since closed for lack of custom. For the moment, it seems as though the Meissen porcelain store is about the only interesting place to shop.

But things look different a few blocks S of Unter den Linden. Several fashion stores have opened up on the handsomely-restored **Gendarmenmarkt**. This area looks like becoming a major shopping district when the gigantic Friedrichstadtpalast shopping mall is completed there in 1995.

Credit cards are widely accepted in Berlin stores, and many accept most of the major cards. But always check before making your purchase. In our recommendations on the following pages, if an establishment is known not to accept any cards, the words "**no cards**" are given.

See also SHOPPING HOURS on page 20 and 59.

What to buy

A SOUVENIR OF BERLIN?

Taking home a chunk of the Berlin Wall, real or fake, is no longer fashionable, but the stuff is still on sale at stalls near the site of Checkpoint Charlie. The KADEWE department store can be counted on to stock frivolous (and pricey) Berlin souvenirs. Look out for their bottled *Berliner Luft* (Berlin air) and *Alt-Berliner Rumtopf.*

If you have space in your suitcase, pick up a replica bust of Nefertiti at the Gipsformerei (plaster-cast workshop) near SCHLOSS CHARLOTTENBURG (see page 199). Russian military relics are traded by street dealers at the Brandenburger Tor, and you can still pick up tacky communist souvenirs in the shop at the foot of the Fernsehturm. LEYSIEFFER sells delicious chocolates, while the delicatessen at the KADEWE will wrap you up a tin of Nuremberg *Lebkuchen* (gingerbread).

But perhaps the best souvenir of Berlin is a book of photographs of the old city (BÜCHERBOGEN has a big selection) or a biography of Marlene Dietrich (try THE BRITISH BOOKSHOP). See BOOKS on page 194.

ANTIQUES

The major antique dealers in Berlin tend to stock German porcelain, Art Nouveau works, Oriental art and furniture. The main shops are found on KURFÜRSTENDAMM and the side streets to the south.

Many minor dealers are based in the BERLINER FLOHMARKT at Bahnhof Friedrichstrasse (see page 98).

ART AUCTIONS

Until 1933, Berlin was one of the world's most important art markets. After decades of isolation, the city is now competing again with Paris, London and New York. Berlin's main strength at present is in 20thC German and Russian art.

Major auctions have been held for several years at the prestigious **Villa Grisebach** *(Fasanenstrasse 25, Charlottenburg, map 2D4 ☎(030) 8826811 Fx(030) 8824145).*

A relatively recent arrival on the scene is **Sotheby's Berlin**, which opened an auction house in East Berlin soon after the Wall came down *(Palais am Festungsgraben, Unter den Linden, Mitte (at the Neue Wache, map 4B8) ☎(030) 3943060).*

The **Orangerie fair** held every two years in Berlin (odd years, next in 1995; see page 67) is now considered Germany's foremost international art and antiques fair, featuring outstanding pieces of medieval sculpture, furniture, photographs, modern German art and the occasional Old Master. For information about the fair, contact the **Association of Berlin Art and Antique Dealers** *(Verband der Berliner Kunst- und Antiquitätenhändler, Fasanenstrasse 25, 10719 Berlin 15 ☎(030) 8826814 Fx(030) 8824145).*

ART GALLERIES

Galleries in Charlottenburg tend to deal in well-established international artists whose work fetches big prices, while the smaller galleries in Kreuzberg promote younger artists who have not yet made their name. Buyers are now venturing into former East Berlin in search of the little art galleries that might be showing the stars of the future.

Most of Berlin's galleries are open Monday to Friday afternoon and Saturday morning, but times are rather erratic and concepts such as opening hours do not necessarily apply in some of the more extreme exhibition spaces. It is always wise to call ahead to check that a gallery is open.

The *Berlin Programm* (available from tourist offices) provides a selective monthly listing of exhibitions, but more detailed information is given in the quarterly *Kunstblatt.* The following list of galleries highlights some of the most interesting or unusual places.

- **Aedes** S-Bahnbogen, Savignyplatz, Charlottenburg. Map **2**D4 ☎(030) 3122598. Gallery located in the arches below S-Bahnhof Savignyplatz, exhibiting architectural plans and scale models ranging from the Acropolis to the Museumsinsel.
- **Brusberg** Kurfürstendamm 213, Charlottenburg. Map **2**D4 ☎(030) 8827682. Major modern Surrealist and Dada artists including Ernst, Dalí, Dubuffet, Miró and Picasso.
- **DAAD** Kurfürstenstrasse 58, Tiergarten. Map **3**D6 ☎(030) 261364. Exhibitions of work by foreign artists, sponsored by the *Deutschen Akademischen Austauschdienstes* (the German academic exchange program). Situated on the first floor of a handsome Old Berlin mansion, above the fashionable Café Einstein.
- **Elefanten Press Galerie** Oranienstrasse 25, Kreuzberg. Map **4**D9

☎(030) 6149036. Bookstore run by alternative Berlin publishing house, with an airy gallery exhibiting radical paintings and photographs.

- **Galerie am Chamissoplatz** Chamissoplatz 6, Kreuzberg. Map **4**E8 ☎(030) 6925381. Gallery situated in a former bakery, mounting shows of critical art including biting cartoons on German unification politics by Gerhard Seyfried. Also occasional readings and concerts.
- **Galerie Eva Poll** Lützowplatz 7, Tiergarten. Map **2**D5 ☎(030) 261709. A gallery that has promoted young German and Russian artists since 1968.
- **Gelbe Musik** Schaperstrasse 11, Wilmersdorf. Map **2**D4 ☎(030) 2113962. Unique gallery and shop specializing in artists' records, tapes and videos.
- **Nierendorf** Hardenbergstrasse 19, Charlottenburg. Map **2**C4 ☎(030) 7856060. Founded during the Weimar Republic, Nierendorf continues to exhibit 1920s German Expressionist art.
- **Pels-Leusden-Galerie** Fasanenstrasse 25, Charlottenburg. Map **2**D4 ☎(030) 8826811. Founded in 1950 by a painter, this elegant gallery is situated in the restored Villa Grisebach. It holds major exhibitions of work by 20thC artists such as Käthe Kollwitz, as well as organizing the Villa Grisebach auctions (see ART AUCTIONS on previous page).
- **Raab** Potsdamerstrasse 58, Tiergarten. Map **3**D6 ☎(030) 2619217. Ingrid Raab's discerning selection of contemporary Berlin artists.
- **Staatliche Kunsthalle Berlin** Budapester Strasse 42, Charlottenburg. Map **2**D5 ☎(030) 2617067. Contemporary Berlin artists are featured in major exhibitions.
- **Weisser Elefant** Almstadtstrasse 11, Mitte. Map **4**B9 ☎(030) 2823908. Situated in a decaying 19th century mustard factory near Alexanderplatz, the Weisser Elefant was formerly a forum for young East Berlin artists such as Wolf Leo — the artist who painted murals on the East side of the Wall.

BODY CARE PRODUCTS

- **The Body Shop** Uhlandstrasse 156, Charlottenburg. Map **2**D4. Sells shampoos and soaps that pamper people without harming animals.
- **Bad + Baden** Uhland-Passage, Charlottenburg. Map **2**D4. Everything for bathing, including luxurious towels, joke sponges, stylish bathing suits, and perhaps Berlin's best selection of clockwork bath toys.

BOOKS

The British Bookshop, located near Checkpoint Charlie *(Mauerstrasse 83, Mitte, map* ***4****C8 ☎(030) 2384680 ℻(030) 2384707, U-Bahn to Stadtmitte),* has an entire section devoted to Berlin. Here you can pick up Isherwood's *Goodbye to Berlin,* or the latest Dietrich biography.

For novels in German, browse in the bookstores clustered around Savignyplatz. **Kiepert** *(Hardenbergstrasse 4-5, Charlottenburg, map* ***2****C4 ☎(030) 31100904)* has a vast stock of German books on all subjects. Glance in the travel department for early 20thC copies of Cook's *Traveller's Handbook to the Rhine* and old maps of Prussia, or head down the street to **Antiquariat Kiepert** *(Knesebeckstrasse 20-21, Charlottenburg,* *map 2 D4 ☎(030) 3135000)* for classic editions of pre-1914 Baedeker guides. For books on Berlin architecture or the movies of Fritz Lang, visit **Bücherbogen** *(Stadtbahnbogen 593, off Savignyplatz, Charlottenburg, map 2 D4 ☎(030) 3121932),* a striking, modern bookstore located in one of the brick arches below S-Bahnhof Savignyplatz, specializing in art, architecture, cinema and photography.

Luxury art books for the collector are sold at **Wasmuth** *(Hardenbergstrasse 9a, Charlottenburg, map 2 C4 ☎(030) 316920).*

CLOTHING AND ACCESSORIES

Clothing sizes are infuriatingly different in the US, the UK and Europe. If in any doubt, turn to the **clothing sizes chart** near the end of the book.

Berlin designers

While many sleek Paris fashion designers have shops in Berlin, the city also offers a good opportunity to check out German designers, many of whom have established a loyal following abroad. Munich, Hamburg and Düsseldorf may still be the main centers of German fashion, but Berlin is beginning to establish a reputation for innovative design.

- **Fifty Fifty** Pariser Strasse 20, Charlottenburg. Map **1**D3 ☎(030) 8839615. Extravagant fashions by seven Berlin designers.
- **Maren Grebe** Kurfürstendamm 190–192. Map **1**D3 ☎(030) 8818864. Crisp creations, displayed in a striking Neoclassical interior.
- **Molotow** Gneisenaustrasse 112, Kreuzberg. Map **4**E8 ☎(030) 6930818. Clothes for men and women, the work of more than 70 Berlin designers.
- **Simone** Uhlandstrasse 170, Charlottenburg. Map **2**D4 ☎(030) 8838662. Women's gowns modeled on the styles of a century ago.

Clothes for women

Women can hunt down clothes by major international designers on Kurfürstendamm or in the big department stores. For the off-beat styles by German designers, it pays to wander down Uhlandstrasse, Fasanenstrasse and Bleibtreustrasse, where some of the most adventurous boutiques are found.

- **Chic im Trachtenlook** Ludwigkirchstrasse 14, Wilmersdorf, map **2**D4. This is one for the Bavarians. Munich fashion houses have been trying for years to turn traditional Bavarian folk costumes *(Trachten)* into designer clothes. Chic im Trachtenlook tries to persuade fashionable Berliners to adopt this new Bavarian look.
- **Ernesto Gugu** Ludwigkirchstrasse 13, Wilmersdorf, map **2**D4. A generally sober collection from a Cologne designer, who has a good eye for blending color tints.
- **Patrick Hellmann** Fasanenstrasse 26, Charlottenburg, map **2**D4. Women who want to turn heads at cocktail parties look for a new dress at this discreet basement boutique near the KÄTHE-KOLLWITZ-MUSEUM. The shop displays a small, carefully-selected collection of clothes, shoes and bags by designers such as Jean-Paul Gaultier,

Calvin Klein and Alaïa. The friendly service and relaxed atmosphere make Hellmann one of the best addresses in Berlin for women's clothes.

- **Horn** Kurfürstendamm 213, Charlottenburg, map **2**D4. This is the place to go for colorful sweaters by Uta Raasch of Düsseldorf and clothes by other German designers.
- **Kookai** Kurfürstendamm 205, Charlottenburg, map **2**D4. Exciting and original clothes for young women with perfect figures.
- **Jil Sander** Kurfürstendamm 48, map **1**D3. German women in tough managerial jobs continue to rely on Jil Sander of Hamburg to provide them with crisp, sober clothes.
- **Schrank** Kurfürstendamm 197, Charlottenburg, map **2**D4. Elegant women's clothes for glitzy dinner parties.
- **Selbach** Kurfürstendamm 195, map **1**D3. Selbach tends to go for safe contemporary fashions by established German or French designers. This is where you would look for something to wear to a dinner party in Zehlendorf.
- **Ralf Setzer** Bleibtreustrasse 19, map **1**D3. A spacious boutique stocked with clothes in rich colors and rare fabrics by Italian and British designers.
- **Soft** Bleibtreustrasse 6, Charlottenburg, map **1**D3. A small boutique with an inspired selection of clothes from the major French fashion houses, including Dorothée Bis, Mugler, Ozbek and Gaultier.

Clothes for men

- **Patrick Hellmann** Bleibtreustrasse 20, Charlottenburg, map **1**D3. Classic men's suits by designer names such as Calvin Klein, Ralph Lauren and Giorgio Armani.
- **Man Store** Uhland-Passage, Charlottenburg, map **2**D4. Stylish and sexy underwear by major designers for the bold among Berlin men.
- **Schrill** Bleibtreustrasse 49, Charlottenburg, map **1**D3. A stylish boutique catering to daring German males who do not recoil at the thought of wearing ties decorated with reproductions of paintings by Van Gogh or Picasso.
- **Sør** Bleibtreustrasse 33, Charlottenburg, map **1**D3. Everything but the name recalls a traditional London tailor's. The interior is decorated with antique wooden cabinets and the odd battered suitcase plastered with stickers of old shipping lines. The clothes are, as you would expect, comfortable cashmere pullovers by Peter Scott, solid shoes by Church's, and classic raincoats by Burberry. The colorful ties by Givenchy strike the only flamboyant note.

Clothes for children

Adults in Berlin often prefer to wear muted colors such as brown and black, but they dress their kids in every color of the rainbow. For something special, start by looking in KADEWE or at one of the following stores.

- **Boom** Uhland-Passage, Charlottenburg, map **2**D4. Children's clothes in styles that have not changed since the age of the Kaisers.

- **Pusteblume** Europa-Center, Charlottenburg, map **2**D5. Attractive and unusual clothes for under-12s.

Clothes for paupers

- **Garage** Ahornstrasse 2, Schöneberg, map **2**D5. Grunge victims looking for old fashions to re-use can rummage here, among the vast stock of second-hand clothes sold by the kilo.
- **Highlights** Hohenzollerndamm 111, Wilmersdorf, map **1**E3. This is the place to snoop for second-hand bargains bearing Jil Sander or Lange labels.

Clothes for everyone

- **Esprit** Kurfürstendamm 26, Charlottenburg, map **2**D4. A large store filled with bright clothes for the young and very young.
- **Hennes & Mauritz** Kurfürstendamm 20, Charlottenburg, map **2**D4; also at Tauentzienstrasse 13A, Charlottenburg, map **2**D5. Young Berliners flock to this Swedish fashion store, known for its inexpensive clothes in bold styles and bright colors. The children's section is especially inspiring.

Shoes, leather goods and other accessories

- **Budapester Schuhe** Kurfürstendamm 199, map **1**D3. Sturdy men's shoes for tramping in the Grunewald, hand-made by Ludwig Reiter of Vienna or Alden of New England, plus chic women's shoes by Pink Flamingo of Zurich.
- **Knopf und Kragen** Oranienstrasse 181, Kreuzberg. Map **4**D9. If you need a button, this shop probably has it, from utilitarian shirt buttons to glitzy gilded pieces for fantasy creations.
- **Moos Grund** Bleibtreustrasse 40, Charlottenburg, map **1**D3. Stylish shoes for special occasions.
- **Sack & Pack** Kantstrasse 48, map **1**D3. Crammed with leather satchels, briefcases, handbags and wallets.
- **Schuhtick** Savignyplatz 11, Charlottenburg, map **2**D4. The shop for shoes in weird styles and wild colors.

Jewelry

The streets around Charlottenburg's Savignyplatz abound in small shops selling exclusive necklaces and rings.

- **Beate Brinkmann** Knesebeckstrasse 29, map **2**D4 ☎(030) 8836740. Necklaces fashioned in elegant and eccentric styles.
- **Covarrubias** Bleibtreustrasse 50, map **1**D3 ☎(030) 3128564. Rare and unusual metal or stone objects, ranging from Balinese stone deities to African necklaces.
- **Lalique** Bleibtreustrasse 47, map **1**D3 ☎(030) 8819762. Innovative jewelry made by hand in Berlin *ateliers*.
- **Maria Makkaroni** Bleibtreustrasse 49, Charlottenburg, map **1**D3 ☎(030) 3128584. This irresistible store sells a bizarre assortment of jewelry, costumes, and accessories which often prove just right for Berlin parties.

COMPACT DISCS AND RECORDS

- **The Virgin Megastore** Gloria-Passage, Kurfürstendamm 14. Map **2**D4 ☎(030) 8800810. Crammed with the latest music, videos and computer games.
- **FNAC** Meinekestrasse 23. Map **2**D4. The French chain offers more of the same in a high-tech interior.

DEPARTMENT STORES

The department store **KaDeWe** (**Ka**ufhaus **de**s **We**stens) ranks second in the world in size (after Harrods of London), with a quarter of a million items spread over six vast floors.

Take the elevator to the delicatessen *(Feinschmeckeretage)* on the 6th floor (see also BERLIN RESTAURANTS A TO Z on page 172), where 25,000 different types of food are irresistibly displayed, including 1,500 cheeses and 400 types of bread. There are rare Japanese delicacies, Alois Dallmayr coffees, Twining teas, Lübeck marzipan and Beluga caviar. Join the Berliners perched on stools at the Lenôtre cake counter before submerging yourself in KaDeWe's other floors.

- **KaDeWe** Tauentzienstrasse 21, Schöneberg. Map **2**D5 ☎(030) 21210.

Berlin's other department stores are eclipsed by KaDeWe, although they can be useful for basic needs such as toothpaste or tights. The main ones to look for are:

- **Hertie** Wilmersdorfer Strasse 118, Charlottenburg. Map **1**D3 ☎(030) 311050.
- **Karstadt** Wilmersdorfer Strasse 109, Charlottenburg. Map **1**D3 ☎(030) 31891. Also in Tegel, Steglitz, Tempelhof, Neukölln and Wedding.
- **Wertheim** Kurfürstendamm 231, Charlottenburg. Map **2**D4 ☎(030) 882061. Good for stylish clothes.

FLEA MARKETS

Berlin has several *Flohmärkte* (flea markets), all packed with evocative souvenirs of the past.

For postcards, old banknotes, tin toys or dolls, go to the bizarre BERLINER FLOHMARKT under the arches of the S-Bahn at Friedrichstrasse station *(map **4**B8)*.

The **Zille-Hof**, under the arches of the S-Bahn at Fasanenstrasse in Charlottenburg *(map **2**D4)*, is named after the Berlin artist Heinrich Zille. It has lost some of its old charm, but still sells a bizarre assortment of dusty dolls, rusty metal advertising signs and faded photographs from the era of the Kaisers.

Of the open-air markets, the **Grosser Berliner Trödelmarkt** *(Strasse des 17 Juni, at S-Bahnhof Tiergarten, map **2**C4; every Sat, Sun 10am-5pm)* has the biggest choice of old objects, but the **Kreuzberger Krempelmarkt** *(Reichpietschufer, at Linkstrasse, map **3**D7; every Sat, Sun 8am-3.30pm; U-Bahn to Kurfürstenstrasse)* is a better place to pick up a bargain.

A browse around the **Berliner Kunst- und Nostalgiemarkt an der**

Museumsinsel *(Am Zeughaus, map* **4***B8; every Sat, Sun 11am-5pm; U-Bahn or S-Bahn to Friedrichstrasse)* might turn up a dusty relic of Old Berlin. The stalls line the Spree waterfront behind the Zeughaus, offering old books, scratched records, lamps, glasses and those battered teddy bears that Berliners love to collect.

For local atmosphere, explore the market held around the ruined 19thC brick church on **Winterfeldtplatz** *(Schöneberg, map* **3***E6; open Wed, Sat 8am-1pm),* where genial young Berliners sell organic vegetables, pottery, books, and pickled herring rolls to munch. The square is surrounded by attractive local cafés, although the curious **Café die Ruine**, which once flourished in a bombed-out apartment, seems to have become a ruin itself. An eccentric market garden nearby, however, continues to thrive in the shell of a prewar building.

FOOD AND DRINK

The biggest choice is to be found at **KaDeWe**'s 6th-floor delicatessen. Take home some Lübeck marzipan or a loaf of German bread, but bear in mind that UK and US regulations forbid the import of meats.

King's Teagarden *(Kurfürstendamm 217, map* **2***D4 ☎(030) 8837059)* stocks more than 170 varieties of tea, some of which can be sampled in an upstairs room overlooking Kurfürstendamm. Creamy Belgian chocolates are sold at **Leonidas** *(Uhland-Passage, Charlottenburg, map* **2***D4),* but perhaps the wickedest chocolates in Berlin are laid out in tempting displays at **Leysieffer** *(Kurfürstendamm 218 ☎(030) 8827820).*

KITCHEN EQUIPMENT

For gleaming German kitchen knives, scissors and cutlery, go to **Zwilling J.A. Henckels** *(Kurfürstendamm 33, map* **2***D4).*

NEWSPAPERS AND MAGAZINES

The attractive Neoclassical **kiosk on Kurfürstendamm** *(at Uhlandstrasse)* sells a wide variety of international newspapers and magazines, but the biggest selection is at the **Europa Presse Center** *(Europa-Center, Charlottenburg, map* **2***D5 ☎(030) 2613003, open daily until 10.45pm).* Look out here for *Vanity Fair, The New Yorker, Cosmopolitan* in six language editions, and maybe even *Village Voice.*

Alternatively, if you fail to find your favorite magazine there, you could try **Internationale Presse** *(Joachimstalerstrasse 1, Charlottenburg, map* **2***D4 ☎(030) 8817256, open daily until 10pm).*

PENS AND PAPER

For stationery, go to **Schaberow** *(Hardenbergstrasse 19, Charlottenburg, map* **2***D4 ☎(030 3124001),* where they have notebooks, elegant pens, artists' paints and wrapping paper.

PLASTER CASTS

Not far from SCHLOSS CHARLOTTENBURG, the **Gipsformerei** (plaster-cast workshop) of the **Staatliche Museen Preussischer Kulturbesitz** *(Sophie-Charlotten-Strasse 17-18, map* **1***C2 ☎(030) 3217011, open Mon-*

Fri 9am-4pm, Wed 9am-6pm) is crammed with plaster-cast models of selected exhibits from the Prussian state museums, including buddhas, Greek gods, and hauntingly beautiful busts of Nefertiti that you may be tempted to ship back home.

PORCELAIN

- **Galerie Lietzow** Knesebeckstrasse 76, map **2**D4. Unusual modern ceramics.
- **Rosenthal Studio** Kurfürstendamm 226, map **2**D4. Porcelain and glass by some of the world's most creative designers.
- **Staatliche Porzellan-Manufaktur** Kurfürstendamm 26a, map **2**D4. Filled with Rococo-style statuettes and imitation Art Deco vases manufactured in the state-owned KPM factory in the Tiergarten district.
- **Yokohama Haus** Kurfürstendamm 214, map **2**D4. Rival Meissen ware.

POSTCARDS

For witty or arty postcards to send home, try **Ararat** *(Kantstrasse 135, Charlottenburg, map **1** D3; also at Bergmannstrasse 99a, Kreuzberg, map **4** E8),* whose vast range of cards is carefully classified by category. You can search the files for everything from cats to curios. Look through the Berlin collection for nostalgic prewar views of the Gedächtniskirche or scenes at the Wall in November 1989.

POSTERS

- **PosterGalerie 200** Kurfürstendamm 200, map **2**D4. Unusual posters, including a gloriously bawdy cartoon titled *Berlinplanzen* (Urinals of Berlin).
- **Nielsen Design** Kantstrasse 41, Charlottenburg, map **1**D3. Artistic German calendars or striking posters.

TOYS

For quality toys to take home, investigate **Heidi's Spielzeugladen** *(Kantstrasse 61, Charlottenburg, map **1** D3),* which is packed with traditional German puppets, wooden train sets and books, or go to **Vogel** *(Uhlandstrasse 137, Charlottenburg, map **2** E4)* for a wide choice of children's toys and games.

It is worth a detour to **Berliner Zinnfiguren** *(Knesebeckstrasse 88, Charlottenburg, map **2** C4)* to take a look at the vast stock of hand-made miniature tin soldiers, including regiments of Prussian soldiers marching in formation.

Berlin for children

For those with children to amuse, Berlin can be a stimulating, if tiring, city. The parks, zoos and lakeside beaches are ideal for a fine day, while many of the museums are crammed with interesting objects.

In SIGHTSEEING, look for the ✱ symbol, which indicates places of interest to children.

• **Beaches and swimming pools** Berlin's numerous sandy beaches provide an unexpected treat for children. The main beach at WANNSEE often gets crowded, but there are countless secret sandy coves on the shores of the GRUNEWALD lakes, easily reached by S-Bahn or U-Bahn.

• **Boat and bus trips** Every child except the most seasickness-prone should be taken on at least one trip on the Havel. Berlin children particularly appreciate jaunts on the *Moby Dick,* a big boat in the shape of a whale that departs from Wannsee pier. A trip on the top floor of a Berlin double-decker bus might also be fun (see page 86).

• **Castles** Berlin's Baroque palaces tend to be rather serious for children, but older kids might enjoy the moated ZITADELLE SPANDAU.

• **Clothes** See CLOTHES FOR CHILDREN in SHOPPING on page 196.

• **Museums and workshops** The MUSEUM FÜR VERKEHR UND TECHNIK is a good place to take older children on a rainy day. There are buttons to push, pulleys to yank, and computers programmed to compose music. The big locomotives can't be climbed on, but there is a marvelous overgrown rail yard at the back, where youngsters love to romp around.

The giant dinosaur skeletons and precious minerals at the MUSEUM FÜR NATURKUNDE might appeal, and the MUSEUM FÜR VOR- UND FRÜHGESCHICHTE has good dioramas of prehistoric settlements.

• **Parks and zoos** *Mit Kind und Kegel 'raus nach Tegel* (Head out to Tegel with a child and a ball), a local preacher urged city dwellers back in 1793. Nowadays children can be kept amused all day at TEGEL, and toys can be rented on the spot. There's miniature golf near the steamer pier on the Greenwichpromenade, while the **Freizeitpark** is a safe place to let off steam, with an adventure playground, trampolines, rowboats, and toys for hire. You can also rent bicycles for adults and children and pedal along the shore to Tegel beach.

The ZOOLOGISCHER GARTEN and the TIERPARK FRIEDRICHSFELDE are well-run modern zoos, with an incredible array of animals kept in natural environments, and the AQUARIUM, with its reptiles and rare fish, may help to engage young imaginations.

At the TIERGARTEN there are boats to rent, and the VIKTORIAPARK has a waterfall and a small zoo. If your kids get fractious on Kurfürstendamm, you might take them to the little playground at the **Uhland-Passage** *(Uhlandstrasse 173).*

• **Planetariums** The spectacle of star-gazing is a possible distraction. See ARCHENHOLDE STERNWARTE, PLANETARIUM AM INSULANER and ZEISS-GROSS-PLANETARIUM.

• **Restaurants and cafés** Restless children are free to romp around in Berlin's beer gardens, some of which have playgrounds. **Loretta in der City** *(details on page 180)* has a magical atmosphere in the evening, when it is lit by thousands of lamps and the Ferris wheel slowly turns.

Farther out of town, the **Chalet Suisse** in the GRUNEWALD (see WALK 4 on page 84) has a rambling garden filled with gurgling fountains, and a large playground complete with a model tractor. Ice cream was one of the rare luxuries in East German life, and the many *Eis Cafés* in Mitte and Prenzlauer Berg are popular places for young families.

- **Sports** See SPORTS AND ACTIVITIES on the following pages.
- **Toys** See TOYS in SHOPPING on page 200.
- **Views** Many youngsters love the thrill of ascending to dizzying heights. The best views can be had from the FRANZÖSISCHER DOM, the FUNKTURM and the FERNSEHTURM, but the SIEGESSÄULE column is perhaps rather risky. Look for the ⋞ symbol.
- **Other events and activities** For details of puppet shows, circuses and other children's activities, look in *Zitty* magazine under *Kinder.*

Sports and activities

The woods and lakes near Berlin offer visitors ample opportunities for walking, cycling, jogging, swimming and boating, while sports centers, stadiums and clubs cater to a wide variety of other leisure activities. In the following pages, all these are listed alphabetically, and a section on **Spectator sports** gives information for those with a more passive interest in sport.

For details of all sporting events and sports associations, contact **Landessportbund Berlin** *(Jesse-Owens-Allee 1-2, Charlottenburg, map* ***5****C3* ☎ *(030) 300020).* The office, near the Olympic stadium, is situated in a street named after the black American athlete who enraged the Nazis by stealing the limelight at the 1936 Olympics.

- **Billiards**

The **Billard Centrum** *(Nollendorfplatz 3-4, Schöneberg, map* ***2****D6* ☎ *(030) 2163361)* is a favored haunt.

- **Boating**

Rowboats can be rented at the Strandbad on the WANNSEE, the Neuer See in the TIERGARTEN, the Schlachtensee in the GRUNEWALD, and the Freizeitpark at TEGEL.

- **Bowling**

Berlin has numerous bowling alleys. The best locations for visitors are **Bowling am Kurfürstendamm** *(Kurfürstendamm 156, Wilmersdorf, map* ***1****D2* ☎ *(030) 8825030)* and **Bowling am Studio** *(Kaiserdamm 80, Charlottenburg, map* ***6****C4* ☎ *(030) 3027094).*

- **Cycling**

Despite Berlin's flat terrain, cycling is not popular, but it is an ideal way to explore the GRUNEWALD and other forests. There is an extensive network of urban cycle lanes (mainly running along the sidewalks), but it is generally wise to take cycles out to the suburbs by S-Bahn or U-Bahn.

For other information, including details on using the S- and U-Bahns, see page 57.

- **Fitness facilities**

City-Fitness *(Uhlandstrasse 185, Charlottenburg, map* ***2****D4* ☎ *(030) 8818688)* is a friendly gym in the heart of the city.

- **Ice-skating**

There are rinks at the **Eissporthalle** *(Jafféstrasse, Charlottenburg, just w of the Funkturm* ☎ *(030) 30381)* and the **Eisstadion** *(Fritz-Wildung-Strasse, Wilmersdorf, map* ***5****D3* ☎ *(030) 8234060)*.

During the winter months, some of the frozen lakes are safe for skating. Take your cue from the locals.

- **Riding**

Certain paths in the GRUNEWALD are marked out for horseback riding. The main school is **Reitschule Onkel Toms Hütte** *(Onkel-Tom-Strasse 172, Zehlendorf, map* **5**E3 ☎ *(030) 8132081)*.

- **Roller-skating**

The main rinks are the **Rollerskating-Center** *(Hasenheide 108, Kreuzberg, map* ***4****E9* ☎ *(030) 6211028)* and, in summer only, the **Rollschuhbahn in Wilmersdorf** *(Fritz-Wildung-Strasse, Wilmersdorf, map* ***6****D4* ☎ *(030) 8234060)*.

- **Running**

The TIERGARTEN is the most central park for running, but you can also limber up before breakfast in the quiet park behind SCHLOSS CHARLOTTENBURG. The GRUNEWALD route described in WALK 4 on page 83 can be taken as an energetic run, as can the Spree route as far as the REICHSTAG (see WALK 1 on page 74).

The annual 50km **Berlin Marathon** is on the first Sunday in October.

- **Skiing and tobogganing**

There are several artificial ski-slopes built on the rubble hills created after World War II. In winter, the **Teufelsberg** in the GRUNEWALD becomes Alpine, with its ski slopes and long toboggan run.

- **Spectator sports**

Berlin has much to offer. The best **soccer games** can be seen at the **Friedrich-Ludwig-Jahn-Sportpark** (home to BFC Dynamo) and the **Stadion an der Wuhlheide** (FC Union Berlin's ground). Blau-Weiss 90 plays at the **Olympic Stadium**. For fixtures, contact the Berlin soccer association, **Berliner Fussballverband** *(☎ (030) 8911047)*. **Ice-hockey** matches often take place at the Eissporthalle.

Rowing regattas take place at the **Hohenzollernkanal**, **Volkspark Jungfernheide** and the Regattastrecke in **Grünau**. **Sailing regattas** are held at the **Tegeler See**, **Gatow** and **Grünau**. Berlin also hosts international **swimming contests** and **tennis tournaments**.

Trotting races are run some Sundays at **Trabrennbahn Karlshorst** or **Trabrennbahn Mariendorf**.

- **Sports centers**

The East German government encouraged its promising athletes to win Olympic medals by building excellent sports centers, such as the **Sport- und Erholungszentrum** *(Landsberger Allee 77, Friedrichshain, map* ***6****C6* ☎ *(030) 42283320, S-Bahn to Landsberger Allee)*, a well-equipped complex with a swimming pool, sauna, gym, roller-skating rink, bowling alley, table-tennis, mini-golf and sports for children.

The leisure center **Meretva** *(Glockenturmstrasse, Charlottenburg, map **5**C3 ☎(030) 3042255)* offers tennis courts, a swimming pool, a sauna and a bowling alley.

- **Swimming**

Many Berlin districts have excellent swimming pools. One that is architecturally spectacular is the **Stadtbad Neukölln** *(Ganghoferstrasse 3-5, Neukölln, map **6**D6 ☎(030) 68092653),* a monumental Neoclassical edifice completed in 1914, with marble and mosaics inspired by the Thermae at Pompeii. **Blub** *(Buschkrugallee 64, Neukölln, map **7**E6 ☎(030) 6066060)* is a modern leisure pool, equipped with wave machines, a slide, whirlpools and a sauna.

To escape the sweltering city, West Berliners take the S-Bahn w to **Strandbad Wannsee** *(Wannseebadweg, map **5**E2 ☎(030) 8035450),* a popular open-air pool, while East Berliners head in the opposite direction to the **Strandbad Müggelsee** *(Fürstenwalder Damm, Rahnsdorf, off map **7**E7; S-Bahn to Rahnsdorf, then a 10min walk through the woods).* For a quieter dip, try the Strandbad at TEGEL.

- **Tennis and squash**

Playing facilities are often filled up way ahead, but you can try to get a court at **Tennis + Squash City** *(Brandenburgische Strasse 53, Wilmersdorf, map **1**E3 ☎(030) 879097).* It has 11 squash courts and seven tennis courts, and you can rent by the hour.

The **Squash Center Alt-Lietzow** *(Alt-Lietzow 15-19, Charlottenburg, map **1**B3 ☎(030) 3421844)* has 12 courts.

For information on other clubs open to nonmembers, contact **Berliner Tennis-Verband** *(☎(030) 8255311).*

- **Walking**

There are excellent forest and lakeside walks, particularly in the **Grunewald**, the **Tegeler Forst**, the **Spandauer Forst**, the **Düppel Forst** and along the **Havel shore**. The S-Bahn gets you to the Grunewald, while the U-Bahn stations at Tegel and Onkel-Toms-Hütte make good starting points for a ramble.

Some half-day walks along the **Spree**, around **Kreuzberg**, the **Old Jewish Quarter** and in the **Grunewald** are given on pages 74–84, and others appear in the entries on UNTER DEN LINDEN, TEGEL and GRUNEWALD. More walks are included in the POTSDAM and DRESDEN sections.

- **Walking tours**

Several organizations in Berlin run walking tours of the city, focusing on architecture, history or politics. **Stattreisen Berlin** *(Stephanstrasse 24 ☎(030) 3953078)* organizes well-researched guided tours in German, taking groups to Potsdam, Wedding district, the abandoned Jewish cemeteries of East Berlin or the eerie wasteland near Potsdamer Platz. Inquire at the **Stattreisenladen** *(Potsdamer Platz, Mitte, map **3**C7, S-Bahn to Potsdamer Platz).*

Potsdam

The Prussian paradise

Potsdam was, until recently, one of the forgotten cities of Europe. Known in past centuries as "the Versailles of Germany," it was once one of Europe's most scintillating Baroque towns, and a major center of the arts, philosophy and science, visited by such famous figures as Voltaire and Einstein. When the Cold War cut Potsdam off from the world, only a trickle of Western tourists were to see its faded Baroque grandeur for almost 50 years. *Die Wende* changed all that, bringing a fresh deluge of tourists to the old Prussian town.

Older than Berlin by more than two centuries, Potsdam began as a Slavic fishing village on the banks of the Havel. Mentioned for the first time in a document dated 993, the village was originally called by a Slavic name, *Poztupimi* (Under the Oaks). Potsdam officially obtained the right to call itself a city in the 14th century, but it was not until the 17th century that it became famous throughout Europe.

A PRUSSIAN ARCADIA

The rise of Potsdam began when the Great Elector Friedrich Wilhelm erected a summer palace near the Havel in 1660. He built a road, lined with lime trees, which began at the royal palace in Berlin. The route crossed a wooden bridge built in 1662, known as the *Glienicker Brücke*. It was the forerunner of the bridge where spies were exchanged during the Cold War.

Potsdam became increasingly courtly and cosmopolitan in the 17th century, especially after the Great Elector enacted the Edict of Potsdam in the royal palace, offering French Huguenot refugees a safe haven in Brandenburg. Some 20,000 Protestants took up the offer, and Potsdam briefly became a symbol of enlightened tolerance.

The Soldier King ended all that. Friedrich Wilhelm I turned Potsdam into a grim military town. He built a gun factory, and several enormous barracks with huge rusticated gateways and stone cannon on the roofs. Some of these monuments to military folly are still standing in the dusty streets of the Old Town. Even the Allied bombs could not shift them.

The town's setting amid hills and lakes appealed immensely to Frederick the Great, and he gave it one of Europe's most dazzling palaces. Graced with the French name of *Sanssouci* (Carefree), it even had a vineyard on the sloping ground in front of the palace. Potsdam became an essential stop on the Grand Tour of Europe—J. S. Bach came to play the organ for Frederick the Great in 1747; Casanova flirted there in the summer of 1764; Voltaire debated philosophy with Frederick in Park Sanssouci in 1750; and Mozart passed this way in 1789.

For more than 200 years, the Hohenzollerns filled the town with handsome buildings, rambling parks and whimsical follies. A pyramid was built to store ice; a steam engine was disguised as a mosque; a reservoir was concealed amid Classical ruins; everything was frivolous and unreal. Potsdam became a place where king and court could briefly escape from the pressures of Berlin, wandering across lawns as green as any in England, soaking in Classical baths as the ancient Romans did.

DECLINE AND FALL

The Potsdam idyll began to fall apart in the 20th century. Its decline started in 1914 when war broke out. The town's barracks supplied vast numbers of troops for the trenches on the Western Front, but the war was lost and the Kaiser had to flee to the Netherlands, leaving Potsdam with a legacy of empty and echoing palaces.

The town found a modest role in the 1920s as a movie city and center of science. But it was not long before the march of boots was heard again on the cobbled streets of the Altstadt. In the wake of the Reichstag fire in 1933, the Nazis chose the Garrison Church in Potsdam as the setting for their first parliament, which led to an exodus of movie directors, Jewish businessmen and scientists. The movie studios at Babelsberg were swallowed up in the Nazi propaganda machine.

Potsdam was bombed toward the end of World War II, but it was a light blow compared with the pounding received by Berlin and Dresden. The Baroque royal palace was hit, as was the town hall. The damage might have been repaired, as in other historic German towns devastated by bombardment, but Potsdam had the bad luck to end up in the Soviet sector. The Potsdam Agreement, which sealed the fate of Europe for almost half a century, was signed in a former Hohenzollern villa on the edge of the town. You can still see the round table where the delegates sat to carve up Germany into four sectors. Thanks to the Potsdam Agreement, the old barracks in Potsdam were soon occupied by Soviet soldiers.

The early communists cared little for the grand palaces of Potsdam. They dynamited its royal palace in 1960, as Berlin's authorities had done ten years earlier with the Berliner Schloss. Eight years on, the Garnisonkirche, where the Nazis held the 1933 parliament, was demolished.

The communists left the Old Town to decay, while they erected tacky apartment blocks along the Havel waterfront. The atmosphere of neglect still lingers on, in the shape of crumbling 19th century apartments with cavernous doorways, and old villas that still bear the scars of the 1945 bombardment.

But then the border was opened, and the Glienicker Bridge became jammed with traffic overnight. A new energy flowed into the city; scaffolding went up, and crumbling buildings were restored and repainted. The Chinese Teahouse at Sanssouci has been freshly gilded; Baroque paintings once patched up with sticky tape are being carefully restored; damaged statues are being repaired, one by one.

Tourism is booming, as two million people tramp through the grounds of Sanssouci each year, making Potsdam's future seem rosy compared with many former East German towns. It is now the state capital of Brandenburg, and many buildings in the old town have been restored for local government offices. The public transport network has been modernized, cycle lanes are being introduced, and bookstores have thrown out their copies of *The Communist Manifesto* to make room for travel guides covering exotic destinations. The movie studios at Babelsberg are booming, and a new university has been established.

Potsdam is one place where *die Wende* has brought about a miraculous transformation.

Landmarks in Potsdam's history

The town of Poztupimi was mentioned for the first time in a charter signed by Kaiser Otto III in **993**.

1664: The attractive setting appealed to the Great Elector, who built a royal palace, the Stadtschloss, near the River Havel. Potsdam became the second Residence of the Electors of Brandenburg, after Berlin.

1685: The Great Elector issued the Edict of Potsdam in the Stadtschloss. This important document guaranteed religious freedom throughout the territories of Brandenburg to Huguenots expelled from France. Encouraged by this enlightened attitude, some hundreds of Protestants settled in Potsdam, bringing new skills and generating a cosmopolitan air that survives to this day.

1713: The reign of Friedrich Wilhelm I, "the Soldier King," began. He turned the gentle and tolerant town of Potsdam into Prussia's foremost military garrison. The Baroque town center was transformed by vast barracks built to accommodate the rapidly multiplying Prussian regiments.

1740: Start of the reign of Frederick the Great. He brought further troops to Potsdam, building the Kleine Kaserne in Charlottenstrasse, the Infanteriekaserne in Hegelallee and the Grosses Militärwaisenhaus (Great Military Orphanage) in Lindenstrasse. **1745–47**: The construction of the summer palace at Sanssouci. **1750–53**: The French philosopher Voltaire was invited to Potsdam by Frederick the Great.

1756–63: Prussia battled with Austria during the Seven Years' War. Prussia's finances were drained, but Frederick the Great began constructing the enormous Neues Palais at the end of the war, to show his enemies that Prussia was still a mighty power. It took six years to build the palace, and it was rarely used.

1806–8: Napoleon garrisoned 6,000 troops in Potsdam.

1840: Start of reign of Friedrich Wilhelm IV. He embellished Potsdam with elegant Neoclassical palaces and landscaped gardens.

1911: Opening of the Filmstadt Babelsberg movie studios.

1914: Kaiser Wilhelm II signed the declaration of war on Russia on August 1, in Potsdam's Neues Palais. **1917**: The movie company UFA was founded at Babelsberg.

1918: Kaiser Wilhelm II abdicated, and fled to Doorn in the Netherlands. His wife left in haste from the Bahnhof Wildpark in Potsdam (now an overgrown ruin behind the S-Bahn station). The royal palaces in Potsdam were confiscated. **1923**: Crown Prince Wilhelm returned to Schloss Cecilienhof in Potsdam.

1926: Fritz Lang filmed *Metropolis* in the world's largest movie studio at Babelsberg. **1929**: Josef von Sternberg filmed *The Blue Angel,* starring Marlene Dietrich, also at Babelsberg.

1933: Uniformed Nazis marched through the streets of Potsdam to the Garrison Church, for the first meeting of the Fascist parliament following the burning of the Reichstag. The event became known as the *Tag von Potsdam* (Potsdam Day) and Potsdam gained the title of the "birthplace of the Third Reich." **1942**: *The Adventures of Baron Münchhausen* was shot at the Babelsberg Studios to mark the 25th anniversary of UFA.

1945: On the night of April 14, Allied planes bombed the center of Potsdam, destroying the Stadtschloss and much of the old town. In the summer of that year, Truman, Churchill, Attlee and Stalin met in Schloss Cecilienhof to sign the Potsdam Agreement, which established the postwar division of Germany. Under the agreement, Potsdam fell within the Soviet sector.

1960: Considered by the communists as a symbol of feudalism, the Stadtschloss was dynamited.

1961: The Berlin Wall was built on August 13. It ran along the northern edge of Potsdam, following the shore of the Havel and Griebnitzsee. The Glienicker Brücke was closed to traffic, cutting Potsdam off from Berlin for the next 28 years. Potsdam declined into a dreary, dilapidated town dominated by a large Soviet military base.

1989: The Berlin Wall came down in November, and the Glienicker Brücke was reopened.

1991: Potsdam's link with Frederick the Great (who had fallen from favor under the communists) was symbolically restored when the king's bones were brought back from Schloss Hechingen, where they had been taken for safety during World War II. They were reburied in the royal crypt on the terrace of Sanssouci, a modest stone slab their memorial.

1993: Potsdam celebrated its 1,000th anniversary. Many of its historic monuments were restored for the occasion.

Potsdam's architecture

The Hohenzollern gave Potsdam almost every style in the architecture books. You can track down a copy of Windsor Castle (SCHLOSS BABELSBERG), a building modeled on London's Banqueting Hall (the Hiller-Brandtsche Häuser), a Russian church (KAPELLE ALEXANDER NEWSKI), a mosque (the MOSCHEE), a tower based on a Frankfurt medieval relic (the Flatowturm), a mock-Roman bathhouse (RÖMISCHER BÄDER) and an entire Dutch quarter (HOLLÄNDISCHES VIERTEL). Potsdam sometimes seems a mere pastiche of other countries, yet it has two architectural styles of its own.

POTSDAM BAROQUE

Potsdam is one of the great Baroque towns of Germany. It was Friedrich Wilhelm I, the barracks builder, who laid out the Baroque grid of streets known as the Neustadt in the 18thC. The character of this quarter is best appreciated in streets like Yorckstrasse and Dortustrasse. The houses have remained virtually intact since they were built in the 1720s. Even the paving stones have survived untouched.

The Potsdam style of Baroque is distinctive. Each house has two floors, with a middle bay flanked by pilasters and topped by a dormer window with a Classical pediment. The houses may be crumbling, but they have at least not been altered. Even the shops along Brandenburgerstrasse have kept their traditional facades, although it may be only a matter of time before commerce begins to ruin the Baroque harmony.

POTSDAM ROCOCO

A change of style came with Frederick the Great. His passion for the elaborate French style of Louis XV led to the creation of Potsdam Rococo. He employed his friend Georg Wenzeslaus Knobelsdorff to design a Rococo music room at the Stadtschloss and a new summer palace called Sanssouci. The music room was destroyed in World War II, but **Schloss Sanssouci** survives. Frederick the Great produced a sketch of the palace he desired. Knobelsdorff quarreled with the king, and eventually gave up the project, bringing his career to an end.

Schloss Sanssouci: the Rococo circular library

The palace contains a series of intimate rooms such as the Music Room, with its mirrors and gilt, and the wood-paneled, circular library with its lavish Rococo decoration.

Later members of the Hohenzollern family added their own favorite styles. While still Crown Prince, Friedrich Wilhelm IV commissioned Schinkel to design **Schloss Charlottenhof** and the **Römische Bäder** (Roman baths). Later, as king of Prussia, he pursued his passion for Italy by building the **Friedenskirche**, a church inspired by the Romanesque basilica of San Clemente in Rome, and the **Orangerie**, a large-scale version of an Italian Renaissance villa.

Energetic visitors can track down **Schloss Lindstedt**, built on a hill to the NW for Friedrich Wilhelm IV, the **Marmorpalais** in the **Neuer Garten**, another Italian-style villa built for Friedrich Wilhelm II, **Schloss Babelsberg**, an imitation of Windsor Castle, to the E, built for the Crown Prince, later Kaiser Wilhelm I, and **Schloss Cecilienhof** to the N, a small palace built for Kaiser Wilhelm II in the style of an English suburban mansion, with half-timbered gables.

THE 19TH AND 20TH CENTURIES

A wealth of 19thC Eclecticism is hidden away in the Potsdam suburbs. You can find mansions bristling with turrets, balconies and belvederes in handsome streets such as Mangerstrasse and Karl-Marx-Strasse. The houses are often dilapidated and the gardens thick with weeds, but this may soon change.

One 20thC building in Potsdam is mentioned in almost any history of architecture: the **Einsteinturm** (Einstein Tower), an extraordinary Expressionist tower designed by Erich Mendelsohn in 1920–21. It was there that Einstein tested the theory of relativity.

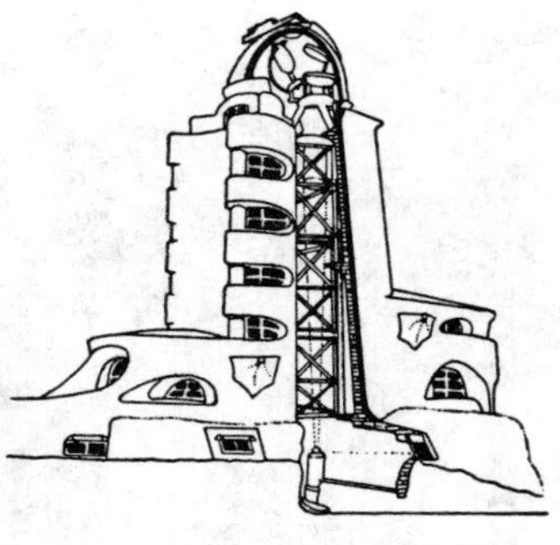
The **Einsteinturm**

The communists made a tragic error when they built modern tower blocks in the bombed-out heart of the old town. These buildings were once the symbols of optimism, but they have aged badly. They now dominate the skyline, somewhat diminishing the Baroque harmony of the city, although at least one monstrosity (the unfinished theater on Am Alten Markt) has already been demolished.

The city's millennium in 1993 was taken as an opportunity to restore the architectural heritage of Potsdam. Among the buildings to benefit were the CHINESISCHES TEEHAUS at Sanssouci and the little temple built by Schinkel on Pfingstberg. The restoration of the old Dutch Quarter (HOLLÄNDISCHES VIERTEL) is another promising sign of urban renewal.

Potsdam: practical information

This section is subdivided as follows:

- **GETTING THERE**, below
- **GETTING AROUND IN POTSDAM**, page 212
- **ON-THE-SPOT INFORMATION**, page 214
- **EMERGENCY INFORMATION**, page 215
- **USEFUL NUMBERS AND ADDRESSES**, page 215

Summaries of subject headings are printed in CAPITALS at the top of most pages. See also **VISITING NORTHERN GERMANY** on page 16.

Getting there

BY RAIL

An increasing number of sleek InterCity and other international trains stop at **Bahnhof Potsdam-Stadt**. The S-Bahn (city railway) from Berlin also terminates at this station.

Once the main station for Potsdam, the **Hauptbahnhof** is now used only for local services. The station is situated on the SW edge of Potsdam, too far from the town center to make an easy walk. Take tram 94 or 96, or (for a more interesting ride) bus 695 (see page 225 for the route).

- For information on train services, contact **Deutsche Reichsbahn** ☎(0331) 4661.

BY CAR

Potsdam is easily reached on the Autobahn network. On the Berliner Ring (A10), leave at Potsdam-Süd for the old town, at Babelsberg for the DEFA studios, and at Potsdam-Nord for PARK SANSSOUCI.

Coming from Berlin, you can drive on the old road to Potsdam (the B1), which takes you across the Glienicker Brücke, but it is quicker to take the AVUS, then Autobahn 115, leaving at the Babelsberg exit.

Traffic gridlock has hit Potsdam now that tourism and trade have begun to boom. It makes sense to avoid using a car in town if possible.

FROM BERLIN TO POTSDAM

Once a bureaucratic and logistic nightmare for visitors from West Berlin, the town now makes an easy side-trip by S-Bahn, bus or boat.

Tickets issued by the Berlin transport authority (BVG) are valid on buses from Berlin to Potsdam, and on the S-Bahn from Wannsee to Potsdam, but not on Potsdam local transport.

From the Berlin airports to Potsdam

- **Berlin-Tegel** Bus 700 runs directly from the airport to Bahnhof Potsdam-Stadt *(from 7.30am–7pm),* but there can be a long wait. Better to take bus 109 from Tegel to S-Bahnhof Charlottenburg, then change to line S3, which terminates at Potsdam-Stadt.
- From **Berlin-Schönefeld** Take the airport shuttle bus *(hourly from 5am-11pm)* to Schönefeld station, then bus 601 to Bassinplatz, in Potsdam center. The journey takes about 90 minutes.

- **Tempelhof** Take the U-Bahn U6 to Mehringdamm, then U7 to S-Bahnhof Charlottenburg, then change to S-Bahn line S3, to Bahnhof Potsdam-Stadt.
- Berlin airport telephone numbers are listed on page 53.

Berlin to Potsdam by S-Bahn

The fastest way to reach Potsdam from Berlin is by S-Bahn. Line S3 runs from central Berlin to Bahnhof Potsdam-Stadt. Trains run every 10 minutes during the day, and every 20 minutes in the evening. The service stops around midnight. You can pick up the S-Bahn at Friedrichstrasse, Bahnhof Zoo and Charlottenburg.

Berlin to Potsdam by bus

Traveling by bus can be a slow way to get to Potsdam, often along old, pot-holed roads, but you will sometimes get interesting glimpses of suburban Potsdam.

Bus 113 runs the 45-minute journey from S-Bahnhof Wannsee to the bus station at Bassinplatz, in the town center.

Bus 116 runs from S-Bahnhof Wannsee to the Glienicke Brücke, where you can walk across the bridge to pick up **tram 93**.

Berlin to Potsdam by steamer

The most romantic way to arrive in Potsdam is to board a Weisse Flotte steamer in Berlin and sail down the Havel, past Pfaueninsel and Schloss Klein-Glienicke. You can set off from Tegel, Spandau or Wannsee. The trip takes you under the Glienicker Brücke and into the Tiefer See. Schloss Babelsberg crowns the wooded hill on the left. The steamer arrives at the Lange Brücke pier, a short walk from Potsdam town center.

- For details of the Weisse Flotte timetable ☎(0331) 21527.

Getting around in Potsdam

GETTING AROUND BY PUBLIC TRANSPORT

Getting from the stations

The station quarter around **Bahnhof Potsdam-Stadt** has been restyled, and bus and tram links into town have been upgraded. You can walk into the town center in about ten minutes from the station. Otherwise, take bus 697 from the station to the town center, or walk up the hill to the tram stop, where you can pick up trams to Schloss Charlottenhof (91, 98), Glienicker Brücke (93) or Luisenplatz, for Schloss Sanssouci (91, 96, 98).

The **Hauptbahnhof**, on the sw edge of the city, is used nowadays for local services. From the station, take tram 94 or 96, or, for a more interesting ride, bus 695 (see page 225 for description).

Trams and buses

Potsdam's public transport network of trams and buses is run by **ViP** *(☎(0331) 22966)*. Since reunification, the service has improved dramatically. There are now smart new glass shelters at most stops, and easy-to-use maps and timetables. Stops are indicated by a sign with a green **H** on a yellow background.

Potsdam's creaky orange **trams** are somewhat old and bumpy, but they get you to outlying places fairly efficiently. You can enter by any of the doors. The driver does not sell tickets, but you can buy any type of ticket at the automatic machine at the front of the tram. There is ample space at the back of trams for luggage.

The **buses** are mostly old, too, although new models are being introduced. You can only enter at the front, showing your pass to the driver, or stamping your ticket in the red *Entwerter.* The driver will also sell you a ticket. It can be difficult to find the button to open the doors. On some buses it is a green button above the door; on others it is marked *Türöffner.* If in doubt, watch other people.

Tickets

The ticket system is similar to Berlin's. At the start of each journey, you must stamp your ticket in the red *Entwerter* inside the tram or bus (tickets from machines are usually automatically stamped). Tickets can be bought at the tourist office, some newspaper stores, or from the automatic machines located in trams.

You can buy a single ticket *(Kurzfahrt),* a multiple ticket *(Sammelkarte 4-Fahrten)* valid for four rides, or a 24-hour ticket *(Potsdam-Ticket).*

A *Kurzfahrt* ticket is valid on the Potsdam public transport network for 30 minutes, but you may find that this does not allow long enough to reach some destinations — the Babelsberg Studios for example. It is not valid on Berlin transport or the S-Bahn.

It is probably cheaper and less worrying to buy a *Potsdam-Ticket,* valid on the ViP network for 24 hours from the time stamped. If you intend to travel in Berlin, or use the S-Bahn, you should buy a *Berlin-Ticket,* which is valid on both Berlin and Potsdam public transport. If in doubt about the validity of your ticket, ask an official.

The tourist office sells a useful *Liniennetzplan* (network map) indicating bus and tram routes.

Ferries

The Potsdam public transport authority **ViP** runs two ferry services. **Line F1** crosses the Havel from Auf dem Kiewitt to the Hermannswerder peninsula every 15 minutes or so. **Line L2** crosses the Jungfernsee from the Glienicker Brücke to Sacrow.

GETTING AROUND BY TAXI

Before reunification, taxis in Potsdam were spluttering Trabants, but every driver has now upgraded to a powerful Western car. There are taxi ranks at Bahnhof Potsdam-Stadt, Bassinplatz, Hauptbahnhof and Luisenplatz. Under a new scheme, passengers on buses or trams can ask the driver to call a taxi to pick them up at a stop along the route.

- To call a taxi in Potsdam ☎(0331) 22231.

On-the-spot information

TOURIST INFORMATION

The local tourist office is **Potsdam-Information** *(Friedrich-Ebert-Strasse 5, 14467 Potsdam ☎ (0331) 21100 or 23385 Fx (0331) 23012. Tram 91, 92, 93, 96, 98 to Alter Markt).* It is open April–October, Monday–Friday 9am–8pm, Saturday, Sunday and holidays 9am–6pm; November–March, Monday–Friday 10am–6pm, Saturday, Sunday and holidays 11am–3pm.

The tourist office sells guidebooks, town maps, public transport tickets and postcards, and has information about concerts, plays and other events.

NAME CHANGES OF POTSDAM STREETS

Some street names have changed in the wake of reunification, although far fewer than in Berlin. The following changes have been made:

- **Bruno-Baum-Strasse** (now **Humboldt Ring**)
- **Johannes-Dieckmann-Allee** (now **Alleestrasse**).
- **Strasse der Junge Pioniere** (now **B. von Suttner-Strasse**)
- **Leninallee** (now **Zeppelinstrasse**)
- **Otto-Nuschke-Strasse** (now **Lindenstrasse**)

Otto-Grotewohl-Strasse, **Karl-Marx-Strasse** and **Hegelallee** are so far unchanged. Some of the old street signs have not yet been replaced, which adds to everyone's confusion. The most reliable map to use is the latest edition of the Falkplan map of Berlin.

MAIL AND GENERAL DELIVERY (POSTE RESTANTE)

The main post office, or *Hauptpostamt,* faces Platz der Einheit *(Am Kanal 16–18, 14467 Potsdam, open Mon-Fri 7am-6pm (7pm Thursday), Sat 8am-11am, Sun 9am-6pm).*

To use the **General Delivery** *(poste restante)* service, send letters to be collected, marked *Hauptpostlagernd,* to the address above.

PUBLIC HOLIDAYS

Shops and banks in Potsdam close on the normal German public holidays (see page 20). Work also stops on *Reformationstag* (31 October), as it does in the rest of Brandenburg *Land,* although it remains a normal working day in Berlin.

SHOPPING HOURS

Shopping hours in Potsdam, as elsewhere in Germany, are tightly controlled. Shops are permitted to open Mon–Fri 9am–6pm, Sat 9am–1pm. On the first Saturday of each month, some shops remain open until 6pm.

Many boutiques in Potsdam do not open until 10am, and some of the smaller shops close for lunch. A few boutiques open on Sundays during the summer season, but don't count on it. Follow the German habit, and get all your weekend shopping done on Saturday morning.

LOCAL PUBLICATIONS

The Berlin magazine *Zitty* provides a brief listing of current events in Potsdam in the daily *Dies & Das* section.

Emergency information

For advice on **automobile accidents**, **lost passport** and **emergency phrases**, see EMERGENCY INFORMATION on page 23.

EMERGENCY SERVICES
Coins are not needed for emergency calls from public telephones.

- **Police** ☎110
- **Fire** ☎112
- **Ambulance** ☎115

MEDICAL AND DENTAL EMERGENCIES

- **Doctors' emergency service** (7pm–7am) ☎(0331) 622157
- **Dentists' emergency service** ☎(0331) 410

HOSPITAL

- **Krankenhaus-Oberlinhaus** Rudolf-Breitscheid-Strasse 24 ☎(0331) 7630.

PHARMACIES
Pharmacies are open during normal shopping hours. A list of those open at night and on Sunday is placed in the window of every pharmacy.

- For information on **all-night pharmacies** ☎(0331) 24069.

CAR BREAKDOWN

- ☎ police (110) or the **ADAC** (road patrol) ☎(033205) 2611.
- See also EMERGENCY INFORMATION on page 23.

LOST PROPERTY
Report all losses to the police immediately, as insurance claims may not be accepted without a police report.

- If you lose something, contact the **Magistrat Potsdam** *(Friedrich-Ebert-Strasse 79–81 ☎(0331) 350).*

Useful numbers and addresses

TELEPHONE SERVICES

- The **area code** for Potsdam is 0331.
- To send a **telegram** ☎13.
- **Directory inquiries** (Germany) ☎180
- **Directory inquiries** (abroad) ☎0117.

AIRLINES
The German airline **Lufthansa** has an office at the MERCURE hotel *(Lange Brücke).*

CAR RENTAL

- **Interrent/Europcar** Rudolf-Breitscheid-Strasse 15 ☎(0331) 75075.

BOAT TOURS

- **Weisse Flotte Potsdam** An der Langen Brücke ☎(0331) 21527 Fx(0331) 21090. Runs regular cruises *(mid-May to mid-Sept)* to the Potsdam lakes, Werder Insel, Brandenburg, Tempelhof, Schloss Petzow, Wannsee, Spandau and Tegel.

GUIDED TOURS

- **Stattreisen** Nansenstrasse 19 ☎(0331) 960894. Walking tours of Potsdam that take tourists off the beaten track.
- **Urania** Haus Wilhelm Foerster, Brandenburger Strasse ☎(0331) 21741 Fx(0331) 23683. Varied program of cultural excursions, and occasional tours of the Einsteinturm and Schloss Lindstedt.

Potsdam: planning your visit

ORIENTATION

Potsdam (population 140,000) is located on the River Havel, 490 meters (1,600 feet) above sea-level, in the *Land* of Brandenburg. The surrounding countryside is primarily lakes and woods. **Berlin** is 24km (15 miles) to the NE; **Brandenburg** is 38km (24 miles) to the W; **Dresden** lies 220km (138 miles) to the SE. The **Polish border** is 114km (71 miles) to the E at Frankfurt/Oder.

WHEN TO GO

With its countless lakes and parks to explore, Potsdam looks its best in the summer months. But bear in mind that the grounds of Sanssouci are teeming with visitors from June to August. Hotel rooms are hard to find, and long lines wait to visit Schloss Sanssouci. Come the autumn, the crowds have thinned, and by winter the town is quiet.

The Potsdam calendar

WINTER

Winters are quiet in Potsdam; the statues in the parks are enclosed in wooden shelters to protect them from the frost, and many of the palaces at Sanssouci are closed from November until May.

MARCH

The arrival of spring is celebrated with a **Frühlingfest** (spring festival), in late March or early April. Look out for posters advertising fairground attractions in Babelsberg park, as well as firework displays on the Havel waterfront.

APRIL
Runners slog through Park Sanssouci and the surrounding hills during the annual **Sanssouci Marathon.**

MAY
Palaces that are closed over winter open again in May, including Schloss Charlottenhof and the Orangerie. • Early May: The steamers of the Weisse Flotte line up in the harbor for the **Flottenparade** (fleet parade) to mark the beginning of the cruise season. Expect brass bands and dancing on board.

JUNE
The **Musikfestspiele Potsdam Sanssouci** (running for several weeks in June) features concerts of classical music in venues dotted around Potsdam and Sanssouci, including Baroque palaces, English parks, and Italianate churches. • Exhibitions of art are staged in galleries, and theater groups perform in the parks during the **Potsdamer Arkadien** (several weeks in June).

AUGUST
The Havel is crammed with boats for the **Potsdamer Hafenfest** (several days in late August). Crowds gather on the quayside near the Weisse Flotte pier to listen to music and eat grilled sausages.

NOVEMBER
Many of the sights at Sanssouci close for the winter.

DECEMBER
The **Weihnachtsmarkt** (Christmas market) is held in the town center, with traditional German wooden toys and Christmas tree decorations on sale.

Organizing your time

Two million visitors tramp through the gardens of Sanssouci each year, and it can be maddening in the summer. Go first thing in the morning, or in the late autumn. Or visit on a rainy Monday morning in February, but don't, if you can help it, go there on a sunny Sunday afternoon in August. You won't see anything for the crowds. Whatever the time of year, you may find a long line of people waiting to get into SCHLOSS SANSSOUCI. Don't despair. There are other sights which tend to be less busy. Try the NEUES PALAIS or the ORANGERIE.

Don't make the mistake of thinking that Sanssouci is the only sight worth visiting in Potsdam. The old town is fascinating to explore. There are still not many attractive hotels in Potsdam, but you should try, if possible, to stay at least one night to allow time to wander around the town and the many parks.

A ONE-DAY VISIT

- Go to **SCHLOSS SANSSOUCI**, arriving as early as possible. Visit the palace, and one or two other sights, but don't kill yourself trying to see the whole lot.
- On a sunny day, you can eat lunch in the beer garden next to the **Historische Windmühle**. Otherwise, you'll probably end up eating in the Old Town, perhaps in a café on Brandenburger Strasse.
- Spend the afternoon walking around the Old Town, then head off into the **NEUER GARTEN** to look at **SCHLOSS CECILIENHOF**. You won't have time to do much more.

A WEEKEND IN POTSDAM

Day 1

- Bear in mind that stores generally close on Saturdays at 1pm. Begin in the morning with a visit to **SCHLOSS SANSSOUCI**, then wander through the gardens, looking at some of the other sights, especially **SCHLOSS CHARLOTTENHOF**.
- Climb up to the **DRACHENHAUS** for lunch, then explore the ruins on **RUINENBERG**. Eat dinner somewhere in the Old Town, but don't rush the meal. There isn't a lot to do in Potsdam after dark, except go to the cabaret or watch a film in German.

Day 2

- Begin with a walk in the Old Town. Look at the **HOLLÄNDISCHES VIERTEL** to see if any new life has come to the quarter, then stroll into the **NEUER GARTEN** to visit **SCHLOSS CECILIENHOF**.
- Finding lunch can be difficult here, but you may like the look of the hotel restaurant located in Schloss Cecilienhof. Otherwise take the bus back into town.
- Take a boat trip in the afternoon if the sun is shining. Go to the **DEFA FILM- UND TV-ERLEBNIS** if it is raining.

A ONE-DAY MOVIE TOUR

- Everyone interested in the movies should take a tour of the **DEFA FILM- UND TV-ERLEBNIS** in the suburb of Babelsberg. That will take up an entire morning, or more.
- You can eat a basic lunch in one of the studio cafés, then go into town to visit the **FILMMUSEUM POTSDAM**. Consult the list of movies in case something takes your fancy.

Potsdam: sightseeing

AN OVERVIEW OF THE CITY

The big attraction in Potsdam is Schloss Sanssouci, just to the west of the town center. You must go there, crowds or not, if only to see Frederick the Great's spectacular Baroque palace poised above its terraced vineyard. But remember the other palaces dotted around Potsdam, for many also have splendid grounds and architectural follies.

Be sure to explore the Baroque town and take the bus to the DEFA film studios. The NEUER GARTEN is not the secret park it used to be, but PARK BABELSBERG remains off the beaten track. The Pfingstberg is quieter still.

See maps of Potsdam and Park Sanssouci on pages 220–21 and 223.

AREA BY AREA

Most tourists go to Potsdam simply to see Schloss Sanssouci, but there is also much to see in the residential suburbs and surrounding hills listed below.

• First ports-of-call

These are the parts of town most likely to be visited by everyone:

OLD TOWN The old town is on the left bank of the Havel. Most of the shops and restaurants are here.

NEUSTADT The Baroque new town created in the 1720s. One of the best examples of Baroque town planning remaining in Europe.

SANSSOUCI The park and palaces to the W of the old town, often teeming with tourists.

• Off the beaten track

Whether handsome or run-down, the suburbs deserve a look:

BABELSBERG The leafy 19thC suburbs to the E of the old town. Handsome villas built in every style of architecture.

BRANDENBURGER VORSTADT Elegant 19thC suburbs to the W of the old town, on the edge of Park Sanssouci. Grand old apartment buildings that have not been repaired since 1945.

NAUENER VORSTADT The handsome 19thC suburbs to the N of the old town. Dotted with eccentric buildings that most tourists miss.

TELTOWER VORSTADT The 19thC suburbs rising up the slopes on the right bank of the Havel.

• High places

BABELSBERG A hill rising to the E of the old town to a height of 65m/213ft. It offers a good view of the Tiefer See.

PFINGSTBERG A hill rising to 38 meters/125 feet to the N of Nauener Vorstadt and surmounted by a ruined belvedere.

THE POTSDAM HILLS The hills around Potsdam are not high, but they offer interesting views in a region that is otherwise mainly flat.

RUINENBERG A hill 73 meters/240 feet high, to the N of Sanssouci, crowned with a curious collection of follies.

TELEGRAPHENBERG On the Havel's right bank, Potsdam's highest summit rises to 93 meters/305 feet. Telegraphenberg is dotted with scientific institutions, including the Einsteinturm and the Meteorological Institute.

The Kleiner Ravensberg hill to the S reaches all of 114 meters/374 feet.

Exploring Potsdam

With its palaces, parks, lakes and other charmingly eccentric buildings, Potsdam is a marvelous town to explore on foot.

The following three walks reveal many elusive delights. The first uncovers the handsome Baroque architecture of the old town; the second takes you through the gardens of Sanssouci, avoiding the crowds; the final walk follows the quiet shores of several lakes, where East German border guards once fired on anyone trying to cross to the West.

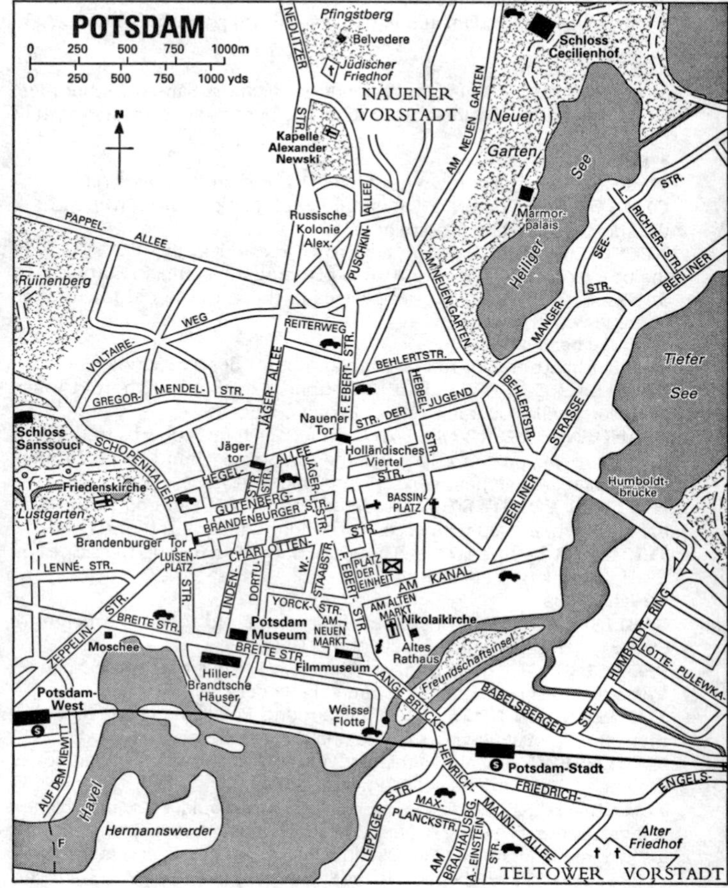

WALK 1: THE TOWN

Tram 91, 92, 93, 96, 98 to Alter Markt. Allow 2hrs.

Potsdam's 18thC Neustadt (New Town) survived the bombs of World War II, and is now one of the finest examples of Baroque town planning in Germany.

Beginning at S-Bahnhof Potsdam-Stadt, cross the Havel by the Lange Brücke. The island on the right, FREUNDSCHAFTSINSEL, has peaceful gardens, fountains and an open-air theater. Turn right to reach the NIKOLAIKIRCHE on the square known as Am Alten Markt.

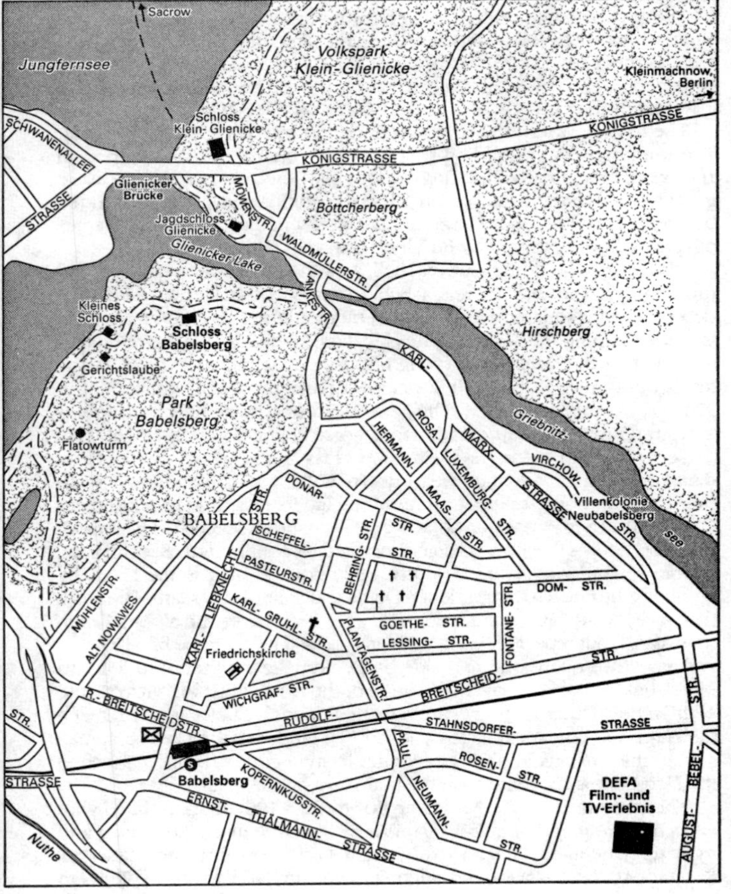

Two bombed buildings on the E side of the square were restored in the 1960s to form a cultural center, the **Haus Marchwitza**, with several restaurants and a café. The **Altes Rathaus**, or former town hall, on the left was built in 1753 by Johann Boumann and Carl Hildebrant. Modeled on a Palladian villa, it has a curious cupola surmounted by a gilded figure of Atlas. The statues symbolizing civic virtues were carved by Johann Heymüller. To the right, the **Knobelsdorff-Haus** is a handsome, pale green Rococo mansion built by Georg Wenzeslaus von Knobelsdorff in 1750. The two caryatides supporting the balcony have the air of typical Prussian *Landsknechte* (mercenaries), with their lank mustaches and ragged costumes.

The bombed Stadtschloss, which formerly stood on the S side of the square, was not saved by the East Germans. The ruins of the royal palace were demolished in 1961, leaving just the solitary Corinthian colonnade designed in 1745 by Knobelsdorff. Known as the **Havelkolonnaden, it** now stands near the steamer landing-stage on the Havel.

The former **Marstall** (royal stables) still stands on the opposite side. The long, red-ocher building was originally built by Johann Nering in 1685 as an orangery overlooking the long-vanished *Lustgarten* (pleasure garden). Converted to stables in 1714, the edifice was greatly extended by Knobelsdorff in 1746. The architrave is crowned with symbolic statues of rearing horses, carved by Friedrich Christian Glume.

Walk along the front of the Marstall, now the FILMMUSEUM POTSDAM, and turn right at the end to reach Schlossstrasse. **Am Neuen Markt**, a deserted, leafy square overshadowed by moldering Baroque mansions, is hidden behind the Marstall. The Neoclassical building in the middle of the square is the **Ratswaage** (weigh-house), constructed in 1836. To the left is the former Kutschstall, a decayed Baroque coach house built in 1787–91 by Andreas Krüger. The gate is festooned with military trophies and surmounted by a *quadriga* (four-horse chariot).

Leave the square on the N side and cross Yorckstrasse, one of Potsdam's filled-in canals, then head down Wilhelm-Staab-Strasse, a well-preserved Baroque street. Continue along Jägerstrasse and turn right into **Brandenburger Strasse**, an attractive pedestrianized street lined with modest 18thC houses that now contain shops and cafés. It leads to **Bassinplatz**, a large square overlooked by dusty gable houses, built in the 18thC by Frederick the Great to tempt skilled Dutch craftsmen to Potsdam. The basin that gave the square its name was dug in 1739 to create the air of a Dutch town canal, but repeated silting problems caused it later to be filled in.

Leave the square on the N side by Benkertstrasse, then turn left into Mittelstrasse. You are now in the heart of the **HOLLÄNDISCHES VIERTEL**, the 18thC model Dutch quarter. Turn right up Friedrich-Ebert-Strasse to reach the **Nauener Tor**, a city gate built in 1755. Frederick the Great commissioned this curious English mock-Gothic-style edifice, which launched the Neo-Gothic movement on the mainland of Europe.

The street leads to the **Nauener Vorstadt**, a 19thC suburb filled with villas that are grand, if rather dilapidated. Turn left along Reiterweg and right up Jägerallee. A lane to the right takes you into the **RUSSISCHE KOLONIE ALEXANDROWKA**, a settlement built in 1826 to house Russian soldiers. At the end of the street, turn left up Puschkinallee, and take the path left through the woods to discover the secluded Russian Orthodox church, **KAPELLE ALEXANDER NEWSKI**.

You can follow Puschkinallee farther to reach the **old Jewish cemetery**. Go up the cobbled road and turn right up the sandy track. The cemetery is on the left, overgrown and abandoned. It is not open to the public, but you can look over the wall at the tombstones. Climb to the top of **Pfingstberg**, a hill landscaped by Peter Lenné in 1849. A gateway leads to the ruins of a summer palace built by Persius in the 1840s for Friedrich Wilhelm IV. Notice the tiny **Pomonatempel**, built in 1801 by Schinkel as his first commission. The building was recently restored.

You have a choice at this stage. Either you go back down the hill and take tram 92 or 95 into town, or you carry on down the far side of the hill. The path leads after about 15 minutes to the terminus of bus 695, not far from SCHLOSS CECILIENHOF. The bus picks up passengers at the shelter.

WALK 2: PARK SANSSOUCI

Tram 91, 94, 96, 98 or bus 692, 695, 697 to Luisenplatz. Allow 2hrs.

The palaces and gardens at Sanssouci cover an extensive area to the w of the old town. The 18th and 19thC landscaped grounds are dotted with an extraordinary variety of palaces, temples, belvederes, statues,

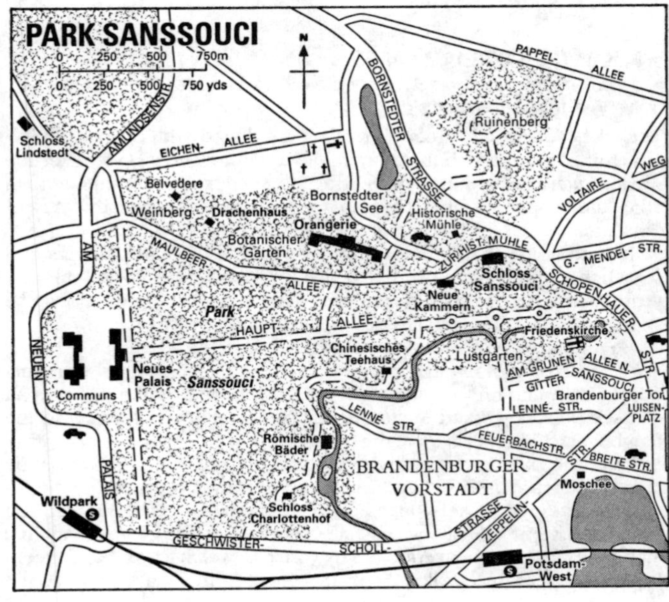

fountains, vineyards and grottos. Frederick the Great gave Sanssouci its Baroque grandeur, commissioning SCHLOSS SANSSOUCI, the NEUES PALAIS and the CHINESISCHES TEEHAUS. In the 19thC, buildings in a more restrained Neoclassical style were added by Friedrich Wilhelm IV, including SCHLOSS CHARLOTTENHOF, the RÖMISCHE BÄDER and the FRIEDENSKIRCHE.

Schloss Sanssouci can be frustrating to visit, as the compulsory guided tours are frequently oversubscribed; the Neues Palais and Schloss Charlottenhof, although just as interesting architecturally, are far less crowded, and the Orangerie and Römische Bäder are frequently almost deserted.

The main entrance to the park is near the **Brandenburger Tor**, built in 1770. Walk down the Allee nach Sanssouci, an almost rural lane which suddenly turns sharp right to give visitors a thrilling first view of the Baroque Schloss. Head toward the palace, then turn left at the pond and follow the **Hauptallee** (main avenue). If you turn left into the woods, you should come upon the bizarre but beautiful **CHINESISCHES TEEHAUS**.

From here, follow the meandering path to the right, past the **Meierei** (dairy) to reach the **Römische Bäder**. Continue to **SCHLOSS CHARLOTTENHOF** and follow the straight path beyond, then turn right along the avenue leading to the **NEUES PALAIS**. Now turn right along the Hauptallee, then left at the circle of statues. Climb up to the **ORANGERIE** for a panorama over the gardens, and, if you feel fit, continue up the hill to the **RUINENBERG**, for a closer look at its curious group of mock ruins. From the summit, you get a good view of Schloss Sanssouci to the S. Descend there to bring an end to the walk.

WALK 3: THE POTSDAM LAKES

See map on page 221. Tram 92, 95 or bus 695 to Am Neuen Garten, then walk along Alleestrasse to enter the park. Allow 3hrs.

The lakes and woods around Potsdam are dotted with overgrown follies, ruined pumping houses and abandoned belvederes. Most of the gardens were created in English Romantic style by Peter Lenné, who in 1833 drew up an ambitious plan to landscape the surroundings of Potsdam.

It used to be that walkers encountered sinister watch towers and stretches of the concrete wall that divided Potsdam from Berlin for 29 years, but almost all traces have now vanished. Our route follows the shores of three lakes, and crosses the old frontier twice.

Beginning in the N at the **NEUER GARTEN**, follow the edge of the Heiliger See to reach a mock ruined temple, once the kitchen of the **Marmorpalais**. Standing on the magnificent terrace in front of the palace, you can see belvederes and teahouses on the far shore, belonging to the flamboyant 19thC villas on Mangerstrasse.

Take the path on to **SCHLOSS CECILIENHOF**, and continue across the lawns where, in 1945, Stalin, Churchill and Truman posed for photographs, seated in wickerwork chairs. Turning right along the Havel, you enter an eerie, wild area once patrolled by East German guards. Continue along the Havel, once overlooked by concrete watch towers, and, keeping close to the river, follow Schwanenallee, formerly a military access road. To the N of here, the white towers of the fake ruined **Schloss** on PFAUENINSEL can be seen across the water.

Cross the Dutch-style canal lined with weeping willows, and continue past decayed summer-houses to the **GLIENICKER BRÜCKE**, an iron suspension bridge where spies were occasionally swapped in Cold War deals. Virtually impossible to cross before 1990, the bridge is now jammed with traffic. On the far side, you come to the entrance to **SCHLOSS KLEIN-GLIENICKE**. Cross the road here to enter a small 19thC park landscaped by Lenné. Following the edge of the Glienicker Lake, you come to a little promontory with a good view of two Schinkel buildings: the NIKOLAIKIRCHE, way off to the SW in Potsdam, and SCHLOSS BABELSBERG on the wooded hill to the S. Continue past **JAGDSCHLOSS GLIENICKE**, a former hunting lodge, then turn left to leave the park.

On Königstrasse turn right, then right again down Möwenstrasse and continue along Waldmüllerstrasse. The villas on the right once had the Berlin Wall running through their back gardens. Now turn right down Lankestrasse, an old cobbled lane leading to **PARK BABELSBERG** across an old bridge that was once heavily guarded. Turn right along the edge of Glienicker Lake to reach the abandoned 19thC pumping house of **Schloss Babelsberg**. Built in the style of a Gothic castle, it later served a genuine defensive role when the East Germans blocked up the windows to prevent escapes during the Cold War. Farther on, you come upon a building, in English Neo-Gothic style, the **Kleines Schloss**, that once housed the ladies-in-waiting employed at Schloss Babelsberg. Make a short detour up a path behind the building to discover a genuine medieval relic, the **Gerichtslaube** (pavilion of the law courts), a folly assembled from fragments of Berlin's old town hall.

Continue along the shore of the Tiefer See to **Strandbad Babelsberg** *(open 9am-7pm),* a lakeside beach with *Strandkörbe* (wickerwork chairs with high, basket-shaped backs to keep off the wind). Follow the path straight ahead, turn left on the paved road and right at a white building. A path ascends to the tram 94 and 95 halt at Humboldt Ring/Nuthestrasse; use the *Zentrum* platform to get back to the town center.

✗ Walking tours of Potsdam are regularly run by **Stattreisen** *(Nansenstrasse 19 ☎ (0331) 960894).*

POTSDAM BY BUS

Guided bus tours of Potsdam leave from Bahnhof Potsdam-Stadt, but you can see many of the palaces and follies around Potsdam by taking local bus 695 from Höhenstrasse to Hauptbahnhof. This trip can be combined with WALK 1, which ends at the terminus of bus 695. Or it can be combined with a visit to SCHLOSS CECILIENHOF. Be sure to have a valid ticket.

Soon after setting off, the bus takes a right turn into the NEUER GARTEN. You see the picturesque gables of **SCHLOSS CECILIENHOF** on the left, and you might glimpse a pyramid tucked away in the trees. The large building on the left, perhaps still covered in scaffolding, is the **Marmorpalais**. Keep looking left to see the handsome **ORANGERIE** and a cluster of Dutch-style houses.

The bus leaves the park and turns down Friedrich-Ebert-Strasse, passing the grand 19thC villas of **Nauener Vorstadt**; some dilapidated, others primly restored, after *die Wende,* to serve as offices for political parties and insurance companies. The lurid yellow building ahead that looks like a medieval tower is the **Nauener Tor**, an 18thC city gate built at a time when English mock-Gothic was the fashion.

The **HOLLÄNDISCHES VIERTEL** is on the left. You may glimpse some of the Dutch-style houses with brick gables and green and white shutters. The bus makes a stop on Bassinplatz before heading down Wilhelm-Pieck-Strasse. It takes a right turn at the **BRANDENBURGER TOR** to head up Schopenhauerstrasse. The church you see on the left is the **FRIEDENSKIRCHE**. The **obelisk** is to your right, designed by Knobelsdorff in 1748 to terminate the main avenue of Sanssouci. An abandoned vineyard stands on the slopes behind. The crumbling ruin decorated with caryatides is the **Winzerhaus** (house of the vine-grower). It stands next to a vineyard planted on the slopes above Sanssouci in 1842 by Friedrich Wilhelm IV. At the foot of the vineyard stands a triumphal gate from the same period.

The bus turns down Zur Historischer Mühle, passing close to Schloss Sanssouci (on the left, behind the gilded gates). Look right to see a cluster of mock ruins crowning the **RUINENBERG**. The bus now crawls around a sharp bend at the **Historische Mühle**, a windmill built in 1796. Keep looking right to see the **ORANGERIE** and the neatly-labeled **Botanischer Garten**. Soon (still looking right) you see the **DRACHENHAUS** in the shape of a pagoda. Just beyond, you can see the **Weinberg**, another of Potsdam's abandoned vineyards, and a ruined belvedere in the throes of restoration.

The next important sight is on the left. It is the **NEUES PALAIS**, bristling with statues. Don't even *try* to count them. For the record, there are a total of 488 figures on the roof and terraces of the palace, some still damaged after World War II. The road curves around the back of the **Communs**, an extravagant building erected by Frederick the Great to accommodate the kitchens of the Neues Palais and guest rooms. The building is now occupied by the newly-created Potsdam University.

The bus stops at Bahnhof Wildpark, a wistful and overgrown railway station used by Kaiser Wilhelm II on his visits to Potsdam. The bus continues through the suburbs to the terminus at Hauptbahnhof. Take tram 94 or 96 to reach the town center, and look out for the romantic Moorish domes of the former pumping station, the **MOSCHEE** on the right, set amid some unlovely modern apartment blocks.

Potsdam: sights and places of interest

HOW TO USE THE A TO Z SECTION

All the sights, including **museums** and **galleries**, **famous buildings** and **monuments**, are arranged alphabetically from pages 227–39.

- Words in SMALL CAPITALS indicate a **cross-reference** to another section of the book or to a full entry in SIGHTSEEING.
- If you only know the name of a museum or other sight in English and cannot find it in the A TO Z OF POTSDAM SIGHTS , try looking it up in the INDEX. Other sights that do not have their own entries may be included in another entry; look these up in the INDEX too.
- The ★ symbol identifies the most important sights.
- The 🏛 symbol indicates buildings of particular architectural interest.
- The ⋞ symbol identifies a good view. There is also a special entry, called VIEWPOINTS, which details the high places.
- The ✱ symbol pinpoints places of special interest for children.
- **For a full explanation of all the symbols used in this book, see page 7.**

A to Z of Potsdam sights

ALTER FRIEDHOF

Heinrich-Mann-Allee (s of Potsdam-Stadt station). Open daily dawn to dusk. Tram 91, 92, 93, 96, 98 to Friedhöfe.

A 19thC Classical temple stands at the entrance to Potsdam's Alter Friedhof (Old Cemetery). The graveyard is strangely empty, with just a few isolated memorials set amid a leafy landscape designed by Lenné. A column topped with an eagle celebrates the soldiers from the Potsdam garrisons who fell in the Napoleonic Wars. Another monument was put up in honor of Eleonore Prohaska, a woman from Potsdam who fought in the Napoleonic Wars disguised as a man.

The **Neuer Friedhof** across the road is a deeply romantic place to wander amid ivy-covered tombstones. The cemetery is thickly planted with trees and shrubs, and dotted with little wooden shelters. The tombs are quite modest, even when they commemorate someone as grand as a general from one of the Potsdam garrisons. The simplest memorials mark the graves of nuns who worked in Potsdam's hospitals and orphanages, sometimes showing nothing more elaborate than a row of wooden crosses.

A small military cemetery near the top of the hill is laid out with the tombs of soldiers from Potsdam who died in the early months of World War I. Other grim tombstones date from the socialist period, when a jagged style of lettering reminiscent of the Nazi era was in vogue.

BILDERGALERIE (Picture Gallery)

In the E wing of Schloss Sanssouci ☎(0331) 22655. Open mid–May to mid–Oct, daily 9am–noon, 12.45–5pm; closed every 4th Wed of month. Tram 91, 94, 96, 98 to Luisenplatz, or bus 695 to Schloss Sanssouci.

The Bildergalerie is Germany's oldest museum, built in 1755–63 by Johann Gottfried Büring to house Frederick the Great's ever-growing collection of Baroque art. The long facade is lined with figures symbolizing the Arts and the Sciences (Painting is shown with brushes in her hand; Geometry supports a globe), while the keystones above the windows are decorated with busts of such artists as Dürer and Cranach.

The care taken to protect the gallery floor (visitors must put on felt slippers) has not been extended to the Baroque paintings, which are in urgent need of repair. But a few appealing works of local interest have survived, such as Julius Schoppe's *Kaiser's Pine in Klein-Glienicke Park,* and Karl Blechens' *Interior of the Palm House on Pfaueninsel,* some of which invest the iron-and-glass structure with a hint of Oriental mystery. A view of the *Spittelmarkt in 1833* by Eduard Gaertner provides a sad glimpse of what is now forever lost.

See also PARK SANSSOUCI for a reminder of what else there is to see while you are at Schloss Sanssouci.

CHINESISCHES TEEHAUS (Chinese Teahouse) ★ 🏛

In the S of Park Sanssouci ☎(0331) 93628. Open mid-May to mid-Oct 9am–noon, 12.45–5pm; closed every 2nd Mon of month. Tram 91, 98 to Schloss Charlottenhof.

Deep in the woods of PARK SANSSOUCI, Frederick the Great's round Chinese teahouse was built to rival the extravagant Rococo buildings of Bavaria.

Designed in 1754–56 by Johann Gottfried Büring, the rotunda is a riot of Frederician Chinoiserie, with gilt tassels hanging from the roof and ornate columns shaped like palm trees. Encircling the teahouse is a terrace dotted with bizarre gilt statues carved by Johann Peter Benckert and Johann Heymüller. A solitary figure holding a parasol is perched on the roof, while whiskered old Chinamen sit with demure European ladies drinking tea or nibbling exotic fruit. The inside, recently restored, contains a profusion of gilt stucco and twisted candlesticks, while the domed ceiling is decorated with pale *trompe l'oeil* frescoes showing Oriental men flirting with Western women amid a landscape of palms, monkeys and parrots.

See also PARK SANSSOUCI for details of other sights within the park.

DEFA FILM- UND TV-ERLEBNIS (DEFA Film and TV Experience) ★
August-Bebel-Strasse 26–52 ☎(0331) 9652755 (compulsory)
Open daily 10am–6pm (ticket office closes 4.30pm). Allow at least 3hrs. S-Bahn to Griebnitzsee, then bus 693 in the direction of Bahnhof Rehbrücke, getting off at the DEFA stop; or bus 690, 691 to Bahnhof Drewitz, then a 10min walk. Note that Potsdam public transport tickets are not valid on the S-Bahn.

The film studios in the Potsdam suburb of Babelsberg saw the making of some of great movies of all time. It was here that Marlene Dietrich posed sexily on a barrel to sing "Falling in Love Again" in the 1930 movie *The Blue Angel.* Four years earlier, Fritz Lang had built the biggest movie studio in the world at Babelsberg, to film his futuristic epic *Metropolis.*

Babelsberg was where the Germany movie industry began. A small film studio called *Deutsche Bioscop Gesellschaft* was set up in a large greenhouse by Guido Seeber in 1911. By 1917, the Babelsberg studios were producing propaganda films for General Ludendorff. The studios, now renamed UFA (Universum-Film-AG), began producing some of the greatest movies of the era. Most of the great early German movies that are still screened today — such as *The Blue Angel* and Fritz Lang's *The Cabinet of Dr Caligari* — were shot at Babelsberg. Under the production director Erich Pommer, they boasted the biggest studios in Europe, with some of the most sophisticated equipment in the world.

Many of the great names in the movies began their careers at the UFA studios, including Josef von Sternberg, Ernst Lubitsch, Billy Wilder, Pola Negri and Greta Garbo. But the Babelsberg dream came to an end on the wet spring day in 1933 when the Nazis marched through Potsdam to hold the first meeting of the Fascist parliament. Before the year was out, most of the directors and stars had left, on liners bound for the US.

The UFA studios fell into the Soviet sector after World War II, becoming the state-run DEFA. For almost half a century, the Babelsberg studios turned out a steady stream of East German television shows and movies. But then the Berlin Wall fell, and many people saw it as the end of the road for the Babelsberg studios. Capitalist hard-liners viewed the vast DEFA movie city as just one more clapped-out communist industry up for grabs.

But a few movie people decided to launch a rescue plan with the aid of *Treuhandanstalt,* the government body for the reconstruction of East German industry. They marketed the movie-making facilities to international directors with the ultimate aim of turning *Medienstadt Babelsberg* (Babelsberg Media City) into the Hollywood of Europe. Nobody knows if the plan will succeed, but the place is beginning to buzz with big names again. During the 1993 Berlin Film Festival, Billy Wilder made an emotional trip back to the studios where his career as a scriptwriter began.

If the goal of a European Hollywood seems a far-off dream, the studios still seem to have a safe future as a tourist attraction. Cinema fans can now tramp around the old sound studios where Marlene sang, and look at the vast shed where 35,000 extras were employed in the shooting of *Metropolis.*

Guided tours are given by enthusiastic old hands brimming with movie gossip. The tours involve a variety of attractions, starting with a short movie titled "Eighty Years of Movie City Babelsberg," narrated by Volker Schlöndorff, the director of *The Tin Drum,* and featuring clips from *Metropolis* and snatches of Dietrich singing *Falling in Love Again.*

You are then taken out on a 30-minute tour of the old studios, beginning with the *Neues Atelier West,* where you can stroll down a replica 1950s street. Visitors then get to look behind the scenes in the **Tonkreuz**, a set of four sound studios in the form of a cross, where Europe's first talking pictures were filmed.

After the tour, you spend as long as you want wandering around the muddy movie lots where several film sets have been preserved. The biggest set is the **Piratenstadt Blackwall**, a mock medieval town where stuntmen in pirate garb stage mock sword fights and demonstrate the art of falling off high buildings. The shows take place in the summer months only; from autumn to spring, the actors stage similar stunts indoors in **Aufnahmehalle 69** (Recording Hall 69).

Another old set features the **Hexenhaus**, a witch's cottage that featured in a long-forgotten movie *Sherlock Holmes and the Seven Dwarfs.* From there, follow signs to the **Kutschenausstellung** where some 40 old carriages and automobiles are on view. The **Bauerndorf** is an old German village, complete with live goats and chickens, which was used in the filming of *Pelle the Conqueror.*

But the highlight of the tour is the **Alt-Berliner Ladenstrasse** (Old Berlin shopping street), a 1920s street with shops, old lampposts and a car. In one shop, kids can dress up in old costumes or sit through a makeup session. Before you leave, try to join the tour of the **Requistenfundus** *(every 15mins),* where more than a million props are stored, including hats, swords, costumes and the world's largest collection of wigs.

DRACHENHAUS

Maulbeerallee ☎(0331) 21594 ⋞ ■ Bus 695 to Drachenhaus.

After a visit to SCHLOSS SANSSOUCI, you might be tempted to hike to the summit of the Klausberg hill to enjoy the view from the café terrace at the Drachenhaus. Modeled on the Oriental pagoda at London's Kew Gardens, the Drachenhaus (dragons' house) was built in 1770 by Karl von Gontard. The eccentric pagoda was the home of a gardener employed by Frederick the Great to tend a vineyard on the slopes of the Klausberg.

See also PARK SANSSOUCI, and café DRACHENHAUS on page 243.

FILMMUSEUM POTSDAM ★

In the Marstall , Schlossstrasse 1 ☎(0331) 23675 ■ (■ on 1st Wed of month). Open Tues–Sun 10am–5pm ■ Tram 91, 92, 93, 96, 98 to Alter Markt.

A cinema museum was established in Potsdam as early as 1922, but the archives were destroyed in a World War II bombing raid. Replaced in 1977–80, the collection is now housed in the former Prussian royal stables *(Marstall)*. Recently renovated, the museum provides a fascinating history of the Potsdam movie industry. Several classic films are screened daily in a comfortable theater inside the Filmmuseum. The selection is international, although foreign movies are normally dubbed into German. The museum café *(open Wed-Sun 11am-6pm)* serves coffee and beer, but not much else, in a pleasant Biedermeier interior decorated with potted plants.

FREUNDSCHAFTSINSEL (Island of Friendship)

Entrances on Lange Brücke and E of Am Alten Markt ▭ ☗ ✱ *Tram 91, 92, 93, 96, 98 to Alter Markt.*

This narrow island on the Havel is still off the beaten track. You can hire a rowboat, or explore the formal gardens laid out by Karl Föster.

FRIEDENSKIRCHE

Am Grünen Gitter ☎*(0331) 23156. Tram 91, 94, 96, 98 or bus 692, 695, 697 to Luisenplatz.*

Inspired by the Romanesque basilica of San Clemente in Rome, King Friedrich Wilhelm IV sketched the plans for the Friedenskirche. The church was built by Persius in 1844–54, on the edge of a small lake. It may be a copy, but, if you can get inside, you will see a genuine Byzantine mosaic in the apse. Bought for the Prussian monarch in 1834, the mosaic comes from a demolished church on the Venetian island of Murano. Friedrich Wilhelm IV and his wife Elisabeth lie buried here.

GLIENICKER BRÜCKE

Berliner Strasse. Tram 93 to Glienicker Brücke (coming from Potsdam); bus 116 to Glienicker Brücke (coming from S-Bahnhof Wannsee in Berlin); steamer to Glienicker Brücke (from Potsdam or Berlin, in summer only).

The Glienicker Brücke used to seem like the end of the world. Marking the frontier between West Berlin and Potsdam, the iron suspension bridge across the Havel was closed to traffic by the Soviet army in 1945. It became a notorious spot soon after the Berlin Wall was built, in February 1962, when the American pilot Gary Powers, shot down over Soviet territory, was exchanged on the bridge for the Russian spy Rudolf Iwanowitsch Abel. Sinister scenes such as this inspired episodes in such spy thrillers as *Funeral in Berlin*. The bridge was opened to traffic when the Wall came down, and immediately became jammed with Mercedes and Trabants.

Standing on the old road from Berlin to Potsdam, the bridge has a long history. The first Glienicker Brücke was a wooden drawbridge, built in 1662 by the Great Elector. It was replaced in 1831 by a monumental Neoclassical bridge designed by Schinkel, but this proved too narrow to cope with 20thC traffic, and an elegant iron suspension bridge was put up in 1907. All that remains of Schinkel's bridge are some Classical columns at the Potsdam end, and a few statues on the Berlin side.

The river near the bridge was patrolled by armed guards in boats during the Cold War. Now it is more festive, and river steamers from Berlin and Potsdam moor at a busy pier on the Berlin side of the bridge.

HOLLÄNDISCHES VIERTEL ★

Mittelstrasse and neighborhood. Tram 92, 95 or bus 695 to Nauener Tor.
A curious Dutch quarter was built by Johann Boumann to the N of Bassinplatz in 1737–42. The idea of creating a Dutch Quarter came to Friedrich Wilhelm I after a trip to Amsterdam. Keen to persuade skilled Dutch builders to settle in Potsdam, he decided to build 134 houses for them in the typical red-brick style of Amsterdam. The plan misfired and only a few Dutch workers took up the king's offer; most of the houses eventually went to Prussian soldiers or local craftsmen.

The East German authorities, unlike the careful Dutch, allowed the houses to fall into ruin, and almost demolished the entire quarter in the 1970s. Now, the houses are being rebuilt with the aid of skilled Berlin squatters. Look out for art galleries, alternative cafés and a fizz of new ideas.

KAPELLE ALEXANDER NEWSKI

W of Puschkinallee in Nauener Vorstadt. Tram 92, 95 to Kapellenberg. Walk up Puschkinallee from the tram stop, then take the path to the left through the trees.
A Russian Orthodox church lies hidden in the Kapellenberg woods. Dedicated to St Alexander Newski, the exotic church with pink walls and onion-shaped domes was designed by Schinkel, following a plan sent from St Petersburg. A little graveyard contains the tombs of expatriate Russians who died in Potsdam. By a strange quirk of history, a large garrison of Soviet troops was, until recently, stationed nearby.

MOSCHEE (Mosque)

Breite Strasse (at Zeppelinstrasse) ☎(0331) 24106. Open Sat, Sun 9am–noon, 1–4pm ✗ available. Tram 91, 94, 96, 98 to Auf dem Kiewitt.

One of Potsdam's most endearing eccentricities is a steam pumping house *(Dampfmaschinenhaus)* disguised as an Oriental mosque, and now standing amid postwar apartment blocks on an inlet of the Havel.

Built for Friedrich Wilhelm IV by Ludwig Persius in 1842, its steam-driven pumps (made at the Berlin Borsig factory) once filled the reservoir on RUINENBERG from which the Sanssouci fountains were supplied. The chimney is disguised as a minaret, and the giant pumps are housed in a domed hall whose Moorish arches and arabesques were based on the Córdoba mosque. The guided tour (in German) includes a demonstration of the restored steam pump, controlled by a regulator that is crowned with a Prussian eagle.

NEUE KAMMERN

To the W of Schloss Sanssouci ☎(0331) 22823. Open Apr–Sept, Sat–Thurs

9am–noon, 12.30pm–5pm; Feb, Mar, Oct until 4pm; Nov–Jan until 3pm. Tram 91, 94, 96, 98 to Luisenplatz, or bus 695 to Schloss Sanssouci.

Built by Knobelsdorff in 1747 as an orangery, the Neue Kammern, to the W of the Schloss, was turned into guest quarters by King Friedrich I. The rooms are richly decorated with Rococo reliefs, and tend to be less crowded than those at SCHLOSS SANSSOUCI.

See also PARK SANSSOUCI for a reminder of what else there is to see while you are within the park.

NEUER GARTEN ★

Am Neuen Gartenstrasse. Tram 92, 95 or bus 695 to Am Neuen Garten, then a 5min walk along Alleestrasse.

Bounded by two lakes, the Neuer Garten was created in 1787–91 as a summer residence for King Friedrich Wilhelm II. With its winding lakeside paths, sweeping lawns and secret follies, it is perhaps Potsdam's most romantic park, yet it remains far less crowded than PARK SANSSOUCI in the summer.

Idyllically sited on the edge of the Heiliger See, the **Marmorpalais** was designed by Karl von Gontard in 1787 as an Italianate villa, and aggrandized a few years later by Carl Langhans. An army museum once located here was quickly closed following the political upheavals of 1989, leaving uncertain the future role of the summer palace.

Linked to the palace by an underground passage, the lakeside kitchen *(Küche)* was designed by Karl von Gontard to evoke a ruined Classical temple sinking into the sand. Fragments of columns dotted among the pine trees enhance the melancholy effect. To the N of the palace, an ice store was built in the shape of a miniature Egyptian pyramid.

Situated on the main avenue, the **Holländisches Etablissement** is another Prussian whimsy: a row of red-brick houses with Dutch gables, built as servants' quarters. Like the Dutch quarter in Potsdam, the houses here have rather Germanic proportions. An orangery — concealed behind the gable houses — was designed in Egyptian style, with mock hieroglyphics and brooding sphinxes. And as if that were not variety enough, **SCHLOSS CECILIENHOF**, near the Jungfernsee, is modeled on an English Tudor manor.

NEUES PALAIS ★ 🏛

Am Neuen Palais (W end of Park Sanssouci) ☎(0331) 973143. Open daily, Apr–Sept, 9am–12.45pm, 1.15–5pm; Feb, Mar, Oct until 4pm; Nov–Jan until 3pm; closed every 2nd and 4th Mon in month 𝒦 available ▀ Bus 695 to Neues Palais.

A stiff walk down the Hauptallee brings you to the Neues Palais, built in 1763–69 by Büring, the architect of the CHINESISCHES TEEHAUS. Frederick the Great apparently commissioned the palace to prove that the Seven Years' War had not bled Prussia dry. He seldom visited the building, however, preferring the more intimate charms of SCHLOSS SANSSOUCI, and its 200 rooms served merely as guest quarters.

An extraordinary collection of 428 statues was carved for the balustrades. Several colossal figures, located on the forecourt and once supporting ornate lamps, revealed cleverly concealed old gas pipes following damage suffered during World War II.

Not content with one extravagant gesture, Frederick commissioned Karl von Gontard to build the palatial servants' quarters to the W, known as the **Communs** after a similar building at Versailles. Two giant wings are linked by a triumphal arch decorated with a sculptural group commemorating the Seven Years' War of 1756–63.

The Neues Palais is far less crowded than Schloss Sanssouci, although its ballrooms and concert halls are just as splendid. The guided tour is not compulsory, but you do have to wear protective footwear — after a long walk down the dusty main avenue it is actually rather pleasant to glide across the parquet ballroom floors in enormous felt slippers.

The rooms are hung with Flemish and Dutch Baroque works, but perhaps the most interesting paintings are historical studies such as Franz Krüger's *Parade on Unter den Linden,* showing the confident swagger of the Prussian army after the victory at Waterloo, and Adolph Menzel's *Coronation of King Wilhelm I at Königsberg in 1861,* depicting jewel-laden princesses, Prussian aristocrats and pompous generals.

The palace boasts a bizarre grotto festooned with elaborate fountains, and sea monsters fashioned from glinting minerals and shells. Elsewhere, there's a theater, and a 19thC bathroom equipped with bells for summoning various servants including the dressmaker *(Schneiderin).*

Frederick the Great sketched the designs for the two Classical temples near the palace, built by Karl von Gontard in 1768. The **Antikentempel** (N of the Hauptallee) was built for the royal collection of antiquities, while the **Freundschaftstempel** (Temple of Friendship) to the S was erected as a memorial to Countess Wilhelmine von Bayreuth.

See also PARK SANSSOUCI for other things to see while you are in the park.

NIKOLAIKIRCHE

Am Alten Markt ☎(0331) 21682 ✗ available. Open Mon–Sat 10am–noon, 2–5pm, Sun 11.30am–5pm. Tram 91, 92, 93, 96, 98 to Alter Markt.

The Neoclassical Nikolaikirche was designed by Karl Friedrich Schinkel and built in 1830–37 by Ludwig Persius. Its lofty dome was added in 1842–50. Bombed in 1945, the church has since been meticulously restored. An information folder is available in many languages.

ORANGERIE

Maulbeerallee (NW of Schloss Sanssouci) ☎(0331) 26189. Open May–Oct, daily 9am–noon, 1–5pm; closed every 4th Thurs of month. Bus 695 to Orangerie.

Dominating the slopes above SCHLOSS SANSSOUCI, the Orangerie was designed by Friedrich Wilhelm IV as an overscaled version of an Italian Renaissance villa. The building was meant to stand on a grand Roman avenue leading to Schloss Lindstedt, but the plan was never realized.

The Orangerie once contained guest quarters occupied by Czar Nicholas I and his wife Charlotte, the daughter of Friedrich Wilhelm III, but it has suffered from years of neglect, and the long, glazed galleries, where tropical palms once flourished, are now dilapidated.

Summer concerts of chamber music are given in the courtyard, and the view of Schloss Sanssouci from the tower *(Turm)* is worth the climb.

See also PARK SANSSOUCI.

PARK BABELSBERG

E of Potsdam. Bus 691 to Babelsberg Nord.

The park around SCHLOSS BABELSBERG was originally laid out by Peter Lenné in 1834 in the same style as SCHLOSS KLEIN-GLIENICKE across the water, but it was later redesigned by Hermann Fürst Pückler-Muskau.

The grounds are dotted with mock-Gothic curiosities, including kitchens linked to the palace by an underground passage. The **Kleines Schloss** down by the water's edge was built in 1841 for Princess Augusta's ladies-in-waiting, but perhaps the most curious building is the **Flatowturm**, a hilltop tower used for guests, modeled on the Frankfurt-am-Main Eschenheimer Tor, which is still standing.

Hidden by trees on a nearby summit, the **Gerichtslaube** is a romantic folly constructed from fragments of Berlin's old town hall on Alexanderplatz, which was demolished in 1871. Its 13thC Gothic arcade, surmounted by a 15thC Renaissance gallery, forms a bizarre architectural puzzle.

PARK SANSSOUCI ★

W of Potsdam. Main entrance at Am Grünen Gitter ☎(0331) 22051 🎫 Tram 91, 94, 96, 98 or bus 692, 695, 697 to Luisenplatz (for main entrance); bus 695 to Orangerie (for Botanical Garden entrance); bus 695 to Neues Palais (for Neues Palais entrance).

SCHLOSS SANSSOUCI is surrounded by vast landscaped gardens created by Frederick the Great and his successors. There is an enormous amount to see, including three separate palaces, a vineyard, a Dutch garden, a Botanical garden, an orangery, a Chinese teahouse, two temples, a Roman bathhouse and a pagoda.

Don't try to see everything. The magic of Sanssouci lies in the gentle landscaping, the mixture of architecture and nature, and the unexpected views. Pick one or two sights to see, and leave the rest for another visit.

Follow the suggested route in WALK 2 if you want to see the main sights, or just stroll off into the park. The main sights are listed in separate entries: see SCHLOSS SANSSOUCI, NEUES PALAIS, SCHLOSS CHARLOTTENHOF, BILDERGALERIE, NEUE KAMMERN, CHINESISCHES TEEHAUS, RÖMISCHE BÄDER, ORANGERIE and DRACHENHAUS. When you feel the need for lunch, you might, if you are lucky, be able to squeeze into the SCHLOSSCAFÉ; otherwise, the best places are the DRACHENHAUS or the beer garden behind the HISTORISCHE MÜHLE: see page 243 for details of these.

POTSDAM-MUSEUM

Breite Strasse 8–12 and 13 ☎(0331) 23782 🎫 (🎫 on first Sun of month) ✱ Open Tues–Sun 9am–5pm. Tram 91, 92, 93, 96, 98 to Alter Markt.

A deserted aquarium, faded photographs of the German royal family at Sanssouci, and a cabinet of *Schuttpflanzen* (plants that thrive amid the rubble of bombed cities) are among the curiosities at Potsdam's excellent local history museum. The extensive collection is housed in two handsome buildings in the old town: the period up to 1900 is in a Baroque mansion constructed by Johann Boumann, while 20thC history occupies a corner of the imposing Hiller-Brandtsche Häuser, an 18thC apartment block modeled on Inigo Jones's Banqueting Hall in London.

The older museum explains the formation of the watery Havel landscape, and the distinctive ecology of postwar bomb sites. Fascinating sections cover Slavonic settlements, local parks, Prussian soldiers' blue and red uniforms, Potsdam porcelain, the 19thC Russian colony, and local shops that supplied the imperial court.

The 20thC museum has a superb map of Potsdam in 1912, showing features that have disappeared, like the Stadtschloss (bombed in World War II), the Dutch canal in Dortustrasse, the numerous *Kaserne* (barracks), the *Kriegsschule* (military academy) in Teltower Vorstadt where World War I officers were trained, and the *Naturtheater für die Heimatspiele* (an open-air amphitheater for staging native German theater).

Old photographs show the Zeppelin base in the Brandenburger Vorstadt, the bizarre Expressionist tower (the Einsteinturm) in Teltower Vorstadt, and the notorious Nazi rally in Potsdam's Garnisonkirche on a wet March day in 1933. Prussian *Pickelhaube* helmets, postage stamps overprinted with Nazi slogans, a cash register overflowing with worthless one-million-Mark notes, and a mock-up of a bombed street, are all strong reminders of Potsdam's troubled history.

RÖMISCHE BÄDER (Roman Baths)

At the S end of Park Sanssouci ☎(0331) 93211. Open mid-May to mid-Oct, 9am–noon and 12.30–5pm; closed every 3rd Mon of month. Tram 91, 98 to Schloss Charlottenhof.

Overlooking a little lake, the mock-Roman Baths are a delightful Neoclassical curiosity designed by Schinkel in 1829. Grouped around an atrium, the intimate rooms are decorated with imitation Pompeian frescoes and Classical landscapes.

An attractive colonnade overlooks a canal in which a gondola prow has been placed to evoke Venice. The Neoclassical pavilion on the water's edge to the S of the baths was once an elegant teahouse.

See also PARK SANSSOUCI, SCHLOSS CHARLOTTENHOF, CHINESISCHES TEEHAUS and SCHLOSS SANSSOUCI.

RUINENBERG

Bus 695 to Schloss Sanssouci, then a 5min climb.

A curious cluster of mock-Classical ruins was built for Frederick the Great in 1748 on the aptly-named Ruinenberg hill that overlooks PARK SANSSOUCI. Its architect was the prolific Knobelsdorff. With its crumbling temple and toppled column, this Frederician folly strangely resembles the ruins of Berlin and Potsdam in 1945.

A pool built as a reservoir to supply Sanssouci's fountains is now eerily stagnant, and the Cyrillic names of Soviet soldiers carved on Classical columns add to the melancholy romance of the spot.

RUSSISCHE KOLONIE ALEXANDROWKA

W of Puschkinallee in Nauener Vorstadt, N Potsdam. Tram 92, 95 to Kapellenberg.

The story of Potsdam's Russian colony is like an old folk tale. In 1812, a group of Russian soldiers from the Singers' Corps was captured and brought to Potsdam. When Russia later became an ally of Prussia, the Czar presented the singers to a Potsdam regiment. Friedrich Wilhelm III then had the delightful idea of creating a mock-Russian village for the musicians, and in 1826 he commissioned Peter Lenné to design 13 identical wooden houses. Surrounded by rambling apple orchards, the habitations, each one bearing the name of a Russian singer, have steep roofs and ornate carved balconies. As at NIKOLSKOE, they reflect Friedrich Wilhelm III's fondness for Russian peasant life, which was sparked off by the marriage of his daughter, Charlotte, to the future Czar Nicholas I. The colony was named Alexandrowka after the Prussian Czarina.

A Russian Orthodox church, the KAPELLE ALEXANDER NEWSKI, lies not far away, hidden in the Kapellenberg woods.

SCHLOSS BABELSBERG

E of Potsdam. Open Tues–Sun 9am–5pm. Bus 691 to Babelsberg Nord.

Situated in a wooded park above the Tiefer See, Schloss Babelsberg was built by Schinkel in 1833 as a summer residence for the Crown Prince, later Kaiser Wilhelm I. Princess Augusta, Wilhelm's consort, asked Schinkel to model the building on Windsor Castle, which she had admired on a tour of Britain in 1826. The rambling Neo-Gothic palace now houses a small museum of local prehistory.

See also PARK BABELSBERG.

SCHLOSS CECILIENHOF ✓

Neuer Garten ☎(0331) 96940 Open daily, 9am–5pm; closed every 2nd and 4th Mon of month compulsory Bus 695 to Cecilienhof.

Built during World War I for the Crown Prince, Schloss Cecilienhof is a rambling country house designed in a typical English suburban style, with ivy-clad brick walls, half-timbered gables and leaded glass windows. It is now a hotel.

The Allied Powers met in this comfortable old mansion in 1945 to discuss the terms of the Potsdam Agreement.

The guided tour takes in the wood-paneled room where the treaty on the postwar division of Germany was signed by Stalin, Churchill and Truman. Looking through the bay window, you can see the Havel river, which, until 1990, formed the boundary between East Germany and West Berlin.

SCHLOSS CHARLOTTENHOF ★

S end of Park Sanssouci ☎(0331) 92774. Open mid-May to mid-Oct 9am–12.30pm, 1–5pm; closed every 4th Mon of month compulsory. Tram 91, 98 to Schloss Charlottenhof.

One of Germany's finest Neoclassical buildings, Schloss Charlottenhof was built by Schinkel in 1826–28 as a summer palace for the Crown Prince, the future Friedrich Wilhelm IV. The intimate rooms are inspired by English domestic interiors, with writing desks equipped with curious gadgets, and bay windows overlooking Peter Lenné's neat English lawns and picturesque ponds.

The walls are crammed with romantic paintings of the Rhine, Italy and the Alps, including Caspar David Friedrich's *Gartenterrasse,* which expresses the German romantic longing for the mountains.

Imitation Pompeian frescoes decorate the dining room, while the breakfast room is painted a deep red. But the most curious part of the villa is the bedroom, where a blue and white awning has been hung above the bed in imitation of a desert tent. The explorer Alexander von Humboldt slept in this bed for a time, dreaming (so it is said) of his far-flung travels in Asia and South America.

See also PARK SANSSOUCI.

SCHLOSS KLEIN-GLIENICKE See BERLIN, page 156.

SCHLOSS SANSSOUCI ★ 🏛

W of Potsdam ☎(0331) 22051. Open Apr–Sept 9am–12.30, 1–5pm; Oct, Feb, Mar until 4pm; Nov–Jan until 3pm; closed every 1st and 3rd Mon of month ✗ (compulsory, lasts 40mins). Tram 91, 94, 96, 98 to Luisenplatz, or bus 695 to Schloss Sanssouci.

Designed in 1744 by Georg Wenzeslaus von Knobelsdorff from an original sketch by Frederick the Great, Schloss Sanssouci was the first summer palace to be built at Potsdam, surrounded by the vast landscaped gardens of PARK SANSSOUCI.

The long, low Baroque building overlooks a terrace, where Frederick tried to give a French air to his country retreat by planting vines. The very name *sans souci* (carefree) suggests that Frederick was trying to escape from the stiff formality of the Prussian court, to enjoy the sensual pleasures depicted by his favored artist, Watteau. But his duties caught up with him, the vines withered, and life at Sanssouci became as dull as in Berlin.

The palace has just 13 rooms, including a circular library with lavish Rococo decoration (illustrated on page 209), and a beautiful music room, decorated with reliefs illustrating Ovid's *Metamorphoses,* where Frederick liked to play the flute. The tour guides will show you the table where Frederick used to work, and the chair in which he died.

The **Damenflügel** *(open mid-May to mid-Oct Wed-Sun 9-11.45am, 12.30-5pm; mid-Oct to mid-May Sat, Sun 9am-noon, 1-4pm)* was added, to the W, by Persius, to accommodate the queen's ladies-in-waiting. The rooms are furnished with Biedermeier cabinets and paintings.

See PARK SANSSOUCI for details of the many other sights in the immediate vicinity of Schloss Sanssouci.

VIEWPOINTS

The rolling hills around Potsdam provide a multitude of views, taking in palaces, castles, lakes and follies. Hike to the top of the **RUINENBERG** for a good view of SCHLOSS SANSSOUCI, or take tram 92 or 95 to Kapellenberg and climb to the ruined belvedere on the top of the **Pfingstberg** for a glimpse of the River Havel.

The belvedere of the **ORANGERIE** offers a view of PARK SANSSOUCI, and yet another belvedere, farther W on the **Klausberg**, lets you admire the park from above. To escape the crowds, ascend the 97-meter/318-foot **Telegraphenberg** to the S, named after a telegraph station installed there in 1832.

For a view of the Glienicker Brücke, climb to the sweeping lawns in front of **SCHLOSS BABELSBERG** known by the English name, the Pleasure Ground.

But possibly the best view of all is to be had from the top of the restored **Flatowturm** on the wooded summit in PARK BABELSBERG, where you can see as far as the GLIENICKER BRÜCKE and SCHLOSS KLEIN-GLIENICKE.

VILLENVIERTEL NEUBABELSBERG

Karl-Marx-Strasse and surrounding streets. Bus 691 to Babelsberg Nord, or S-Bahn to Griebnitzsee.

Old and crumbling villas in many flamboyant architectural styles line the shores of the Griebnitzsee. Built by a property speculator in 1872, this became a rich retreat for the Berlin elite in the early years of the German Empire. During the 1920s, the extravagant architecture appealed to the actors and directors who worked at the nearby film studios at Babelsberg.

The appeal was lost when Hitler seized power in 1933. Many of the owners fled abroad. Others were murdered. At the end of the war, the neighborhood was briefly occupied by the parties to the Potsdam Accord. Three villas in the neighborhood were taken over, to house the leaders of the three powers. The now overgrown **Villa Müller-Grote** *(Karl-Marx-Strasse 2)* was the residence of President Truman, and subsequently became known locally as the *Kleines Weisses Haus* (Little White House). It was here that Truman signed the orders to drop the atom bombs on Hiroshima and Nagasaki.

The **Villa Herpich** *(Karl-Marx-Strasse 27)* was Stalin's residence during the 1945 conference, while Winston Churchill was based nearby in the **Villa Urbig** *(Virchowstrasse 2),* a building designed by Mies van der Rohe in 1915. Architecture enthusiasts should note, before they hop on a bus to take a look, that Van der Rohe was still deeply stuck in the German Romantic rut at this date.

After the war, the villas were converted by the East Germans into state institutions such as kindergartens, schools and asylums. The Berlin Wall ran along the edge of the Griebnitzsee, passing through the back gardens of the villas on Karl-Marx-Strasse. After the Wall came down, this forgotten quarter was slowly rediscovered by historians and architecture enthusiasts.

The history of the neighborhood is neatly summed up by the name changes of the main street. Originally, it was the Kaiserstrasse, grand and imperial. It became the Strasse der SA in 1934, in honor of the brutish Nazi Stormtroopers. After the war, new street signs went up with the name Karl-Marx-Strasse. Many people thought the name would change again after 1989, but the authorities have so far resisted the temptation. Germans have learned from experience to be a tad more cautious about making sweeping changes.

Where to stay in Potsdam

Many people travel to Potsdam for the day from Berlin. You can easily do so, now that the S-Bahn line S3 runs directly from central Berlin to Potsdam-Stadt station. Yet you may well find that you want to linger for several days in the town to explore the many sights.

These days, the hotels in Potsdam have become far more customer-friendly and efficient. The main problem now is that there are too few hotels, and those that exist are mostly the drab legacy of the communist era.

CHOOSING A HOTEL

Potsdam is a small town with a reasonably good public transport network. Most hotels are not far from the main sights, although in some suburban locations you will require a car for getting around. Prices have risen sharply in the past couple of years as demand has soared, and it can be hard to find inexpensive rooms in the town center.

A room in town One large hotel, the MERCURE, is located in the old town, close to the main sights and restaurants. For many people, this is the most convenient place to stay. To meet the increased demand, a former ship moored nearby, the HOTELSCHIFF FRIEDRICH DER GROSSE, has been converted into a hotel. The accommodation is as comfortable as any hotel room, and perhaps more appealing.

A room in the country Potsdam's leafy suburbs are dotted with old mansions dating from the turn of the century. A few hotels are located in these quiet parts of town, although you sometimes need a car to get out to them. Those traveling with a car might be tempted to stay in one of the country hotels outside Potsdam, such as the HAKEBURG.

A room with a family As in other former Eastern European towns, you can stay with a local family in Potsdam. The rates are extremely cheap, although the locations are often out of town, making a car necessary to get around. Contact the Potsdam tourist information office *(details on page 214)*.

Symbols For an explanation of our symbols, see page 7. Our **price category symbols** are explained in WHERE TO STAY IN BERLIN, page 163.

RESERVATIONS

Once a quiet backwater of Eastern Europe, Potsdam is now a favorite destination. You should reserve your room well ahead, especially in the summer months. The **tourist office** *(Friedrich-Ebert-Strasse 5, 14467 Potsdam ☎(0331) 23385 or 21100)* will do its best to find you a room, but it may only be able to offer a location far out of town.

BAYRISCHES HAUS
Im Wildpark 1, 14471 Potsdam ☎(0331) 973192 Fx(0331) 972329 24 rms
Location: In the Potsdamer Wildpark woods, 4km (2½ miles) w of the old town. This is the most romantic hotel in Potsdam. The main building is a mock Alpine chalet built by Friedrich Wilhelm IV in 1847 as a birthday present for his wife, Countess Elisabeth Luise of Bavaria. A popular country inn in the 1920s and '30s, it recently opened as a small hotel. The location is ideal for walks in the woods, although a car is certainly needed to get into Potsdam.

HAKEBURG
Zehlendorfer Damm 185, 14532 Kleinmachnow. Map **5**F3 *(033203) 22858 (033203) 22212 to 18 rms No cards Bus 117 from S-Bahnhof Zehlendorf, or bus 601 from Bassinplatz in Potsdam, then a 10min walk.*
Location: In a leafy suburb 13km (8 miles) E of Potsdam. A solid mansion in the style of a medieval fortress, built in 1906 for the aristocrat Dietloff von Hake. Converted into a hotel in 1990, the Hakeburg offers quite basic rooms (some without bathrooms). The furniture dates from the communist era, but the lakeside setting is rather appealing. You can get around by bus, but a car is more than useful.

HOTELSCHIFF FRIEDRICH DER GROSSE
Kai der Weissen Flotte, Am Hinzenberg, 14467 Potsdam. Reservations are made through the RESIDENCE hotel (0331) 8760 (0331) 872006 49 cabins Tram 91, 92, 93, 96, 98 to Alter Markt.
Location: Moored on the Havel next to the Mercure Hotel. This unusual and appealing hotel occupies two converted cruise ships moored on the river near the center of the old town. It was recently opened to cope with the surge in demand for accommodation. The cabins are bright and stylish, although perhaps a little cramped for two. The style is modern and functional, with unusual, jaggedly-shaped mirrors above the beds. Rooms on the top deck have large windows, while the slightly cheaper rooms on the lower deck have small portholes. The cabins facing the river have the best views.

MERCURE
Lange Brücke, 14467 Potsdam (0331) 4631 (0331) 23496 208 rms Tram 91, 92, 93, 96, 98 to Alter Markt.
Location: On the edge of the old town, on the Havel. This modern high-rise hotel spoils the Potsdam skyline, but, if you can live with that, the Mercure offers a high level of comfort. Once part of the East German Interhotel organization and known as the Hotel Potsdam, the hotel is now run on Western lines by a French group. The rooms are comfortable and well-equipped, with views of the old town or the Havel. Weisse Flotte cruise ships depart from the pier beside the hotel, and the main sights in Potsdam are within easy walking distance. The hotel stands on the site of the royal pleasure gardens, but the only vestige that has survived is a row of Classical columns beside the river.

RESIDENCE
Otto-Grotewohl-Strasse 60, 14478 Potsdam (0331) 8760 (0331) 872006 248 rms Tram 91 or 93 to Erich-Weinert-Strasse, then 5mins farther on foot.
Location: In a leafy setting, 4km ($2\frac{1}{2}$ miles) S of the old town. This modern hotel is a long way out, but prices are considerably lower than you pay elsewhere. The rooms are modern and functional, with a choice of simple or luxury decor. The Residence is Potsdam's biggest hotel, with the best conference facilities in town, so you may sometimes find the breakfast room swarming with astrophysicists. Getting into town by tram is easy, but allow about 30 minutes.

SCHLOSS CECILIENHOF
Am Neuen Garten, 14469 Potsdam (0331) 23141 (0331) 22498 40 rms Bus 695 to Cecilienhof.
Location: In a quiet setting in the Neuer Garten, 3km (1 mile) from the town center. History was made in this comfortable mock-Tudor country house on the edge of Potsdam. The Allied leaders met here, in 1945, to carve up postwar Germany. Now a hotel, Schloss Cecilienhof offers tranquil lodgings in a romantic park dotted with palaces and follies. The bedrooms are quiet, but not luxurious. Some have views across the rolling lawns where Truman, Churchill and Stalin once posed for press photographers. A car is useful for getting to the hotel.

Eating and drinking in Potsdam

The restaurants in Potsdam are steadily improving, but you must not expect grand cuisine. The local cooking *(Märkische Küche)* is plain and hearty. Fish caught locally is worth a try; look out for *Zander* (pike) and *Karpfen* (carp). Bear in mind that the revolution is still young. The local economy of Potsdam is in a state of flux, and restaurants frequently change owners, move premises, or fail financially. You can either take a chance on finding somewhere, or reserve ahead.

Symbols For an explanation of our symbols, see page 7. Our **price category symbols** are explained in EATING IN BERLIN on page 170.

RESTAURANTS

MINSK ***Traditional German***
Max-Planck-Strasse 10 ☎(0331) 23636
VISA Tram 91, 92, 93, 96, 98 to Schwimmhalle am Brauhausberg.
This modern restaurant stands on a hillside overlooking the spires and tower blocks of the old town. The menu features Havelland regional fish specialities such as eel and pike. You may also find the occasional Russian dish on offer. The restaurant has a large terrace where you can watch the sun go down on summer evenings.

TATORT ***Traditional German***
Strasse der Jugend 34 ☎(0331) 23861
AE VISA Tram 92, 95 or bus 695 to Nauener Tor.
This friendly restaurant and bar is located in the basement of an old villa near the Heiliger See. With its wood paneling, chandeliers and candles, it makes an inviting place to linger on a winter evening. You can eat hearty local dishes accompanied by a local Rex beer. Tatort attracts a youngish crowd of students and artists, who sit around the wooden tables chatting quietly.

VILLA KELLERMANN ***Italian***
Mangerstrasse 34–36 ☎(0331) 21572
No cards. Closed Mon and lunch Tues–Fri. Tram 92, 95 or bus 695 to Nauener Tor, then a 10min walk.
An Italian restaurant located in a vast, echoing mansion on the shores of the Heiliger See. The menu features classic Umbrian regional cooking, served with homemade pasta. The children's dishes such as *penette ai Ferri* have appeal for young eaters. In summer, you can eat in the garden, at tables overlooking the lake. The shiny BMWs with Berlin license plates tell you that this is a fashionable place to eat. Reserve ahead.

ZUM ATLAS ***Traditional German***
Am Kanal ☎(0331) 25246 Any tram to Platz der Einheit.
A modern restaurant from the socialist era, furnished in a comfortable, if somewhat chilly style. The fare is hearty — Brandenburg style, with chicken, lamb, and pork — the sort of food that goes well with a glass of the local Rex beer. This may not be a place for a romantic dinner, but the food is decent enough.

BREAKFAST

The young of Potsdam have taken up the Berlin habit of lavish breakfasts. There are now several places where you can eat a breakfast of rye bread, cold meats, cheese and strong coffee. The restaurant ZUM ATLAS serves breakfast from 7am, but it's livelier at the art gallery café STAUNDENHOF.

CAFÉS

Gone are the days when Potsdam's cafés were all dire State-run institutions. Several attractive new ones have opened up to cater to tourists and locals. They may not all survive, but you are sure to find somewhere pleasant to pause. Here are some addresses to check out.

CAFÉ ARTHUR
Dortustrasse (at Brandenburgerstrasse). Open Tues–Fri 10am–6pm, Sun 10am–2pm.
An elegant little café with whitewashed walls and dangling tendrils of greenery. All kinds of people squeeze in here to drink coffee or herb tea in the romantic candlelit interior.

CAFÉ IM FILMMUSEUM
Schlossstrasse 1. Open Tues–Thurs 2pm–5pm, Fri–Sun noon–5pm.
An intimate café furnished in Biedermeier style, with potted plants and a piano. The café is located in the former royal stables, next to the Filmmuseum-Potsdam.

DRACHENHAUS
Maulbeerallee. Open daily Apr–Oct 11am–6.30pm, Nov–Mar 11am–5.30pm.
An Oriental-style pagoda on a hill above Sanssouci, where you can drink a beer and eat basic food.

HISTORISCHE MÜHLE
Maulbeerallee. Open daily 10am–6pm (until 5pm in winter months).
An extensive beer garden where you can fill up on *Weissbier* and *Bratwurst*, or *Kaffee und Kuchen*, while chickens cluck around your feet. The establishment has several antiquated weighing machines for those who are beginning to worry about the effects of too much hearty German food.

SCHLOSSCAFÉ
In the Neues Palais. Open daily 11am–6pm (Apr–Oct to 7pm).
Tourists who made the long trek out to the Neues Palais used to find empty and echoing rooms, and nowhere to eat. But everything has changed these days, and the palace now has a spectacular café occupying one of its 18thC rooms. You'll find stylish pink tablecloths, Baroque paintings, glittering chandeliers, and, most likely, every table occupied.

STAUNDENHOF
Am Alten Markt 10. Open daily 9am–late.
A small café attached to an art gallery where local artists display their works. A youngish crowd of students and artists meet here for coffee or a glass of *Glühwein*. The café is a popular place for breakfast, which comes with crisp rolls and strong coffee. You can choose between French, American, Russian, Balkan, and even a "Breakfast for the Rich," which comes with caviar and a bottle of Sekt sparkling wine. The candles flicker here until late in the night, long after the rest of Potsdam is in bed.

FAST FOOD

Stands selling *Wurst* are dotted everywhere. One of the best is **Mayer's Schmalzbäckerei** on Bassinplatz *(open Mon-Sat 7.30am-midnight, Sun 11am-midnight),* a wooden cabin next to the market, where you can eat *Thüringer Bratwurst* served in a crisp roll with mustard.

ICE CREAM

The **Café am Kanal** *(Am Kanal 54)* is a modern ice cream parlor dating from the days when *tutti-frutti* was the ultimate socialist luxury. Sample ice cream on the terrace of MINSK (see opposite) in the summer.

BEER GARDENS

Several leafy beer gardens situated around the perimeter of Park Sanssouci may be worth tracking down on summer days. A lane leads off Zur Historischer Mühle *(near the old windmill behind Schloss Sanssouci)* to the **Historische Mühle beer garden**.

Shopping

Several years after reunification, Potsdam still does not have many interesting shops. Most of the shops from the socialist era — the ones with simple names like *Obst und Gemüse* (Fruit and Vegetables) — have by now closed down, but the new shops are as yet a little disappointing. For the moment, the best shopping strategy is to take the S-Bahn from Potsdam-Stadt to Savignyplatz in Berlin. This gets you to the heart of Berlin's most attractive shopping district in about half an hour.

Potsdam's main shopping street is Brandenburgerstrasse, an attractive car-free street running from Bassinplatz to Potsdam's Brandenburger Tor. The street is lined with attractive 18thC houses containing small shops and cafés. One of the blessings of the sluggish socialist economy is that most of the buildings have preserved their dignified Baroque facades. It remains to be seen if the new owners will respect the architecture.

The more enterprising shops now accept credit cards, but it is still more common in Potsdam to pay with a Eurocheque or with cash.

BOOKSTORES

One of the first signs of *die Wende* in Potsdam was the restocking of bookstores. Out went the dull Marxist tomes and Russian grammars; in came stacks of guidebooks covering countries that were previously impossible to visit. Now at several good bookstores you can buy a detailed guide to Potsdam, or maps for planning walks in the nearby forests.

- **Alexander von Humboldt Buchhandlung** Am Alten Markt ☎(0331) 22539. Stocks German literature, local maps for walking or cycling, and appealing postcards.
- **Das Internationale Buch** Friedrich-Ebert-Strasse 16 ☎(0331) 21496. Travel books, Potsdam guides and postcards.

CLOTHES

The dreary styles and colors of pre-*Wende* Potsdam have gone, to be replaced by American jackets, Hawaiian shirts and French underwear.

- **Benetton** Charlottenstrasse 84 AE MC VISA Satisfies the urge to dress in bright colors.
- **Erich Goebel** Brandenburger Strasse MC VISA Imports classy and saucy French underwear for men and women.

DEPARTMENT STORE

Potsdam's one and only department store, **Horten** *(Brandenburger Strasse),* is the place to go for necessities like shoelaces and umbrellas. It is chaotic, crowded and cheap.

MARKETS

A small market is held on **Bassinplatz** *(Mon-Sat, 8am-6pm).* Stalls sell local vegetables, fruit, flowers and cheap clothes, but not much else.

PHARMACY

The pharmacy that supplied the Prussian court and the German Kaisers is still standing. Founded in 1735, the **Apotheke "Zum Goldenen Hirsch"** *(Lindenstrasse 40 ☎(0331) 23084)* remains an attractive shop to buy cough medicine or suntan oil.

PORCELAIN
Clou & Classic *(Mittelstrasse 13, open Tues-Sun)* sells Prussian porcelain from the KPM factory in Berlin.

RECORDED MUSIC
Young East Germans flocked to buy Western music when the Wall came down. **City-Music** *(Brandenburger Strasse 62)* meets the demand with the latest rock CDs. It occupies a shop once grandly called **Musikhaus Carl Philipp Emanuel Bach**.

SPORTS EQUIPMENT
There are endless opportunities around Potsdam for walking, boating, fishing and swimming. If you lack a vital piece of equipment, go to **Intersport** *(Am Alten Markt ☎(0331) 22781 AE Ⓓ MC VISA)*, which has a vast stock of hiking boots, rucksacks, bathing suits and skis.

TOYS
The biggest toy store is **Kid's Corner** *(Charlottenstrasse)*. Nowadays, it is crammed with Lego and Fisher-Price products.

Potsdam after dark

Socialism has left a lasting imprint on the nocturnal habits of the people of Potsdam. After the shops close, the streets become virtually deserted, apart from a few German and French tourists looking for the action. The truth is that the real action is 24 kilometers (15 miles) to the NE of here, in Berlin.

Local people do not eat out very often, or even go to bars. There are a few cinemas, mainly small (although the programs are interesting), a cabaret, a few theaters — and that's about it.

In the summer months, it is pleasant strolling through the old town, but in winter the streets seem very quiet. You may end up looking at the *Fernsehen* (TV) listings in the local newspaper, or striking out by S-Bahn to the bright lights of Berlin.

For those willing to try their luck in Potsdam, here follow some addresses to investigate.

TICKETS
Tickets for concerts and plays in Potsdam are sold at the **tourist office** *(address on page 214)*. You can also pick up tickets for pop concerts at **City-Music** *(Brandenburger Strasse 62)*.

Most *Theaterkassen* in Berlin sell tickets for Potsdam events (see page 181 for addresses).

CABARET

- **Kabarett am Obelisk** Schopenhauerstrasse 27 ☎(0331) 21069. This cabaret-theater is the liveliest spot in town after nightfall. Late-night shows and cabaret for kids take place one floor up in **Café Klatsch**.

CINEMAS

Cinemas in Potsdam are small and simple, but they often show excellent movies, ranging from Babelsberg classics to new Hollywood releases.

- **DEFA-Studiokino** August-Bebel-Strasse 26–53 ☎(0331) 723424. A two-screen cinema located next to the Babelsberg DEFA Studios. The big cinema tends to show recent Hollywood movies (dubbed into German more often than not). The small screen might be running an art film season if you're lucky.
- **Kino im Filmmuseum** Schlossstrasse 4 ☎(0331) 23675. A small and comfortable cinema located in the FILMMUSEUM-POTSDAM. The best movies turn up here eventually.
- **Melodie-Lichtspiele** Friedrich-Ebert-Strasse 12 ☎(0331) 22917. This is the kind of small-town movie house shot by Wim Wenders in *Kings of the Road*. The decor is run-down, but the movies (usually dubbed) are good.

CLASSICAL CONCERTS

The people of Potsdam share with other Germans a deep love of music. The city has been a center of musical creativity ever since Frederick the Great brought some of the great musicians of the day to Sanssouci. The summer is the time to catch the best concerts in churches, parks and palaces.

- **Schlosstheater** Neues Palais, Park Sanssouci ☎(0331) 92910. Concerts of classical music are occasionally held in the intimate Baroque theater at the NEUES PALAIS. Listening to Mozart in this soft red velvet cocoon is an unforgettable experience.
- **Theaterhaus am Alten Markt** Am Alten Markt ☎(0331) 23038. The Brandenburgische Philharmonie Potsdam perform the classics in a makeshift building in front of the Nikolaikirche.
- **Gaststätte "Historische Mühle"** Zur Historischer Mühle. Jazz and classical concerts often take place in summer, in the beer garden next to the reconstructed windmill known as the Historische Mühle.

DISCOS AND DANCING

You need to look hard to find places to romp and stomp in Potsdam. The restaurant MINSK *(Max-Planck-Strasse 10)* organizes dances for singles and old-timers on Friday and Saturday, and a disco on Sunday.

ROCK CONCERTS

The main rock venue is the **Lindenpark** *(Stannsdorferstrasse 76-78 ☎(0331) 78944),* next to the DEFA Studios at Babelsberg.

THEATER

The monstrous concrete theater in front of the Nikolaikirche was recently demolished. The most exciting theater in Potsdam is now staged on the same site, in the temporary **Theaterhaus Am Alten Markt** *(Am Alten Markt ☎ (0331) 23038)*.

Sports and activities in Potsdam

The forests around Potsdam are ideal for rambling, running and bike rides. Potsdam is also well supplied with swimming pools, race tracks and arenas.

CYCLING
Before the Wall came down, bicycles were a rare sight in Potsdam, but many locals are now discovering the pleasures of cycling in the flat Brandenburg landscape. The main problems are bumpy cobblestones, pot-holed roads and a lack of cycle lanes.

Bikes can be rented from **Detlef Bels** *(Röhrenstrasse 4 ☎ (0331) 622113)*.

ROWBOATS
Rowboats can be rented in the summer months on Freundschaftsinsel.

SPECTATOR EVENTS
The East German government pumped massive sums into sports facilities to train Olympic winners. Potsdam's legacy is several modern stadiums for indoor and outdoor events. The **Karl-Liebknecht-Stadion** is the principal outdoor stadium for soccer and hockey matches.

SWIMMING
None of Potsdam's hotels has a swimming pool, but you will find a modern municipal pool on the slopes above the old town: **Schwimmhalle "Am Brauhausberg"** *(Am Brauhausberg ☎ (0331) 4691)*.

WALKING
Those keen on walking will find countless forest trails and lakeside walks around Potsdam. For an easy half-day ramble, follow WALK 3 through the Neuer Garten, Volkspark Klein-Glienicke and Park Babelsberg. For a longer walk, buy a map of the region, and set off into the woods from Bahnhof Wildpark *(reached from the town center by bus 695)*.

Walking tours of Potsdam are run regularly by **Stattreisen** *(Nansenstrasse 19 ☎ (0331) 960894)*.

Dresden

The ruins, the riches, the rebuilding

Dresden is a difficult city to visit. It was once one of the most beautiful Baroque cities in Europe. Picturesquely sited on the banks of the Elbe, its skyline bristled with spires and domes; and its museums were crammed with Baroque paintings, Meissen porcelain and precious jewelry.

The German Romantics fell in love with Dresden. They painted moody views of the city skyline at sunset, and climbed the nearby peaks in search of solitary grandeur. The Romantic spirit is preserved in a little museum located at the top of a house on the Hauptstrasse, and in the melancholy paintings by Caspar David Friedrich in the Albertinum.

Foreigners were equally captivated by Dresden, which became one of the essential stops on the Grand Tour of Europe. By the end of the 19th century, the city boasted more than 10,000 expatriate residents. Most lived in the See-Vorstadt near the Hauptbahnhof, where there were once four foreign churches (English, American, Scottish and Russian). The poet Johann Gottfried von Herder was so struck by the city's art and architecture that he declared it to be "the Florence on the Elbe."

THE FIRESTORMS

The Florence on the Elbe was destroyed in one night. Early in 1945, the Royal Air Force hit Dresden in two separate raids on the night of February 13. The old town was engulfed by terrifying firestorms. Most of the Baroque palaces and Neoclassical museums were reduced to smoldering ruins. The 19th century churches of the English, Scottish and American communities were all destroyed; only the Russian chapel survived.

The firestorm that swept through Dresden was a nightmare that the old still remember, and the young are not allowed to forget. Many other European cities had been bombed, but the scale of destruction in Dresden was unprecedented. At least 35,000 people died, although some put the figure as high as 135,000. At the time, the city was crammed with refugees fleeing from the Soviet army. They had come thinking it a safe haven.

TODAY

You cannot visit Dresden without feeling a deep sense of loss. The ruins and the rubble are still there. The town center is still an incoherent jumble of gutted buildings, weed-infested bomb sites and signs of hasty postwar construction. Scores of bombed-out ruins have been left untouched since the war. The postcard stands are mainly stocked with views of bombed buildings, or nostalgic old photographs of prewar Dresden.

But Dresden is changing. The end of the Cold War has brought a new vitality to the city. The old town is now bristling with cranes, as several ruined buildings are restored, including the vast Residenzschloss and the Frauenkirche, which was, until recently, a heap of rubble.

You will be disappointed if you come to Dresden in search of the Florence of the North — the Pompeii of the North is nearer the truth. The city has had to be built again from scratch; this enormous task was begun by communists, but it will probably be completed by capitalists. There is much still to be done: the parks are overgrown, the shops are mostly drab, and good restaurants are hard to find.

New hotels are being built in the suburbs, and the dilapidated Czech trams are gradually being replaced by the latest West German models. But it will take many years before the city is whole again. The target of 2006 has been set as the completion date for the restoration of the Residenzschloss and Frauenkirche. The other ruins may remain until well into the next century.

AT THE TURNING POINT

But it is still well worth visiting Dresden at this turning point in its history. There are three unmissable sights: the Zwinger, the Gemäldegalerie Alte Meister and the Grünes Gewölbe, and other attractions that are well worth a trip, including Schloss Pillnitz, the Fürstenzug and the Hofkirche. It is interesting to a visitor simply to watch the painstaking restoration of the Frauenkirche.

You might even find that Dresden still has a strangely romantic allure. You can spend the night on a riverboat moored on the Elbe, or stroll along the Brühlsche Terrasse on a moonlit evening. There are paddle steamer trips to Meissen, and classical concerts in the gardens of Baroque palaces and secret amphitheaters. The energetic can wander through the wistfully abandoned old spa town of Weisser Hirsch, or even go for a hike in the vineyards above the Elbe.

Vineyards? You probably didn't expect that, but there are old vines planted on the northern slopes of the Elbe. They are among the most northerly vineyards in the world, producing an elegant dry white wine. You can taste it in one of the dark wine cellars in Dresden, served in a heavy green glass.

There are other sights that come as a surprise to many visitors. Dresden has a 100-year-old funicular railway, a fleet of old paddle steamers, and an abandoned tobacco factory disguised as a mosque. It also has a Russian church, a miniature railway, and a "glass woman" who is almost as famous as the Zwinger.

Dresden is a surprising city, with more to offer than many people expect. Yet it is likely to remain an uncomfortable place to visit until well into the next century. No other city in Germany, not even Berlin, has so many tangible relics of the war. But no other city in Europe has such a mixture of riches and ruins.

Landmarks in Dresden's history

EARLY TIMES

1206: Dresden was mentioned for the first time in a document. **1234**: A chapel was constructed to contain a relic of the Cross. **1275**: The first stone bridge was built across the Elbe, replacing an older wooden one destroyed by fire. **1285**: First written mention of the existence of a castle in Dresden.

FEUDAL SAXONY

Late 13thC: The cultured Margrave Heinrich der Erlauchte built a castle at Dresden. The first city wall was built. **1349**: Jews were expelled from Dresden.

1403: The town of Altendresden on the right bank of the Elbe was granted a charter. **1409**: The Hussites came to Dresden from Prague to preach for radical reforms in the church, but were expelled three years later.

1464: The brothers Albrecht and Ernst, who ruled Saxony jointly, moved to Dresden from Meissen. Dresden became the official residence of the Wettins. **1485**: Under the terms of the Leipzig Division, Saxony was split into two regions governed by the Duke Albrecht and Duke Ernst. Albrecht remained in Dresden. **1491**: Much of Dresden was destroyed by a fire.

RENAISSANCE AND REFORMATION

1517: Martin Luther preached for sweeping reforms in the church, in Dresden's Schlosskapel. Although the Elector did not adopt Lutheranism, Dresden became a Protestant city in 1539. The Kreuzkirche was converted to a Lutheran church. **1547**: Moritz became Elector of Saxony. He began to transform Dresden into a northern Renaissance city.

1548: The Hoforkest (court orchestra) was founded, later to become the famous Dresden State Orchestra. **1560**: An art gallery was established in the Residenzschloss. **1563**: The *Zeughaus* (arsenal) was built (now the Albertinum).

16thC: The towns of Dresden and Altendresden (on the right bank of the Elbe) merged. **1618–48**: The Thirty Years' War led to economic slump. **1676**: The Grosser Garten was landscaped in Baroque style. **1685**: Altendresden was destroyed by a fire. A plan was drawn up by W. C. von Klengel to create a new town. This became the Neustadt.

DRESDEN'S GOLDEN AGE

1694: Frederick Augustus (Augustus the Strong) became Elector of Saxony. This marked the beginning of Dresden's golden age, which saw the construction of the Zwinger, the Frauenkirche and Schloss Pillnitz. **1697**: Augustus the Strong converted to Catholicism to enable him to be crowned king of Poland. Combined with the extensive Polish territories, Saxony briefly became one of the great powers of Europe.

1708: Johann Friedrich Böttger invented European hard porcelain in a secret laboratory under the Brühlsche Terrasse. The same year saw the completion of Johann Melchior Dinglinger's *Imperial Household of the*

Great Mogul (the centerpiece of the Grünes Gewölbe). **1710**: The Meissen porcelain factory was founded by Augustus the Strong. Work began on the construction of the Zwinger in the same year, although it was not completed until 1732. **1726**: Work began on the construction of the Frauenkirche.

1733: Death of Augustus the Strong. He was succeeded by his son Augustus III. **1736**: The statue of Augustus the Strong was placed on the Neustädtischer Markt. **1738**: The Catholic Hofkirche was begun by Gaetano Chiaveri.

1751: Canaletto (the Younger) was invited to Dresden from Venice by Augustus III. He was commissioned to paint 14 views of the city over six years. The paintings now hang in the Gemäldegalerie Alte Meister. **1754**: Augustus III bought the *Sistine Madonna* for his collection in Dresden.

1756–63: The Seven Years' War. Saxony joined Austria, France and Russia in a joint attack on Prussia. **1760**: Dresden was bombarded by the Prussians, led by Frederick the Great. **1763**: The Seven Years' War ended in victory for Prussia. Saxony was forced to pay reparations to Prussia.

1764: The Academy of Art was founded in Dresden. **1770**: A camellia was brought from Japan and planted in the gardens of Schloss Pillnitz. It is now the oldest living camellia in Europe. **1785–87**: Schiller lived in Dresden, and completed *Don Carlos* in a summerhouse in Loschwitz belonging to the Körner family.

ROMANTICS AND REVOLUTIONARIES

1806: Napoleon conquered Saxony. In **1809** he ordered the demolition of the city ramparts. **1813**: Napoleon won his final victory at the Battle of Bautzen, near Dresden. He captured Dresden, but was defeated later that year at the Battle of Leipzig, after which came exile on Elba.

1815: The Treaty of Vienna was signed following the final defeat of Napoleon at Waterloo. Saxony was forced to surrender more than half of its territory to its old enemy Prussia.

1817: Carl Maria von Weber was appointed Court Director of Music. **1828**: The royal art collections were shown to the public for the first time. **1839**: The first long-distance railway line in Germany was opened, between Dresden and Leipzig.

1842: Wagner's opera *Rienzi* was premiered in Dresden. **1843**: Wagner was appointed director of the Staatsoper in Dresden. His opera *The Flying Dutchman* was first performed there that year. **1845**: Wagner's romantic opera *Tannhäuser* was premiered in Dresden. **1847–54**: Gottfried Semper completed the Zwinger by adding the long gallery on Theaterplatz (now the Gemäldegalerie and the Rüstkammer).

1849: A rebellion in Dresden was put down by Saxon and Prussian troops. Semper and Wagner were forced to flee from Dresden because of their revolutionary activities. Cancellation of the Dresden premiere of Wagner's *Lohengrin,* which Wagner had composed in the city.

RUINS AND REBIRTH

1905: The artist's group *Die Brücke* (The Bridge) was founded in Dresden by Ernst Kirchner, Karl Schmitt-Rottluff and Erich Heckel.

1911: The First International Hygiene Exhibition was held in Dresden.

1914: Start of World War I. **1918**: The monarchy was abolished at the end of World War I. Dresden became capital of the Free State of Saxony.

1933: The Nazis seized power. Dresden's Jews were persecuted: those who fled from Dresden included the painter Otto Dix and the conductor of the State Orchestra Fritz Busch. **1937**: The Nazis staged an exhibition of "degenerate" art in the town hall, which included paintings by *Die Brücke* artists.

February 13–14, 1945: Dresden was bombed by the RAF in a raid code-named "Thunderclap." Most of the old city was devastated and at least 35,000 people died. **1945**: Dresden fell under Soviet control.

1952: The communist regime abolished the old German states. Saxony ceased to exist, and Dresden lost its role as capital. **1953**: The reconstruction of the Altmarkt was begun in monumental Stalinist Neo-classicism, but this style gave way to a bland modernism in the 1960s. **1956**: Reopening of the Gemäldegalerie. **1959**: The communists decided to leave the Frauenkirche as a permanent ruin. **1981**: The Hofkirche became a cathedral.

1989: Huge demonstrations were held in Dresden in October at the Hauptbahnhof and the Frauenkirche. On **November 9**, the frontier between East and West Germany was opened. **1990**: The state of Saxony was restored, with Dresden as its capital.

1993: German politicians protested when a statue was unveiled in London commemorating Sir Arthur ("Bomber") Harris, who planned the air attack on Dresden. Russian and German representatives met at Dresden to sign an agreement securing the return to Germany of works of art stolen during World War II.

2006: Dresden will celebrate its 800th anniversary, by which time the Frauenkirche and the Residenzschloss should have been restored to their prewar splendor.

Who's who in Dresden

The lives of some of those whose names are linked with Dresden are briefly sketched below. Many were composers who worked for the Staatsoper; others were painters who taught at the Academy of Art.

• **Brühl, Count** The Prime Minister of Augustus III, Count Brühl was famous for his extravagant lifestyle. At one time he owned 200 pairs of shoes, 800 dressing gowns and 1,500 wigs. The Brühlsche Terrasse stands on the site of Count Brühl's palace.

• **Canaletto** His real name was Bernardo Bellotto, but he called himself Canaletto. Born in Venice in 1720, he was the nephew of the more famous Canaletto who painted views of Venice and London. The younger Canaletto took over his uncle's style, as well as his name. He became the court painter in Dresden in 1747, producing a series of precise views of the city. The Gemäldegalerie still has some 14 of these paintings on display. Canaletto moved to Warsaw in 1767, and died there in 1780. His paintings of Warsaw were so detailed that they were used in the postwar reconstruction of the old town, but the same did not happen in Dresden, where the modernists had their way.

• **Dix, Otto** One of the great modern German painters, Otto Dix was born in Thuringia in 1891. After serving on the Western Front in World War I, he studied at Dresden Academy of Art, and later became a leading figure of the *Neue Sachlichkeit* (New Objectivity) movement, which insisted on absolute realism. Dix took up a teaching post at Dresden Academy of Art in 1929, but he was dismissed by the Nazis in 1933. He died in 1969.

• **Friedrich, Caspar David** The great German Romantic painter lived for much of his life in Dresden. Born in 1774 in Greifswald, near the Baltic coast, he studied art for four years in Copenhagen before moving to Dresden in 1798. He lived with his wife Caroline in a house overlooking the Elbe. Friedrich joined the Dresden Academy of Art in 1816 and was appointed professor of art in 1824. His paintings were suffused with a melancholy spirit, featuring misty landscapes, cemeteries under snow, jagged Gothic ruins and craggy mountains.

The solitary human figures in his paintings seem dwarfed by the immensity of nature. He died in Dresden in 1840 and was buried in the city's Trinitatis Friedhof. A few of Friedrich's paintings hang in the GEMÄLDEGALERIE NEUE MEISTER in Dresden; others are in the GALERIE DER ROMANTIK in Berlin.

• **Kokoschka, Oskar** The Austrian painter Oskar Kokoschka found himself in Dresden in 1915 after being wounded in World War I. He was professor at the Dresden Academy of Art from 1919–24. During his Dresden period, Kokoschka painted several Expressionist views of the Elbe from his studio on the Brühlsche Terrasse.

• **Krone, Hermann** Born in 1827, Krone was one of the pioneers of photography. He opened a studio in Dresden in 1852, taking photographs of Dresden streets and the landscape of Saxon Switzerland. His collection of cameras and photographs is now owned by the Dresden Technical University, where he taught as professor of photography. He died in 1916.

• **Richter, Adrian Ludwig** The Romantic painter Richter was born in 1803 in the prosperous Dresden suburb of Friedrichstadt. His early work was influenced by Italian landscape painting, but he converted to a Germanic style after a mystical experience on the Elbe.

• **Schumann, Robert** The Romantic German composer Robert Schumann was born in Zwickau in 1810. He fell in love with Clara Wieck, the daughter of his piano teacher, and they married in 1840. Clara Schumann (whose portrait appears on the current DM100 banknote) was an accomplished pianist, and Schumann lived with her in Dresden from 1845–50, where he composed many of his greatest works, including the A-minor piano concerto. Schumann later suffered a nervous breakdown and died in a Dresden asylum in 1856. Clara died in Frankfurt in 1896.

• **Vonnegut Jr, Kurt** The American novelist (born in 1922) was a prisoner of war near Dresden in 1945 and witnessed the destruction caused by the historic raid. His most famous novel, *Slaughterhouse-Five,* is a fantasy based partially on his war experiences.

• **Wagner, Richard** Most people link Wagner with Ludwig, King of Bavaria, but the German composer equally had contacts with the King of Saxony. Wagner studied in Dresden, and his first successful opera *(Rienzi)* was premiered in the Dresden opera house. He was appointed *Kapellmeister* at the Staatsoper in 1843, and wrote several of his greatest works in Dresden, including *Tannhäuser* and *Lohengrin,* but was forced to flee the city in 1848 after siding with the revolutionaries. The *Lohengrinhaus* near Pillnitz, where Wagner composed *Lohengrin* in the spring of 1846, is now preserved as a museum.

• **Weber, Carl Maria von** The German Romantic composer was born near Lübeck in 1786. He moved to Prague in 1813 to direct the opera, but the King of Saxony persuaded him to settle in Dresden in 1816 to direct the Staatsoper. Many of his operas were premiered in Dresden. He died in London in 1826, but his friend Wagner paid for his body to be brought back to Dresden, for burial in the ALTER KATHOLISCHER FRIEDHOF.

• **The Wettin rulers** Just as Berlin had its long line of Hohenzollern Friedrichs, Dresden has been ruled by one Augustus or another for much of its history. The main names to get straight are: **Elector Augustus**, who built the arsenal (now the Albertinum) in the 16thC; **Augustus the Strong** (also known as **Friedrich Augustus I**), who built the Zwinger in the early 18thC; and his son **Augustus II** of Saxony (Augustus III of Poland), who built up the Gemäldegalerie collection. Another important figure was **Elector Moritz**, the father of **Elector Augustus**, who founded the Grünes Gewölbe in the 16thC.

Architecture in Dresden

Prepare yourself for the worst. Most of Dresden was hastily built in the 1950s and '60s, in a tacky modern style. The city once dubbed "the Florence on the Elbe" now sometimes looks more like a Moscow on the Elbe. Some of the buildings of the socialist era on Prager Strasse and Altmarkt are worthy of a glance, but most of the architecture is in the doggedly dreary Communist Party mold.

A BAROQUE FLOURISH

But, don't abandon hope. Dresden still has some extraordinary architecture to be admired, much of which was carefully restored at the same time as the concrete apartment blocks were being built. Dresden owes almost all its grandeur to one man: King Augustus the Strong (1694–1733). The town had been capital of the Kingdom of Saxony since 1485, but it only assumed a royal grandeur under Augustus. Most of the buildings that visitors admire today are the legacy of Augustus: the **Zwinger**, **Schloss Pillnitz** and the **Japanisches Palais** were his pet projects. The **Frauenkirche** was another of his grand ideas.

Matthäus Daniel Pöppelmann (1662–1736) was Augustus the Strong's favorite architect. He came to Dresden in 1686, eventually rising to the post of chief architect in 1705.

His first commission was to construct the **Taschenberg Palais** for Augustus the Strong's mistress, but his greatest triumph was the **Zwinger**, designed in an airy Baroque style. Pöppelmann traveled to Italy and Vienna to find out the latest Baroque styles, but the Zwinger is no mere copy. It is a unique building featuring a vast courtyard enclosed by long galleries and billowing corner pavilions, entered by gateways laden with sculptural decoration.

The sculpture was carved by Balthasar Permoser, who worked closely with Pöppelmann to achieve a dazzling effect. The vast courtyard enclosed by curvaceous buildings looks like a palace, but it was intended simply as a backdrop for festivities and flirting. Some of the pavilions now lie empty, but others contain some of the city's most important museums. Scintillating interiors decorated with marble can still be found in the **Mathematisch-Physicalischer Salon** and the **Porzellansammlung**, but the most thrilling space to visit is the upper room adjoining the **Gemäldegalerie**, where paintings by Van Eyck and Dürer are on view.

Pöppelmann went on to design other palaces for Augustus the Strong, but they lack the dramatic impact of the Zwinger. An insatiable passion for porcelain led Augustus the Strong to commission two palaces on the Elbe with roofs in the Chinoiserie style, modeled on the buildings seen in paintings on imported Japanese dishes. The first was **Schloss Pillnitz** (1720–23), followed by the **Japanisches Palais**.

Pöppelmann worked on the early designs of Schloss Moritzburg, a splendid Baroque summer palace used for celebrations. He also designed several Baroque churches in Dresden, including the **Dreikönigskirche** in the Neustadt.

EXUBERANT ROMANTICISM

The Berlin architect Karl Friedrich Schinkel designed a neat little Neoclassical building on Theaterplatz in 1830 (originally a guard house, now a theater box office), but the experiment was not repeated.

Dresden's exuberant romanticism was better served by Gottfried Semper (1803–79), a dashing figure who had fled from Germany after fighting a duel in Munich. He spent three years studying the Classical architecture of Italy and Greece, and eventually settled in Dresden in 1834 as professor of architecture at the Academy of Art.

His first building in Dresden was the Neo-Renaissance royal opera house (1838–41), which was destroyed by fire in 1871. He later completed the **Zwinger** by adding the wing on Theaterplatz currently occupied by the Gemäldegalerie Alte Meister and the Rüstkammer (1847–54). Semper, like Wagner, was forced to flee from Dresden after the 1848 revolution, settling first in Paris and eventually in London, where he was involved in the design of the Victoria and Albert Museum. He was invited in 1871 to design a new opera house in Dresden after a fire destroyed his original building. The opera house, named in his honor the **Semperoper**, repeated the semicircular front of the old building, but in a more Baroque style.

ENGINEERING AND ECCENTRICITIES

Semper's grand Neo-Renaissance was widely copied in the prosperous 19thC suburbs such as Blasewitz, Loschwitz and Weisser Hirsch. Virtually untouched in 1945, these districts are still dotted with rambling villas decorated with flamboyant turrets, romantic friezes, statues and balconies.

A handful of eccentricities were built in Dresden in the late 19thC. You will see a building that looks like a mosque (originally a tobacco factory), and a castle (Schloss Eckberg) built on the slopes above the Elbe in English Neo-Gothic style.

Several spectacular engineering projects were carried out at the turn of the century, including the **Blaues Wunder bridge** and the **Loschwitz funicular** and cable railway. In the 1920s, the ideas of the Bauhaus influenced the design of the **Deutsches Hygiene-Museum**, but the rise of the Nazis put an end to such visionary architecture.

AFTER THE THUNDERCLAP

The British air raid on February 13–14 (code-named "Thunderclap") devastated the heart of the old town. The Zwinger was gutted and the dome of the Frauenkirche collapsed.

The main priority after the war was to build new homes as fast as possible, and the results, although dull, are no worse than similar postwar developments elsewhere in Europe. The reconstruction of Prager Strasse resembles the Lijnbaan in Rotterdam, with a mixture of high-rise and low buildings occupied by hotels, shops, movie theaters and restaurants. For a relic of heroic Stalinist architecture, look for the huge concrete power station (if it is still standing), built in 1951 on Weisseritzstrasse (at Magdeburger Strasse). An inscription carved on the facade reads: "Built in the first year of the five-year plan."

The communists were diligent in repairing old buildings such as the Zwinger and the Albertinum, but they neglected the royal palace and deliberately left the Frauenkirche as a heap of ruins.

Since the 1989 revolution, Western firms have taken over the task of rebuilding Dresden. The skyline is now bristling with cranes, but the task of repairing the city will go on well into the next century. Until the work is done, Dresden can be considered the most fascinating building site in Europe.

Books about Dresden

• **Slaughterhouse-five** *(1969)* A slim novel with a Dresden theme, Kurt Vonnegut Jr's *Slaughterhouse-five* was made into a movie by George Roy Hill in 1972. Vonnegut was held as a prisoner of war near Dresden and actually saw the ruined city after the 1945 air raid. The novel is a fantasy, based loosely on Vonnegut's wartime experiences, although it cannot be described as a simple war story.
• **Utz** *(1988)* Another fascinating book that won't weigh down your suitcase is Bruce Chatwin's *Utz*. Mainly set in Prague, this slim novel is the story of a collector fascinated by Meissen porcelain. Chatwin has some interesting passages about Augustus the Strong's consuming passion for porcelain.
• **The Destruction of Dresden** *(1963)* There are few general histories of Dresden, but the 1945 air raid is covered in David Irving's controversial book.

> Dresden was one big flame. The one flame ate everything organic, everything that would burn.
>
> It wasn't safe to come out of the shelter until noon the next day. When the Americans and their guards did come out, the sky was black with smoke. The sun was an angry little pinhead. Dresden was like the moon now, nothing but minerals. The stones were hot. Everybody else in the neighborhood was dead.
>
> So it goes.
>
> (*Slaughterhouse-five,* 1969, Kurt Vonnegut, Jr.)

Dresden: practical information

This section is subdivided as follows:

- **BEFORE YOU GO**, below
- **GETTING THERE**, below
- **GETTING AROUND IN DRESDEN**, opposite
- **ON-THE-SPOT INFORMATION**, page 261
- **BUSINESS IN DRESDEN**, page 261
- **USEFUL NUMBERS AND ADDRESSES**, page 262
- **EMERGENCY INFORMATION**, page 263

Summaries of subject headings are printed in CAPITALS at the top of most pages. See also **VISITING NORTHERN GERMANY** on page 16.

Before you go

TOURIST INFORMATION

German national tourist offices stock some information about Dresden, but the best source for planning a trip is the Dresden tourist office: **Tourist-Information**, Prager Strasse 10, 01069 Dresden ☎(0351) 4955025 [Fx](0351) 4951276.

Getting there

BY AIR

- **Dresden-Klotzsche** airport *(☎(0351) 58903080)* is located 9km ($5\frac{1}{2}$ miles) to the N of the city. The airport is small, and most scheduled services are short-hop flights to other German cities. The main direct international connections are to Paris, Zurich, Moscow and Budapest.
- A bus runs from the airport to the Dresden Hauptbahnhof (main station), stopping at Bahnhof Neustadt, the Maritim Hotel Bellevue and the Dresden Hilton. The journey takes 30 minutes. For times ☎(0351) 4328043.

BY RAIL

- Railway services to Dresden are operated by **Deutsche Reichsbahn**. Direct **InterCity (IC)** trains run to many German cities including Hamburg and Frankfurt-am-Main. Direct international **EuroCity (EC)** services run to Paris, Prague, Vienna, Bucharest and Copenhagen. Long-distance trains stop at two main railway stations: **Dresden-Hauptbahnhof** and **Dresden-Neustadt**.

BY ROAD

- The E40 autobahn links Dresden with Ostend, Brussels and Cologne. The E55 links Dresden with Berlin and Rostock.

BY SHIP

- The most romantic way to arrive is to take a cruise ship down the Elbe from Hamburg to Dresden. This new inland route was opened soon after German reunification. The seven-day trip takes you through former East Germany, past the historic towns of Wittenberg and Meissen. The service is operated by **Köln-Düsseldorfer (KD)**, *(Frankenwerft 15, 50667 Köln ☎(0221) 20880 ℻(0221) 2088231).*

Getting around in Dresden

GETTING FROM THE AIRPORT TO THE CITY

See GETTING THERE BY AIR, opposite.

GETTING AROUND BY PUBLIC TRANSPORT

Dresden has an extensive public transport network run by **Regionalverkehr Dresden (RVD)**.

- For information about services ☎(0351) 4955012.

Buses

Buses provide a fast service to some of the outlying suburbs such as Pillnitz. Following privatization, the old fleet of buses is gradually being replaced by sleek, new West German models.

Main stations

- **Dresden-Hauptbahnhof** *(☎(0351) 4710600, switchboard 6am-8pm)* is the main station, situated S of the old town. Destroyed in 1945, it has now been restored to its former grandeur. This is the best station to use for getting to addresses in central Dresden or the southern suburbs. You can take a tram from the station into the old town, or out to the suburbs. It takes about ten minutes to walk into town along the attractive Prager Strasse (leave the station by *Durchgang 2*). The **Mitropa** station restaurant is a relic of the communist era probably best avoided. There are better places to eat on Prager Strasse.
- **Dresden-Neustadt** *(☎(0351) 51185, switchboard 7am-6pm).* Dresden's second station lies to the NW of the old town, in the Neustadt district. Grand and grimy, it is convenient for getting to addresses in the Neustadt. Trams run from the station to the Hauptbahnhof, the old town and Weisser Hirsch.

SV-Bahn

Dresden has a network of suburban trains known as the *Stadt-Vorortbahn,* or SV-Bahn for short. They provide a fast and enjoyable means of access to some of the picturesque sights around Dresden, such as Saxon Switzerland, the Dresden Heath and the Meissen wine route.

Trams

Antiquated trams *(Strassenbahn)* built in Prague still form the backbone of the service, trundling along the wide socialist boulevards of central Dresden, rumbling out the old roads to Loschwitz and Radebeul, and even toiling up the hill to Weisser Hirsch. The tram journey to Weisser Hirsch makes an interesting trip on its own (see DRESDEN BY TRAM, page 276, for a route description).

Tickets and other practicalities

Buses and trams provide a frequent service Monday to Friday, from early morning until about 6pm. At other times, the service is less frequent, and you might sometimes wish you had the use of a car, even a stuttering old Trabant with bad suspension, to get you out into the mountains.

Tickets can be bought at the public transport kiosk in front of the Hauptbahnhof or at newspaper shops displaying a *Fahrkarten* sign in the window. There are also efficient automatic ticket machines at most public transport stops. You can buy a *Kurzfahrt* ticket for a single journey, or a *Sammelfahrausweise* valid for seven journeys. The simplest option is to buy a *24-Stunden Karte,* valid on trams and buses in Dresden for 24 hours.

Be sure to stamp all tickets at the start of the journey in the *Entwerter* machine (placed near the doors on trams and buses). The doors on trams and buses are normally opened by a button labeled *Türöffner.* Network maps are displayed in most bus and tram shelters.

FUNICULAR RAILWAY AND CABLE RAILWAY

A **funicular railway**, the *Stadseilbahn,* runs regularly from Talstation Körnerplatz (Körnerplatz Valley Station) to Bad Weisser Hirsch. A **cable railway** *(Schwebebahn)* runs from Körnerplatz to the Loschwitzhöhe.

GETTING AROUND BY TAXI

The main taxi stand is in front of the Hauptbahnhof (main station). Otherwise you can find a cab in the street.

A taxi called by telephone will arrive within a few minutes *(☎(0351) 4312, 24hrs).*

RENTING A CAR

A car is unnecessary within Dresden, but you may find it useful to rent one to explore the surrounding countryside. Several major international car rental firms have branches at Klotzsche airport or in Dresden. Payment is almost always made by charge or credit card. Some car rental firms do not allow their cars to be driven in Eastern European countries; check with the rental company before you set off on a trip to the nearby Czech Republic.

- **Europcar Klotzsche airport** ☎(0351) 5894591; Liebstädter Strasse 5 ☎(0351) 2323399.
- **Hertz Klotzsche airport** ☎(0351) 5894591; Maritim-Hotel Bellevue ☎(0351) 56628.
- **Kreisel Maritim-Hotel Bellevue** ☎(0351) 5662615. Chauffeur-driven limousines.
- **Sixt Klotzsche airport** ☎(0351) 5894570; Dresden Hilton ☎(0351) 4841696; Hotel Mercure Newa ☎(0351) 4951059.

NAME CHANGES OF DRESDEN STREETS

Juri-Gagarin-Platz has survived *die Wende,* but many other street names from the communist era have disappeared. The former **Strasse der Be-**

freiung (Street of Liberation) has reverted to plain **Hauptstrasse** (High Street). About 100 controversial street names have been purged, including **Ho-Chi-Minh-Strasse**, **Leninplatz** and **Karl-Marx-Platz**.

If buying a map, be sure to check that the new street names are given. The most reliable map is the latest (5th) edition of Falkplan Dresden.

- Maps of Dresden within this section can be found on pages 266–67, 271, 275 and color maps **8** & **9** at the back of the book.

On-the-spot information

BANKS AND CURRENCY EXCHANGE

Most banks in Dresden are open Monday to Friday 8.30am–12.30pm and 2–4pm. The banks accept all major currencies. The branch of the **Deutsche Verkehrsbank** at the Hauptbahnhof is open Monday to Friday 7am–7.30pm, Saturday 8am–4pm.

SHOPPING HOURS

Shops are open Monday to Friday 9am–6.30pm. Most remain open on Thursday until 8.30pm, but close on Saturday at about 2pm, except on the first Saturday in the month, when they open until 6pm in winter and 4pm in summer.

MAIL AND GENERAL DELIVERY (POSTE RESTANTE)

The main post office is **Postamt 1** *(Am Queckbrunnen 1, 01067 Dresden ☎(0351) 4953017, open Mon-Fri 8am-7pm).* There is another post office on Prager Strasse *(open Mon-Fri 8am-6pm, Sat 9am-noon).*

If you wish to use the **General Delivery** *(poste restante)* service, letters to be collected should be marked *Hauptpostlagernd* and sent to the main post office.

LOCAL PUBLICATIONS

Two monthly magazines, *Sax* and *Dresdner,* provide full listings of cultural events in Dresden, including movies, theater, music and dance. Both are excellent.

Business in Dresden

Dresden is rapidly becoming an important business center, and hotels and conference organizations can now offer a sophisticated range of facilities.

HOTELS

The DRESDEN HILTON has the best conference facilities in town, including a "Meeting 2000" service, which provides for just about every possible conference need. The hotel has a congress center seating 150, and several intimate salons for smaller meetings.

CONGRESS CENTERS

Dresden has two main congress centers. The larger is the **Kulturpalast**, a postwar building on the Altmarkt with a large hall seating 2,400.

The other venue is the **Deutsches Hygiene-Museum**, which has two halls, seating 1,000 and 500 participants.

CONFERENCE ORGANIZATION

CPO Hanser Service *(Oehmestrasse 5, 01277 Dresden ☎(0351) 32169 Fx(0351) 32169)* organizes conferences and excursions in Dresden for groups.

Useful numbers and addresses

TOURIST INFORMATION

The main tourist information office is a five-minute walk from the Hauptbahnhof, and is located at Prager Strasse 10, 01069 Dresden *(map 8E3 ☎(0351) 4955025 Fx(0351) 4951276)*. It is open April to October, Monday to Saturday 9am–8pm, Sunday and holidays 9am–noon; November to March, Monday to Saturday 9am–6pm, Sunday and holidays 9am–noon.

A second tourist information office is located in the Neustadt at Neustädter Markt *(map 9C4 ☎(0351) 53539 Fx(0351) 53539)*. It is open Monday to Friday 9am–6pm, Saturday 9am–4pm, Sunday 11am–4pm.

American Express Travel Service Bellevue Arkade, in the Maritim Hotel Bellevue, Grosse Meissner Strasse 15, map **9**C4 ☎(0351) 5662865 Fx(0351) 5662870. A useful source of information for any traveler, whether a Cardholder or not, in need of advice or emergency aid. It is open Monday to Friday 9am–noon, 1–5.30pm, Saturday 9am–noon.

BOAT TOURS

- **Weisse Flotte Dresden** Terrassenufer 2. Map **9**C4 ☎(0351) 5022611 Fx(0351) 4956436. Regular sailings April–October. Tram 4 to Theaterplatz. The steamers of the Weisse Flotte (some more than 100 years old) run regular trips on the Elbe, to such destinations as Meissen and Pillnitz.

BUS TOURS

- **Hamburger Hummelbahn** Parked at Postplatz. Map **8**D3 ☎(0351) 4123687. Departs April to October daily at 10am, noon, 2pm and 4pm; November to March daily at 10am, noon and 2pm. Tram 1, 2, 4, 7, 8, 11, 12, 14 to Postplatz. Two 1920s Hamburg railway carriages with wooden seats are pulled through the streets by a tractor. It plods along at about the speed of a Trabant, crossing the Grosser Garten and chugging along the Elbe waterfront.

Emergency information

For advice on **automobile accidents**, **lost passport** and **emergency phrases**, see EMERGENCY INFORMATION on page 23.

EMERGENCY SERVICES

- **Police** ☎110
- **Fire** ☎112
- **Ambulance** ☎115

HOSPITAL

The main hospital in Dresden is the **Krankenhaus Dresden-Friedrichstadt** *(Friedrichstrasse 41).*

MEDICAL EMERGENCIES

- **Medical emergencies** ☎(0351) 52251

DENTAL EMERGENCIES

- **Zentraler Zahnärztlicher Notdienst** St Petersburger Strasse 15 ☎(0351) 4954141, open Monday to Friday 7am–10pm.
- For information on weekends ☎0011500.

ALL-NIGHT PHARMACIES

- For information about 24-hour pharmacy services ☎0011500.

CAR BREAKDOWNS

- ☎ police (110) or the **ADAC** 24-hour breakdown service: ☎(0351) 4353444.
- See also EMERGENCY INFORMATION on page 23.

LOST PROPERTY

- If you have lost something in the city, go to **Fundbüro der Stadt Dresden** *(Hamburgerstrasse 19a ☎(0351) 4884280).*
- For property lost on a train, go to **Fundbüro der Deutschen Reichsbahn** *(Lohrmannstrasse 4 ☎(0351) 4614630).*

Dresden: planning your visit

ORIENTATION

Dresden (population 500,000) is located on the River Elbe, 105 meters (344 feet) above sea-level, in the *Land* of Saxony. The countryside around is rocky and wooded, but sometimes scarred by industry.

Berlin is 198km (123 miles) to the N, **Meissen** is 23km (14 miles) to the NW, and **Leipzig** is 111km (69 miles) to the W. The Czech border lies 43km (28 miles) to the S at **Altenberg**, and **Prague** is 152km (95 miles) to the SE. The Polish border lies 98km (61 miles) to the E at **Görlitz**.

WHEN TO GO

Dresden looks its best in the summer, from about May to September, when the paddle steamers are running, and classical concerts take place in the ZWINGER courtyard. If you come in the winter months, you will still be able to visit the museums and picture galleries, but you may find the city rather desolate in the evening. Yet there can be attractive days in winter, when snow covers the statues in the Zwinger.

Looking ahead to the future, consider being in Dresden in 2006 for the 800th anniversary celebrations, when the RESIDENZSCHLOSS and the FRAUENKIRCHE should be restored to their original splendor.

The Dresden visitor's calendar

JANUARY

The New Year tends to begin with a concert of classical music. • Some hotels offer a special **Advent Weekend**, combining a hotel room, dinner and ticket for an Advent concert.

FEBRUARY

February 13: **Memorial services** are often held to commemorate the bombing of Dresden in 1945.

MARCH

The **Dresdner Citylauf** (Dresden City Run) usually takes place one day in March.

APRIL

Paddle steamers flying the Weisse Flotte flag begin scheduled services. Several hotels offer special Easter weekend packages, combining accommodation and excursions. • April/May: The **Dresdner Frühlingsfest** (Dresden Spring Fair) is held in the Volksfestgelände in Johannstadt. • Late April: Dresden's **Filmfest** (Film Festival).

MAY

The **little railways of Saxony** begin running regular trips. • Several days in May: The **Internationales Dixielandfestival** brings dozens of jazz bands to Dresden. • Some hotels offer special **Whitsun package deals**. • Late May/early June: The **Dresdner Musikfestspiele** (Dresden Music Festival) brings opera and classical music to venues throughout the city.

JUNE
Start of the summer season; occasional **open-air concerts** on Theaterplatz and elsewhere. • Several days in late June: The **Internationales Tanzfestival Dresden** (Dresden International Dance Festival) brings in dance groups from various countries. • Also for several days in late June: **Elbhangfest** (Elbe Waterside Festival) — a music festival held on the banks of the Elbe.

JULY
Several days in early July: The **Country-Festival** brings international Country & Western singers to the Kulturpalast. • Early July: **Sommerfestival der Volksmusik** (Summer Festival of Folk Music). • Early July to mid-August: During the warm summer nights, **movies** are screened after dark on the Elbe waterfront. • Most of July: A boisterous **fairground** takes over the Volksfestgelände in Johannstadt.

SEPTEMBER
Several days in late September: The **Sächsisches Volkstanzfest** features performances of traditional Saxony folk dancers.

OCTOBER
Several days in early October: **Festival of contemporary music**. • End of October: The **little railways of Saxony** end regular services.

NOVEMBER
Beginning of the winter season. • Late November until a few days before Christmas: **Striezelmarkt**, a traditional Christmas market.

DECEMBER
December 31: The year often ends with a **Silvesterball** (New Year Ball).

Organizing your time

Dresden is not an impossibly big city, but it has an enormous wealth of art treasures to see. You have to visit the **ZWINGER**, and it will take you an entire day, or even more, to see everything. Don't miss the **GEMÄLDEGALERIE ALTE MEISTER**, the **PORZELLANSAMMLUNG**, the **Nymphenbad** and the **MATHEMATISCH-PHYSICALISCHER SALON**. It may sound a lot, but it will be worth the effort. You must also go to the **ALBERTINUM**, if only to see the treasures of the **GRÜNES GEWÖLBE**.

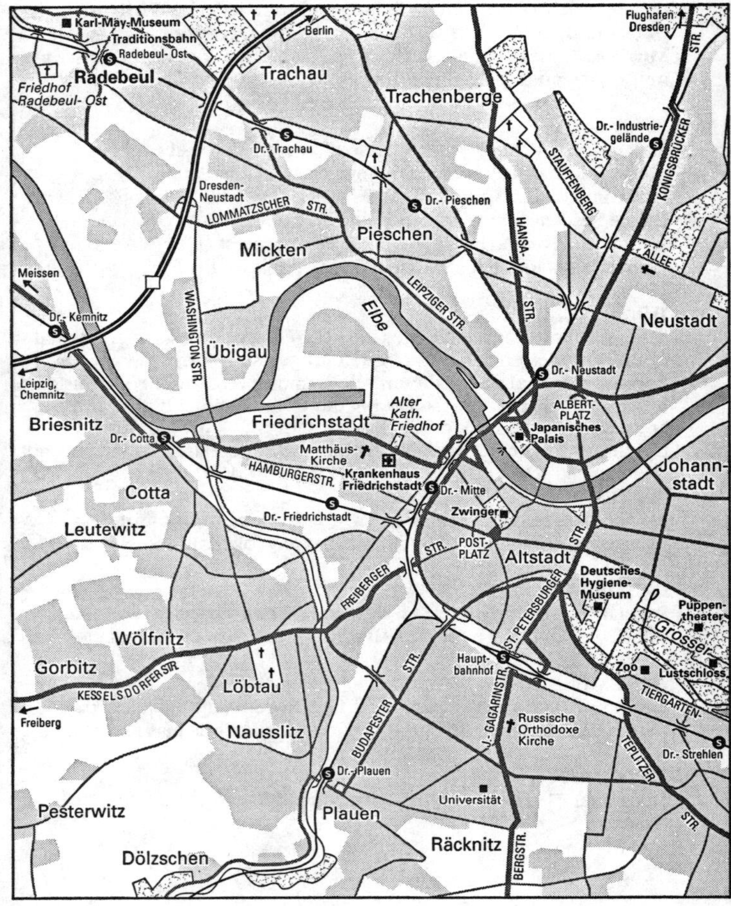

And then what? Some people think they have seen it all, and they take the next train out to Prague or Berlin, but it's worth staying on for at least one more day, to see some of the outlying districts of Dresden, which were not destroyed in the war.

WHAT TO SEE AND DO

You may not manage everything, but as well as the main attractions, you should try to see one or two of the following sights: the Hauptstrasse, the GROSSER GARTEN, the MUSEUM ZUR DRESDNER FRÜHROMANTIK, SCHLOSS

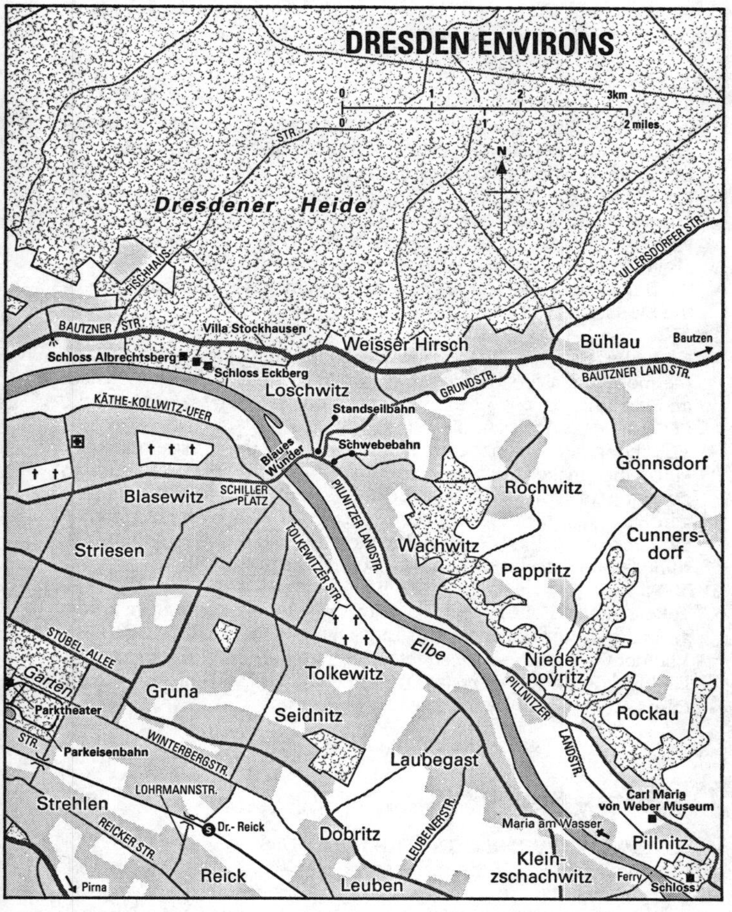

ALBRECHTSBERG, SCHLOSS PILLNITZ and the bizarre KARL-MAY-MUSEUM. In years to come, you might also regret not getting a glimpse of the famous BLAUES WUNDER bridge, or taking the old funicular up to WEISSER HIRSCH.

These are the sights, but there are other pleasures that should not be missed. Try, if you can, to sample a glass of white Meissen wine in a local wine cellar; eat an ice cream on Hauptstrasse; and stroll beside the Elbe.

One last thing. On the night before you leave, make a point of strolling along the BRÜHLSCHE TERRASSE after dinner. A more romantic spot is hard to find.

The following suggested three-day visit brings together Dresden's essential viewing.

DAY 1

- Spend the day at the ZWINGER. Go to the GEMÄLDEGALERIE as soon as it opens. Spend the morning looking at paintings, then eat lunch somewhere nearby, perhaps at the RESTAURANT IM SCHAUSPIELHAUS, an attractive restaurant on the second floor of the theater.
- Go back to the Zwinger in the afternoon to look at the PORZELLANSAMMLUNG, or, if porcelain is not quite your thing, the MATHEMATISCH-PHYSICALISCHER SALON. Before you leave, climb the steps to the terraces, and hunt for the Nymphenbad (most people miss it).
- Eat dinner in one of the restaurants on Münzgasse (most are part of the DRESDEN HILTON).

DAY 2

- Go to the ALBERTINUM in the morning. Look at the GRÜNES GEWÖLBE and the modern masters on the top floor. Cross the river to the Neustadt and eat lunch in one of the restaurants on Hauptstrasse, perhaps the KÜGELGENHAUS, for example.
- Visit the MUSEUM ZUR DRESDNER FRÜHROMANTIK, or the MUSEUM FÜR VOLKSKUNST, then make your way to the JAPANISCHES PALAIS, not necessarily to go inside (the collection is not too interesting) but to walk through the gardens behind, where you get a spectacular view of the old town.
- Go back across the bridge and explore the old town, looking at the ruined FRAUENKIRCHE, the FÜRSTENZUG and the HOFKIRCHE.

DAY 3

- Take a tram (#1 or 6) to Schillerplatz. Cross the BLAUES WUNDER bridge and take the funicular up to WEISSER HIRSCH (see WALK 2, page 274). Wander through the leafy streets to admire the 19thC villas.
- Eat lunch in one of the restaurants on Bautzner Landstrasse. Take the tram (#10) back to the old town.

Dresden: sightseeing

AN OVERVIEW OF THE CITY: THE DISTRICTS

For an understanding of the shape of the city, see the DRESDEN ENVIRONS map on pages 266–67, or color maps **8** & **9**. There are also maps accompanying WALK 1, the heart of the city, and WALK 2, beyond the Blaues Wunder bridge to the funicular railway.

• First ports-of-call

ALTSTADT (Old Town) The historic heart of Dresden lies on the left bank of the Elbe. This is where you will find the Baroque palaces, the shops, the restaurants — and the crowds.

FRIEDRICHSTADT An old industrial quarter to the W of the Altstadt. The bombs hardly touched this area, and Friedrichstrasse still retains much of its 18thC architecture.

NEUSTADT (New Town) The quarter on the right bank of the Elbe. War damage was relatively light, and many old buildings survive, some neatly restored by the communists.

• **The suburbs**

BLASEWITZ A leafy suburb to the E of the old town. The 1945 firestorm hardly touched this district, and many grand 19thC Neoclassical villas survive, but only just. The houses have been left to decay, and the rhododendrons desperately need pruning.

DRESDENER HEIDE A vast forest to the N of Dresden.

JOHANNSTADT A 19thC suburb to the E of the old town. Some bombs fell here in 1945, but the firestorm was less intense. Many dilapidated villas survive, amid overgrown ruins and unlovely modern apartment blocks. The Jewish cemetery and synagogue are here, tucked away behind a grimy factory.

LOSCHWITZ An elegant 19thC suburb on the slopes to the E of the old town. Loschwitz stands on the right bank of the Elbe, linked to Blasewitz by the Blaues Wunder bridge and to the Weisser Hirsch by two funicular railways. The hillside is dotted with 19thC villas built in more fanciful styles than those of Blasewitz, but the gardens are every bit as wild.

WEISSER HIRSCH A former spa town built on the hill to the N of the Elbe. Now rather wistful and derelict, but still dotted with romantic villas from the turn of the century.

Exploring Dresden

Dresden is a city of hidden treasures. With a little guidance, you can track down handsome old streets, attractive waterfront views and rambling 19th century suburbs.

The following two walks take you to the parts of Dresden that have retained their romantic allure. An excursion by tram takes you farther afield, out to the spa resort of WEISSER HIRSCH.

WALK 1: HEART OF DRESDEN – RUINS AND RECONSTRUCTION

*See map on page 271, and color maps **8** & **9**. Allow 2hrs to complete this walk.*

It sometimes seems as if there isn't much left of the old town, but you can still find many historic buildings, and you may even find a view reminiscent of a Canaletto painting in the Gemäldegalerie Alte Meister. Remember that Dresden is a city in the throes of an enormous reconstruction program. Walking in the Altstadt isn't easy, and it is unlikely to get much easier until the major buildings have been reconstructed early next century. Yet there are important sights to be found amid the building sites and rubble.

Begin in front of the **Hauptbahnhof** (main station). If you have been here before, you may feel that something is missing: the statue of Lenin has gone. The founding father of Communism became a political embarrassment after *die Wende,* and he was hoisted from his plinth.

Now walk up **Prager Strasse**. Old photographs reveal that this was once a handsome street, lined with grand hotels and stores. It is now a modern shopping precinct. This quarter lay at the heart of the firestorm, and everything was leveled after the war to make a new start. The mix of tall and low buildings is reminiscent of Rotterdam's Lijnbaan (which was built after the Germans had destroyed the heart of Rotterdam). Prager Strasse has three large (and virtually indistinguishable) tower hotels, a tourist office, one department store and some shops. The round movie theater on the right was built on the site of an old cinema. You can catch the latest Hollywood blockbusters here, but dubbed into German.

After crossing **Dr.-Külz-Ring**, you find yourself on the vast **Altmarkt**, where the communist government staged May Day parades. It is good for nothing much now except a car park. The church on the right is the **Kreuzkirche**. The interior has been left unrestored, as a reminder of the war. The arcaded building opposite was once a communist showpiece. It was built in the Stalinist 1950s in a solemn Neo-Baroque style. A few cafés set out tables under the arches, and a night club from the communist era still stages old-fashioned Parisian-style floor shows.

Cross Wilsdruffer Strasse and go up **Schlossstrasse**. This narrow street was once lined with elegant shops that supplied the royal court. Look at it now. The bleak **Kulturpalast** stands on the right. The ruins of the RESIDENZSCHLOSS are straight ahead. It may not look very impressive now, but come back in the year 2006. The entire palace should have been restored by that date.

Now turn right (you have little choice) alongside the construction site. You will see a curious Renaissance portal propped up with concrete (on the left). There's nothing to tell you so, but this was once the entrance to the royal chapel. The chapel has gone, and all that remains is this portal and some relics in the Residenzschloss.

The building beyond has been restored to its original state. Known as the JOHANNEUM, it has served many functions, the latest being as a museum of transport. Turn left on **Neumarkt** and you'll come to a gateway on the left. Go into the courtyard to look at the Renaissance gallery of the STALLHOF (on the right). The entrance to the transport museum is opposite. Dive in if you find old trams irresistible, but otherwise leave the courtyard and turn left down **Augustusstrasse**.

The mural running along the left side of the street calls for an explanation. Known as the FÜRSTENZUG, it shows the rulers of the house of Wettin marching along on horseback. The leading figure is King Albrecht. The rest you will have to guess. The final 93 figures represent famous artists and scientists. The aim of the frieze is to glorify Saxony. Judge the results for yourself as you walk down the lane toward **Schlossplatz**.

On entering the square, you'll see another wing of the sprawling RESIDENZSCHLOSS (on the left). The building straight ahead is the HOFKIRCHE. The church is somewhat bare inside, but you ought to enter if only to look at the exhibition of photographs showing the bombing of Dresden.

Once outside, walk down to the Terrassenufer quayside and turn right.

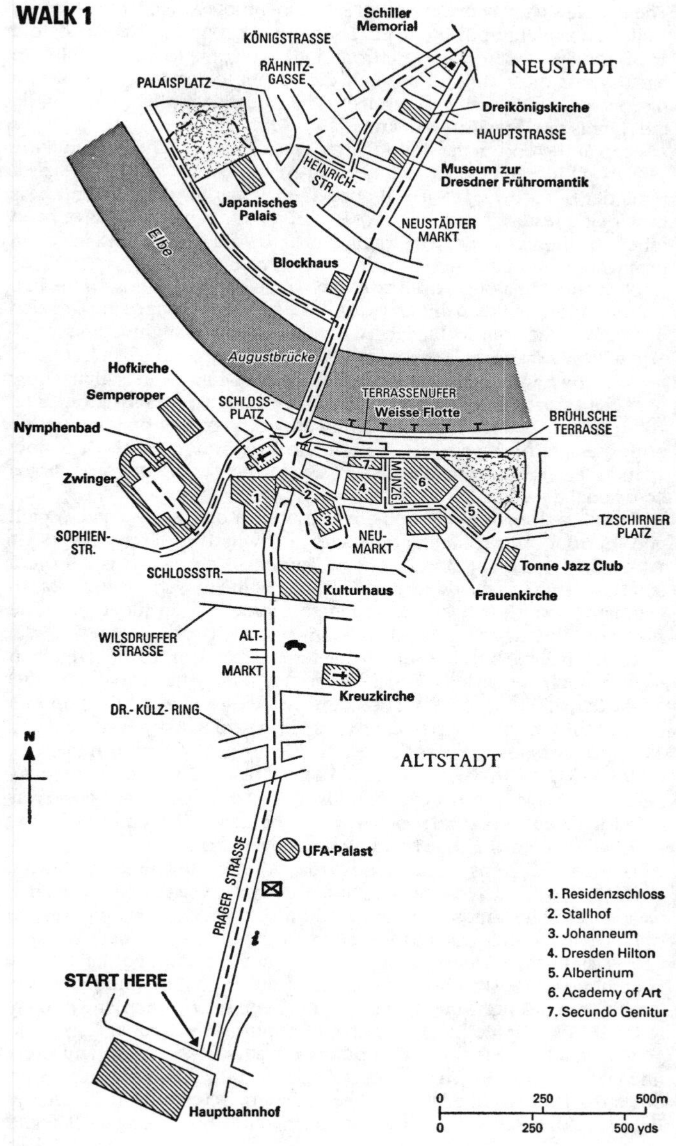
WALK 1
Schiller Memorial
KÖNIGSTRASSE
NEUSTADT
RÄHNITZ-GASSE
PALAISPLATZ
Dreikönigskirche
HAUPTSTRASSE
HEINRICH-STR.
Museum zur Dresdner Frühromantik
Japanisches Palais
Elbe
NEUSTÄDTER MARKT
Blockhaus
Augustbrücke
Hofkirche
Semperoper
SCHLOSS-PLATZ
TERRASSENUFER
Weisse Flotte
Nymphenbad
BRÜHLSCHE TERRASSE
Zwinger
MÜNZG.
SOPHIEN-STR.
NEU-MARKT
TZSCHIRNER PLATZ
Tonne Jazz Club
SCHLOSSSTR.
Kulturhaus
Frauenkirche
WILSDRUFFER STRASSE
ALT-MARKT
Kreuzkirche
DR.-KÜLZ-RING
N
ALTSTADT
UFA-Palast
PRAGER STRASSE
1. Residenzschloss
2. Stallhof
3. Johanneum
4. Dresden Hilton
5. Albertinum
6. Academy of Art
7. Secundo Genitur
START HERE
Hauptbahnhof
0 250 500m
0 250 500 yds

The paddle steamers of the WEISSE FLOTTE are moored below the old town walls. You might spot the aged *Dresden*, recently restored to its old splendor. Stroll along the waterfront until you come to traffic lights. Go back across the road and through the tunnel to reach **Münzgasse**, a narrow lane lined with café terraces. The attractive modern building on the right is the **Dresden Hilton**.

Stop at the end of the lane. The FRAUENKIRCHE stood nearby until the 1945 bombing. It was left as a heap of rubble by the communists as a reminder of the war, but it will not stay that way for much longer. It is now being restored, stone by stone, and the church should have been rebuilt by the year 2006. The fragments of the old church are stacked in neat rows behind the reconstructed church clock.

Now turn left along **Töpferstrasse**. There are more ruins on the left. The enormous building thickly overgrown with ivy was once the Dresden Academy of Art. Some of the great German Romantics taught at this school. The wistfully overgrown school looks like just their kind of subject.

After the ruins, you come to the ALBERTINUM, a former arsenal that now contains a wealth of art treasures. Go straight ahead to **Tzschirner Platz**, and turn left. You may be wondering about the ruined building on the opposite side of the street. This was the **Kurländer Palais**. It is now abandoned, apart from the cellars where the JAZZ CLUB TONNE holds occasional concerts.

Turn left along the side of the Albertinum and cross the road. A path goes in front of the building opposite. Follow it to reach the BRÜHLSCHE TERRASSE, once Count Brühl's private gardens. Very likely, you'll see a couple kissing in a shady corner. This, one of the most romantic spots in Germany, was turned into a tree-lined promenade in the 19thC. The shady benches and views of the Elbe may tempt you.

Climb the little hill at the end of the terrace for a view of the river, then walk through the gardens. You'll see the KUNSTAKADEMIE (Academy of Art) on the left, the ships of the WEISSE FLOTTE on the right, and, on the opposite bank of the Elbe, the former Ministry of Finance of Saxony. After crossing over **Münzgasse**, you pass the restored **Secundo Genitur** (on the left), built in 1897 on the site of Count Brühl's library. The Latin name may need to be explained. It means literally "the second born": the palace was built for the king's second son. It now belongs to the Dresden Hilton, and is linked to the main hotel building by a covered bridge.

Go down the steps at the far end to reach the **Schlossplatz** once again. This time, walk across the **Augustusbrücke** to reach the NEUSTADT. Despite its solid sandstone construction, the Baroque building on the opposite bank (on the left as you cross) is known as the *Blockhaus* (log cabin). It stands on the site of a wooden hut. Go through the subway (watching out for skateboarders spinning out of control) and follow the signs to **Neustädter Markt**. The first thing you see on emerging is likely to be the 18thC gilt equestrian statue of Augustus the Strong.

Go straight ahead down **Hauptstrasse**, a traffic-free shopping street lined with trees. This was once a fashionable 18thC quarter where court officials and artists liked to live. The communists renamed it Strasse der Befreiung (Liberation Street), but it's back to its old name again. The old houses near the river were bombed in the war, but some Baroque mansions survived farther down the street, including the handsome MUSEUM ZUR DRESDNER FRÜHROMANTIK *(#13)*. Take note of the restaurant KÜGELGENHAUS on the ground floor of the building; it is one of the best eating places in town.

Farther down the street, you will see a church on the left. What was a church, that is — for it is now a conference hall. This is the **Dreikönigskirche**, designed by Pöppelmann. Stroll to the end of the street and turn left through a small garden, stopping a moment to look at the curious Schiller memorial standing in a circular enclosure. The walls are decorated with scenes from his tragedies.

Now go back toward the river down **Königstrasse**, a handsome street lined with 18thC mansions, where everything — even the massive paving stones — remains intact. Head for the fountain at the end of the street, but not by the shortest route. It's worth taking a little detour down an attractive and little-known lane called **Rähnitzgasse**. It runs off at an angle (on the left) from a small square behind the Dreikönigskirche.

Follow the lane through every twist and turn, to **Heinrichstrasse**. Turn right here, to reach a square with a fountain. It used to be called Karl-Marx-Platz, but it's back to being **Palaisplatz**. The Palais is straight ahead. Although called the JAPANISCHES PALAIS, the Japanese influence is limited to the roof. It was intended by Augustus the Strong to hold porcelain, and nothing but porcelain — a dream that was never realized.

Wait for a break in the traffic to cross the road, and go inside the palace, if you can, to look at the Oriental statues in the hall and courtyard. The ethnographic museum on the first floor isn't much of a collection at the moment. Leaving the palace, turn left. Very soon, you'll find a gate (on the left) leading into the palace gardens.

Before you do anything else, look for the path on the right. It takes you to the top of a little hill where you have one of the best views of Dresden. Now walk down to the terrace near the river and look toward the old town. You may recognize the view. It was here that Canaletto set up his easel to paint a view of Dresden now in the GEMÄLDEGALERIE ALTE MEISTER. All that is missing today is the dome of the Frauenkirche (but even that should soon rise again above the rooftops). Look right and you'll see a curious Oriental dome that wasn't there in Canaletto's day. It belongs to the old cigarette factory, the YENIDZE TABAKSKONTOR.

Walk along the river bank. You might seek out another Canaletto viewpoint, under the bridge; otherwise, climb the steps leading up to the Augustusbrücke. Cross the river to **Schlossplatz**, and turn right in front of the church. You will soon see the SEMPEROPER on the right and, nearby, a waterfront restaurant (now closed down) called Italienisches Dörfchen. The restaurant dates from 1913 and stands on the site of the 18thC settlement where Italian craftsmen lived while working on the Hofkirche. Now go down **Sophienstrasse**, past the RESIDENZSCHLOSS (on the left), still probably wrapped in scaffolding (it will probably remain so until early in the next century).

Cross the road near the Hotel Taschenberg Palais and look for the gateway leading through the **Glockenspiel Pavillon**, which takes you into the ZWINGER courtyard. Find a quiet bench and sit down. This is the best vantage point for admiring the Zwinger, or for listening to the classical street musicians who often perform here.

The building straight ahead is the **Wallpavillon**. A hidden flight of steps inside the pavilion leads to the upper terraces. To end the walk, go up the steps and turn right at the top. You'll discover a secret courtyard known as the Nymphenbad. Sit down by the cool fountains. You have just found the best of Old Dresden.

WALK 2: ROMANTIC DRESDEN

See map opposite and DRESDEN ENVIRONS map on pages 266–67. Allow 2hrs.

This walk takes you away from the bombed quarters of Dresden to a leafy suburb dotted with grand 19thC villas. It is perhaps a walk for a Sunday afternoon, after you have been to the Zwinger and seen the Old Masters.

Begin by taking the tram *(#1, 6)* to Schillerplatz. The route takes you through the 19thC suburb of Blasewitz, past dusty Neoclassical villas half-hidden by wild rhododendron bushes. When you step off at **Schillerplatz**, you will see, on the left, an iron suspension bridge painted blue. The official name is the **Loschwitzer Brücke**, but it's known to everyone in Dresden as the BLAUES WUNDER, the "blue miracle." Before you cross the bridge, you might be tempted to stop off at the elegant café TOSCANA, next to the bridge. Opposite is a famous old restaurant, the **Schiller Garten**, which has now closed.

The route takes you up the slopes behind the bridge, but most of the ascent is by funicular railway. Look left as you cross the bridge. You won't see Dresden, which is hidden beyond the bend in the river, but you can spot the twin towers of SCHLOSS ALBRECHTSBERG on the summit.

Once across the bridge, pause for a moment on **Körnerplatz**. Blot out the heavy traffic and this square gives you a good impression of the architecture of prewar Dresden. The solid red brick buildings and the ornate gables were once typical. You can even spot a faded advertisement on the wall of a building at the end of Körnerstrasse, giving the address of a long-vanished porcelain shop.

The lower station of the funicular (known as the STANDSEILBAHN) is on the far side of **Schillerstrasse**. Buy a one-way ticket and, for the best view, sit in the carriage looking back toward the bridge. The ancient yellow funicular creakingly ascends the steep hillside above Loschwitz, plunging into a tunnel before emerging among orchards and rambling gardens. As it nears the top, it plunges into another tunnel, moving so slowly that you begin to worry that it might not reach the top. But it does, as it has done for more than 100 years, and everyone gets off and heads straight for the restaurant LUISENHOF, cannily built opposite the upper station in 1895.

Another building nearby often attracts the curious. Decorated with a lofty tower, it is known as the **Villa San Remo**. The walk continues up **Bergbahnstrasse** (there is no alternative), past rambling gardens and old villas built on the slopes above the Elbe. This is an area that has hardly been touched since the war, although you now occasionally hear a whining saw or see a smart car parked next to a worn-out Trabant —

WALK 2

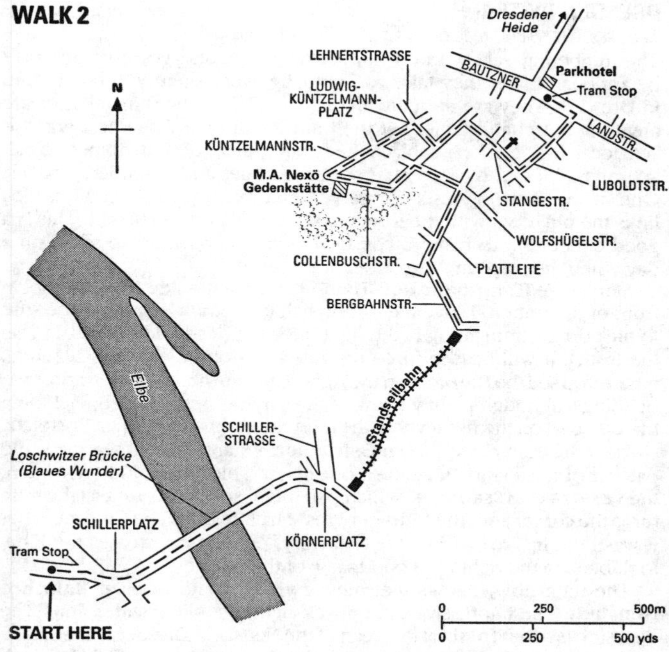

proof that changes are imminent. Continue up **Plattleite**, past an observatory *(on the left at #31),* built by Baron Manfred van Ardenne.

Turn left along **Wolfshügelstrasse**, looking out for the fresco on the wall of a house called *Abendstern.* Now turn left down Collenbuschstrasse, to a secret little park with a view of distant bluish hills. The road bends around to the right, taking you past the **M.A. Nexö Gedenkstätte** *(Collenbuschstrasse 4),* a house where the Danish poet Nexö lived.

Now turn right up Küntzelmannstrasse. On **Ludwig-Küntzelmann-Platz**, you'll see **Villa Gitta**, a mansion dating from 1893. The front of the villa is painted with lengthy texts in Gothic script recounting the history of Weisser Hirsch from 1686 to 1932. Turn right down Lehnertstrasse, left up Collenbuschstrasse and right along Stangestrasse. You pass an attractive old Lutheran church in this street.

Go left up **Luboldtstrasse** to reach the old Parkhotel. Don't expect to eat lunch in the hotel; it closed down a few years ago. The only places serving food are in the center of WEISSER HIRSCH, reached by turning right along Bautzner Landstrasse. If you still feel energetic, head off into the **Dresdener Heide** down the lane next to the hotel.

To return to the city center, pick up tram 11 at the Plattleite halt, in front of the Parkhotel.

DRESDEN BY TRAM

See *DRESDEN ENVIRONS map on page 267.* *Tram 11. Allow 2hrs.*

The lumbering yellow trams built several decades ago in Prague may be antiquated, but they take you virtually everywhere you need to go in Dresden. They are not particularly fast, and the hard metal seats are anything but comfortable, but the tram is still one of the best ways to see local life. You pass blackened war ruins, golden domes, bleak apartment blocks, recently abandoned factories and untended gardens. One of the most interesting trips you can make is on tram 11, which links the old town with the former spa resort of WEISSER HIRSCH. This is a good expedition to make if you have a couple of hours to spare on a day when the museums are closed.

Start at the **Hauptbahnhof**. Tram 11 stops at the side entrance, not in front of the station. Leave the station hall by *Durchgang 1* and be sure to pick up the tram going in the right direction (it should say **Bühlau** on the front). It will head off into the Altstadt, stopping at Dr.-Külz-Ring, where you see the **Rathaus** on the right. The tram continues past postwar buildings, although plainly a few of the earlier ones survived, including the ZWINGER, on the right where the tram slows down to stop at Postplatz.

Next the tram passes down **Ostraallee**, where you still see ruins and patches of wasteland. But there is one remarkable relic of 19thC Dresden, the **YENIDZE TABAKSKONTOR**, which you might spot on the left as the tram turns the corner after the Haus der Presse halt. It looks like a mosque, but it was built in 1907 as a cigarette factory. As the tram crosses the Elbe, look back to the right for a good view of the old city.

The tram now follows the railway viaduct, and stops at **Bahnhof Neustadt**. The impressive old railway station is black with grime. The next stop is **Albertplatz** at the heart of the Neustadt. Dresden's alternative rebels live an increasingly threatened existence in this neighborhood. The ruined building on the right was once the Schauspielhaus, where plays were performed in prewar years.

The tram now rumbles along **Bautzner Strasse**, which would be an attractive street if the buildings were repaired. Many of the little neighborhood shops have gone out of business in the wake of reunification, and the future here remains uncertain. This could become a fashionable shopping street — or a slum.

Once the tram starts to climb the hill from the Nordstrasse halt, try to look back to see the distant spires of Dresden. At the next stop, **Angelikastrasse**, you will see a modern building on the right. This was the headquarters of the Stasi secret police. Some local radicals want it turned into a memorial to the victims of totalitarianism; others would prefer to forget the whole sad episode in their history. Soon after this stop, the tram plunges into the woods of the Dresdener Heide. Notice the several footpaths on the left going off into the woods.

Look right just after the tram leaves the Wilhelminenstrasse halt to see SCHLOSS ALBRECHTSBERG, the first of three 19thC Elbe castles. The other two (on the right after the Schloss Albrechtsberg halt) are buried in the trees, invisible except for the gatehouses. The next stop is **Mordgrundbrücke**, not far from a dank valley with a stream tumbling down into the Elbe.

The tram now enters the former spa town of WEISSER HIRSCH. You will see flamboyant 19thC villas with turrets and balconies, no two alike. The houses are crumbling now, and the once-grand Parkhotel (on the left at the Plattleite halt) is derelict. Get off at the next stop (Am Weissen Adler). The tram goes on farther, but there is little more to see.

Not far from the tram halt, the **Hubertusgarten** *(Bautzner Landstrasse 89)* is a rustic old restaurant specializing in game dishes. Take tram 11 back to Dresden, or, if you want to see more of Weisser Hirsch, walk down the steep Rissweg to reach Loschwitz (where you can pick up tram #1 or 6).

Dresden: sights and places of interest

USEFUL TO KNOW

- **Opening hours** Dresden museums tend to be open six days a week, but not all keep the same hours. Some stay open an extra hour on one particular day. It is worth calling ahead to check, if you are particularly keen to visit a particular collection.
- **Tickets** A *Tageskarte* (day pass) can be bought, giving entry to the ALBERTINUM, RESIDENZSCHLOSS, GEMÄLDEGALERIE ALTE MEISTER, RÜSTKAMMER, PORZELLANSAMMLUNG, MUSEUM FÜR VOLKSKUNST, SCHLOSS PILLNITZ and other lesser museums. It is excellent value if you have the stamina to race through several museums in one day.

HOW TO USE THE A TO Z SECTION

All the sights, including **museums**, **galleries** and **famous buildings**, are arranged alphabetically from pages 278–304.

- Words in SMALL CAPITALS indicate a **cross-reference** to another section of the book or to a full entry in SIGHTSEEING.
- If you only know the name of a museum or other sight in English and cannot find it in the A TO Z OF DRESDEN SIGHTS, try looking it up in the INDEX. Other sights that do not have their own entries may be included elsewhere; look these up in the INDEX too.
- The ★ symbol identifies the most important sights.
- The 🏛 symbol indicates buildings of particular architectural interest.
- The ⋞ symbol identifies a good view. There is also a special entry, called VIEWPOINTS, which details the high places.
- The ✱ symbol pinpoints places of special interest for children.
- **A full explanation of all the symbols in this book is given on page 7.**

A to Z of Dresden sights

ALBERTINUM ★

*Georg-Treu-Platz. Map **9**D4 ☎(0351) 4953056 ▭ (Tageskarte valid). Open 10am–6pm; closed Thurs ▬ Tram 3, 5, 7, 8 to Rathenauplatz.*

Tucked away behind the Brühlsche Terrasse, the massive Albertinum currently houses a sculpture collection (SKULPTURENSAMMLUNG) in the main hall, the "Green Vault" (GRÜNES GEWÖLBE) and coin collection (Münzsammlung) on the first floor, and the New Masters Picture Gallery (GEMÄLDEGALERIE NEUE MEISTER) on the second floor.

Yet the building was never intended to be an art gallery. It was built in 1563 as the city Zeughaus (arsenal) by Kaspar Voigt, in a rusticated Renaissance style, and was for a time the largest arsenal in Europe. The vaulted hall that now houses Classical sculpture was once crammed with 600 heavy guns.

The change of function happened in the 19thC, when massive new barracks were built in the Albertstadt. The old arsenal was converted to house the Saxon state archives and sculpture collection. The Albertinum was gutted by fire in 1945, and was one of the first museums to be restored. Opened in 1964, the building was originally crammed with paintings, sculpture, jewelry and coins, but the overcrowding was alleviated recently when the paintings from the Gemäldegalerie Alte Meister were returned to the Zwinger.

The museum will become less cluttered still when the GRÜNES GEWÖLBE collection is moved back to the RESIDENZSCHLOSS in time for 2006. Until then, you have to accept a certain amount of inconvenience if you want to admire the great works of Western art in the Albertinum.

ALTER KATHOLISCHER FRIEDHOF

*Friedrichstrasse 54. Map **8**B1. Open 8am–7pm in summer (closes earlier in winter). Tram 9 to Krankenhaus Friedrichstadt.*

Surrounded by factories and hospital buildings, the Old Catholic Cemetery is hard to find, yet it is worth visiting this rambling cemetery with its pine trees and rose bushes, established as a Catholic burial ground by Augustus the Strong in 1721. His Hapsburg daughter-in-law Maria Josepha had died in Dresden, just two years after the spectacular wedding celebrations held in the Zwinger, and the cemetery was created for her tomb.

This cemetery became the main burial ground for Catholics living in Dresden. A list at the gatehouse pinpoints the many famous people buried here. Some were Italian craftsmen who came to Dresden to work on the Hofkirche; others were Russian and Czech exiles. The German musician Carl Maria von Weber was buried in 1826 at the far end of the graveyard under a sober Neoclassical tomb designed by Gottfried Semper.

Look out also for the blackened statue of a woman holding a shield bearing the initials J.B.C. This is the tomb of Johann Baptist Cassanova, not *the* Cassanova, but his brother, who died in Dresden in the winter of 1795. Johann Baptist taught painting at the Dresden Academy of Art and, according to the inscription on the tomb, "his works are immortal."

In fact, it was his brother's deeds that were to prove immortal.

The saddest tomb in the churchyard stands nearby. Look for the sarcophagus with the statue of a young woman lying as if asleep. The inscription on one side says: "To my first wife, Caroline, who died at the age of 32." But now look around the other side, where a later inscription reads: "To my second wife Juliana, who died at the age of 26."

BLAUES WUNDER ★

To the E of the old town. See *DRESDEN ENVIRONS map (pages 266–67) and WALK 2 map (page 275)* *Tram 1, 6 to Schillerplatz.*

The people of Dresden are immensely proud of the iron suspension bridge known as the *Blaues Wunder* (blue miracle). The 141-meter/ 462-foot bridge was built across the Elbe in 1890–93 to link the districts of **Basewitz** and **Loschwitz**.

The SS tried to demolish the bridge in 1945 to halt the Soviet advance, but two plucky locals foiled the plan by cutting the detonator wires.

BRÜHLSCHE TERRASSE

Left bank of the Elbe. Map ***9C4*** *Tram 4 to Theaterplatz, or tram 3, 5, 7, 8 to Rathenauplatz.*

The Brühlsche Terrasse is one of the most romantic spots in Dresden. Sometimes grandly called "the balcony of Europe," it stands above the Elbe on the site of the private garden of Count Brühl, Prime Minister of Augustus III. The terrace was turned into a public park in 1814 by the Russian military commander Prince Repnin. It became a fashionable place to stroll, with views across the Elbe to the Neustadt. As you wander among the trees, look out for the statues of the painter Caspar David Friedrich and the architect Gottfried Semper.

DEUTSCHES HYGIENE-MUSEUM

Lingnerplatz 1. Map ***9E4*** *☎(0351) 48460 Open 9am–5pm; closed Mon. Tram 10, 13, 26 to Hygiene-Museum.*

It might not sound too exciting, but the German Museum of Hygiene is actually fascinating. Built between 1926–30 in a clinical Bauhaus style, the Museum of Hygiene looks rather like a run-down hospital. A large statue in front of the museum depicts the sort of muscular nude athlete idolized by the Germans in the 1930s.

The museum was largely funded by the Dresden industrialist Karl August Lingner, who had a big stake in early 20thC hygiene. If Odol mouthwash seems to crop up rather frequently among the exhibits, it is perhaps because Lingner owned the Odol factory. Yet even if it does sometimes seem like an Odol museum, it is interesting to see the range of Odol packaging, the early 20thC advertisements based on Romantic German paintings, and the other memorabilia connected with Dresden's most famous export.

The museum has various old snapshots showing the world's first International Hygiene Exhibition, which was held in Dresden in 1911. Long lines of women wearing flamboyant hats waited to look at exhibitions about the human body and disease. But the exhibit that every visitor in 1911 most wanted to see was the "glass woman" — a life-sized body made of transparent plastic, with veins and organs illuminated by colored lights. It is now displayed in the museum on a revolving stand, accompanied by a lengthy recorded commentary telling you everything you ever wanted to know about the female body, and then some.

The glass woman is not the only transparent model. You can also examine a horse and a pregnant woman. Some of the other exhibits are less easy to stomach. The museum puts a great deal of emphasis on disfiguring diseases and incurable conditions such as AIDS, but a light-hearted note is sometimes introduced by special exhibitions organized on off-beat sociological topics like "The Bath" or "One Hundred Years of Odol Mouthwash."

FRAUENKIRCHE (Church of Our Lady) ★

An der Frauenkirche (opposite the Dresden Hilton). Map ***9D4****. Tram 1, 2, 4, 12, 14 to Altmarkt.*

A heap of rubble in the center of Dresden is all that remains of the Frauenkirche. Commissioned by Augustus the Strong, the vast Baroque church was built over a period of 19 years by George Bähr, and was finally completed in 1745. Its dome, which reached a height of 95 meters (310 feet), dominated the city skyline in Canaletto's views of Dresden. In its time, it was the largest Lutheran church in Europe.

But no more. The Frauenkirche was set alight in the 1945 firestorm. Two days after the raid, the dome collapsed. All that remained standing were two solitary fragments of the outer wall.

The **Frauenkirche** — as it was, and will be again

The communists took the decision to retain the heap of rubble rather than rebuild the church, so that it could stand as a reminder of the horrors of 1945. That way of thinking has now been abandoned. In response to local anger at the neglect of the city's architectural heritage, the authorities recently began to reconstruct the edifice, using Bähr's original plans. Donations have poured in from all over the world, and the old stones are now being removed to a special site on the Altmarkt, where they are tagged and neatly stacked on wooden racks. About half the original material is to be used in the reconstruction.

While the work goes on, you can peer through the security fence to observe workers sifting through rubble that has remained untouched since 1945. A temporary cabin next to the ruins contains a model of the church and some old photographs. But the most interesting feature so far is the reconstructed clock, on temporary scaffolding on the Altmarkt. It was restored by a local clock factory, and gives the time exactly.

If the project is completed on time, the dome of the Frauenkirche will once again rise above the Elbe when the city celebrates its 800th anniversary in 2006. It is likely to be a proud moment for Dresden.

FRIEDRICHSTADT

*W of the old town. Off map **8**A1–B1, and see* DRESDEN ENVIRONS *map, pages 266–67.* *Tram 9 to Krankenhaus Friedrichstadt.*

A fascinating and forgotten corner of Dresden lies beyond the railway lines in the western district of Friedrichstadt. The district was hardly hit during the February 13 raid, and still preserves something of the look of Old Dresden.

As you walk down the crumbling Friedrichstrasse, you come upon an unexpected Baroque palace (now a large hospital, the Krankenhaus Friedrichstadt). This handsome, pale yellow building was once the **Marcolini Palais**, built by Johann Christoph Naumann in 1728 for the Duchess of Teschen. She did not live long in the palace, and in 1736 it was converted into a summer retreat for the fastidious Count Brühl. Count Camillo Marcolini bought the palace in 1774, and Napoleon stayed there in the spring of 1813 after driving the Russian army out of the city.

The palace was also home to Richard Wagner from 1847–49. Employed as *Kapellmeister,* he worked here on the scores of *Lohengrin* and *Siegfried's Death.*

Carl Maria von Weber is buried in the **Catholic churchyard** opposite the hospital (see ALTER KATHOLISCHER FRIEDHOF, page 278). The attractive Baroque **Matthäuskirche** (Church of St Matthew) next to the hospital was built in 1728–30 by Matthäus Daniel Pöppelmann, architect of the Zwinger. He was buried in the church in 1736.

The overgrown and melancholy **Protestant cemetery** behind the church *(entrance at Friedrichstrasse 43)* contains the tomb of Wilhelm Walther, the artist who created the FÜRSTENZUG. There are no weeping angels or Greek temples in the Protestant cemetery; the graves are far more austere than the Catholic ones across the street.

Before leaving Friedrichstadt, you should take a look at the YENIDZE TABAKSKONTOR, a mosque-shaped building and former tobacco factory that miraculously survived the 1945 air attack.

FÜRSTENZUG (Procession of Princes)

*Augustusstrasse. Map **8**D3. Tram 4 to Theaterplatz.*

The outside wall of the 16thC STALLHOF is decorated with a curious mosaic more than 100 meters (328 feet) long. It shows the dukes of the House of Wettin in a long horseback procession stretching back to Margrave Konrad. The first in line is King Albrecht, who ruled Saxony at the time the work was commissioned. The Wettins are followed by 93 Saxon scientists, scholars and artists. The last figure in the procession is the painter, Wilhelm Walther, who produced the work in 1872–76.

Walther's craftsmanship was not first-class, for the original *sgraffito* work began to disintegrate within a few decades. Not to be robbed of this masterpiece, the authorities took it down, shipped it to the Meissen porcelain factory, and had the entire work transferred to some 25,000 tiny tiles. By 1907, the procession had been restored to its full glory. Eleven years later, the history of the Wettins ended for good with the abolition of the monarchy.

GEMÄLDEGALERIE ALTE MEISTER (Old Masters Picture Gallery) ★ 🏛

*Zwinger, Semperbau. Map **8**C3 ☎(0351) 4840120 🎫 (Tageskarte valid). Open 10am–6pm; closed Mon. Tram 1, 2, 4, 7, 8, 11, 12, 14 to Postplatz.*

The Old Masters Gallery contains one of the world's greatest collections of paintings. For many years, the collection was crammed into a few gloomy rooms at the ALBERTINUM, but it is now back where it belongs, in the restored 19thC building known as the **Semperbau**.

The Semperbau was built in 1847–54 by Gottfried Semper, to enclose the E side of the Zwinger. Gutted by fire in 1945, it was among the first buildings to be reconstructed. The building was closed a few years ago to allow a major renovation, but it has now reopened.

The paintings are superbly displayed against red and green velvet walls, in rooms flooded with daylight. There is an attractive art bookstore in the basement and a spacious new entrance hall. Despite a few pompous touches (the octagonal hall with the inscription *Wilkommen im Heiligthume der Kunst* [Welcome to the Sanctuary of Art] is particularly daunting), this is essentially an easy gallery to visit, with occasional distracting views of the old town through the windows, and an abundant supply of thick leather sofas. Even the staff seem more friendly these days, except if anyone strays too close to one of the paintings.

Orientation

This is not a museum to rush. It will take you at least two hours to see the main collection. It pays to arrive early, a few hours ahead of the crowds. Leave your bag in the cloakroom, buy a ticket or a *Tageskarte* (explained on page 277), and head up to the first floor. Go straight into the **Gobelinsaal** (tapestry room), sit down on a chair and read the description that follows.

History

The Gemäldegalerie collection represents the taste of one man. It was not Augustus the Strong, but his son, who gave the Gemäldegalerie its greatest works. Augustus the Strong had assembled a modest collection of 500 or so works in the Johanneum, including Giorgione's *Slumbering Venus,* but it was Augustus III who sent his agents to the great art fairs in Antwerp and Paris, to buy Baroque and Renaissance paintings in bulk. They shipped back a hundred works from the collection of the Duke of Modena, 69 paintings from the Imperial Gallery in Prague and a further 268 canvases from the Wallenstein collection in Schloss Dux.

Augustus III's collection is still almost intact. Most of the works reflect his fondness for the Baroque. You will see rosy-cheeked Madonnas, plump Flemish nudes, and placid Dutch landscapes, but not many Italian

Gothic paintings. This is mainly a collection of northern art, robust and rich in style.

The collection

Go into the first room **(#2)**, off the Gobelinsaal. In the past, the visit would begin with the early Italian paintings, but the new arrangement achieves far greater impact. The first paintings you come upon are 18thC views of Dresden by Canaletto. Before World War I, these works were tucked away in a dark corner of the building, but they are now given prominent exposure. Many people make the mistake of thinking that this is the Canaletto who painted the canals of Venice, but he is a different (although related) artist. The Venice Canaletto (real name Antonio Canal) was born in 1697, whereas the Dresden Canaletto (real name Bernardo Bellotto) was his nephew and pupil. The Gemäldegalerie has some paintings of Venice by the older Canaletto tucked away on the top floor **(rm 207)**, but the Dresden views are the more interesting: seven in this section **(rms 2, 3)** and a further seven elsewhere.

The Canalettos are given star treatment. They are hung on red velvet walls in a series of rooms looking out onto the Zwinger courtyard. Don't go too quickly, for these paintings provide precise documentaries of 18thC Dresden. The town was in the throes of construction when Canaletto arrived in 1747, and the Hofkirche was still being built. Canaletto painted it covered with scaffolding, looking much as it does nowadays (it is still being restored). The streets were strewn with rubble in Canaletto's day, but the Zwinger was more or less complete. One of Canaletto's views shows the wooden bridge across the Zwinger moat (the bridge you cross nowadays is still made of wood).

Canaletto's views of the Altmarkt are the most poignant. Now a bleak urban space, it appears in Canaletto's view as a bustling square surrounded by handsome Baroque houses. Yet disaster struck the city in 1760. The Prussians bombarded the town during the Seven Years' War, and destroyed 500 buildings including the KREUZKIRCHE. Canaletto painted the ruins of the church in 1765. Look closely and you'll see a figure on top of the broken tower. Others are sifting through the rubble. Many people are struck by this painting's eerie resemblance to the ruins of Dresden in 1945.

Another room **(#4)** has some of Canaletto's views of Pirna, a town on the Elbe, but you may be more interested in the views of the ZWINGER in 1722 by Thiele. They show horsemen and human statues engaged in mock battles. The room you are standing in looks out on the courtyard, which still appears much as it did in the reign of Augustus the Strong, although fountains have since been added.

Now go up the stairs, pausing to admire the handsome vaulted ceilings. Remember that all this was a heap of ruins in 1945. One of the best features of the restored gallery are the plump leather sofas placed in strategic positions. You can sit down on one in the next room **(#107)** to admire Canaletto's 1751 view of the FRAUENKIRCHE. This is the church that is now just rubble on the Neumarkt. The other painting in this room shows the Kreuzkirche, the same church that Canaletto painted a few years later in ruins. It was rebuilt, but not in the old style.

There are more Canalettos in the long gallery (**#102**). Look at the view of the Neustädter Markt in 1751. You will see the golden statue of the Augustus the Strong, which still stands on the square. The avenue lined with trees is the Hauptstrasse. The houses were mostly destroyed in 1945.

The most famous view of Dresden hangs in this room: the Altstadt in 1748 from the right bank of the Elbe, not far from the JAPANISCHES PALAIS. The view today has changed, but not *too* much. WALK 1 (page 273) guides you to the spot where Canaletto stood. Before leaving the Canalettos, look for the view of the Zwinger, painted before the Semperbau was built.

The next rooms (**#104**, **105**) immerse you in the grand Baroque style of 17thC Flanders. Most of the works are by Rubens, including the famed *Wild Boar Hunt* acquired from the Prague collection. The larger canvases by Rubens have gone out of fashion, but there are still those who admire the dramatic gusto of "Neptune Soothes the Waves." Most people, however, are now more comfortable with intimate works such as the *Portrait of a Woman with Curly Blonde Hair.*

Rembrandt is the other great northern Baroque painter represented in the collection. Augustus III failed to get hold of any of his major works, but he managed to acquire three portraits of Saskia, Rembrandt's first wife. Hung side-by-side, they provide a poignant chronicle of her declining health. The first shows Rembrandt posing as the prodigal son with Saskia. It is a playful work, full of youthful swagger, painted in 1635. Saskia died just seven years later, and the portrait showing her holding a red flower was painted just before her death.

The next room (**#108**) is crammed with 17thC Dutch paintings. Dutch artists like Steen and Dou churned out paintings like pulp novels. They are full of bawdy humor and lusty women, but they were rushed works. One painting hidden away among them is different. It is Vermeer's *Girl Reading a Letter by an Open Window.* Vermeers are a rare thing, and this is one of the best. Look at the girl's reflection in the open window, and the texture of the carpet in the foreground. Another Vermeer, *The Procuress,* is also in this room. Dutch artists were fond of painting brothel scenes full of innuendo, but Vermeer broke the mould by including himself as a somewhat bashful onlooker (on the left).

Enter now the most spectacular room in the Gemäldegalerie. Part of the original Zwinger, it is decorated in the original Baroque style, with marble floors and large Rococo windows looking down on the courtyard. The paintings — mainly by Flemish and German artists — jump back in time to the 15thC. There is a small altarpiece of the *Madonna with Sts Catharine and Michael,* painted by Jan van Eyck in 1437. You have to peer closely to see the significant details, such as the view through a window (a new theme in those days). The inscription is difficult to read even in the excellent lighting conditions.

The Dresden Gemäldegalerie is not the place to see the greatest German paintings — for those you must go to Berlin and Munich — but this room holds a few important German Renaissance paintings. The most famous is Albrecht Dürer's *Dresden Altar,* painted in an Italian style. His portrait of *Bernhard van Reesen* was painted during Dürer's six-month stay in Antwerp in 1521. Lucas Cranach the Elder was court painter to three successive Electors of Saxony, yet nothing much is to be seen in Dresden, apart from one of his many studies of *Adam and Eve*.

The gallery does not lead anywhere. You have to go back into the Semperbau and through the Vermeers room to reach the rest of the Dutch collection, which occupies a series of intimate rooms (**#109–111**). The 17thC Dutch artists set out to please their customers, and their works still have immense appeal. Some people are fascinated by Pieter Claes' still-life studies of oyster shells; others are pleasantly surprised to find views of Amsterdam and Haarlem by Gerrit Berckheyde. The 17thC French paintings (**rm #112**) do not have the same pull, and even Poussin's svelte nudes are unjustly ignored by most visitors.

The next three rooms (**#113–5**) are hung with 17thC Italian paintings. You then come to a room full of 15thC Italian works (**#116**), but one is missing. You may have heard about the famous Raphael of Dresden, but you will have to wait for it a little longer. The Gemäldegalerie has kept its best painting to the last.

Many visitors are horrified at this point to discover that there remains an entire floor still to visit, but don't despair. You can go straight past a lot of the paintings, which tend to be minor 18thC German works, although it would be a pity to leave Dresden without seeing the charming portraits by Pietro Graf Rotardi (**rm #203**), and the little works by Watteau (**rm #202**). You'll also find some interesting views of Venice by *the* Canaletto (**rm #207**), alongside one view by his nephew.

But the main reason for climbing to the top floor is to see the Pastels Collection in the last room (**#201**). Every visitor is taken aback by the sight of the famous *Maid Carrying Chocolate* by Jean-Etienne Liotard, acquired by Augustus III in 1741.

Now go back to the stairs near the Canalettos. You descend into a huge hall where an inscription pompously welcomes you to the sanctuary of art. Go through the door marked *Wilkommen*. The most famous painting in Dresden is at the far end, beyond the Titians and the Correggios. The paintings in these rooms include Titian's *Tribute Money,* painted in about 1514, but most people by now have their eyes fixed on the painting hanging on the far wall.

This is Raphael's *Sistine Madonna,* the pride of the collection. The work was brought to Dresden in 1753 from a monastery in Piacenza, and almost immediately inspired a cult of adoration. Romantic German poets and painters flocked to Dresden in the 18thC to gaze on the tender face of The Virgin. The artist Philipp Otto Runge stated that in its presence he "forgot entirely where he was." We live in a less romantic age, and people are unlikely to be enraptured by the painting, although almost everyone is captivated by the two dreaming angels peering out at the bottom of the picture.

GEMÄLDEGALERIE NEUE MEISTER (New Masters Picture Gallery)

Albertinum, Georg-Treu-Platz. Map **9**D4 ☎ *(0351) 4953056* ▣ *(Tageskarte valid). Open 10am–6pm; closed Thurs. Tram 3, 5, 7, 8 to Rathenauplatz.*

Dresden's Picture Gallery of New Masters occupies the upper floor of the ALBERTINUM, next door to the Art Academy where some of the New

Masters once studied. From the café window you can see the ruined academy, with an inscription carved in stone. *Den Bildenden Kuensten zu Nutz und Frommen,* it declares. It was a typical Saxon idea. The visual arts were "useful and advantageous."

The name "New Masters" may be misleading, as the majority of the paintings date from the 19thC. But the works by German Romantics and French Impressionists were new and daring when this collection was founded by the art historian Karl Woermann.

The highlight is a room of moody Romantic works by Caspar David Friedrich. He spent much of his life in Dresden, although not painting the townscape. He was drawn to solitary churches, remote mountain tops, prehistoric tombs — virtually anywhere that felt isolated. His paintings are gloomy, to say the least. The *Cross in the Mountains* (1808) is one of his most famous works, set in a Neo-Gothic frame like a medieval altarpiece.

Other 19thC Dresden artists took up the same melancholy themes. The next few rooms are crowded with lonely forest scenes, ruined churches, and funerals in the mist. After some time with the Romantics, you may feel the urge to head off to a crowded beer garden and listen to some Dixieland jazz. But there is worse to come.

The largest painting in the collection is Otto Dix's *War Triptych.* Dix fought on the Western Front in World War I — and it shows. His painting (in the style of a Gothic altarpiece) depicts trench warfare in all its sickening realism, with mutilated bodies gruesomely posed like medieval martyrs. Other paintings by Dix depict German families in the 1920s, psychologically twisted by the experience of war. Dix taught at the Dresden Academy of Art from 1927 until 1933.

Hans Grundig tried something akin to Dix's *War Triptych* in his triptych of the *Thousand Year Reich,* which hangs opposite. Notice also Bernhard Kreutzschamer's painting of the *Synagogue in Dresden* in the 1920s. This building stood near the Albertinum until it was burned down in 1938. Nothing remains, not a single stone. Just a plaque at the end of the Brühlsche Terrasse marks the site.

The next rooms come as something of a relief. They contain some major works by French Impressionists, including Monet's *Seine near Lavacourt* and works by Degas, Gauguin and Toulouse-Lautrec.

The gallery should have a large collection of paintings by *Die Brücke,* the group that briefly flourished in Dresden from 1905–10. It doesn't. Their paintings were targeted by Hitler as examples of "decadent" art. The works were sold or destroyed, the artists harangued. All that now remains on show are five paintings: one by Pechstein, one by Nolde and three by Schmidt-Rottluff. The works are hung like rejects at the top of the staircase and most people pass them by without a second glance.

Yet they are important reminders of an extraordinary art movement with its roots in Dresden. The works were often bold, exciting and strangely primitive, inspired sometimes by the masks in Dresden's Ethnographic Museum. Although forgotten in Dresden, *Die Brücke* is celebrated in Berlin, where the group lasted for three years, from 1910–13. The BRÜCKE-MUSEUM (described on pages 103–4) is the best place to find out more about this forgotten period in German art.

GROSSER GARTEN (Great Garden)

Main entrance on Lennéstrasse. Map **9**E5–F6, *and see* DRESDEN ENVIRONS *map, pages 266–67* *Park open continuously. Tram 10, 13, 26 to Hygiene-Museum.*

The Grosser Garten was created outside the city walls as a royal park in 1676. It was redesigned in the 18thC in formal French style, with long straight avenues and ornamental gardens dotted with statues. Some of the park was later landscaped in the 19thC in the more rambling style of English gardens. The grounds have become somewhat neglected and overgrown, and the botanical garden seems to have been left to grow wild, but it is still a pleasant place to stroll on a summer day.

The Hauptallee (main avenue) leads to the **Lustschloss**, a handsome Baroque summer palace built in 1678–83 by Johann Georg Starcke. The palace was patchily restored after it was bombed in 1945, and now lies empty. Of the eight villas that once surrounded the palace, only four survived the war intact.

A small **zoo** (listen for the screeching of peacocks) is tucked away in a corner of the park (☎*(0351) 4715445* *open in summer 8.30am-7pm; in winter 9am-5pm; last tickets sold one hour before closing time* *tram 9, 13 to Zoo).*

Other attractions include an **open-air theater** (it may look abandoned, but still features performances by local groups in the summer) and a children's **puppet theater** (see DRESDEN FOR CHILDREN, page 318). You might even track down a sculpture garden hidden amid the trees.

The Grosser Garten had several cafés and restaurants in its heyday. Only one survived the austere years of communism. Find it in a building called the Carolaschlösschen, with a terrace overlooking a small lake.

GRÜNES GEWÖLBE (Green Vault) ★

Albertinum, entrance at Georg-Treu-Platz. Map **9**D4 ☎*(0351) 4953056* *(Tageskarte is valid). Open 10am–6pm; closed Thurs. Tram 3, 5, 7, 8 to Rathenauplatz.*

Take a deep breath. The "Green Vault" contains one of the world's greatest collections of jewels and curiosities. Once buried in a secure vault in the depths of the RESIDENZSCHLOSS, the Grünes Gewölbe was one of the most famous sights in Dresden.

Elector Augustus founded the collection in 1560 as a private museum of treasures. Augustus the Strong rebuilt the treasure chamber in a flamboyant Rococo style, complete with green walls (which gave the vault its name), gilt mirrors and elaborate display shelves.

The collection was rehoused after 1945. Some but not all of the objects can now be seen on the first floor of the ALBERTINUM, while the double doors that enclosed the vault are now in the RESIDENZSCHLOSS. The Grünes Gewölbe is to be reconstructed within the Residenzschloss, but that is unlikely until the year 2006. Until then, you need to use your imagination to conjure up the splendor of the treasure room. It is not quite so impressive these days, but some of the works on display are still dazzling.

The collection is displayed in four rooms. You get an idea of the interior of the original green vault on entering the **Silver Room (#1)**. A green Rococo display cabinet with gilt mirrors and elaborate consoles occupies an entire wall. It is filled with bizarre objects from the Rococo age, such as goblets, sea shells, reliquaries and chalices. Most of the work is German, and much of it is laden with decoration. But is it beautiful? Opinions vary, but everyone agrees that the craftsmanship is remarkable.

The **Ivory Room (#2)** contains a cabinet made entirely from amber, which was presented to Augustus the Strong by Friedrich Wilhelm I of Prussia (the Soldier King) in 1728.

A display case in the middle of the next room **(#3)** contains the most famous object of all. It was made by the Saxon jeweler Johann Melchior Dinglinger and depicts *The Court of the Grand Mogul Aurungzebe at Delhi.* Set in a miniature palace, it shows the Mogul's birthday celebrations, with 132 tiny movable figures made from solid enameled gold, and more than 5,000 diamonds and other precious jewels. Dinglinger also produced an enormous gold coffee set for Augustus the Strong, decorated with jewels and miniature figures.

The final room **(#4)** contains the crown jewels of Saxony, which have survived virtually intact. A room beyond contains the **Münzsammlung**, a collection of coins dating back to the 16thC.

HOFKIRCHE (Court Church)

*Schlossplatz. Map **8**C3 ▣ Open daily 9am–5pm. Tram 4 to Theaterplatz.*

The handsome Hofkirche (elevated to a cathedral in 1980, although still known by its old name) stands close to the Elbe, its 85-meter/280-foot Baroque spire dominating the Dresden skyline. It seems an essential part of the city, yet for many years the plans to build this Catholic church were shrouded in secrecy.

Politics were to blame. Augustus the Stong had converted to Catholicism in 1697 so that he could be crowned King of Poland. His son, Augustus III, was a genuine Catholic, and he wanted to build a Catholic church to rival the Lutheran FRAUENKIRCHE built during his father's reign. This notion was not likely to win much support among the Lutheran majority in Dresden, and so the project had to be organized in secret.

The Italian architect Gaetano Chiaveri was brought to design the church. He insisted on Italian craftsmen, who were put up in a temporary village built on the waterfront. A restaurant (recently closed) called **Italienisches Dörfchen** stands on the site of the village.

The project was plagued by problems. Chiaveri left Dresden in 1743 and three German architects had to be brought in to supervise the work. By 1747, when Canaletto painted the church (the view is in the GEMÄLDEGALERIE), the tower was almost built. The church was eventually consecrated in 1751, but construction work went on for another four years.

The Hofkirche was gutted in 1945, but the bulk of the damage has now been repaired. The interior looks rather bleak, but there are a few interesting features, such as a Baroque pulpit and an 18thC organ. Several generations of the Wettin family lie buried in the crypt, although not Augustus the Strong, who lies in Cracow, Poland. Only his heart was brought back to Dresden, to be kept in a copper casket in the crypt.

Most visitors tend to linger over the photographs of Dresden displayed in a chapel. Many of the photographs are likely to be familiar to visitors who have spent time in the city; they turn up on postcard stands and in countless books. A few of the photographs show truly harrowing scenes of the aftermath of the firestorm. Like the Frauenkirche ruins, the Hofkirche has become a symbol of war's destruction. A Meissen porcelain *pietà* in the church commemorates the unknown number of victims who died on February 13, and the victims of unjust violence throughout the world.

JAPANISCHES PALAIS (Japanese Palace)

*Palaisplatz. Map **8**B3 ☎(0351) 52591 ▣ Museum open Sat–Thurs 10am–5pm; closed Fri. Tram 4, 5 to Palaisplatz.*

The name is an enigma. The Japanese Palace does not look at all Japanese, apart from the slightly wavy rooflines. This palace on the right bank of the Elbe was originally built for Count Flemming in 1715 in a straightforward Baroque style. Augustus the Strong bought it in 1717, and some years later conceived a grandiose plan to turn it into a vast museum of porcelain.

Four of Dresden's greatest Baroque architects were enlisted to convert the Baroque mansion into a Japanese palace: Pöppelmann (who built the Zwinger), Jean de Bodt, Johann Christoph Knöffel and Zacharias Longuelune. They worked on the project from 1727–33, restyling the roof and incorporating other Oriental details such as the four giant Chinese caryatides in the entrance hall. A new courtyard was also added, with 24 Oriental figures supporting the balcony.

Augustus the Strong died before the building was completed, and his porcelain collection ended up after World War II in the PORZELLANSAMMLUNG at the ZWINGER. The Japanese Palace remains dusty and dilapidated, although a few of the rooms on the first floor were restored to their old marbled splendor.

The rooms currently contain a small selection from Dresden's famous ethnographic collection (see STAATLICHES MUSEUM FÜR VÖLKERKUNDE), but the objects on show are hardly worth the climb. The rest of the building remains empty and dilapidated, although the courtyard is worth a glance.

JOHANNEUM

*Neumarkt. Map **9**D4 ▣ to Verkehrsmuseum ✱ Open 10am–5pm; closed Mon. Tram 1, 2 4, 12 14 to Altmarkt.*

The Johanneum was originally built in the 16thC as the royal stables and armory. It was redesigned in Baroque style in the 18thC and turned into a picture gallery. The building has served various other purposes, including a weapons museum and a temporary home for the Dresden porcelain collection. Rebuilt after 1945, it now contains the VERKEHRSMUSEUM.

KARL-MAY-MUSEUM

Karl-May-Strasse 5, Radebeul. See DRESDEN ENVIRONS map, pages 266–67 ☎(0351) 762723 ▣ Open daily 9am–4.30pm. Tram 5 to Schildenstrasse. Turn left at the traffic lights down Schildenstrasse. Karl-May-Strasse is the first street on the right.

You know you're in the right place when you see the sign pointing to Sam's Saloon. The saloon is located in the garden of an old villa in a street of dilapidated houses. The villa is no different from any other except for the name. Look up and you'll see *Villa Shatterhand* in large gold letters.

This was once the home of the bestselling Western writer Karl May. The house is now a museum, but the garden contains the biggest surprise of all. Tucked away in the trees is a mock log cabin called **Villa Bärenfett**. It is crammed with Karl May's collection of Indian relics, including tomahawks, costumes and scalps. It now looks like an old-fashioned folk museum, but the local people love it.

For many years, this museum provided East Germans with a rare glimpse of America. Now that there are American movies showing at all the cinemas, and cheap package tours to the US, the Karl-May-Museum may have lost some of its exotic allure, but it is still a popular sight. The collection of Karl May souvenirs displayed in the house provides a glimpse of this romantic Saxon who loved to dress up in cowboy garb. It was often difficult to separate May from the cowboy hero he created. "Old Shatterhand — that's me," he once said.

May is buried nearby in the Friedhof Radebeul-Ost (turn right on leaving the house, left down Schumannstrasse, right on Pestalozzistrasse, following the track of the narrow gauge railway, left down Wasserstrasse, and then take the right fork down Friedhofstrasse). It doesn't take much to find Old Shatterhand's tomb — it's by far the biggest monument in the cemetery, built in the style of a Greek temple and decorated with a frieze depicting angels at the gates of Heaven. It comes as something of a disappointment after Villa Shatterhand. You expect a mock wigwam at the very least.

KASEMATTEN (Casemates)

*Georg-Treu-Platz. Map **9**D4 ☎(0351) 2371008 ✗ (compulsory, begins on the hour) ▣ Only Sats 9am–5pm. Tram 3, 5, 7, 8 to Rathenauplatz.*

A network of 16thC underground passages still survives beneath the Brühlsche Terrasse. Johann Böttger is said to have invented porcelain somewhere in this murky network of casemates. Abandoned for years, they are now being excavated by local archeologists.

You can now occasionally join a guided tour through the secret tunnels led by an enthusiastic local expert.

KREUZKIRCHE

*Altmarkt. Map **9**D4 ▣ Tram 1, 2, 4, 12, 14 to Altmarkt.*

The Kreuzkirche has had an unlucky history. A church was built on this site in the 13thC, but not a trace of it remains. This building was destroyed during the Prussian bombardment of Dresden in 1760. A new church in Late Baroque style was begun in 1764 (a painting by Canaletto in the GEMÄLDEGALERIE shows the rubble being cleared for this project), but it was not finally completed until 1792. In its turn, this church was destroyed in 1945.

The outside structure was carefully rebuilt, but the interior was left bare as a constant reminder of the bombardment. The famous Kreuzkirche boys' choir gives a weekly concert in the austere and bleak interior.

KUNSTAKADEMIE (Academy of Art)

*Brühlsche Terrasse. Map **9**D4. Tram 3, 5, 7, 8 to Rathenauplatz.*

A curious glass dome surmounts the old Saxon Academy of Art next to the Brühlsche Terrasse. Its nickname (if you haven't already guessed) is "the lemon squeezer." The dome used to loom over the life-drawing class of one of Germany's greatest art schools. This overbearing building was designed in 1891–94 by Constantin Lipsius.

Fire ripped through the building in 1945, and much of it still remains in ruins, with weeds growing out of the cornices and ivy smothering the walls. Melancholy and mouldering, the academy is now being restored, but slowly, and no target date has been set for its completion.

The art academy of Saxony dates back to 1764. An early director was Giovanni Battista Casanova, brother of the notorious womaniser. It became a breeding ground of German Romanticism in the 19thC, with pupils including Anton Graff and Ludwig Richter. Oskar Kokoschka was director from 1919–24, and Otto Dix worked under the "lemon squeezer" during his spell as an art teacher from 1927–33. A few paintings by former students still hang in the nearby GEMÄLDEGALERIE NEUE MEISTER.

KUPFERSTICHKABINETT (Engravings Collection)

*Güntzstrasse 34. Map **9**D6 ☎(0351) 4593813 ▣ (Tageskarte valid). Open Mon, Wed, Fri 9am–4pm, Tues, Thurs 9am–6pm. Tram 13 to Dürerstrasse.*

Augustus the Strong founded the Dresden engravings collection in 1720. Within a few years, it had grown into one of the foremost collections of prints and engravings in Europe. Most of the collection is out of bounds to the casual visitor, but you can often catch temporary exhibitions featuring works by major artists such as Dürer, Grünewald, Cranach and Goya.

MATHEMATISCH-PHYSIKALISCHER SALON (Mathematics and Physical Science Collection) ★

*Zwinger. Map **8**C3 ☎(0351) 4951364 ▣ (Tageskarte is not valid). Open 9.30am–5pm; closed Thurs and 12.15–1pm Sat and Sun. Tram 1, 2, 4, 7, 8, 11, 12, 14 to Postplatz.*

Don't be put off by the daunting name. This is one of the most interesting museums of scientific instruments in Europe. Elector Augustus founded the collection in 1560, and Augustus the Strong moved it to a Baroque pavilion in the corner of the Zwinger in 1728. The collection is still displayed in the pavilion, which is filled with sunlight streaming through the Baroque windows.

Crammed into the ground floor is a fascinating assortment of antique telescopes, globes, weights and spectacles. The upper floor contains a collection of old and sometimes bizarre clocks, no two showing the same time, and only one (next to the door) showing the right time. The clocks chime at different times, or remain stopped. One automatic clock made in Nuremberg is called *Verkehrte Welt* (the world turned on its head); but the most amazing instrument is the *Weltzeituhr* made in Dresden by Andreas Gartner in about 1700, which has 360 miniature clocks indicating the time in different cities of the world. The museum interior is rather old-fashioned, but this adds further charm to the place.

MUSEUM FÜR VOLKSKUNST (Folk Museum)

*Köpckestrasse 1. Map **9C4** ☎(0351) 570817 ▣ (Tageskarte valid). Open 10am–6pm; closed Mon. Tram 3, 5, 7, 8 to Carolaplatz.*

An old Renaissance hunting lodge survives amid a cluster of postwar apartment blocks in Neustadt. The building was bombed in 1945, like everything else around, but it alone was considered worth rebuilding.

The *Jägerhof* (hunting lodge) was turned into a Saxon folk museum back in 1913. The vaulted rooms are now filled with a miscellaneous collection of painted cupboards, rustic beds and local porcelain. The presentation is uninspired, but you may be impressed by the elaborate chandeliers or the mechanical wooden models representing Biblical episodes such as Christ's entry into Jerusalem and (a rather tasteless notion) the Crucifixion. The upstairs room contains a collection of wooden toys from Saxony.

MUSEUM ZUR DRESDNER FRÜHROMANTIK (Museum of Early Romanticism in Dresden)

*Kügelgenhaus (2nd floor), Hauptstrasse 13. Map **9B4** ☎(0351) 54760 ▣ Open 10am–6pm (last entry 5.30pm); closed Mon, Tues. Tram 4, 5 to Neustädter Markt, or tram 3, 6, 7, 8, 11, 26 to Albertplatz.*

You may remember this, one of the quietest museums in Dresden, with fondness long after you have gone home. The museum is located on the second floor of an old house in the Neustadt that was scarcely touched by the firestorm in 1945. The building by some miracle has even retained painted wooden beams dating back to the 17thC.

A minor artist called Gerhard von Kügelgen (1772–1820) rented these rooms in the early 19thC. You may not find Von Kügelgen mentioned in many art histories, but he was an important figure in his day, painting portraits of Schiller and Goethe. His house was visited by many great artists and musicians.

The intimate rooms are now occupied by a museum dedicated to Early Romanticism in Dresden. You will find letters, portraits and mementoes of the Romantic artists linked with Dresden in the early 19thC. The rooms are elegantly furnished with Biedermeier cabinets, paintings of the Elbe, photographs of Old Dresden, porcelain vases and odd little trinkets that evoke the spirit of the age. It helps if you know German, as there are long quotations to read.

One room contains some works by Caspar David Friedrich — not originals, but interesting all the same. Other rooms contain souvenirs of Wagner and Kleist. Look out for the room containing a few mementoes salvaged from the Körner Museum, which once stood nearby on Körnerstrasse. This house — once the home of the poet Christian Gottfried Körner — was not as fortunate as Von Kügelgen's in 1945. The neighborhood was hit by the bombers, and most of the buildings were razed after the war to make way for the new Hotel Bellevue. Schiller stayed in Körner's house in 1786–87. Other famous guests included Mozart, Goethe, Herder and the Humboldt brothers.

One little room is particularly romantic. It contains a careful reconstruction of Von Kügelgen's studio, based on an 1811 drawing done by a fellow artist (displayed in the room). This, more than any other room in Dresden, recaptures the spirit of a golden age in German history. On the ground floor is a good restaurant: see KÜGELGENHAUS on page 309.

PARKEISENBAHN

*Grosser Garten, Lennéstrasse. Map **9**E5–F5 ▣ Train leaves from Strassburger Platz. Regular services Apr–Oct ✱ Tram 1, 2, 4, 10, 12, 13, 14, 26 to Strassburger Platz.*

The idyllic peace of the GROSSER GARTEN public park is occasionally shattered when a miniature steam train chugs through the rhododendron bushes. Rusty iron bells jangle and level crossing barriers descend as the train approaches. There are even four miniature stations along the 5km/3-mile route through the park.

The miniature railway was built in the 1930s to carry visitors attending exhibitions at the nearby *Ausstellungshalle.* The communist youth organization ran the trains until 1990.

PILLNITZ

SE of the old town, on the Elbe. See DRESDEN ENVIRONS map, pages 266–67. Tram 9, 14 to Kleinzschachwitz (terminus), then a 10min walk down Berthold-Haupt-Strasse to the Elbe, and a 5min ferry crossing; or bus 85 to Pillnitz (terminus).

The former village of Pillnitz has long been a favorite excursion from Dresden. It's possible to get there by city tram or bus, but the more romantic route is to take the Weisse Flotte steamer downriver from the Brühlsche Terrasse, past the three Elbe castles and under the BLAUES WUNDER bridge.

The main attraction is SCHLOSS PILLNITZ, which stands in beautiful gardens on the right bank of the Elbe. You get the best view of the palace from the left bank (reached by tram). From here, you see the Schloss to the right of the pier, with its Japanese roofs rising above the trees. The little church with the Baroque dome (to the left) is **Maria am Wasser** (Maria on the Water), a local chapel, founded in the 16thC for the Elbe boatmen and rebuilt in Baroque style in 1704.

Pillnitz is dotted with interesting buildings, many of which belonged to the vineyards that once covered the slopes. The **Weinbergkirche** (vineyard church) above Schloss Pillnitz was built in the midst of the vineyards by Matthäus Daniel Pöppelmann in 1725. A former winegrower's house in Pillnitz was used as a summer retreat by the composer Carl Maria von Weber from 1818–24. It now contains a collection of Weber memorabilia *(Dresdner Strasse 44, open Wed-Sun 1-6pm).*

PORZELLANSAMMLUNG (Porcelain Collection) ★

*Zwinger (entrance on Sophienstrasse). Map **8**D3 ☎(0351) 4840127 ▣ (Tageskarte valid). Open 10am–6pm; closed Thurs. Tram 1, 2, 4, 7, 8, 11, 12, 14 to Postplatz.*

Augustus the Strong had many passions, but collecting porcelain was his greatest obsession. He bullied Böttger into discovering the secret process for its manufacture, and set up a factory at Meissen which he hoped would enjoy a monopoly.

It is difficult to imagine a better setting for one of the world's greatest collections of porcelain than this pavilion of the Zwinger. Yet it was never Augustus' plan to display his collection there; he had the much grander notion of creating a palace full of porcelain (the JAPANISCHES PALAIS) on the right bank of the Elbe. But the plan fell through after his death, and the collection of some 20,000 porcelain objects ended up, after many years of neglect, in the JOHANNEUM. The move to its current location in the Zwinger happened in 1962.

The airy Baroque rooms are flooded with light, glinting on the smooth white surfaces of porcelain elephants and highlighting the elaborate decoration on soup tureens. Most of the works were manufactured in Meissen, although some were shipped from China, Japan, Italy and France. A few of the dinner services were designed for the royal families of Europe.

Many of the pieces have their own history, but the most famous legend concerns the monumental blue pieces known as the "Dragoon Vases." The story goes that the military-minded Friedrich Wilhelm I of Prussia gave these vases to Augustus the Strong in exchange for a regiment of dragoon guards. It sounds like just the sort of cynical deal that the Soldier King would strike.

RESIDENZSCHLOSS 🏛

Sophienstrasse. Map ***8D3*** *☎(0351) 4953110 🎫 (Tageskarte valid). Open 10am–6pm; closed Thurs. Tram 1, 2, 4, 7, 8, 11, 12, 14 to Postplatz.*

The Residenzschloss stands in ruins in the heart of Dresden. The palace dates back to the late 15thC, when Dresden became the capital of Albertine Saxony (the territory given to Albrecht when Saxony was split in 1485). The original building was transformed into a bristling German Renaissance palace in 1548–56 under Duke Moritz, and the STALLHOF was added a few decades later in the more graceful Renaissance style of Tuscany. A fire ripped through the building in 1701, and the palace was rebuilt by Augustus the Strong in Baroque style.

The Residenzschloss was rebuilt yet again at the end of the 19thC when the city was busy celebrating 800 years of Wettin family rule. The reconstruction was done in Neo-Renaissance style, so that the building now looks closer to Duke Moritz's palace.

The royal palace was gutted by fire in 1945, and the communist government left it in ruins for many years. Palaces and other aristocratic buildings came at the bottom of the list of priorities, and were often simply demolished. By the 1980s, the communists were less tough-minded, and reconstruction work was begun in 1986. It is now hoped that the work will be completed by the year 2006, when the city celebrates its 800th anniversary, and the GRÜNES GEWÖLBE and the RÜSTKAMMER will be proudly displayed in the palace. Until then, much of the palace is likely to be hidden by scaffolding.

There isn't much to see inside at the moment, although a few rooms are open to the public. A scale model of the palace gives an idea of the grandeur of the edifice, its roof bristling with gables and turrets. You will also see fragments of the old building, a few blackened statues, and the restoration plan, drawn up when the communists were still in power.

You can stand in front of a stern-looking full-length portrait of Elector Augustus painted by Hans Krell. Look in the corner for the scrap of paper dating the painting to 1561. This was one year after Augustus had founded the Grünes Gewölbe in the Residenzschloss.

Augustus also built the *Schlosskapelle* (palace chapel) in Renaissance style. The chapel was destroyed in 1945, and all that stands is the Renaissance portal next to the Johanneum known as the SCHÖNE PFORTE. The Residenzschloss contains a few fragments from inside the chapel that were saved, including the shattered, and partly reconstructed, remains of the *Taufstein* (font). If you peer through the tiny windows of the scale model of the chapel, you will see the font in its original location.

The most famous part of the Residenzschloss was the GRÜNES GEWÖLBE. The collection is currently in the ALBERTINUM, but the massive bronze doors can be seen in a room of the Residenzschloss, along with a small collection of treasures such as miniature Roman emperors. Many people are puzzled by the little Baroque room enclosed by glass (in a corner of the main hall). This was the *Eck-Kabinett* (corner room) of the Grünes Gewölbe, richly decorated with wood paneling and frescoes. It was built to display jewels and trinkets. The figure standing inside the corner room represents Augustus the Strong in his Coronation garb. The face was modeled in plaster from the dead king's features.

RUSSISCH-ORTHODOXE KIRCHE (Russian Orthodox Church)

Juri-Gagarin-Strasse. See DRESDEN ENVIRONS map, pages 266–67. Tram 5, 11 to Reichenbachstrasse.

A 19thC Russian Orthodox church stands amid a cluster of postwar apartment blocks to the S of the main station. With its painted domes and pastel tints, the church is one of the last mementoes of 19thC Dresden's Russian community, standing on a street ironically renamed Juri-Gagarin-Strasse in honor of the Russian cosmonaut.

RÜSTKAMMER (Armory)

*Zwinger, Semperbau. Map **8C3** ☎(0351) 4840126 ▣ (Tageskarte valid). Open 10am–6pm; closed Mon. Tram 1, 2, 4, 7, 8, 11, 12, 14 to Postplatz.*

A collection of weapons — beautiful and ornate, but utterly deadly — is displayed in the **Semper wing** of the ZWINGER. The glinting steel pikes and flamboyant breast-plates used by Saxon armies in European wars are superbly displayed in two large halls. The hall at the back has an interesting exhibit showing a 16thC jousting tournament in full armor.

Most of the pieces were acquired by Elector Moritz and Elector Augustus in the 16thC. The aim was to glorify the Wettins by amassing a collection equal to that of the Hapsburgs in Vienna. The Rüstkammer is now the greatest armory in Germany, although only a fraction of the collection is currently on display. Many more weapons will be on view when the collection moves to the RESIDENZSCHLOSS in about 2006.

SCHLOSS ALBRECHTSBERG ☆

Bautzner Landstrasse 130. See DRESDEN ENVIRONS map, page 267 ☎(0351) 55655 ▢ (gardens) ▣ (Schloss) ✗ compulsory (every hour). Open Tues–Sat

1–5pm, Sun 10am–2pm ⚞ *Tram 11 to Schloss Albrechtsberg, then a 5min walk down the hill.*

Schloss Albrechtsberg, along with Schloss Eckberg and VILLA STOCKHAUSEN, is a 19thC castle built on the hill above the Elbe to the E of Dresden. The three castles give the Elbe valley something of the romance of the Rhine.

Schloss Albrechtsberg was built by Prince Albrecht, a brother of King Friedrich Wilhelm IV. Prince Albrecht decided to quit Berlin when the Prussian court snubbed his second wife because of her humble origins. He bought an old vineyard on the slopes of the Elbe and commissioned Adolph Lohse to build him a grand villa. Lohse was a pupil of Schinkel, and the building is a textbook example of Berlin Classicism. Constructed from 1851–54, the project included terraces and ponds cut into the hillside.

The villa survived the war intact and was used by the communist young pioneers until 1989. You can now take a guided tour of the Schloss, although the main thing to see is the frescoed ballroom. You have to imagine the rooms as they once looked, filled with heavy German sofas and Romantic oil paintings.

The garden has been left untended for many years, and the view of Dresden is now blocked by thick trees, but you can still stand on the terrace looking upstream to the BLAUES WUNDER bridge. Classical concerts are regularly given in the Kronensaal on Sundays.

SCHLOSS PILLNITZ ★

Pillnitz (E of Dresden). See DRESDEN ENVIRONS map, pages 266–67 ☎(0351) 39325 ▣ (Tageskarte valid). Open daily 9.30am–5.30pm (Bergpalais closed Mon, Wasserpalais closed Tues). Bus 85 to Pillnitz, or tram 9, 14 to Kleinzschachwitz, then a 10min walk to the Elbe waterfront, where a ferry crosses to Pillnitz.

A Renaissance palace was built at Pillnitz by Elector Johann Georg IV for the use of his mistress. Augustus the Strong subsequently acquired the palace for his own mistress Countess Constantia von Cosel. Inspired by the buildings he had seen painted on Oriental porcelain, Augustus commissioned Pöppelmann to redesign the building in "Chinoiserie" style.

The palace now contains a small museum of arts and crafts, founded in 1876. Much of the collection was destroyed in World War II, but there remain sizeable displays of glass, pottery, pewter and furniture.

SCHÖNE PFORTE (Beautiful Portal)

*Neumarkt. Map **9**D4. Tram 1, 2 4, 12 14 to Altmarkt.*

The royal chapel has gone, but the portal is still standing, looking somewhat misplaced, next to the JOHANNEUM in the heart of Dresden. Considered one of the greatest works of German Renaissance architecture, it was built in about 1555 by Juan Maria de Padua and Hans Walther the Younger. The relief above the doorway shows the raising of Lazarus.

Nothing else remains of the Schlosskapelle except for some fragments displayed in the RESIDENZSCHLOSS.

SCHWEBEBAHN (Cable Railway) ★

Pillnitzer Landstrasse, Loschwitz. See *DRESDEN ENVIRONS map, pages 266–67* *Mon–Fri 6am–8pm; Sat, Sun, hols 8am–8pm. Runs every 15mins. The trip takes about 3mins Tram 1, 6 to Schillerplatz, then a 10min walk across the Blaues Wunder bridge, or bus 61, 84, 93 to Körnerplatz.*

The world's first cable railway was built in 1901 to connect Loschwitz with the spa town of Weisser Hirsch. After being shut down for many years, the old-fashioned cable cars are again running regular services on the 280-meter/918-foot track.

The view of the Elbe becomes increasingly striking as the cable car slowly makes the 84-meter/80-foot ascent. Sit looking backward, to enjoy the sweeping landscape.

SEMPEROPER (Semper Opera House)

Theaterplatz 2. Map ***8****C3* ☎*(0351) 48420 (☎ to reserve tickets). Tram 4 to Theaterplatz.*

Gottfried Semper built an opera house in 1841, but it was gutted by fire in 1869. He had fled from Dresden because of his part in the 1849 revolution, but was invited to design a new opera house. The construction was supervised on site by his son Manfred in 1871–78.

The Semperoper — named in honor of the architect — is designed in a solemn Renaissance style, with a projecting curved front surmounted by a *quadriga.* Few people notice that the chariot is being pulled by four black panthers. Opera audiences enter through a portal flanked by statues of Goethe and Schiller.

The Semperoper is one of the foremost opera houses in Germany. Its audiences have witnessed the premieres of some of the great operas of the 19th and early 20thC, such as Richard Strauss' *Salome.*

SKULPTURENSAMMLUNG

Albertinum, entrance at Georg-Treu-Platz. Map ***9****D4* ☎*(0351) 4953056 (Tageskarte valid). Open 10am–6pm; closed Thurs. Tram 3, 5, 7, 8 to Rathenauplatz.*

Dresden has Augustus the Strong to thank for one of the greatest collections of Classical sculpture in Europe. Part of the collection is currently displayed in the vaulted hall of the ALBERTINUM, but many other works will remain in storage until the Grünes Gewölbe collection moves out of the Albertinum in about the year 2006.

The sculpture comes from various private collections bought up by Augustus the Strong. A large collection of Roman busts once formed the "Brandenburg Collection" of King Friedrich Wilhelm I of Prussia. Other works came from collections built up by Duke Agostini Chigi and Cardinal Albani. Stop to admire the Greek gods and warriors, now missing heads and arms. The three *Herkulanerinnen* (women of Herculaneum) have survived the centuries virtually intact. These three life-sized female figures were dug from the ruins of Herculaneum.

The collection was expanded in the 19thC by Georg Treu, a friend of Rodin and the Belgian sculptor Constantin Meunier. A few of the modern works acquired by Treu are upstairs in the GEMÄLDEGALERIE NEUE MEISTER; the rest are in storage.

STAATLICHES MUSEUM FÜR MINERALOGIE UND GEOLOGIE

(Museum of Mineralogy and Geology)

*Augustusstrasse 2. Map **9**C4 ☎(0351) 4952446 ▣ Open 10am–1pm, 2–4pm; closed Mon, Tues. Tram 4 to Theaterplatz.*

This collection of minerals dates back to 1560, when Elector Moritz established a "cabinet of curiosities" in the Residenzschloss. The collection grew inexorably, and at the most recent count boasted 350,000 fossils and 50,000 minerals.

The bulk of the finds were chipped off rock faces in Saxony and Central Europe, but some of the exhibits have come from the planet's remoter regions.

STAATLICHES MUSEUM FÜR TIERKUNDE (Museum of Zoology)

*Zwinger (entrance at the Kronentor). Map **8**C3 ☎(0351) 4952503 ▣ (Tageskarte is not valid). Open daily 9am–4pm. Tram 1, 2, 4, 7, 8, 11, 12, 14 to Postplatz.*

Elector Moritz began collecting stuffed animals for his "cabinet of curiosities" back in the mid-16thC. The collection originally muddled together animals, rocks and paintings, but the animals were hived off to a separate collection in the 18thC.

The present zoology collection is vast, and only a fraction of the exhibits are displayed in the Zwinger building.

STAATLICHES MUSEUM FÜR VÖLKERKUNDE (Museum of Ethnography)

*Japanisches Palais, Palaisplatz. Map **8**B3 ☎(0351) 52591 ▣ Open 10am–5pm; closed Fri. Tram 4, 5 to Palaisplatz.*

The Museum of Ethnography was established in the 19thC to house a variety of exotic objects brought back by local explorers from remote regions of the world. The brightly painted Polynesian masks were a major inspiration for the early 20thC artists of *Die Brücke* group. Originally housed in the Zwinger, the ethnography collection is now kept in the JAPANISCHES PALAIS on the right bank of the Elbe, but only a fraction of the exhibits are currently on show.

STADTMUSEUM (Dresden City Museum)

Wilsdruffer Strasse 2. Map ***9****D4 ☎(0351) 4952302 ▣ Open 10am–6pm (Wed until 8pm); closed Fri. Tram* ***1, 2, 3, 4, 5, 7, 8, 12 14*** *to Pirnaischer Platz.*

The communist dogma has been purged, but the city museum still offers a rather plodding view of Dresden's history. The museum was established in 1965 in a handsome 18thC Baroque building where the Saxon parliament used to debate. The building was gutted in the 1945 firestorm, but painstakingly restored by the communists to contain the museum of local history.

The collection takes up the top three floors of the building. The most logical approach is to take the sweeping Baroque staircase to the top floor to look at the **medieval rooms**, then return to the ground floor passing through various rooms devoted to the **18thC and 19thC** (second floor) and **20thC** (first floor).

The **medieval collection** is in the attic, but only the most solid objects have survived. There are iron locks, tombstones, armor, some bloodthirsty weapons, and a few statues, but virtually no books or paintings. You might learn something about the development of Dresden from the scale model of the medieval town, but nothing is explained.

One floor down, you plunge into the **18thC**. You won't find out much about the construction of the Zwinger, or the development of porcelain, but you do get the impression that a lot of fighting was going on at the same time. There are old uniforms, tin soldiers set out in mock battle scenes, and, for light relief, 18thC portraits of aristocratic women.

The **19thC room** is good for an understanding of the industrialization of Dresden, but less interesting on Romanticism. There's an attractive reconstruction of a Biedermeier interior. Hygiene, however, is well documented. The advertisements for Odol mouthwash, and the photographs of the 1911 International Hygiene Exhibition won't be new to those who have already been to the DEUTSCHES HYGIENE-MUSEUM.

World War I is summed up by a single glass case of relics, and the Nazi years (one floor down) are hardly touched on (there is a woman's white vest with a stitched-on Swastika, and a few other isolated relics). But the bombing of Dresden is covered in all its gruesome detail. The photographs are mostly familiar. You see the shattered Wallpavillon of the Zwinger and the roofless Schloss. Pictures like this appear in every postcard shop, alongside faded photographs of Dresden at the turn of the century. But some of the photographs don't appear on the postcard racks. They show the bodies of the victims on the morning after the attack. Those are hard images to forget.

The final section deals with the awkward period from 1945 to 1989. Gone are the grand declarations about the triumphs of communism. They were ruthlessly purged — as was the museum director — soon after *die Wende.* Instead, you see glass cases filled with everyday objects such as Russian phrase books and cheap toys. The museum ends with some photographs of the demonstrations in Dresden that eventually toppled the communist leaders in 1989. They offer a glimmer of hope at the end of a hideous century.

STALLHOF 🏛

*Neumarkt. Map **8**D3. Tram 4 to Theaterplatz.*

The Stallhof (stable yard) was added to Dresden castle by Duke Moritz in 1548–56. A long arcade known as the Langer Gang was built in Tuscan Renaissance style, probably by Giovanni Maria Nosseni. This is the one building in Dresden where the epithet "Florence on the Elbe" still holds true. The gallery was decorated with the coats-of-arms of the regions of Saxony, an elaborate sundial, and (this you would never see in Florence) rows of deer antlers. The outside wall of the Langer Gang was decorated in the 19thC with a mosaic, the FÜRSTENZUG.

STANDSEILBAHN (Funicular Railway) ★

Körnerplatz, Loschwitz. See DRESDEN ENVIRONS map, pages 266–67 and WALK 2 map on page 275 🎫 Runs daily every 20mins from early morning until 11.30pm. Trip takes about 5mins ✱ ⋞ Tram 1, 6 to Schillerplatz, then a 10min walk across the Blaues Wunder bridge, or bus 61, 84, 93 to Körnerplatz.

A trip on the funicular railway has been a favorite excursion since it opened in 1895. The antiquated yellow cabin creaks slowly up the hillside, from Loschwitz to the former spa town of WEISSER HIRSCH. Two counterbalanced cable cars powered by electricity run along the 547-meter/1,795-foot track, passing through two tunnels and across a 102-meter/334-foot bridge. The best views are gained by sitting on one of the wooden benches, facing backward.

TASCHENBERG PALAIS

*Sophienstrasse. Map **8**D3. Tram 1, 2, 4, 7, 8, 11, 12, 14 to Postplatz.*

Augustus the Strong had many mistresses, but his favorite was Constantia von Cosel. He was generous to her in the early years of their affair, building her the TASCHENBERG PALAIS in 1705–08 (linked to the Residenzschloss by a covered passage) and buying her SCHLOSS PILLNITZ on the banks of the Elbe. The relationship soured when Augustus, following the advice of his prime minister, acquired a new Polish mistress to win support in his new territories to the E. The relationship with Constantia was brutally terminated, and she was imprisoned in Burg Stolpen for the remaining 49 years of her life.

Taschenberg Palais was gutted by fire in 1945, and left in ruins until a few years ago. It is now being rebuilt as a hotel (see page 305).

TRADITIONSBAHN RADEBEUL

Radebeul. See DRESDEN ENVIRONS map, pages 266–67 ☎(0351) 4614100 ✱ Regular trips May–Oct. Special trips for groups can be booked at other times. S-Bahn to Radebeul-Ost or tram 4 to Weisses Ross.

This is a genuine old train, unlike the miniature locomotives that run in the Grosser Garten. It rumbles along a narrow-gauge track from Radebeul-Ost station to Radeburg, passing along quiet suburban streets and sounding its whistle at every road junction. Passengers sit in old carriages with hard wooden seats for the short ride. The train makes a stop at Baroque Schloss Moritzburg.

VERKEHRSMUSEUM (Museum of Transport)

Johanneum, Neumarkt (entrance at back of building, reached through the Stallhof). Map ***9D4*** *☎(0351) 4953002 ✱ Open 10am–5pm; closed Mon. Tram 1, 2 4, 12 14 to Altmarkt.*

The handsome Baroque JOHANNEUM has been occupied by a succession of museums devoted to armor, paintings and porcelain, but it is now crammed with a bewildering assortment of old vehicles. You squeeze between ancient Dresden trams, bicycles, steam locomotives (the 1861 *Muldenthal* is a favorite), an 1885 carriage from the Saxon Royal Train (complete with waxwork effigies of the royal family), early Daimler cars, motor cycles and model ships. Everything is crammed together, but, for the transport enthusiast, such inconveniences matter little when you are in the presence of a 1902 model 309 Dresden tram.

VIEWPOINTS

An elevator takes visitors to an observation deck near the top of the 98-meter/320-foot town hall tower, the **Rathausturm** *(entrance on Kreuzstrasse, map 9D4)*. From this tower a famous photograph was taken of Dresden following the 1945 air raid. Pick up a postcard showing the scene in February, 1945, and compare it with the view now.

For a less dizzying and depressing view, stand on the BRÜHLSCHE TERRASSE or climb to the upper terrace of the ZWINGER. For the views that captivated Canaletto, cross the Augustusbrücke and walk through the meadows (either to the left or right of the bridge). If you ignore the cranes and the modern apartment blocks, the view has hardly changed.

For more sweeping views of the Elbe, walk through the garden of SCHLOSS ALBRECHTSBERG to the stone terrace above the river. The view from this vantage point has hardly changed since the 19thC, nor has the view of the BLAUES WUNDER bridge from the Loschwitz heights, near the upper station of the SCHWEBEBAHN cable railway.

For the best view of SCHLOSS PILLNITZ, take the tram *(#9 or 14)* to Kleinzschachwitz and stroll down to the river. Germans are fond of erecting restaurants on spots with picturesque views. There are two near Dresden: the restaurant LUISENHOF is perched on the slopes above Loschwitz, and the Spitzhaus stands in the hills above Radebeul.

VILLA STOCKHAUSEN

Bautzner Strasse 132. See DRESDEN ENVIRONS *map, page 267. Tram 11 to Schloss Albrechtsberg.*

Hidden away in an overgrown garden, Villa Stockhausen is a sadly forgotten relic of 19thC Dresden. The second of the Elbe castles, it was built by Adolph Lohse in the same style as SCHLOSS ALBRECHTSBERG. The house, originally owned by Baron von Stockhausen, Prince Albrecht's chamberlain, was later bought by Walther Naumann, the enormously wealthy owner of the Seigel & Naumann sewing machine factory.

The house was sold in 1906 to Karl August Lingner, a name that will be familiar to anyone who has visited the DEUTSCHES HYGIENE-MUSEUM. Lingner made his fortune from Odol mouthwash, and put up the money to build the Hygiene-Museum. The museum is filled with Odol advertisements and photographs of Lingner, including some old shots of the interior of his Elbe castle.

WEISSE FLOTTE DRESDEN

*Terrassenufer 2. Map **9**D4 ☎(0351) 5022611 Fx(0351) 4956436 ♣ ■ Regular sailings Apr–Oct. Tram 4 to Theaterplatz.*

Dresden's fleet of historic paddle steamers lie moored below the BRÜHLSCHE TERRASSE. The fleet of steamers is the largest and oldest in the world, and one vessel, the *Stadt Wehlen,* has been plying the River Elbe since 1879.

A steamer trip on the River Elbe is an idyllic way to discover something of the landscape of Saxony. The ships depart from the Terrassenufer in the summer months at the times posted on the notice boards. You can take a trip downstream to Meissen, or upstream to Schloss Pillnitz or Saxon Switzerland.

WEISSER HIRSCH

E of Dresden. See DRESDEN ENVIRONS map, pages 266–67. Tram 11 to Plattleite, or funicular railway from Körnerplatz.

Sited on the slopes above the BLAUES WUNDER bridge, Weisser Hirsch was once a fashionable 19thC spa town. Its winding leafy lanes are now lined with dilapidated mansions from the turn of the century, decorated with mock-Alpine wooden balconies, English Tudor half-timbering, and Art Nouveau stained glass. Almost all are begging to be repaired. Some of the houses are abandoned, while others only look that way, with rusted Trabants buried in the rhododendrons.

The rot set in after World War II when the Soviet army took over the famous Lahmann Sanatorium for use as a military hospital. The whole area is now sad and forgotten, the gardens wild. Occasionally you pass a crumbling mansion where someone is playing Schumann on the piano, and the Romantic sadness is almost too much to bear. Weisser Hirsch does in fact have a vague claim to Romanticism; Friedrich Wieck, father of Clara Schumann (who married the Romantic composer Robert Schumann) lived in a house at Friedrich-Wieck-Strasse 10.

The old villas may be crumbling, but the funicular and cable railway that run from Loschwitz to Weisser Hirsch are still in perfect working order. And now the streets are being dug up to lay new pipes. The elegiac mood may not last much longer.

YENIDZE TABAKSKONTOR (Yenidze Cigarette Factory) 🏛

*Magdeburger Strasse (at Weisseritzstrasse). Map **8**B2. Tram 9, 12, 26 to Maxstrasse.*

A bizarre building in the shape of a mosque stands next to the main railway line in FRIEDRICHSTADT district. This was formerly the Yenidze cigarette factory, built in 1907 to project the company's Oriental image.

The building is now abandoned, like many factories in East Germany, but there are vague plans to turn it into a hotel.

ZWINGER ★ 🏛

*Entrances on Ostraallee, Sophienstrasse and Theaterplatz. Map **8**C3–D3* 🆓 *(courtyard and upper terraces)* 💰 *(buildings). Tram 1, 2, 4, 7, 8, 11, 12, 14 to Postplatz.*

The Zwinger is one of the most extraordinary buildings in Germany. It looks like a palace, but was originally intended as a simple orangery. The name Zwinger (inner courtyard) refers to its site next to the city walls. The lake next to the Zwinger was once part of the city moat.

Augustus the Strong sketched a plan for the Zwinger as early as 1709, but most of the work was still unfinished when he died, and the complex was not finally completed until the late 19thC. He sent the architect Matthäus Daniel Pöppelmann on a grand tour of Europe in 1710 to pick up the latest trends in architecture. Pöppelmann returned with his head full of the frothy Baroque of Italy, Austria and Bohemia. Work on the Zwinger began later that year.

Orientation

Go through one of the three gates leading into the Zwinger courtyard. They are easily identified. Enter from Sophienstrasse by the gate under the **Glockenspielpavillon** (Carillon Pavilion) for the best view. Or cross the wooden bridge leading from Ostraallee for the **Kronentor** (Crown Gate) entrance. Most people, however, tend to arrive from Theaterplatz through the gate in the **Semperbau**.

Sit down on one of the benches facing the Wallpavillon *(directly opposite the Carillon Pavilion).* You are now in one of the most elegant courtyards in Europe. The architecture is German Baroque, grand and full of gusto, but with a hint, too, of a lighter Rococo touch. On most days in the summer months, you will hear music students playing classical works. Sometimes there are half a dozen groups playing in different spots (the best acoustics are in the Semperbau arch). The repertoire is strictly confined to the classics. If you want Dixieland tunes, you'll have to go out to the beer garden on Postplatz.

The courtyard is open free of charge. With its cool fountains and architectural exuberance, it makes the perfect spot to read a novel, write a letter, or (to be truly Baroque) flirt with a friend. Almost all the damage caused in 1945 has been skillfully repaired, apart from a few blackened statues tucked away in odd corners.

The courtyard was intended by Augustus the Strong as a setting for festivities. He wanted the complex to be completed in time for his son's wedding in 1719 with the Hapsburg princess Maria Josepha. But Pöppelmann failed to meet the deadline, and some of the buildings, such as the Glockenspielpavillon, had to be built hastily from wood.

Most of the Zwinger was built in the 18thC, but one wing remained unfinished. Later generations did not have the enthusiasm to complete the ensemble until the 19thC, when Gottfried Semper added a wing in Neoclassical style. It sits uncomfortably alongside Pöppelmann's work, looking rather too grave.

The original plan to create an orangery was abandoned in 1728, and Augustus decided instead to use the Zwinger as a museum for the royal art collections. The building currently contains five major collections: the MATHEMATISCHE-PHYSICALISCHER SALON (in the Baroque pavilion to the left of the Glockenspielturm), the STAATLICHES MUSEUM FÜR TIERKUNDE (in the long wing on your left, entered from the Kronentor), the PORZELLANSAMMLUNG (behind you, between the Glockenspielpavillon and the Kronentor, entered from outside the courtyard), the GEMÄLDEGALERIE (on the right side, in the far section of the Neoclassical wing) and the RÜSTKAMMER (in the near section of the Neoclassical wing).

Each of the collections deserves a visit (although you can skip *Tierkunde* (zoology) if need be, or the *Porzellansammlung* if ornate porcelain doesn't thrill you. Don't tire yourself out slogging through each of the museums. It is equally important to take time to savor the voluptuous Baroque architecture.

The **Wallpavillon** is not open to the public, but it conceals a Baroque staircase that leads up to the roof terraces. Many visitors fail to discover the upper terraces, which are shaded by trees and cooled by fountains. You can sit on a bench looking down on the courtyard, or inspect the mason's yard where statues damaged in 1945 are still being repaired.

One secret corner of the Zwinger can only be reached from the upper terraces. The **Nymphenbad** (nymphs' bath) can be spied from the terrace next to the Wallpavillon. A sweeping flight of steps leads down to a cool quadrangle. Water tumbles down a rusticated mock waterfall, splashing onto cavorting maidens and bearded Greek gods. It enters a basin where various jets of water produce soft gurgling sounds (known as *Stille Musik*). The fountain is surrounded by 16 shapely nymphs carved by Balthasar Permoser and his assistants.

Where to stay in Dresden

Forget about finding an old hotel in Dresden. They were virtually all destroyed in 1945. The modern hotels built in the postwar period tend to be well-located and functional, but that's about all. The decor can often resemble that of a funeral parlor, with beige walls and brown leather chairs. New hotels are being built all the time, but although they are more attractive, they are often located less conveniently.

For a time, it was difficult to find a room in Dresden, but not any more. When the Wall came down, tourists flooded into Eastern European cities such as Dresden and Prague, and chronic shortages followed. Visitors are still flocking to Prague in great numbers, and some are even settling there, although Dresden has lost some of its initial allure. The city currently hosts about six million visitors a year.

In the meantime, several new business hotels have opened in Dresden, and dozens more are planned. You are therefore not likely to have any problem finding a room, although it is always wise to reserve ahead, as the city might just happen to be hosting a major conference.

CHOOSING A HOTEL

Most visitors will find a hotel in the old town best suits their needs, although a few travelers may prefer a location in one of the leafy suburbs.

A room in the old town

Several large hotels are located in the old town, within walking distance of the Zwinger. Many occupy modern, concrete buildings dating from the communist era; rooms are comfortable and well-equipped, but have little character.

A cabin on a hotel ship

To meet the demand for hotel rooms, four former ships were converted into hotels (known as *Hotelschiffe*). They lie moored on the Elbe, E of the Carolabrücke (see ELBRESIDENZ). As comfortable as normal hotels, the ships are often rather romantic, but don't expect them to be cheap. Allow ten minutes to walk into the old town.

A room in the suburbs

Dresden's leafy suburbs have preserved much of their turn-of-the-century grandeur, and a few hotels are located in these quiet parts of town. You may need a car to get around.

A room in the country

Dresden is surrounded by rolling hills dotted with villages. If you have a car, you might be tempted to look for a hotel out of town. Some of the most attractive hotels are located in Saxon Switzerland, a mountainous region to the SE.

A room with a family

As in other former Eastern European towns, you can stay with a Dresden family. The rates are extremely cheap, although the locations are often out of town, and the beds might creak in the small hours.

NEW HOTELS

At the last count, some sixty new hotels were in the pipeline. Although many projects are being held up by lingering disputes over land ownership, some are already being built. One bold plan to create a new hotel in the disused tobacco factory YENIDZE TABAKSKONTOR does not seem to be progressing, but another project to convert the crumbling brick ruins of the TASCHENBERG PALAIS into a luxury hotel is going ahead.

If all proceeds according to plan, the Grand Hotel Taschenberg Palais Kempinski will open in late 1994 in a complex next to the RESIDENZSCHLOSS. It is expected to contain 214 hotel rooms, luxury boutiques, several restaurants and a conference center.

Elsewhere, work should begin in 1994 on a hotel next to the LUISENHOF restaurant. This hotel should enjoy spectacular views of the Elbe.

RESERVATIONS

It makes sense to reserve ahead, even though the chronic room shortage of past years no longer exists. The **tourist office** *(☎(0351) 4955025)* will do its best to obtain a room in the required price bracket.

WEEKEND DEALS

Several large hotels offer special weekend deals, combining a room, meals and excursions. The MERCURE NEWA offers a weekend discovering Meissen; the Hotel Königstein has a special Advent weekend deal, with a ticket to a concert in the KREUZKIRCHE; the MARITIM HOTEL BELLEVUE has a Whitsun package, featuring a wine tour and a Polynesian evening in the hotel restaurant.

The DRESDEN HILTON, in common with other Hilton hotels, sometimes offers a special weekend deal of two nights for the price of one.

HOW TO USE THIS CHAPTER

The following list of recommended hotels uses symbols to show price categories, charge/credit cards and other useful features. For a full explanation of our **symbols**, see page 7. For equivalent values of our **price category symbols**, see WHERE TO STAY IN BERLIN on page 163.

COVENTRY COTTAGE & GARDENS
Hülssestrasse 1, 01237 Dresden. See map on page 267 ☎(0351) 2743175 Fx(0351) 2743014 46 rms Tram 9, 13 to Hülssestrasse.

Location: SE of the city center, 20 minutes by tram from the Hauptbahnhof. One of the newest hotels in Dresden, named in honor of the British city bombed in World War II. The interior design is light years ahead of the official communist style that you still find elsewhere in Dresden. The lobby is filled with paintings and quirky Post-Modern chairs, while the bedrooms have stylish sofas and zany, abstract curtains. The bathrooms are large and luxurious, although not every gadget is totally rational (a common German failing). Each room has a spacious balcony, but the one drawback is the suburban location. There aren't any places to eat in the neighborhood, although the hotel restaurant itself is good. The tram services to central Dresden and Pillnitz are efficient, but most people staying here use a car to get around.

DRESDEN HILTON
An der Frauenkirche 5, 01067 Dresden. Map ***9****D4 ☎(0351) 48410 Fx(0351) 4841700 333 rms Tram 1, 2, 4, 12, 14 to Altmarkt.*

Location: In the historic heart of Dresden, next to the Frauenkirche ruins. Occupying an attractive low-rise courtyard building near the Brühlsche Terrasse, the Hilton has brought considerable vitality to a quarter that was once lifeless. The bedrooms are furnished in a modern style, with the usual wide range of facilities deemed needful by Hilton to pamper its guests. Some rooms look out on the ragged profile of the ruined Frauenkirche, others face a quiet courtyard. The hotel has several good restaurants and an attractive pool. It remains lively long after dark, with its high-tech disco, big dinner parties and a plush piano bar.

ELBRESIDENZ
Terrassenufer (near the Carolabrücke), 01069 Dresden. Map ***9****C5 ☎(0351) 4595003 Fx(0351) 4595137 181 rms (open-air) Tram 3, 5, 7, 8 to Rathenauplatz, then a 5min walk along the waterfront.*

Location: A cruise ship moored next to the Carolabrücke, ten minutes' walk from the old town. A sleek ship of the Köln-Düsseldorfer line is permanently moored on the Elbe. It used to cruise down the Rhine from Rotterdam to Lake Constance, but is now in use as a hotel. There is no longer a pressing need to stay on a ship, as hotel rooms are now in plentiful supply, but it is still one of Dresden's most romantic locations. The cabins are small, but comfortable enough for two people, although the bathrooms (all with showers) are rather basic. For the best view, try asking for a room on the river side. The ship was built in 1964, and the wooden furnishings are now rather dated, but there's nowhere else in Dresden where you can wake up in the morning to see an old paddle steamer passing by your window. The upper deck has a swimming pool, deckchairs and a giant game of chess. You get an excellent buffet breakfast on board, with five types of cereal, six types of bread, seven different pots of jam, yogurt, bacon, scrambled egg, sausage and croissants. Possibly the best feature of the hotel ship is its closeness to the heart of the old town.

MARITIM HOTEL BELLEVUE

Grosse Meissner Strasse 15, 01097 Dresden. Map **9**C4 *☎(0351) 56620 Fx(0351) 55997 328 rms Tram 4, 5 to Neustädter Markt.*

Location: On the right bank of the Elbe, near the Japanisches Palais. The Bellevue Hotel has been a Dresden landmark since the 19thC. Destroyed in World War II, the hotel was partly rebuilt in its original Neo-Baroque style, but on the opposite bank of the river, facing the old town. The Bellevue aims to be a grand hotel, with a host of facilities including several restaurants (one serving Polynesian dishes amid a South Sea Island decor), a beer cellar, wine bar, casino, and a sizeable swimming pool.

MERCURE NEWA

Prager Strasse 34, 01069 Dresden. Map **8**E3 *☎(0351) 4814109 Fx(0351) 4955137 312 rms Tram 3, 5, 9, 10, 11, 26 or airport bus to Hauptbahnhof.*

Location: On Prager Strasse, directly opposite the main rail station. The Mercure group has taken over several hotels in former East Germany, including Dresden's Newa. This bleak tower will never enhance Dresden's skyline, but the interior has been attractively redecorated, using pale woods and zany fabrics. The views from the hotel are not ravishing, although you may be amused to spot an old neon sign on a nearby tower block advertising *Moskwitsch Lada.* The location opposite the main station makes it a useful base for expeditions by train, to Meissen or the peaks of Saxon Switzerland.

SCHLOSS ECKBERG

Bautzner Strasse 134, 01099 Dresden. See map on page 267 ☎(0351) 52571 Fx(0351) 55379 85 rms Tram 11 to Schloss Albrechtsberg, then a 5min walk up the hill.

Location: In Loschwitz, 5km/3 miles NE *of the city center.* Built in 1859–61 for the Dresden merchant John Daniel Souchay, Schloss Eckberg is the most romantic of the three Elbe castles. The architect Christian Friedrich Arnold, a pupil of Semper's, created an English Gothic mansion complete with mock cloisters and turrets. The building was recently converted from a youth hostel into a hotel. You may be fortunate enough to get one of the 19 bedrooms in the Schloss; otherwise you will be given one of 62 rooms in a modern annex built near the gatehouse. Wherever you stay, you have to park your car at the gatehouse (where the reception desk is located). You can then stroll up the driveway or hop on a little buggy that takes guests and their luggage around the grounds. Meals are served in the Schloss, while the fitness center is in the annex. You can wander in rambling English-style gardens with a pond and greenhouse, or look down from the terrace on the sweeping bend of the Elbe. There are forest trails in the nearby Dresdener Heide, and the old spa town of Weisser Hirsch is just a ten-minute walk away.

Eating and drinking in Dresden

Don't go to Dresden expecting to find a wonderful restaurant in a quiet back street of the old city. There aren't any, at least not yet. The firestorm destroyed most of the old restaurants, and the subsequent years of communist dogma killed off any lingering desire to cook well. You may despair of finding anywhere good to eat, but the situation is not as bad as it at first seems.

WHERE TO EAT

New restaurants are springing up all the time. The best areas to hunt for good food are the **Münzgasse** (a lane near the Frauenkirche ruins) and the **Neustadt** district on the right bank (especially along **Hauptstrasse** and the nearby side streets).

Some restaurants still behave as if they are part of the communist state apparatus, but they are unlikely to survive much longer. As competition increases, restaurants will have to improve or go to the wall. You will find good, if not spectacular, cooking at the KÜGELGENHAUS and the RESTAURANT IM SCHAUSPIELHAUS. Outside the old town, you can enjoy the spectacular setting of the LUISENHOF.

HOTEL RESTAURANTS

Some of the most reliable restaurants in Dresden are located in the large hotels. For a special meal, you might try one of the many restaurants in the MARITIM HOTEL BELLEVUE. Saxon specialities are served in the elegant **Palais** restaurant overlooking the Elbe, or, for a change from pork and dumplings, you might be drawn to **Buri-Buri**, a Polynesian restaurant with creaking cane chairs, and waitresses with flowers in their hair. The restaurant **Canaletto** *(closed Sun, Mon, lunch)* offers sophisticated French cooking, while the Bellevue's **wine cellar** serves simple German dishes.

The new DRESDEN HILTON is an even better bet. You can eat quite sophisticated German food at the **Bistro De Saxe**, Italian cuisine at the **Rossini**, or simple German fare in the **Wettiner Keller**.

WHAT TO EAT

Traditional Dresden restaurants offer food in the Central European style. The specialities are similar to those of Prague, Vienna and Berlin. The art of cooking in these parts has not advanced much since the Middle Ages. Good things tend to be simple, like beer, bread and sausages. Bad things generally involve strange sauces or weird recipes.

Among the local specialities are pork prepared in a dozen different ways, heavy stews, well-made noodles and plump dumplings. This is not a weight-watcher's diet, but you will often find locally-caught fish on the menu (pike is common).

Saxon specialities are not particularly memorable, although dishes labelled *Lausitzer Art* are often worth a try. One local speciality is *Eiskaffee* (vanilla ice cream served with cold coffee and cream). It is an acquired taste.

WINE CELLARS

Many visitors are surprised to discover that Dresden lies in a wine-growing region. The slopes of the Elbe do not produce large quantities of wine, and most of it is drunk locally. You can sample the dry white wines from Radebeul and Meissen in several *Weinkeller* (wine cellars). These are generally located in the vaulted cellars of old buildings. The wine cellars usually offer food, but only basic German dishes.

HOW TO USE THIS CHAPTER

The following list of recommended restaurants uses symbols to show price categories, charge/credit cards and other useful features. For a full explanation of our **symbols**, see page 7. For equivalent values of our **price category symbols**, see EATING IN BERLIN on page 170.

BISTRO DE SAXE ***Traditional German***
Dresden Hilton: enter on Münzgasse. Map ***9****D4 ☎(0351) 48410 ▭▭ 🚗 AE ⦿ ⦿ VISA Tram 1, 2, 4, 12, 14 to Altmarkt.*

This is a mock-French bistro, complete with round marble table tops and a black and white tiled floor. The restaurant is part of the DRESDEN HILTON, which ensures a high standard of service and good wines. The atmosphere is relaxed and the prices are reasonable. The German cooking may not please fickle Parisians, but most people are thrilled to find *anywhere* that's this sophisticated in Dresden. The menu might include steaks, fish or *tortellini alla panna* served with crab in a cream sauce. There are some interesting Saxon specialities such as *Kalbfleisch-Sülze* (veal in aspic), but the *Dresdner Sauerbraten Apfelrotkohl und Kartoffelklösse* is best left to the locals.

KÜGELGENHAUS ***Traditional German***
Hauptstrasse 13. Map ***9****B4 ☎(0351) 54518 ▭ to ▭▭ 🚘 AE ⦿ ⦿ VISA Tram 4, 5 to Neustädter Markt.*

A friendly restaurant in the heart of the Neustadt, where you can eat well-prepared Saxon specialities. The restaurant occupies three vaulted rooms on the ground floor of an 18thC mansion. The Romantic artist Gerhard von Kügelgen once rented the apartment on the second floor (now the MUSEUM ZUR DRESDNER FRÜHROMANTIK). The walls of the restaurant are hung with charcoal portraits by Von Kügelgen and old prints of his country house at Loschwitz. The solid wooden furniture looks utilitarian, but tablecloths and candles help to create a convivial atmosphere. The food is mainly Central European in style, with a heavy emphasis on pork, stews, dumplings and noodles. Several Saxon specialities are on offer, including a tasty *Schweinsrücken Lausitzer Art* (pork slices served with stewed prunes). The house beer is Radeberger Pilsner, a tempting local brew, but many Germans consider it more fitting to sample a glass of Meissen white wine. The restaurant has a terrace overlooking the leafy Hauptstrasse; you can eat cakes there in the afternoon.

LA SCALA ***Italian***
Rähnitzgasse 24. Map ***9****B4 ☎(0351) 5022376 ▭ AE VISA Tram 4, 5 to Neustädter Markt.*

A friendly Italian restaurant, located on a quiet lane next to one of Pöppelmann's Baroque churches. Expect plain Italian trattoria cooking, including pizza, tortellini and the like. Not a sophisticated place, but lively and relaxed.

LUISENHOF ***Traditional German***
Bergbahnstrasse 8 (next to the Standseilbahn upper station). See map page 267 ☎(0351) 36842 ▭▭ 🚘 ≪ AE ⦿ ⦿ VISA Closed Mon. Tram 4, 10 to Schillerplatz. Walk across the Blaues Wunder bridge, then take the funicular from Körnerplatz to the upper station.

This is the most romantic setting in Dresden, where courting couples have come since the days of the Kaiser. Built in 1895 on the heights above the Elbe, it is reached by funicular railway from Loschwitz (although you can arrive more prosaically by car). You can go here for a simple coffee in the lounge, or a full lunch. Expect plain German cooking served in elegant surroundings. The views are superb, taking in the spires of Dresden and the distant hills. The restaurant has a terrace, and a tower which can sometimes be climbed. A new hotel is currently being built nearby.

MEISSNER WEINKELLER ***Traditional German***
Hauptstrasse 1b. Map ***9****B4 ☎(0351) 55814 ▭ ≡ AE ⊕ ◉ VISA Closed lunch. Tram 4, 5 to Neustädter Markt.*
This restaurant occupies the vaulted cellars of the Neustadt town hall, which was destroyed in 1945. The interior is dark, rustic and rather gloomy, even when the people at the next table are cracking jokes at a ripping pace. The food is well-prepared and inventive, if rather expensive. Specialities on offer include *Meissner Weinfleisch* (beef marinated in Meissen wine and served with sour cream). The wine cellar is well stocked with bottles from France and Italy, but most people go for the local Meissen wine, which is dry and subtle.

RESTAURANT IM SCHAUSPIELHAUS ***Traditional German***
Ostraallee 2 (2nd floor of Schauspielhaus theater). Map ***8****D3 ☎(0351) 4956131 ▭ to ▭ No cards. Tram 1, 2, 4, 7, 8, 11, 12, 14 to Postplatz.*
This elegant restaurant is well worth the climb. Decorated with mirrors and Neoclassical mouldings, it is located on the second floor of the restored theater, next to the Upper Circle. The chef is particularly fond of such Bohemian specialities as goulash with dumpling, although there are Saxon dishes as well. The restaurant is conveniently close to the Zwinger, if all that fine art has left you with an appetite.

ROSSINI ***Italian***
An der Frauenkirche 5 (in Dresden Hilton, 1st floor). Map ***9****D4 ☎(0351) 48410 ▭ ➡ AE ⊕ ◉ VISA Tram 1, 2, 4, 12, 14 to Altmarkt.*
An elegant Italian restaurant with a wide-ranging menu, from simple pastas to sophisticated Tuscan dishes. The setting is just right for a business lunch, and the prices are not unduly high.

WETTINER KELLER ***Traditional German***
Secundo Genitur, Brühlsche Terrasse (a covered bridge links the Secundo Genitur with the Dresden Hilton, An der Frauenkirche 5). Map ***9****C4 ☎(0351) 48410 ▭ ➡ ≡ AE ⊕ ◉ VISA Tram 1, 2, 4, 12, 14 to Altmarkt.*
An attractive wine cellar in the vaults of the *Secundo Genitur*. This Neo-Baroque palace was built on the Brühlsche Terrasse in 1897, and is part of the Dresden Hilton, linked to the main building by a covered bridge. Decorated with light wood and halogen lamps, this wine cellar is less gloomy than most. The kitchen produces traditional Saxon dishes with plenty of flair. The *Eisbeinsülze* (pig's feet in aspic) is good, although you can find that in Berlin. For something more regional, try the traditional Dresden-style stuffed cabbage. Wine is served by the glass or bottle. The list includes Rhineland wines and some French bottles, but it is worth trying one of the dry white wines from the Radebeul vineyards near Dresden.

CAFÉS

Cafés in Dresden are not as grand or as old as those in Prague, but many now offer good coffee and sinful cakes. Most cafés serve the local speciality *Dresdner Eierschecke*, a type of cheese cake.

CAFÉ PÖPPELMANN
In the Maritim Hotel Bellevue, Grosse Meissner Strasse. Map ***9****C4 ☎(0351) 56620. Open Sat, Sun, hols, 2–6pm.*
This tea room looking out on the Elbe makes an elegant setting for the Sunday ritual of *Kaffee und Kuchen*. It remains one of Dresden's most romantic spots.

CAFÉ SCHAUSPIEL
*Schauspielhaus, Ostraallee. Map **8**D3.*
A small café with marble-topped tables and vases of flowers, set on a terrace under an arcade with a fine view of the Zwinger. In truth, the view is dominated by cranes and scaffolding, but you still see the golden domes and spires. A good place to go when visiting the Zwinger.

EISCAFÉ VENEZIA
*Hauptstrasse 2a. Map **9**B4. Open daily 9am–10pm.*
An airy, modern café on the right bank of the Elbe, where you can indulge in moist Italian *Sachertorte,* or the best ice cream in town. The terrace fills quickly on balmy summer evenings.

TOSCANA
Schillerplatz 1, Blasewitz. See map on page 267. Open Mon–Sat 7am–10pm, Sun, hols 1–10pm.
An elegant modern café decorated with fabrics casually draped over suspended tree branches. Some people come for the delicious cakes; others for the superb view of the Blaues Wunder.

BEER GARDEN
The **Biergarten am Postplatz** *(map 8D3)* is a friendly beer garden situated on a patch of wasteland opposite the Zwinger. You can pick up a tasty *Bratwurst* at a rustic stall, and order a local beer from a genial waiter. The management is fond of playing loud German Country and Western songs. While not totally in keeping with the Baroque architecture across the street, the place seems to have many fans. How long it will remain on this prime site is impossible to predict, but don't be surprised if you find a more modern building has driven out the Stetsons.

Dresden entertainment

Dresden tends to be quiet after dark. The old city doesn't have many jazz clubs or discos — nor does anywhere else in Saxony. If you want a wild time, you'll have to take the train to Berlin or Prague (each about 3 hours away). So what do you do? You might come across someone playing the piano in the HILTON bar, or a jazz band busking on the Brühlsche Terrasse. Otherwise, the main entertainment in Dresden is classical music, which you can hear in concert halls, gardens and churches.

For those who speak German, there are two good theaters, two cabaret-theaters, and some cinemas. It doesn't add up to a lively city, and you won't find much happening after midnight, but it is still more exciting than any other city in the parts of Germany once under communist rule.

TICKETS
The tourist office on Prager Strasse is the most convenient place to reserve tickets for concerts and theater, but the assistant will probably shake her head if you ask about places for the opera. Seats tend to sell out months ahead, although you might succeed in picking up a last-minute ticket at the main advance booking office, **Zentrale Vorverkaufskasse**, *(Theaterplatz, map **8**C3 ☎(0351) 48420, open Mon-Fri noon-5pm (Thurs 6pm), Sat 10am-1pm).* The ticket office is located in a former guard house built by Schinkel. It handles reservations for the Staatsoper, the Staatsoperette and major theaters.

Performing arts in Dresden

Dresden is particularly famous for its opera and classical concerts, although you can also find adventurous theater and the latest movies. Music has the advantage, of course, of transcending language boundaries for those who don't speak fluent German.

CABARET

Dresden has two regular cabaret-theaters within heckling distance of each other, offering a lively mixture of satire, music and clowning. It helps if you can follow the local dialect.

- **Die Herkuleskeule** Sternplatz, map **8**E2 ☎(0351) 4951446
- **Dresdner Brettl** Maternistrasse 17, map **8**D2 ☎(0351) 4954123

CINEMA

Dresden's seven cinemas screen a wide range of international films, but almost invariably dubbed into German. If you are unfazed by the idea of Woody Allen talking German in *Mach's Noch Einmal, Sam,* turn to the "film index" in *Sax* magazine for a complete listing of the month's movies. Otherwise, the nearest cities with films in English are Prague and Berlin. The most interesting movie houses are listed below.

- **Casablanca** Friedenstrasse 23, off map **9**A4 ☎(0351) 571652. Screens recent arthouse movies.
- **Hauptbahnhof** Wiener Platz (in front of the railway station), map **8**E3 ☎(0351) 4710532. A blackened relic of Old Dresden, this small Neoclassical cinema is attached to the 19thC main railway station. There are weeds sprouting from the roof, yet this old cinema shows some of the best recent alternative films from the US and Europe (usually dubbed). A haunt of dedicated young movie fans.
- **Programmkino Ost** Schandauer Strasse 73 ☎(0351) 333782. Shows a careful selection of international movies.
- **UFA-Palast** Prager Strasse, map **8**E3 ☎(0351) 4952025. A modern multiscreen cinema on the main street. Hollywood blockbusters.

CLASSICAL MUSIC

Dresden was once one of the great European cities for classical music and opera. The city's reputation declined after World War II, but it is now slowly rebuilding its musical traditions. Dresden boasts several large concert halls, but they are not always the most attractive of buildings. Some of the most enjoyable performances take place out of the city center, in 19thC castles or Baroque gardens.

The most likely venues for classical concerts are:

- **Dreikönigskirche** Hauptstrasse 23, map **9**B4 ☎(0351) 5624101. Occasional concerts happen in this Baroque church in the Neustadt.
- **Dresdner Zentrum für Zeitgenössische Musik** Schevenstrasse 7, see map on page 267 ☎(0351) 378281. The Dresden Center of Contemporary Music regularly puts on performances of avant-garde music in a wistful old villa in Loschwitz.

- **Hofkirche** Schlossplatz, map **8**C3 ☎(0351) 4955135. The Hofkirche organist occasionally gives recitals in the restored Baroque church next to the RESIDENZSCHLOSS.
- **Kongresshalle** Deutsches Hygiene-Museum, Lingnerplatz 1, map **9**E4 ☎(0351) 48460. Classical concerts, jazz and modern dance sometimes take place in the rather lugubrious conference hall of the German Hygiene Museum.
- **Kreuzkirche** Kreuzstrasse 7, map **9**D4 ☎(0351) 4951435. The *Dresdner Kreuzchor* (Choir of the Dresden Kreuzkirche) has been giving recitals in the Kreuzkirche for more than 750 years. One of the most famous boys' choirs in Europe, it still regularly performs during church services. The best way to catch the choir is to attend *Vesper* (Evensong) on Saturdays at 6pm.
- **Kulturpalast** Schlossstrasse 2, map **8**D3 ☎(0351) 4866333. Dresden Philharmonic concerts are normally given in a modern concert hall on the Altmarkt.
- **Schloss Albrechtsberg** Bautzner Strasse 130, see map on page 267 ☎(0351) 55655. Concerts take place on Sundays at 4pm in an attractive 19thC villa overlooking the Elbe.

MUSIC IN THE OPEN AIR

Classical concerts are often held in the summer months, in Dresden's parks and palace gardens. Look out for concerts in the Zwinger courtyard, the gardens of Schloss Pillnitz, the Loschwitzer Elbwiese and the Roman Baths at Schloss Albrechtsberg. Here are two venues you might see advertised.

- **Canaletto Hof** Maritim Hotel Bellevue, in the inner courtyard of the old building, map **9**C4. Chamber music concerts are occasionally held on summer evenings in an intimate Renaissance courtyard filled with geraniums. Tickets are expensive, but the price includes a buffet supper served in the courtyard.
- **Schloss Pillnitz** Schlosshof, in the palace courtyard, Pillnitz, see map on page 267. Concerts in the summer take place on Sundays at 5pm. Take a Weisse Flotte steamer to Pillnitz, or bus 85 to Pillnitz. Performances by orchestras and brass bands are regularly held in an exotic outdoor courtyard, amid whimsical Japanese architecture and giant potted ferns.

OPERA

Dresden was once one of the great opera cities of Europe, and major works by Richard Wagner and Richard Strauss were premiered there.

- **Semperoper** Theaterplatz 2, map **8**C3 ☎(0351) 4842393. The SEMPEROPER is one of the great opera houses of Europe (see page 297). Gutted in 1945, it was carefully restored to its original Neoclassical splendor. It is now the setting for opera, ballet and classical concerts by the Saxon State Orchestra.
- **Staatsoperette** Pirnaer Landstrasse 131 ☎(0351) 2238763. Classical operetta by Mozart and Offenbach, plus the occasional Broadway hit by the likes of Stephen Sondheim.

THEATER

Released from decades of state censorship, theater audiences in Dresden were keen to catch up on Western plays that had once been banned. Brecht went briefly out of fashion as audiences lapped up Agatha Christie and Paul Simon, but the people with money to spend (mostly *Wessis*) now want more Brecht and less Broadway.

- **Kleines Haus** Glacisstrasse 28, map **9**B5 ☎(0351) 52631. A serious theater with a program of works by Ibsen, Brecht and young German dramatists.
- **Schauspielhaus** Ostraallee 1, map **8**D3 ☎(0351) 4842429. The main theater in Dresden, restored to its old splendor after the war. The plays are mainly classics by "greats" such as Brecht and Shakespeare.

OPEN-AIR THEATER

Look out in the summer for performances at the **Felsenbühne Rathen** staged by the *Landesbühnen Sachsen* (Regional Theater of Saxony). This is an open-air amphitheater in the heart of Saxon Switzerland. Don't expect Shakespeare or Schiller; the most popular works here are adaptations of Karl May's Wild West stories.

Tickets can be booked at the **Zentrale Vorverkaufskasse** on Dresden's Theaterplatz, but you will need a car to get to Rathen.

Dresden by night

Be patient. Dresden used to be dead after dark. It now shows increasing signs of life, especially around the Münzgasse and in the Neustadt. If you've just come from Berlin, things will seem tame, but there's plenty to do if you hunt around.

BARS

Not many bars in Dresden look inviting. The piano bar at the DRESDEN HILTON is a quiet place for a drink with a business colleague. Otherwise, a stroll down Münzgasse takes you past some of the upmarket places where you can drink an expensive beer.

Fashionable *Szene* bars tend to be located in the Neustadt, but they lead precarious lives. Look in *Sax* magazine under *Szene,* or ask someone who knows. A few Neustadt bars have now been around for several years, including **Planwirtschaft** *(Louisenstrasse 15)* and **Die 100** *(Alaunstrasse 100).* Even if they close down, there are other good places in the neighborhood.

COUNTRY MUSIC

Country and Western music has a big following in Dresden. The chances are high that you'll hear *Die Schönste Frau von Texas (The Yellow Rose of Texas)* at least once before you leave Dresden. If you are keen to catch Saxony's answer to Johnny Cash, try the BIERGARTEN AM POSTPLATZ (see BEER GARDENS on page 311).

DISCOS

Dresden's students gather to dance in the smoky catacombs under the Brühlsche Terrasse, at **Bärenzwinger** *(Brühlscher Garten ☎(0351) 4951409).* The dancing is less wild, and the dress more mainstream at the disco **Alibi** *(Münzgasse)* in the basement of the DRESDEN HILTON.

JAZZ

Jazz is big in Dresden, but it's not the same bluesy jazz that you hear in Berlin. The bands that play Dresden are faithful Dixieland followers. You'll hear it in the bars on Münzgasse and in the beer garden on Postplatz. For serious jazz, you have to go to one of the alternative cafés in Neustadt, or the cellar jazz club near the Albertinum.

The following addresses are worth checking out.

BIERHAUS DAMPFSCHIP
Dresden Hilton (entrance on Münzgasse). Map ***9****D4 ☎(0351) 4841776.*
Jazz groups play Dixieland favorites in a beer cellar next to Brühlsche Terrasse.

JAZZ CLUB TONNE
Tzschirnerplatz 3. Map ***9****D4 ☎(0351) 4951354. Concerts 9pm; doors open 8pm.*
It isn't easy to find, and it isn't always open, but Tonne stages some of the best jazz concerts in town. The club is located in the basement of a ruined building next to the Albertinum. However, in these unstable times, such places can vanish overnight.

Shopping

You don't go to Dresden for smart shops. The local economy is still too fragile to support more than a handful of luxury stores, and most of these are located in expensive hotels such as the DRESDEN HILTON and the MARITIM HOTEL BELLEVUE. **Prager Strasse** is the main shopping street for basic necessities, but some of the more interesting stores are on the other side of the river, along the increasingly attractive **Hauptstrasse**.

DEPARTMENT STORE

Most everyday goods can be found at **Karstadt** *(Prager Strasse 17, map* ***8****E3 ☎(0351) 48470, open Mon-Fri 9am-6.30pm (to 8.30pm on Thurs), Sat 9am-2pm (to 4pm on 1st Sat of month), tram 7, 8, 11 to Webergasse).* The store has a large food department, basic clothes (including Esprit fashions) and a well-stocked newsstand.

FASHION

Germans go to Berlin or Munich for fashion, but not Dresden. Most people in Dresden still don't have the money to buy Karl Lagerfeld or Jil Sander clothes. The only fashion chain that has set up in Dresden is **Benetton**. The feisty Italian group has opened up a spacious store packed with the inevitable bright fashions, in a huge 19thC Neustadt building that survived the bombing *(Hauptstrasse 36, map* ***9****B4).*

A second Benetton store, much smaller, stands on Körnerplatz in Loschwitz.

NEWSPAPERS AND MAGAZINES

Large hotels such as the DRESDEN HILTON and the MARITIM HOTEL BELLEVUE have newsstands selling some international newspapers, but the biggest selection in town is at the **Karstadt** department store, which usually stocks the *International Herald Tribune, The Guardian* and even Prague's weekly English newspaper *Prague Post.*

You can buy the local listings magazines *Sax* or *Dresdner* at most newsagents, tourist offices, hotel desks and museums.

PORCELAIN

Meissen porcelain is the one luxury item that has always been in plentiful supply in Dresden. The **Meissen Porzellanshop** is the most reliable source (a porcelain plaque displayed in the window certifies that it is all genuine Meissen ware). You will find a small outlet in the **Bellevue Arkade** *(at the Maritim Hotel Bellevue),* and there is a much bigger selection in the shopping arcade at the DRESDEN HILTON *(An der Frauenkirche 5, map 9D4 ☎ (0351) 4841871* AE Φ ● VISA*).*

The shops sell blue-and-white porcelain, imitation Japanese dishes painted with dragon motifs, and vases decorated with views of Dresden. A porcelain pepper pot is probably the cheapest item on offer — whereas a Meissen porcelain chess set has to be looked on as a long-term investment.

SOUVENIRS

Porcelain is the obvious souvenir to take home, although you might find it interesting to buy a book of photographs of Old Dresden. Attractive wooden toys from the Erzgebirge region are on sale in many shops, but perhaps the most unusual memento is a *Fürstenzug* candle, which is decorated with the procession of princes that line the outer wall of the Stallhof in Augustusstrasse.

The **Miacz** store (AE Φ ● VISA) in the DRESDEN HILTON arcade has a good selection of local souvenirs. Look out for the limited-edition wristwatches incorporating fragments of FRAUENKIRCHE rubble, which went on sale recently in aid of the Frauenkirche restoration fund.

Sports and activities

Pack boots and a bathing suit if you want to be energetic. Dresden makes an excellent base for walking, mountaineering and skiing.

CYCLING

You don't see many bicycles in Dresden yet, but if you feel brave, you can rent a sturdy bike for the day at the DRESDEN HILTON or the MARITIM HOTEL BELLEVUE.

The best route for beginners is to follow the Elbe upstream from the old town to the BLAUES WUNDER bridge (see WALKING, on opposite page, for route description).

MOUNTAINEERING

Dresden is one of the main centers in Germany for serious rock climbers. The most challenging climbs within a reasonable distance are in Saxon Switzerland.

RUNNING

Runners can follow the gravel paths in the Grosser Garten, or cut across the meadows beside the Elbe.

SKIING

The main center for winter sports is the small town of Altenberg, 43km/27 miles S of Dresden. The resort has ski runs and cross-country skiing routes.

Further information from the tourist office *(Verkehrsamt, Rathaus, Platz des Bergmanns 2, 01773 Altenberg ☎ (035056) 4240 Fx (035056) 4263).*

SWIMMING

Dresden has a good number of swimming pools, both indoor and outdoor. One of the best located outdoor pools for serious swimming is the Georg-Arnhold-Bad, next to the HYGIENE-MUSEUM.

WALKING

A favorite local walk goes through the meadows on the left bank of the Elbe from the Altstadt to Blasewitz. You can then cross the BLAUES WUNDER bridge and return to town along the right bank, following the Körnerweg.

Other attractive walks can be done in the nearby Dresdener Heide, taking tram 11 to Mordgrundbrücke and heading off into the woods. Armed with a good map, you might be tempted to try the 11-kilometer/7-mile hike from Loschwitz to Pillnitz, beginning from the upper station of the SCHWEBEBAHN. See also WALKS 1 and 2 on pages 269 and 274.

Spectator sports

HORSE RACES

The **Galopprennbahn Dresden-Seidnitz** *(Oskar-Röder-Strasse 1 ☎ (0351) 2371103)* stages regular race meetings.

SOCCER

Dresden's team **FC Dynamo Dresden** play at the modern **Rudolf Harbig Stadion** *(Lennéstrasse, opposite the Grosser Garten, map 9E4–F4).* The young fans are not always angelic.

TOBOGGAN RUN

The **Bobbahn Altenberg** *(Altenberg ☎ (035056) 5120)* organizes toboggan contests in the winter months.

Dresden for children

It may seem, at first glance, as if there isn't a lot for children to do in Dresden unless they adore museums. Here are a few ideas for keeping your offspring entertained.

MUSEUMS

Children may well groan at the thought of visiting the ZWINGER or the GEMÄLDEGALERIE, but they might at least enjoy the scientific instruments collection (MATHEMATISCH-PHYSIKALISCHER SALON), the medieval weapons hall (RÜSTKAMMER) or the zoology museum (STAATLICHES MUSEUM FÜR TIERKUNDE).

The other museum worth suggesting is the DEUTSCHES HYGIENE-MUSEUM. They might think it sounds boring, but try telling them about the full-size glass models of a woman and a horse. That should get them curious.

PARKS AND PLAYGROUNDS

Once you are at the HYGIENE-MUSEUM, it takes no time to reach the GROSSER GARTEN. The main attraction for children is the small zoo.

Children's playgrounds are hard to find, and not too well equipped. The small play area in the Grosser Garten might, at best, keep a child amused for ten minutes.

PUPPET THEATER

Another children's attraction in the Grosser Garten is the **Puppentheater Sonnenhäusel** *(Herkulesallee, off map 9E6, or see map on page 266).* This children's puppet theater is located in a magical little Baroque pavilion tucked away in the trees. The publicity poster may get them interested; it says: "Our puppet theater welcomes people big and small, fat and thin, young and not so young, with blonde, brown, black or green hair."

Be prepared for dialogue in German, although the plot of Hansel and Gretel is fairly easy to follow in any language.

MINIATURE RAILWAYS

Dresden has several antiquated miniature railways that are kept running by bands of enthusiasts.

A ride on the little railway in the Grosser Garten might keep a child amused for half an hour (see PARKEISENBAHN, page 293). The little train that runs out to Schloss Moritzburg (TRADITIONSBAHN RADEBEUL) makes a fun excursion lasting several hours.

EXCURSIONS

The city doesn't offer that much for kids to do, but several exciting excursions can be suggested. Take a paddle steamer trip (see WEISSE FLOTTE DRESDEN, page 262), or a ride on the world's oldest mountain railway, the SCHWEBEBAHN.

If all else fails, take them for a look at the ruins of the FRAUENKIRCHE and explain their significance. Children ought to know.

German in a nutshell

German does not appear easy, because it has a complex sentence structure and compound words. A simple conversation is not difficult, though, as every word is pronounced as written. English is widely spoken in former West Berlin, but in parts of what was East Berlin you are more likely to meet people whose second language, if any, is Russian.

In written German, nouns are always written with an initial capital letter. The old script form of ss (ß) can still be seen.

BASIC COMMUNICATION

Yes / no ja / nein
Please bitte *(informal),* bitte schön *(formal)*
Thank you danke
Thanks very much danke schön
You're welcome bitte sehr
No, thank you nein, danke
Excuse me entschuldigen Sie
Sorry es tut mir leid
Excellent! prima!
Hello guten Tag
Good morning / evening / night guten Morgen / Abend / Nacht
Goodbye auf Wiedersehen *(formal),* auf Wiederhören *(on the telephone)*
Mr / Mrs Herr / Frau
Miss Fräulein
Ladies Damen
Gentlemen Herren
This one / that one dieses / jenes
Big / small gross / klein
With / without mit / ohne
Hot / cold heiss / kalt
Cheap billig
Expensive teuer
Good / bad gut / schlecht
Rest room / toilet Toiletten / WC
I speak English ich spreche Englisch
Do you speak English? sprechen Sie Englisch?
I don't speak German ich spreche kein Deutsch
I don't understand ich verstehe nicht
I don't know ich weisse nicht
I am American / British ich bin Amerikaner / Engländer (*female:* Amerikanerin / Engländerin)
Where is?... wo ist?...
Do you have?... haben Sie?...
I'd like... ich möchte...
How much?... wieviel?...

Numbers: **0** – null **1** – eins **2** – zwei **3** – drei **4** – vier **5** – fünf **6** – sechs **7** – sieben **8** – acht **9** – neun **10** – zehn **11** – elf **12** – zwölf **13** – dreizehn **14** – vierzehn **15** – fünfzehn **16** – sechzehn **17** – siebzehn **18** – achtzehn **19** – neunzehn **20** – zwanzig **21** – einundzwanzig **22** – zweiundzwanzig **30** – dreissig **40** – vierzig **50** – fünfzig **60** – sechzig **70** – siebzig **80** – achtzig **90** – neunzig **100** – hundert **500** – funf hundert **1,000** – tausend

1994/95/96 – neunzehn hundert vier/funf/sechs und neunzig

The calendar: **Day** – Tag **Month** – Monat **Year** – Jahr
Today – Heute **Yesterday** – Gestern **Tomorrow** – Morgen
Monday – Montag **Tuesday** – Dienstag **Wednesday** – Mittwoch
Thursday – Donnerstag **Friday** – Freitag **Saturday** – Samstag *or* Sonnabend **Sunday** – Sonntag
January – Januar **February** – Februar **March** – März
April – April **May** – Mai **June** – Juni **July** – Juli **August** – August
September – September **October** – Oktober **November** – November
December – Dezember

Time: **. . . o' clock** – . . . Uhr **quarter past. . .** – viertel nach. . .
half-past five – halb sechs *(i.e., half of six)* **quarter to. . .** – viertel vor. . .
What time is it? – wie spät ist es?

SIGN DECODER

Achtung beware
Anmeldung reception
Aufzug elevator
Ausgang exit
Auskunft information
Ausverkauf clearance sale
Baden verboten no swimming
Besetzt full / occupied
Betreten verboten no trespassing
Betriebsferien closed for vacation
Bitte nicht stören do not disturb
Denkmal memorial
Dom cathedral
Dorf village
Drücken push
Eingang entrance
Eintritt frei admission free
Einwurf insert
Erdgeschoss / Parterre ground floor
Etage floor
Erste hilfe first aid
Feiertags geschlossen closed on holidays
Fernsprecher telephone
Feuermelder fire alarm
Flughafen airport
Frei vacant
Freibad open-air swimming pool
Friedhof cemetery
Fussgängerzone pedestrian mall
Gasse lane
Gefahr danger
Geöffnet / offen open
Geschlossen closed
Gesperrt out of order
Hof courtyard
Insel island
Kirche church
Krankenhaus hospital
Lebensgefahr danger
Nicht berühren do not touch
Notausgang emergency exit
Polizei police
Privatgrundstück private property
Rathaus town hall
Rauchen verboten no smoking
Rolltreppe escalator
Ruhetag closed all day
Schloss castle / palace
Selbstbedienung self-service
Sonderangebot special offer
Stadt city
Strasse street
Tor gate
Turm tower
Verkehrsamt / Verkehrsverein tourist office
Viertel district / quarter
Wald forest
Wechsel currency exchange
Ziehen pull
Zutritt verboten no admission

PUBLIC TRANSPORT

Abfahrt departures
Ankunft arrivals
Bahnhofsmission travelers' aid
Bahnsteig track / platform
Bushaltestelle bus stop
Einsteig vorn / hinten enter at front / rear
Entwerter ticket-stamping machine
Fahrkarten ticket office
Gepäckaufbewahrung checked (left) luggage
Gleis track / platform
Hauptbahnhof (Hbf) main railway station
Liegewagen couchette
Nichtraucher nonsmoking car
Raucher smoking car
Reserviert reserved
Schlafwagen sleeping car
Schliessfächer checked-luggage (left-luggage) lockers
Speisewagen restaurant car

SHOPPING

Laden shop
Apotheke dispensing pharmacy
Bäckerei baker
Buchhandlung bookstore
Drogerie pharmacist / chemist
Friseur hairdresser
Geschenkartikel gifts
Juwelier jeweler
Kaufhaus department store
Konditorei pastry store
Kunstgewerbe craft store
Postamt post office
Reisebüro travel agency
Schuhgeschäft shoe store

Food and drink

Waiter / waitress Herr Ober / Fräulein
Snacks Erfrischungen
Breakfast Frühstück
Lunch Mittagessen
Dinner Abendessen
The bill, please die Rechnung, bitte
Menu Speisekarte
Snack bar Schnellimbiss
Glass / bottle Glas / Flasche
Carafe Karaffe
Draft beer Bier vom Fass
Light ale Helles Bier
Brown ale Dunkles Bier
Lager / bitter Pilsener / Altbier
Red wine Rotwein
White wine Weisswein
Dry / sweet trocken / süss
Mineral water Mineralwasser
Orange juice Orangensaft
Apple juice Apfelsaft
Milk Milch
Salt / pepper Salz / Pfeffer
Mustard / oil Senf / Öl
Vinegar Essig
Bread / roll Brot / Brötchen
Butter / cheese Butter / Käse
Fruit Obst
Coffee / tea Kaffee / Tee
Chocolate Schokolade
Sugar Zucker

MENU DECODER

Angemacht in a special dressing
Auflauf soufflé
Aufschnitt sliced cold meats
Bauernbrot coarse rye bread
Bauernomelett omelet + bacon + onions
Bismarckhering pickled herring
Blau steamed, with butter
Blutig rare
Bockwurst large, boiled sausage
Boulette cold hamburger
Bratkartoffeln fried potatoes

Bratwurst fried sausage
Brühe broth
Brust breast
Durchgebraten well done
(Gekochtes) Ei (boiled) egg
Eisbein knuckle of pig
Ente duck
Erbensuppe thick pea soup
Fasan pheasant
Fleisch meat
Forelle trout
Frühlingssuppe vegetable soup
Gänseleberpastete goose liver pâté
Gebacken baked
Gedämpft steamed
Gefrorene ice cream
Gefüllt stuffed
Gegrillt grilled
Gekocht boiled
Gelee jelly
Gemischt mixed
Gemüse vegetables
Gepökelt pickled
Geräuchert smoked
Geschmort stewed, braised
Halbdurch medium
Hausfrauenart with apple, onions + sour cream
Hausgemacht homemade
Holländisch with mayonnaise
Holstein served with anchovies and topped with a fried egg
Jägerart in a red wine sauce with mushrooms
Kaiserschmarren shredded pancake served with raisins and almonds
Kartoffelpuffer crisp potato and onion pancakes sprinkled with sugar
Kartoffelsalat potato salad
Klösse / Knödel dumplings
Kompott stewed fruit
Kräuter herbs
Lachs salmon
Leberwurst liver pâté
Linsensuppe lentil soup
Matjeshering small, cured herring
Müllerin baked in butter, and topped with breadcrumbs and egg
Ochsenschwanzsuppe oxtail soup
Pfannkuchen pancake
Rahm cream
Räucheraal smoked eel
Rauchwurst smoked sausage
Roh raw
Rosenkohl Brussels sprouts
Röst fried
Rotkraut red cabbage
Sahne cream
Salat lettuce / salad
Sauerbraten beef marinated in vinegar, sugar and spices, and then braised
Sauerkraut pickled white cabbage
Schinken ham
Schwarzbrot brown rye bread
Schweinshaxe knuckle of pork
Schnitzel veal escalope
Soleier pickled egg
Sosse sauce
Spargel asparagus
Speck bacon
Spiess skewered
Sülze jellied pressed meat
Suppe soup
Topf stew
Truthahn turkey
Überbacken au gratin
Wiener Schnitzel veal escalope fried in breadcrumbs
Zwiebel onion

Index

Page numbers in **bold** type indicate main entries. *Italic* page numbers indicate illustrations and maps. See also the LIST OF STREET NAMES on page 336.

Abdul Hamid, Sultan, 140
Abel, Rudolf Iwanowitsch, 231
Academy of Art *see* Kunstakademie
Accidents, 23
Addresses and telephone numbers:
Berlin, **61–2**
Dresden, **262**
Potsdam, **215–16**
Adenauer, Konrad, 35
Admiralpalast, 82
Aedes gallery, 70, 177, 193
Ägyptisches Museum, 69, 89, 90, 91, **92**, 95, 100, 137, 145
Air Ministry, 78
Air travel/airports:
Berlin, 19, 53, 62, 162
Dresden, 19, 258
Potsdam, 215
Airlift monument, 80
Albertinum, 248, 256, 265, 268, 272, 277, **278**, 282, 285, 287, 295, 298
Albrecht, Prinz, 143, 296
Albrecht III, Duke of Saxony, 250, 270, 294
Albrecht the Bear, 159
Alcohol, duty-free allowances, 18
Alexander I, Czar, 92
Alexanderplatz, 68, 80, 85, 87, **92**
Allotments, **92–3**
Alte Königliche Bibliothek, 43, **154**
Alte Nationalgalerie, 15, 48, 70, 76, 89, 91, **93–4**, 109, 117, 134, 135, *135*
Altenberg, 264, 317
Alter Friedhof, **227**
Alter Katholischer Friedhof, 254, **278–9**
Alternative centers, **181–2**
Altes Museum, 44, *44*, 69, 76, 81, 87, **94**, 111, 125, 129, 134, *135*
Altes Rathaus (Potsdam), 222
Altstadt (Dresden), **268**, 269, 284
Ambulances:
Berlin, 64
Dresden, 263
Potsdam, 215
American Express:
charge cards, 17
mail-holding service, 59
medical insurance, 17
MoneyGram®, 17
Travel Service, 61, 262
travelers checks, 17, 23, 64
Amerika-Gedenkbibliothek, 80
Anhalter Bahnhof, 78, **94**, 99
Antikenmuseum, 89, 90, 91, 92, **95**, 145
Antikensammlung, **95**
Antikentempel, 234
Antiques, **192**
Aquarium, 86, **95**, 201
Archenhold-Sternwarte, **95**, 201
Architecture:
Berlin, **42–6**, **69–70**
Dresden, **254–6**
Potsdam, **208–10**
Ardenne, Baron Manfred van, 275
Arnim, Ferdinand von, 156
Arnold, Christian Friedrich, 307
Art, **47–8**, 70
Art auctions, **193**
Art Deco, 15, 103, 124, 200
Art Galleries, **193**
Art Nouveau, 15, 45, 103, 124, 192
see also Jugendstil
Arts and Crafts, Museum of *see* Kunstgewerbemuseum
Attlee, Clement, 208
Auctions, **193**
Augusta, Princess, 235, 237
Augustus, Elector of Saxony, **254**, 287, 291, 295
Augustus II, Elector of Saxony, **254**
Augustus III, Elector of Saxony, 251, 282, 284, 285, 288
Augustus the Strong, 14, 250, 251, **254–5**, 272, 273, 278, 280, 282, 284, 287, 288, 289, 291, 293–4, 295, 296, 298, 300, 303–4
Avus, 116, 211

Babelsberg, **48–9**, 50, 219
Babelsberg Studios, **48–9**, 50, 182, 206, 207, 208, 229
Bach, J.S., 66, 205
Bahnhof Friedrichstrasse, 56, 75
Bahnhof Lichtenberg, 57
Bahnhof Zoologischer Garten, 56, 182
Bähr, George, 280
Ballet, **185**
Baluschek, Hans, 128
Banks, 20
Berlin, 59
Dresden, 261
Baroque architecture, **42–3**, **209**, **254–5**
Bars:
Berlin, **187–9**
Dresden, **314**
Bauer, Felice, 164
Bauhaus, 15, **45**, 96, 103, 256
Bauhaus-Archiv, 45, 90, **96**
Bayreuth, Countess Wilhelmine von, 234
Beaches:
Berlin, 91, **201**
Potsdam, 225
Wannsee, 158
Beck, General Ludwig, 34
Beckmann, Max, 97, 137
Beer halls and beer gardens:
Berlin, **179–80**
Dresden, **311**
Potsdam, **243**
Beethoven, Ludwig van, 28
Begas, Reinhold, 136
Behrens, Peter, **36**, 45
Benckengraff, Johann, 14
Benckert, Johann Peter, 228
Benz, Karl, 132
Berckheyde, Gerrit, 285
Berger, Ines, 129

Bergman, Ingmar, 49
Berlin, **25–204**
airports, 19
beer halls and beer gardens, **179–80**
cafés, **175–9**
children in, **201–2**
history, **27–8**, **31–6**
hotels, **161–8**
maps, *76–77, 79, 81, 83*
nightlife, **181**, **187–91**
performing arts, **181–7**
planning, **65–70**
porcelain, **14–15**
restaurants, **168–75**
shopping, **191–200**
sights and places of interest, **88–160**
sports, **202–4**
tourist information, **53–64**
walks, **74–8**, **154–5**, **157**, **204**
Berlin Airlift, 35, 80
Berlin Blockade, 35
Berlin Film Festival, 35, 36, 66, 182, 229–30
Berlin Green Head, 92
Berlin Hauptbahnhof, 56
Berlin Marathon, 67, 203
Berlin-Museum, 15, 48, 70, 79, 84, 89, 90, **96–7**, 98, 121, 124
"Berlin painter," 95
Berlin-Pavillon, 75, **97**, 149
Berlin Philharmonic Orchestra, 66, 67, 183, 184
Berlin-Schönefeld Airport, 53, 162, 211
Berlin-Tegel Airport, 53, 162, 211
Berlin-Tempelhof Airport, 35, 53, 80, 162, 212
Berlin University, 30
Berlin Wall, 11, 25–6, 28, 29, 30, 35, 36, 46, 48, 49, 55, 56, 71, 72, 74, 78, 85, 86, 87, 89, 96, 97, **98**, 102, 105, **117–18**, 122, 123, 126, 142, 143, 151, 152, 153, 157, 186, 192, 208, 224, 225, 229, 231, 239, 304
Berliner Ensemble, 76, 102, **186**
Berliner Flohmarkt, 82, **98**, 192, 198
Berliner Kinomuseum, 50, **98**, 182
Berliner Panoptikum, **98–9**
Berliner Schloss, 43, **99**, 149
Berliner Secession, 47
Beuys, Joseph, 94
Bicycles, 57, **202**, **247**, **316**
Biedermeier era, 27, 93, 124
Bildergalerie, **228**
Biller family, 125
Billiards, **202**
Biographies, **36–41**, **252–4**
Bismarck, Otto von, 33, **36–7**, 93, 125–6, 151
Bladelin, Pieter, 113
Blasewitz, 256, **269**, 274, 279
Der Blaue Engel (The Blue Angel), **51**, 208, 229
Blaues Wunder, 256, 267, 268, 274, **279**, 293, 296, 301, 302, 316, 317
Blechens, Karl, 228
Blockhaus Nikolskoe, **138**, 171
Blücher, General von, 32
Boats, 61
Elbe cruises, 20, 259
Havel river trips, **87–8**, 118, **201**, 212
hotel ships, 305
Müggelsee cruises, 130
Potsdam ferries, 213
rowboats, 202, **203**, 247
sailing, 203
Wannsee, 157–8
Weisse Flotte Dresden, 216, 262, 272, 293, **302**, 318
Böcklin, Arnold, 137
Bode, Wilhelm von, 99, 100, 140, 148
Bode-Museum, 26, 43, 76, 82, 85, 89, 91, 94, **99–101**, 111, 131, 134, 135, *135*, 137, 148, 155
Bodt, Jean de, 289
Body care products, **194**
Books:
bookstores, **194–5**, **244**
reading lists, **52**, **257**
Borsig, August, 82, 94, 106, 132
Botanischer Garten, 86, **101**, 226
Böttger, Johann Friedrich, 14, 250, 290, 293
Botticelli, Sandro, 112
Boumann, Johann, 43, 222, 232, 236
Bousset, Johannes, 153
Bowling, **202**
Brandenburg, 118, 216
Brandenburg, Electors of, 27, **31–2**
Brandenburger Tor (Brandenburg Gate, Berlin), 25, 28, 29, 30, 43, 68, 87, **101–2**, *101*, 127, 150, 154, 155
Brandenburger Tor (Potsdam), 224, 226
Brandenburger Vorstadt, 219
Brandt, Willy, 35, **37**
Braun, Eva, 38
Breakfast, 163, **175–6**, 242
Brecht, Bertolt, 28, 34, **37**, 40, 76, 82, **102**, 106, 120, 171, 186, 314
Brecht-Weigel-Haus, 82, **102**
Breitscheidplatz, **102**
Brendel, Johann, 141
Britz, **102–3**, 183
Britzer Garten, 103
Broadcasting Museum *see* Deutsches Rundfunk-Museum
Bröhan, Karl, 103
Bröhan-Museum, 15, **103**, 145
Die Brücke, 47, **103–4**, 251, 252, 286, 298
Brücke-Museum, 26, 48, 67, 69, 70, 90, **103–4**, 286
Bruegel, Pieter the Elder, 114, 125
Brühl, Count, **252**, 272, 279, 281
Brühlsche Terrasse, 252, 267, 272, **279**, 290, 301, 302
Bundestag, 36
Bureaux de change, 20
Büring, Johann Gottfried, 43, 228, 233
Busch, Fritz, 252
Buses:
Berlin, 55, 61–2, 86–7, 201
Dresden, 259, 260, 262
Potsdam, 212–13, 225–6
Business facilities:
Berlin, **63**
Dresden, **261–2**

Cabaret:
Berlin, **190**
Dresden, **312**
Potsdam, **246**
Cabinet of Dr. Caligari, The, 48, 50, 51, 98, 229
Cable railway, 260, **297**, 302

Café terraces, **176**
Cafés:
  Berlin, **175–9**
  children in, 201
  dance, **189–90**
  Dresden, **310–11**
  Potsdam, **242–3**
  women-only, 60
Caine, Michael, 49
Calendar of events:
  Berlin, **65–7**
  Dresden, **264–5**
  Potsdam, **216–17**
Canaletto (Antonio Canal), 112, 283, 285
Canaletto (Bernardo Bellotto), 251, **252–3**, 269, 273, 280, 283–4, 285, 288, 290, 301
Canova, Antonio, 148
Carove, Giovanni, 125
Cars, 22
  accidents, 23
  in Berlin, 57
  breakdowns, 23, 64, 215, 263
  documents, 16
  driving to Dresden, 258
  driving to Potsdam, 211
  renting, 57, 216, 260
Casanova, Giacomo Girolamo, 206
Casanova, Giovanni Battista, 278–9, 291
Casino, 107, **190**
Castles, listed, 90
Cemeteries:
  Alter Friedhof, **227**
  Alter Katholischer Friedhof, **278–9**
  Dorotheenstädtischer Friedhof, **106**
  Französischer Friedhof, 106
  Friedrichstadt, 281
  Neuer Friedhof, **227**
  Old Jewish, 223
  Russischer Orthodoxe, **144**
Cézanne, Paul, 93
Chagall, Marc, 93
Chaplin, Charlie, 182
Charge cards, 17, 23
Charlotte, Princess (Czarina Alexandra), 138, 171, 234, 237
Charlottenburg, 42, **72**, 86, **104**, 161
Chatwin, Bruce, 257
Checkpoint Charlie, 25, 29, 70, 78, **117–18**, 192
Chemists *see* Pharmacies
Chiaveri, Gaetano, 251, 288
Children:
  in Berlin, **201–2**
  clothes, **196–7**
  in Dresden, **318**
  in hotels, 162–3
  toy stores, **200**, **245**
Chinesisches Teehaus, 43, 70, 206, 224, **228–9**, *228*
Christmas, 67, 217, 265
Christus, Petrus, 113
Churches, 62
  in Berlin, listed, 90
  see also individual churches
Churchill, Winston, 208, 224, 237, 239, 241
Cinema, 27, **48–51**
  Babelsberg Studios, **48–9**, 50, 182, 206, 207, 208, 229, 239
  Berlin, **182–3**
  Berlin Film Festival, 66, 182, 229–30
  Berliner Kinomuseum, **98**, 182
  DEFA Film- und TV-Erlebnis, 50, 211, 218, 219, **229–30**
  Dresden, **312**
  Filmmuseum Potsdam, 218, 222, **230–1**
  Potsdam, **246**
Circus, Berlin, **183**
Citny, Kiddy, 97
Claes, Pieter, 285
Clärchens Ballhaus, 82, 189
Classical Antiquities Collection *see* Antikensammlung
Clay, General Lucius D., 35
Climate, 18–19
Clothes, 19
  stores, **195–7**, **244**, **315**
Coach travel, 20, 54
Cobra group, 94
Coffee and cake, **176**
Cold War, 27, 35, 45, 49, 52, 71, 88, 102, 117, 153, 161, 186, 205, 225, 231, 249
Communs, 226, 234
Compact discs, **198**, **245**
Conference hotels, 63, 162
Congress centers, 262
Conrad, Carl, 157
Consulates, 62
Cook, Captain James, 133
Cosel, Constantia von, 296, 300
Country and Western music, **314**
Courbet, Gustave, 137
Cranach, Lucas the Elder, 112, 119, 125, 159, 228, 284–5, 291
Credit cards, 17, 192
  lost, 23
Crime, 68
Cultural institutions, **184**
Currency, 17
Currency exchange, 20
  Berlin, 59
  Dresden, 261
Customs allowances, 18
Cycling, 57
  Berlin, **202**
  Dresden, **316**
  Potsdam, **247**

Dada, 47
Dahlem, 25, **73**, 89, **104–5**, 135, 153
Dahlem-Dorf, 153
Dahme River, 71, 122
Daimler, Gottlieb, 132
Daimler-Benz, 46, 122
Damenflügel, 238
Dampfmaschinenhaus, 232
Dance, Potsdam, **246**
Dance cafés, **189–90**
David, Jacques Louis, 146
DEFA Film- und TV-Erlebnis, 50, 211, 218, 219, **229–30**
Degas, Edgar, 286
Deighton, Len, 49, **52**
Dentists:
  Berlin, 64
  Dresden, 263
  Potsdam, 215
Department stores, 20
  Berlin, **198**
  Dresden, **315**
  Potsdam, **244**
Derossi, Pietro, 78
Descartes, René, 31
Desiderio da Settignano, 148
Destruction of Dresden, The, 257
Deutsche Bundesbahn (DB), 19, 54
Deutsche Reichsbahn (DR), 19, 54
Deutsche Staatsbibliothek, 155
Deutscher Dom, 43, 107, 115
Deutscher Werkbund, 129
Deutsches Historisches Museum, 43, 48, 70, 77–8, 87, 90, 98, **105**, 155, 183

Deutsches Hygiene-Museum, 256, 262, **279–80**, 299, 302, 313, 318
Deutsches Rundfunk-Museum, **106**
Dialing codes, 21
Dietrich, Marlene, 27, 28, 34, 36, **37**, 48, 50, 51, 69, 96, 106, 182, 186–7, 192, 195, 208, 229, 230
Dinglinger, Johann Melchior, 250–1, 288
Disabled visitors, 60
Discos:
Berlin, **190–1**
Dresden, **315**
Potsdam, **246**
Districts:
Berlin, **72–4**, 91
Dresden, **268–9**
Potsdam, **219**
Dix, Otto, 28, 47–8, 125, 137, 139, 252, **253**, 286, 291
Döblin, Alfred, **52**, 92
Doctors, 17, 64
Documents required, 16
Doesburg, Theo van, 45
Dom, 74, 76, 81, 87, 94, **106**, 149
Donatello, 101
Dorotheenstadt, 42
Dorotheenstädtischer Friedhof, 82, 102, **106**
Dou, Gerard, 284
Drachenhaus, 218, 226, **230**, 235
Dreikönigskirche, 255, 273
Dresden, 65, 216, **248–318**
architecture, **254–6**
calendar of events, **264–5**
children in, **318**
food and drink, **308–11**
history, **250–2**
hotels, **304–7**, 308
maps, *266–7*, *271*, *275*
nightlife, **314–15**
performing arts, **311–13**
shopping, **315–16**
sports, **316–17**
tourist information, **258–63**
tram tours, **276–7**
walks, **269–75**
Dresden Academy of Art *see* Kunstakademie
Dresden City Museum *see* Stadtmuseum
Dresden-Klotzsche airport, 19, 258
Dresdener Heide, **269**, 276, 317
Driver's licenses, 16
Dröste-Hülshoff, Annette von, 17
Düppel Forst, 204
Duquesnoy, François, 101
Dürer, Albrecht, 112, 125, 228, 255, 284, 291
Duris, 95
Dutch East India Company, 77–8
Duty-free allowances, 18

Ebert, Friedrich, 33
Edel, Ulrich, 50
Egyptian Museum *see* Ägyptisches Museum
Einstein, Albert, **37**, 205, 210
Einsteinturm, 210, *210*, 236
Eiserne Brücke, 76
Eiswerder, 87
Elbe, River, 20, 77, 118, 248, 249, 259, 264, 272, 279, 296, 302, 305, 316, 317
Electric current, 22
Elisabeth Luise, Countess of Bavaria, 231, 240
Emergency information, **23**
Berlin, **64**
Dresden, **263**
Potsdam, **215**
Engels, Friedrich, 155
Englischer Garten, 151
Engravings Collection *see* Kupferstichkabinett
Ephraim, Veitel Heine, 106
Ephraimpalais, **106–7**, 138
Ermelerhaus, 77
Ernst, Duke of Saxony, 250
Ethnography, Museums of *see* Museum für Völkerkunde; Staatliches Museum für Völkerkunde
Etiquette, 22
Eurocheques, 17
Europa-Center, 102, **107**, 155, 169
Eurotunnel, 19, 54
Exhibitions, business, 63
Expressionism, 28, 47, 48, 49, 97, 104
Eyck, Jan van, 112–13

Families, staying with, 240, 305
Fashion stores, **195–6**, **315**
Fassbinder, Rainer Werner, 50
Fast food, **176–7**, **243**
Faxes, 21, 60, 63
Feininger, Lyonel, 97
Felixmüller, Conrad, 129
Ferdinand III, Kaiser, 148
Fernsehturm, 85, 87, **107**, 127, 133, 155, 202
Ferries, 20, 54, 55, 56, 213
Festivals *see* Calendar of events
Fetting, Rainer, 97
Fichte, Johann Gottlieb, **37**, 106
Filmmuseum Potsdam, 218, 222, **230–1**
Films *see* Cinema
Filmstadt Babelsberg, **48–9**
Fire services:
Berlin, 64
Dresden, 263
Potsdam, 215
Firestorms, Dresden, **248**, 257, 280
First aid, Berlin, 64
Fischerinsel, 77
Fitness facilities, **203**
Flatowturm, 235, 239
Flea markets, 82, **98**, **198–9**
Flemming, Count, 289
Folk Museum *see* Museum für Volkskunst
Folk music, **184–5**
Food and drink:
bars, **87–9**
Berlin, **168–80**
beer halls and beer gardens, **179–80**, **243**, **311**
breakfast, 163, **175–6**
cafés, **175–9**, **242–3**, **310–11**
Dresden, **308–11**
fast food, **176–7**, **243**
ice cream, **176**, **243**
Potsdam, **242–3**
shops, **199**
Football, **203**, 247, 317
Foreign exchange, 17, 20
Forests, 91
Fosse, Bob, 49
Föster, Karl, 231
Franz Ferdinand, Archduke, 33, 164
Französischer Dom, 43, 69, **107–8**, 115, 155, 202
Französischer Friedhof, 106
Frauenkirche, 249, 254, 256, 264, 268, 272, 273, **280–1**, *280*, 283, 288, 318

Frederick the Great, 14, 27, 32, **41**, 43, 44, 99, 101, 106, 121, 125, 136, 137, 145, 146, 150, 154, 205–6, 207, 208, 209, 219, 222, 224, 226, 228, 230, 233–4, 235, 236, 238, 246, 251
Freie Universität, 105
Freizeitpark, 150, 201
Freundschaftsinsel, 221, **231**
Freundschaftstempel, 234
Freybrücke, 87
Friedenskirche, 210, 224, 226, **231**
Friederike, Princess, 15, 93
Friedländer, Max, 112
Friedrich, Caspar David, 27, 109, 238, 248, **253**, 279, 286, 292
Friedrich, Prince, 124
Friedrich I, Elector, 31
Friedrich I, King (Elector Friedrich III), 31, 32, **41**, 42, 43, 115, 125, 145, 150, 233
Friedrich II, Elector, 31
Friedrich II, Kaiser, 41
Friedrich III, Elector *see* Friedrich I, King Friedrich
Karl, Prince, 118
Friedrich Wilhelm, Great Elector, 31, **41**, 42, 43, 76, 118, 125, 133, 146, 153–4, 205, 207, 231
Friedrich Wilhelm I, King, 27, 32, **41**, 43, 80, 96, 125, 154, 205, 207, 209, 232, 288, 294, 298
Friedrich Wilhelm II, King, 32, **41**, 140, 141, 151, 210, 233
Friedrich Wilhelm III, King, 32, **41**, 88, 94, 138, 140, 141, 143, 146, 171, 237
Friedrich Wilhelm IV, King, 27, 33, **41**, 100, 121, 134, 137, 160, 207, 210, 223, 224, 226, 231, 232, 234, 237, 240
Friedrichsbrücke, 76
Friedrichsfelde, 183
Friedrichshagen, **108**, 122
Friedrichshain, 72
Friedrichstadt, 42, **268**, **281**, 302
Friedrichstadt-Passagen, **108**
Friedrichswerder, 42
Friedrichswerdersche Kirche, 44, 69, **108–9**, 129, 146
Friseurmuseum, **142**
Fuller, Sam, 49
Funicular railway, 256, 260, 274, **300**, 302
Funkturm, 106, **109**, 155, 202
Fürstenzug, 249, 268, 270, **281–2**, 300

Gaertner, Eduard, 97, 109, 128, 146, 228
Galerie der Romantik, 69, 70, 91, **109–10**, 145, 253
Galleries, 90, **193–4**
Garbo, Greta, 229
Gardens *see* Parks
Garrison Church, 206, 208
Gartner, Andreas, 291
Gatow, 118
Gatower Heide, **74**
Gauguin, Paul, 104, 286
Gay, Peter, **52**
Gedenkstätte Deutscher Widerstand, **110**
Gedenkstätte Haus der Wannsee-Konferenz, **110**
Gedenkstätte Plötzensee, **111**
Gemäldegalerie, 26, 67, 69, 70, 100, 105, **111–15**
Gemäldegalerie Alte Meister, 249, 255, 256, 265, 268, 273, 277, 278, **282–5**, 290, 304, 318
Gemäldegalerie Neue Meister, 253, 278, **285–6**, 291, 298
Gendarmenmarkt, 12, 26, 67, 69, 72, 107, **115–16**, *115*, 120, 129, 192
General delivery, 19
  Berlin, 59
  Dresden, 261
  Potsdam, 214
Georg-Kolbe Museum, **116**
George IV of England, 141
Gerichtslaube, 225, 235
Gerickesteg, 75
German Folklore, Museum of *see* Museum für Deutsche Volkskunde
German History, Museum of *see* Deutsches Historisches Museum
German language, 319–22
German National Tourist Offices, 16
German Resistance Memorial *see* Gedenkstätte Deutscher Widerstand
Germany, map, *13*
Gertrauden Brücke, 77
Gestapo, 143, 152
Gilly, Friedrich, 43–4
Giorgione, 282
Gipsformerei, 199–200
"Glass woman," 280
Gleisdreieck, 78, 122
Glienicker Brücke, 88, 118, 157, 158, 205, 206, 208, 212, 225, **231**, 239
Glinka, Mikhail, 144, 150
Glockenspielpavillon, 273–4, 303
Glockenturm, 139
Glume, Friedrich Christian, 222
Godeau, Simon, 146
Goebbels, Dr Joseph, 34, **37**, 51, 141
Goes, Hugo van der, 114
Goethe, Eosander von, 145
Goethe, Johann Wolfgang von, 150, 151, 292, 297
Gontard, Karl von, 43, 107, 115, 120, 121, 230, 233, 234
Göring, Hermann, 34
Gorki, Maxim, 178
Görlitz, 264
Gotzkowsky, Johann, 14
Goya, Francisco José de, 93, 291
Goyen, Jan van, 115
Graff, Anton, 291
Greenwichpromenade, 149
Grenander, Alfred, 153
Griebnitzsee, 88
Gropius, Martin, 128
Gropius, Walter, 45, 96, 103, 128
Grosser Garten, 266, **287**, 293, 318
Grosser Müggelsee, 130
Grosses Militärwaisenhaus, 207
Grossfürstenplatz, 75, 87
Grosz, Georg, 47–8
Grotewohl, Otto, 35
Grundig, Hans, 286
Grünes Gewölbe, 249, 265, 268, 278, **287–8**, 294, 295, 298
Grunewald, 26, 27, 57, 69, 73, **74**, **83–4**, 86, 87, 104, **116–17**, 118, 126,

201, 202, 203, 204
hotels, 162
map, *83*
Grünewald, Matthias, 125, 291
Grunewaldsee, 84
Grunewaldturm, 87–8, **116**
Guided tours:
Berlin, 61–2
Dresden, 262
Potsdam, 216

Haarlem School, 119
Hagemeister, Karl, 103
Hairdressers' Museum *see* Friseurmuseum
Hamburg, 65, 259
Hamburger Bahnhof, 98, **117**, 132
Hans Walther the Younger, 296
Hansabrücke, 75
Hansaviertel, 45, 85, 97, **117**, 149
Hanseatic League, 31
Harris, Sir Arthur ("Bomber"), 252
Haus am Checkpoint Charlie, 70, 78, 90, **117–18**
Haus der Kulturen der Welt, **121**
Haus Marchwitza, 222
Havel River, 55, 56, 71, 77, **87–8**, 116, 117, **118**, 140, 148, 149, 156, 157, 159, 201, 204, 205, 213, 216, 217, 224, 231, 238
Havelkolonnaden, 222
Heartfield, John, 47, 106, 139
Hebbel-Theater, 30
Heckel, Erich, 103, 104, 137, 251
Hegel, Georg Wilhelm Friedrich, **37–8**, 106
Heinersdorf, 72
Heinrich, Prince, 155
Heinrich der Erlauchte, Margrave, 250
Helm, Brigitte, 27
Hemessen, Jan van, 114
Henselmann, Hermann, 120
Herder, Johann Gottfried von, 248, 292
Herrmann, Curt, 97
Herzog, Werner, 50
Hess, Rudolf, 35, **38**
Heymüller, Johann, 222, 229
Hildebrant, Carl, 222
Hill, George Roy, 257
Hiller-Brandtsche Häuser, 208, 236
Hindenburg, General Field Marshal von, 34
Hintze, 146
Historische Mühle, 218, 226, 235, 243
History:
Berlin, **27–8**, **31–6**
Dresden, **250–2**
Potsdam, **207–8**
Hitchcock, Alfred, 49
Hitler, Adolf, 12, 34, **38**, 45, 47, 48, 51, 102, 105, 106, 110, 144, 147, 150, 191, 239, 286
Hockey, 247
Hoffmann, Ernest Theodor Amadeus, **38**
Hoffmann, Friedrich, 106
Hofkirche, 249, 268, 270, 283, **288–9**
Hohenschönhausen, 72
Hohenzollern dynasty, 27, **41**, 133, 134, 136, 153, 206, 208
Hohenzollernplatz, 153
Holbein, Hans the Younger, 112
Holidays, public, 20, 214
Holländisches Etablissement, **233**
Holländisches Viertel, 208, 218, 222, 226, **232**
Holocaust, 110
Holy Roman Empire, 32, 33
Honecker, Erich, 36
Horse racing, **317**
Horseback riding, **203**
Hospitals, 215, 263
Hotels:
Berlin, **161–8**
conference hotels, 63, 261
Dresden, **304–7**, 308
hotel ships, 305
Potsdam, 162, **240–1**
Huelsenbeck, Richard, 47
Huguenots, 27, 31, 42, 43, 106, 107, 115, 205, 207
Humann, Carl, 139
Humboldt, Alexander von, **38**, 147, 238, 292
Humboldt, Wilhelm von, **38**, 44, 147, 155, 292
Humboldt-Universität, 75, 82, 87, 131, **155**
Hummel, Johann Erdmann, 93, 110
Hundekehlefenn nature reserve, 84
Hundekehlesee, 83
Hussites, 250

IAMAT, 17
IBA architecture, **46**, 79, 121, 149
Ice cream, **176**, **243**
Ice-hockey, 203
Ice-skating, **203**
Identity cards, 16
Ihne, Ernst von, 99, 155
Impressionism, 47, 286
Indian Art, Museum of *see* Museum für Indische Kunst
Infanteriekaserne, 207
Insel Brücke, 77
Insurance, 16–17
Internationales Congress Centrum (ICC), 63
Irving, David, 257
Isherwood, Christopher, 24, 27, **38**, 49, **52**, 116, 150
Islamic Art, Museum of *see* Museum für Islamische Kunst
Islamisches Museum, **140**
Isozaki, Arata, 79

Jacobi, Johann, 145
Jaeckel, Willy, 103
Jagdschloss Glienicke, **118**, 157, 225
Jagdschloss Grunewald, 26, 42, 70, 84, 104, 116, **119**
Jägertor, 157
Jannings, Emil, 49
Jannowitzbrücke, 77, 86
Japanisch-Deutsches Zentrum, 150–1
Japanisches Palais, 254, 255, 268, 273, 284, **289**, 294, 299
Jazz, 66, 67, **185**, 246, **315**
Jewelry stores, **197**
Jewish Quarter, 73, 74, **80–3**, 204
map, *81*
Jews, 34, 110, 111, 143
Jüdische Abteilung des Berlin Museums, **129**
Neue Synagogue, 74, 80, 81, 82, 121, **137**
Old Jewish Cemetery, 223
Prenzlauer Berg cemetery, 143
see also Jewish Quarter
Joachim II, Elector, 31, 42, 101, 116, 119, 122, 159
Johann Georg IV, Elector of Saxony, 296

Johanneum, 270, 282, **289**, 294, 296, 301
Johannstadt, **269**
Jones, Inigo, 236
Joyce, James, 52
Juan Maria de Padua, 296
Jüdische Abteilung des Berlin Museums, **129**
Jugendstil, 15, 75, 86
Jungfernbrücke, 77

KaDeWe, 17, 59, 66, 68, 69, 153, 169, 171–3, 176, 177, 192, 196, **198**, 199
Kafka, Franz, 94, 164
Kaiser-Wilhelm-Gedächtniskirche, 29, 68, 86, 102, 116, **119–20**, *119*, 125, 126
Kammergericht, **121**
Kammermusiksaal, 46, 123
Kandinsky, Wassily, 34, 45, 96, 125
Kapelle Alexander Newski, 208, 223, **232**, 237
Kapellenberg, 238
Kapp Putsch, 33
Karajan, Herbert von, **39**, 183, 184
Karl-Marx-Allee, 117, **120**
Karl-May-Museum, 267, **289–90**
Karl von Preussen, Prince, 156, 157
Kasematten, **290**
Käthe-Kollwitz-Museum, **120**
Kavalerhaus, 141
Kennedy, John F., 35, **38**
Kirche St Peter und Paul, **138**
Kirchner, Ernst Ludwig, 47, 97, 103, 104, 251
Kitchen equipment, **199**
Kladow, 88, 118
Klausberg, 230, 239
Klee, Paul, 45, 96
Klein, César, 47
Kleine Kaserne, 207
Kleines Schloss, 225, 235
Kleist, Heinrich von, **39**, 120–1, 158, 292
Kleistpark, 86, 101, **120–1**
Klengel, W.C. von, 250
Klosterhof, 156–7
Knobelsdorff, Georg Wenzeslaus von, 43, 145, 154, 209, 222, 226, 233, 236, 238
Knobelsdorff-Haus, 222
Knoblauch, Armand, 121
Knoblauch, Eduard, 121, 137
Knoblauch, Johann, 121
Knoblauchhaus, **121**, 138
Knöffel, Johann Christoph, 289
Kokoschka, Oskar, 93, **253**, 291
Kolbe, Georg, 116
Kollwitz, Käthe, **39**, **120**, 139, 143, 194
Kongresshalle, 75, 87, **121–2**, 151
Köpenick, 25, 72, **73**, 108, **122**, 124–5, 130, 149
Köpjohan Stiftung, 75
Körner Museum, 292
KPM porcelain, 14–15, **97**, 103, 124, 128, 146, 200, 245
Kranzler, Johann, 96–7
Krell, Hans, 295
Kreutzschamer, Bernhard, 286
Kreuzberg, 26, 46, 57, **72**, 74, **122–3**, 156, 204
hotels, 161
map, *79*
walks, **78–80**
Kreuzkirche, 270, 283, **290**, 313
Krone, Hermann, **253**
Kronprinzen Ufer, 75
Krüger, Andreas, 222
Krüger, Franz, 234
Krumme Lanke, 84
Kügelgen, Gerhard von, **292–3**, 309
Kultur-Forum, 46, 73, 89, 91, 94, 109, 111, **123**, 124, 125, 135, 136
Kulturpalast, 262
Kunckel, Johann, 140
Kunstakademie, 272, **291**
Kunstgewerbemuseum Schloss Köpenick, 122, 123, **124–5**
Kunstgewerbemuseum Tiergarten, 15, 91, **123–5**, 128
Künstlerhaus Bethanien, 122–3
Kupferstichkabinett, 94, 105, 123, **125**, **291**
Kurfürstendamm, 25, 68, 71, 72, 96, 104, 107, **125–6**, 149, 182
hotels, 161
shops, 191
Kurländer Palais, 272

Lang, Fritz, 28, 34, **39**, 49, 51, 208, 229
Langes Luch nature reserve, 84
Langevelt, Rutger van, 124
Langhans, Carl Gotthard, 43, 102, 127, 145, 146, 154, 233
Language, 23, 319–22
Lapidarium, 78, 122, **126**, 159
Laurana, Francesco, 148
Lavatories, 22
Laws and regulations, 22
Leather goods, **197**
Leibnitz, Gottfried Wilhelm, 31, 32, 145
Leipzig, 264
Leistikow, Walter, 84
Lenbach, Franz von, 93
Lenin, 12, 36, 269–70
Lenné, Peter, **39**, 118, 140, 143, 146, 150, 151, 156, 157, 160, 223, 224, 225, 227, 235, 237, 238
Leo, Wolf, 194
Leo, Ludwig, 85
Lessing, Gotthold Ephraim, 75, 151
Lessingbrücke, 75
Libraries, Berlin, 62
Lichtenau, Countess, 140
Lichtenberg, 72
Lichterfelde, 86, 162
Liebermann, Max, 47, 93, 157
Liebknecht, Karl, 39–40, 99, 105, 155
Lilienthal, Otto, **39**
Lindenufer, 87
Lindwerder, 88, 158
Lingner, Karl August, 279, 302
Liotard, Jean-Etienne, 285
Lipsius, Constantin, 291
Local publications, 60, 214, 261
Lohse, Adolph, 296, 301
Longuelune, Zacharias, 289
Lorre, Peter, 51
Loschwitz, 256, **269**, 274, 277, 279, 297, 300, 301, 317
Loschwitzer Brücke *see* Blaues Wunder
Lost property, 23
Berlin, 64
Dresden, 263
Potsdam, 215
Louis XIV of France, 27
Louis Philippe of France, 33
Lübars, **126**

Lubitsch, Ernst, 49, 229
Ludendorff, General, 34, 229
Luise, Princess, 15, 93
Luise, Queen, 141, 146, 151
Lustgarten, 42, 87, 154
Lustschloss, 287
Luther, Martin, 17, 31, 250
Luther Brücke, 75, 85
Lutherans, 115, 288
Luxemburg, Rosa, **39–40**, 50
Lynar, Graf Rochus von, 159

M, **51**
McEwan, Ian, **52**
Magazines, **199**, **316**
Mail services, 21
  Berlin, 59
  Dresden, 261
  Potsdam, 214
Manet, Edouard, 137
Mann, Heinrich, 51, 106
Männlich, Daniel, 138
Maps, 58
  Berlin-Museum, 96
  Dresden, 261
Marathons, 67, 203, 217
Märchenbrunnen, 156
Marcolini, Count Camillo, 281
Marcolini Palais, 281
Maria am Wasser, 293
Maria Josepha, Princess, 278, 303
Maria Regina Martyrum, 111, **127**
Marienkirche, 42, 87, 96, **127**, 136
Markets:
  Berlin, 91, **98**, **198–9**
  Potsdam, **244**
Märkisches Museum, 15, 70, 77, 85, 89, 96, 107, **127–8**, 132, 138, 149
Marmion, Simon, 113
Marmorpalais, 210, 224, 225, **233**
Marschallbrücke, 75
Marstall, 222
Martin-Gropius-Bau, 78, 90, 123, 124, **128–9**, 152
Marx, Karl, 30, 105, 155
Marzahn, 72
Mathematisch-Physikalischer Salon, 255, 265, 268, **291**, 304, 318
Matthäuskirche, 281
Maxim Gorki Theater, 155
Maximilian, Elector of Bavaria, 148
May, Karl, **290**, 314
Medical emergencies:
  Berlin, 64
  Dresden, 263
  Potsdam, 215
Medical insurance, **16–17**
Mehringplatz, 80
Meierei, 141
Meissen, 14, 20, 249, 259, 264, 293, 302
Meissen porcelain, **14**, 32, 192, 251, 282, 289, 293–4, 316
Memling, Hans, 113
Memorials in Berlin, listed, 90
Mendelsohn, Erich, 186, 210
Menzel, Adolph, 128, 137, 234
Messegelände, 63, 155, 163
Metropolis, **51**, 208, 229, 230
Metsys, Quinten, 114
Mexicoplatz, 86
Middlebrook, Martin, **52**, 160
Mies van der Rohe, Ludwig, 45, *46*, 137, 239
Miller, Wolfgang, 103
Miniature railways, 293, 300–1, 318
Minnelli, Liza, 49
Mitlijanskij, Daniel, 118
Mitte, **72**, **129**, 161
Moabiter Brücke, 75
Modern Movement, 45
Moholy-Nagy, Laszlo, 96
Moltke, Count Helmuth von, 33, 75, 151
Moltke Brücke, 75
Monbijou Brücke, 76
Monet, Claude, 137, 286
Money, 17
Moorlake, 88, 157
Moritz, Elector, 250, **254**, 294, 295, 298, 300
Morris, William, 45
Moschee, 208, 226, **232**, *232*
Mountaineering, **317**
Movies *see* Cinema
Mozart, W.A., 206, 292
Mueller, Otto, 103
Müggelberge, **74**
Müggelsee, 71, 108, 122, **130**
Müggelturm, 130
Mühlendamm-Schleuse, **77**
Munch, Edvard, 47, 104, 128
Münzgasse, 12
Münzsammlung, 288
Murnau, F.W., 51
Museum Berliner Arbeiterleben um 1900, **142**
Museum für Deutsche Volkskunde, 105, **130**
Museum zur Dresdner Frühromantik, 266, 268, 273, **292–3**
Museum für Indische Kunst, **130–1**
Museum für Islamische Kunst, **131**
Museum für Naturkunde, **131**, 201
Museum für Ostasiatische Kunst, **131**
Museum für Verkehr und Technik, 67, 117, 128, **131–3**, 201
Museum für Völkerkunde, 105, **133**
Museum für Volkskunde, **140**
Museum für Volkskunst, 268, 277, **292**
Museum für Vor- und Frühgeschichte, 91, 101, **133–4**, 145, 201
Museums:
  for children, **201**, 318
  in Berlin, listed, 90
  opening hours, 21, 90, 277
  see also individual museums
Museumsdorf Düppel, **134**
Museumsinsel, 70, 72, 74, 76, 80–1, 83, 85, 87, 89, 91, 93, 94, 99, 104, 105, 129, **134–5**, *135*, 136, 137, 148, 149
Music:
  classical, **183–4**, **246**, **312–13**
  compact disk and record stores, **198**, **245**
  Country and Western, **314**
  discos, **190–1**, **246**, **315**
  festivals, 66
  folk, **184–5**
  jazz, 66, 67, **185**, 246, **315**
  opera and ballet, **185**, **313**
  rock, **246**
Musikinstrumenten-Museum, 91, 123, **136**

Nagel, Otto, 94, 139
Napoleon I, Emperor, 32, 44, 99, 102, 207, 251, 281

Napoleon III, Emperor, 33
National identity cards, 16
Nationalgalerie, *135*, **136**, 137, 139
see also Alte Nationalgalerie; Neue Nationalgalerie
Natural Science, Museum of *see* Museum für Naturkunde
Naturdenkmal "Alte Potsdamer Strasse," **136**
Nauener Tor, 222, 226
Nauener Vorstadt, 219, 222, 226
Naumann, Johann Christoph, 281
Naumann, Walther, 301
Nazis, 26, 28, **34–5**, 45, 47, 48, 49, 51, 70, 73, 80, 92, 93, 94, 104, 105, 110, 111, 127, 128, 137, 139, 141, 143, 149, 152, 154, 186, 202, 206, 208, 229, 236, 252, 299
Nebuchadnezzar, King, 140
Nefertiti, 67, **92**, 137, 192, 200
Negri, Pola, 49, 182, 186, 229
Neighborhoods, Berlin, **73–4**
Neoclassical architecture, **43–4**
Neptunsbrunnen (Neptune Fountain), **136**, 146
Nering, Johann Arnold, 42, 43, 105, 124, 145, 222
Neue Kammern, **232–3**
Neue Nationalgalerie, 45, *46*, 48, 70, 89, 91, 123, **136–7**
Neue Sachlichkeit, 47–8
Neue Secession, 47
Neue Synagogue, 74, 80, 81, 82, 121, **137**
Neue Wache, 44, 87, **155**
Die Neue Wilden, 48
Neuer Friedhof, **227**
Neuer Garten, 210, 218, 219, 224, 225, **233**
Neues Museum, 76, 80, 95, 100, 125, 134, 135, *135*, **137**
Neues Palais, 207, 217, 224, 226, **233–4**, 246
Neukölln, 72
Neumann, Balthasar, 17
Neustadt (Dresden), **269**, 272, 308
Neustadt (Potsdam), 219, 221
Neustädter Markt, 272
New German Cinema, 50
Newspapers, **199**, **316**
Nexö, M.A., 275
Nicholas I, Czar, 121, 138, 171, 234, 237
Nicolai, Friedrich, **40**
Nicolai, Otto, **40**
Nightlife:
Berlin, **181**, **187–91**
Dresden, **314–15**
Potsdam, **245–7**
Nikolaikirche (Berlin), 42, 96, **138**
Nikolaikirche (Potsdam), 44, 221, 225, **234**
Nikolaiviertel, 68, **73**, 76, 85, 106, 121, 129, **138**
Nikolskoe, 88, **138**, 157, 237
Nolde, Emil, 47, 286
Nosferatu, **51**
Nosseni, Giovanni Maria, 300
Novembergruppe, 47
Nudist sunbathing, 22
Nuremberg Trials, 35
Nymphenbad, 265, 268, 274, 304

Observatory, Archenhold-Sternwarte, **95**, 201
Oder, River, 77
Odol, 279, 299, 302
Oesteld, Carl, 96
Offenbach, Jacques, 38
Old Jewish Cemetery, 223
Old Town (Potsdam), 219
Olympia, **51**
Olympia-Stadion, **139**
Opening hours:
banks, 20, 59, 261
museums, 21, 90, 277
shops, 20, 261
Opera, **185**, 297, **313**
Operation "Thunderclap," **252**, 256
Orangerie, 67, 210, 217, 224, 225, 226, **234–5**, 239
Oriental Art, Museum of *see* Museum für Ostasiatische Kunst
Otto III, Kaiser, 207
Otto-Nagel-Haus, 77, **139**
Owens, Jesse, 34, 202

Palaces in Berlin, listed, 90
Palais des Prinzen Heinrich, 43, 155
Palais Unter den Linden, 154
Palast der Republik, 76, 99, 155
Parkeisenbahn, **293**
Parks and gardens:
allotments, **92–3**
Berlin, **74**, 91
Botanischer Garten, 86, **101**, 226
Britzer Garten, 103
for children, **201**, 318
Englischer Garten, 151
Freizeitpark, 150, 201
Freundschaftsinsel, 221, 231
Grosser Garten, 266, **287**, 293, 318
Jagdschloss Glienicke, 118, 157
Kleistpark, 86, 101, **120–1**
Neuer Garten, 210, 218, 219, 224, 225, **233**
Park Babelsberg, 88, 219, 225, **235**, 239
Park Sanssouci, 219, **223–4**, 228, 233, **235**, 236, 238, 239
Schloss Albrechtsberg, 296, 301
Tiergarten, 26, 57, 65, 67, 69, 72, **73**, **74**, 86, **150–1**, 201, 202, 203
Tierpark Friedrichsfelde, 151
Treptower Park, **152**
Viktoriapark, 80, 122, **155–6**, 176, 201
Volkspark Friedrichshain, **156**
Volkspark Klein-Glienicke, 44, 88, **156–7**
Zwinger, 304
Passports, 16, 23
Pechstein, Max, 47, 286
Performing arts:
Berlin, **181–7**
Dresden, **311–13**
Potsdam, **245–7**
Pergamon-Museum, 26, 68, 76, 82, 85, 89, 91, 95, 130, 131, 133, 135, *135*, **139–40**, 153
Permoser, Balthasar, 255, 304
Persius, Ludwig, 157, 223, 231, 232, 234, 238
Pfaueninsel, 29, 88, 118, **140–1**, *141*, 146, 157, 158, 212, 225
Pfingstberg, 219, 223, 238

Pharmacies:
Berlin, 64
Dresden, 263
Potsdam, 215, 244–5
Philharmonie, 46, 123, 136, 181, **184**
Picasso, Pablo, 94
Pillnitz, **293**, 317
Piscator, Erwin, 186
Planetariums:
Archenhold-Sternwarte, **95**, 201
Planetarium am Insulaner, **141–2**, 201
Zeiss-Grossplanetarium, **158**, 201
Plaster casts, **199–200**
Playgrounds, 318
Poland, 65, 216, 264
Police, 23
Berlin, 64
Dresden, 263
Potsdam, 215
Pommer, Erich, 229
Pommern-Stettin, Duke of, 124
Pomonatempel, 223
Pöppelmann, Matthäus Daniel, 255, 273, 281, 289, 293, 296, 303
Porcelain, **14–15**, 255
Meissen, **14**, 32, 192, 251, 282, 289, 293–4, 316
Porzellansammlung, **293–4**
stores, **200**, **245**, **316**
Porzellansammlung, 15, 255, 265, 268, 277, 289, **293–4**, 304
Post offices, 21
Berlin, 59
Dresden, 261
Potsdam, 214
Postcards, **200**
Postcodes, 21, 59
Poste restante *see* General delivery
Posters, **200**
Postmuseum, **142**
Potsdam, 65, 118, **205–47**
architecture, 70, **208–10**
bus tour, **225–6**
calendar of events, **216–17**
food and drink, **242–3**
history, **207–8**
hotels, 162, **240–1**
maps, *220–21, 223*
nightlife, **245–7**
orientation, **216**
shopping, **244–5**
sports, **247**
tourist information, **211–17**
walks, **220–5**
Potsdam Agreement (1945), 35, 206, 208, 237, 239
Potsdam Hills, 219
Potsdam lakes, **224–5**
Potsdam Museum, **235–6**
Potsdam University, 226
Potsdamer Platz, 30, 46, 136, **142**
Poussin, Nicolas, 285
Powers, Gary, 231
Prague, 264
Praunheim, Rosa von, 50
Prehistory and Early History, Museum of *see* Museum für Vor- und Frühgeschichte
Prenzlauer Berg, 57, **72–3**, **142–3**, 153
Prince Albrecht Palace, 143
Prinz-Albrecht-Gelände, 78, 128, 137, **143**, 151–2
Prinzessinnenpalais, 154
Prohaska, Eleonore, 227
Prussia, history, **32–3**
Prussian Cultural Foundation, 89
Public holidays, 20, 214
Public lavatories, 22
Publications, local, 60, 214, 261
Pückler-Muskau, Hermann Fürst, 235
Puppet theaters, 318

Quellien, Artus the Elder, 127

Rahnsdorf, 122
Rail services, 19
Berlin, 54, **84–6**
cable, 260, **297**, 302
Dresden, 258, 259
funicular, 256, 260, 274, **300**, 302
miniature, 293, 300–1, 318
Potsdam, 211
Raphael, 112, 285
Rathaus (Dresden), 276
Rathaus Schöneberg, 30
Rathausbrücke, 76
Rathausturm, 301
Rathenau, Walther, 33, 128
Ratswaage, 222
Rauch, Christian, 93, 146
Reed, Carol, 49
Reformation, 31
Reichstag, 30, 70, 74, **75**, 85, 87, **143–4**, 147
Reinhardt, Max, **40**, 186
Reinickendorf, 72
Rembrandt, 115, 125, 284
Renting:
bicycles, 57, 247, 316
cars, 57, 216, 260
Repnin, Prince, 279
Residenzschloss, 249, 264, 270, 273, 277, 278, 287, **294**, 295, 296
Rest rooms, 22
Restaurants:
Berlin, **168–75**
children in, 201–2
Dresden, **308–10**
Potsdam, **242**
tipping, 22, 170
Reuter, Ernst, 35
Richter, Adrian Ludwig, **253**, 291
Riding, **203**
Riefenstahl, Leni, 51, 139
Riehmer, Wilhelm, 80, 167
Riehmers Hofgarten, 80, 167
Riemeisterfenn, 84
Riemenschneider, Tilman, 100, 148
Rieselfelder, 149
Rinderstall, 141
Rizzo, Antonio, 101
Rock concerts, **246**
Rococo architecture, 43, **209–10**
Rodin, Auguste, 93
Roller-skating, **203**
Romantic Movement, 248, **255–6**, 272, 286, **292–3**
Romantic Painting, Gallery of *see* Galerie der Romantik
Römische Bäder, 208, 210, 224, **236**
Rossellini, Roberto, 49
Rossi, Aldo, 144
Rostock, 65
Rotardi, Pietro Graf, 285
Rote Rathaus, 30
Rowboats, 202, **203**, **247**
Royal Air Force, 248, 252
Rubens, Peter Paul, 100, 114, 115, 125, 284
Ruinenberg, 218, 219, 224, 226, 232, **236**, 238
Ruisdael, Jacob van, 115
Runge, Philipp Otto, 285
Running, **203**, **317**

Russisch-Orthodoxe Kirche (Dresden), **295**
Russische Kolonie Alexandrowka, 222–3, **237**
Russischer Orthodoxe Friedhof, **144**, 150
Rüstkammer, 256, 277, 294, **295**, 304, 318
Ruttmann, Walter, 50

S-Bahn, 29, 55, **84–6**, 212
Safety, 68
Sailing, 203
St Annen, 104
St Hedwigs-Kathedrale, 43, **154**
St Matthäi-Kirche, 123
St Nikolai-Kirche, 148
Sammlung Ludwig, **94**
Sanssouci *see* Schloss Sanssouci
Savignyplatz, **73**, 86
Schadow, Johann Gottfried, 15, 93, 102, 106, 109, 128
Schadow, Rudolf, 109
Scharoun, Hans, 46, 123, 184
Schauspielhaus, 44, 107, **115–16**, *115*
Scheib, Hans, 129
Scheunenviertel, **73–4**, **80–3**
Schiller, J.C.F. von, 251, 273, 292, 297
Schinkel, Karl Friedrich, 38, **40**, **44**, 45, 69, 70, 77, 87, 88, 94, 97, 106, 107, 108, 109, 111, 115, 120, 128, 129, 134, 141, 143, 144, 146, 147, 154, 155, 156, 157, 210, 223, 231, 232, 234, 236, 237, 255, 296
Schinkel-Pavillon, 44, 109, **146**
Schinkelmuseum, 69, **109**
Schlachtensee, 84, 86
Schlemmer, Oskar, 96
Schleusenbrücke, 77
Schliemann, Heinrich, 101, 134
Schlöndorff, Volker, 230
Schloss Albrechtsberg, 266–7, 274, 276, **295–6**, 301, 313
Schloss Babelsberg, 44, 157, 208, 210, 212, 225, 235, **237**, 239
Schloss Bellevue, 43, 75, 86, 150
Schloss Britz, 103
Schloss Brücke, 77, 154
Schloss Cecilienhof, 210, 218, 223, 224, 225, 233, **237**
Schloss Charlottenburg, 14, 15, 26, 27, 42–3, *42*, 44, 67, 69, 72, 87, 89, 91, 95, 99, 104, 109, 134, 135, 136, 141, **144–6**, 149, 183, 192, 203
Schloss Charlottenhof, 44, 70, 210, 217, 218, 224, **237–8**
Schloss Eckberg, 296, 307
Schloss Friedrichsfelde, **147**, 151
Schloss Klein-Glienicke, 118, 138, **156–7**, 158, 212, 225, 235, 239
Schloss Köpenick, **124–5**
Schloss Lindstedt, 210, 234
Schloss Moritzburg, 255, 318
Schloss Pillnitz, 249, 254, 255, 267, 277, 293, **296**, 300, 301, 302, 313
Schloss Sanssouci, 43, 146, 183, 205, 206–7, 208, 209, *209*, 211, 216, 217, 218, 219, **223–4**, 233, 234, 235, **238**
Schloss Tegel, 44, **147**
Schlüter, Andreas, 32, 43, 76, 99, 100, 105, 138, 145, 155
Schmettau, Joachim, 102
Schmidt-Rottluff, Karl, 103, 104, 251, 286
Schmuz-Baudiss, Theodor Hermann, 15
Schöne Pforte, 295, **296**
Schöneberg, 72
Schoppe, Julius, 228
Schumann, Clara, **253**, 302
Schumann, Robert, **253**, 302
Schwanenwerder, **158**
Schwebebahn, **297**, 301, 318
Schwechten, Franz, 97
Science museums in Berlin, listed, 91
Sea travel, 20, 54
Secundo Genitur, 272, 310
Seeber, Guido, 229
Semper, Gottfried, 251, 255–6, 278, 279, 282, 297, 303
Semper, Manfred, 297
Semperbau, 282, 303
Semperoper, 256, 273, **297**, *297*, 313
Seyfried, Gerhard, 194
Shoe shops, **197**
Shopping:
  Berlin, 91, **191–200**
  Dresden, **315–16**
  opening hours, 20, 59, 214, 261
  Potsdam, **244–5**
Siegessäule, 85, 86, **147**, *147*, 155, 202
Siemens, Werner von, **40**
Sineck, Major, 96
Sint Jans, Geertgen tot, **114**
Skarbina, Franz, 93
Skating, **203**
Skiing, **203**, **317**
Skladanowsky, Max, 48
Skulpturengalerie, 70, 100, 105, **148**
Skulpturensammlung, 278, **297–8**
Slaughterhouse-five, 257
Soccer, **203**, 247, **317**
Social Democratic Party (SPD), 33
Solly, Edward, 111
Sophie Charlotte, Queen, 31, 42, 104, 145
Sophienkirche, 81
Souvenirs, 192, **316**
Sowjetisches Ehrenmal, 151, 152
Spandau, 28, 72, **73**, 87, 118, 129, **148–9**, 158, 159
Spandauer Forst, 204
Spar, Otto von, 127
Spartacus revolt, 33, 39–40, 82, 99
Spectrum exhibition, 133
Speer, Albert, 35, **40**, 45, 75, 126
Sperlingsgasse, 68
Sports:
  Berlin, **202–4**
  Dresden, **316–17**
  Potsdam, **247**
Sports equipment stores, **245**
Spree, River, 65, 69, 71, **74–8**, 87, 108, 122, 148, **149**, 159, 204
  map, *76–7*
Spreeinsel, 149
Spreetunnel, 108
Springer, Axel, 78
Squash, **204**

Staatliche Museen
  Preussischer Kulturbesitz, 89, 90, 91, **199–200**
Staatliche
  Porzellan-Manufaktur, 15
Staatliches Museum für
  Mineralogie und Geologie, **298**
Staatliches Museum für
  Tierkunde, **298**, 304, 318
Staatliches Museum für
  Völkerkunde, **298–9**
Staatsbibliothek, 46, 123
Staatsoper, 43, 87, **154**, **185**
Staatsrat, 99, 155
Stadtmuseum, **299–300**
Stadtschloss, 43
Stalin, Joseph, 12, 30, 120, 208, 224, 237, 239, 241
Stallhof, 270, 281, 294, **300**
Standseilbahn, 274, **300**
Starcke, Johann Georg, 287
Stasi secret police, 276
Stationery stores, **199**
Stations:
  Berlin, 56–7
  Dresden, 258
  Potsdam, 212
Stauffenberg, Colonel von, 34, 52, 110, 111
Steen, Jan, 284
Steglitz, 72, 86
Stemmle, Robert, 49
Sternberg, Josef von, 51, 208, 229
Stockhausen, Baron von, 301
Stoker, Bram, 51
Strade, Heinrich, 147
Strandbad Babelsberg, 225
Strandbad Müggelsee, 204
Strandbad Tegel, 150
Strandbad Wannsee, **158**, 204
Strauss, Richard, 297, 313
Street name changes:
  Berlin, 58
  Dresden, 260–1
  Potsdam, 214
Street numbers, Berlin, 71–2
Streetlamps, **149**
Stubbins, Hugh, 121
Stüler, Friedrich August, 92, 123, 134, 137, 138, 145
Subway, 55, **152–3**
Sunbathing, nudist, 22
SV-Bahn, 259

Swimming:
  Berlin, **201**, 203, **204**
  Dresden, **317**
  Potsdam, **247**
Synagogue, Neue, 80, 81, 82, **137**
Die Szene, **187**

Taschenberg Palais, 255, **300**, 305
Taut, Bruno, 84
Taxis, 22
  Berlin, 57
  Dresden, 260
  Potsdam, 213
Teahouse, Chinese *see* Chinesisches Teehaus
Tegel, 28, **73**, 87, 118, **149–50**, 201, 202, 204
  hotels, 162
Tegeler Forst, 204
Tegeler See, 27, 87
Telegrams, 21, 61
Telegraphenberg, 219, 239
Telephones, 21
  Berlin, 59–60, 61
  Potsdam, 215
Television Tower *see* Fernsehturm
Teltower Vorstadt, 219
Teltowkanal, 71
Tempelhof, 72
Tempelhofer Feld, 27
Tennis, 203, **204**
Terraces, café, **176**
Teschen, Duchess of, 281
Teufelsberg, **116**, 203
Teufelsbrücke, 157
Teufelsee, 130
Theater:
  Berlin, **186–7**
  Dresden, **314**
  Potsdam, **246–7**
Theater des Westens, 85, 187
Theiss, Caspar, 119
Thiele, 283
Tickets:
  entertainments, 181, 245, 311
  museums, 91, 277
  public transport, 56, 211, 213, 260
Tieck, Christian, 109
Tiede, August, 131
Tiergarten, 26, 57, 65, 67, 69, 72, **73**, **74**, 86, **150–1**, 201, 202, 203
Tierpark Friedrichsfelde, 89, 147, **151**, 201
Time zones, 18

Tipping, 22, 170
Titian, 285
Tobacco, duty-free allowances, 18
Tobogganing, **203**, **317**
Topographie des Terrors, 78, 143, **151–2**
Toulouse-Lautrec, Henri de, 286
Tourist information, **16–23**
  Berlin, **53–64**
  Dresden, **258–63**
  Potsdam, **211–17**
Tourist offices:
  Berlin, 61
  Dresden, 258, 262
  Potsdam, 214
  Worldwide, 16
Toy stores, **200**, **245**
Traditionsbahn Radebeul, **300–1**, 318
Trains *see* Rail services
Trams:
  Berlin, 22, 55
  Dresden, 259, 260, **276–7**
  Potsdam, 212–13
Tränenpalast, 50, 82, **152**
Transport and Technology, Museum of *see* Museum für Verkehr und Technik
Travel:
  air, 19, 53, 62, 258
  bicycles, 57, **202**, **247**
  boat trips, 20, 61, **87–8**, 118, 130, 157–8, 212, 259, 216, 262, **302**
  buses, 55, 61–2, **86–7**, 201, 212–13, 225–6, 259, 260
  cable railway, **297**, 302
  cars, 22, 57, 211, 258
  coaches, 20, 54
  ferries, 20, 54, 55, 56, 213
  funicular railway, 256, 260, 274, **300**, 302
  insurance, 16
  Parkeisenbahn, **293**
  Potsdam, 211–13
  rail services, 19, 54, 211, 258, 259
  S-Bahn, 29, 55, **84–6**, 212
  taxis, 22, 57, 213, 260
  tickets, 56
  Traditionsbahn Radebeul, **300–1**, 318
  trams, 22, 55, 212–13, 259, 260, **276–7**
  U-Bahn, 55, **152–3**
Travelers checks, 17
  lost, 17, 23, 64
Treptow, 72, 87

Treptower Park, **152**
Treu, Georg, 298
Treuhandanstalt, 78, 229
Trotta, Margarethe von, 50
Trotting races, 203
Truman, Harry S., 208, 224, 237, 239, 241

U-Bahn, 55, **152–3**
Ulbricht, Walter, 35, 155
Underground railway, 55, **152–3**
Unger, Christian, 43
Universal Film AG (UFA), 33, 49, 207, 229
Unter den Linden, 25, 26, 30, 42, 43, 65, 67, 68, 69, 70, 71, 72, 77, 87, **153–5**, 192
Ury, Lesser, 47, 84, 93–4, 97, 129
Utz, 257

Value-Added Tax (VAT), 18
Van Eyck, Jan, 255, 284
Van Gogh, Vincent, 47, 104, 129
Vassiltchikov, Marie, **52**
Vehicle registration certificates, 16
Velde, Esaias van de, 115
Velde, Henry van der, 45, 103
Verkehrsmuseum, 289, **301**
Vermeer, Jan, 114, 284
Viewpoints, listed:
  in Berlin, **155**, **202**
  in Dresden, **301**
  in Potsdam, **238–9**
Viktoria-Versicherung, 79
Viktoriapark, 80, 122, **155–6**, 176, 201
Villa Bärenfett, 290
Villa Gitta, 275
Villa Herpich, 239
Villa Kamecke, 43, 100
Villa Müller-Grote, 239
Villa San Remo, 274
Villa Shatterhand, **290**
Villa Stockhausen, 296, **301–2**
Villa Urbig, 239
Villenviertel Neubabelsberg, **239**
Vineyards, 249
Voigt, Kaspar, 278
Volkspark Friedrichshain, **156**
Volkspark Klein-Glienicke, 44, 88, **156–7**
Voltaire, 41, 205, 206, 207
Vonnegut, Kurt, Jr., **253–4**, 257
Vorderasiatisches Museum, **140**
Vostell, Wolf, 129, 164

Wagener, Joachim, 93
Wagner, Richard, 93, 251, **254**, 256, 281, 292, 313
Waldbühne, **139**
Walks:
  Berlin, 57–8, **74–84**, **154–5**, **157**, **204**
  Dresden, **269–75**, **317**
  in Potsdam, **220–5**, **247**
Wallot, Paul, 143
Wallpavillon, 274, 304
Walther, Wilhelm, 281, 282
Wannsee, 26, 29, 55, 86, 87, 88, 110, 118, 130, **157–8**, 201, 202
Wannsee Conference, **110**
Watteau, Jean-Antoine, 14, 27, 146, 238, 285
Weather, 18–19
Weber, Carl Maria von, 251, **254**, 278, 281 293
Wedding, 72, **73**, 94
Wegeley, Wilhelm Caspar, 14
Weidendammer Brücke, 76
Weigel, Helene, **40**, 102, 106, 171
Weill, Kurt, 27, **40**
Weimar Republic, 15, 28, **33–4**, 48, 49, 50, 52, 92
Weinberg, 226
Weinbergkirche, 293
Weisse Flotte Dresden, 216, 262, 272, 293, **302**, 318
Weissensee, 72
Weisser Hirsch, 249, 256, 259, 267, 268, **269**, 275, 276, 277, 297, 300, **302**
Wellington, Duke of, 15
Weltkugelbrunnen, 102
Die Wende (the turning point), 11, 12, 36, 205, 207, 270, 299
Wenders, Wim, **40**, 51
Werkbund-Archiv, **129**
Wettins, 250, **254**, 270, 281–2, 288, 294, 295
Weyden, Roger van der, 113
Wieck, Friedrich, 302
Wiene, Robert, 51
Wilder, Billy, 34, 36, 49, 51, 229–30
Wilhelm, Crown Prince, 208
Wilhelm I, Kaiser, 33, **41**, 116, 119, 146, 154, 210, 237
Wilhelm II, Kaiser, 30, 33, **41**, 99, 106, 119, 123, 126, 140, 206, 207–8, 210, 226
Wilhelmine architecture, **44–5**
Wilmersdorf, 72, **73**
Wine cellars, **309**
Winterfeldtplarz, **74**
Winzerhaus, 226
Wisniewski, Edgar, 136
Wittenberg, 20, 31, 259
Woermann, Karl, 286
Women's organizations, 60
Words and phrases, 319–22
  emergencies, 23
World War I, 33, 47, 48, 120, 159, 206, 207–8, 227
World War II, 28, 34, 42, 45, 89, 93, 99, 111, 126, 142, 148, 152, 160, 206, 208, 248–9, 299

Yenidze Tabakskontor, 273, 276, 281, **302–3**, 305
York, Michael, 49

Zehlendorf, 28, 72, 86
Zeiss-Grossplanetarium, **158**, 201
Zeughaus, 43, 87, 105, 179
Zhukhov, Marshal, 34
Zille, Heinrich, **158–9**, 198
Zille-Museum, 90, 98, **158–9**
Zitadelle Spandau, 129, 148, **159**, 201
Zoology, Museum of *see* Staatliches Museum für Tierkunde
Zoos:
  Dresden, 287, 318
  in Berlin, listed, 91
  Tierpark Friedrichsfelde, 89, **151**
  Zoologischer Garten, 69, 73, 85, 86, 89, 95, 141, 150, **159–60**, 201
Zuckmayer, Carl, 122
Zwinger, 47, 249, 254, 255, 255, 256, 264, 265, 268, 274, 276, 282, 283, 284, 289, 291, 293, 295, 298, 301, **303–4**, 313, 318

List of street names

- Listed below are all streets mentioned in the text that fall within the areas covered by our color maps of Berlin (maps **1** to **4**) and Dresden (maps **8** and **9**).
- Map numbers are printed in **bold** type. Some smaller streets are not named on the maps, but the map reference given below will help you locate the correct neighborhood.

BERLIN

Adenauerplatz, **1**D3
Ahornstr., **2**D5
Alexanderplatz, **4**B9
Almstadtstr., **4**B9
Altonaer Str., **2**C5
Alt-Lietzow, **1**B3
Am Berlin Museum, **4**D8
Am Köllnischen Park, **4**C9
Am Kupfergraben, **4**B8
Am Rathaus, **2**F5
Am Weidendamm, **4**B8
An der Spandauer Brücke, **4**B9
Askanischer Platz, **3**D7
Augsburgerstr., **2**D4–5
Auguststr., **4**B8–A9

Bebelplatz, **4**C8
Behrenstr., **3**C7–**4**C8
Bellevue Ufer, **3**B5
Bergmannstr., **4**E8–9
Bernburger Str., **3**C7–D7
Bertolt-Brecht-Platz, **4**B8
Bismarckstr., **1**C2–3
Bleibtreustr., **1**D3
Blücherplatz, **4**E8
Bodestr., **4**B8–9
Brandenburgische Str., **1**D3–E3
Breitscheidplatz, **2**D4
Budapester Str., **2**D5
Burgstr., **4**B9

Carmerstr., **2**C4
Chamissoplatz, **4**E8
Chausseestr., **3**A7–**4**A8
Clara-Zetkin-Str., **3**B7–**4**B8

Damaschkestr., **1**D2
Dudenstr., **3**F7

Eiserne Brücke, **4**B8
Eislebener Str., **2**D4
Eosanderstr., **1**B2–3
Ernst-Reuter-Platz, **2**C4

Fasanenstr., **2**C4–D4
Französischer Str., **4**C8
Franz-Klühs-Str., **4**D8
Friedrichs Brücke, **4**B9
Friedrichstr., **4**B8–D8

Gendarmenmarkt, **4**C8
Georgenstr., **4**B8
Gertrauden Brücke, **4**C9
Gleisdreieck, **3**D7
Gloria-Passage, **2**D4
Gneisenaustr., **4**E8–9
Goltzstr., **3**E6
Grolmanstr., **1**C3–**2**D4
Grossbeerenstr., **3**E7–D8
Grosse Hamburger Str., **4**A8–B8
Grossfürstenplatz, **3**C6
Grossgörschenstr., **3**E6
Grosser Stern, **2**C5

Hagelbergerstr., **3**E7
Hallesches Ufer, **3**D7–**4**D8
Hansabrücke, **2**B5
Hansaplatz, **2**B5
Hardenbergplatz, **2**D4
Hardenbergstr., **2**C4–D4
Hasenheide, **4**E9–F10
Hauptstr., **3**E6–F6
Hausvogteiplatz, **4**C8
Haydnstr., **2**B5
Henriettenplatz, **1**E2
Heubnerweg, **1**B2
Hirtenstr., **4**B9
Hohenzollerndamm, **1**F2–**2**E4
Hohenzollernplatz, **2**E4
Holsteiner Ufer, **2**B5
Holtzendorffplatz, **1**D2
Holzhauser Str., **6**B4
Hütten Weg, **5**E3

In den Zelten, **3**B6
Insel Brücke, **4**C9
Invalidenstr., **3**B6–A7

Jannowitzbrücke, **4**C10
Jägerstr., **4**C8
Joachimstalerstr., **2**D4
Jungfernbrücke, **4**C9
John-Foster-Dulles-Allee, **3**C6–B7

Kantstr., **1**D3–**2**D4
Kaiserdamm, **1**C1–2
Kaiser-Friedrichstr., **1**B2–D2
Karl-Liebknecht-Str., **4**B9
Karl-Marx-Allee, **4**B10
Kemperplatz, **3**C7
Klausener Platz, **1**B2
Kleine Alexanderstr., **4**B9
Klingelhöferstr., **3**D6
Klopstockstr., **2**C5
Knesebeckstr., **2**C4–D4
Kochstr., **4**D8
Koenigs Allee, **5**D3
Körnerstr., **3**D6
Kuno-Fischer-Str., **1**D2

Krausnickstr., **4**B8
Kreuzbergstr., **3**E7–8
Kronprinzendamm, **1**D1
Kronprinzen Ufer, **3**B7
Kupfergraben, **4**B8
Kurfürstendamm, **1**E1–**2**D4
Kurfürstenstr., **2**D5–**3**D6

Lehniner Platz, **1**D2
Leibnitzstr., **1**C3–D3
Leipziger Platz, **3**C7
Leipzigerstr., **3**C7–**4**C8
Lessingbrücke, **2**B5
Lietzenburgerstr., **1**D3–**2**D5
Lietzensee Ufer, **1**C2
Lindenstr., **4**D8–C9
Linkstr., **3**C7–D7
Los-Angeles-Platz, **2**D4
Ludwigkirchstr., **2**D4
Luftbrücke, Platz der, **4**F8
Luisenplatz, **1**B2
Lustgarten, **4**C8
Luther Brücke, **2**B5
Lützowplatz, **2**D5–**3**D6
Lützowufer, **2**D5–**3**D6

Mansteinstr., **3**E6
Marburgerstr., **2**D4–5
Märkisches Ufer, **4**C9
Marschallbrücke, **3**B7
Matthäikirchstr., **3**C6
Mauerstr., **3**C7–**4**C8
Mehringdamm, **4**E8–F8
Mehringplatz, **4**D8
Meinekestr., **2**D4
Methfesselstr., **3**F7
Moabiter Brücke, **2**B6
Möckernbrücke, **3**D7
Mohrenstr., **4**C8
Moltke Brücke, **3**B7
Monbijou Brücke, **4**B8
Monbijoustr., **4**B8
Münzstr., **4**B9

Nassauische Str., **2**E4–F4

Neue Schönhauser Str., **4**B9
Nikolaikirchplatz, **4**C9
Nollendorfplatz, **2**D6
Nürnbergerstr., **2**D5

Oberwasserstr., **4**C9
Oranienburger Str., **4**B8
Oranienplatz, **4**D9
Oranienstr., **4**D8–10

Pariser Platz, **3**C7
Pariser Str., **1**D3
Pestalozzistr., **1**C2–3
Pohlstr., **3**D6–7
Poststr., **4**C9
Potsdamer Platz, **3**C7
Potsdamer Str., **3**E6–D6

Rathausbrücke, **4**C9
Rathausstr., **4**B9
Rathenauplatz, **1**E1
Regensburgerstr., **2**E4–5
Reichpietschufer, **3**D7
Reichstagufer, **3**B7–**4**B8
Republik, Platz der, **3**B7
Richard-Wagner-Platz, **1**C3
Rolandufer, **4**C9
Rosenthaler Str., **4**A9–B9

Sächsische Str., **1**D3–E3
Savignyplatz, **2**D4
Savigny-Passage, **2**D4
Schaperstr., **2**D4
Schiffbauerdamm, **3**B7–**4**B8
Schillstr., **2**C5
Schleswiger Ufer, **2**B5
Schleusenbrücke, **4**C9
Schlossbrücke, **1**B2
Schlossbrücke, **4**B9
Schloss-Str., **1**B2–C2
Schlüterstr., **1**C3–E3
Schönebergerstr., **3**D7
Schumannstr., **3**B7
Siegesallee, **3**C6
Siegmunds Hof, **2**B5
Sophienstr., **4**B8–9
Sophie-Charlotten-Str./Platz, **1**C2
Spandauer Damm, **1**B2
Spielhagenstr., **1**C2
Spreeufer, **4**C9
Spreeweg, **3**C5–6
Stauffenbergstr., **3**C6
Steinplatz, **2**C4
Str. des 17. Juni, **2**C4–**3**C7
Stresemannstr., **3**C7–**4**D8

Tauentzienstr., **2**D5
Tegeler Weg, **1**A2–B2
Tempelhofer Ufer, **3**D7
Tiergartenstr., **3**C6
Toleranzstr., **3**C7–D8
Trebbiner Str., **3**D7
Tucholskystr., **4**A8–B8

Uhland-Passage, **2**D4
Uhlandstr., **2**C4–F4
Universitätsstr., **4**B8
Unter den Linden, **3**C7–**4**B8

Viktoria-Luise-Platz, **2**E5
Vorbergstr., **3**E6

Waisenstr., **4**C9
Weidendammer Brücke, **4**B8
Welserstr., **2**D5–E5
Werderstr., **4**C8–9
Wilhelmstr., **4**C8
Wilmersdorfer Str., **1**C3–D3
Windscheidstr., **1**C2–D2
Winterfeldplatz, **2**E5
Wittenbergplatz, **2**D5

Yorckstr., **3**E7

Zimmerstr., **4**C8

DRESDEN

Alaunstr., **9**B4–A5
Albertbrücke, **9**C5
Albertplatz, **9**B4
Altmarkt, **8**D3
Am Queckbrunnen, **8**C2
Am Zwingerteich, **8**C3
An der Frauenkirche, **9**D4
Antonstr., **8**B3–**9**B4
Augustusstr., **9**D4
Augustusbrücke, **8**C3–**9**C4

Bautzner Str., **9**B4–6
Brühlsche Ter., **9**C4
Brühlscher Garten, **9**D4
Bürgerwiese, **9**E4
Budapester Str., **8**E2–3

Carolabrücke, **9**C4

Dr.-Külz-Ring, **8**D3–**9**D4
Dürerstr., **9**D5–6

Friedrichstr., **8**B1–C2

Georg-Treu-Platz, **9**D4
Glacisstr., **9**B5
Grosse Meissner Str., **8**B3–**9**B4
Güntzstr., **9**E5–C6

Hauptallee, **9**E4–F6
Hauptstr., **9**B4
Heinrichstr., **9**B4
Herkulesallee, **9**E5–F6

Königstr., **9**B4
Königsbrücker Str., **9**A4–B4
Könneritzstr., **8**D2–B2
Köpckestr., **9**C4
Kreuzstr., **9**D4

Lennéstr., **9**F4–E5
Lingnerplatz, **9**E4
Louisenstr., **9**A5–6

Magdeburger Str., **8**B1–C2
Marienbrücke, **8**B3
Maternistr., **8**D2–E2
Münzgang, **9**D4

Neue Herkulesallee, **9**E4–5
Neumarkt, **9**D4
Neustädter Markt, **9**B4–C4

Ostraallee, **8**C2–D3

Palaisplatz, **8**B3–**9**B4
Parkstr., **9**E4–F4
Pillnitzer Str., **9**D4–6
Pirnaischer Platz, **9**D4
Postplatz, **8**D3
Prager Str., **8**E3

Rähnitzgasse, **9**B4
Rathenauplatz, **9**D4

Schlossplatz, **8**C3
Schlossstr., **8**D3
Schweriner Str., **8**C2–D3
Sophienstr., **8**D3–C3
St. Petersburger Str., **8**F3–**9**C4
Sternplatz, **8**E2
Strassburger Platz, **9**E5

Terrassenufer, **8**C3–**9**C5
Theaterplatz, **8**C3
Töpferstr., **9**D4
Tzschirner Platz, **9**D4

Waisenhausstr., **8**E3–**9**E4
Weisseritzstr., **8**C1–B2
Wiener Platz, **8**E3
Wilsdruffer Str., **8**D3–**9**D4

Clothing sizes chart

LADIES

Suits and dresses

Australia	8	10	12	14	16	18	
France	34	36	38	40	42	44	
Germany	32	34	36	38	40	42	
Italy	38	40	42	44	46		
Japan	7	9	11	13			
UK	6	8	10	12	14	16	18
USA	4	6	8	10	12	14	16

Shoes

USA	6	6½	7	7½	8	8½
UK	4½	5	5½	6	6½	7
Europe	38	38	39	39	40	41

MEN

Shirts

USA, UK	14	14½	15	15½	16	16½	17
Europe, Japan Australia	36	37	38	39.5	41	42	43

Sweaters/T-shirts

Australia, USA, Germany	S		M		L		XL
UK	34		36-38		40		42-44
Italy	44		46-48		50		52
France	1		2-3		4		5
Japan			S-M		L		XL

Suits/Coats

UK, USA	36	38	40	42	44
Australia, Italy, France, Germany	46	48	50	52	54
Japan	S	M	L	XL	

Shoes

UK	7	7½	8½	9½	10½	11
USA	8	8½	9½	10½	11½	12
Europe	41	42	43	44	45	46

CHILDREN

Clothing

UK						
Height (ins)	43	48	55	60	62	
Age	4-5	6-7	9-10	11	12	13
USA						
Age	4	6	8	10	12	14
Europe						
Height (cms)	125	135	150	155	160	165
Age	7	9	12	13	14	15

What the papers say:

- "The expertly edited American Express series has the knack of pinpointing precisely the details you need to know, and doing it concisely and intelligently." ***(The Washington Post)***

- "*(Venice)* . . . the best guide book I have ever used." ***(The Standard* — London)**

- "Amid the welter of guides to individual countries, American Express stands out . . . . " ***(Time)***

- "Possibly the best . . . guides on the market, they come close to the oft-claimed 'all you need to know' comprehensiveness, with much original experience, research and opinions." ***(Sunday Telegraph* — London)**

- "The most useful general guide was *American Express New York* by Herbert Bailey Livesey. It also has the best street and subway maps." ***(Daily Telegraph* — London)**

- " . . . in the flood of travel guides, the *American Express* guides come closest to the needs of traveling managers with little time." ***(Die Zeit* — Germany)**

What the experts say:

- "We only used one guide book, Sheila Hale's *AmEx Venice,* for which she and the editors deserve a Nobel Prize." **(travel writer Eric Newby, London)**

- "Congratulations to you and your staff for putting out the best guide book of *any* size *(Barcelona & Madrid).* I'm recommending it to everyone." **(travel writer Barnaby Conrad, Santa Barbara, California)**

- "If you're only buying one guide book, we recommend American Express . . . . " ***(Which?* — Britain's leading consumer magazine)**

- "The judges selected *American Express London* as the best guide book of the past decade — it won the competition in 1983. [The guide] was praised for being 'concise, well presented, up-to-date, with unusual information.' " **(News release from the London Tourist Board and Convention Bureau)**

KEY TO MAP PAGES

1–4 BERLIN CITY

5–7 BERLIN ENVIRONS

8–9 DRESDEN

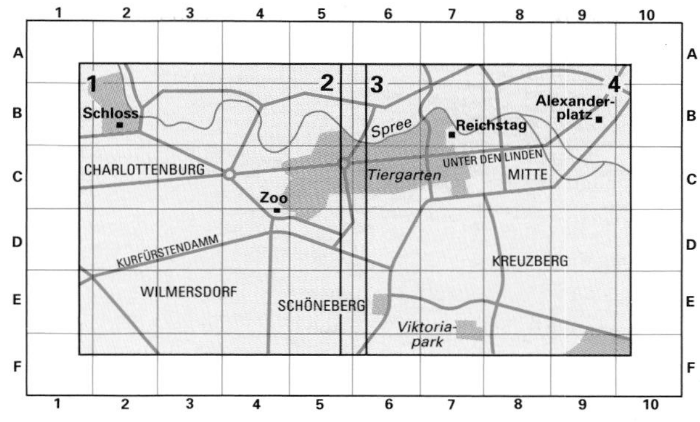

KEY TO MAP SYMBOLS

City Maps

- Major Place of Interest
- Other Important Building
- Built-up Area
- Park
- Cemetery
- Church
- Synagogue
- Hospital
- Hotel
- Information Office
- Post Office
- Police Station
- Parking Lot / Garage
- U-Bahn Station
- S-Bahn Station
- One-way Street
- No Entry
- Adjoining Page No.

0 250 500 750m

0 250 500 750 yds

For maps 1-4 only

Environs Maps

- Place of Interest
- Built-up Area
- Wood or Park
- Cemetery
- Autobahn (with access point)
- Main Road / Four-lane Highway
- Other Main Road
- Secondary Road
- Other Road
- Railroad
- Long-distance Station
- International Airport
- Other Airport
- River Boat Route
- Landing Stage
- F Ferry

BERLIN
1
CHARLOTTENBURG
WILMERSDORF
Schloss Charlottenburg
SCHLOSS-
GARTEN
Belvedere
Mausoleum
Schinkel-Pavillon
Mus. f. Vor- u. Frühgeschichte
Gal. der Romantik
Gipsformerei
Westend
Antikenmuseum
Ägyptisches Museum
Bröhan-Museum
Tegeler Weg
SPANDAUER DAMM
OTTO-SUHR-ALLEE
KAISERIN-AUGUSTA-
MIERENDORFF-PLATZ
Schloss-br.
Caprivi-br.
Röntgen-br.
Rathaus
RICH. WAGNER PLATZ
Deutsche Oper
DEUTSCHE OPER
Schiller-Theater
BISMARCKSTR.
KAISER-DAMM
BISMARCK-STRASSE
SOPHIE-CHARLOTTE-PLATZ
Lietzensee
NEUE KANTSTRASSE
KANTSTRASSE
WILMERSDORFER STRASSE
Charlottenburg
Savignyplatz
Westkreuz
KURFÜRSTENDAMM
ADENAUER PLATZ
OLIVAER PLATZ
LEHNINER PLATZ
HENRIETTEN-PLATZ
Halensee
RATHENAU-PLATZ
HOCHMEISTER-PLATZ
WESTFÄLISCHE STRASSE
KONSTANZER STRASSE
PREUSSEN-PARK
FEHRBELLINER PLATZ
STADTRING
Hohenzollern-damm
HOHENZOLLERN-DAMM
Russische Kirche
BERLINERSTRASSE
10
104

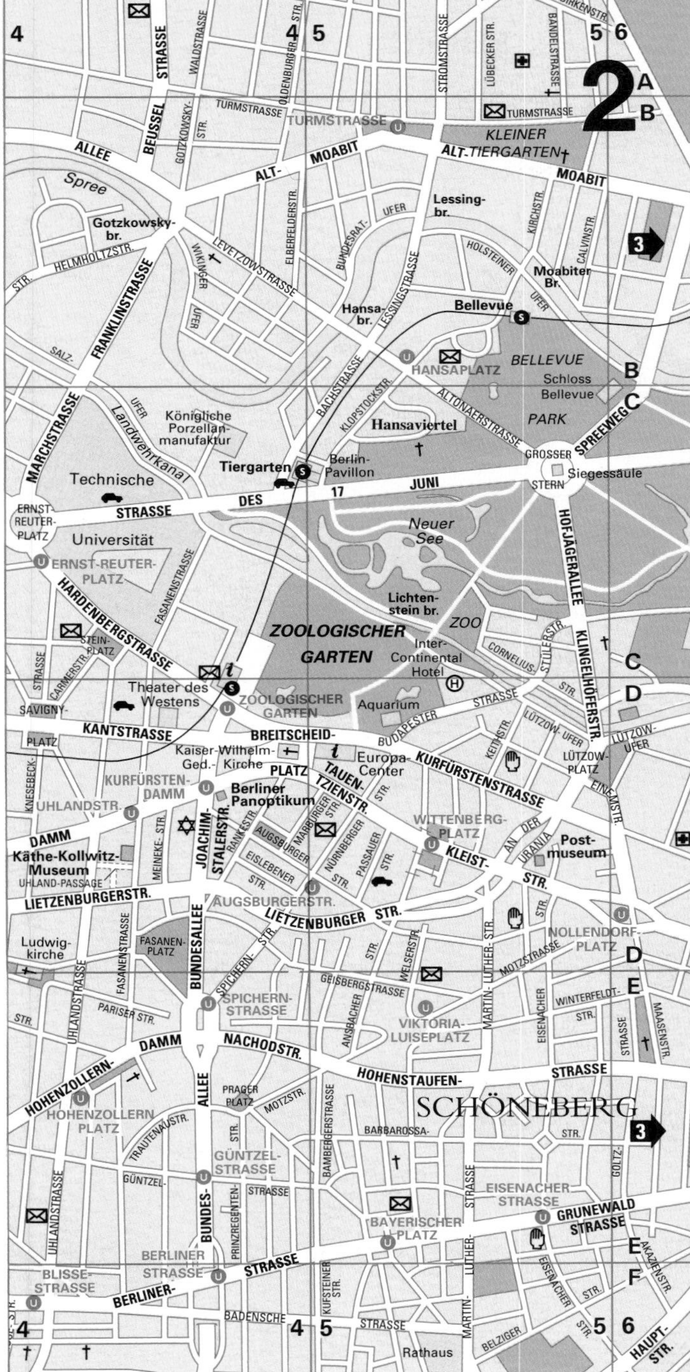

2
SCHÖNEBERG
Spree
Landwehrkanal
TURMSTRASSE
KLEINER TIERGARTEN
BELLEVUE
HANSAPLATZ
Schloss Bellevue
BELLEVUE PARK
Hansaviertel
Königliche Porzellanmanufaktur
Tiergarten
Berlin-Pavillon
GROSSER STERN
Siegessäule
STRASSE DES 17 JUNI
Technische Universität
ERNST-REUTER-PLATZ
Neuer See
Lichtenstein br.
ZOOLOGISCHER GARTEN
ZOO
Inter-Continental Hotel
Aquarium
Theater des Westens
KANTSTRASSE
BREITSCHEID-PLATZ
Kaiser-Wilhelm-Ged.-Kirche
Europa-Center
KURFÜRSTENSTRASSE
KURFÜRSTENDAMM
UHLANDSTR.
Berliner Panoptikum
WITTENBERGPLATZ
Käthe-Kollwitz-Museum
Post-museum
LIETZENBURGERSTR.
AUGSBURGERSTR.
NOLLENDORFPLATZ
Ludwigkirche
FASANENPLATZ
SPICHERNSTRASSE
VIKTORIA-LUISEPLATZ
HOHENZOLLERNDAMM
NACHODSTR.
HOHENSTAUFENSTRASSE
HOHENZOLLERNPLATZ
GÜNTZELSTRASSE
EISENACHERSTRASSE
GRUNEWALDSTRASSE
BAYERISCHER PLATZ
BERLINER STRASSE
BLISSESTRASSE
BERLINER STRASSE
Rathaus
HAUPTSTR.

BERLIN
3
PARK FRITZ-SCHLOSS-
KLEINER TIERGARTEN
Museum für Naturkunde
Brecht-Weigel-Haus
DOROTHEEN. FRIEDHOF
Hamburger Bahnhof
Lehrter Stadtbahnhof
INVALIDENSTRASSE
Charité
Deutsches Theater
ALT-MOABIT
PAULSTRASSE
Moltke-br.
MOLTKE-STR.
Spree
Kongresshalle
Reichstag
Luther-br.
Schloss Bellevue
JOHN-FOSTER-DULLES-ALLEE
Sowjet Ehrenmal
PARISER PLATZ
UNTER
Brandenburger Tor
Unter den Linden
Berliner Ensemble
Marschall-br.
US Embassy
British
SPREEWEG
GROSSER STERN
Siegessäule
STRASSE DES 17 JUNI
TIERGARTEN
HOFJÄGERALLEE
ENTLASTUNGSSTR.
EBERTSTRASSE
VOSS-STRASSE
TIERGARTENSTRASSE
Kunstgewerbe-museum
Musik.-mus.
Potsdamer Platz
Kulturforum
Philharmonie
Gedenkstätte Deutscher Widerstand
St-Matthäus-K.
POTSDAMER PLATZ
Bauhaus-Archiv
Neue National-galerie
Staats Bibliothek
M.-Gropius-
PRINZ-AL GELÄNDE
LÜTZOWPLATZ
LÜTZOW-UFER
REICHPIETSCH-UFER
SCHÖNEBERGER-
Anhalter Bahnhof
Lapidarium
GLEISDREIECK
KURFÜRSTENSTRASSE
POHLSTRASSE
NOLLENDORFPLATZ
BÜLOW-STRASSE
Museum für Verkehr und Technik
MÖCKERNBRÜCKE
TEMPELHOFER-UFER
HALLESCHES-UFER
WINTERFELDT-PLATZ
POTSDAMER-STRASSE
PALLASSTRASSE
GOEBENSTRASSE
YORCKSTRASSE
Riehmers Hofgarten
Kinomuseum
KLEIST-PARK
KLEISTPARK
Grossgörschen-strasse
GRUNEWALDSTRASSE
HAUPT-STRASSE
MONUMENTEN-STR.
KREUZBERGSTR.
VIKTORIA-PARK
DUDEN-STRASSE
KOLONNEN-STRASSE
METHFESSELSTRASSE

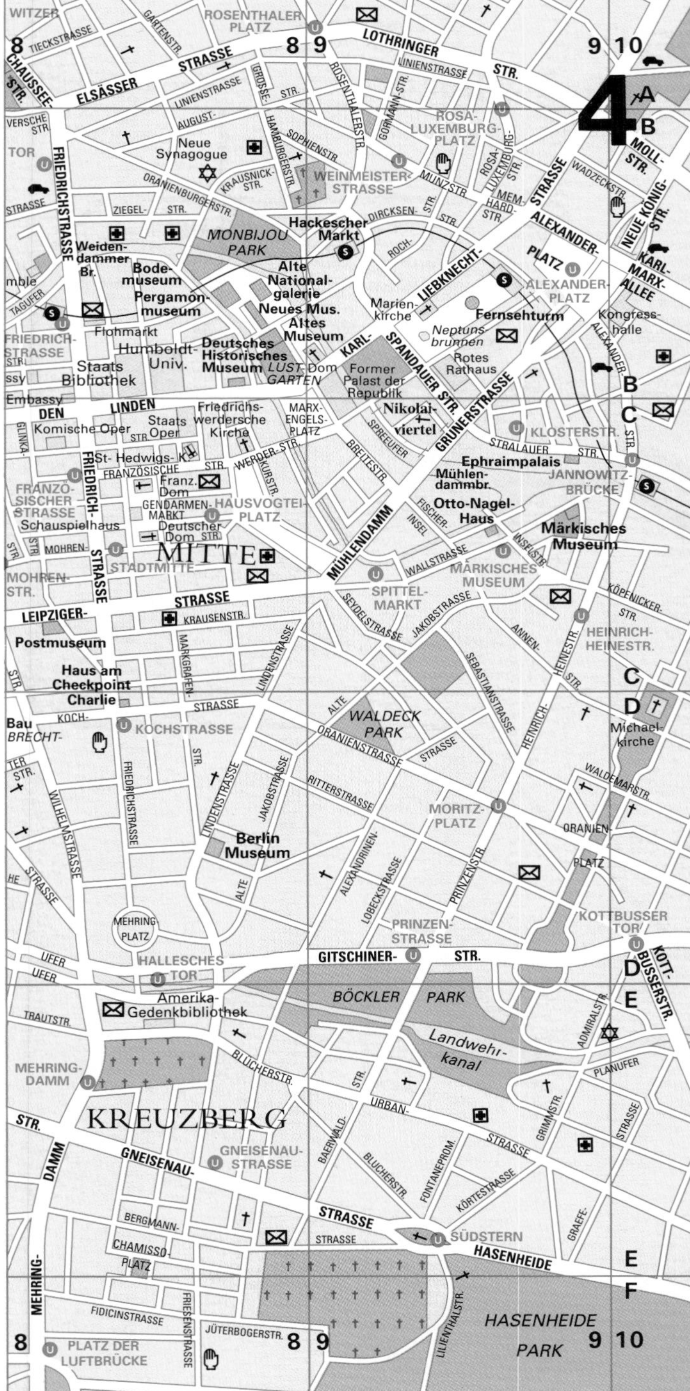

4
A
B
C
D
E
F
8
9
10
WITZER
TIECKSTRASSE
GARTENSTR.
ROSENTHALER PLATZ
LOTHRINGER
STR.
LINIENSTRASSE
STRASSE
CHAUSSEE-STR.
ELSÄSSER
GROSSE-
ROSENTHALERSTR.
GORMANN-STR.
ROSA-LUXEMBURG-PLATZ
AUGUST-
HAMBURGERSTR.
SOPHIENSTR.
VERSCHE STR.
TOR
FRIEDRICHSTRASSE
Neue Synagogue
KRAUSNICK-STR.
WEINMEISTER-STRASSE
MÜNZSTR.
ROSA-LUXEMBURG-STR.
MEM-HARD-STR.
MOLL-STR.
WADZECKSTR.
NEUE KÖNIG-STR.
ORANIENBURGERSTR.
ZIEGEL-
Hackescher Markt
DIRCKSEN-
ALEXANDER-
PLATZ
MONBIJOU PARK
Weiden-dammer Br.
Bode-museum
Pergamon-museum
Alte National-galerie
Neues Mus.
Altes Museum
ROCH-
LIEBKNECHT-
KARL-MARX-ALLEE
ALEXANDER-PLATZ
Kongress-halle
TAGUFER
Flohmarkt
Marien-kirche
Fernsehturm
FRIEDRICH-STRASSE
Humboldt-Univ.
Deutsches Historisches Museum
KARL-
SPANDAUER STR.
Neptuns-brunnen
Staats Bibliothek
LUST-GARTEN
Dom
Former Palast der Republik
Rotes Rathaus
ALEXANDER-STR.
Embassy
DEN
LINDEN
Friedrichs-werdersche Kirche
MARX-ENGELS-PLATZ
Nikolai-viertel
GRUNERSTRASSE
KLOSTERSTR.
Komische Oper
Staats Oper
SPREEUFER
STRALAUER
STR.
GLINKA-
St- Hedwigs- K.
WERDER-STR.
BREITESTR.
Ephraimpalais
JANNOWITZ-BRÜCKE
FRANZÖSISCHE
KURSTR.
Mühlen-dammbr.
FRANZÖ-SISCHER STRASSE
Franz. Dom
GENDARMEN-MARKT
HAUSVOGTEI-PLATZ
Otto-Nagel-Haus
FISCHER-
INSEL
Schauspielhaus
Deutscher Dom
Märkisches Museum
MÜHLENDAMM
MOHREN-
MITTE
WALLSTRASSE
INSELSTR.
STADTMITTE
MÄRKISCHES MUSEUM
MOHREN-STR.
SPITTEL-MARKT
KÖPENICKER-STR.
LEIPZIGER-
KRAUSENSTR.
SEYDELSTRASSE
JAKOBSTRASSE
HEINRICH-HEINESTR.
Postmuseum
MARKGRAFEN-
LINDENSTRASSE
SEBASTIANSTRASSE
ANNEN-
HEINESTR.
Haus am Checkpoint Charlie
Michael-kirche
KOCH-
KOCHSTRASSE
ALTE
WALDECK PARK
HEINRICH-
Bau
BRECHT-
ORANIENSTRASSE
WALDEMARSTR.
RITTERSTRASSE
WILHELMSTRASSE
JAKOBSTRASSE
MORITZ-PLATZ
ORANIEN-
PLATZ
Berlin Museum
ALEXANDRINEN-
PRINZENSTR.
LOBECKSTRASSE
KOTTBUSSER TOR
MEHRING-PLATZ
PRINZEN-STRASSE
UFER
GITSCHINER-
KOTT-BUSSERSTR.
HALLESCHES TOR
BÖCKLER
PARK
Amerika-Gedenkbibliothek
ADMIRALSTR.
Landwehr-kanal
TRAUTSTR.
BLÜCHERSTR.
PLANUFER
MEHRING-DAMM
URBAN-
GRIMMSTR.
KREUZBERG
BAERWALD-
FONTANEPROM.
GNEISENAU-
GNEISENAU-STRASSE
KÖRTESTRASSE
DAMM
BERGMANN-
GRAEFE-
CHAMISSO-PLATZ
SÜDSTERN
HASENHEIDE
MEHRING-
LILIENTHALSTR.
FIDICINSTRASSE
FRIESENSTRASSE
JÜTERBOGERSTR.
HASENHEIDE PARK
PLATZ DER LUFTBRÜCKE

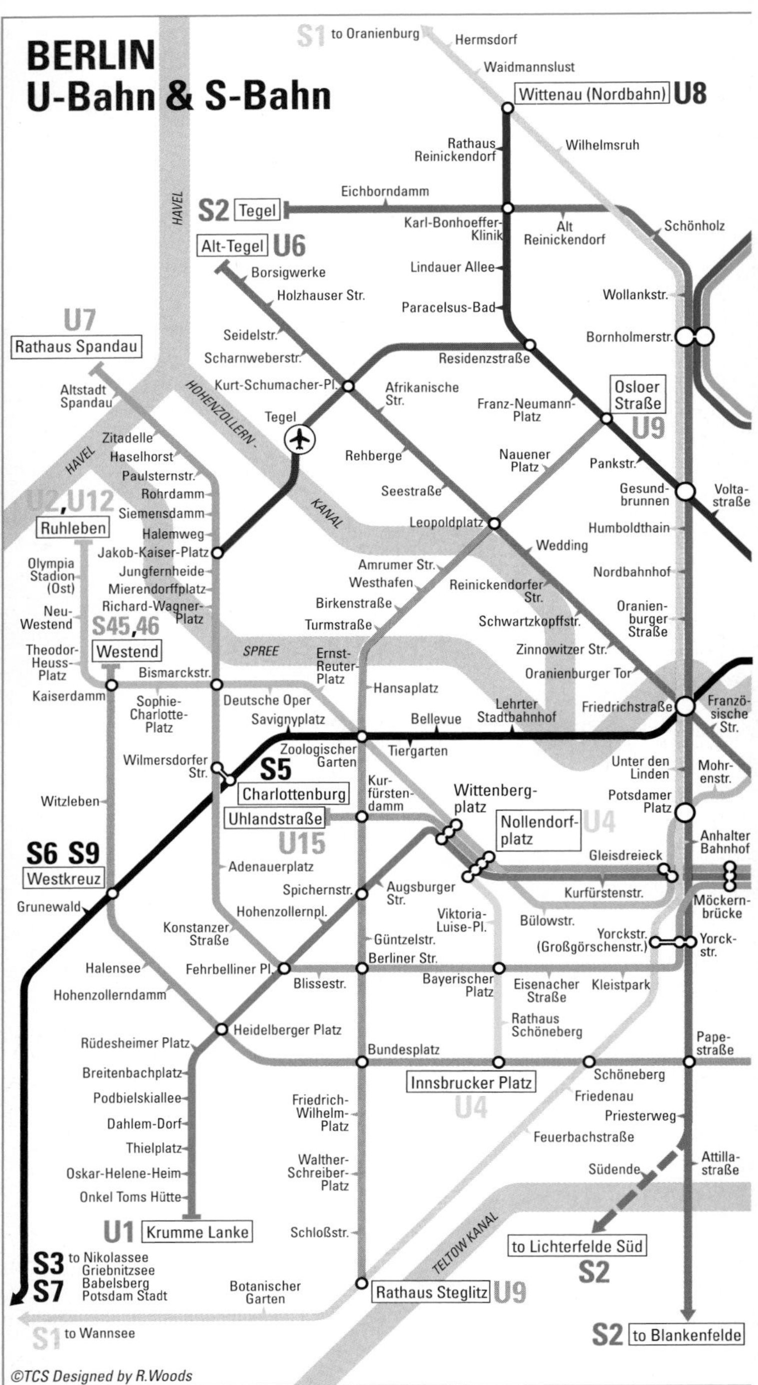
BERLIN
U-Bahn & S-Bahn
S1 to Oranienburg
Hermsdorf
Waidmannslust
Wittenau (Nordbahn) U8
Rathaus Reinickendorf
Wilhelmsruh
Eichborndamm
S2 Tegel
Karl-Bonhoeffer-Klinik
Alt Reinickendorf
Schönholz
Alt-Tegel U6
Borsigwerke
Lindauer Allee
Holzhauser Str.
Wollankstr.
Paracelsus-Bad
U7
Rathaus Spandau
Seidelstr.
Scharnweberstr.
Residenzstraße
Bornholmerstr.
Altstadt Spandau
Kurt-Schumacher-Pl.
Afrikanische Str.
Osloer Straße
Franz-Neumann-Platz
U9
HAVEL
HOHENZOLLERN-
KANAL
Tegel
Zitadelle
Haselhorst
Paulsternstr.
Rohrdamm
Siemensdamm
Halemweg
Jakob-Kaiser-Platz
Rehberge
Nauener Platz
Pankstr.
Seestraße
Gesund-brunnen
Volta-straße
U2,U12
Ruhleben
Leopoldplatz
Humboldthain
Wedding
Olympia Stadion (Ost)
Jungfernheide
Mierendorffplatz
Richard-Wagner-Platz
Amrumer Str.
Westhafen
Nordbahnhof
Neu-Westend
Reinickendorfer Str.
Birkenstraße
Oranien-burger Straße
S45,46
Westend
Turmstraße
Schwartzkopffstr.
Theodor-Heuss-Platz
SPREE
Ernst-Reuter-Platz
Zinnowitzer Str.
Oranienburger Tor
Bismarckstr.
Hansaplatz
Kaiserdamm
Sophie-Charlotte-Platz
Deutsche Oper
Lehrter Stadtbahnhof
Friedrichstraße
Französische Str.
Savignyplatz
Bellevue
Zoologischer Garten
Tiergarten
Wilmersdorfer Str.
S5
Charlottenburg
Unter den Linden
Mohrenstr.
Kurfürstendamm
Wittenberg-platz
Potsdamer Platz
Witzleben
Uhlandstraße
Nollendorf-platz
U4
U15
Anhalter Bahnhof
S6 S9
Westkreuz
Gleisdreieck
Adenauerplatz
Spichernstr.
Augsburger Str.
Kurfürstenstr.
Grunewald
Möckern-brücke
Hohenzollernpl.
Viktoria-Luise-Pl.
Bülowstr.
Konstanzer Straße
Yorckstr. (Großgörschenstr.)
Yorck-str.
Güntzelstr.
Berliner Str.
Halensee
Fehrbelliner Pl.
Blissestr.
Bayerischer Platz
Eisenacher Straße
Kleistpark
Hohenzollerndamm
Rathaus Schöneberg
Heidelberger Platz
Rüdesheimer Platz
Bundesplatz
Pape-straße
Breitenbachplatz
Schöneberg
Innsbrucker Platz
Podbielskiallee
Friedrich-Wilhelm-Platz
Friedenau
U4
Priesterweg
Dahlem-Dorf
Feuerbachstraße
Thielplatz
Walther-Schreiber-Platz
Südende
Attilla-straße
Oskar-Helene-Heim
Onkel Toms Hütte
TELTOW KANAL
U1 Krumme Lanke
Schloßstr.
to Lichterfelde Süd
S2
S3 to Nikolassee
S7 Griebnitzsee
Babelsberg
Potsdam Stadt
Botanischer Garten
Rathaus Steglitz U9
S1 to Wannsee
S2 to Blankenfelde
©TCS Designed by R.Woods

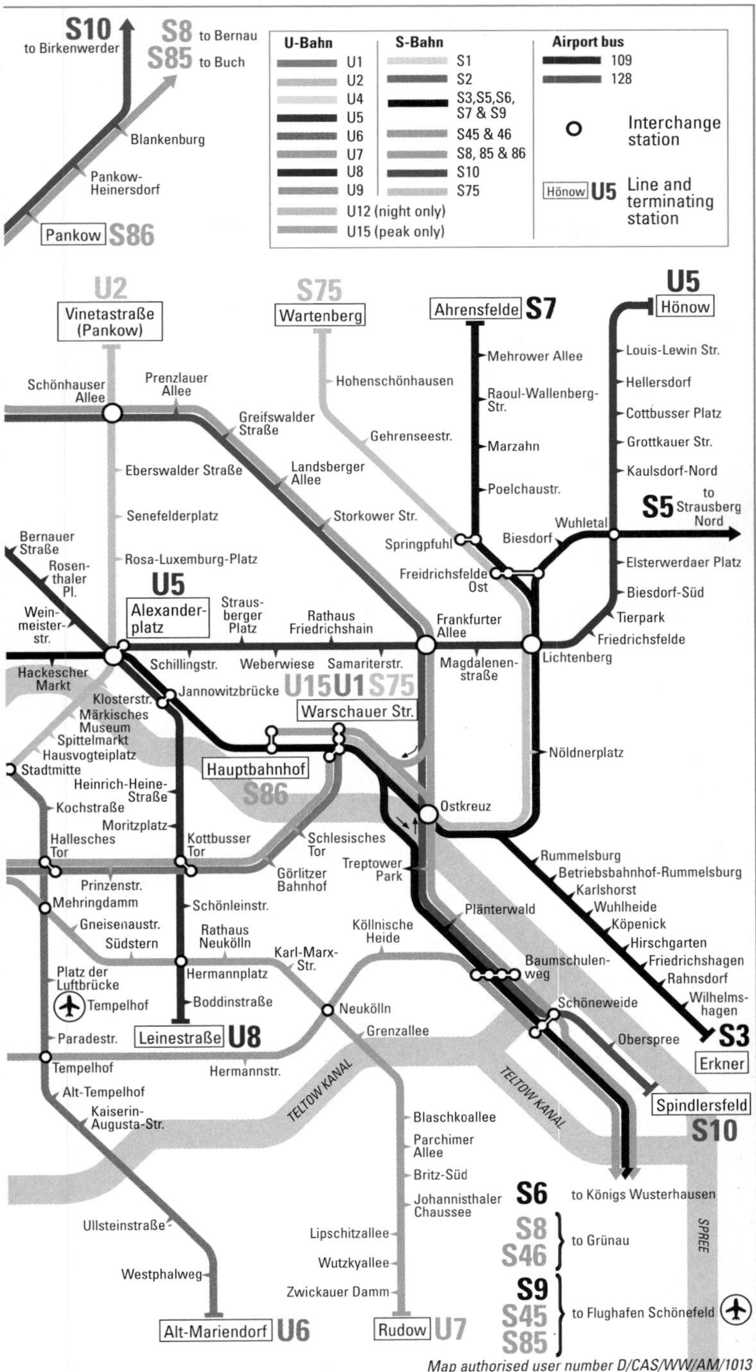

Map authorised user number D/CAS/WW/AM/1013

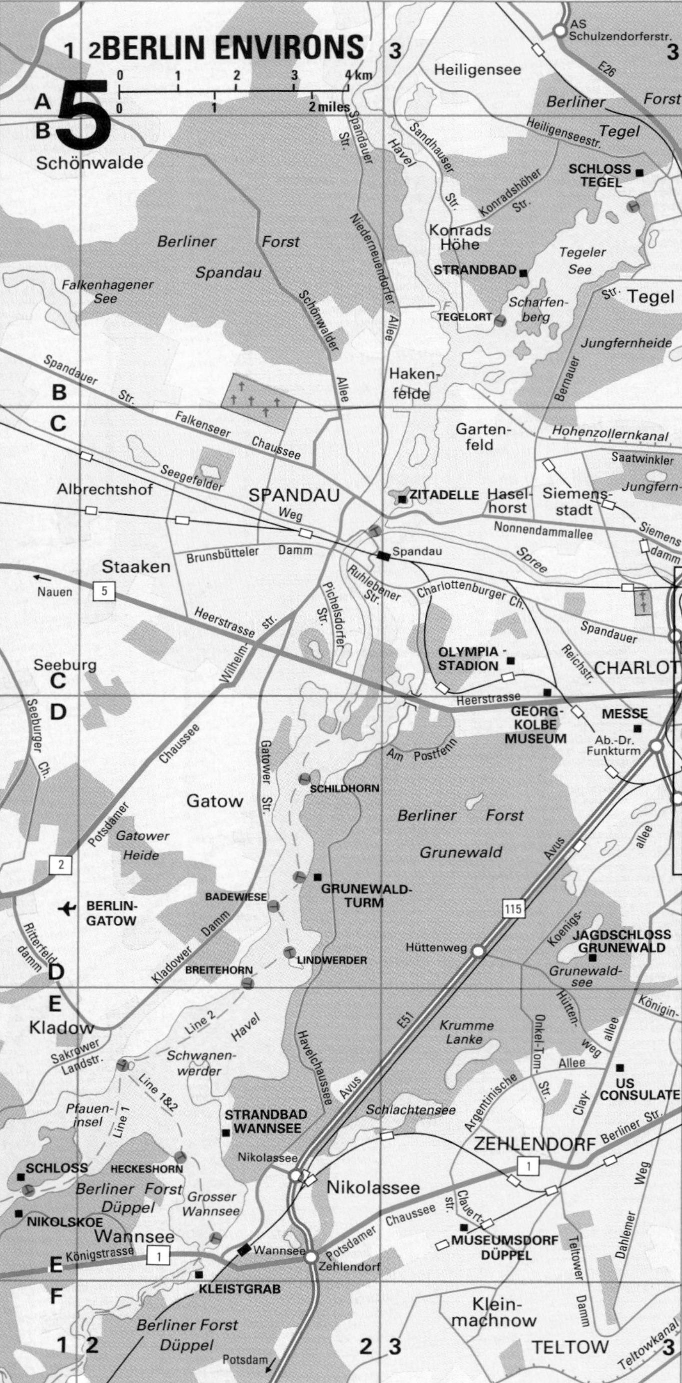
BERLIN ENVIRONS
5
0 1 2 3 4 km
0 1 2 miles
Schönwalde
Berliner Forst
Spandau
Falkenhagener See
Heiligensee
Berliner Forst
Tegel
SCHLOSS TEGEL
Konrads Höhe
STRANDBAD
TEGELORT
Scharfenberg
Tegeler See
Tegel
Jungfernheide
Hakenfelde
Gartenfeld
Hohenzollernkanal
Saatwinkler
Jungfern-
Albrechtshof
SPANDAU
ZITADELLE
Haselhorst
Siemensstadt
Nonnendammallee
Spandau
Spree
Staaken
Nauen
Heerstrasse
Charlottenburger Ch.
OLYMPIA-STADION
CHARLOT
Seeburg
GEORG-KOLBE MUSEUM
MESSE
Ab.-Dr. Funkturm
Gatow
SCHILDHORN
Berliner Forst
Grunewald
Gatower Heide
BERLIN-GATOW
BADEWIESE
GRUNEWALD-TURM
Hüttenweg
JAGDSCHLOSS GRUNEWALD
Grunewaldsee
BREITEHORN
LINDWERDER
Kladow
Havel
Schwanenwerder
Krumme Lanke
US CONSULATE
Pfaueninsel
STRANDBAD WANNSEE
Schlachtensee
ZEHLENDORF
SCHLOSS
HECKESHORN
Nikolassee
Berliner Forst Düppel
Grosser Wannsee
NIKOLSKOE
Wannsee
Königstrasse
Zehlendorf
MUSEUMSDORF DÜPPEL
KLEISTGRAB
Kleinmachnow
Berliner Forst Düppel
Potsdam
TELTOW
Teltowkanal

6
A
B
Hermsdorf
Lübars
Stralsund
Blankenfelde
Waidmannslust
Märkisches Viertel
Rosenthal
Buchholz
Wittenau
Wilhelmsruh
Niederschönhausen
REINICKENDORF
Course of Former Wall
Schlosspark
PANKOW
Berlin- Tegel
Volkspark Rehberge
Plötzensee
WEDDING
Volkspark Humboldthain
Nordbahnhof
ZEISS-GROSS PLANETARIUM
GEDENK. PLÖTZENSEE
Charlottenburg
SCHLOSS CHARLOTTENBURG
MITTE
Volkspark Friedrichshain
Friedrichstr.
TIERGARTEN
Tiergarten
Unter den Linden
Karl-Marx-Allee
Spree
Zoo
BERLIN
Halensee
Kurfürstendamm
WILMERSDORF
KREUZBERG
Hasenheide
AREA COVERED BY MAPS 1-4
SCHÖNEBERG
Schmargendorf
Berlin-Tempelhof
NEUKÖLLN
Friedenau
TEMPELHOF
Botanischer Garten
DAHLEM MUSEUMS
PLANETARIUM AM INSULANER
STEGLITZ
Britz
Mariendorf
Lichterfelde
Britzer Garten
Lankwitz
Marienfelde
Seehof
Rangsdorf

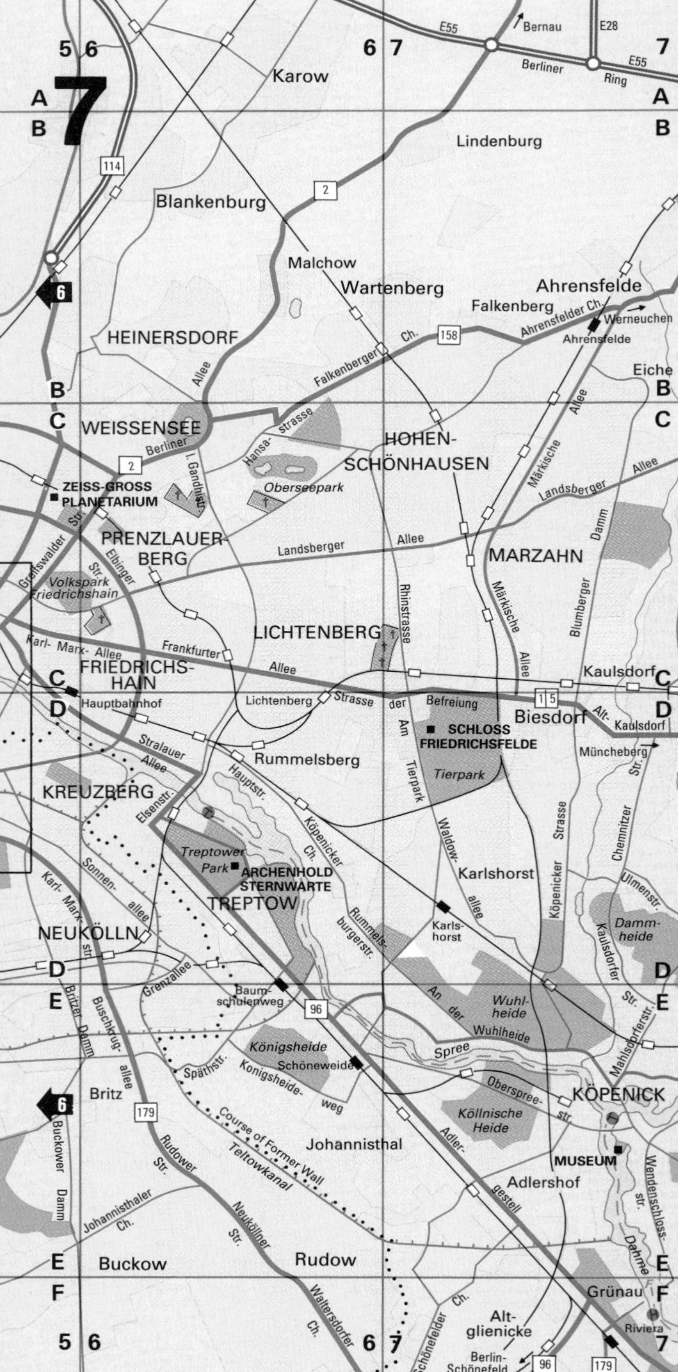

7
Karow
Bernau
E55
E28
Berliner Ring
Lindenburg
114
2
Blankenburg
Malchow
Wartenberg
Ahrensfelde
Falkenberg
Ahrensfelder Ch.
Werneuchen
HEINERSDORF
158
Falkenberger Ch.
Eiche
WEISSENSEE
HOHEN-SCHÖNHAUSEN
Berliner
Hansastrasse
ZEISS-GROSS PLANETARIUM
Oberseepark
Landsberger Allee
PRENZLAUER-BERG
MARZAHN
Volkspark Friedrichshain
Rhinstrasse
Märkische Allee
Blumberger Damm
LICHTENBERG
Frankfurter Allee
Karl-Marx-Allee
FRIEDRICHS-HAIN
Kaulsdorf
Hauptbahnhof
Lichtenberg
Strasse der Befreiung
Biesdorf
Alt-Kaulsdorf
SCHLOSS FRIEDRICHSFELDE
Tierpark
Am Tierpark
Stralauer Allee
Rummelsberg
Müncheberg
KREUZBERG
Elsenstr.
Hauptstr.
Köpenicker Ch.
Waldowallee
Köpenicker Strasse
Chemnitzer Str.
Treptower Park
ARCHENHOLD STERNWARTE
TREPTOW
Karlshorst
Ulmenstr.
Dammheide
Sonnenallee
Karl-Marx-Str.
NEUKÖLLN
Rummelsburgerstr.
Kaulsdorfer Str.
Grenzallee
Baumschulenweg
96
An der Wuhlheide
Wuhlheide
Britzer Damm
Buschkrugallee
Königsheide
Spree
Mahlsdorferstr.
Schöneweide
Späthstr.
Konigsheideweg
Oberspreestr.
KÖPENICK
Britz
6
179
Course of Former Wall
Köllnische Heide
Buckower Damm
Rudower Str.
Teltowkanal
Johannisthal
Adlergestell
MUSEUM
Wendenschlossstr.
Johannisthaler Ch.
Neuköllner Str.
Adlershof
Dahme
Buckow
Rudow
Grünau
Waltersdorfer Ch.
Schönefelder Ch.
Altglienicke
Riviera
Berlin-Schönefeld

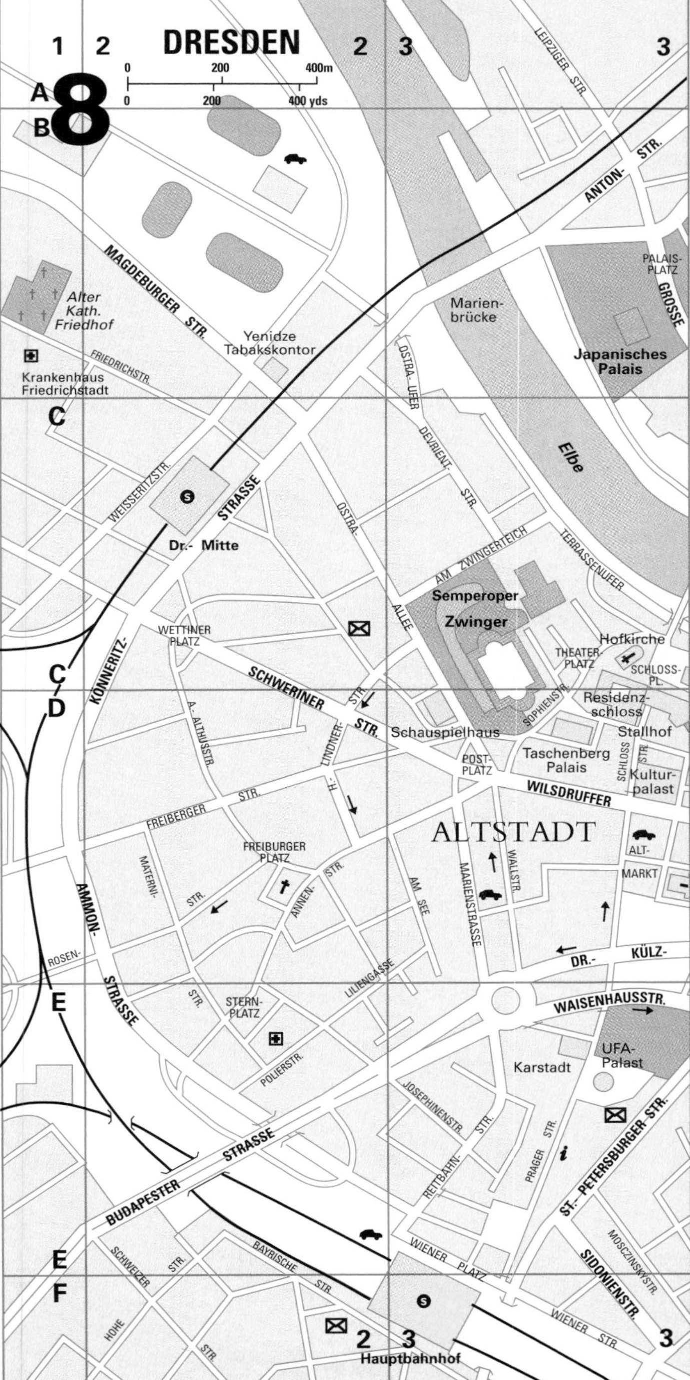
DRESDEN
8
0
200
400m
400 yds
Magdeburger Str.
Alter Kath. Friedhof
Friedrichstr.
Krankenhaus Friedrichstadt
Yenidze Tabakskontor
Leipziger Str.
Anton-Str.
Palais-Platz
Grosse
Marienbrücke
Japanisches Palais
Ostra-Ufer
Devrient-Str.
Elbe
Weisseritzstr.
Strasse
Dr.- Mitte
Ostra-Allee
Am Zwingerteich
Terrassenufer
Semperoper
Zwinger
Hofkirche
Theater-Platz
Schloss-Pl.
Wettiner Platz
Schweriner Str.
Könneritz-
Sophienstr.
Residenzschloss
Schauspielhaus
Stallhof
A.-Althusstr.
Lindner-Str.
Post-Platz
Taschenberg Palais
Schloss-Str.
Kulturpalast
Freiberger Str.
H.-
Wilsdruffer
ALTSTADT
Alt-Markt
Materni-Str.
Freiburger Platz
Annen-Str.
Am See
Marienstrasse
Wallstr.
Ammon-Strasse
Rosen-Str.
Dr.-Külz-
Waisenhausstr.
Stern-Platz
Liliengasse
UFA-Palast
Karstadt
Polierstr.
Josephinenstr.
Prager Str.
St.-Petersburger Str.
Reitbahn-Str.
Budapester Strasse
Mosczinskystr.
Sidonienstr.
Wiener Platz
Schweizer Str.
Bayrische Str.
Wiener Str.
Hohe Str.
Hauptbahnhof

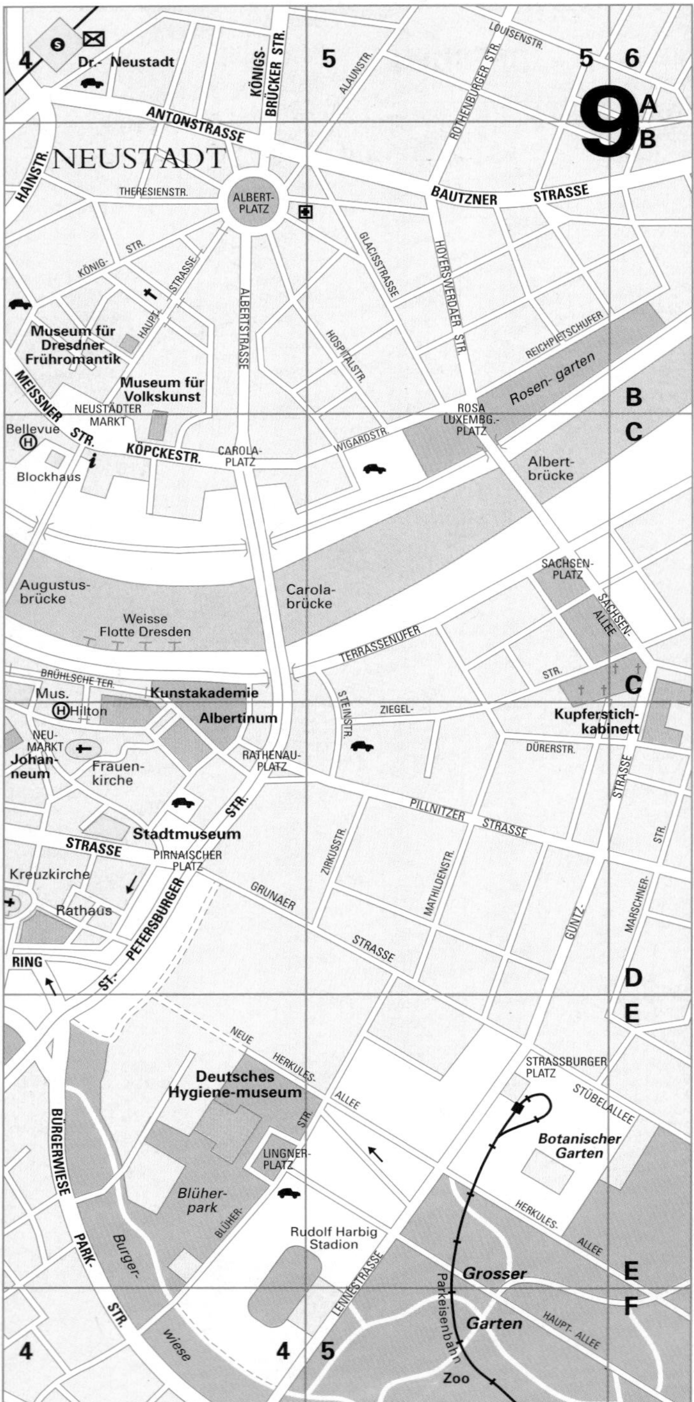

9 A B
4
5
5 6
Dr.- Neustadt
KÖNIGSBRÜCKER STR.
ALAUNSTR.
LOUISENSTR.
ROTHENBURGER STR.
ANTONSTRASSE
NEUSTADT
HAINSTR.
THERESIENSTR.
ALBERT-PLATZ
BAUTZNER STRASSE
GLACISSTRASSE
HOYERSWERDAER STR.
KÖNIG-STR.
HAUPT-STRASSE
ALBERTSTRASSE
HOSPITALSTR.
REICHPIETSCHUFER
Rosen-garten
Museum für Dresdner Frühromantik
Museum für Volkskunst
MEISSNER STR.
NEUSTÄDTER MARKT
ROSA LUXEMBG.-PLATZ
B
C
Bellevue
KÖPCKESTR.
CAROLA-PLATZ
WIGARDSTR.
Albert-brücke
Blockhaus
Augustus-brücke
Carola-brücke
SACHSEN-PLATZ
SACHSEN-ALLEE
Weisse Flotte Dresden
TERRASSENUFER
BRÜHLSCHE TER.
STR.
Mus.
Kunstakademie
Hilton
Albertinum
STEINSTR.
ZIEGEL-
Kupferstich-kabinett
NEU-MARKT
Johan-neum
Frauen-kirche
RATHENAU-PLATZ
DÜRERSTR.
STRASSE
PILLNITZER STRASSE
Stadtmuseum
STR.
STRASSE
PIRNAISCHER PLATZ
ZIRKUSSTR.
MATHILDENSTR.
Kreuzkirche
GRUNAER STRASSE
GÜNTZ-
MARSCHNER-
Rathaus
ST. PETERSBURGER STR.
RING
D
E
NEUE HERKULES-ALLEE
STRASSBURGER PLATZ
STÜBELALLEE
Deutsches Hygiene-museum
BÜRGERWIESE
STR.
LINGNER-PLATZ
Botanischer Garten
Blüher-park
BLÜHER-
HERKULES-ALLEE
PARK-STR.
Burger-wiese
Rudolf Harbig Stadion
LENNÉSTRASSE
Grosser Garten
Parkeisenbahn
HAUPT-ALLEE
F
4
4 5
Zoo